OREGON CAMPING

TOM STIENSTRA

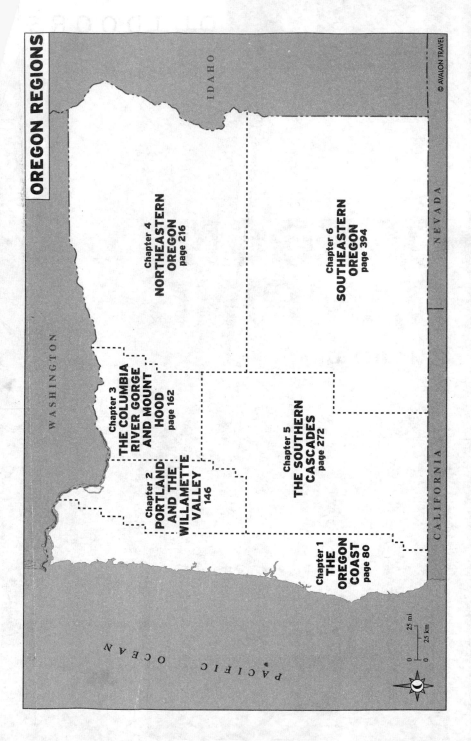

OREGON REGIONS

WASHINGTON

IDAHO

PACIFIC OCEAN

Chapter 3
THE COLUMBIA RIVER GORGE AND MOUNT HOOD
page 162

Chapter 4
NORTHEASTERN OREGON
page 216

Chapter 2
PORTLAND AND THE WILLAMETTE VALLEY
146

Chapter 5
THE SOUTHERN CASCADES
page 272

Chapter 6
SOUTHEASTERN OREGON
page 394

Chapter 1
THE OREGON COAST
page 80

NEVADA

CALIFORNIA

0   25 mi
0   25 km

© AVALON TRAVEL

Contents

How to Use This Book

ABOUT THE CAMPGROUND PROFILES

The campgrounds are listed in a consistent, easy-to-read format to help you choose the ideal camping spot. If you already know the name of the specific campground you want to visit, or the name of the surrounding geological area or nearby feature (town, national or state park, forest, mountain, lake, river, etc.), look it up in the index and turn to the corresponding page. Here is a sample profile:

Campground name and number →

1 SOMEWHERE USA CAMPGROUND

Icons noting activities and facilities at or nearby the campground

General location of the campground in relation to the nearest major town or landmark →

Scenic rating: 10

south of Somewhere USA Lake

Rating of scenic beauty on a scale of 1-10 with 10 the highest rating

Map 1.2, page 4   **BEST (**

Map the campground can be found on and page number the map can be found on

Each campground in this book begins with a brief overview of its setting. The description typically covers ambience, information about the attractions, and activities popular at the campground.

Symbol indicating that the campground is listed among the author's top picks

Campsites, facilities: This section notes the number of campsites for tents and RVs and indicates whether hookups are available. Facilities such as restrooms, picnic areas, recreation areas, laundry, and dump stations will be addressed, as well as the availability of piped water, showers, playgrounds, stores, and other amenities. The campground's pet policy and wheelchair accessibility is also mentioned here.

Reservations, fees: This section notes whether reservations are accepted, and provides rates for tent sites and RV sites. If there are additional fees for parking or pets, or discounted weekly or seasonal rates, they will also be noted here.

Directions: This section provides mile-by-mile driving directions to the campground from the nearest major town or highway.

Contact: This section provides an address, phone number, and website, if available, for the campground.

ABOUT THE ICONS

The icons in this book are designed to provide at-a-glance information on activities, facilities, and services available on-site or within walking distance of each campground.

- Hiking trails
- Biking trails
- Swimming
- Fishing
- Boating
- Canoeing and/or kayaking
- Winter sports

- Hot Springs
- Pets permitted
- Playground
- Wheelchair accessible
- 5% Club
- RV sites
- Tent sites

ABOUT THE SCENIC RATING

Each campground profile employs a scenic rating on a scale of 1 to 10, with 1 being the least scenic and 10 being the most scenic. A scenic rating measures only the overall beauty of the campground and environs. The scenic rating, whether a 1 or a 10, does not take into account noise level, facilities, maintenance, recreation options, or campground management. The setting of a campground with a lower scenic rating may simply not be as picturesque as that of a higher rated campground. However, other factors, such as noise or recreation access, can still affect your camping trip.

If the noise levels or cleanliness of a campground—even a higher rated one—are unacceptable, it's best to contact the campground manager with your concerns. But because these elements can change from day to day, or simply with a new employee hired, these issues are not factored into the ratings. Consider both the scenic rating and the profile description before deciding which campground is perfect for you.

MAP SYMBOLS

Expressway	80	Interstate Freeway	✗	Airfield
Primary Road	101	U.S. Highway	✗	Airport
Secondary Road	21	State Highway	O	City/Town
Unpaved Road	66	County Highway	▲	Mountain
Ferry		Lake	▲	Park
National Border		Dry Lake	)(	Pass
State Border		Seasonal Lake	◉	State Capital

ABOUT THE MAPS

This book is divided into chapters based on major regions in the state; an overview map of these regions precedes the table of contents. Each chapter begins with a map of the region, which is further broken down into detail maps. Campgrounds are noted on the detail maps by number.

Reference to adjacent region

Detail map number and page number

Grid line divides region into detail maps

Region border

REGION/CHAPTER MAP EXAMPLE

MAP 11.1 page 497

MAP 11.2 page 498

MAP 11.3 page 499

MAP 11.4 page 500

No Campgrounds

see Yosemite and Mammoth Lakes page 439

see Death Valley page 575

see San Joaquin Valley page 16

see The Southern Deserts page 7

Locates region within state

Detail map 11.4 shown on next page

Indicates
adjacent detail
maps within region

Locates detail
map within
region

Map
number → **Map 11.4**

Sites shown
on detail map
and the page
range where
those sites are
listed

Campgrounds 105-117
Pages 564-570

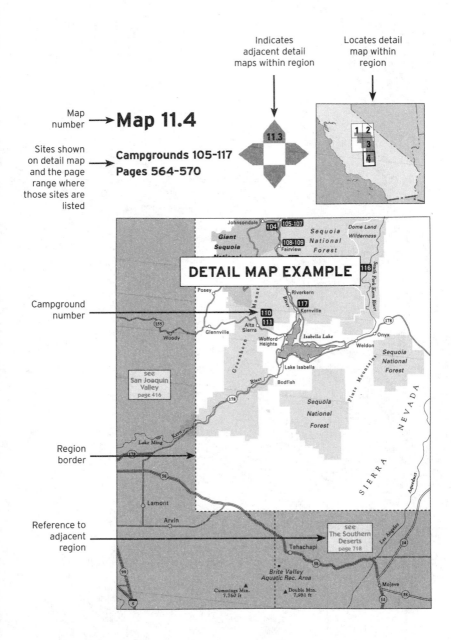

Campground
number →

Region
border →

Reference to
adjacent
region →

DETAIL MAP EXAMPLE

INTRODUCTION

© JILL REID/123rf.com

Author's Note

When my family and friends throughout Oregon heard I was writing this book, they all instantly hated me! They figured their favorite spots would be revealed to all. But after reading the book, they don't hate me anymore (except for this one cousin). That is because they have discovered, as I have, that Oregon is filled with beautiful, little-used campgrounds that are perfect jump-off points for adventure—and there are hundreds of outstanding destinations, in addition to their sprinkling of personal favorites.

Looking for *mystery?* There are hundreds of hidden, rarely used campgrounds listed and mapped in this book that most people have never dreamed of. *Excitement?* At many of them, you'll find the sizzle with the steak: the hike to a great lookout or the big fish at the end of your line. *Fun?* The Camping Tips section of this book can help you take the futility out of your trips and put the fun back in. Add it up, put it in your cash register, and you can turn a camping trip into the satisfying adventure it's meant to be, whether it's just an overnight quickie or a month-long expedition.

Going on a camping trip can be like trying to put hiking boots on an octopus. You've tried it too, eh? Instead of a relaxing and fun trip full of adventure, it turns into a scenario called "You Against the World." You might as well try to fight a volcano. But it doesn't have to be that way, and that's what this book is all about. If you give it a chance, the information herein can remove the snarls, confusion, and occasional, volcanic temper explosions that keep people at home, locked away from the action.

It's estimated that 95 percent of American vacationers use only 5 percent of the country's available recreation areas. With this book, you can leave the herd, wander, and be free. You can join the inner circle, the Five Percenters who know the great hidden areas used by so few people. To join the Five Percent Club, take a hard look at the maps for the areas you wish to visit and the corresponding campground listings. As you study the camps, you'll start to feel a sense of excitement building, a feeling that you are about to unlock a door and venture into a world that is rarely viewed. When you feel that excitement, act on it. Parlay that energy into a great trip.

The campground maps and listings can serve in two ways: 1) If you're on the road late in the day and you're stuck for a spot for the night, you can likely find one nearby; or 2) if you are planning a trip, you can tailor a vacation to fit exactly into your plans rather than heading off and hoping—maybe praying—it turns out all right.

For the latter, you may wish to obtain additional maps, particularly if you are venturing into areas governed by the U.S. Forest Service or Bureau of Land Management. Both are federal agencies that offer low-cost maps detailing all hiking trails, lakes, streams, and backcountry camps reached via logging roads. The Resource Guide at the back of this book details how to obtain these and other maps.

Backcountry camps listed in this book are often in primitive and rugged settings but provide the sense of isolation that you may want from a trip. They also provide good jump-off points for backpacking trips, if that's your calling. These camps are often free, and I have listed hundreds of them.

At the other end of the spectrum are the developed parks for RVs. They offer a home away from home, with everything from full hookups to a grocery store and laundry room. Instead of isolation, an RV park provides a place to shower and get outfitted for food and clean clothes. For RV cruisers, it's a place to stay in high style while touring the area. RV parks range in price, depending on location, and an advance deposit may be necessary in summer.

Somewhere between the two extremes are hundreds and hundreds of campgrounds that provide a compromise: beautiful settings and some facilities, with a small overnight fee. Piped water, vault toilets, and picnic tables tend to come with the territory. Fees for these sites are usually in the $10–35 range, with the higher-priced sites located near population centers. Because they offer a bit of both worlds, they are in high demand. Reservations are usually advised, and at state parks, particularly during the summer season, you can expect company. This doesn't mean you need to forgo them in hopes of a less confined environment. For one thing, most state parks have set up quotas so that visitors don't feel as if they've been squeezed in with a shoehorn. For another, the same parks are often uncrowded during the off-season and on weekdays.

Before your trip, you'll want to get organized, and that's when you must start putting boots on that giant octopus. The trick to organization for any task is breaking it down to its key components and then solving each element independent of the others. Remember the octopus. Grab a moving leg, jam on a boot, and make sure it's on tight before reaching for another leg. Do one thing at a time, in order, and all will get done quickly and efficiently.

Now you can become completely organized for your trip in just one week, spending just a little time each evening on a given component. Getting organized is an unnatural act for many. By splitting up the tasks, you take the pressure out of planning and put the fun back in.

As you might figure, this is not a hobby for me, as it is for some part-time writers who publish books. This is my full-time job. Because I spend up to 200 days a year in the field, I understand how seriously people take their fun, what they need to know to make their trips work, as well as their underlying fears that they might get stuck for the night without a spot. I get tons of emails and letters, and I read each one carefully. These have been of great benefit. In the process, I have incorporated dozen of suggestions from readers to make this the book they want it to be. Your comments and questions are always welcome and appreciated. As a full-tome outdoors writer, the question I am asked more than any other is: "Where are you going this week?"

All of the answers are in this book.

KEEP IT WILD

"Enjoy America's country and leave no trace." That's the motto of the Leave No Trace program, and I strongly support it. Promoting responsible outdoor recreation through education, research, and partnerships is its mission. Look for the Keep It Wild Tips, developed from the policies of Leave No Trace, throughout the Camping Tips portion of this book. This copyrighted information has been reprinted with permission from the Leave No Trace Center for Outdoor Ethics. For more information or materials, please visit www.LNT.org or call 303/442-8222 or 800/332-4100.

Best Campgrounds

Can't decide where to stay? Here are my picks for the best Oregon campgrounds in seven different categories.

❰ Most Scenic

Honey Bear Campground & RV Resort, The Oregon Coast, page 133.
Long Bow Group, Portland and the Willamette Valley, page 157.
Piety Island Boat-In, The Columbia River Gorge and Mount Hood, page 201.
Cove Creek, The Columbia River Gorge and Mount Hood, page 202.
Paul Dennis, The Columbia River Gorge and Mount Hood, page 205.
Anthony Lakes, Northeastern Oregon, page 252.
Scott Lake Walk-In, The Southern Cascades, page 297.
North Waldo, The Southern Cascades, page 312.
Lava Lake, The Southern Cascades, page 334.
Squaw Lake Hike-In, The Southern Cascades, page 387.

❰ Best for Families

Fort Stevens State Park, The Oregon Coast, page 86.
Honey Bear Campground & RV Resort, The Oregon Coast, page 133.
Cascade Locks Marine Park, The Columbia River Gorge and Mount Hood, page 177.
Hoover Group Camp, The Columbia River Gorge and Mount Hood, page 202.
Twin Lakes Resort, The Southern Cascades, page 340.
Indian Mary Park, The Southern Cascades, page 358.
Abbott Creek, The Southern Cascades, page 367.
Lake of the Woods Resort, The Southern Cascades, page 377.
Drews Creek, Southeastern Oregon, page 415.

❰ Best for Fishing

Waldport/Newport KOA, The Oregon Coast, page 105.
Port of Siuslaw RV Park and Marina, The Oregon Coast, page 111.
Carter Lake, The Oregon Coast, page 113.
Trillium Lake, The Columbia River Gorge and Mount Hood, page 186.
Gone Creek, The Columbia River Gorge and Mount Hood, page 192.
Pelton, The Columbia River Gorge and Mount Hood, page 209.
Belknap Hot Springs Resort, The Southern Cascades, page 286.
Mallard Marsh, The Southern Cascades, page 334.
Trapper Creek, The Southern Cascades, page 350.
Drews Creek, Southeastern Oregon, page 415.

❰ Best for Hiking

Nehalem Falls, The Oregon Coast, page 89.
Cape Lookout State Park, The Oregon Coast, page 94.
Cape Blanco State Park, The Oregon Coast, page 127.
Eagle Creek, The Columbia River Gorge and Mount Hood, page 176.
Toll Gate, The Columbia River Gorge and Mount Hood, page 183.

Belknap Hot Springs Resort, The Southern Cascades, page 286.
Boulder Flat, The Southern Cascades, page 321.
Natural Bridge, The Southern Cascades, page 367.
Aspen Point, The Southern Cascades, page 378.

◖ Best for Waterfalls

Nehalem Falls, The Oregon Coast, page 89.
Alsea Falls, The Oregon Coast, page 107.
Ainsworth State Park, The Columbia River Gorge and Mount Hood, page 169.
Salmon Creek Falls, The Southern Cascades, page 312.
Susan Creek, The Southern Cascades, page 318.
Steamboat Falls, The Southern Cascades, page 319.
Hemlock Lake, The Southern Cascades, page 326.

◖ Best Waterfront Campgrounds

Loon Lake Recreation Area, The Oregon Coast, page 120.
Laird Lake, The Oregon Coast, page 129.
Lost Lake, The Columbia River Gorge and Mount Hood, page 180.
Trillium Lake, The Columbia River Gorge and Mount Hood, page 186.
Meditation Point, The Columbia River Gorge and Mount Hood, page 194.
Jubilee Lake, Northeastern Oregon, page 235.
Wallowa Lake State Park, Northeastern Oregon, page 240.
Bull Prairie Lake, Northeastern Oregon, page 248.
Middle Fork, Northeastern Oregon, page 256.
Driftwood, The Southern Cascades, page 299.
Hemlock Lake, The Southern Cascades, page 326.
Gold Lake, The Southern Cascades, page 347.
Bolan Lake, The Southern Cascades, page 366.
Campbell Lake, Southeastern Oregon, page 412.
Dog Lake, Southeastern Oregon, page 415.

◖ Best for Wildlife-Viewing

Cape Lookout State Park, The Oregon Coast, page 94.
Seal Rocks RV Cove, The Oregon Coast, page 103.
Port of Siuslaw RV Park and Marina, The Oregon Coast, page 111.
Harris Beach State Park, The Oregon Coast, page 139.
Pelton, The Columbia River Gorge and Mount Hood, page 209.
Penland Lake, Northeastern Oregon, page 227.
Crooked River Ranch RV Park, The Southern Cascades, page 296.
Bolan Lake, The Southern Cascades, page 366.
Mount Ashland, The Southern Cascades, page 388.
Jackson Creek, Southeastern Oregon, page 408.

Camping Tips

FOOD AND COOKING GEAR

It was a warm, crystal clear day, the kind of day when, if you had ever wanted to go skydiving, you would go skydiving. That was exactly the case for my old pal Foonsky, who had never before tried the sport. But a funny thing happened after he jumped out of the plane and pulled on the rip cord: His parachute didn't open.

In total free fall, Foonsky watched the earth below getting closer and closer. Not one to panic, he calmly pulled the rip cord on the emergency parachute. Again, nothing happened. No parachute, no nothing.

The ground was getting ever closer, and as he tried to search for a soft place to land, Foonsky detected a small object shooting up toward him, growing larger as it approached. It looked like a camper.

Figuring this was his last chance, Foonsky shouted as they passed in midair, "Hey, do you know anything about parachutes?"

The other fellow just yelled back as he headed off into space, "Do you know anything about lighting camping stoves?"

Well, Foonsky got lucky and his parachute opened. As for the other guy, well, he's probably in orbit like a NASA weather satellite. If you've ever had a mishap while lighting a camping stove, you know exactly what I'm talking about.

When it comes to camping, all gear is not created equal. Nothing is more important than lighting your stove easily and having it reach full heat without feeling as if you're playing with a short fuse to a miniature bomb. If your stove does not work right, your trip can turn into a disaster, regardless of how well you have planned the other elements. In addition, a bad stove will add an underlying sense of foreboding to your day. You will constantly have the inner suspicion that your darn stove is going to foul up again.

Camping Stoves

If you are buying a camping stove, remember this one critical rule: Do not leave the store with a new stove unless you have been shown exactly how to use it.

Know what you are getting. Many stores that specialize in outdoor recreation equipment now staff experienced campers/employees who will demonstrate the use of every stove they sell. While they're at it, they'll also describe the stoves' respective strengths and weaknesses.

An innovation by Peak 1 is a two-burner backpacking stove that allows you to boil water and heat a pot of food simultaneously. While that has long been standard for car campers using Coleman's legendary camp stove, it was previously unheard of for wilderness campers in high-elevation areas.

A stove that has developed a cultlike following is the little Sierra, which burns small twigs and pinecones, then uses a tiny battery-driven fan to develop increased heat and cooking ability. It's an excellent alternative for long-distance backpacking trips, as it solves the problem of carrying a fuel bottle, especially on expeditions for which large quantities of fuel would otherwise be needed. Some tinkering with the flame (a very hot one) is required, and they are legal and functional only in the alpine zone where dry wood is available. Also note that in years with high fire danger, the U.S. Forest Service enacts rules prohibiting open flames, and fires are also often prohibited above an elevation of 10,000 feet.

For expeditions, I prefer a small, lightweight stove that uses white gas so I can closely gauge fuel consumption. My pal Foonsky uses one with a butane bottle because it lights so easily. We have contests to see who can boil a pot of water faster, and the difference is usually negligible. Thus, other factors are important when choosing a stove.

Of these, ease of cleaning the burner is the most important. If you camp often, especially with a smaller stove, the burner holes will eventually become clogged. Some stoves have a built-

Stoves are available in many styles and burn a variety of fuels. These are three typical examples. Top left: **White gas stoves** are the most popular because they are inexpensive and easy to find; they do require priming and can be explosive. Top right: **Gas canister stoves** burn propane, butane, isobutane, and mixtures of the three. These are the easiest to use but have two disadvantages: 1) Because the fuel is bottled, determining how much fuel is left can be difficult. 2) The fuel is limited to above-freezing conditions. Bottom: **Liquid fuel stoves** burn Coleman fuel, denatured alcohol, kerosene, and even gasoline; these fuels are economical and have a high heat output, but most must be primed.

in cleaning needle: a quick twist of the knob and you're in business. Others require disassembly and a protracted cleaning session using special tools. If a stove is difficult to clean, you will tend to put off the tiresome chore, and your stove will sputter and pant while you watch that pot of water sitting there, staying cold.

Before making a purchase, have the salesperson show you how to clean the burner head. Except in the case of large, multi-burner family-style camping stoves, which rarely require cleaning, this run-through can do more to determine the long-term value of a stove than any other factor.

Fuels for Camping Stoves

White gas and butane have long been the most popular camp fuels, but a newly developed fuel could dramatically change that.

LPG (liquid petroleum gas) comes in cartridges for easy attachment to a stove or lantern. At room temperature, LPG is delivered in a combustible gaseous form. When you shake the cartridge, the contents sound liquid; that is because the gas liquefies under pressure, which is why it is so easy to use. Large amounts of fuel can be compressed into small canisters.

While convenience has always been the calling card for LPG, recent innovations have allowed it to become a suitable choice for winter and high-altitude mountaineering expeditions, and it now comes close to matching white gas performance specs. For several years now, Camping Gaz, Coleman, Epi (Coleman), Markill, MSR, Primus, and other makers have been mixing propane, butane, and isobutane to improve performance capabilities.

The industry has leaped two important hurdles that stood in the way of LPG's popularity. Coleman, working in cooperation with the U.S. Postal Service, has developed a program in which three-packs of 170-gram Coleman Max fuel cartridges can be shipped by mail to any address or post office in the 50 states and Puerto Rico. Also, each Coleman Max fuel cartridge is now made of aluminum and comes with a special device that allows the consumer to puncture the cartridge safely once the fuel is gone and then toss it into any aluminum recycling container.

The following summaries detail the benefits and drawbacks of other available fuels:

• **Butane:** You don't have to worry about explosions when using stoves that burn bottled butane fuel. Butane requires no pouring, pumping, or priming, and butane stoves are the easiest to light. Just turn a knob and light—that's it. On the minus side, because it comes in bottles, you never know precisely how much fuel you have left. And when a bottle is empty, you have a potential piece of litter. (Never litter. Ever.)

The other problem with butane is that it just plain does not work well in cold weather or when there is little fuel left in the cartridge. Since you cannot predict mountain weather in spring or fall, you might wind up using more fuel than originally projected. That can be frustrating, particularly if your stove starts wheezing when there are still several days left to go. In addition, with most butane cartridges, if there is any chance of the temperature falling below freezing, you often have to sleep with the cartridge to keep it warm. Otherwise, forget about using it come morning.

• **Butane/Propane:** This blend offers higher octane performance than butane alone, solving the cold temperature doldrums somewhat. However, propane burns off before butane, so there's a performance drop as the fuel level in the cartridge lowers.

• **Coleman Max Performance Fuel:** This fuel offers a unique approach to solving the consistent burn challenge facing all pressurized gas cartridges: operating at temperatures at or below 0°F. Using a standard propane/butane blend for high-octane performance, Coleman gets around the drop-off in performance other cartridges experience by using a version of fuel injection. A hose inside the cartridge pulls liquid fuel into the stove, where it vaporizes—a switch from the standard approach of pulling only a gaseous form of the fuel into a stove. By drawing liquid out of the cartridge, Coleman gets around the tendency of propane to burn off first and allows each cartridge to deliver a consistent mix of propane and butane to the stove's burners throughout the cartridge's life.

• **Denatured alcohol:** Though this fuel burns cleanly and quietly and is virtually explosion-proof, it generates much less heat than pressurized or liquid gas fuels.

• **Kerosene:** Never buy a stove that uses kerosene for fuel. Kerosene is smelly and messy, generates low heat, needs priming, and is virtually obsolete as a camp fuel in the United States. As a test, I once tried using a kerosene stove. I could scarcely boil a pot of water. In addition, some kerosene leaked out when the stove was packed, ruining everything it touched. The smell of kerosene never did go away. Kerosene remains popular in Europe only because most campers there haven't yet heard much about white gas. When they do, they will demand it.

• **Primus Tri-Blend:** This blend is made up of 20 percent propane, 70 percent butane, and 10 percent isobutane and is designed to burn with more consistent heat and efficiency than standard propane/butane mixes.

• **Propane:** Now available for single-burner stoves using larger, heavier cartridges to accommodate higher pressures, propane offers the very best performance of any of the pressurized gas canister fuels.

• **White gas:** White gas is the most popular camp fuel in the United States because it is inexpensive and effective—not to mention, sold at most outdoor recreation stores and many supermarkets. It burns hot, has virtually no smell, and evaporates quickly when spilled. If you are caught in wet, miserable weather and can't get a fire going, you can use white gas as an emergency fire starter; however, if you do so, use it sparingly and never on an open flame.

White gas is a popular fuel both for car campers who use the large, two-burner stoves equipped with a fuel tank and a pump and for hikers who carry a lightweight backpacking stove. On the latter, lighting can require priming with a gel called priming paste, which some people dislike. Another problem with white gas is that it can be extremely explosive.

As an example, I once almost burned my beard completely off in a mini-explosion while lighting one of the larger stoves designed for car camping. I was in the middle of cooking dinner when the flame suddenly shut down. Sure enough, the fuel tank was empty, and after refilling it, I pumped the tank 50 or 60 times to regain pressure. When I lit a match, the sucker ignited from three feet away. The resulting explosion was like a stick of dynamite going off, and immediately the smell of burning beard was in the air. In a flash, my once thick, dark beard had been reduced to a mass of little, yellow, burned curlicues.

My error? After filling the tank, I forgot to shut the fuel cock off while pumping up the pressure in the tank. As a result, the stove burners were slowly emitting the gas/air mixture as I pumped the tank, filling the air above the stove. Then, strike a match from even a few feet away and ka-boom!

Building Fires

One summer expedition took me to the Canadian wilderness in British Columbia for a 75-mile canoe trip on the Bowron Lake Circuit, a chain of 13 lakes, six rivers, and seven portages. It is one of the greatest canoe trips in the world, a loop that ends just a few hundred feet from its starting point. But at the first camp at Kibbee Lake, my stove developed a fuel leak at the base of the burner, and the nuclear-like blast that followed just about turned Canada into a giant crater.

As a result, we had to complete the final 70 miles of the trip without a stove, cooking instead on open fires each night. The problem was compounded by the weather. It rained eight of the 10 days. Rain? In Canada, raindrops the size of silver dollars fall so hard they actually bounce on the lake surface. We had to stop paddling a few times to empty the rainwater out of the canoe. At the end of the day, we'd make camp and then face the critical decision: either make a fire or go to bed cold and hungry.

Equipped with an ax, at least we had a chance for success. Although the downed wood was soaked, I was able to make my own fire-starting tinder from the chips of split logs; no matter how hard it rains, the inside of a log is always dry.

In miserable weather, matches don't stay lit long enough to get tinder started. Instead, we used either a candle or the little waxlike fire-starter cubes that remain lit for several minutes. From those, we could get the tinder going. Then we added small, slender strips of wood that had been axed from the interior of the logs. When the flame reached a foot high, we added the logs, their dry interior facing in. By the time the inside of the logs had caught fire, the outside was drying from the heat. It wasn't long before a royal blaze was brightening the rainy night.

That's a worst-case scenario, and I hope you will never face anything like it. Nevertheless, being able to build a good fire and cook on it can be one of the more satisfying elements of a camping trip. At times, just looking into the flames can provide a special satisfaction at the end of a good day.

KEEP IT WILD TIP 1: CAMPFIRES

1. Fire use can scar the backcountry. If a fire ring is not available, use a lightweight stove for cooking.
2. Where fires are permitted, use existing fire rings away from large rocks or overhangs.
3. Don't char rocks by building new rings.
4. Gather sticks from the ground that are no larger than the diameter of your wrist.
5. Don't snap branches of live, dead, or downed trees, which can cause personal injury and also scar the natural setting.
6. Put the fire "dead out" and make sure it's cold before departing. Remove all trash from the fire ring and sprinkle dirt over the site.
7. Remember that some forest fires can be started by a campfire that appears to be out. Hot embers burning deep in the pit can cause tree roots to catch fire and burn underground. If you ever see smoke rising from the ground, seemingly from nowhere, dig down and put the fire out.

However, never expect to build a fire for every meal or, in some cases, even to build one at all. Many state and federal campgrounds have been picked clean of downed wood. During the fire season, the danger of forest fires can force rangers to prohibit fires altogether. In either case, you must use your camp stove or go hungry.

But when you can build a fire and the resources for doing so are available, it will enhance the quality of your camping experience. Of the campgrounds listed in this book, those where you are permitted to build fires will usually have fire rings. In primitive areas where you can make your own fire, you should dig a ring eight inches deep, line the edges with rock, and clear all the needles and twigs in a five-foot radius. The next day, when the fire is dead, you can scatter the rocks, fill over the black charcoal with dirt, and then spread pine needles and twigs over it. Nobody will even know you camped there. That's the best way I know to keep a secret spot a real secret.

When you start to build a campfire, the first thing you will notice is that no matter how good your intentions, your fellow campers will not be able to resist moving the wood around. Watch. You'll be getting ready to add a key piece of wood at just the right spot, and

your companion will stick his mitts in, confidently believing he has a better idea. He'll shift the fire around and undermine your best-thought-out plans.

So I enforce a rule on camping trips: One person makes the fire while everybody else stands clear or is involved with other camp tasks, such as gathering wood, getting water, putting up tents, or planning dinner. Once the fire is going strong, then it's fair game; anyone adds logs at his or her discretion. But in the early, delicate stages of the campfire, it's best to leave the work to one person.

Before a match is ever struck, you should gather a complete pile of firewood. Then, start small, with the tiniest twigs you can find, and slowly add larger twigs as you go, crisscrossing them like a miniature tepee. Eventually, you will get to the big chunks that produce high heat. The key is to get one piece of wood burning into another, which then burns into another, setting off what I call the chain of flame. Conversely, single pieces of wood set apart from each other will not burn.

On a dry summer evening at a campsite where plenty of wood is available, about the only way you can blow the deal is to get impatient and try to add the big pieces too quickly. Do that and you'll get smoke, not flames, and it won't be long before every one of your fellow campers is poking at your fire. It will drive you crazy, but they just won't be able to help it.

Cooking Gear

I like traveling light, and I've found that all I need for cooking is a pot, small frying pan, metal pot grabber, fork, knife, cup, and matches. If you want to keep the price of food low and also cook customized dinners each night, a small pressure cooker can be just the ticket. (See *Keeping the Price Down* in this chapter.) I store all my gear in one small bag that fits into my pack. If I'm camping out of my four-wheel-drive rig, I can easily keep track of the little bag of cooking gear. Going simple, not complicated, is the key to keeping a camping trip on the right track.

You can get more elaborate by buying complete kits with plates, a coffeepot, large pots, and other cookware, but what really counts is having a single pot that makes you happy. It needs to be just the right size, not too big or small, and stable enough so it won't tip over, even if it is at a slight angle on a fire, filled with water at a full boil. Mine is just six inches wide and 4.5 inches deep. It holds better than a quart of water and has served me well for several hundred camp dinners.

The rest of your cook kit is easy to complete. The frying pan should be small, light-gauge aluminum, and Teflon-coated, with a fold-in handle so it's no hassle to store. A pot grabber is a great addition. This little aluminum gadget clamps to the edge of pots and allows you to lift them and pour water with total control and without burning your fingers. For cleanup, take along a plastic scrubber and a small bottle filled with dish soap, and you're in business.

A sierra cup, a wide aluminum cup with a wire handle, is an ideal item to carry because you can eat out of it as well as use it for drinking. This means no plates to scrub after dinner, so washing up is quick and easy. In addition, if you go for a hike, you can clip its handle to your belt.

If you opt for a more formal setup, complete with plates, glasses, silverware, and the like, you can end up spending more time preparing and cleaning up after meals than enjoying the country you are exploring. In addition, the more equipment you bring, the more loose ends you will have to deal with, and loose ends can cause plenty of frustration. If you have a choice, go simple.

Remember what Thoreau said: "A man is rich in proportion to what he can do without."

Food and Cooking Tricks

On a trip to the Bob Marshall Wilderness in western Montana, I woke up one morning, yawned, and said, "What've we got for breakfast?"

The silence was ominous. "Well," finally came the response, "we don't have any food left."

"What!?"

"Well, I figured we'd catch trout for meals every other night."

On the return trip, we ended up eating wild berries, buds, and, yes, even roots (not too tasty). When we finally landed the next day at a suburban pizza parlor, we nearly ate the wooden tables.

Running out of food on a camping trip can do more to turn reasonable people into violent grumps than any other event. There's no excuse for it, not when figuring meals can be done precisely and with little effort. You should not go out and buy a bunch of food, throw it in your rig, and head off for yonder. That leaves too much to chance. And if you've ever been really hungry in the woods, you know it's worth a little effort to guard against a day or two of starvation. Here's a three-step solution:

1. Draw up a general meal-by-meal plan and make sure your companions like what's on it.

2. Tell your companions to buy any specialty items (such as a special brand of coffee) on their own and not to expect you to take care of everything.

3. Put all the food on your living room floor and literally plan out every day of your trip, meal by meal, putting the food in plastic bags as you go. That way, you will know exact food quotas and you won't go hungry.

Fish for your dinner? There's one guarantee as far as that goes: If you expect to catch fish for meals, you will most certainly get skunked. If you don't expect to catch fish for meals, you will probably catch so many they'll be coming out of your ears. I've seen it a hundred times.

Keeping the Price Down

"There must be some mistake," I said with a laugh. "Whoever paid $750 for camp food?"

But the amount was as clear as the digital numbers on the cash register: $753.27.

"How is this possible?" I asked the clerk.

"Just add it up," she responded, irritated.

Then I started figuring. The freeze-dried backpack dinners cost $6 apiece. A small pack of beef jerky went for $2, the beef sticks for $0.75, granola bars for $0.50. Multiply it all by four hungry men, including Foonsky, for 21 days. This food was to sustain us on a major expedition—four guys hiking 250 miles over three weeks from Mount Whitney to Yosemite Valley.

The dinners alone cost close to $500. Add in the usual goodies—candy, coffee, dried fruit, granola bars, jerky, oatmeal, soup, and Tang—and I felt as if an earthquake had struck when I saw the tab.

A lot of campers have received similar shocks. In preparation for their trips, campers shop with enthusiasm. Then they pay the bill in horror.

Well, there are solutions, lots of them. You can eat gourmet-style in the outback without having your wallet cleaned out. But it requires do-it-yourself cooking, more planning, and careful shopping. It also means transcending the push-button, I-want-it-now attitude that so many people can't leave behind when they go to the mountains.

The secret is to bring along a small pressure cooker. A reader in San Francisco, Mike Bettinger, passed this tip on to me. Little pressure cookers weigh about two pounds, which may sound like a lot to backpackers and backcountry campers. But when three or four people are on a trip, it actually saves weight.

The key is that it allows campers to bring items that are normally difficult to cook at high altitudes, such as brown and white rice; red, black, pinto, and lima beans; and lentils. You pick one or more for a basic staple and then add a variety of freeze-dried ingredients to make a complete dish. Packets of garlic, meat, onions, shallots, and vegetables are available. Sun-dried tomatoes, for instance, reconstitute wonderfully in a pressure cooker. Add herbs, spices, and maybe a few rainbow trout and you will be eating better out of a backpack than most people do at home.

"In the morning, I have used the pressure cooker to turn dried apricots into apricot sauce to put on the pancakes we made with sourdough starter," Bettinger said. "The pressure cooker is also big enough for washing out cups and utensils. The days when backpacking meant eating terrible freeze-dried food are over. It doesn't take a gourmet cook to prepare these meals, only some thought beforehand."

Now when Foonsky, Mr. Furnai, Rambob, and I sit down to eat such a meal, we don't call it "eating." We call it "hodgepacking" or "time to pack your hodge." After a particularly long day on the trail, you can do some serious hodgepacking.

If your trip is a shorter one, say for a weekend, consider bringing more fresh food to add some sizzle to the hodge. You can design a hot soup/stew mix that is good enough to eat at home.

Start by bringing a pot of water to a full boil, and then add pasta, ramen noodles, or macaroni. While it simmers, cut in a potato, carrot, onion, and garlic clove, and cook for about 10 minutes. When the vegetables have softened, add in a soup mix or two, maybe some cheese, and you are just about in busi-

HOW TO MAKE BEEF JERKY IN YOUR OWN KITCHEN

Start with a couple of pieces of meat: lean top round, sirloin, or tritip. Cut them into 3/16-inch strips across the grain, trimming out the membrane, gristle, and fat. Marinate the strips for 24 hours in a glass dish. The fun begins in picking a marinade. Try two-thirds teriyaki sauce, one-third Worcestershire sauce. You can customize the recipe by adding pepper, ground mustard, bay leaf, red wine vinegar, garlic, and, for the brave, Tabasco sauce.

After a day or so, squeeze out each strip of meat with a rolling pin, lay them in rows on a cooling rack over a cookie sheet, and dry them in the oven at 125°F for 12 hours. Thicker pieces can take as long as 18-24 hours.

That's it. The hardest part is cleaning the cookie sheet when you're done. The easiest part is eating your own homemade jerky while sitting at a lookout on a mountain ridge. The do-it-yourself method for jerky may take a day or so, but it is cheaper and can taste better than any store-bought jerky.

– my thanks to Jeff Patty for this recipe

ness. But you can still ruin it and turn your hodge into slodge. Make sure you read the directions on the soup mix to determine cooking time. It can vary widely. In addition, make sure you stir the whole thing up; otherwise, you will get those hidden dry clumps of soup mix that taste like garlic sawdust.

How do I know? Well, it was up near Kearsage Pass in the Sierra Nevada, where, feeling half-starved, I dug into our nightly hodge. I will never forget that first bite—I damn near gagged to death. Foonsky laughed at me, until he took his first bite (a nice big one) and then turned green.

Another way to trim food costs is to make your own beef jerky, the trademark staple of campers for more than 200 years. A tiny packet of beef jerky costs $2, and for that 250-mile expedition, I spent $150 on jerky alone. Never again. Now we make our own and get big strips of jerky that taste better than anything you can buy.

If all this still doesn't sound like your idea of a gourmet but low-cost camping meal, well, you are forgetting the main course: rainbow trout. Remember: If you don't plan on catching them for dinner, you'll probably snag more than you can finish in one night's hodgepacking.

Some campers go to great difficulties to cook their trout, bringing along frying pans, butter, grills, tinfoil, and more, but all you need is some seasoned salt and a campfire.

Rinse the gutted trout, and while it's still wet, sprinkle on a good dose of seasoned salt, both inside and out. Clear any burning logs to the side of the campfire, then lay the trout right on the coals, turning it once so both sides are cooked. Sound ridiculous? Sound like you are throwing the fish away? Sound like the fish will burn up? Sound like you will have to eat the campfire ash? Wrong on all counts. The fish cooks perfectly, the ash doesn't stick, and after cooking trout this way, you may never fry trout again.

If you can't convince your buddies, who may insist that trout should be fried, then make sure you have butter to fry them in, not oil. Also make sure you cook them all the way through, so the meat strips off the backbone in two nice, clean fillets. The fish should end up looking like one that Sylvester the Cat just drew out of his mouth—only the head, tail, and a perfect skeleton.

You can supplement your eats with sweets, nuts, freeze-dried fruits, and drink mixes. In any case, make sure you keep the dinner menu varied. If you and your buddies look into your dinner cups and groan, "Ugh, not this again," you will soon start dreaming of cheeseburgers and french fries instead of hiking, fishing, and finding beautiful campsites.

If you are car camping and have a big ice chest, you can bring virtually anything to eat and drink. If you are on the trail and don't mind paying the price, the newest freeze-dried dinners provide another option.

Some of the biggest advances in the outdoors industry have come in the form of freeze-dried dinners. Some of them are almost good enough to serve in restaurants. Sweet-and-sour pork over rice, tostadas, Burgundy chicken—it sure beats the poopy goop we used to eat, like the old soupy chili-mac dinners that tasted bad and looked so unlike food that consumption was nearly impossible, even for my dog, Rebel. Foonsky usually managed to get it down, but just barely.

To provide an idea of how to plan a menu, consider what my companions and I ate while hiking 250 miles on California's John Muir Trail:

• Breakfast: instant soup, oatmeal (never get plain), one beef or jerky stick, coffee or hot chocolate.

• Lunch: one beef stick, two jerky sticks, one granola bar, dried fruit, half cup of pistachio nuts, Tang, one small bag of M&Ms.

• Dinner: instant soup, one freeze-dried dinner (split between two people), one milk bar, rainbow trout.

What was that last item? Rainbow trout? Right! Unless you plan on it, you can catch them every night.

CLOTHING AND WEATHER PROTECTION

What started as an innocent pursuit of the perfect campground evolved into one heck of a predicament for Foonsky and me.

We had parked at the end of a logging road and then bushwhacked our way down a canyon to a pristine trout stream. On my first cast—a little flip into the plunge pool of a waterfall—I caught a 16-inch rainbow trout, a real beauty that jumped three times. Magic stuff.

Then, just across the stream, we saw it: The Perfect Camping Spot. On a sandbar on the edge of the forest, there lay a flat spot, high and dry above the river. Nearby was plenty of downed wood collected by past winter storms that we could use for firewood. And, of course, this beautiful trout stream was bubbling along just 40 yards from the site.

But nothing is perfect, right? To reach it, we had to wade across the river, although it didn't appear to be too difficult. The cold water tingled a bit, and the river came up surprisingly high, just above the belt. But it would be worth it to camp at The Perfect Spot.

Once across the river, we put on some dry clothes, set up camp, explored the woods, and fished the stream, catching several nice trout for dinner. But late that afternoon, it started raining. What? Rain in the summertime? Nature makes its own rules. By the next morning, it was still raining, pouring like a Yosemite waterfall from a solid gray sky.

That's when we noticed The Perfect Spot wasn't so perfect. The rain had raised the river level too high for us to wade back across. We were marooned, wet, and hungry.

"Now we're in a heck of a predicament," said Foonsky, the water streaming off him.

Getting cold and wet on a camping trip with no way to warm up is not only unnecessary and uncomfortable, it can be a fast ticket to hypothermia, the number one killer of campers in the woods. By definition, hypothermia is a condition in which body temperature is lowered to the point that it causes illness. It is particularly dangerous because the afflicted are usually unaware it is setting in. The first sign is a sense of apathy, then a state of confusion, which can lead eventually to collapse (or what appears to be sleep), then death.

You must always have a way to get warm and dry in short order, regardless of any conditions you may face. If you have no way of getting dry, then you must take emergency steps to prevent hypothermia. (See the steps detailed in *First Aid and Insect Protection* in this chapter.)

But you should never reach that point. For starters, always have spare sets of clothing tucked away so no matter how cold and wet you might get, you have something dry to put on. On hiking trips, I always carry a second set of clothes, sealed to stay dry, in a plastic garbage bag. I keep a third set waiting back at the truck.

If you are car camping, your vehicle can cause an illusory sense of security. But with an extra set of dry clothes stashed safely away, there is no illusion. The security is real. And remember, no matter how hot the weather is when you start your trip, always be prepared for the worst. Foonsky and I learned the hard way.

So both of us were soaking wet on that sandbar. With no other choice, we tried holing up in the tent for the night. A sleeping bag with Quallofil or another polyester fiberfill can retain warmth even when wet, because the fill is hollow and retains its loft. So as miserable as it was, the night passed without incident.

The rain stopped the next day and the river dropped a bit, but it was still rolling big and angry. Using a stick as a wading staff, Foonsky crossed about 80 percent of the stream before he was dumped, but he made a jump for it and managed to scramble to the riverbank. He waved for me to follow. "No problem," I thought.

It took me 20 minutes to reach nearly the same spot where Foonsky had been dumped. The heavy river current was above my belt and pushing hard. Then, in the flash of an instant, my wading staff slipped on a rock. I teetered in the river current and was knocked over like a bowling pin. I became completely submerged. I went tumbling down the river, heading right toward the waterfall. While underwater, I looked up at the surface, and I can remember how close it seemed yet how out of control I was. Right then, this giant hand appeared, and I grabbed it. It was Foonsky. If it weren't for that hand, I would have sailed right over the waterfall.

My momentum drew Foonsky right into the river, and we scrambled in the current, but I suddenly sensed the river bottom under my knees. On all fours, the two of us clambered ashore. We were safe.

"Thanks, ol' buddy," I said.

"Man, we're wet," he responded. "Let's get to the rig and get some dry clothes on."

The Art of Layering

The most important element for enjoying the outdoor experience in any condition is to stay dry and warm. There is no substitute. You must stay dry and you must stay warm.

Thus comes the theory behind layering, which suggests that as your body temperature fluctuates or the weather shifts, you simply peel off or add available layers as needed—and have a waterproof shell available in case of rain.

The introduction of a new era of outdoor clothing has made it possible for campers to turn choosing clothes into an art form. Like art, it's much more expensive than throwing on a pair of blue jeans, a T-shirt, and some flannel, but, for many, it is worth the price.

In putting together your ideal layering system, there are some general considerations. What you need to do is create a system that effectively combines elements of breathability, durability, insulation, rapid drying, water repellence, wicking, and wind resistance, while still being lightweight and offering the necessary freedom of movement, all with just a few garments.

The basic intent of a base layer is to manage moisture. Your base layer will be the first article of clothing you put on and the last to come off. Since your own skin will be churning out the perspiration, the goal of this second skin is to manage the moisture and move it away from you. The best base layers are made of bicomponent knits, that is, blends of polyester and cotton, which provide wicking and insulating properties in one layer.

The way it works is that the side facing your skin is water-hating, while the side away from your skin is water-loving; thus, it pulls or "wicks" moisture through the material. You'll stay dry and happy, even with only one layer on, something not possible with old single-function weaves. The best include Capilene, Driclime, Lifa, Polartec 100, and Thermax. The only time that cotton should become a part of your base layer is if you wish to keep cool, not warm, such as in a hot desert climate where evaporative cooling becomes your friend, not your enemy.

Stretch fleece and microdenier pile also provide a good base layer, though they can be used as a second layer as well. Microdenier pile can be worn alone or layered under or over other pieces; it has excellent wicking capability as well as more windproof potential.

The next layer should be a light cotton shirt or a long-sleeved cotton/wool shirt, or both, depending on the coolness of the day. For pants, many just wear blue jeans when camping, but blue jeans can be hot and tight, and once wet, they tend to stay that way. Putting on wet blue jeans on a cold morning is a torturous way to start the day. (I tell you this from experience, since I have suffered that fate a number of times.) A better choice is pants made from a cotton/canvas mix, which are available at outdoors stores. They are light, have a lot of give, and dry quickly. If the weather is quite warm, shorts that have some room to them can be the best choice.

Finally, you should top the entire ensemble off with a thin, windproof, water-resistant layer. You want this layer to breathe like crazy, yet not be so porous that rain runs through it like floodwater through a leaking dike. Patagonia's Velocity shell is one of the best. Its outer fabric is treated with DWR (durable water-repellent finish), and the coating is by Gore. Patagonia calls it Pneumatic (Gore now

calls it Activent, while Marmot, Moonstone, and North Face all offer their own versions). Though condensation will still build up inside, it manages to get rid of enough moisture.

It is critical to know the difference between "water-resistant" and "waterproof." (This is covered under the *Rain Gear* section in this chapter.)

But hey, why does anybody need all this fancy stuff just to go camping? Fair question. Like the introduction of Gore-Tex years ago, all this fabric and fiber mumbo jumbo has its skeptics, including me. You don't have to opt for this aerobic-function fashion statement; it is unnecessary on many camping trips. But the fact is you must be ready for anything when you venture into the outdoors. Truth be told, the new era of outdoor clothing works, and it works better than anything that has come before.

Regardless of what you choose, weather should never be a nuisance or cause discomfort. Instead it should provide a welcome change of pace.

Hats

Another word of advice: Always pack along a warm hat for those times when you need to seal in warmth. You lose a large percentage of heat through your head. I almost always wear a wide-brimmed hat, something like those that the legendary outlaws wore 150 years ago. There's actually logic behind it: My hat is made of waterproof canvas, is rigged with a lariat (it can be cinched down when it's windy), and has a wide brim that keeps the tops of my ears from being sunburned (years ago, they burned to a red crisp on a trip when I was wearing a baseball hat). But to be honest, I like how I look in it, kind of like my pal Waylon Jennings.

HEAD LIGHT

I've tried many head lights and the Trail Torch Hat Light is my favorite (www.halibut.net, $9.95). It comes with five white and green LED lights in a horizontal row that clips under the bill of your hat. For the best option, order the set with three green lights (for night vision) and two white lights. (At night you'll look like a jet coming in for a landing.)

Vests and Parkas

In cold weather, you should take the layer system one step further with a warm vest and a parka jacket. Vests are especially useful because they provide warmth without the bulkiness of a parka. The warmest vests and parkas are either filled with down or Quallofil, or they are made with a cotton/wool mix. Each has its respective merits and problems. Down fill provides the most warmth for the amount of weight, but becomes useless when wet, closely resembling a wet dishrag. Quallofil keeps much of its heat-retaining quality even when wet, but it is expensive. Vests made of cotton/wool mixes are the most attractive and also are quite warm, but they can be as heavy as a ship's anchor when wet.

Sometimes, the answer is combining a parka with a vest. One of my best camping companions wears a good-looking cotton/wool vest and a parka filled with Quallofil. The vest never gets wet, so weight is not a factor.

Rain Gear

One of the most miserable nights of my life was on a camping trip for which I hadn't brought my rain gear or a tent. Hey, it was early August, the temperature had been in the 90s for weeks, and if anybody had said it was going to rain, I would have told him to consult a brain doctor. But rain it did. And as I got wetter and wetter, I kept saying to myself, "Hey, it's summer, it's not supposed to rain." Then I remembered one of the 10 commandments of camping: Forget your rain gear and you can guarantee it will rain.

To stay dry, you need some form of water-repellent shell. It can be as simple as a $5 poncho made out of plastic or as elaborate as a $300 Gore-Tex jacket-and-pants set. What counts is not how much you spend, but how dry you stay.

The most important thing to realize is that waterproof and water-resistant are completely different things. In addition, there is no such thing as rain gear that is both waterproof and breathable. The more waterproof a jacket is, the less it breathes. Conversely, the more breathable a jacket is, the less waterproof it becomes.

If you wear water-resistant rain gear in a downpour, you'll get soaked. Water-resistant rain gear is appealing because it breathes and will keep you dry in the light stuff, such as mist, fog, even a little splash from a canoe paddle. But in rain? Forget it.

So what is the solution?

I've decided that the best approach is a set of fairly light but 100 percent–waterproof rain gear. I recently bought a hooded jacket and pants from Coleman, and my assessment is that it is the most cost-efficient rain gear I've ever had. All I can say is, hey, it works: I stay dry, it doesn't weigh much, and it didn't cost a fortune.

You can also stay dry with any of the waterproof plastics and even heavy-duty rubber-coated outfits made for commercial anglers. But these are uncomfortable during anything but a heavy rain. Because they are heavy and don't breathe, you'll likely get soaked anyway (that is, from your own sweat), even if it isn't raining hard.

On backpacking trips, I still stash a super-lightweight, water-repellent slicker for day hikes and a poncho, which I throw over my pack at night to keep it dry. But, otherwise, I never go anywhere—*anywhere*—without my rain gear.

Some do just fine with a cheap poncho, and note that ponchos can serve other uses in addition to a raincoat. Ponchos can be used as a ground tarp, as a rain cover for supplies or a backpack, or can be roped up to trees in a pinch to provide a quick storm ceiling if you don't have a tent. The problem with ponchos is that in a hard rain, you just don't stay dry. First your legs get wet, then they get soaked. Then your arms follow the same pattern. If you're wearing cotton, you'll find that once part of the garment gets wet, the water spreads until, alas, you are dripping wet, poncho and all. Before long, you start to feel like a walking refrigerator.

One high-cost option is buying a Gore-Tex rain jacket and pants. Gore-Tex is actually not a fabric, as is commonly believed, but a laminated film that coats a breathable fabric. The result is lightweight, water-repellent, breathable jackets and pants. They are perfect for campers, but they cost a fortune.

Some hiking buddies of mine have complained that the older Gore-Tex rain gear loses its water-repellent quality over time. However, manufacturers insist that this is the result of water seeping through seams, not leaks in the jacket. At each seam, tiny needles have pierced the fabric, and as tiny as the holes are, water will find a way through. An application of Seam Lock, especially at major seams around the shoulders of a jacket, can usually fix the problem.

If you don't want to spend the big bucks for Gore-Tex rain gear but want more rain protection than a poncho affords, a coated nylon jacket is the compromise that many choose. They are inexpensive, have the highest water-repellency of any rain gear, and are warm, providing a good outer shell for your layers of clothing. But they are not without fault. These jackets don't breathe at all, and if you zip them up tight, you can sweat a river.

My brother Rambob gave me a nylon jacket before a mountain-climbing expedition. I wore that $20 special all the way to the top with no complaints; it's warm and 100 percent waterproof. The one problem with nylon comes when temperatures drop below freezing. It gets so stiff that it feels as if you are wearing a straitjacket. But at $20, it seems like a treasure, especially compared to a $180 Gore-Tex jacket.

There's one more jacket-construction term to know: DWR, or durable water-repellent finish. All of the top-quality jackets these days are DWR-treated. The DWR causes water to bead up on the shell. When the DWR wears off, even a once-waterproof jacket will feel like a wet dishrag.

Also note that ventilation is the key to coolness. The only ventilation on most shells is often the zipper. But waterproof jackets need additional openings. Look for mesh-backed pockets and underarm zippers, as well as cuffs, waists, and hems that can be adjusted to open wide. Storm flaps (the baffle over the zipper) that close with hook-and-loop material or snaps let you leave the zipper open for airflow into the jacket.

Other Gear

What are the three items most commonly forgotten on a camping trip? A hat, sunglasses, and lip balm.

A hat is crucial, especially when you are visiting high elevations. Without one you are constantly exposed to everything nature can give you. The sun will dehydrate you, sap your energy, sunburn your head, and in worst cases, cause sunstroke. Start with a comfortable hat. Then finish with sunglasses, lip balm, and sunscreen for additional protection. They will help protect you from extreme heat.

To guard against extreme cold, it's a good idea to keep a pair of thin ski gloves stashed away with your emergency clothes, along with a wool ski cap. The gloves should be thick enough to keep your fingers from stiffening up, but pliable enough to allow full movement so you don't have to take them off to complete simple tasks, like lighting a stove. An alternative to gloves is glovelets, which look like gloves with no fingers. In any case, just because the weather turns cold doesn't mean that your hands have to.

And if you fall into a river as Foonsky and I did—well, I hope you have a set of dry clothes waiting back at your rig. Oh, and a hand reaching out to you.

HIKING AND FOOT CARE

We had set up a nice little camp in the woods, and my buddy, Foonsky, was strapping on his hiking boots, sitting against a big Douglas fir.

"New boots," he said with a grin. "But they seem pretty stiff."

We decided to hoof it down the trail for a few hours, exploring the mountain wildlands that are said to hide Bigfoot and other strange creatures. After just a short while on the trail, a sense of peace and calm seemed to settle in. The forest provides the chance to be purified with clean air and the smell of trees, freeing you from all troubles.

But it wasn't long before a look of trouble was on Foonsky's face. And no, it wasn't from seeing Bigfoot.

"Got a hot spot on my toe," he said.

Immediately, we stopped. He pulled off his right boot, then his sock, and inspected the left side of his big toe. Sure enough, a blister had bubbled up, filled with fluid, but hadn't popped. From his medical kit, Foonsky cut a small piece of moleskin to fit over the blister and taped it to hold it in place. In a few minutes we were back on the trail.

A half hour later, there was still no sign of Bigfoot. But Foonsky stopped again and pulled off his other boot. "Another hot spot." On the little toe of his left foot was another small blister, over which he taped a Band-Aid to keep it from further chafing against the inside of his new boot.

In just a few days, ol' Foonsky, a strong, 6-foot-5, 200-plus-pound guy, was walking around like a sore-hoofed horse that had been loaded with a month's worth of supplies and ridden over sharp rocks. Well, it wasn't the distance that had done Foonsky in; it was those blisters. He had them on eight of his 10 toes and was going through Band-Aids, moleskin, and tape like a walking emergency ward. If he'd used any more tape, he would've looked like a mummy from an Egyptian tomb.

If you've ever been in a similar predicament, you know the frustration of wanting to have a good time, wanting to hike and explore the area where you have set up a secluded camp, only to be held up by several blisters. No one

is immune—all are created equal before the blister god. You can be forced to bow to it unless you get your act together.

What causes blisters? In almost all cases, it is the simple rubbing of a foot against the rugged interior of a boot. That can be worsened by several factors:

1. A very stiff boot or one in which your foot moves inside as you walk, instead of a boot that flexes as if it were another layer of skin.

2. Thin, ragged, or dirty socks. This is the fastest route to blisters. Thin socks will allow your feet to move inside your boots, ragged socks will allow your skin to chafe directly against the boot's interior, and dirty socks will wrinkle and fold, also rubbing against your feet instead of cushioning them.

3. Soft feet. By themselves, soft feet will not cause blisters, but in combination with a stiff boot or thin socks, they can cause terrible problems. The best way to toughen up your feet is to go barefoot. In fact, some of the biggest, toughest-looking guys you'll ever see, from Hells Angels to pro football players, have feet that are as soft as a baby's butt. Why? Because they never go barefoot and don't hike much.

The Perfect Boot

Every hiker eventually conducts a search for the perfect boot in the mission for ideal foot comfort and freedom from blisters. While there are many entries in this search—in fact, so many that it can be confusing—there is a way to find that perfect boot for you.

To stay blister-free, the most important factors are socks and boot flexibility. If there is any foot slippage from a thin sock or a stiff boot, you can rub up a blister in minutes. For instance, I never wear stiff boots and I always wear two fresh sets of SmartWools ($18 a pop).

My search for the perfect boot included discussions with the nation's preeminent long-distance hikers, Brian Robinson of Mountain View (7,200 miles in 2001) and Ray Jardine of Oregon (2,700 miles of Pacific Crest Trail in three months). Both believe that the weight of a boot (or athletic shoe, as they often use) is the defining factor when selecting hiking footwear. They both go as light as possible, believing that heavy boots will eventually wear you out by forcing you to pick up several pounds on your feet over and over again. A compatriot at the *San Francisco Chronicle,* outdoors writer Paul McHugh, offers the reminder that arch support may be even more vital, especially for people who hike less frequently and thus have not developed great foot strength as have Robinson and Jardine.

It is absolutely critical to stay away from very stiff boots and thin socks. Always wear the right style boots for what you have in mind and then protect your feet with carefully selected socks. If you are still so unfortunate as to get a blister or two, it means knowing how to treat them fast so they don't turn your walk into a sore-footed endurance test.

Selecting the Right Boots

When I hiked the John Muir Trail, I hiked 400 miles in three months—that is, 150 miles in a two-month general-training program, then 250 miles in three weeks from Mount Whitney to Yosemite Valley. In that span, I got just one blister, suffered on the fourth day of the 250-miler. I treated it immediately and suffered no more. One key is wearing the right boot, and for me, that means a boot that acts as a thick layer of skin that is flexible and pliable to my foot. I want my feet to fit snugly in them, with no interior movement.

There are four kinds of hiking footwear, most commonly known as: 1. Hiking boots; 2. Hunting boots; 3. Mountaineering boots; 4. Athletic shoes. Select the right one for you or pay the consequences.

One great trick when on a hiking vacation is to bring all four, and then for each hike, wear different footwear. This has many benefits. By changing boots, you change the points of stress for your feet and legs, greatly reducing soreness and the chance of creating a hot spot on a foot. It also allows you to go light on flat trails and heavy on steep trails, where additional boot weight can help with traction in downhill stretches.

HIKING BOOTS

Hiking boots can resemble low-cut leather/ Gore-Tex hunting boots or Gore-Tex walking shoes. They are designed for day walks or short backpacking trips. Some of the newer models are like rugged athletic shoes, designed with a Gore-Tex top for lightness and a Vibram sole for traction. These are perfect for people who like to walk but rarely carry a heavy backpack. Because they are flexible, they are easy to break in, and with fresh socks, they rarely cause blister problems. Because they are light, general hiking fatigue is greatly reduced.

On the negative side, because hiking boots are light, traction can be far from good on steep, slippery surfaces. In addition, they provide less than ideal ankle support, which can be a problem in rocky areas, such as along a stream where you might want to go trout fishing. Turn your ankle and your trip can be ruined.

For day hiking, they are the footwear of choice for most.

HUNTING BOOTS

Hunting boots are also called backpacking boots, super boots, or wilderness boots. They feature high ankle support, deep Vibram lug sole, built-in orthotics and arch support, and waterproof exterior. Many larger backpackers and those carrying heavy packs prefer them because of the additional support they provide. They also can stand up to hundreds of miles of wilderness use, constantly being banged against rocks and walked through streams while supporting 200 pounds.

On the negative side, hunting boots can be quite hot, weigh a ton, and if they get wet, take days to dry. Because they are heavy, they can wear you out. Often, the extra weight can add days to long-distance expeditions, cutting into the number of miles a hiker is capable of on a daily basis.

MOUNTAINEERING BOOTS

Mountaineering boots are identified by mid-range tops, laces that extend almost as far as the toe area, and ankle areas that are as stiff as a board. The lack of "give" is what endears them to mountaineers. Their stiffness is preferred when rock-climbing, walking off-trail on craggy surfaces, or hiking along the edge of streambeds where walking across small rocks can cause you to turn your ankle. Because these boots don't give on rugged, craggy terrain, they reduce ankle injuries and provide better traction.

The drawback to stiff boots is that if you don't have the proper socks and your foot starts slipping around in the boot, blisters will inevitably follow. If you just want to go for a walk or a good tromp with a backpack, then hiking shoes or hunting boots will serve you better.

ATHLETIC SHOES

Athletic shoes are built so well these days that they often can serve as good hiking footwear. They are frequently featherlight, so the long-term wear on your legs is minimal. For many short walks, they are ideal. For those with very strong feet and arches, they are popular even on multi-day trips that require only a small pack.

But there can be many problems with such a shoe. On steep sections, you can lose your footing, slip, and fall. If you stub your toe, you have little protection, and it hurts like heck. If you try to carry a backpack and don't have a strong arch, your arch can collapse or, at the minimum, overstress your ankles and feet. In addition, heavy socks usually are not a good fit in these lightweight shoes; if you go with a thin cotton sock and it folds over, you can rub up a blister in minutes.

AT THE STORE

There are many styles, brands, and price ranges to choose from. If you wander about comparing all their many features, you will get as confused as a kid in a toy store.

Instead, go into the store with your mind clear about what you want, find it, and buy it. If you want the best, expect to spend $85–200 for hiking boots, $100–250 for hunting boots, $250–300 for mountaineering boots, and $90–120 for athletic shoes. If you go much cheaper, well, then you are getting cheap footwear.

This is one area where you don't want to scrimp, so try not to yelp about the high cost. Instead, walk into the store believing you deserve the best, and that's exactly what you'll pay for.

You don't always get what you pay for, though. Once, I spent $250 for hiking boots custom-made in Germany. I wore them for close to 2,000 miles, yet they weighed four pounds each! Another time, trying to go light, I spent $185 on some low-cut hiking boots; they turned out to be miserable blister makers. Even after a year of trying to get my money's worth, I never felt they worked right on the trail. They now occupy a dark place deep in my closet.

If you plan to use the advice of a shoe salesperson, first look at what kind of boots he or she is wearing. If the salesperson isn't even wearing boots, then their advice may not be worth much. Most people I know who own quality boots, including salespeople, wear them almost daily if their jobs allow, since boots are the best footwear available. However, even these well-meaning folks can offer sketchy advice. Plenty of hikers claim to wear the world's greatest boot! Instead of asking how great the boot is, ask, "How many blisters did you get when you hiked 12 miles a day for a week?"

Enter the store with a precise use and style in mind. Rather than fish for suggestions, tell the salesperson exactly what you want, try two or three brands of the same style, and always try on both boots in a pair simultaneously so you know exactly how they'll feel. If possible, walk up and down stairs with them. Are they too stiff? Are your feet snug yet comfortable, or do they slip? Do they have that "right" kind of feel when you walk?

KEEP IT WILD TIP 2: TRAVEL LIGHTLY

1. Visit the backcountry in small groups.
2. Below tree line, always stay on designated trails.
3. Don't cut across switchbacks.
4. When traveling cross-country where no trails are available, follow animal trails or spread out with your group so no new routes are created.
5. Read your map and orient yourself with landmarks, a compass, and an altimeter. Avoid marking trails with rock cairns, tree scars, or ribbons.

If you get the appropriate answers to those questions, then you're on your way to blister-free, pleasure-filled days of walking.

Socks

People can spend so much energy selecting the right kind of boots that they virtually overlook wearing the right kind of socks. One goes with the other.

Your socks should be thick enough to cushion your feet as well as fit snugly. Without good socks, you might tie your bootlaces too tight—and that's like putting a tourniquet on your feet. You should have plenty of clean socks on hand, or plan on washing what you have on your trip. As socks are worn, they become compressed, dirty, and damp. If they fold over, you'll rub up a blister in minutes.

My companions believe I go overboard when it comes to socks, that I bring too many and wear too many. But it works, so that's where the complaints stop. So how many do I wear? Well, it varies. On day hikes, I have found a sock called a SmartWool that makes my size 13s feel as if they're walking on pillows. I always wear two of them; that is, two on each foot.

Do not wear cotton socks. Your foot can get damp and mix with dirt, which can cause a hot spot to start on your foot. Eventually, you get blisters, lots of them.

SmartWool socks and other similar socks are a synthetic composite. They can partially wick moisture away from the skin.

The exterior sock can be wool or its equivalent. This will cushion your foot, provide that just-right snug fit in your boot, and give you some additional warmth and insulation in cold weather. It is critical to keep the sock clean. If you wear a dirty wool sock over and over again, it will compact, lose its cushion, and start wrinkling while you hike. Then your feet will catch on fire from the blisters that start popping up. Of course, when wearing multiple socks, especially a wool composite, you will likely need to go up a boot size so they fit comfortably.

A Few More Tips

If you are like most folks—that is, if the bottoms of your feet are rarely exposed and quite soft—you can take additional steps in their care. The best tip is keeping a fresh foot pad made of sponge rubber in your boot. But note that brand-new foot pads are often slippery for a few days, which can cause blisters. Just like new boots, they need to be broken in before an expedition.

Another cure for soft feet is to get out and walk or jog on a regular basis before your camping trip. On one trip on the Pacific Coast Trail, I ran into the long-distance master Jardine. He swore that going barefoot regularly is the best way to build up foot strength and arch support, while toughening up the bottom of your feet.

If you plan to use a foot pad and wear two heavy socks, you will need to use these items when sizing boots. It is an unforgiving error to wear thin cotton socks when buying boots and later try to squeeze all that stuff, plus your feet, into them. There just won't be enough room.

Treating Blisters

The key to treating blisters is fast work at the first sign of a hot spot. If you feel a hot spot, never keep walking, figuring that the problem will go away or that you will work through it. Wrong! Stop immediately and go to work.

Before you remove your socks, check to see if the sock has a wrinkle in it, a likely cause of the problem. If so, either change socks or pull them tight, removing the tiny folds, after taking care of the blister.

To take care of the blister, cut a piece of moleskin to cover the offending toe, securing the moleskin with white medical tape. If moleskin is not available, small Band-Aids can do the job, but these have to be replaced daily, and sometimes with even more frequency. At night, clean your feet and sleep without socks. That will allow your feet to dry and heal.

Tips in the Field

Two other items that can help your walking are an Ace bandage and a pair of gaiters.

For sprained ankles and twisted knees, an Ace bandage can be like an insurance policy to get you back on the trail and out of trouble. In many cases, a hiker with a twisted ankle or sprained knee has relied on a good wrap with a four-inch bandage for the added support to get home. Always buy the Ace bandages that come with the clips permanently attached, so you don't have to worry about losing them.

Gaiters are leggings made of Gore-Tex that fit from just below your knees, over your calves, and attach under your boots. They are of particular help when walking in damp areas or in places where rain is common. As your legs brush against ferns or low-lying plants, gaiters deflect the moisture. Without them, pants get soaking wet in short order.

Another tip: Should your boots become wet,

never try to force-dry them. Some well-meaning folks will try to dry them quickly at the edge of a campfire or actually put the boots in an oven. While this may dry the boots, it can also loosen the glue that holds them together, ultimately weakening them until one day they fall apart in a heap.

A better bet is to treat the leather so the boots become water-repellent. Silicone-based liquids are the easiest to use and least greasy of the treatments available.

A final tip is to have another pair of lightweight shoes or moccasins that you can wear around camp and, in the process, give your feet the rest they deserve.

SLEEPING GEAR

On an eve long ago in the mountain pines, my dad, brother, and I had rolled out our sleeping bags and were bedded down for the night. After the pre-trip excitement, a long drive, an evening of trout fishing, and a barbecue, we were like three tired doggies who had played too much.

But as I looked up at the stars, I was suddenly wide awake. I was still wired. A half hour later? No change—wide awake.

And as little kids can do, I had to wake up ol' Dad to tell him about it. "Hey, Dad, I can't sleep."

"This is what you do," he said. "Watch the sky for a shooting star and tell yourself that you cannot go to sleep until you see at least one. As you wait and watch, you will start getting tired, and it will be difficult to keep your eyes open. But tell yourself you must keep watching. Then you'll start to really feel tired. When you finally see a shooting star, you'll go to sleep so fast you won't know what hit you."

Well, I tried it that night and I don't even remember seeing a shooting star, I went to sleep so fast.

It's a good trick, and along with having a good sleeping bag, ground insulation, maybe a tent, or a few tricks for bedding down in a pickup truck or motor home, you can get a good night's sleep on every camping trip.

More than 20 years after that camping episode with my dad and brother, we made a trip to the planetarium at the Academy of Sciences in San Francisco to see a show on Halley's Comet. The lights dimmed, and the ceiling turned into a night sky, filled with stars and a setting moon. A scientist began explaining phenomenas of the heavens.

After a few minutes, I began to feel drowsy. Just then, a shooting star zipped across the planetarium ceiling. I went into such a deep sleep, it was like I was in a coma. I didn't wake up until the show was over, the lights were turned back on, and the people were leaving.

Feeling drowsy, I turned to see if Dad had liked the show. Oh yeah? Not only had he gone to sleep too, but he apparently had no intention of waking up, no matter what. Just like a camping trip.

Sleeping Bags

Question: What could be worse than trying to sleep in a cold, wet sleeping bag on a rainy night without a tent in the mountains?

Answer: Trying to sleep in a cold, wet sleeping bag on a rainy night without a tent in the mountains when your sleeping bag is filled with down.

Water will turn a down-filled sleeping bag into a mushy heap. Many campers do not like a high-tech approach, but a state-of-the-art polyfiber sleeping bag can keep you warm even when wet. That factor, along with temperature rating and weight, is key when selecting a sleeping bag.

A sleeping bag is a shell filled with heat-retaining insulation. By itself, it is not warm. Your body provides the heat, and the sleeping bag's ability to retain that heat is what makes it warm or cold.

The old-style canvas bags are heavy, bulky, cold, and, when wet, useless. With other options available, their function is limited. Anybody who sleeps outdoors or backpacks should choose otherwise. Use a sleeping bag filled with down or one of the quality poly-fills. Down is light, warm, and aesthetically pleasing to those who don't think camping and technology mix. If you choose a down bag, be sure to keep it double wrapped in plastic garbage bags on your trip to keep it dry. Once it's wet, you'll spend your nights howling at the moon.

The polyfiber-filled bags are not necessarily better than those filled with down, but they can be. Their one key advantage is that even when wet, some poly-fills can retain up to 85 percent of your body heat. This allows you to sleep and get valuable rest even in miserable conditions. In my camping experience, no matter how lucky you may be, there will come

Even with the warmest sleeping bag in the world, if you just lay it down on the ground and try to sleep, you will likely get as cold as a winter cucumber. That is because the cold ground will suck the warmth right out of your body. The solution? A sleeping pad.

a time when you will get caught in an unexpected, violent storm and everything you've got will get wet, including your sleeping bag. That's when a poly-fill bag becomes priceless. You either have one and can sleep, or you don't have one and suffer. It is that simple. Of the synthetic fills, Quallofil made by DuPont is the industry leader.

But just because a sleeping bag uses a high-tech poly-fill doesn't necessarily make it a better bag. There are other factors.

The most important are a bag's temperature rating and weight. The temperature rating of a sleeping bag refers to how cold it can get outside before you start actually feeling cold. Many campers make the mistake of thinking, "I only camp in the summer, so a bag rated at 30 or 40°F should be fine." Later, they find out it isn't so fine, and all it takes is one cold night to convince them of that. When selecting the right temperature rating, visualize the coldest weather you might ever confront, and then get a bag rated for even colder weather.

For instance, if you are a summer camper, you may rarely experience a night in the low 30s or high 20s. A sleeping bag rated at 20°F would be appropriate, keeping you snug, warm, and asleep. For most campers, I advise bags rated at 0 or 10°F.

If you buy a poly-filled sleeping bag, never leave it squished in your stuff sack between camping trips. Instead, keep it on a hanger in a closet or use it as a blanket. One thing that can reduce a poly-filled bag's heat-retaining qualities is if the tiny hollow fibers that make up the fill lose their loft. You can avoid this with proper storage.

The weight of a sleeping bag can also be a key factor, especially for backpackers. When you have to carry your gear on your back, every ounce becomes important. Sleeping bags that weigh just three pounds are available, although they are expensive. But if you hike much, it's worth the price to keep your weight to a minimum. For an overnighter, you can get away with a 4- or 4.5-pound bag without much stress. However, bags weighing five pounds and up should be left back at the car.

I have two sleeping bags: a seven-pounder that feels like a giant sponge, and a four-pounder. The heavy-duty model is for pickup-truck camping in cold weather and doubles as a blanket at home. The lightweight bag is for hikes. Between the two, I'm set.

Insulation Pads

Even with the warmest sleeping bag in the world, if you just lay it down on the ground and try to sleep, you will likely get as cold as a winter cucumber. That is because the cold ground will suck the warmth right out of your body. The solution is to have a layer of insulation between you and the ground. For this, you can use a thin Insulite pad, a lightweight Therm-a-Rest inflatable pad, a foam pad or mattress, an air bed, or a cot. Here is a capsule summary of each:

• **Insulite pads:** They are light, inexpensive, roll up quickly for transport, and can double as a seat pad at your camp. The negative side is that in one night, they will compress, making you feel like you are sleeping on granite.

• **Therm-a-Rest pads:** These are a real luxury because they do everything an Insulite pad does, but they also provide a cushion. The negative side is that they are expensive by comparison, and if they get a hole in them, they become worthless without a patch kit.

• **Foam mattresses, air beds, and cots:** These are excellent for car campers. The new line of air beds, especially the thicker ones, are outstanding and inflate quickly with an electric motor inflator that plugs into a power plug or cigarette lighter in your vehicle. Foam mattresses are also excellent—in fact, the most comfortable of all—but their size precludes many from considering them. I've found that cots work great, too. I finally wore out an old wood one and replaced it immediately with one of the new high-tech, light metal ones. For camping in the back of a pickup truck with a camper shell, the cots with three-inch legs are best, of course.

A Few Tricks

When surveying a camp area, the most important consideration should be to select a good spot for sleeping. Everything else is secondary. Ideally, you want a flat area that is wind-sheltered and on ground soft enough to drive stakes into. Yeah, and I want to win the lottery, too.

Sometimes, the ground will have a slight slope to it. In that case, always sleep with your head on the uphill side. If you sleep parallel to the slope, every time you roll over, you'll find yourself rolling down the hill. If you sleep with your head on the downhill side, you'll get a headache that feels as if an ax is embedded in your brain.

When you've found a good spot, clear it of all branches, twigs, and rocks, of course. A good tip is to dig a slight indentation in the ground where your hip will fit. Since your body is not flat, but has curves and edges, it will not feel comfortable on flat ground. Some people even get severely bruised on the sides of their hips when sleeping on flat, hard ground. For that reason alone, they learn to hate camping. What a shame, especially when the problem is solved easily with a Therm-a-Rest pad, foam insulation, an air bed, or a cot.

After the ground is prepared, throw a ground cloth over the spot, which will keep much of the morning dew off you. In some areas, particularly where fog is a problem, morning dew can be heavy and get the outside of your sleeping bag quite wet. In that case, you need overhead protection, such as a tent or some kind of roof, like a poncho or tarp with its ends tied to trees.

Tents and Weather Protection

All it takes is to get caught in the rain once without a tent and you will never go anywhere without one again. A tent provides protection from rain, wind, and mosquito attacks. In exchange, you can lose a starry night's view, though some tents now even provide moon roofs.

A tent can be as complex as a four-season, tubular-jointed dome with a rain fly or as simple as two ponchos snapped together and roped up to a tree. They can be as cheap as a $10 tube tent, which is nothing more than a hollow piece of plastic, or as expensive as a $500 five-person deluxe expedition dome model. They vary greatly in size, price, and assembly time. For those who camp infrequently and want to buy a tent without paying much, off-brand models are available at considerable price discounts. My experience in field-testing outdoor gear, though, is that these tents often rip at the seams if subjected to regular use. If you plan on getting a good one, plan on doing plenty of shopping and asking lots of questions. With a little bit of homework, you can get the right answers to these questions:

WILL IT KEEP ME DRY?

On many one-person and two-person tents, the rain fly does not extend far enough to keep water off the bottom sidewalls of the tent. In a driving rain, water can also drip from the rain fly and onto those sections of the tent. Eventually, the water can leak through to the inside, particularly through the seams.

You must be able to stake out your rain fly so it completely covers all of the tent. If you are tent shopping and this does not appear possible, then don't buy the tent. To prevent potential leaks, use a seam waterproofer, such as Seam Lock, a gluelike substance that can close potential leak areas on tent seams. For large umbrella tents, keep a patch kit handy. Note that as of 2003, Coleman tents are guaranteed to keep campers dry.

Another way to keep water out of your tent is to store all wet garments outside the tent, under a poncho. Moisture from wet clothes stashed in the tent will condense on the interior tent walls. If you bring enough wet clothes into the tent, by the next morning you'll feel as if you're camping in a duck blind.

HOW HARD IS IT TO PUT UP?

If a tent is difficult to erect in full sunlight, you can just about forget it at night, especially the first night out. Some tents can go up in just a few minutes, without requiring help from another camper. This might be the kind of tent you want.

The way to compare put-up times when shopping for tents is to count the number of connecting points from the tent poles to the tent and the number of stakes required. The fewer, the better. Think simple. My two-person-plus-a-dog tent has seven connecting points and, minus the rain fly, requires no stakes. It goes up in a few minutes.

My bigger family tent, which has three rooms with walls, so we can keep our two kids, Jeremy and Kris, isolated on each side, takes about a half hour to put up. That's without anybody's help. With their help, add about 15 minutes. Heh, heh.

Another factor is the tent poles themselves. Some small tents have poles that are broken into small sections that are connected by bungee cords. It takes only an instant to convert them to a complete pole.

Some outdoor shops have tents on display on their showroom floors. Before buying the tent, have the salesperson take the tent down and put it back up. If it takes him more than five minutes, or he says he doesn't have time, then keep looking.

IS IT ROOMY ENOUGH?

Don't judge the size of a tent on floor space alone. Some tents that are small on floor space can give the illusion of roominess with a high ceiling. You can be quite comfortable and snug in them.

But remember that a one-person or two-person tent is just that. A two-person tent has room for two people plus gear. That's it. Don't buy a tent expecting it to hold more than it is intended to.

HOW MUCH DOES IT WEIGH?

If you're a hiker, this becomes the preeminent question. If it's much more than six or seven pounds, forget it. A 12-pound tent is bad enough, but get it wet and it's like carrying a piano on your back. On the other hand, weight is scarcely a factor if you camp only where you can take your car. My dad, for instance, used to have this giant canvas umbrella tent that folded down to a neat little pack that weighed about 500 pounds.

Family Tents

It is always worth spending the time and money to buy a tent you and your family will be happy with.

Many excellent family tents are available for $125–200, particularly from Cabela's, Coleman, Eureka!, North Face, Remington, and Sierra Designs. Guide-approved expedition tents for groups cost more, generally $350–600. Here is a synopsis of some of the best out there:

CABELA

Alaskan Guide Model
Deluxe Backwoods Three-Room Cabin
800/237-4444
www.cabelas.com

The Alaskan Guide series is based around a dome tent that can be connected by a tube to another dome tent. In use, it looks like a giant caterpillar, with dome tents that sleep four, or six to eight, on each end of a connector tube. It allows privacy without having to buy separate tents. A favorite for both families and professionals.

The beautiful forest-green, three-room cabin tent features a 10- by 20-foot floor available in different configurations with removable interior walls. Three doors mean everybody doesn't tromp through the center room for access to the side rooms. It will stand up to wind, rain, and frequent use.

COLEMAN

Sundome
Weathermaster
800/835-3278
www.coleman.com

Coleman Sundome tents are available in six different single- and multi-room designs.

The pole structure is unique, with two upright poles shock-corded together for an integrated system that makes setup extremely fast and easy. Mesh panels in the ceiling are a tremendous plus for ventilation.

The Weathermaster series features tents with multiple rooms, walls, and ample headroom, and they are guaranteed to keep rain out. The 17- by 9-foot model sleeps six to eight, has a 76-inch ceiling, and has zippered dividers. Since the dividers are removable, you can configure the tent in multiple layouts. The frame is designed with poles adjustable to three different heights to accommodate uneven ground.

Eureka
800/572-8822
www.EurekaTent.com

Eureka has some of the best new tents yet created in the 21st century. Most feature 2–3 poles and go up quickly, with strategically placed mesh panels and multiple hooded vents. The result is maximum airflow and little condensation build-up, even with four people. Tents come in multiple sizes, are lightweight, and feature plenty of space.

Kelty
800/423-2320
www.kelty.com

Kelty's top-of-the-line tents are based on a sleek dome profile. This is a great package, with mesh sides, tops, and doors, along with a full awning fly and coverage for weather protection. Clip sleeves and rubber-tipped poles for easy slide during setup are nice bonuses.

With the world going high-tech, **tents** of today vary greatly in complexity, size, price, and put-up time. And they wouldn't be fit for this new millennium without offering options such as moon roofs, rain flies, and tent wings. Be sure to buy the one that's right for your needs.

Bivouac Bags

If you like going solo and choose not to own a tent at all, a bivy bag, short for bivouac bag and pronounced "bivvy" as in dizzy, not "bivy" as in ivy, can provide the extremely lightweight weather protection you require. A bivy bag is a water-repellent shell in which your sleeping bag fits. It is light and tough, and for some is the perfect alternative to a heavy tent. My own bivy weighs 31 ounces and cost me $240; it's made by OR (Outdoor Research), and I just plain love the thing on expeditions. On the downside, however, it can be a bit difficult getting settled just right in it, and some say they feel claustrophobic in such close quarters. Once you get used to a bivy, spend a night in a tent; the tent will feel like a room at the Mirage.

The idea of riding out a storm in a bivy can be quite worrisome. You can hear the rain hitting you, and sometimes even feel the pounding of the drops through the bivy bag. For some, it can be unsettling to try to sleep under such circumstances. On the other hand, I've always looked forward to it. In cold weather, a bivy also helps keep you warm. I've had just one miserable night in mine. That was when my sleeping bag was a bit wet when I started the night. By the middle of the night, the water was condensing from the sleeping bag on the interior walls of the bivy, and then soaking the bag, like a storm cycle. The night hit only about 45°F but I just about froze to death anyway. Otherwise, I've used it on multi-week expeditions with great results: warm, dry quarters and deep, restful sleeps by night, and a pack lightened without carrying a tent by day.

Pickup Truck Campers

If you own a pickup truck with a camper shell, you can turn it into a self-contained campground with a little work. This can be an ideal way to go: It's fast, portable, and you are guaranteed a dry environment.

But that does not necessarily mean it is a warm environment. In fact, without insulation from the metal truck bed, it can be like trying to sleep on an iceberg. The metal truck bed will get as cold as the air temperature, which is often much colder than the ground temperature. Without insulation, it can be much colder in your camper shell than it would be on the open ground.

When I camp in my rig, I use a large piece of foam for a mattress and insulation. The foam measures four inches thick, 48 inches wide, and 76 inches long. It makes for a bed as comfortable as anything one might ask for. In fact, during the winter, if I don't go camping for a few weeks because of writing obligations, I sometimes will throw the foam on the floor, lay down the old sleeping bag, light a fire, and camp right in my living room. It's in my blood, I tell you. Air beds and cots are also extremely comfortable and I've used both many times. Whatever you choose, just make sure you have a comfortable sleeping unit. Good sleep makes for great camping trips.

KEEP IT WILD TIP 3: CAMP WITH CARE

1. Choose an existing, legal site. Restrict activities to areas where vegetation is compacted or absent.
2. Camp at least 75 steps (200 feet) from lakes, streams, and trails.
3. Always choose sites that won't be damaged by your stay.
4. Preserve the feeling of solitude by selecting camps that are out of view when possible.
5. Don't dig trenches or build structures or furniture.

RVs

The problems RVers encounter come from two primary sources: lack of privacy and light intrusion.

The lack of privacy stems from the natural restrictions of where a land yacht can go. Without careful use of the guide section of this book, motor-home owners can find themselves in parking-lot settings, jammed in with plenty of neighbors. Because RVs often have large picture windows, you lose your privacy, causing some late nights; then, come daybreak, light intrusion forces an early wake up. As a result, you get shorted on your sleep.

The answer is to carry inserts to fit over the inside of your windows. These close off the outside and retain your privacy. And if you don't want to wake up with the sun at daybreak, you don't have to. It will still be dark.

FIRST AID AND INSECT PROTECTION

Mountain nights don't get any more perfect, I thought as I lay in my sleeping bag.

The sky looked like a mass of jewels and the air tasted sweet and smelled of pines. A shooting star fireballed across the sky, and I remember thinking, "It just doesn't get any better."

Just then, as I was drifting into sleep, a mysterious buzz appeared from nowhere and deposited itself inside my left ear. Suddenly awake, I whacked my ear with the palm of my hand, hard enough to cause a minor concussion. The buzz disappeared. I pulled out my flashlight and shined it on my palm, and there, lit in the blackness of night, lay the squished intruder: a mosquito, dead amid a stain of blood.

Satisfied, I turned off the light, closed my eyes, and thought of the fishing trip planned for the next day. Then I heard them. It was a squadron of mosquitoes making landing patterns around my head. I tried to grab them with an open hand, but they dodged the assault and flew off. Just 30 seconds later, another landed in my left ear. I promptly dispatched the invader with a rip of the palm.

Now I was completely awake, so I got out of my sleeping bag to retrieve some mosquito repellent. But en route, several of the buggers swarmed and nailed me in the back and arms. After I applied the repellent and settled snugly again in my sleeping bag, the mosquitoes would buzz a few inches from my ear. After getting a whiff of the poison, they would fly off. It was like sleeping in a sawmill.

The next day, drowsy from little sleep, I set out to fish. I'd walked but 15 minutes when I brushed against a bush and felt a stinging sensation on the inside of my arm, just above the wrist. I looked down: A tick had his clamps in me. I ripped it out before he could embed his head into my skin.

After catching a few fish, I sat down against a tree to eat lunch and just watch the water go by. My dog, Rebel, sat down next to me and stared at the beef jerky I was munching as if it were a T-bone steak. I finished eating, gave him a small piece, patted him on the head, and said, "Good dog." Right then, I noticed an itch on my arm where a mosquito had drilled me. I unconsciously scratched it. Two days later, in that exact spot, some nasty red splotches started popping up. Poison oak. By petting my dog and then scratching my arm, I had transferred the oil residue of the poison oak leaves from Rebel's fur to my arm.

When I returned home, Foonsky asked me about the trip.

"Great," I said. "Mosquitoes, ticks, poison oak. Can hardly wait to go back."

"Sorry I missed out," he answered.

Mosquitoes, No-See-Ums, Horseflies

On a trip to Canada, Foonsky and I were fishing a small lake from the shore when suddenly a black horde of mosquitoes could be seen moving across the lake toward us. It was like when the French army looked across the Rhine and saw the Wehrmacht coming. There was a buzz in the air. We fought them off for a few minutes, then made a fast retreat to the truck and jumped in, content the buggers had been foiled. But in some way still unknown to us, the mosquitoes gained entry to the truck. In 10 minutes, we squished 15 of them as they attempted to plant their oil drills into our skins. Just outside the truck, the black horde waited for us to make a tactical error, such as rolling down a window. It finally took a miraculous hailstorm to squelch the attack.

When it comes to mosquitoes, no-see-ums, gnats, and horseflies, there are times when there is nothing you can do. However, in most situations, you can muster a defense to repel the attack.

The first key with mosquitoes is to wear clothing too heavy for them to drill through. Expose a minimum of skin, wear a hat, and tie a bandanna around your neck, preferably one that has been sprayed with repellent. If you try to get by with just a cotton T-shirt, you will be declared a federal mosquito sanctuary.

So, first, your skin must be well covered, with only your hands and face exposed. Second, you should have your companion spray your clothes with repellent. Third, you should dab liquid repellent directly on your skin.

At night, the easiest way to get a good sleep without mosquitoes buzzing in your ear is to sleep in a bug-proof tent. If the nights are warm and you want to see the stars, new tent models are available that have a skylight covered with mosquito netting. If you don't like tents on summer evenings, mosquito netting rigged with an air space at your head can solve the problem. Otherwise, prepare to get bitten, even with the use of mosquito repellent.

If your problems are with no-see-ums or biting horseflies, then you need a slightly different approach.

No-see-ums are tiny black insects that look like nothing more than a sliver of dirt on your skin. Then you notice something stinging, and when you rub the area, you scratch up a little no-see-um. The results are similar to mosquito bites, making your skin itch, splotch, and, when you get them bad, swell.

In addition to using the techniques described to repel mosquitoes, you should go one step further.

The problem is that no-see-ums are tricky little devils. Somehow, they can actually get under your socks and around your ankles, where they will bite to their hearts' content all night long while you sleep, itch, sleep, and itch some more. The best solution is to apply a liquid repellent to your ankles, then wear clean socks.

Horseflies are another story. They are rarely a problem, but when they get their dander up, they can cause trouble you'll never forget.

One such episode occurred when Foonsky and I were paddling a canoe along the shoreline of a large lake. This giant horsefly, about the size of a fingertip, started dive-bombing the canoe. After 20 minutes, it landed on Foonsky's thigh. He immediately slammed it with an open hand, then let out a blood-curdling "Yeeeee-ow!" that practically sent ripples across the lake. When Foonsky whacked it, the horsefly had somehow turned around and bit him on the hand, leaving a huge red welt.

In the next 10 minutes, that big fly strafed the canoe on more dive-bomb runs. I finally got my canoe paddle, swung it as if it were a baseball bat, and nailed that horsefly as if I'd hit a home run. It landed about 15 feet from the boat, still alive and buzzing in the water. While I was trying to figure what it would take to kill this bugger, a large rainbow trout surfaced and snatched it out of the water, finally avenging the assault.

If you have horsefly or yellow jacket problems, you'd best just leave the area. One, two, or a few can be dealt with. More than that and your fun camping trip will be about as fun as being roped to a tree and stung by an electric shock rod.

On most trips, you will spend time doing everything possible to keep from getting bitten by mosquitoes or no-see-ums. When your attempts fail, you must know what to do next, and fast, especially if you are among those ill-fated campers who get big, red lumps

KEEP IT WILD TIP 4: SANITATION

If no refuse facility is available:

1. Deposit human waste in "cat holes" dug 6–8 inches deep. Cover and disguise the cat hole when finished.

2. Deposit human waste at least 75 paces (200 feet) from any water source or camp.

3. Use toilet paper sparingly. When finished, carefully burn it in the cat hole, then bury it.

4. If no appropriate burial locations are available, such as in popular wilderness camps above tree line in granite settings, then all human refuse should be double-bagged and packed out.

5. At boat-in campsites, chemical toilets are required. Chemical toilets can also solve the problem of larger groups camping for long stays at one location where no facilities are available.

6. To wash dishes or your body, carry water away from the source and use small amounts of biodegradable soap. Scatter dishwater after all food particles have been removed.

7. Scour your campsites for even the tiniest piece of trash and any other evidence of your stay. Pack out all the trash you can, even if it's not yours. Finding cigarette butts, for instance, provides special irritation for most campers. Pick them up and discard them properly.

8. Never litter. Never. Or you become the enemy of all others.

---

from a bite inflicted from even a microscopic mosquito.

A fluid called After Bite or a dab of ammonia should be applied immediately to the bite. To start the healing process, apply a first-aid gel (not a liquid), such as the one made by Campho-Phenique.

DEET

What is DEET? You're not likely to find the word DEET on any repellent label. That's because DEET stands for N,N diethyl-m-toluamide. If the label contains this scientific name, the repellent contains DEET. Despite fears of DEET-associated health risks and the increased attention given natural alternatives, DEET-based repellents are still acknowledged as by far the best option when serious insect protection is required.

What are the health risks associated with using DEET? A number of deaths and a number of medical problems have been attributed in the press to DEET in recent years—

events that those in the DEET community vehemently deny as being specifically DEET-related, pointing to reams of scientific documentation as evidence. It does seem logical to assume that if DEET can peel paint, melt nylon, destroy plastic, wreck wood finishes, and damage fishing line, then it must be hell on the skin—perhaps worse.

On one trip, I had a small bottle of mosquito repellent in the same pocket as a Swiss army knife. Guess what happened? The mosquito repellent leaked a bit and literally melted the insignia right off the knife. DEET will also melt synthetic clothes. That is why, in bad mosquito country, I'll expose a minimum of skin, just hands and face (with full beard), apply the repellent only to my cheeks and the back of my hands, and perhaps wear a bandanna sprinkled with a few drops as well. That does the trick, with a minimum of exposure to the repellent.

Although nothing definitive has been published, a growing number in the scientific community believe that repeated applications of products containing low percentages of DEET can be potentially dangerous. It is theorized that this actually puts consumers at a greater risk for absorbing high levels of DEET into the body than if they had just used one application of a 30–50 percent DEET product with an efficacy of 4–6 hours. Also being studied is the possibility that low levels of DEET, which might not otherwise be of toxicological concern, may become hazardous if they are formulated with solvents or diluters (considered inert ingredients) that may enhance the absorption rate.

"NATURAL" REPELLENTS

Are natural alternatives a safer choice than DEET? To imply that essential oils are completely safe because they are natural products is not altogether accurate. Essential oils, while derived from plants that grow naturally, are chemicals too. Some are potentially hazardous if ingested, and most are downright painful if they find their way into the eyes or onto mucus membranes. For example, pennyroyal is perhaps the most toxic of the essential oils used to repel insects and can be deadly if taken internally. Other oils used include cedarwood, citronella (perhaps the most common, it's extracted from an aromatic grass indigenous to Southern Asia), eucalyptus, and peppermint.

Three citronella-based products—Avon's Skin-So-Soft, Buzz Away (manufactured by Quantum), and Natrapel (manufactured by Tender)—have received EPA registration and approval for sale as repellents against flies, gnats, midges, and mosquitoes.

How effective are natural repellents? While there are numerous studies cited by those on both the DEET and citronella sides of the fence, the average effective repelling time of a citronella product appears to range from 1.5 to two hours. Tests conducted at Cambridge University, England, comparing Natrapel to DEET-based Skintastic (a low-percentage DEET product) found citronella to be just

as effective in repelling mosquitoes. The key here is effectiveness and the amount of time until reapplication.

Citronella products work for up to two hours and then require reapplication (the same holds true for other natural formulations). Products using a low-percentage level of DEET also require reapplication every two hours to remain effective. So, if you're going outside for only a short period in an environment where insect bites are more an irritant than a hazard, you would do just as well to go natural.

What other chemical alternatives are there? Another line of defense against insects is the chemical permethrin, used on clothing, not on skin. Permethrin-based products are designed to repel and kill arthropods or crawling insects, making them a preferred repellent for ticks. The currently available products remain effective—repelling and killing chiggers, mosquitoes, and ticks—for two weeks and through two launderings.

Ticks

Ticks are nasty little vermin that will wait in ambush, jump on unsuspecting prey, and then crawl to a prime location before filling their bodies with their victim's blood.

I call them Dracula bugs, but by any name they can be a terrible camp pest. Ticks rest on grass and low plants and attach themselves to those who brush against the vegetation (dogs are particularly vulnerable). Typically, they can be found no more than 18 inches above ground, and if you stay on the trails, you can usually avoid them.

There are two common species of ticks. The common coastal tick is larger, brownish in color, and prefers to crawl around before putting its clamps on you. The feel of any bug crawling on your skin can be creepy, but consider it a forewarning of assault; you can just pick the tick off and dispatch it. The coastal tick's preferred destination is usually the back of your neck, just where the hairline starts. The other species, the wood tick, is small and black, and when he puts his clamps in, it's immediately painful. When a wood tick gets into a dog for a few days, it can cause a large red welt. In either case, ticks should be removed as soon as possible.

If you have hiked in areas infested with ticks, it is advisable to shower as soon as possible, washing your clothes immediately. If you just leave your clothes in a heap, a tick can crawl out and invade your home. They like warmth, and one way or another, they can end up in your bed. Waking up in the middle of the night with a tick crawling across your chest can be unsettling, to put it mildly.

Once a tick has its clampers in your skin, you must determine how long it has been there. If it has been a short time, the most painless and effective method for removal is to take a pair of sharp tweezers and grasp the little devil, making certain to isolate the mouth area, then pull him out. Reader Johvin Perry sent in the suggestion to coat the tick with Vaseline, which will cut off its oxygen supply, after which it may voluntarily give up the hunt.

If the tick has been in longer, you may wish to have a doctor extract it. Some people will burn a tick with a cigarette or poison it with lighter fluid, but neither is advisable. No matter how you do it, you must take care to remove all of the tick, especially its clawlike mouth.

The wound, however small, should then be cleansed and dressed. First, apply liquid peroxide, which cleans and sterilizes, and then apply a dressing coated with a first-aid gel, such as First-Aid Cream, Campho-Phenique, or Neosporin.

Lyme disease, which can be transmitted by the bite of a deer tick, is rare but common enough to warrant some attention. To prevent tick bites, some people tuck their pant legs into their hiking socks and spray tick repellent, called Permamone, on their pants.

The first symptom of Lyme disease is a bright red, splotchy rash that develops around the bite area. Other possible early symptoms include headache, nausea, fever, and/or a stiff neck. If any of these happen, or if you have any doubts, you should see your doctor immediately. If you do get Lyme disease, don't panic. Doctors say it is easily treated in the early stages with simple antibiotics. If you are nervous about getting Lyme disease, carry a small plastic bag with you when you hike. If a tick manages to get his clampers into you, put the tick in the plastic bag after you pull it out. Then give it to your doctor for analysis to see if the tick is a carrier of the disease.

During the course of my hiking and camping career, I have removed ticks from my skin hundreds of times without any problems. However, if you are worried about ticks, you can buy a tick removal kit from any outdoors store. These kits allow you to remove ticks in such a way that their toxins are guaranteed not to enter your bloodstream.

If you are particularly wary of ticks or perhaps even have nightmares of them, wear long pants that are tucked into your socks, as well as a long-sleeved shirt tucked securely into your pants and held with a belt. Clothing should be light in color, making it easier to see ticks, and tightly woven so ticks have trouble hanging on. On one hike with my mom, Eleanor, I brushed more than 100 ticks off my blue jeans in less than an hour, while she did not pick up a single one on her polyester pants.

Perform tick checks regularly, especially on the back of the neck. The combination of DEET insect repellents applied to the skin and permethrin repellents applied directly to clothing is considered to be the most effective line of defense against ticks.

Poison Oak

After a nice afternoon hike, about a five-miler, I was concerned about possible exposure to poison oak, so I immediately showered and put on clean clothes. Then I settled into a chair with my favorite foamy elixir to watch the end of a baseball game. The game went 18 innings; meanwhile, my dog, tired from the hike, went to sleep on my bare ankles.

A few days later, I had a case of poison oak. My feet looked as though they had been on fire and put out with an ice pick. The lesson? Don't always trust your dog, give him a bath as well, and beware of extra-inning ball games.

You can get poison oak only from direct contact with the oil residue from the plant's leaves. It can be passed in a variety of ways, as direct as skin-to-leaf contact or as indirect as leaf to dog, dog to sofa, sofa to skin. Once you have it, there is little you can do but feel horribly itchy. Applying Caladryl lotion or its equivalent can help because it contains antihistamines, which attack and dry the itch.

My pal Furniss offers a tip that may sound crazy but seems to work. You should expose the afflicted area to the hottest water you can stand, then suddenly immerse it in cold water. The hot water opens the skin pores and gets the "itch" out, and the cold water then quickly seals the pores.

In any case, you're a lot better off if you don't get poison oak to begin with. Remember that poison oak can disguise itself. In the spring, it is green; then it gradually turns reddish in the summer. By fall, it becomes a bloody, ugly-looking red. In the winter, it loses its leaves altogether and appears to be nothing more than the barren, brown sticks of a small plant. However, at any time and in any form, its contact with skin can quickly lead to infection.

Some people are more easily afflicted than others, but if you are one of the lucky few who aren't, don't cheer too loudly. While some people can be exposed to the oil residue of poison oak with little or no effect, the body's resistance can gradually be worn down with repeated exposure. At one time, I could practically play in the stuff and the only symptom would be a few little bumps on the inside of my wrist. Now, more than 15 years later, my resistance has broken down. If I merely brush against poison oak now, in a few days the exposed area can look as if it were used for a track meet.

So regardless of whether you consider your-

Avoiding Poison Oak: Remember the old Boy Scout saying: "Leaves of three, let them be."

self vulnerable or not, you should take heed to reduce your exposure. That can be done by staying on trails when you hike and making sure your dog does the same. Remember, the worst stands of poison oak are usually brush-infested areas just off the trail. Also protect yourself by dressing so your skin is completely covered, wearing long-sleeved shirts, long pants, and boots. If you suspect you've been exposed, immediately wash your clothes and then wash yourself with aloe vera, rinsing with a cool shower.

And don't forget to give your dog a bath as well.

Sunburn

The most common injury suffered on camping trips is sunburn, yet some people wear it as a badge of honor, believing that it somehow enhances their virility. Well, it doesn't. Neither do suntans. Too much sun can lead to serious burns or sunstroke.

Both are easy enough to avoid. Use a high-level sunscreen on your skin, apply lip balm, and wear sunglasses and a hat. If any area gets burned, apply first-aid cream, which will soothe and provide moisture to the parched skin.

The best advice is not to get even a suntan. Those who tan are involved in a practice that can eventually ruin their skin and possibly lead to cancer.

Giardia and Cryptosporidium

You have just hiked in to your backwoods spot, you're thirsty and a bit tired, but you smile as you consider the prospects. Everything seems perfect—there's not a stranger in sight, and you have nothing to do but relax with your pals.

You toss down your gear, grab your cup, dip it into the stream, and take a long drink of that ice-cold mountain water. It seems crystal pure and sweeter than anything you've ever tasted. It's not till later that you find out it can be just like drinking a cup of poison.

Whether you camp in the wilderness or not, if you hike, you're going to get thirsty. And if your canteen runs dry, you'll start eyeing any water source. Stop! Do not pass Go. Do not drink.

By drinking what appears to be pure mountain water without first treating it, you can ingest a microscopic protozoan called *Giardia lamblia*. The ensuing abdominal cramps can make you feel like your stomach and intestinal tract are in a knot, ready to explode. With that comes long-term diarrhea that is worse than even a bear could imagine.

Doctors call the disease giardiasis, or giardia for short, but it is difficult to diagnose. One friend of mine who contracted giardia was told he might have stomach cancer before the proper diagnosis was made.

Drinking directly from a stream or lake does not mean you will get giardia, but you are taking a giant chance. There is no reason to assume such a risk, potentially ruining your trip and enduring weeks of misery.

A lot of people are taking that risk. I made a personal survey of campers in the Yosemite National Park wilderness, and found that roughly only one in 10 was equipped with some kind of water-purification system. The result, according to the Public Health Service, is that an average of 4 percent of all backpackers and campers suffer giardiasis. According to the Parasitic Diseases Division of the Center for Infectious Diseases, the rates range from 1 percent to 20 percent across the country.

But if you get giardia, you are not going to care about the statistics. "When I got giardia, I just about wanted to die," said Henry McCarthy, a fellow camper. "For about 10 days, it was the most terrible thing I have ever experienced. And through the whole thing, I kept thinking, 'I shouldn't have drunk that water, but it seemed all right at the time.'"

That is the mistake most campers make. The stream might be running free, gurgling over boulders in the high country, tumbling into deep, oxygenated pools. It looks pure. Then in a few days, the problems suddenly start. Drinking untreated water from mountain streams is a lot like playing Russian roulette. Sooner or later the gun goes off.

FILTERS

There's really no excuse for going without a water filter: Handheld filters are getting more compact, lighter, easier to use, and often less expensive. Having to boil water or endure chemicals that leave a bad taste in the mouth has been all but eliminated.

With a filter, you just pump and drink. Filtering strains out microscopic contaminants, rendering the water clear and somewhat pure. How pure? That depends on the size of the filter's pores—what manufacturers call pore-size efficiency. A filter with a pore-size efficiency of one micron or smaller will remove protozoa, such as *Giardia lamblia* and cryptosporidium, as well as parasitic eggs and larva, but it takes a pore-size efficiency of less than 0.4 micron to remove bacteria. All but one of the filters recommended here do that.

Water filters are a wise investment since all wilderness water should be considered contaminated. Make sure the filter can be easily cleaned or has a replaceable cartridge. The filter pores must be 0.4 micron or less to remove bacteria.

A good backcountry water filter weighs less than 20 ounces, is easy to grasp, simple to use, and a snap to clean and maintain. At the very least, buy one that will remove protozoa and bacteria. (A number of cheap, pocket-sized filters remove only *Giardia lamblia* and cryptosporidium. That, in my book, is risking your health to save money.) Consider the flow rate, too: A liter per minute is good.

All filters will eventually clog—it's a sign that they've been doing their job. If you force water through a filter that's becoming difficult to pump, you risk injecting a load of microbial nasties into your bottle. Some models can be back-washed, brushed, or, as with ceramic elements, scrubbed to extend their useful lives. And if the filter has a pre-filter to screen out the big stuff, use it: It will give your filter a boost in mileage, which can then top out at about 100 gallons per disposable element. Any of the filters reviewed here will serve well on an outing into the wilds, providing you always play by the manufacturer's rules. They cost about $35–75, up to more than $200, depending on the volume of water they are constructed to filter.

• **First Need:** The First Need water filters from General Ecology (www.generalecology.com) do something no other handheld filter will do: It removes protozoa, bacteria, and viruses without using chemicals. Such effectiveness is the result of a fancy three-stage matrix system. Unfortunately, if you drop the filter and unknowingly crack the cartridge, all the little nasties can get through. General Ecology's solution is to include a bottle of blue dye that indicates breaks. The issue hasn't scared off too many folks, though: The First Need has been around since 1982. A final note: The filter pumps smoothly and puts out more than a liter per minute. A favorite of mine.

• **Katadyn Mini:** The Mini Filter is a much more compact version of Katadyn's (www.katadyn.com) venerable Pocket Filter. This one weighs just eight ounces, ideal for the minimalist backcountry traveler, and it effectively removes protozoa and bacteria. A palm-of-the-hand-size filter, however, makes it challenging to put any kind of power behind the pump's tiny handle, and the filtered water comes through at a paltry half-liter per minute. It also requires more cleaning than most filters—though the good news is that the element is made of long-lasting ceramic. Ironically, one option lets you buy the Mini Filter with a carbon element instead of the ceramic. The pumping is easier and the flow rate is better, but I'd only go that route if you'll be pumping from clear mountain streams.

• **MSR SweetWater WalkAbout:** The SweetWater (http://cascadedesigns.com) is perfect for the day hiker or backpacker who obsesses on lightening the load. The filter weighs just 11 ounces, is easily cleaned in the field, and removes both protozoa and bacteria: a genuine bargain. There are some trade-offs, however, for its diminutiveness. Water delivery is a tad slow at just under a liter per minute, but redesigned filter cartridges are good for up to 100 gallons.

• **MSR MiniWorks:** Like the MSR SweetWater, the reasonably priced MiniWorks (http://cascadedesigns.com) has a bigger and more expensive water-filtering brother. But in this case, the differences are harder to discern: The 14.6-ounce MiniWorks looks similar to the MSR WaterWorks II and, like the WaterWorks, is fully field-maintainable, while guarding against protozoa, bacteria, and chemicals. But the Mini is the best-executed, easiest-to-use ceramic filter on the market, and it attaches directly to a standard one-quart Nalgene water bottle. Too bad it takes 90 seconds to filter that quart.

• **PentaPure:** The PentaPure Water Purification System (www.pentapure.net) from WTC/Ecomaster offers drinkable water with a twist: You squeeze and sip instead of pumping. Weighing 6.5 ounces, the system packages a three-stage filter inside a 21-ounce-capacity sport bottle with an angled and sealing drinking nozzle, ideal for mountain bikers. The filter removes and/or kills protozoa, bacteria, and viruses, so it's also suitable for world travel. It's certainly convenient: Just fill the bottle with untreated water, screw on the cap, give it a firm squeeze (don't expect the easy flow of a normal sport bottle; there's more work being done), and sip. The Oasis only runs into trouble if the water source is shallow; you'll need a cup for scooping.

The big drawback with filters is that if you pump water from a mucky lake, the filter can clog in a few days. Therein lies the weakness. Once plugged up, it is useless, and you have to replace it or take your chances. One trick to extend the filter life is to fill your cook pot with water, let the sediment settle, then pump from there. As an insurance policy, always have a spare filter canister on hand.

BOILING WATER

Except for water filtration, this is the only treatment that you can use with complete confidence. According to the federal Parasitic Diseases Division, it takes a few minutes at a rolling boil to be certain you've killed *Giardia lamblia.* At high elevations, boil for 3–5 minutes. A side benefit is that you'll also kill other dangerous bacteria that live undetected in natural waters.

But to be honest, boiling water is a thorn for most people on backcountry trips. For one thing, if you boil water on an open fire, what should taste like crystal-pure mountain water tastes instead like a mouthful of warm ashes. If you don't have a campfire, it wastes stove fuel. And if you are thirsty *now,* forget it. The water takes hours to cool.

The only time boiling always makes sense, however, is when you are preparing dinner. The ash taste will disappear in whatever freeze-dried dinner, soup, or hot drink you make.

WATER-PURIFICATION PILLS

Pills are the preference for most backcountry campers, and this can get them in trouble. At just $3–8 per bottle, which can figure up to just a few cents per canteen, they do come cheap. In addition, they kill most of the bacteria, regardless of whether you use iodine crystals or potable aqua iodine tablets. The problem is they just don't always kill *Giardia lamblia,* and that is the one critter worth worrying about on your trip. That makes water-treatment pills unreliable and dangerous.

Another key element is the time factor. Depending on the water's temperature, organic content, and pH level, these pills can take a long time to do the job. A minimum wait of 20 minutes is advised. Most people don't like waiting that long, especially when they're hot and thirsty after a hike and thinking, "What the heck, the water looks fine."

And then there is the taste. On one trip, my water filter clogged and we had to use the iodine pills instead. It doesn't take long to get tired of iodine-tinged water. Mountain water should be one of the greatest tasting beverages of the world, but the iodine kills that.

No Treatment

This is your last resort and, using extreme care, can be executed with success. One of my best hiking buddies, Michael Furniss, is a nationally renowned hydrologist, and on wilderness trips he has shown me the difference between safe and dangerous water sources.

Long ago, people believed that just finding water running over a rock was a guarantee of its purity. Imagine that. What we've learned is that the safe water sources are almost always small springs in high, craggy mountain areas. The key is making sure no one has been upstream from where you drink. We drink untreated water only when we can see the source, such as a spring.

Furniss mentioned that another potential problem in bypassing water treatment is that even in settings free of *Giardia lamblia,* you can still ingest other bacteria that cause stomach problems.

Hypothermia

No matter how well planned your trip might be, a sudden change in weather can turn it into a puzzle for which there are few answers. Bad weather or an accident can set in motion a dangerous chain of events.

Such a chain of episodes occurred for my brother Rambob and me on a fishing trip one fall day just below the snow line. The weather had suddenly turned very cold, and ice was forming along the shore of the lake. Suddenly, the canoe became terribly imbalanced, and, just that quickly, it flipped. The little life vest seat cushions were useless, and using the canoe as a paddleboard, we tried to kick our way back to shore where my dad was going crazy at the thought of his two sons drowning before his eyes.

It took 17 minutes in that 38-degree water, but we finally made it to shore. When they pulled me out of the water, my legs were dead, not strong enough even to hold up my weight. In fact, I didn't feel so much cold as tired, and I just wanted to lie down and go to sleep.

I closed my eyes, and my brother-in-law, Lloyd Angal, slapped me in the face several times, then got me on my feet and pushed and pulled me about.

In the celebration over our making it to shore, only Lloyd had realized that hypothermia was setting in. Hypothermia is the condition in which the temperature of the body is lowered to the point that it causes poor reasoning, apathy, and collapse. It can look like the afflicted person is just tired and needs to sleep, but that sleep can be the first step toward a coma.

Ultimately, my brother and I shared what little dry clothing remained. Then we began hiking around to get muscle movement, creating internal warmth. We ate whatever munchies were available because the body produces heat by digestion. But most important, we got our heads as dry as possible. More body heat is lost through wet hair than any other single factor.

A few hours later, we were in a pizza parlor replaying the incident, talking about how only a life vest can do the job of a life vest. We decided never again to rely on those little flotation seat cushions that disappear when the boat flips.

We had done everything right to prevent hypothermia: Don't go to sleep, start a physical activity, induce shivering, put dry clothes on, dry your head, and eat something. That's how you fight hypothermia. In a dangerous situation, whether you fall in a lake or a stream or get caught unprepared in a storm, that's how you can stay alive.

After being in that ice-bordered lake for almost 20 minutes and then finally pulling ourselves to the shoreline, we discovered a strange thing. My canoe was flipped right-side up and almost all of its contents were lost: tackle box, flotation cushions, and cooler. But remaining were one paddle and one fishing rod, the trout rod my grandfather had given me for my 12th birthday.

Lloyd gave me a smile. "This means that you are meant to paddle and fish again," he said with a laugh.

Getting Unlost

I could not have been more lost. There I was, a guy who is supposed to know about these things, transfixed by confusion, snow, and hoofprints from a big deer.

I discovered that it is actually quite easy to get lost. If you don't get your bearings, getting found is the difficult part. This occurred on a wilderness trip where I'd hiked in to a remote lake and then set up a base camp for a deer hunt.

"There are some giant bucks up on that rim," confided Mr. Furnai, who lives near the area. "But it takes a mountain man to even get close to them."

That was a challenge I answered. After four-wheeling it to the trailhead, I tromped off with pack and rifle, gut-thumped it up 100 switchbacks over the rim, then followed a creek drainage up to a small but beautiful lake. The area was stark and nearly treeless, with bald granite broken only by large boulders. To keep from getting lost, I marked my route with piles of small rocks to act as directional signs for the return trip.

But at daybreak the next day, I stuck my head out of my tent and found eight inches of snow on the ground. I looked up into a gray sky filled by huge, cascading snowflakes.

Visibility was about 50 yards, with fog on the mountain rim. "I better get out of here and get back to my truck," I said to myself. "If my truck gets buried at the trailhead, I'll never get out."

After packing quickly, I started down the mountain. But after 20 minutes, I began to get disoriented. You see, all the little piles of rocks I'd stacked to mark the way were now buried in snow, and I had only a smooth white blanket of snow to guide me. Everything looked the same, and it was snowing even harder now.

Five minutes later, I started chewing on some jerky to keep warm, then suddenly stopped. Where was I? Where was the creek drainage? Isn't this where I was supposed to cross over a creek and start the switchbacks down the mountain?

Right then, I looked down and saw the tracks of a huge deer, the kind Mr. Furnai had talked about. What a predicament: I was

To keep from getting lost (above tree line or in sparse vegetation), mark your route with **trail ducks,** small piles of rock that act as directional signs for the return trip.

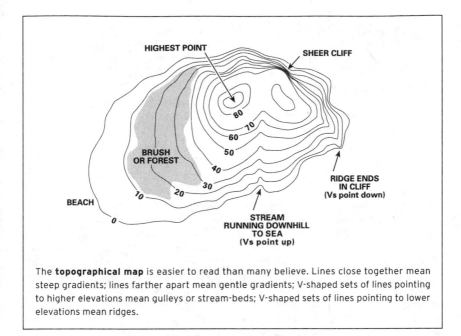

HIGHEST POINT   SHEER CLIFF

80
70
60
50
BRUSH
OR FOREST
40
30
10   20
BEACH
RIDGE ENDS
IN CLIFF
(Vs point down)
0
STREAM
RUNNING DOWNHILL
TO SEA
(Vs point up)

The **topographical map** is easier to read than many believe. Lines close together mean steep gradients; lines farther apart mean gentle gradients; V-shaped sets of lines pointing to higher elevations mean gulleys or stream-beds; V-shaped sets of lines pointing to lower elevations mean ridges.

lost and snowed in and seeing big hoofprints in the snow. Part of me wanted to abandon all safety and go after that deer, but a little voice in the back of my head won out. "Treat this as an emergency," it said.

The first step in any predicament is to secure your present situation, that is, to make sure it does not get any worse. I unloaded my rifle (too easy to slip, fall, and have a misfire), took stock of my food (three days' worth), camp fuel (plenty), and clothes (rain gear keeping me dry). Then I wondered, "Where the hell am I?"

I took out my map, compass, and altimeter, then opened the map and laid it on the snow. It immediately began collecting snowflakes. I set the compass atop the map and oriented it to north. Because of the fog, there was no way to spot landmarks, such as prominent mountaintops, to verify my position. Then I checked the altimeter, which read 4,900 feet. Well, the elevation at my lake was 5,320 feet. That was critical information.

I scanned the elevation lines on the map and was able to trace the approximate area of my position, somewhere downstream from the lake, yet close to a 4,900-foot elevation. "Right here," I said, pointing to a spot on the map with my finger. "I should pick up the switchback trail down the mountain somewhere off to the left, maybe just 40 or 50 yards away."

Slowly and deliberately, I pushed through the light, powdered snow. In five minutes, I suddenly stopped. To the left, across a 10-foot depression in the snow, appeared a flat spot that veered off to the right. "That's it! That's the crossing."

In minutes, I was working down the switchbacks, on my way, no longer lost. I thought of the hoofprints I had seen, and now that I knew my position, I wanted to head back and spend the day hunting. Then I looked up at the sky, saw it filled with falling snowflakes, and envisioned my truck buried deep in snow. Alas, this time logic won out over dreams.

In a few hours, now trudging through more than a foot of snow, I was at my truck at a spot called Doe Flat, and next to it was a giant, all-terrain U.S. Forest Service vehicle and two rangers.

"Need any help?" I asked them.

They just laughed. "We're here to help you," one answered. "It's a good thing you filed a trip plan with our district office in Gasquet. We wouldn't have known you were out here."

"Winter has arrived," said the other. "If we don't get your truck out now, it will be stuck here until next spring. If we hadn't found you, you might have been here until the end of time."

They connected a chain from the rear axle of their giant rig to the front axle of my truck and started towing me out, back to civilization. On the way to pavement, I figured I had gotten some of the more important lessons of my life. Always file a trip plan and have plenty of food, fuel, and a camp stove you can rely on. Make sure your clothes, weather gear, sleeping bag, and tent will keep you dry and warm. Always carry a compass, altimeter, and map with elevation lines, and know how to use them, practicing in good weather to get the feel of it.

And if you get lost and see the hoofprints of a giant deer, well, there are times when it is best to pass them by.

CATCHING FISH, AVOIDING BEARS, AND HAVING FUN

Feet tired and hot, stomachs growling, we stopped our hike for lunch beside a beautiful little river pool that was catching the flows from a long but gentle waterfall. My brother Rambob passed me a piece of jerky. I took my boots off, then slowly dunked my feet into the cool, foaming water.

I was gazing at a towering peak across a canyon when suddenly, Wham! There was a quick jolt at the heel of my right foot. I pulled my foot out of the water to find that, incredibly, a trout had bitten it.

My brother looked at me as if I had antlers growing out of my head. "Wow!" he exclaimed. "That trout almost caught himself an outdoors writer!"

It's true that in remote areas trout sometimes bite on almost anything, even feet. On one high-country trip, I caught limits of trout using nothing but a bare hook. The only problem is that the fish will often hit the splitshot sinker instead of the hook. Of course, fishing isn't usually that easy. But it gives you an idea of what is possible.

America's wildlands are home to a remarkable abundance of fish and wildlife. Deer browse with little fear of man, bears keep an eye out for your food, and little critters, such as squirrels and chipmunks, are daily companions. Add in the fishing, and you've got yourself a camping trip.

Your camping adventures will evolve into premium outdoor experiences if you can work in a few good fishing trips, avoid bear problems, and occasionally add a little offbeat fun with some camp games.

Trout and Bass

He creeps up on the stream as quietly as an Indian scout, keeping his shadow off the water. With his little spinning rod he'll zip his lure within an inch or two of its desired mark, probing along rocks, the edges of riffles, pocket water, or wherever he can find a change in river habitat. Rambob is trout fishing, and he's a master at it.

In most cases, he'll catch a trout on his first or second cast. After that, it's time to move up the river, giving no spot much more than five minutes' due. Stick and move, stick and move, stalking the stream like a bobcat zeroing in on an unsuspecting rabbit. He might keep a few trout for dinner, but mostly he releases what he catches. Rambob doesn't necessarily fish for food. It's the feeling that comes with it.

You don't need a million dollars' worth of fancy gear to catch fish. What you need is the right outlook, and that can be learned. That goes regardless of whether you are fishing for trout or bass, the two most popular fisheries in the United States. Your fishing tackle selection should be as simple and clutter-free as possible.

At home, I've got every piece of fishing tackle you might imagine, more than 30 rods and many tackle boxes, racks and cabinets filled with all kinds of stuff. I've got one lure that looks like a chipmunk and another that resembles a miniature can of beer with hooks. If I hear of something new, I want to try it and usually do. It's a result of my lifelong fascination with the sport.

But if you just want to catch fish, there's an easier way to go. And when I go fishing, I take that path. I don't try to bring everything. It would be impossible. Instead, I bring a relatively small amount of gear. At home, I scan my tackle boxes for equipment and lures, make my selections, and bring just the essentials. Rod, reel, and tackle will fit into a side pocket of my backpack or a small carrying bag.

So what kind of rod should be used on an outdoor trip? For most camper/anglers, I suggest the use of a light, multipiece spinning rod that will break down to a small size. The lowest-priced, quality six-piece rod on the market is the Daiwa 6.5-foot pack rod, number 6752, which is made of a graphite/glass composite that gives it the quality of a much more expensive model. And it comes in a hard plastic carrying tube for protection. Other major rod manufacturers, such as Fenwick, offer similar premium rods. It's tough to miss with any of them.

The use of graphite/glass composites in fishing rods has made them lighter and more sensitive, yet stronger. The only downside to graphite as a rod material is that it can be brittle. If you rap your rod against something, it can crack or cause a weak spot. That weak spot can eventually snap under even light pressure, like setting a hook or casting. Of course, a bit of care will prevent that from ever occurring.

If you haven't bought a fishing reel in some time, you will be surprised at the quality and price of micro spinning reels on the market. The reels come tiny and strong, with rear-control drag systems. Among others, Abu, Cardinal, Shimano, Sigma all make premium reels. They're worth it. With your purchase, you've just bought a reel that will last for years and years.

The one downside to spinning reels is that after long-term use, the bail spring will weaken. As a result, after casting and beginning to reel, the bail will sometimes not flip over and allow the reel to retrieve the line. Then you have to do it by hand. This can be incredibly frustrating, particularly when stream fishing, where instant line pickup is essential. The solution is to have a new bail spring installed every few years. This is a cheap, quick operation for a tackle expert.

You might own a giant tackle box filled with lures but, on your fishing trip, you are better off to fit just the essentials into a small container. One of the best ways to do that is to use the Plano Micro-Magnum 3414, a tiny two-sided tackle box for trout anglers that fits into a shirt pocket. In mine, I can fit 20 lures in one side of the box and 20 flies, splitshot, and snap swivels in the other. For bass lures, which are bigger, you need a slightly larger box, but the same principle applies.

There are more fishing lures on the market than you can imagine, but a few special ones can do the job. I make sure these are in my box on every trip. For trout, I carry a small black Panther Martin spinner with yellow spots, a small gold Kastmaster, a yellow Roostertail, a gold Z-Ray with red spots, a Super Duper, and a Mepps Lightning spinner.

You can take it a step further using insider's wisdom. My old pal Ed "the Dunk" showed me his trick of taking a tiny Dardevle spoon, spray painting it flat black, and dabbing five tiny red dots on it. It's a real killer, particularly in tiny streams where the trout are spooky.

The best trout catcher I've ever used on rivers is a small metal lure called a Met-L Fly. On days when nothing else works, it can be like going to a shooting gallery. The problem is that the lure is nearly impossible to find. Rambob and I consider the few we have remaining so valuable that if the lure is snagged on a rock, a cold swim is deemed mandatory for its retrieval. These lures are as hard to find in tackle shops as trout can be to catch without one.

For bass, you can also fit all you need into a small plastic tackle box. I have fished with many bass pros, and all of them actually use just a few lures: a white spinner bait, a small jig called a Gits-It, a surface plug called a Zara Spook, and plastic worms. At times, like when the bass move into shoreline areas during the spring, shad minnow imitations like those made by Rebel or Rapala can be dynamite. My favorite is the one-inch, blue-silver Rapala. Every spring as the lakes begin to warm and the fish snap out of their winter doldrums, I like to float and paddle around in my small raft. I'll cast that little Rapala along the shoreline and catch and release hun-dreds of bass, bluegill, and sunfish. The fish are usually sitting close to the shoreline, await-ing my offering.

Fishing Tips

There's an old angler's joke about how you need to think like a fish. But if you're the one getting zilched, you may not think it's so funny.

The irony is that it is your mental approach, what you see and what you miss, that often determines your fishing luck. Some people will spend a lot of money on tackle, lures, and fishing clothes, and that done, just saunter up to a stream or lake, cast out, and wonder why they are not catching fish. The answer is their mental outlook. They are not attuning themselves to their surroundings.

Basic Steps to Cleaning a Fish: First, slit belly from anal vent to gills. Then sever lower junctions of gills. Next, pull out innards and gills. And last but not least, run thumbnail along cavity to clean out dark matter.

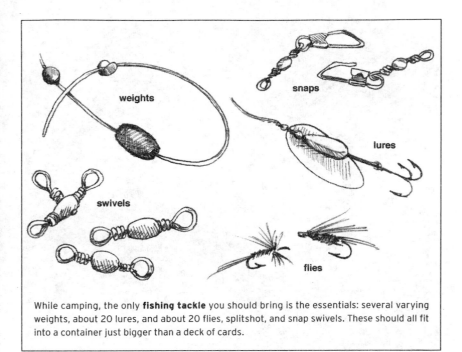

While camping, the only **fishing tackle** you should bring is the essentials: several varying weights, about 20 lures, and about 20 flies, splitshot, and snap swivels. These should all fit into a container just bigger than a deck of cards.

You must live on nature's level, not your own. Try this and you will become aware of things you never believed even existed. Soon you will see things that will allow you to catch fish. You can get a head start by reading about fishing, but to get your degree in fishing, you must attend the University of Nature.

On every fishing trip, regardless of what you fish for, try to follow three hard-and-fast rules:

1. Always approach the fishing spot so you will be undetected.

2. Present your lure, fly, or bait in a manner so it appears completely natural, as if no line was attached.

3. Stick and move, hitting one spot, working it the best you can, then moving to the next.

APPROACH

No one can just walk up to a stream or lake, cast out, and start catching fish as if someone had waved a magic wand. Instead, give the fish credit for being smart. After all, they live there.

Your approach must be completely undetected by the fish. Fish can sense your presence through sight and sound, though these factors are misinterpreted by most people. By sight, fish rarely actually see you; more often, they see your shadow on the water or the movement of your arm or rod while casting. By sound, they don't necessarily hear you talking, but they do detect the vibrations of your footsteps along the shore, a rock being kicked, or the unnatural plunking sound of a heavy cast hitting the water. Any of these elements can spook them off the bite. In order to fish undetected, you must walk softly, keep your shadow off the water, and keep your casting motion low. All of these key elements become easier at sunrise or sunset, when shadows are on the water. At midday, the sun is at its peak, causing a high level of light penetration in the water. This can make the fish skittish to any foreign presence.

Like a hunter, you must stalk the spots. When my brother Rambob sneaks up on a

The rule of the wild is that wildlife will congregate wherever there is a distinct change in habitat. To find where fish are hiding, look where a riffle pours into a small pond, where a rapid plunges into a deep hole and flattens, and around submerged trees, rock piles, and boulders in the middle of a long riffle.

fishing spot, he is like a burglar sneaking through an unlocked window.

PRESENTATION

Your lure, fly, or bait must appear in the water as if no line were attached, so it looks as natural as possible. My pal Mo Furniss has skin-dived in rivers to watch what the fish see when somebody is fishing.

"You wouldn't believe it," he said. "When the lure hits the water, every trout within 40 feet, like 15, 20 trout, will do a little zigzag. They all see the lure and are aware something is going on. Meanwhile, onshore the guy casting doesn't get a bite and thinks there aren't any fish in the river."

If your offering is aimed at fooling a fish into striking, it must appear as part of the natural habitat, like an insect just hatching or a small fish looking for a spot to hide. That's where you come in.

After you have sneaked up on a fishing spot, you should zip your cast upstream and start your retrieval as soon as it hits the water. If you let the lure sink to the bottom and then start the retrieval, you have no chance. A minnow, for instance, does not sink to the bottom, then start swimming. On rivers, the retrieval should be more of a drift, as if the "minnow" is in trouble and the current is sweeping it downstream.

When fishing on trout streams, always hike and cast upriver and retrieve as the offering drifts downstream in the current. This is effective because trout will sit almost motionless, pointed upstream, finning against the current. This way, they can see anything coming their direction, and if a potential food morsel arrives, all they need to do is move over a few inches, open their mouths, and they've got an easy lunch. Thus, you must cast upstream.

Conversely, if you cast downstream, your retrieval will bring the lure from behind the fish, where he cannot see it approaching. And I've never seen a trout that had eyes in its tail. In addition, when retrieving a downstream lure, the river current will tend to sweep your lure inshore to the rocks.

FINDING SPOTS

A lot of anglers don't catch fish, and a lot of hikers never see any wildlife. The key is where they are looking.

The rule of the wild is that fish and wildlife will congregate wherever there is a distinct change in the habitat. This is where you should begin your search. To find deer, for instance, forget probing a thick forest, but look for where it breaks into a meadow or a clearcut has splayed a stand of trees. That's where the deer will be.

In a river, it can be where a riffle pours into a small pool, a rapid plunges into a deep hole and flattens, a big boulder in the middle of a long riffle, a shoreline point, a rock pile, a submerged tree. Look for the changes. Conversely, long, straight stretches of shoreline will not hold fish—the habitat is lousy.

On rivers, the most productive areas are often where short riffles tumble into small oxygenated pools. After sneaking up from the downstream side and staying low, you should zip your cast so the lure plops gently into the white water just above the pool. Start your retrieval instantly; the lure will drift downstream and plunk into the pool. Bang! That's where the trout will hit. Take a few more casts and then head upstream to the next spot.

With a careful approach and lure presentation and by fishing in the right spots, you have the ticket to many exciting days on the water.

Of Bears and Food

The first time you come nose-to-nose with a bear can make your skin quiver.

Even the sight of mild-mannered black bears, the most common bear in America, can send shock waves through your body. They weigh 250–400 pounds and have large claws and teeth that are made to scare campers. When they bound, the muscles on their shoulders roll like ocean breakers.

Bears in camping areas are accustomed to sharing the mountains with hikers and campers. They have become specialists in the food-raiding business. As a result, you must be able to bear-proof your camp or be able to scare the fellow off. Many campgrounds provide bear- and raccoon-proof food lockers. In most wilderness areas, bear-proof food canisters are required. Never leave your food or trash in your car!

If you are staying at one of the backpack sites listed in this book, there will be no food lockers available. Your car will not be there, either. The solution is to make a bear-proof food hang, suspending all of your food wrapped in a plastic garbage bag from a rope in midair, 10 feet from the trunk of a tree and 20 feet off the ground. (Counterbalancing two bags

with a rope thrown over a tree limb is very effective, but finding an appropriate limb can be difficult.)

The food hang is accomplished by tying a rock to a rope, then throwing it over a high but sturdy tree limb. Next, tie your food bag to the rope and hoist it in the air. When you are satisfied with the position of the food bag, tie off the end of the rope to another tree. In an area frequented by bears, a good food bag is a necessity—nothing else will do.

I've been there. On one trip, my pal Foonsky and my brother Rambob left to fish. I was stoking up an evening campfire when I felt the eyes of an intruder on my back. I turned

minimum 10 feet

minimum diameter 1 inch

minimum diameter 4 inch

heavy stick

minimum 22 feet to ground

food wrapped in plastic bags

minimum 20 feet to food bags

In an area frequented by bears, a good **bear-proof food hang** is a must. Food should be stored in a plastic bag 10 feet from the trunk of the tree and at least 20 feet from the ground.

around and saw a big bear heading straight for our camp. In the next half hour, I scared the bear off twice, but then he got a whiff of something sweet in my brother's pack.

The bear rolled into camp like a truck, grabbed the pack, ripped it open, and plucked out the Tang and the Swiss Miss. The 350-pounder then sat astride a nearby log and lapped at the goodies like a thirsty dog drinking water.

Once a bear gets his mitts on your gear, he considers it his. I took two steps toward the pack, and that bear jumped off the log and galloped across the camp right at me. Scientists say a man can't outrun a bear, but they've never seen how fast I can go up a granite block with a bear on my tail.

Shortly thereafter, Foonsky returned to find me perched on top of the rock and demanded to know how I could let a bear get our Tang. It took all three of us, Foonsky, Rambob, and me, charging at once and shouting like madmen, to clear the bear out of camp and send him off over the ridge. We learned never to let food sit unattended.

The Grizzly

When it comes to grizzlies, well, my friends, you need what we call an attitude adjustment. Or that big ol' bear may just decide to adjust your attitude for you, making your stay at the park a short one.

Grizzlies are nothing like black bears. They are bigger, stronger, have little fear, and take what they want. Some people believe there are many different species of this critter, such as Alaskan brown, silvertip, cinnamon, and Kodiak, but the truth is they are all grizzlies. Any difference in appearance has to do with diet, habitat, and life habits, not speciation. By any name, they all come big.

The first thing you must do is determine if there are grizzlies in the area where you are camping. That can usually be done by asking local rangers. If you are heading into Yellowstone or Glacier National Park, or the Bob Marshall Wilderness of Montana, well, you don't have to ask. They're out there, and they're the biggest and potentially most dangerous critters you could run into.

One general way to figure the size of a bear is from his footprint. Take the width of the footprint in inches, add one to it, and you'll have an estimated length of the bear in feet. For instance, a nine-inch footprint equals a 10-foot bear. Any bear that big is a grizzly. In fact, most grizzly footprints average about 9–10 inches across, and black bears (though they may be brown in color) tend to have footprints only 4.5–6 inches across.

Most encounters with grizzlies occur when hikers fall into a silent march in the wilderness with the wind in their faces, and they walk around a corner and right into a big, unsuspecting grizzly. If you do this and see a big hump just behind its neck, don't think twice. It's a grizzly.

And then what should you do? Get up a tree, that's what. Grizzlies are so big that their claws cannot support their immense weight, and thus they cannot climb trees. And although young grizzlies can climb, they rarely want to get their mitts on you.

If you do get grabbed, every instinct in your body will tell you to fight back. Don't believe it. Play dead. Go limp. Let the bear throw you around a little. After awhile, you'll become unexciting play material and the bear will get bored. My grandmother was grabbed by a grizzly in Glacier National Park and, after a few tosses and hugs, was finally left alone to escape.

Some say it's a good idea to tuck your head under his chin, since that way the bear will be unable to bite your head. I'll take a pass on that one. If you are taking action, any action, it's a signal that you are a force to be reckoned with, and he'll likely respond with more aggression. And bears don't lose many wrestling matches.

What grizzlies really like to do, believe it or not, is to pile a lot of sticks and leaves on you.

GRIZZLY BEAR TERRITORY

If you are hiking in a wilderness area in Canada or Alaska that may have grizzlies, it is necessary to wear bells on your pack (grizzlies are not a problem in California, but you do not want to attract the native bears either). That way the bear will hear you coming and likely get out of your way. Keep talking, singing, or maybe even debating the country's foreign policy, but do not fall into a silent hiking vigil. And if a breeze is blowing in your face, you must make even more noise (a good excuse to rant and rave about the government's domestic affairs). Noise is important because your smell will not be carried in the direction you are hiking. As a result, the bear will not smell you coming.

If a bear can hear you and smell you, it will tend to get out of the way and let you pass without your knowing it was even close by. The exceptions are if you are carrying fish or lots of sweets in your pack or if you are wearing heavy, sweet deodorants or makeup. All of these are bear attractants.

Just let them, and keep perfectly still. Don't fight them; don't run. And when you have a 100 percent chance (not 98 or 99) to dash up a nearby tree, that's when you let fly. Once safely in a tree, you can hurl down insults and let your aggression out.

In a wilderness camp, there are special precautions you should take. Always hang your food at least 100 yards downwind of camp and get it high; 30 feet is reasonable. In addition, circle your camp with rope and hang the bells from your pack on it. Thus, if a bear walks into your camp, he'll run into the rope, the bells will ring, and everybody will have a chance to get up a tree before ol' griz figures out what's going on. Often, the unexpected ringing of bells is enough to send him off in search of a quieter environment.

You see, more often than not, grizzlies tend to clear the way for campers and hikers. So be smart, don't act like bear bait, and always have a plan if you are confronted by one.

My pal Foonsky had such a plan during a wilderness expedition in Montana's northern Rockies. On our second day of hiking, we started seeing scratch marks on the trees 13–14 feet off the ground.

"Mr. Griz made those," Foonsky said. "With spring here, the grizzlies are coming out of hibernation and using the trees like a cat uses a scratch board to stretch the muscles."

The next day, I noticed Foonsky had a pair of track shoes tied to the back of his pack. I just laughed.

"You're not going to outrun a griz," I said. "In fact, there's hardly any animal out here in the wilderness that man can outrun."

Foonsky just smiled.

"I don't have to outrun a griz," he said. "I just have to outrun you!"

Fun and Games

"Now what are we supposed to do?" the young boy asked his dad.

"Yeah, Dad, think of something," said another son.

Well, Dad thought hard. This was one of the first camping trips he'd taken with his sons and one of the first lessons he received was that kids don't appreciate the philosophic release of mountain quiet. They want action and lots of it. With a glint in his eye, Dad searched around the camp and picked up 15 twigs, breaking them so each was four inches long. He laid them in three separate rows, three twigs in one row, five twigs in another, and seven in the other.

"OK, this game is called 3-5-7," said Dad.

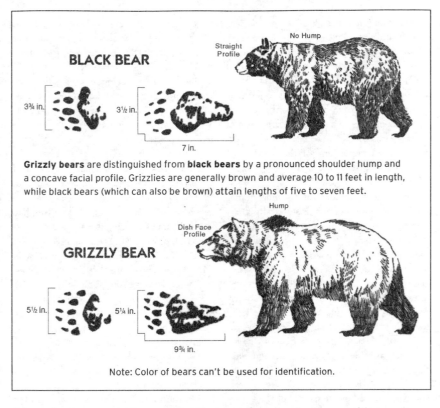

BLACK BEAR

Straight Profile

No Hump

3¾ in.

3½ in.

7 in.

Grizzly bears are distinguished from **black bears** by a pronounced shoulder hump and a concave facial profile. Grizzlies are generally brown and average 10 to 11 feet in length, while black bears (which can also be brown) attain lengths of five to seven feet.

Hump

Dish Face Profile

GRIZZLY BEAR

5½ in.

5¼ in.

9¾ in.

Note: Color of bears can't be used for identification.

"You each take turns picking up sticks. You are allowed to remove all or as few as one twig from a row, but here's the catch: You can pick only from one row per turn. Whoever picks up the last stick left is the loser."

I remember this episode well because those two little boys were my brother Bobby, as in Rambobby, and I. And to this day, we still play 3-5-7 on campouts, with the winner getting to watch the loser clean the dishes. What I have learned in the span of time since that original episode is that it does not matter what your age is: Campers need options for camp fun.

Some evenings, after a long hike or ride, you feel too worn out to take on a serious romp downstream to fish or a climb up to a ridge for a view. That is especially true if you have been in the outback for a week or more. At that point, a lot of campers will spend their time resting and gazing at a map of the area, dreaming of the next day's adventure, or just take a seat against a rock, watching the colors of the sky and mountain panorama change minute by minute. But kids in the push-button video era, and a lot of adults too, want more. After all, "I'm on vacation. I want some fun."

There are several options, such as the 3-5-7 twig game, and they should be just as much a part of your trip planning as arranging your gear.

For kids, plan on games, the more physically challenging the competition, the better. One of the best games is to throw a chunk of wood into a lake and challenge the kids to hit it by throwing rocks. It wreaks havoc on the fishing, but it can keep kids totally absorbed for some time. Target practice with a wrist-rocket slingshot—firing rocks at small targets, like pinecones set on a log—is also all-consuming for kids.

You can also set kids off on little missions near camp, such as looking for the footprints of wildlife, searching out good places to have a "snipe hunt," picking up twigs to get the evening fire started, or having them take the water purifier to a stream to pump some drinking water into a canteen. The latter is an easy, fun, yet important task that will allow kids to feel a sense of equality they often don't get at home.

For adults, the appeal should be more to the intellect. A good example is star and planet identification, and while you are staring into space, you're bound to spot a few asteroids or shooting stars. A star chart can make it easy to find and identify many distinctive stars and constellations, such as Pleiades (the Seven Sisters), Orion, and others from the zodiac, depending on the time of year. With a little research, this can add a unique perspective to your trip. You could point to Polaris, one of the most easily identified of all stars, and note that navigators in the 1400s used it to find their way. Polaris, of course, is the North Star and is at the end of the handle of the Little Dipper. Pinpointing Polaris is quite easy. First find the Big Dipper and then find the outside stars of the ladle of the Big Dipper. They are called the "pointer stars" because they point right at Polaris.

A tree identification book can teach you a few things about your surroundings. It is also a good idea for one member of the party to research the history of the area you have chosen and another to research the geology. With shared knowledge, you end up with a deeper love of wild places.

Another way to add some recreation into your trip is to bring a board game, a number of which have been miniaturized for campers. The most popular are chess, checkers, and cribbage. The latter comes with an equally miniature set of playing cards. And if you bring those little cards,

that opens a vast set of other possibilities. With kids along, for instance, just take three queens out of the deck and you can play Old Maid.

But there are more serious card games, and they come with high stakes. Such occurred on one high-country trip where Foonsky, Rambob, and I sat down for a late-afternoon game of poker. In a game of seven-card stud, I caught a straight on the sixth card and felt like a dog licking on a T-bone. Already, I had bet several Skittles and peanut M&Ms on this promising hand.

Then I examined the cards Foonsky had face up. He was showing three sevens, and acting as happy as a grizzly with a pork chop—or a full house. He matched my bet of two peanut M&Ms, then raised me three SweetTarts, one Starburst, and one sour apple Jolly Rancher. Rambob folded, but I matched Foonsky's bet and hoped for the best as the seventh and final card was dealt.

Just after Foonsky glanced at that last card, I saw him sneak a look at my grape stick and beef jerky stash.

"I raise you a grape stick," he said.

Rambob and I both gasped. It was the highest bet ever made, equivalent to a million dollars laid down in Las Vegas. Cannons were going off in my chest. I looked hard at my cards. They looked good, but were they good enough?

Even with a great hand like I had, a grape stick was too much to gamble, my last one with 10 days of trail ahead of us. I shook my head and folded my cards. Foonsky smiled at his victory.

But I still had my grape stick.

Old Tricks Don't Always Work

Most people are born honest, but after a few camping trips, they usually get over it.

I remember some advice I got from Rambob, normally an honest soul, on one camping trip. A giant mosquito had landed on

KEEP IT WILD TIP 5:
KEEP THE WILDERNESS WILD

1. Let nature's sound prevail. Avoid loud voices and noises.
2. Leave radios and tape players at home. At drive-in camping sites, never open car doors with music playing.
3. Careful guidance is necessary when choosing any games to bring for children. Most toys, especially any kind of gun toys with which children simulate shooting at each other, shouldn't be allowed on a camping trip.
4. Control pets at all times or leave them with a sitter at home.
5. Treat natural heritage with respect. Leave plants, rocks, and historical artifacts where you find them.

my arm and he alerted me to an expert bit of wisdom.

"Flex your arm muscles," he commanded, watching the mosquito fill with my blood. "He'll get stuck in your arm, then he'll explode."

For some reason, I believed him. We both proceeded to watch the mosquito drill countless holes in my arm.

Alas, the unknowing face sabotage from their most trusted companions on camping trips. It can arise at any time, usually in the form of advice from a friendly, honest-looking face, as if to say, "What? How can you doubt me?" After that mosquito episode, I was a little more skeptical of my dear old brother. Then the next day, when another mosquito was nailing me in the back of the neck, out came this gem:

"Hold your breath," he commanded. I instinctively obeyed. "That will freeze the mosquito," he said, "then you can squish him."

But in the time I wasted holding my breath, the little bugger was able to fly off without my having the satisfaction of squishing him. When he got home, he probably told his family, "What a dummy I got to drill today!"

Over the years, I have been duped numerous times with dubious advice:

On a grizzly bear attack: "If he grabs you, tuck your head under the grizzly's chin; then he won't be able to bite you in the head." This made sense to me until the first time I saw a nine-foot grizzly 40 yards away. In seconds, I was at the top of a tree, which suddenly seemed to make the most sense.

On coping with animal bites: "If a bear bites you in the arm, don't try to jerk it away. That will just rip up your arm. Instead, force your arm deeper into his mouth. He'll lose his grip and will have to open it to get a firmer hold, and right then you can get away." I was told this in the Boy Scouts. When I was 14, I had a chance to try it out when a friend's dog bit me as I tried to pet it. What happened? When I shoved my arm deeper into his mouth, he bit me three more times.

On cooking breakfast: "The bacon will curl up every time in a camp frying pan. So make sure you have a bacon stretcher to keep it flat." As a 12-year-old Tenderfoot, I spent two hours looking for the bacon stretcher until I figured out the camp leader had forgotten it. It wasn't for several years that I learned that there is no such thing.

On preventing sore muscles: "If you haven't hiked for a long time and you are facing a rough climb, you can keep from getting sore muscles in your legs, back, and shoulders by practicing the 'Dead Man's Walk.' Simply let your entire body go slack, and then take slow, wobbling steps. This will clear your muscles of lactic acid, which causes them to be so sore after a rough hike." Foonsky pulled this one on me. Rambob and I both bought it and tried it while we were hiking up Mount Whitney, which requires a 6,000-foot elevation gain in six miles. In one 45-minute period, about 30 other hikers passed us and looked at us as if we were suffering from some rare form of mental aberration.

Fish won't bite? No problem: "If the fish are not feeding or will not bite, persistent anglers can still catch dinner with little problem. Keep casting across the current, and eventually, as they hover in the stream, the line will feed across their open mouths. Keep reeling and you will hook the fish right in the side of the mouth. This technique is called 'lining.' Never worry if the fish will not bite, because you can always line 'em." Of course, heh, heh, heh, that explains why so many fish get hooked in the side of the mouth.

On keeping bears away: "To keep bears away, urinate around the borders of your campground. If there are a lot of bears in the area, it is advisable to go right on your sleeping bag." Yeah, surrrrrre.

On disposing of trash: "Don't worry about packing out trash. Just bury it. It will regenerate into the earth and add valuable minerals." Bears, raccoons, skunks, and other critters will dig up your trash as soon as you depart, leaving one huge mess for the next camper. Always pack out everything.

Often the advice comes without warning. That was the case after a fishing trip with a female companion, when she outcaught me two to one, the third such trip in a row. I explained this to a shopkeeper, and he nodded, then explained why.

"The male fish are able to detect the female scent on the lure, and thus become aroused into striking."

Of course! That explains everything!

Getting Revenge

I was just a lad when Foonsky pulled the old snipe-hunt trick on me. It took nearly 30 years to get revenge.

You probably know about snipe hunting.

The victim is led out at night in the woods by a group, and then is left holding a bag.

"Stay perfectly still and quiet," Foonsky explained. "You don't want to scare the snipe. The rest of us will go back to camp and let the woods settle down. Then when the snipe are least expecting it, we'll form a line and charge through the forest with sticks, beating bushes and trees, and we'll flush the snipe out right to you. Be ready with the bag. When we flush the snipe out, bag it. But until we start our charge, make sure you don't move or make a sound or you will spook the snipe and ruin everything."

I sat out there in the woods with my bag for hours, waiting for the charge. I waited, waited, and waited. Nothing happened. No charge, no snipe. It wasn't until well past midnight that I figured something was wrong. When I finally returned to camp, everybody was sleeping.

Well, I tell ya, don't get mad at your pals for the tricks they pull on you. Get revenge. About 25 years later, on the last day of a camping trip, the time finally came.

"Let's break camp early," Foonsky suggested to Mr. Furnai and me. "Get up before dawn, eat breakfast, pack up, and be on the ridge to watch the sun come up. It will be a fantastic way to end the trip."

"Sounds great to me," I replied. But when Foonsky wasn't looking, I turned his alarm clock ahead three hours. So when the alarm sounded at the appointed 4:30 A.M. wake-up time, Mr. Furnai and I knew it was actually only 1:30 A.M.

Foonsky clambered out of his sleeping bag and whistled with a grin. "Time to break camp."

"You go ahead," I answered. "I'll skip breakfast so I can get a little more sleep. At the first sign of dawn, wake me up, and I'll break camp."

"Me, too," said Mr. Furnai.

Foonsky then proceeded to make some coffee, cook a breakfast, and eat it, sitting on a log in the black darkness of the forest, waiting for the sun to come up. An hour later, with still no sign of dawn, he checked his clock. It now read 5:30 A.M. "Any minute now we should start seeing some light," he said.

He made another cup of coffee, packed his gear, and sat there in the middle of the night, looking up at the stars, waiting for dawn. "Anytime now," he said. He ended up sitting there all night long.

Revenge is sweet. Before a fishing trip at a lake, I took Foonsky aside and explained that the third member of the party, Jimbobo, was hard of hearing and very sensitive about it. "Don't mention it to him," I advised. "Just talk real loud."

Meanwhile, I had already told Jimbobo the same thing. "Foonsky just can't hear very good."

We had fished less than 20 minutes when Foonsky got a nibble.

"GET A BITE?" shouted Jimbobo.

"YEAH!" yelled back Foonsky, smiling. "BUT I DIDN'T HOOK HIM!"

"MAYBE NEXT TIME!" shouted Jimbobo with a friendly grin.

Well, they spent the entire day yelling at each other from the distance of a few feet. They never did figure it out. Heh, heh, heh.

That is, I thought so, until we made a trip salmon fishing. I got a strike that almost knocked my fishing rod out of the boat. When I grabbed the rod, it felt as if Moby Dick were on the other end. "At least a 25-pounder," I said. "Maybe bigger."

The fish dove, ripped off line, and then bulldogged. "It's acting like a 40-pounder," I announced, "Huge, just huge. It's going deep. That's how the big ones fight."

Some 15 minutes later, I finally got the "salmon" to the surface. It turned out to be a coffee can that Foonsky had clipped on the line with a snap swivel. By maneuvering the boat, he made the coffee can fight like a big fish.

This all started with a little old snipe hunt years ago. You never know what your pals will try next. Don't get mad. Get revenge.

CAMPING OPTIONS
Boat-In Seclusion

Most campers would never think of trading in their cars, pickup trucks, or RVs for a boat, but people who go by boat on a camping trip enjoy virtually guaranteed seclusion and top-quality outdoor experiences.

Camping with a boat is a do-it-yourself venture in living under primitive circumstances. Yet at the same time, you can bring along any luxury item you wish, from giant coolers, stoves, and lanterns to portable gasoline generators. Weight is almost never an issue.

Many outstanding boat-in campgrounds in beautiful surroundings are available. The best are on the shores of lakes accessible by canoe or skiff, and at offshore islands reached by saltwater cruisers. Several boat-in camps are detailed in this book.

If you want to take the adventure a step further and create your own boat-in camp, perhaps near a special fishing spot, this is a go-for-it deal that provides the best way possible to establish your own secret campsite. But most people who set out freelance style forget three critical items for boat-in camping: a shovel, a sunshade, and an ax. Here is why these items can make a key difference in your trip:

• **Shovel:** Many lakes and virtually all reservoirs have steep, sloping banks. At reservoirs subject to drawdowns, what was lake bottom in the spring can be a campsite in late summer. If you want a flat area for a tent site, the only answer is to dig one out yourself. A shovel gives you that option.

• **Sunshade:** The flattest spots to camp along lakes often have a tendency to support only sparse tree growth. As a result, a natural shield from sun and rain is rarely available. What? Rain in the summer? Oh yeah, don't get me started. A light tarp, set up with poles and staked ropes, solves the problem.

• **Ax:** Unless you bring your own firewood, which is necessary at some sparsely wooded reservoirs, there is no substitute for a good, sharp ax. With an ax, you can almost always find dry firewood, since the interior of an otherwise wet log will be dry. When the weather turns bad is precisely when you will most want a fire. You may need an ax to get one going.

In the search to create your own personal boat-in campsite, you will find that the flattest areas are usually the tips of peninsulas and points, while the protected back ends of coves are often steeply sloped. At reservoirs, the flattest areas are usually near the mouths of the feeder streams and the points are quite steep. On rivers, there are usually sandbars on the inside of tight bends that make for ideal campsites.

Almost all boat-in campsites developed by government agencies are free of charge, but you are on your own. Only in extremely rare cases is piped water available.

Any way you go, by canoe, skiff, or power cruiser, you end up with a one-in-a-million campsite you can call your own.

Desert Outings

It was a cold, snowy day in Missouri when 10-year-old Rusty Ballinger started dreaming about the vast deserts of the West.

"My dad was reading aloud from a Zane Grey book called *Riders of the Purple Sage*," Ballinger said. "He would get animated when he got to the passages about the desert. It wasn't long before I started to have the same feelings."

That was in 1947. Ballinger, now in his 60s, has spent a good part of his life exploring the West, camping along the way. "The deserts are the best part. There's something about the uniqueness of each little area you see," Ballinger said. "You're constantly surprised. Just the time of day and the way the sun casts a different color. It's like the lady you care about. One time she smiles, the next time she's pensive. The desert is like that. If you love nature, you can love the desert. After awhile, you can't help but love it."

A desert adventure is not just an antidote for a case of cabin fever in the winter. Whether you go by RV, pickup truck, car, or on foot, it provides its own special qualities.

If you go camping in the desert, your approach has to be as unique as the setting. For starters, don't plan on any campfires, but bring a camp stove instead. And unlike in the mountains, do not camp near a water hole. That's because an animal, such as a badger, coyote, or desert bighorn, might be desperate for water, and if you set up camp in the animal's way, you may be forcing a confrontation.

In some areas, there is a danger of flash floods. An intense rain can fall in one area, collect in a pool, then suddenly burst through a narrow canyon. If you are in its path, you could be injured or drowned. The lesson? Never camp in a gully.

"Some people might wonder, 'What good is this place?'" Ballinger said. "The answer is that it is good for looking at. It is one of the world's unique places."

CAMP ETHICS AND POLITICS

The perfect place to set up a base camp turned out to be not so perfect. In fact, according to reader Doug Williams, it did not even exist.

Williams and his son, James, had driven deep into Angeles National Forest, prepared to set up camp and then explore the surrounding area on foot. But when they reached their destination, no campground existed.

"I wanted a primitive camp in a national forest where I could teach my son some basics," said the senior Williams. "But when we got there, there wasn't much left of the camp, and it had been closed. It was obvious that the area had been vandalized."

It turned out not to be an isolated incident. A lack of outdoor ethics practiced by a few people using the unsupervised campgrounds available on national forestland has caused the U.S. Forest Service to close a few of them and make extensive repairs to others.

In setting up camp, always be mindful of potential ecological disturbances. Pitch tents and dispose of human waste at least 200 feet from the water's edge. In grizzly bear territory, increase the distance between your tent and your cooking area, food-hang, and the water's edge threefold. In other words, if you're in grizzly country, do all your cooking 100 yards (not feet) downwind of your sleeping area. If you can establish an escape tree nearby, all the better.

"There have been sites closed," said David Flohr, regional campground coordinator for the U.S. Forest Service. "It's an urban type of thing, affecting forests near urban areas. They get a lot of urban users and they bring with them a lot of the same ethics they have in the city. They get drinking and they're not afraid to do things. They vandalize and run. Of course, it is a public facility, so they think nobody is getting hurt."

But somebody is getting hurt, starting with the next person who wants to use the campground. And if the ranger district budget doesn't have enough money to pay for repairs, the campground is then closed for the next arrivals. Just ask Doug and James Williams.

In an era of considerable fiscal restraint for the U.S. Forest Service, vandalized campgrounds could face closure instead of repair.

Williams had just a taste of it, but Flohr, as camping coordinator, gets a steady diet.

"It starts with behavior," Flohr said. "General rowdiness, drinking, partying, and then vandalism. It goes all the way from the felt-tip pen things (graffiti) to total destruction, blowing up toilet buildings with dynamite. I have seen toilets destroyed totally with shotguns. They burn up tables, burn barriers. They'll burn up signs for firewood, even the shingles right off the roofs of the bathrooms. They'll shoot anything, garbage cans, signs. It can get a little hairy. A favorite is to remove the stool out of a toilet building. We've had people fall in the open hole."

The National Park Service had similar problems some years back, especially with rampant littering. Park Director Bill Mott responded by creating an interpretive program that attempts to teach visitors the wise use of natural areas, and to have all park workers set examples by picking up litter and reminding others to do the same.

The U.S. Forest Service has responded with a similar program, making Recreation Opportunity Guides available that detail the wise use of national forests. The four most popular brochures are: Camping, General Wilderness Information, Recreational Sites, and Safe Drinking Water. These include details on campfires, drinking water from lakes or streams, hypothermia, safety, and outdoor ethics. The brochures are available for download at http://www.fs.fed.us/r5/sierra/recreation/rogsheets/index.shtml.

Flohr said even experienced campers sometimes cross over the ethics line unintentionally. The most common example, he said, is when campers toss garbage into the outhouse toilet, rather than packing it out in a plastic garbage bag.

"They throw it in the vault toilet bowls, which just fills them up," Flohr said. "That creates an extremely high cost to pump it. You know why? Because some poor guy has to pick that stuff out piece by piece. It can't be pumped."

At most backcountry sites, the U.S. Forest Service has implemented a program called "Pack it in, pack it out," even posting signs that remind all visitors to do so. But a lot of people don't do it, and others may even uproot the signs and burn them for firewood.

On a trip to a secluded lake near Carson Pass in the Sierra Nevada, I arrived at a small, little-known camp where the picnic table had been spray painted and garbage had been strewn about. A pristine place, the true temple of God, had been defiled.

Getting Along with Fellow Campers

The most important thing about a camping, fishing, or hunting trip is not where you go, how many fish you catch, or how many shots you fire. It often has little to do with how beautiful the view is, how easily the campfire lights, or how sunny the days are.

Oh yeah? Then what is the most important factor? The answer: The people you are with. It is that simple.

Who would you rather camp with? Your enemy at work or your dream mate in a good mood? Heh, heh. You get the idea. A camping trip is a fairly close-knit experience, and you can make lifetime friends or lifelong enemies in the process. That is why your choice of companions is so important. Your own behavior is equally consequential.

Yet most people spend more time putting together their camping gear than considering why they enjoy or hate the company of their chosen companions. Here are 10 rules of behavior for good camping mates:

1. **No whining:** Nothing is more irritating than being around a whiner. It goes right to the heart of adventure, since often the only difference between a hardship and an escapade is simply whether or not an individual has the spirit for it. The people who do can turn a rugged day in the outdoors into a cherished memory. Those who don't can ruin it with their incessant sniveling.

2. **Activities must be agreed upon:** Always have a meeting of the minds with your companions over the general game plan. Then everybody will possess an equal stake in the outcome of the trip. This is absolutely critical. Otherwise they will feel like merely an addendum to your trip, not an equal participant, and a whiner will be born (see number one).

3. **Nobody's in charge:** It is impossible to be genuine friends if one person is always telling another what to do, especially if the orders involve simple camp tasks. You need to share the space on the same emotional plane, and the only way to do that is to have a semblance of equality, regardless of differences in experience. Just try ordering your mate around at home for a few days. You'll quickly see the results, and they aren't pretty.

KEEP IT WILD TIP 6: RESPECT OTHER USERS

1. Horseback riders have priority over hikers. Step to the downhill side of the trail and talk softly when encountering horseback riders.

2. Hikers and horseback riders have priority over mountain bikers. When mountain bikers encounter other users even on wide trails, they should pass at an extremely slow speed. On very narrow trails, they should dismount and get off to the side so hikers or horseback riders can pass without having their trip disrupted.

3. Mountain bikes aren't permitted on most single-track trails and are expressly prohibited in designated wilderness areas and all sections of the Pacific Crest Trail. Mountain bikers breaking these rules should be confronted and told to dismount and walk their bikes until they reach a legal area.

4. It's illegal for horseback riders to break off branches that may be in the path of wilderness trails.

5. Horseback riders on overnight trips are prohibited from camping in many areas and are usually required to keep stock animals in specific areas where they can do no damage to the landscape.

4. **Equal chances at the fun stuff:** It's fun to build the fire, fun to get the first cast at the best fishing spot, and fun to hoist the bagged food for a bear-proof food hang. It is not fun to clean the dishes, collect firewood, or cook every night. So obviously, there must be an equal distribution of the fun stuff and the not-fun stuff, and everybody on the trip must get a shot at the good and the bad.

5. **No heroes:** No awards are bestowed for achievement in the outdoors, yet some guys treat mountain peaks, big fish, and big game as if they are prizes in a trophy competition. Actually, nobody cares how wonderful you are, which is always a surprise to trophy chasers. What people care about is the heart of the adventure, the gut-level stuff.

6. **Agree on a wake-up time:** It is a good idea to agree on a general wake-up time before closing your eyes for the night, and that goes regardless of whether you want to sleep in late or get up at dawn. Then you can proceed on course regardless of what time you crawl out of your sleeping bag in the morning, without the risk of whining (see number one).

7. **Think of the other guy:** Be self-aware instead of self-absorbed. A good test is to count

the number of times you say, "What do you think?" A lot of potential problems can be solved quickly by actually listening to the answer.

8. **Solo responsibilities:** There are a number of essential camp duties on all trips, and while they should be shared equally, most should be completed solo. That means that when it is time for you to cook, you don't have to worry about me changing the recipe on you. It means that when it is my turn to make the fire, you keep your mitts out of it.

9. **Don't let money get in the way:** Of course everybody should share equally in trip expenses, such as the cost of food, and it should be split up before you head out yonder. Don't let somebody pay extra, because that person will likely try to control the trip. Conversely, don't let somebody weasel out of paying a fair share.

10. **Accordance on the food plan:** Always have complete agreement on what you plan to eat each day. Don't figure that just because you like Steamboat's Sludge, everybody else will, too, especially youngsters. Always, always, always check for food allergies, such as nuts, onions, or cheese, and make sure each person

brings his or her own personal coffee brand. Some people drink only decaffeinated; others might gag on anything but Burma monkey beans.

Obviously, it is difficult to find companions who will agree on all of these elements. This is why many campers say that the best camping buddies they'll ever have are their mates, who know all about them and like them anyway.

OUTDOORS WITH KIDS

How do you get a youngster excited about the outdoors? How do you compete with the television and remote control? How do you prove to a kid that success comes from persistence, spirit, and logic, which the outdoors teaches, and not from pushing buttons?

The answer is in the Ten Camping Commandments for Kids. These are lessons that will get youngsters excited about the outdoors and that will make sure adults help the process along, not kill it. I've put this list together with the help of my own kids, Jeremy and Kris, and their mother, Stephani. Some of the commandments are obvious, some are not, but all are important:

1. Take children to places where there is a guarantee of action. A good example is camping in a park where large numbers of wildlife can be viewed, such as squirrels, chipmunks, deer, and even bears. Other good choices include fishing at a small pond loaded with bluegill or hunting in a spot where a kid can shoot a .22 at pinecones all day. Boys and girls want action, not solitude.

2. Enthusiasm is contagious. If you aren't excited about an adventure, you can't expect a child to be. Show a genuine zest for life in the outdoors, and point out everything as if it is the first time you have ever seen it.

3. Always, always, always be seated when talking to someone small. This allows the adult and child to be on the same level. That is why fishing in a small boat is perfect for adults and kids. Nothing is worse for youngsters than having a big person look down at them and give them orders. What fun is that?

4. Always *show* how to do something, whether it is gathering sticks for a campfire, cleaning a trout, or tying a knot. Never tell—always show. A button usually clicks to "off" when a kid is lectured. But kids can learn behavior patterns and outdoor skills by watching adults, even when the adults are not aware they are being watched.

5. Let kids be kids. Let the adventure happen, rather than trying to force it within some preconceived plan. If they get sidetracked watching pollywogs, chasing butterflies, or sneaking up on chipmunks, let them be. A youngster can have more fun turning over rocks and looking at different kinds of bugs than sitting in one spot, waiting for a fish to bite.

6. Expect short attention spans. Instead of getting frustrated about it, use it to your advantage. How? By bringing along a bag of candy and snacks. Where there is a lull in the camp activity, out comes the bag. Don't let them know what goodies await, so each one becomes a surprise.

7. Make absolutely certain the child's sleeping bag is clean, dry, and warm. Nothing is worse than discomfort when trying to sleep, but a refreshing sleep makes for a positive attitude the next day. In addition, kids can become quite scared of animals at night. A parent should not wait for any signs of this, but always play the part of the outdoor guardian, the one who will take care of everything.

8. Kids quickly relate to outdoor ethics. They will enjoy eating everything they kill, building a safe campfire, and picking up all their litter, and they will develop a sense of pride that goes with it. A good idea is to bring extra plastic garbage bags to pick up any trash you come across. Kids long remember when they do something right that somebody else has done wrong.

9. If you want youngsters hooked on the outdoors for life, take a close-up photograph of them holding up fish they have caught, blow-

ing on the campfire, or completing other camp tasks. Young children can forget how much fun they had, but they never forget if they have a picture of it.

10. The least important word you can ever say to a kid is "I." Keep track of how often you are saying "Thank you" and "What do you think?" If you don't say them very often, you'll lose out. Finally, the most important words of all are: "I am proud of you."

PREDICTING WEATHER

Foonsky climbed out of his sleeping bag, glanced at the nearby meadow, and scowled hard.

"It doesn't look good," he said. "Doesn't look good at all."

I looked at my adventure companion of 20 years, noting his discontent. Then I looked at the meadow and immediately understood why: *When the grass is dry at morning light, look for rain before the night.*

"How bad you figure?" I asked him.

"We'll know soon enough, I reckon," Foonsky answered. *Short notice, soon to pass. Long notice, long it will last.*

When you are out in the wild, spending your days fishing and your nights camping, you learn to rely on yourself to predict the weather. It can make or break you. If a storm hits the unprepared, it can quash the trip and possibly endanger the participants. But if you are ready, a potential hardship can be an adventure.

You can't rely on TV weather forecasters,

people who don't even know that when all the cows on a hill are facing north, it will rain that night for sure. God forbid if the cows are all sitting. But what do you expect from TV's talking heads?

Foonsky made a campfire, started boiling some water for coffee and soup, and we started to plan the day. In the process, I noticed the smoke of the campfire: It was sluggish, drifting and hovering.

"You notice the smoke?" I asked, chewing on a piece of homemade jerky.

"Not good," Foonsky said. "Not good." He knew that sluggish, hovering smoke indicates rain.

"You'd think we'd have been smart enough to know last night that this was coming," Foonsky said. "Did you take a look at the moon or the clouds?"

"I didn't look at either," I answered. "Too busy eating the trout we caught." You see, if the moon is clear and white, the weather will be good the next day. But if there is a ring around the moon, the number of stars you can count inside the ring equals the number of days until the next rain. As for clouds, the high, thin ones—called cirrus—indicate a change in the weather.

We were quiet for a while, planning our strategy, but as we did so, some terrible things happened: A chipmunk scampered past with his tail high, a small flock of geese flew by very low, and a little sparrow perched on a tree limb quite close to the trunk.

"We're in for trouble," I told Foonsky.

"I know, I know," he answered. "I saw 'em,

KEEP IT WILD TIP 7:
PLAN AHEAD AND PREPARE

1. Learn about the regulations and issues that apply to the area you're visiting.
2. Avoid heavy-use areas.
3. Obtain all maps and permits.
4. Bring extra garbage bags to pack out any refuse you come across.

too. And come to think of it, no crickets were chirping last night either."

"Damn, that's right!"

These are all signs of an approaching storm. Foonsky pointed at the smoke of the campfire and shook his head as if he had just been condemned. Sure enough, now the smoke was blowing toward the north, a sign of a south wind. *"When the wind is from the south, the rain is in its mouth."*

"We'd best stay hunkered down until it passes," Foonsky said.

I nodded. "Let's gather as much firewood now as we can, get our gear covered up, then plan our meals."

"Then we'll get a poker game going."

As we accomplished these camp tasks, the sky clouded up, then darkened. Within an hour, we had gathered enough firewood to make a large pile, enough wood to keep a fire going no matter how hard it rained. The day's meals had been separated out of the food bag so it wouldn't have to be retrieved during the storm. We buttoned two ponchos together, staked two of the corners with ropes to the ground, and tied the other two with ropes to different tree limbs to create a slanted roof/shelter.

As the first raindrop fell with that magic sound on our poncho roof, Foonsky was just starting to shuffle the cards.

"Cut for deal," he said.

Just as I did so, it started to rain a bit harder. I pulled out another piece of beef jerky and started chewing on it. It was just another day in paradise.

Weather lore can be valuable. Here is the list I have compiled over the years:

When the grass is dry at morning light,
Look for rain before the night.

Short notice, soon to pass.
Long notice, long it will last.

When the wind is from the east,
'Tis fit for neither man nor beast.

When the wind is from the south,
The rain is in its mouth.

When the wind is from the west,
Then it is the very best.

Red sky at night, sailors' delight.
Red sky in the morning, sailors take warning.

When all the cows are pointed north,
Within a day rain will come forth.

Onion skins very thin, mild winter coming in.
Onion skins very tough, winter's going to be very rough.

When your boots make the squeak of snow,
Then very cold temperatures will surely show.

If a goose flies high, fair weather ahead.
If a goose flies low, foul weather will come instead.

Small signs provided by nature and wildlife can also be translated to provide a variety of weather information:

• A thick coat on a woolly caterpillar means a big, early snow is coming.

• Chipmunks will run with their tails up before a rain.

• Bees always stay near their hives before a rainstorm.

• When the birds are perched on large limbs near tree trunks, an intense but short storm will arrive.

• On the coast, if groups of seabirds are flying a mile inland, look for major winds.

• If crickets are chirping very loudly during the evening, the next day will be clear and warm.

• If the smoke of a campfire at night rises in a thin spiral, good weather is assured for the next day.

• If the smoke of a campfire at night is sluggish, drifting and hovering, it will rain the next day.

• If there is a ring around the moon, count the number of stars inside the ring, and that is how many days until the next rain.

• If the moon is clear and white, the weather will be good the next day.

• High, thin clouds, or cirrus, indicate a change in the weather.

• Oval-shaped lenticular clouds indicate high winds.

• Two levels of clouds moving in different directions indicate changing weather soon.

• Huge, dark, billowing clouds, called cumulonimbus, suddenly forming on warm afternoons in the mountains mean that a short but intense thunderstorm with lightning can be expected.

• When squirrels are busy gathering food for extended periods, it means good weather is ahead in the short term, but a hard winter is ahead in the long term.

And God forbid if all the cows are sitting down....

CAMPING GEAR CHECKLIST

Cooking Gear
- Camp stove and fuel
- Dish soap and scrubber
- Fire-starter cubes
- Heavy-duty paper plates
- Ice chest and drinks
- Itemized food, separated by groups
- Knife, fork, cup
- Large, heavy-duty garbage bags
- Matches stored in resealable (such as Ziploc) bags
- One lighter for each camper
- Paper towels
- Plastic spatula and stir spoon
- Pot grabber or pot holder
- Salt, pepper, spices
- Two pots and no-stick pan
- Water jug or lightweight plastic "cube"

Optional Cooking Gear
- Aluminum foil
- Ax or hatchet
- Barbecue tongs
- Can opener
- Candles
- Dustpan
- Grill or hibachi
- Plastic clothespins
- Tablecloth
- Whisk broom
- Wood or charcoal for barbecue

Clothing
- Cotton/canvas pants
- Gore-Tex parka or jacket
- Gore-Tex rain pants
- Lightweight, breathable shirt
- Lightweight fleece jacket
- Medium-weight fleece vest
- Polypropylene underwear
- Rain jacket and pants, or poncho
- Sunglasses
- Waterproofed, oilskin wide-brimmed hat

Optional Clothing
- Gloves
- Shorts
- Ski cap
- Swimsuit

Hiking Gear
- Backpack or daypack
- Hiking boots
- Fresh bootlaces
- Innersole or foot cushion (for expeditions)
- Moleskin and medical tape
- SmartWool (or equivalent) socks
- Water-purification system

Optional Hiking Gear
- Backup lightweight shoes or moccasins
- Gaiters
- Water-repellent boot treatment

Sleeping Gear
- Ground tarp
- Sleeping bag
- Tent or bivy bag
- Therm-a-Rest pad

Optional Sleeping Gear
- Air bed
- Cot
- Catalytic heater
- Foam pad for truck bed

- Mosquito netting
- Mr. Heater and propane tank (for use in pickup truck camper shell)
- Pillow (even in wilderness)
- RV windshield light screen
- Seam Lock for tent stitching

First Aid
- Ace bandage
- After-Bite for mosquito bites (before you scratch them)
- Aspirin
- Biodegradable soap
- Caladryl for poison oak
- Campho-Phenique gel for bites (after you scratch them)
- Mosquito repellent
- Lip balm
- Medical tape to affix pads
- Neosporin for cuts
- Roller gauze
- Sterile gauze pads
- Sunscreen
- Tweezers

Optional First Aid
- Athletic tape for sprained ankle
- Cell phone or coins for phone calls
- Extra set of matches
- Mirror for signaling
- Thermometer

Fishing/Recreation Gear
- All required permits and licenses
- Fishing reel with fresh line
- Fishing rod
- Knife

- Leatherman tool or needle-nose pliers
- Small tackle box with flies, floats, hooks, lures, snap swivels, and splitshot

Optional Recreation Gear
- Backpacking cribbage board
- Deck of cards
- Folding chairs
- Guidebooks
- Hammock
- Mountain bike
- Reading material

Other Necessities
- Duct tape
- Extra plastic garbage bags
- Flashlight and batteries
- Lantern and fuel
- Maps
- Nylon rope for food hang
- Spade for cat hole
- Toilet paper
- Toothbrush and toothpaste
- Towelettes
- Wristwatch

Other Optional Items
- Altimeter
- Assorted bungee cords
- Binoculars
- Camera with fresh battery and digital card or film
- Compass
- Feminine hygiene products
- GPS unit
- Handkerchief
- Notebook and pen

THE OREGON COAST

© STEVE ESTVANIK/123rf.com

BEST CAMPGROUNDS

❮ Most Scenic
Honey Bear Campground & RV Resort, **page 133.**

❮ Families
Fort Stevens State Park, **page 86.**
Honey Bear Campground & RV Resort, **page 133.**

❮ Fishing
Waldport/Newport KOA, **page 105.**
Port of Siuslaw RV Park and Marina, **page 111.**
Carter Lake, **page 113.**

❮ Hiking
Nehalem Falls, **page 89.**
Cape Lookout State Park, **page 94.**
Cape Blanco State Park, **page 127.**

❮ Waterfalls
Nehalem Falls, **page 89.**
Alsea Falls, **page 107.**

❮ Waterfront Campgrounds
Loon Lake Recreation Area, **page 120.**
Laird Lake, **page 129.**

❮ Wildlife-Viewing
Cape Lookout State Park, **page 94.**
Seal Rocks RV Cove, **page 103.**
Port of Siuslaw RV Park and Marina, **page 111.**
Harris Beach State Park, **page 139.**

If you want to treat yourself to vacation memories

you'll treasure forever, take a drive and then set up camp along U.S. 101 on the Oregon Coast. Here you'll see some of the most dramatic coastal frontage in North America: tidewater rock gardens, cliff-top views that seem to stretch to forever, vast sand dunes, protected bays, beautiful streams with giant salmon and steelhead (in fall and winter), and three major national forests. I prefer cruising north to south, in the right lane close to the coastline and with the wind behind me; it often seems I'm on the edge of Never Never Land.

If you're heading down from Washington, you'll cross the Columbia River on the border of Oregon and Washington. The river is so wide here that it looks like an inland sea. I find that the best way to appreciate this massive waterway is to get off the main highway and explore the many coastal streams by two-lane road. There are numerous routes, from tiny Highway 15 on the Little Nestucca River to well-known Highway 38 along the beautiful Umpqua.

The most spectacular region on the coast may be the Oregon Dunes National Recreation Area, which spans roughly from Coos Bay north past Florence to near the mouth of the Siuslaw River. Whenever I visit, I feel like I'm instantly transported to another universe. I have a photo of the dunes in my office. While I'm writing, I often look at the image of a lone raptor soaring past a pyramid of sand – it's my window to this wonderful otherworld.

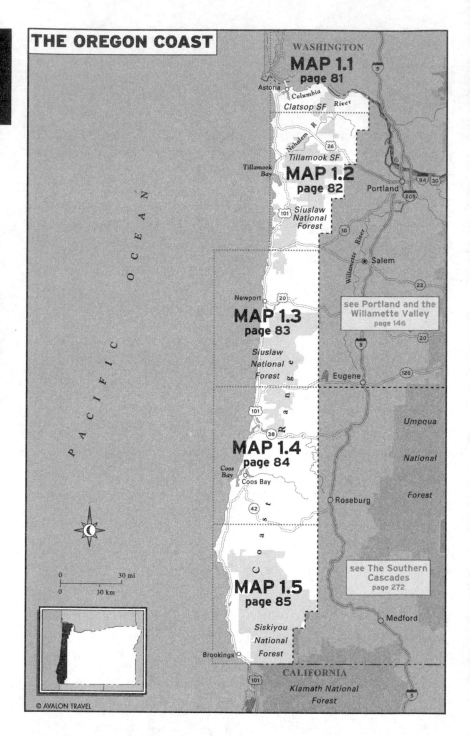

THE OREGON COAST

WASHINGTON

MAP 1.1
page 81

Astoria

Columbia River

Clatsop SF

Nehalem R.

26

Tillamook SF

Tillamook
Bay

MAP 1.2
page 82

Portland

84 30

205

101

Siuslaw
National
Forest

18

Willamette River

Salem

22

P A C I F I C   O C E A N

Newport

20

MAP 1.3
page 83

Siuslaw
National
Forest

see Portland and the
Willamette Valley
page 146

5

20

126

Eugene

Umpqua

101

38

National

MAP 1.4
page 84

Coos
Bay

Coos Bay

Forest

C o a s t   R a n g e

42

Roseburg

see The Southern
Cascades
page 272

Medford

0   30 mi

0   30 km

MAP 1.5
page 85

Siskiyou

National

Brookings

Forest

CALIFORNIA

Klamath National
Forest

101

5

© AVALON TRAVEL

Map 1.1

Campgrounds 1-3
Pages 86-87

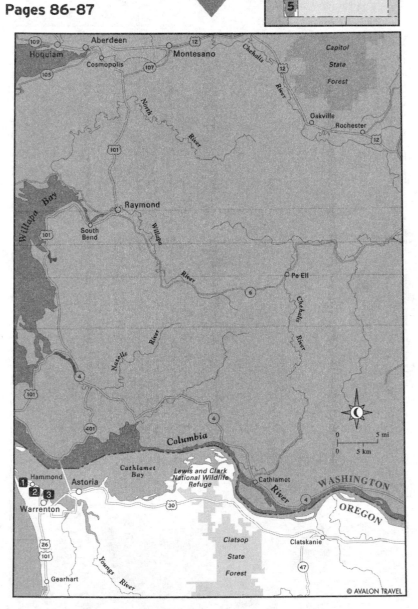

Map 1.2

Campgrounds 4-32
Pages 87-99

Map 1.3

Campgrounds 33-59
Pages 99-110

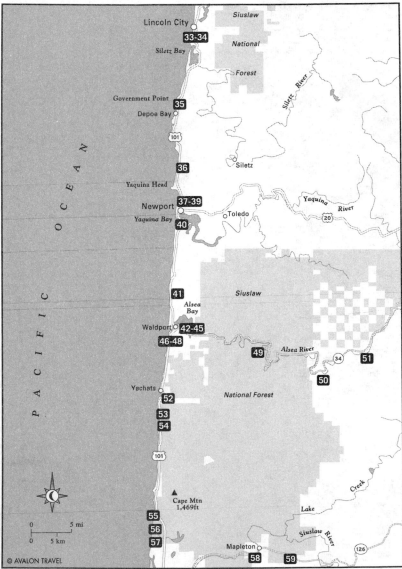

Map 1.4

Campgrounds 60-95

Pages 110-126

Map 1.5

Campgrounds 96-130
Pages 126-141

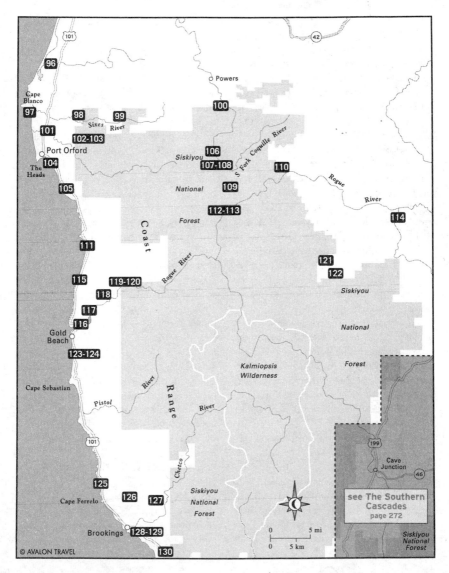

1 FORT STEVENS STATE PARK

🏃 🚲 🏊 ⛵ ⛴ 🦌 🏕 ♿ 🚐 ⛺

Scenic rating: 8

at the mouth of the Columbia River

Map 1.1, page 81　　　　**BEST (**

This classic spot is set at the northern tip of Oregon, right where the Columbia River enters the Pacific Ocean. At 3,700 acres, the park offers nine miles of biking trails, six miles of hiking trails, swimming, boating, fishing, and wildlife-viewing in a landscape of forests, wetlands, and dunes. The trailhead for the Oregon Coast Trail is here as well. History buffs will find a museum, tours of the fort and artillery batteries, and the remains of the *Peter Iredale* shipwreck.

Campsites, facilities: There are 476 sites with full or partial hookups for tents or RVs up to 60 feet long, 19 sites for tents or small RVs (no hookups), a camping area for hikers and bicyclists, and 15 yurts. Picnic tables and fire grills are provided. Drinking water, restrooms with flush toilets and showers, dump station, a transfer and recycling station, two picnic shelters, firewood, and a playground are available. Boat docks and launching facilities are nearby. Some facilities are wheelchair accessible. Leashed pets are permitted.

Reservations, fees: Reservations are accepted at 800/452-5687 or www.oregonstateparks.org ($8 reservation fee). RV sites are $18–27 per night, tent sites are $13–21 per night, $4–6 per night per person for hikers/bikers, yurts are $30–41 per night, $5 per night per additional vehicle. Some credit cards are accepted. Open year-round.

Directions: From Portland, turn west on U.S. 26 and drive 73 miles to the junction with U.S. 101. Turn right (north) on U.S. 101 and drive about 15 miles (about 0.25 mile past the Camp Rilea Army Base). Turn west on Perkins Road/Highway 104 at the sign for Fort Stevens State Park and drive about one mile to Ocean View Cemetery Road. Turn left and drive about 2.5 miles (Ocean View Cemetery Road becomes Ridge Road) to the park entrance.

Contact: Fort Stevens State Park, 503/861-1671 or 800/551-6949, www.oregonstateparks.org.

2 ASTORIA/WARRENTON SEASIDE KOA

🏃 🚲 🏊 ⛵ ⛴ 🏊 🦌 🏕 ♿ 🚐 ⛺

Scenic rating: 3

near Fort Stevens State Park

Map 1.1, page 81

This campground is nestled in a wooded area adjacent to Fort Stevens State Park, and tours of that historical military site can be arranged. This camp provides an excellent alternative if the state park campground is full. A host of activities are available in the immediate area, including beachcombing, bicycling, deep-sea fishing, hiking, and kayaking. Horse stables are within 10 miles.

Campsites, facilities: There are 311 sites with full or partial hookups for tents or RVs of any length, 54 cabins, and two lodges. Some sites are pull-through. Picnic tables and fire pits are provided. Cable TV, 30- and 50-amp service, modem hookups, wireless Internet service, restrooms with showers, security, public phone, coin laundry, meeting room, firewood, limited groceries, ice, snack bar, RV supplies, propane gas, and a picnic area are available. Recreational facilities include a playground, game room, recreation field, bicycle rentals, miniature golf, horseshoe pits, spa, and a heated indoor swimming pool. Some facilities are wheelchair accessible. Leashed pets are permitted with some restrictions.

Reservations, fees: Reservations are accepted at 800/562-8506. Sites are $39.55–199 per night, $6.50 per person per night for more than two people, $2 per pet per night, $5 per night per additional vehicle unless towed. Some credit cards are accepted. Open year-round.

Directions: From Portland, turn west on U.S. 26 and drive 73 miles to the junction with U.S. 101. Turn right (north) on U.S. 101 and drive about 15 miles (about 0.25 mile past the Camp Rilea Army Base). Turn west on Perkins Road/Highway 104 at the sign for Fort Stevens State Park and drive about one mile to Ocean View Cemetery Road. Turn left and drive about 2.5 miles (Ocean View Cemetery Road becomes Ridge Road) to the campground directly across from the state park.

Contact: Astoria/Warrenton Seaside KOA, 503/861-2606, fax 503/861-3209, www.koa.com.

3 KAMPERS WEST RV PARK

Scenic rating: 7

near Fort Stevens State Park

Map 1.1, page 81

Just four miles from Fort Stevens State Park, this privately run camp offers full RV services. Nearby recreation possibilities include an 18-hole golf course, hiking trails, and marked bike trails.

Campsites, facilities: There are 163 sites with full or partial hookups for RVs of any length, a small area for tents only, and three park-model cabins. Drinking water and picnic tables are provided, and some sites have fire pits. Restrooms with flush toilets and showers, propane gas, dump station, coin laundry, and ice are available. A store and a café are within one mile. Leashed pets are permitted.

Reservations, fees: Reservations are accepted. RV sites are $36 per night, and tent sites are $28 per night. Some credit cards are accepted. Open year-round.

Directions: From Portland, turn west on U.S. 30 and drive 105 miles north and west to Astoria and the junction of U.S. 101. Turn south and drive 6.5 miles to the Warrenton/Hammond Junction. Turn right (west) on

Warrenton and drive 1.5 miles to the campground on the right.

Contact: Kampers West RV Park, 503/861-1814, fax 503/861-3620, www.kamperswest.com.

4 VENICE RV PARK

Scenic rating: 3

on the Neawanna River

Map 1.2, page 82

This park along the Neawanna River—one of two rivers running through Seaside—is less than a mile from the beach. A great bonus: Crab pot rentals are available. Seaside offers beautiful ocean beaches for fishing and surfing, moped and bike rentals, shops, and a theater. The city provides swings and volleyball nets on the beach. An 18-hole golf course is nearby.

Campsites, facilities: There are 26 sites for RVs of any length (full hookups, some pull-through) and six tent sites. Drinking water, cable TV, and picnic tables are provided. Restrooms with flush toilets and showers, picnic area and a coin laundry are available. A store and a café are within one mile. Leashed pets are permitted.

Reservations, fees: Reservations are accepted. RV sites are $27.25 per night (with camp membership), tent sites are $18 per night, $2 per person per night for more than two people, $2 per night per additional vehicle, and $2 per pet per night. Some credit cards are accepted. Open year-round.

Directions: From Portland on I-5, turn west on U.S. 26 and drive 73 miles to the junction with U.S. 101. Turn north on U.S. 101 and drive 5.25 miles to Seaside. Continue to the north end of town and bear left (west) on 24th Avenue. The campground is on the corner (do not cross the bridge) at 1032 24th Avenue.

Contact: Venice RV Park, 503/738-8851, www.shopseaside.com/vrv.

5 SEA RANCH RV PARK

Scenic rating: 9

in Cannon Beach

Map 1.2, page 82

This park is set in a wooded area with nearby access to the beach. Activities at the camp include stream fishing, horseback riding, and swimming on the seashore. A golf course is six miles away, and the historic Lewis and Clark Trail is nearby. Elk hunters camp here in season. The beach and the town of Cannon Beach are within walking distance of the park.

Campsites, facilities: There are 80 sites with full or partial hookups for tents or RVs up to 40 feet long and seven cabins. Picnic tables and fire rings are provided. Restrooms with showers, horse rentals, and a dump station are available. Supplies are available within two miles. Leashed pets are permitted.

Reservations, fees: Reservations are accepted. RV sites are $30–90 per night, tent sites are $23 per night; and it costs $2 per person per night for more than two people, $3 per night per additional vehicle, and $10 per pet per night. Some credit cards are accepted. Open year-round.

Directions: From Portland on I-5, turn west on U.S. 26 and drive 73 miles to the junction with U.S. 101. Turn south on U.S. 101 and drive three miles to the Cannon Beach exit. Take that exit and drive on Fir Street for 0.3 mile to the park on the left.

Contact: Sea Ranch RV Park, 503/436-2815, www.searanchrv.com.

6 RV RESORT AT CANNON BEACH

Scenic rating: 9

near Ecola State Park

Map 1.2, page 82

This private resort is located about seven blocks from one of the nicest beaches in the region and about two miles from Ecola State Park. From the town of Cannon Beach, you can walk for miles in either direction. Nearby recreational facilities include marked bike trails, a riding stable, and tennis courts. The city shuttle service stops here.

Campsites, facilities: There are 100 sites with full hookups for RVs of any length; some are pull-through sites. Picnic tables and fire pits are provided. Restrooms with flush toilets and showers, cable TV, propane gas, firewood, recreation hall, playground, horseshoe pits, basketball court, convenience store, spa, coin laundry, ice, gasoline, playground, and a heated swimming pool (year-round) are available. Leashed pets are permitted.

Reservations, fees: Reservations are accepted at 800/847-2231. Sites are $32–44 per night, $3 per person per night for more than two people, $3 per night per additional vehicle. Some credit cards are accepted. Open year-round.

Directions: From Portland on I-5, turn west on U.S. 26 and drive 73 miles to the junction with U.S. 101. Turn south on U.S. 101 and drive four miles to the second Cannon Beach exit at Milepost 29.5. Exit on the left (east) and drive 200 feet to the resort.

Contact: RV Resort at Cannon Beach, 503/436-2231, fax 503/436-1527, www.cbrvresort.com.

7 SADDLE MOUNTAIN STATE NATURAL AREA

Scenic rating: 7

on Saddle Mountain

Map 1.2, page 82

This inland camp offers a good alternative to the many beachfront parks. A 2.5-mile trail climbs to the top of Saddle Mountain, a great lookout on clear days. The park is a real find for the naturalist interested in rare and unusual varieties of plants, many of which have established themselves along the slopes of this isolated mountain.

Campsites, facilities: There are 10 primitive tent sites, a grassy overflow area for tents, and a parking lot camping area for RVs. Drinking water, garbage bins, picnic tables, and fire grills are provided. Vault toilets and a picnic area are available. Leashed pets are permitted.

Reservations, fees: Reservations are not accepted. Sites are $5–10 per night, $5 per night per additional vehicle. Open March–October.

Directions: From Portland, turn west on U.S. 26 and drive about 63 miles to just before Necanicum Junction and Saddle Mountain Road. Turn right (north) on Saddle Mountain Road and drive seven miles to the park. The road dead-ends at the park.

Contact: Ecola State Park, 503/436-2844 or 800/551-6949 (this number reaches Ecola State Park, which manages Saddle Mountain), www.oregonstateparks.org.

8 NEHALEM BAY STATE PARK

Scenic rating: 7

on Nehalem Bay

Map 1.2, page 82

This state park on a sandy point separating the Pacific Ocean from Nehalem Bay features six miles of beach frontage. There is no ocean view from the campsites, but the sites are about 150 yards from the ocean. In 2008, beachcombers discovered a pair of historic cannons at low tide, likely dating back to an 1846 shipwreck. Crabbing and fishing on the bay are popular. The Oregon Coast Trail passes through the park. A horse camp with corrals and a 7.5-mile equestrian trail are available. There is also a two-mile bike trail. The neighboring towns of Manzanita and Nehalem offer fine dining and shopping. An airport is adjacent to the park, and there are airstrip fly-in campsites.

Campsites, facilities: There are 265 sites with partial hookups for tents or RVs up to 60 feet long, a camping area for hikers and bicyclists, and six primitive fly-in sites next to the airport. There are also 18 yurts and 17 equestrian sites with stock corrals. Drinking water, picnic tables, and fire grills are provided. Restrooms with flush toilets and showers, dump station, playgrounds, firewood, and a meeting hall are available. Boat-launching facilities are nearby on Nehalem Bay, and an airstrip is adjacent to the park. Some facilities are wheelchair accessible. Leashed pets are permitted.

Reservations, fees: Reservations are accepted at 800/452-5687 or www.oregonstateparks.org ($8 reservation fee). Sites are $16–24 per night, $5 per night per additional vehicle, and $4–5 per person per night for hikers/bikers. Yurts are $27–36 per night; horse sites are $12–19 per night. Fly-in sites are $8–10 per night, not including tie-down. Some credit cards are accepted. Open year-round.

Directions: From Portland, drive west on U.S. 26 for 73 miles to the junction with U.S. 101. Turn south on U.S. 101 and drive 19 miles to Manzanita. Continue south on U.S. 101 for 0.75 mile to Necarney City Road. Turn right and drive 0.2 mile to a stop sign. Turn right and drive 0.75 mile to the park entrance.

Contact: Nehalem Bay State Park, 503/368-5154 or 800/551-6949, www.oregonstateparks.org.

9 NEHALEM FALLS

Scenic rating: 10

in Tillamook State Forest

Map 1.2, page 82   BEST (

This beautiful campground, amid old-growth hemlock and spruce, is located within a two-minute walk of lovely Nehalem Falls. Note that swimming in the pool below the falls is hazardous and not advised. A half-mile loop trail follows the Nehalem River, where fishing and swimming are options.

Campsites, facilities: There are 14 sites for tents or RVs up to 40 feet long, four walk-in tent sites, and one group site for up to 20 people. Drinking water, picnic tables, garbage bins, recycling center, fire grills, and vault toilets are available. A camp host is on-site. Some facilities are wheelchair accessible. Leashed pets are permitted.

Reservations, fees: Reservations are accepted only for the group site at 503/842-2545. Sites are $10 per night, $2 per night per additional vehicle, walk-in sites are $5 per night, and the group site is $25 per night. Open May–October.

Directions: From Tillamook on U.S. 101 northbound, drive 22 miles to Highway 53. Turn right (east) and drive 1.3 miles to Miami Foley Road. Turn right (south) and drive one mile to Foss Road (narrow and rough). Turn left and drive seven miles to the campground on the left.

Contact: Tillamook State Forest, Tillamook District, 503/842-2545, fax 503/842-3143, www.oregon.gov.

10 BARVIEW JETTY PARK

Scenic rating: 7

near Garibaldi

Map 1.2, page 82

This Tillamook County park covers 160 acres and is located near the beach, in a wooded area adjacent to Tillamook Bay. The sites are set on grassy hills. Nearby recreation options include an 18-hole golf course, surf and scuba fishing, and a full-service marina.

Campsites, facilities: There are 224 tent sites, 69 sites for tents or RVs of any length (full hookups), and four hiker/bicyclist sites. Some sites are pull-through. Drinking water, picnic tables, and fire pits are provided. Restrooms with flush toilets and showers, a dump station, fish-cleaning station, and day-use area are available. Groups can be accommodated. Propane gas, store, café, and ice are within one mile. Some facilities are wheelchair accessible. Leashed pets are permitted.

Reservations, fees: Reservations are accepted ($5 reservation fee) at 503/322-3522 or www.co.tillamook.or.us. Sites are $10–30 per night, $3–5 per night per each additional vehicle or tent, $5 per person per night for hikers/bikers. Some credit cards are accepted. Open year-round.

Directions: From Tillamook, drive north on U.S. 101 for 12 miles to the park on the left (two miles north of the town of Garibaldi).

Contact: Barview Jetty Park, Tillamook County, 503/322-3522, www.co.tillamook.or.us/gov/parks.

11 BIAK-BY-THE-SEA RV PARK

Scenic rating: 7

on Tillamook Bay

Map 1.2, page 82

This park along the shore of Tillamook Bay is a prime retreat for beachcombing, clamming, crabbing, deep-sea fishing, scuba diving, and surf fishing. The nearby town of Tillamook is home to a cheese factory and a historical museum. Cape Meares State Park, where you can hike through the national wildlife preserve and see how the seabirds nest along the cliffs, makes a good side trip. There is also a golf course nearby. Note that most of the sites are monthly rentals.

Campsites, facilities: There are 45 pull-through sites with full hookups for RVs of any length and a grassy area for tents. Drinking water and cable TV are provided. Restrooms with flush toilets and coin showers and a coin laundry are available. Propane gas, a store, café, and ice are within one mile. Boat docks, launching facilities, and rentals are nearby. Leashed pets are permitted.

Reservations, fees: Reservations are accepted. Sites are $25 per night. Some credit cards are accepted. Open year-round.

Directions: From Tillamook and U.S. 101,

drive north for 10 miles to 7th Street. Turn left on 7th Street and drive to the park on the left (just over the tracks).

Contact: Biak-by-the-Sea RV Park, 503/322-2111.

1.2 KILCHIS RIVER PARK

Scenic rating: 8

on the Kilchis River

Map 1.2, page 82

Riverfront campsites are the highlight at this Tillamook County campground. The campground is forested and gets moderate use. Hiking trails are available. Other recreational options include boating, fishing, and swimming.

Campsites, facilities: There are 63 sites for tents or RVs of any length (no hookups), hiker/bicyclist sites, and group sites. Picnic tables, drinking water, flush toilets, and fire pits are provided. A playground, garbage bins, boat launch, day-use area, pay phone, coin showers, dump station, basketball court, and a volleyball court are available. A camp host is on-site. Leashed pets are permitted.

Reservations, fees: Reservations are accepted ($5 reservation fee) at 503/842-6694 or www.co.tillamook.or.us. Sites are $12–15 per night, $3 per night per additional vehicle, and $5 per person per night for hikers and bicyclists. Open May–September.

Directions: From Tillamook and U.S. 101, take the Alderbrook Loop/Kilches Park exit. Turn onto Alderbrook Loop and drive northeast for approximately one mile to Kilches River Road. Turn right and drive approximately four miles to the park at the end of the road.

Contact: Kilchis River Park, Tillamook County, 503/842-6694, www.co.tillamook.or.us/gov/parks.

1.3 JONES CREEK

Scenic rating: 7

on the Wilson River in Tillamook State Forest

Map 1.2, page 82

Set in a forest of alder, fir, hemlock, and spruce, campsites here are spacious and private. The adjacent Wilson River provides opportunities for steelhead and salmon fishing (artificial lures only). A scenic 3.8-mile trail runs along the riverfront. The camp fills up on weekends July–Labor Day.

Campsites, facilities: There are 29 sites for tents or RVs (27 sites are 50 feet long and one is 72 feet long and pull-through), nine walk-in tent sites, and one group site for up to 80 people. Drinking water, picnic tables, and fire grills are provided. Vault toilets, garbage bins, firewood, and a horseshoe pit are available. A camp host is on-site. Some facilities are wheelchair accessible. Leashed pets are permitted.

Reservations, fees: Reservations are accepted only for the group site at 503/842-2545. Sites are $10 per night, $2 per night per additional vehicle, walk-in sites are $5 per night, and the group site is $25 per night. Open May–October.

Directions: From Portland, turn west on U.S. 26 and drive 24 miles to Highway 6. Turn west on Highway 6 and drive 28 miles to Milepost 22.7 and North Fork Road. Turn right and drive 0.25 mile to the campground on the left.

Contact: Tillamook State Forest, Tillamook District, 503/842-2545, fax 503/842-3143, www.oregon.gov.

1.4 ELK CREEK WALK-IN

Scenic rating: 7

on Elk Creek in Tillamook State Forest

Map 1.2, page 82

This small campground is set among alder, fir, and maple on Elk Creek and borders the

Wilson River. The Elk Mountain trailhead is here and a good swimming hole is nearby. Note that Elk Creek is closed to fishing; call ahead for fishing information on the Wilson River, as regulations often change.

Campsites, facilities: There are 15 walk-in tent sites. Drinking water, picnic tables, fire grills, and vault toilets are available. Garbage must be packed out. Some facilities are wheelchair accessible. Leashed pets are permitted.

Reservations, fees: Reservations are not accepted. Sites are $5 per night, $2 per night per additional vehicle. Open early May–October.

Directions: From Portland, turn west on U.S. 26 and drive 24 miles to Highway 6. Turn west on Highway 6 and drive 23 miles to Milepost 28 and the campground entrance road on the right. Turn right on Elk Creek Road and drive 0.5 mile to the campground on the left.

Contact: Tillamook State Forest, Forest Grove District, 503/357-2191, www.oregon.gov.

15 JORDAN CREEK OHV

Scenic rating: 6

near Jordan Creek in Tillamook State Forest

Map 1.2, page 82

This off-highway vehicle (OHV) camp is set at the bottom of a scenic, steep canyon next to Jordan Creek. Wooded campsites are clustered around a central parking area, and the park caters to OHV campers. There are almost 40 miles of OHV trails, varying from moderate to difficult. Note that in order to ride an ATV on roads, you need an ATV sticker, a driver's license, and a spark arrestor. There's no fishing in Jordan Creek.

Campsites, facilities: There are six sites for tents or RVs of any length. Overflow RV camping is allowed in the main parking lot. There is no drinking water. Picnic tables, fire grills, garbage bins, and vault toilets are available. Leashed pets are permitted.

Reservations, fees: Reservations are not accepted. Sites are $10 per night, $2 per night per additional vehicle. Open March–November.

Directions: From Tillamook on U.S. 101, turn east on Highway 6 and drive 17.9 miles to Jordan Creek Road. Turn right and drive 2.2 miles to the campground on the right.

Contact: Tillamook State Forest, Tillamook District, 503/842-2545, fax 503/842-3143, www.oregon.gov.

16 GALES CREEK

Scenic rating: 7

on Gales Creek in Tillamook State Forest

Map 1.2, page 82

Gales Creek runs through this heavily forested camp. The Gales Creek Trailhead is accessible from camp, providing access to hiking and mountain biking opportunities. A day-use picnic area is also available.

Campsites, facilities: There are 19 sites for tents or RVs up to 35 feet long and four walk-in tent sites. Drinking water, picnic tables, fire grills, garbage bins, and vault toilets are available. Some facilities are wheelchair accessible. Leashed pets are permitted.

Reservations, fees: Reservations are not accepted. RV sites are $10 per night, walk-in tent sites are $5 per night, and an additional vehicle is $2 per night. Open early May–October.

Directions: From Portland, turn west on U.S. 26 and drive 24 miles to Highway 6. Turn west on Highway 6 and drive 17 miles to the campground entrance road (Rogers Road) on the right at Milepost 35. Turn right on Rogers Road and drive one mile to the campground.

Contact: Tillamook State Forest, Forest Grove District, 503/357-2191, www.oregon.gov.

17 BROWNS CAMP OHV

Scenic rating: 6

in Tillamook State Forest

Map 1.2, page 82

This camp is located next to the Devil's Lake Fork of the Wilson River and has sites with and without tree cover. Surrounded by miles of OHV trails, it caters to off-highway vehicle campers. Don't expect peace and quiet. No fishing is allowed here.

Campsites, facilities: There are 29 sites for tents or RVs up to 45 feet long. Drinking water, picnic tables, fire grills, garbage bins, and vault toilets are available. Some facilities are wheelchair accessible. Leashed pets are permitted.

Reservations, fees: Reservations are not accepted. Sites are $10 per night, $2 per night per additional vehicle. Open March–November.

Directions: From Portland, turn west on U.S. 26 and drive 24 miles to Highway 6. Turn west on Highway 6 and drive 19 miles to Beaver Dam Road. Turn left (south) and drive 2.5 miles to Scoggins Road. Turn left (southeast) and drive 0.5 mile to the campground.

Contact: Tillamook State Forest, Forest Grove District, 503/357-2191, www.oregon.gov.

18 TRASK RIVER PARK

Scenic rating: 7

on the Trask River

Map 1.2, page 82

This is a popular campground and park that gets moderate use primarily from the locals in Tillamook County. Some campsites are shaded. Fishing for trout and steelhead is available in season; check current fishing regulations.

Campsites, facilities: There are 63 sites for tents or RVs of any length (no hookups) and a hiker/bicyclist area. Picnic tables, garbage service, and fire pits are provided. Drinking water, vault toilets, and a day-use area are available. A camp host is on-site. Some facilities are wheelchair accessible. Leashed pets are permitted.

Reservations, fees: Reservations are accepted ($5 reservation fee) at 503/842-4559 or www.co.tillamook.or.us. Sites are $10–15 per night, $3 per night for additional vehicle, and $5 per person per night for hikers/bicyclists. Some credit cards are accepted. Open year-round.

Directions: From Tillamook and U.S. 101, turn east on 3rd Street. Drive 2.5 miles to Trask River Road. Turn right and drive 1.5 miles, turning left to stay on Trask River Road. Continue 10 miles to the park.

Contact: Trask River Park, Tillamook County, 503/842-4559, www.co.tillamook.or.us/gov/parks.

19 NETARTS BAY RV PARK & MARINA

Scenic rating: 8

on Netarts Bay

Map 1.2, page 82

This camp is one of three on the east shore of Netarts Bay. A golf course is eight miles away. Sunsets and wildlife-viewing are notable here. Some sites are filled with rentals for the summer season.

Campsites, facilities: There are 88 sites with full hookups for RVs of any length; some are pull-through sites. Drinking water and picnic tables are provided, and fire rings are available at some sites. Restrooms with flush toilets and showers, propane gas, a meeting room, coin laundry, playground, horseshoe pits, crab-cooking facilities, crab bait, and ice are available. Boat docks, launching facilities, and rentals are available on-site. A store and a café are within one mile. Leashed pets are permitted, with a two-pet maximum.

Reservations, fees: Reservations are recommended. Sites are $28–35 per night, $5 per night per additional vehicle. Some credit cards are accepted. Monthly rentals are available. Open year-round.

Directions: From Tillamook and Netarts Highway/Highway 131, drive west on Netarts Highway for six miles to the campground entrance.

Contact: Netarts Bay RV Park & Marina, 503/842-7774, www.netartsbay.com.

20 PLEASANT VALLEY RV PARK

Scenic rating: 8

on the Tillamook River

Map 1.2, page 82

Pleasant Valley RV Park sits along the Tillamook River. The park is very clean and provides easy access to many recreation options in the immediate area.

Campsites, facilities: There are 10 tent sites and 76 pull-through sites with full or partial hookups for RVs of any length, plus two cabins. Drinking water and picnic tables are provided and some sites have fire rings. Restrooms with flush toilets and showers, propane gas, dump station, firewood, a meeting room, cable TV, modem access, convenience store, coin laundry, ice, and a playground are available. Boat-launching facilities are nearby. Leashed pets are permitted.

Reservations, fees: Reservations are accepted. RV sites are $28-32 per night, tent sites are $18 per night, $2 per person per night for more than two people; cabins are $29 per night. Some credit cards are accepted. Open year-round.

Directions: From Tillamook and U.S. 101, drive south on U.S. 101 for 7 miles to the campground entrance on the right (west).

Contact: Pleasant Valley RV Park, 503/842-4779, fax 503/842-2293, www.pleasantvalleyrvpark.com.

21 CAPE LOOKOUT STATE PARK

Scenic rating: 8

near Netarts Bay

Map 1.2, page 82   BEST (

This park is set on a sand spit between Netarts Bay and the Pacific. There are more than eight miles of wooded trails, including the Cape Lookout Trail which follows the headland for more than two miles. Another walk will take you out through a variety of estuarine habitats along the five-mile sand spit that extends between the ocean and Netarts Bay. With many species to view, this area is a paradise for bird-watchers. You might also catch the local hang gliders and paragliders that frequent the park. Fishing is another option here.

Campsites, facilities: There are 173 sites for tents or RVs (no hookups), 38 sites with full hookups for RVs up to 60 feet long, a tent camping area for hikers and bicyclists, two group tent sites for up to 25 people each, three cabins, and 13 yurts. Picnic tables and fire grills are provided. Restrooms with flush toilets and showers, dump station, garbage bins, meeting hall and picnic shelter, summer interpretive programs, and firewood are available. Some facilities are wheelchair accessible. Leashed pets are permitted.

Reservations, fees: Reservations are accepted at 800/452-5687 or www.oregonstateparks.org ($8 reservation fee). RV sites are $16-24 per night, tent sites are $12-19 per night, $4-5 per person per night for hikers/bikers, $40-71 per night for group sites, $45-76 per night for cabins, and $27-36 per night for yurts, $5 per night per additional vehicle. Some credit cards are accepted. Open year-round.

Directions: From Tillamook and U.S. 101, turn east on 3rd Street (becomes Netarts Highway). Drive approximately five miles to Whiskey Creek Road. Turn left and drive approximately seven miles to the park on the right.

Contact: Cape Lookout State Park, 503/842-4981, www.oregonstateparks.org.

22 WHALEN ISLAND PARK

Scenic rating: 6

in the Sandlake Estuary

Map 1.2, page 82

This park is located in the Sandlake Estuary and is close to the beach and Nestucca Bay. The campground is fairly open and has a few trees.

Campsites, facilities: There are 34 sites for tents or RVs of any length (no hookups) and two hiker/bicyclist sites. Picnic tables and fire pits are provided. Drinking water, flush and chemical toilets, dump station, a day-use area, and a boat launch are available. A camp host is on-site during the summer. Some facilities are wheelchair accessible. Leashed pets are permitted.

Reservations, fees: Reservations are accepted ($5 reservation fee). Sites are $10–15 per night, $3 per night per additional vehicle, and $5 per person per night for hikers and bicyclists. Open March–November; check for current status at other times of year.

Directions: From Tillamook and U.S. 101, drive south for 11 miles to Sand Lake Road. Turn right (west) and drive approximately 55 miles to a stop sign. Turn left to stay on Sand Lake Road. Continue 4.75 miles south to the park entrance road on the right.

Contact: Whalen Island Park, Tillamook County, 503/965-6085, www.co.tillamook.or.us/gov/parks.

23 SANDBEACH, EAST DUNES, AND WEST WINDS OHV

Scenic rating: 5

in Siuslaw National Forest

Map 1.2, page 82

Sandbeach campground is set along the shore of Sand Lake, which is actually more like an estuary than a lake since the ocean is just around the bend. This area is known for

its beaches with large sand dunes, which are popular with off-road-vehicle enthusiasts. It's noisy and can be windy. East Dunes and West Winds, which used to be the overflow parking area, are nearby. This is the only coastal U.S. Forest Service camping area for many miles, and it's quite popular. If you're planning a trip for midsummer, be sure to reserve far in advance. Holiday permits are required ($10 at the district office) for three-day holiday weekends.

Campsites, facilities: At Sandbeach, there are 101 sites for tents or RVs; West Winds has 51 sites for tents or RVs; and East Dunes has 51 sites for tents or RVs. There are no hookups and RV length limit is 60 feet long. Picnic tables and fire pits are provided. Drinking water, garbage bins, and flush toilets are available. A camp host is on-site at each campground. Leashed pets are permitted.

Reservations, fees: Reservations are accepted during the summer season at 877/444-6777 or www.recreation.gov ($10 reservation fee). Sites at Sandbeach are $20 per night; sites at East Dunes and West Winds are $15 per night. Additional vehicles cost $8 per night at all campgrounds. Open year-round.

Directions: From Tillamook on U.S. 101, drive south for 11 miles to County Road 8. Turn right (west) on County Road 8 and drive approximately 12 miles to the campground.

Contact: Siuslaw National Forest, Hebo Ranger District, 503/392-3161, fax 503/392-4203, www.fs.fed.us.

24 CAMPER COVE RV PARK AND CAMPGROUND

Scenic rating: 6

on Beaver Creek

Map 1.2, page 82

This small, wooded campground along Beaver Creek is set just far enough off the highway to provide quiet. The park can be used as a base camp for anglers, with seasonal steelhead and salmon fishing in the nearby Nestucca River. It gets crowded here, especially in the summer, so be sure to make a reservation if possible. Ocean beaches are four miles away.

Campsites, facilities: There are 50 sites with full hookups for RVs up to 40 feet long, five tent sites, and three cabins. Drinking water, fire pits, and picnic tables are provided. Restrooms with flush toilets and coin showers, dump station, firewood, recreation hall, coin laundry, and ice are available. Leashed pets are permitted.

Reservations, fees: Reservations are accepted. RV sites are $28 per night, tent sites are $20 per night, $3 per person per night for more than two people and $3 per night per additional vehicle. Open year-round.

Directions: From Tillamook and U.S. 101, drive south on U.S. 101 for 12 miles to the park entrance on the right (west), three miles north of Beaver.

Contact: Camper Cove RV Park and Campground, 503/398-5334, www.campercovecampground.com.

25 ROCKY BEND

Scenic rating: 5

on the Nestucca River in
Siuslaw National Forest

Map 1.2, page 82

This campground along the Nestucca River is a little-known, secluded spot that provides guaranteed peace and quiet. There isn't much in the way of recreational activities out here, but clamming, fishing, hiking, and swimming are available along the coast, a relatively short drive away.

Campsites, facilities: There are six tent sites. Picnic tables and fire pits are provided. Vault toilets are available. There is no drinking water and garbage must be packed out. Leashed pets are permitted.

Reservations, fees: Reservations are not accepted. There is no fee for camping. Open year-round.

Directions: On U.S. 101 southwest of Portland, drive to the tiny town of Beaver and Blaine Road. Turn east on Blaine Road (keep right; Blaine Road turns into Nestucca River Access Road) and drive 15.5 miles to the campground on the right.

Contact: Siuslaw National Forest, Hebo Ranger District, 503/392-5100, fax 503/392-5143, www.fs.fed.us.

26 DOVRE, FAN CREEK, ALDER GLEN

Scenic rating: 5

on the Nestucca River

Map 1.2, page 82

This is a series of three BLM campgrounds set along the Nestucca River. The camps, separated by alder trees and shrubs, are near the river, and some have river views. Tourists don't know about these spots. The Nestucca is a gentle river, with the water not deep enough for swimming.

Campsites, facilities: Dovre has 10 sites, Fan Creek has 11 sites, and Alder Glen has 11 sites—all for tents or small RVs. Picnic tables and fire grills are provided. Drinking water and vault toilets are available. Garbage must be packed out. Some facilities, including a fishing pier at Alder Glen, are wheelchair accessible. Leashed pets are permitted.

Reservations, fees: Reservations are not accepted. Sites are $10 per night, $4 per night per additional vehicle with a limit of two vehicles per site. Open year-round.

Directions: On U.S. 101 southwest of Portland, drive to the tiny town of Beaver and Blaine Road. Turn east on Blaine Road (keep right; Blaine Road turns into Nestucca River Access Road) and drive 17.5 miles to Alder Glen. Continue east for seven more miles to reach Fan Creek and nine more miles to reach Dovre.

Contact: Bureau of Land Management, Salem District, 503/375-5646, fax 503/375-5622, www.blm.gov.

27 WOODS COUNTY PARK

🚶🏼 🚲 🛶 🐕 🚐 ⛺

Scenic rating: 6

on the Kilchis River

Map 1.2, page 82

This small Tillamook County park is not well known outside the local area and gets fairly light use. The campground is grassy with few trees. Salmon fishing is a possibility; check current regulations.

Campsites, facilities: There are seven tent sites and five sites for RVs up to 40 feet long. Picnic tables and fire pits are provided. Drinking water, flush toilets, garbage containers, and a day-use area are available. A camp host is on-site. Leashed pets are permitted.

Reservations, fees: Reservations are accepted ($5 reservation fee) at 503/965-5001 or www. co.tillamook.or.us. Sites are $15–25 per night, $3 per night per additional vehicle. Open May–October, weather permitting.

Directions: From Tillamook and U.S. 101, drive approximately 25 miles south to Resort Drive. Turn right (west) and drive three miles (road changes to Brooten Drive) to the park on the right.

Contact: Woods County Park, Tillamook County, 503/965-5001, www.co.tillamook. or.us/gov/parks.

28 CAPE KIWANDA RV RESORT

🚶🏼 🚲 🏊 🛶 🚤 🎣 🐕 🚐 ⛺

Scenic rating: 8

near Cape Kiwanda State Park

Map 1.2, page 82

This park is set a short distance from Cape Kiwanda State Park, which is open for day use only. Highlights at the park include a boat launch and hiking trails that lead out to the cape. Four miles south at Nestucca Spit, there is another day-use park, providing additional recreational options. The point extends about three miles and is a good spot

for bird-watching. The campsites do not have ocean views, but the ocean is across the road and within walking distance. Surfing is an option.

Campsites, facilities: There are 150 sites with full hookups for RVs up to 65 feet long, 13 tent sites, and 14 camping cabins. Some sites are pull-through. Drinking water, fire rings, and picnic tables are provided. Restrooms with flush toilets and showers, dump station, modem access, a heated swimming pool (year-round), hot tub, an exercise room, firewood, a recreation hall, coin laundry, propane, a seafood market, deli, gift shop, automated teller machine (ATM), sandboard rentals, and a playground are available. Gasoline, a store, and a café are within one mile. Boat docks, launching facilities, and rentals are nearby. Leashed pets are permitted.

Reservations, fees: Reservations are accepted. RV sites are $40.95–43.95 per night, tent sites are $26 per night, $2–4 per person per night for more than two people, and $4 per night per additional vehicle. Some credit cards are accepted. Open year-round.

Directions: From Tillamook and U.S. 101, drive south on U.S. 101 for 25 miles to the Pacific City exit and Brooten Road. Turn right on Brooten Road and drive three miles toward Pacific City and Three Capes Drive. Turn left, cross the bridge, and bear right on Three Capes Drive. Continue one mile north to the park on the right.

Contact: Cape Kiwanda RV Resort, 503/965-6230, fax 503/965-6235, www.capekiwandarvpark.com.

29 WEBB PARK

🚶🏼 🚲 🛶 🐕 🚐 ⛺

Scenic rating: 7

near Cape Kiwanda

Map 1.2, page 82

This public campground provides an excellent alternative to the more crowded commercial RV parks off U.S. 101. Although not as developed, it offers a quiet, private setting and access to the ocean. Fishing and swimming are among your options here. The camp is adjacent to Cape Kiwanda and provides convenient access to the beach.

Campsites, facilities: There are 31 sites for tents or RVs (no hookups), seven sites with partial hookups for RVs up to 40 feet long, and a hiker/bicyclist site. Picnic tables and fire pits are provided. Drinking water, a dump station, fish-cleaning station, and restrooms with flush toilets and showers are available. Beach launching is nearby. Leashed pets are permitted.

Reservations, fees: Reservations are accepted ($5 reservation fee) at 503/965-5001 or www.co.tillamook.or.us. Sites are $15–25 per night, $3 per night per additional vehicle, and $5 per person per night for hikers/bikers. Some credit cards are accepted. Open May–September.

Directions: From Tillamook and U.S. 101, drive south on U.S. 101 for 25 miles to the Pacific City exit and Highway 30. From Pacific City, turn right (north) and drive to the four-way stop at McPhillips Drive. Turn left on McPhillips Drive and drive 0.5 mile to Cape Kiwanda and the park on the right.

Contact: Webb Park, Tillamook County Parks, 503/965-5001, www.co.tillamook.or.us/gov/parks.

30 HEBO LAKE

Scenic rating: 7

on Hebo Lake in Siuslaw National Forest

Map 1.2, page 82

This U.S. Forest Service campground along the shore of Hebo Lake is a secluded spot with sites nestled under trees. The trailhead for the eight-mile-long Pioneer-Indian Trail is located in the campground. The trail around the lake is wheelchair accessible.

Campsites, facilities: There are 15 sites for tents or RVs up to 18 feet long. Picnic tables and fire pits are provided. Drinking water,

garbage bins, and vault toilets are available. Boats with electric motors are allowed on the lake, but gas motors are not. Some facilities are wheelchair accessible. Leashed pets are permitted.

Reservations, fees: Reservations are not accepted. Sites are $12 per night, $5 per night per additional vehicle. Open from mid-April to mid-November, weather permitting.

Directions: On U.S. 101 southwest of Portland, drive to the town of Hebo and Highway 22. Turn east on Highway 22 and drive 0.25 mile to Forest Road 14. Turn left (east) and drive five miles to the campground on the right.

Contact: Siuslaw National Forest, Hebo Ranger District, 503/392-5100, fax 503/392-5143, www.fs.fed.us.

31 CASTLE ROCK

Scenic rating: 4

on Three Rivers in Siuslaw National Forest

Map 1.2, page 82

This tiny spot along Three Rivers provides tent campers with an inland alternative to the large beachfront RV parks popular on the Oregon coast. Fishing can be good here. Though primitive, this camp is located along the edge of the highway and can fill up quickly.

Campsites, facilities: There are four tent sites. Picnic tables, garbage bins, and a vault toilet are provided. There is no drinking water. Leashed pets are permitted.

Reservations, fees: Reservations are not accepted. There is no fee for camping. Open year-round, weather permitting.

Directions: On U.S. 101 southwest of Portland, drive to the town of Hebo and Highway 22. Turn east on Highway 22 and drive five miles to the campground on the right.

Contact: Siuslaw National Forest, Hebo Ranger District, 503/392-5100, fax 503/392-5143, www.fs.fed.us.

32 WANDERING SPIRIT RV PARK

Scenic rating: 6

on Rock Creek

Map 1.2, page 82

The major draw here is the nearby casino, but there is the added benefit of shaded sites next to Rock Creek, which provides fishing and swimming options. The Yamhill River is 0.5 mile away. Fishing is good for steelhead and salmon in season. Golf courses and wineries are available within 10 miles. There is a combination of monthly rentals and overnighters at this park.

Campsites, facilities: There are 129 sites with full hookups for RVs up to 45 feet long, 10 tent sites, and four park-model cabins. Some sites are pull-through. Drinking water, cable TV, wireless Internet service, modem access, restrooms with showers, dump station, coin laundry, RV storage, RV supplies, and a convenience store are available. Propane, a clubhouse, basketball hoop, an exercise room, and a game room are also available on-site. A 24-hour free bus shuttles campers to and from the Spirit Mountain Casino, restaurants, and shops less than two miles away. Some facilities are wheelchair accessible. Leashed pets are permitted.

Reservations, fees: Reservations are accepted at 800/390-6980. RV sites are $26 per night, tent sites are $16 per night, $2 per person per night for more than two people. Monthly rates are available. Some credit cards are accepted. Open year-round.

Directions: From Salem, drive west on Highway 22 about 25 miles to Highway 18. Turn west on Highway 18 and drive seven miles to the park on the left.

Contact: Wandering Spirit RV Park, 503/879-5700, fax 503/879-5171.

33 DEVIL'S LAKE STATE PARK

Scenic rating: 7

on Devil's Lake

Map 1.3, page 83

Oregon's only coastal camp in the midst of a city, Devil's Lake is the center of summertime activity. A take-your-pick deal: You can boat, canoe, fish, kayak, or water ski. A walking path extends from the campground to the boat launch 0.25 mile away. For something different, head west and explore the seven miles of beaches. Lincoln City also has a number of arts and crafts galleries and a weekend farmers market during the summer. East Devil's Lake is two miles east and offers a boat ramp and picnic facilities.

Campsites, facilities: There are 54 sites for tents or small RVs (no hookups), 33 sites for tents or RVs up to 55 feet long (full hookups), 10 yurts, and a separate area for hikers and bikers. Picnic tables and fire grills are provided. Drinking water, cable TV, garbage bins, restrooms with flush toilets and showers, an amphitheater, and firewood are available. Boat docks and launching facilities are nearby. Some facilities are wheelchair accessible. Leashed pets are permitted.

Reservations, fees: Reservations are accepted at 800/452-5687 or www.oregonstateparks. org ($8 reservation fee). RV sites are $17–23 per night, $5 per night per additional vehicle, tent sites are $13–17 per night, $4 per person per night for hikers/bikers, and yurts are $29 per night. Boat mooring is $7 per night. Some credit cards are accepted. Open year-round.

Directions: From Lincoln City and U.S. 101, take the 6th Street exit. Drive east on 6th Street for one block to the park on the right.

Contact: Devil's Lake State Park, 503/994-2002 or 800/551-6949, www.oregonstate parks.org.

34 KOA LINCOLN CITY

Scenic rating: 7

on Devils Lake

Map 1.3, page 83

This area offers opportunities for beach-combing, fishing, and tidepool-viewing along a seven-mile stretch of beach. Nearby recreation options include a casino, factory outlets, a golf course, skateboard park, and tennis courts.

Campsites, facilities: There are 15 tent sites and 81 sites with full or partial hookups for RVs up to 60 feet long, including some pull-through sites, and 30- and 50-amp service is available. There are also 14 cabins. Picnic tables and fire pits are provided. Drinking water, cable TV, modem access, restrooms with flush toilets and showers, dump station, public phones, convenience store, snack bar, gift shop, propane gas, ice, RV supplies, video and DVD rentals, game room, coin laundry, meeting room, firewood, and a playground are available. Leashed pets are permitted.

Reservations, fees: Reservations are accepted at 800/562-2791. RV sites are $20–32 per night, tent sites are $20–25 per night, $3 per person per night for more than two people, $7.50 per night per additional vehicle. Some credit cards are accepted. Open year-round.

Directions: From Portland, drive south on Highway 99 West to Highway 18. Turn west on Highway 18 and drive 47 miles to U.S. 101. Turn south on U.S. 101 and drive 1.5 miles to East Devil's Lake Road. Turn east on East Devil's Lake Road and drive one mile to the park on the left.

Contact: KOA Lincoln City, 541/994-2961, fax 541/994-9454, www.koa.com.

35 SEA AND SAND RV PARK

Scenic rating: 9

near Siletz Bay

Map 1.3, page 83

Beachcombing for fossils and agates is popular at this oceanfront park near Gleneden Beach on Siletz Bay. Some sites have ocean views and pleasant terraces. The Siletz River and numerous small creeks are in the area. The park is located 3.5 miles north of Depoe Bay.

Campsites, facilities: There are 109 sites with full hookups for RVs up to 35 feet long. Drinking water, cable TV, fire pits, and picnic tables are provided. Restrooms with flush toilets and showers, dump station, firewood, and a coin laundry are available. A store, café, and ice are within one mile. Leashed pets are permitted.

Reservations, fees: Reservations are accepted. Sites are $29–57 per night, $2 per person per night for more than two people, and $5 per night per additional vehicle unless towed. Open year-round.

Directions: From Lincoln City and U.S. 101, drive south for nine miles on U.S. 101 to the park entrance (on the beach side of the highway).

Contact: Sea and Sand RV Park, 541/764-2313.

36 BEVERLY BEACH STATE PARK

Scenic rating: 7

near Newport

Map 1.3, page 83

This beautiful campground is set in a wooded, grassy area on the east side of U.S. 101. Treed campsites sit along Spencer Creek. A tunnel leads under the roadway to a beach that stretches from Yaguna Head to the Otter Rock headlands. A one-mile hiking trail is available. Just a mile to the north lies a small day-use state park called Devil's Punchbowl, named for an unusual bowl-shaped rock formation with caverns under it where the waves rumble about. For some great ocean views, head north one more mile to the Otter Crest Wayside. The Oregon Coast Aquarium is within a few minutes' drive.

Campsites, facilities: There are 128 sites for tents or small RVs, 128 sites with full or partial hookups for tents or RVs up to 65 feet long, a special camping area for hikers and bicyclists, and five group sites for tents or RVs (no hookups) that can accommodate up to 25 people each. There is also a village of 21 yurts. Picnic tables and fire grills are provided. Drinking water, restrooms with flush toilets and showers, cable TV, a playground, a day-use area, garbage bins, and a dump station are available. Some facilities are wheelchair accessible. Leashed pets are permitted.

Reservations, fees: Reservations are accepted at 800/452-5687 or www.oregonstateparks.org ($8 reservation fee). Sites are $13–26 per night, $5 per night per additional vehicle, $4–6 per person per night for hikers/bikers, $30–40 per night for yurts, and $44–77 for group sites. Some credit cards are accepted. Open year-round.

Directions: From Newport and U.S. 101, drive north on U.S. 101 for seven miles to the park entrance on the east side.

Contact: Beverly Beach State Park, 541/265-9278 or 800/551-6949, www.oregonstateparks. org.

37 AGATE BEACH RV PARK

Scenic rating: 6

near Newport

Map 1.3, page 83

This park is located about half a mile from Agate Beach Wayside, a small state park with beach access. Agate hunting can be good. Sometimes, a layer of sand covers the agates, and you have to dig a bit. But other times, wave action clears the sand, unveiling the agates at low tides. Beverly Beach State Park is 4.5 miles north. About half of the sites are filled with monthly rentals. There are no ocean views from the campsites.

Campsites, facilities: There are 32 sites with full or partial hookups for RVs up to 40 feet long. Drinking water, cable TV, and picnic tables are provided. Restroom with flush toilets and showers, dump station, and a coin laundry room are available. A store and ice are within one mile. Leashed pets are permitted, with some restrictions.

Reservations, fees: Reservations are accepted. Sites are $22.50 per night, $1 per person per night for more than two people, and $1 per night per additional vehicle. Some credit cards are accepted. Open year-round.

Directions: From Newport and U.S. 101, drive to the north end of town. The park is on the east side of the road.

Contact: Agate Beach RV Park, 541/265-7670.

38 HARBOR VILLAGE RV PARK

Scenic rating: 6

on Yaquina Bay

Map 1.3, page 83

This wooded and landscaped park is set near the shore of Yaquina Bay. Nearby recreation options include clamming, crabbing, deep-sea fishing, an 18-hole golf course, hiking trails, and a full-service marina.

Campsites, facilities: There are 40 sites with full hookups for RVs up to 35 feet long. Note that there are also 100 sites for full-time renters and a mobile-home park for ages 55 and up. Drinking water, cable TV, wireless Internet service, modem access, and picnic tables are provided. Restrooms with flush toilets and showers and a coin laundry are available. Propane gas, a store, and a café are within one mile. Boat docks, launching facilities, and rentals are nearby. Leashed pets are permitted.

Reservations, fees: Reservations are accepted at 888/818-0002. Sites are $30 per night, $5 per person per night for more than two people. Some credit cards are accepted. Open year-round.

Directions: In Newport, drive south on John Moore Road for 0.5 mile to the bay and Bay Boulevard. Bear left and drive a short distance to the park entrance on the left.

Contact: Harbor Village RV Park, 541/265-5088, fax 541/265-5895, www.harborvillag-ervpark.com.

39 PORT OF NEWPORT MARINA AND RV PARK

Scenic rating: 7

on Yaquina Bay

Map 1.3, page 83

This public park is set along the shore of Yaquina Bay near Newport, a resort town that offers a variety of attractions. Among them are ocean fishing, a museum and aquarium at the nearby Hatfield Marine Science Center, the Undersea Garden, the Waxworks, Ripley's Believe It or Not, and the Lincoln County Historical Society Museum. Nearby recreation options include an 18-hole golf course, hiking trails, and a full-service marina.

Campsites, facilities: There are 143 sites with full hookups for RVs up to 45 feet long. Restrooms with flush toilets and showers, cable TV, Wi-Fi, modem access, dump station, convenience store, coin laundry, fish-cleaning station, and ice are available. A marina with boat docks and launching facilities is available on-site. Some facilities are wheelchair accessible. Leashed pets are permitted.

Reservations, fees: Reservations are accepted at 541/867-3321. Sites with hookups are $29.73–40.78 per night, sites without hookups are $17.68 per night, $1 per person per night for more than two people. Weekly rates

are available. Some credit cards are accepted. Open year-round.

Directions: From Newport and U.S. 101, drive south for 0.5 mile (over the bridge) to Marine Science Drive. Turn right (east) and drive 0.5 mile to the park entrance on the left.

Contact: Port of Newport Marina and RV Park, 541/867-3321, fax 541/867-3352, www.portofnewport.com.

40 SOUTH BEACH STATE PARK

Scenic rating: 7

near Newport

Map 1.3, page 83

This park along the beach offers opportunities for beachcombing, boating, crabbing, fishing, hiking, and windsurfing. The Oregon Coast Trail passes right through the park. A nature trail circles the campground, and there are hiking and bicycling trails to the beach. A primitive hike-in campground is also available. A naturalist provides campground talks during the summer season. Kayak trips are an option during the summer. The park is within walking distance of Oregon Aquarium. Newport attractions include the Hatfield Marine Science Center, the Undersea Garden, the Waxworks, Ripley's Believe It or Not, and the Lincoln County Historical Society Museum.

Campsites, facilities: There are 228 sites with partial hookups for tents or RVs up to 45 feet long, six primitive tent sites, a dispersed camping area (without designated sites) for hikers and bicyclists, and an overflow area for RVs. There are also three group sites for up to 25 people each and 27 yurts. Picnic tables and fire grills are provided. Drinking water, restrooms with flush toilets and showers, garbage bins, recycling, a dump station, Wi-Fi, horseshoe pits, playground, a day-use area, meeting hall, and firewood are available. A camp host is on-site. Some facilities are wheelchair accessible. Leashed pets are permitted.

Reservations, fees: Reservations are accepted at 800/452-5687 or www.oregonstateparks. org ($8 reservation fee). Sites are $18–27 per night, $5 per night per additional vehicle, $4–6 per person per night for hikers/bicyclists (three-night limit), $10 for primitive tent sites, $44–77 per night for group sites, and $30–40 per night for yurts. Some credit cards are accepted. Open year-round.

Directions: From Newport and U.S. 101, drive south for three miles to the park entrance on the right.

Contact: South Beach State Park, 541/867-4715 or 800/551-6949, www.oregonstateparks. org.

41 SEAL ROCKS RV COVE

Scenic rating: 8

near Seal Rock State Park

Map 1.3, page 83   BEST

This RV park is situated on the rugged coastline near Seal Rock State Park (open for day use only), where you may find seals, sea lions, and a variety of birds. The ocean views are stunning, and some sites have views.

Campsites, facilities: There are 28 sites with full hookups for RVs of any length and 16 tent sites with electricity. Drinking water, picnic tables, and fire rings are provided. Firewood and restrooms with flush toilets and showers are available. A store, a café, and ice are within one mile. Leashed pets are permitted.

Reservations, fees: Reservations are accepted. RV sites are $29–36 per night, tent sites are $20–24 per night, $1–3 per person per night for more than two people, and there's a $3 one-time fee for an additional vehicle unless towed. Winter rates are available. Open year-round.

Directions: From Newport and U.S. 101, drive south for 10 miles to the town of Seal Rock. Continue south on U.S. 101 for 0.25 mile to the park entrance on the left.

Contact: Seal Rocks RV Cove, 541/563-3955, www.sealrocksrv.com.

42 DRIFT CREEK LANDING

Scenic rating: 6

on the Alsea River

Map 1.3, page 83

Drift Creek Landing is set along the shore of the Alsea River in a heavily treed and mountainous area. The Oregon Coast Aquarium is 15 miles away, and an 18-hole golf course is nearby. There are 10 mobile homes with long-term renters on this property, and more than one-third of the RV sites are taken by monthly renters.

Campsites, facilities: There are 49 sites with full hookups for RVs of any length, five sites for tents, and three cabins. Drinking water and picnic tables are provided. Restroom with flush toilets and showers, cable TV, propane gas, recreation hall, convenience store, snack bar, coin laundry, boat docks, boat rentals, and launching facilities are available. Leashed pets are permitted.

Reservations, fees: Reservations are accepted. RV sites are $22 per night, and tent sites are $15 per night; it's $2 per person per night for more than two people and $5 per night per additional vehicle. Some credit cards are accepted. Open year-round.

Directions: From Newport and U.S. 101, drive south for 14 miles to Waldport and Highway 34. Turn east on Highway 34 and drive 3.8 miles to the campground.

Contact: Drift Creek Landing, 541/563-3610, fax 541/563-5234.

43 FISHIN' HOLE RV PARK & MARINA

Scenic rating: 6

on the Alsea River

Map 1.3, page 83

This campground is one of several along the shore of the Alsea River. Kayaking and canoeing are popular. Some of the sites here are filled with monthly rentals.

Campsites, facilities: There are 24 sites with full or partial hookups for RVs of any length, six sites for tents, one rental home, and one cabin. Drinking water and picnic tables are provided, and fire pits are available on request. Restrooms with flush toilets and showers, coin laundry, recreation room, bait and tackle, boat docks, boat rentals, and launching facilities are available. Leashed pets are permitted.

Reservations, fees: Reservations are accepted at 877/770-6137. Tent sites are $17 per night, RV sites are $21–23 per night, and it's $5 person per night for more than two people and $5 per night per additional vehicle. Some credit cards are accepted. Open year-round.

Directions: From Newport and U.S. 101, drive south for 14 miles to Waldport and Highway 34. Turn east on Highway 34 and drive four miles to the entrance on the left.

Contact: Fishin' Hole RV Park & Marina, 541/563-3401.

44 CHINOOK RV PARK
🏊 🎣 🚐 🦌 🚗 🏕

Scenic rating: 7

on the Alsea River

Map 1.3, page 83

This park is set along the shore of the Alsea River, about 3.5 miles from the ocean. The park is filled primarily with monthly rentals, although several RV sites are reserved for short-term campers. Campsites are rented on a space-available basis.

Campsites, facilities: There are six sites for tents and 34 sites with full or partial hookups for RVs up to 40 feet long. Picnic tables are provided. Drinking water, cable TV, wireless Internet service, restrooms with flush toilets and showers, a picnic area, ice, and a coin laundry are available. A store is within 1.5 miles. Boat docks are nearby. Propane gas and boat launching facilities are available 3.5 miles away. Leashed pets are permitted.

Reservations, fees: Reservations are accepted. RV sites are $22–27 per night, tent sites are $15.75–17.50 per night, $3 per person per night for more than two people. Open year-round.

Directions: From Newport and U.S. 101, drive south for 14 miles to Waldport and Highway 34. Turn east on Highway 34 and drive 3.3 miles to the park entrance on the left.

Contact: Chinook RV Park, 541/563-3485, www.chinookrvpark.com.

45 TAYLOR'S LANDING RV PARK
🚶 🏊 🎣 🚐 🦌 🚗 🏕

Scenic rating: 9

on the Alsea River

Map 1.3, page 83

This wooded campground is set along the scenic Alsea River. Fall, when the salmon fishing is best, is the prime time here, and the park often fills up. Recreation options include hiking trails, marked bike trails, the Oregon Coast Aquarium, the Sea Lion Caves, and a marina.

Campsites, facilities: There are 81 sites for tents or RVs of any length (full hookups). Drinking water, cable TV, and picnic tables are provided. Restrooms with flush toilets and showers, propane gas, a café, coin laundry, community fire ring, and boat docks and rentals are available. Boat launching facilities are nearby. Leashed pets are permitted.

Reservations, fees: Reservations are accepted. Sites are $27 per night, $1 per person per night for more than two people. Monthly rates are available. Open year-round.

Directions: From Newport and U.S. 101, drive south for 14 miles to Waldport and Highway 34. Turn east on Highway 34 and drive seven miles to the entrance on the right.

Contact: Taylor's Landing RV Park, phone/fax 541/528-3388, www.taylorslandingrvpark-marina.com.

46 WALDPORT/NEWPORT KOA

Scenic rating: 8

on Alsea Bay

Map 1.3, page 83   BEST (

This pretty park, set amid some of the oldest pine trees in Oregon, is located within walking distance of the beach, the bay, and downtown Waldport—and to top it off, some of the campsites have beautiful ocean views. Alsea Bay's sandy and rocky shoreline makes this area a favorite with anglers. The crabbing and clamming can also be quite good. Kite flying is popular. South Beach State Park, about five miles north on U.S. 101, offers more fishing and a boat ramp along Beaver Creek. It's open for day use only. Other nearby recreation options include hiking trails, marked bike trails, the Oregon Coast Aquarium, the Sea Lion Caves, and a marina.

Campsites, facilities: There are 10 tent sites and 66 sites for RVs up to 45 feet long (full hookups), and 15 cabins. Picnic tables and fire pits are provided; drinking water and cable TV are also available. Restrooms with flush toilets and showers, wireless Internet service, modem access, recreation room, propane gas, dump station, store, café, coin laundry, playground, and ice are available. Boat docks, launching facilities, and boat rentals are nearby. A café is within one mile. Leashed pets are permitted, with certain restrictions.

Reservations, fees: Reservations are accepted at 800/562-3443. RV sites are $46.50–59.50 per night, tent sites are $25–26 per night, $2–5 per person per night for more than two people. Some credit cards are accepted. Open year-round.

Directions: From Newport and U.S. 101, drive south for approximately 14 miles to Milepost 155 at the north end of the Alsea Bay Bridge. The park is on the west side of the bridge.

Contact: Waldport/Newport KOA, 541/563-2250, fax 541/563-4098, www.koa.com.

47 BEACHSIDE STATE RECREATION SITE

Scenic rating: 7

near Alsea Bay

Map 1.3, page 83

This state park offers about nine miles of beach and is not far from Alsea Bay and the Alsea River. Sites are close to the beach. Nearby attractions include clamming, crabbing, and fishing, as well as hiking and driving tours, tidepools, an aquarium, three lighthouses, science centers, and visitors centers. South Beach State Park, about five miles north on U.S. 101, offers more fishing and a boat ramp along Beaver Creek (day use only).

Campsites, facilities: There are 42 sites for tents, 32 sites with partial hookups for RVs up to 30 feet long, two yurts, and a special camping area for hikers and bicyclists. Picnic tables and fire grills are provided. Drinking water, garbage bins, restrooms with flush toilets and showers, recycling, and firewood are available. A horseshoe pit is available nearby. Some facilities are wheelchair accessible. Leashed pets are permitted.

Reservations, fees: Reservations are accepted at 800/452-5687 or www.oregonstateparks. org ($8 reservation fee). RV sites are $18–21 per night, $5 per night per additional vehicle, tent sites are $13–17 per night, $4 per person per night for hikers/bicyclists, and yurts are $30 per night. Some credit cards are accepted. Open mid-March–October, weather permitting.

Directions: From Newport and U.S. 101, drive south for 16 miles to Waldport. Continue south on U.S. 101 for four miles to the park entrance on the west side of the road.

Contact: Beachside State Recreation Site, 541/563-3220, fax 541/563-3657, www.oregonstateparks.org.

48 TILLICUM BEACH
🏃 🛶 🐕 🏕 🚐 ⛺

Scenic rating: 8

in Siuslaw National Forest

Map 1.3, page 83

Oceanview campsites are a big draw at this campground just south of Beachside State Park. Since it's just off the highway and along the water, this camp fills up very quickly in the summer, so expect crowds. Nearby forest roads provide access to streams in the mountains east of the beach area.

Campsites, facilities: There are 61 sites for tents or RVs up to 60 feet long; some sites have partial hookups. Picnic tables and fire grills are provided. Flush toilets, garbage bins, firewood, and drinking water are available. Leashed pets are permitted.

Reservations, fees: Reservations are accepted at 877/444-6777 or www.recreation.gov ($10 reservation fee). Sites are $22 per night, $6 per night per additional vehicle. Open year-round, with reduced capacity in winter.

Directions: From Newport and U.S. 101, drive south for 14 miles to Waldport. Continue south on U.S. 101 for 4.5 miles to the campground entrance on the right.

Contact: Siuslaw National Forest, Waldport Ranger District, 541/563-3211 or 541/547-3679 (concessionaire), fax 541/563-8449, www.fs.fed.us.

49 CANAL CREEK
🏃 🏕 🐕 🚐 ⛺

Scenic rating: 5

on Canal Creek in Siuslaw National Forest

Map 1.3, page 83

There's one key thing you must know: Vehicles must be able to cross a small creek to access this site. That accomplished, this pleasant little campground is just off the beaten path in a large, wooded, open area along Canal Creek. It feels remote because of the creek that runs through the campground and the historic

homesites nearby, with old fruit trees on the grounds. Yet it has easy access and is close to the coast and all the amenities. The climate here is relatively mild, but, on the other hand, there is the rain in winter—lots of it.

Campsites, facilities: There are 11 sites for tents or RVs up to 22 feet long, plus a group area for up to 100 people. Picnic tables and fire grills are provided. Vault toilets are available. There is no drinking water and garbage must be packed out. The group site has a picnic shelter and a play area. Leashed pets are permitted.

Reservations, fees: Reservations are not accepted for family sites but are required for group sites at 877/444-6777 or www.recreation.gov ($10 reservation fee). Sites are $17 per night, $6 per night per additional vehicle; group sites are $115–165 per night. Open year-round for individual camping. The group sites are open mid-May–mid-September.

Directions: From Albany, drive west on U.S. 20 for 15 miles to Philomath and Highway 34. Turn south on Highway 34 and drive 52 miles to Forest Road 3462. Turn left (south) and drive four miles to the camp.

Contact: Siuslaw National Forest, Waldport Ranger District, 541/563-3211 or 541/547-3679, fax 541/563-3124, www.fs.fed.us.

50 BLACKBERRY
🏃 🛶 🚣 🏕 🚐 ⛺

Scenic rating: 7

on the Alsea River in Siuslaw National Forest

Map 1.3, page 83

Blackberry makes a good base camp for a fishing trip on the Alsea River. The U.S. Forest Service provides boat launches and picnic areas at several spots along this stretch of river. Often, there is a camp host who can give you inside information on nearby recreational opportunities. Large fir trees and lawns separate the sites.

Campsites, facilities: There are 32 sites for tents or RVs of any length. Picnic tables and fire grills are provided. Drinking water, garbage bins, and flush toilets are available. There is no firewood. A boat ramp is on-site. Leashed pets are permitted.

Reservations, fees: Reservations are not accepted. Sites are $20 per night, $6 per night per additional vehicle. Open year-round.

Directions: From Albany, drive west on U.S. 20 for 15 miles to Philomath and Highway 34. Turn south on Highway 34 and drive 41 miles to the campground entrance on the left.

Contact: Siuslaw National Forest, Waldport Ranger District, 541/563-3211, fax 541/563-3124, www.fs.fed.us.

51 ALSEA FALLS

Scenic rating: 8

adjacent to the south fork of the Alsea River

Map 1.3, page 83   **BEST (**

Enjoy the beautiful surroundings of Alsea Falls by exploring the trails that wander through this park and lead to a picnic area by the falls. Trails to McBee Park and Green Peak Falls are accessible from the campground along the south fork of the river. The campsites are situated in a 40-year-old forest of Douglas fir and vine maple. On a warm day, Alsea Falls offers cool relief along the river. The area was named after its original inhabitants, the Alsea people.

Campsites, facilities: There are 16 sites for tents or RVs up to 30 feet long. Picnic tables and fire pits are provided. Drinking water, vault toilets, and garbage bins are available. Leashed pets are permitted.

Reservations, fees: Reservations are not accepted. Sites are $10 per night, $5 per night per additional vehicle. Open late May-early September.

Directions: From Albany, drive west on U.S. 20 for nine miles to Corvallis. Turn left (south) onto Highway 99 and drive 15 miles to County Road 45120. Turn right (west) and drive five miles to Alpine Junction. Continue along the South Fork Alsea Access Road for nine miles to the campground on the right.

Contact: Bureau of Land Management, Salem District Office, 503/375-5646, fax 503/375-5622, www.blm.gov.

52 CAPE PERPETUA

Scenic rating: 8

on Cape Creek in Siuslaw National Forest

Map 1.3, page 83

This U.S. Forest Service campground is set along Cape Creek in the Cape Perpetua Scenic Area. The visitor information center provides hiking and driving maps to guide you through this spectacular region; maps highlight the tidepools and picnic spots. The coastal cliffs are perfect for whale-watching December–March. Neptune State Park is just south and offers additional rugged coastline vistas.

Campsites, facilities: There are 38 sites for tents or RVs up to 45 feet long, plus one group site that can accommodate up to 50 people and 12 vehicles. Picnic tables and fire grills are provided. Flush toilets, drinking water, dump station, firewood, and garbage bins are available. A camp host is on-site. Some facilities are wheelchair accessible. Leashed pets are permitted.

Reservations, fees: Reservations are accepted at 877/444-6777 or www.recreation.gov ($10 reservation fee). Sites are $22 per night, $6 per night per additional vehicle; group sites are $115 per night. Open May–September.

Directions: From Newport and U.S. 101, drive south for 23 miles to Yachats. Continue three miles south on U.S. 101 to the entrance on the left.

Contact: Siuslaw National Forest, Waldport Ranger District, 541/563-3211 or 541/547-3676 (concessionaire), fax 541/563-3124, www.fs.fed.us; Cape Perpetua Visitors Center, 541/547-3289.

53 SEA PERCH RV PARK

Scenic rating: 8

near Cape Perpetua

Map 1.3, page 83

Sea Perch sits right in the middle of one of the most scenic areas on the Oregon coast. This private park just south of Cape Perpetua has sites 75 feet from the beach and lawn areas, plus its own shell museum and gift shop. Surf fishing and windsurfing are options here, or head to Cape Perpetua for whale-watching and tidepooling. Big rigs are welcome here.

Campsites, facilities: There are 29 sites with full or partial hookups for RVs of any length. Some sites are pull-through. Drinking water and picnic tables are provided. Restrooms with flush toilets and coin showers, dump station, firewood, recreation hall, coin laundry, ice, convenience store, wireless Internet access, modem hookups, picnic area, and a beach are available. Leashed pets are permitted.

Reservations, fees: Reservations are accepted. Sites are $45–60 per night, $5 per person per night for more than four, $15 per night for an additional vehicle if it cannot be parked on your site. Some credit cards are accepted. Open year-round.

Directions: From Newport and U.S. 101, drive south for 23 miles to Yachats. Continue south on U.S. 101 for 6.5 miles to the campground at Milepost 171 on the right.

Contact: Sea Perch RV Park, 541/547-3505, fax 541/547-3368, www.seaperchrvpark.com.

54 ROCK CREEK

Scenic rating: 7

on Rock Creek in Siuslaw National Forest

Map 1.3, page 83

This little campground is set along Rock Creek just 0.25 mile from the ocean. It's a premium spot for coastal-highway travelers, although it can get packed very quickly. An excellent side trip is to Cape Perpetua, a designated scenic area a few miles up the coast. The cape offers beautiful ocean views and a visitors center that will supply you with information on nature trails, picnic spots, tidepools, and where to find the best viewpoints in the area.

Campsites, facilities: There are 15 sites for tents or RVs up to 22 feet long. Fire grills and picnic tables are provided. Flush toilets, garbage bins, and drinking water are available. Leashed pets are permitted.

Reservations, fees: Reservations are not accepted. Sites are $22 per night, $6 per night per additional vehicle. Open mid-May–September.

Directions: From Newport and U.S. 101, drive south for 23 miles to Yachats. Continue south on U.S. 101 for 10 miles to the campground entrance on the left.

Contact: Siuslaw National Forest, Waldport Ranger District, 541/563-3211 or 541/547-3679 (concessionaire), fax 541/563-3124, www.fs.fed.us.

55 CARL G. WASHBURNE STATE PARK

Scenic rating: 7

near Florence

Map 1.3, page 83

Even though busy Highway 101 lies right next to Washburne State Park, a bank of native plants shields campers from most road noise, so you hear the roar of the ocean instead of traffic. Sites are spacious, with some abutting China Creek, and elk are frequent visitors. Short hikes lead from the campground to a two-mile-long beach, extensive tidepools along the base of the cliffs, and a three-mile trail to Heceta Head Lighthouse. Just three miles south of the park are the Sea Lion Caves, where an elevator takes visitors down into a cavern for an insider's view of the life of a sea lion.

Campsites, facilities: There are 56 sites for

tents or RVs up to 45 feet long (full hookups), seven primitive walk-in sites, two yurts, and a hiker/biker camping area. Picnic tables, fire pits, drinking water, garbage bins, and a dump station are provided. Firewood and restrooms with flush toilets and showers are available. Leashed pets are permitted.

Reservations, fees: Reservations are not accepted, except for yurts. RV sites are $17–26 per night, tent sites are $13–21 per night, $4–5 per person per night for hikers/bicyclists, and yurts are $29–39 per night; $5 per night per additional vehicle. Some credit cards are accepted. Open year-round.

Directions: From Florence and U.S. 101, drive north for 12.5 miles to the park entrance road (it is well signed, 10 miles south of the town of Yachats). Turn east and drive a short distance to the park.

Contact: Carl G. Washburne State Park, 541/547-3416 or 800/551-6949, www.oregonstateparks.org.

56 ALDER DUNE

Scenic rating: 7

near Alder Lake in Siuslaw National Forest

Map 1.3, page 83

This wooded campground is situated near four lakes—Alder Lake, Dune Lake, Mercer Lake (the largest), and Sutton Lake. A boat launch is available at Sutton Lake. An excellent recreation option is to explore the expansive sand dunes in the area by foot (there is no off-road-vehicle access here). Side trips include the Sea Lion Caves, Darlington State Park, Jessie M. Honeyman Memorial State Park, and the Indian Forest, just four miles north.

Campsites, facilities: There are 39 sites for tents or self-contained RVs (no hookups) up to 62 feet long. Picnic tables and fire grills are provided. Flush toilets, garbage bins, and drinking water are available. Leashed pets are permitted.

Reservations, fees: Reservations are accepted at 877/444-6777 or www.recreation.gov ($10 reservation fee). Sites are $20 per night. Open year-round, weather permitting.

Directions: From Florence and U.S. 101, drive north for eight miles to the campground on the left.

Contact: Siuslaw National Forest, Reedsport Ranger District, 541/271-6000, fax 541/271-1563, www.fs.fed.us.

57 SUTTON

Scenic rating: 7

near Sutton Lake in Siuslaw National Forest

Map 1.3, page 83

This campground is located adjacent to Sutton Creek, not far from Sutton Lake. Vegetation provides some privacy between sites. Holman Vista on Sutton Beach Road offers a beautiful view of the dunes and ocean. Wading and fishing are both popular. A hiking trail system leads from the camp out to the dunes. There is no off-road-vehicle access here. An alternative camp is Alder Dune to the north.

Campsites, facilities: There are 80 sites, 20 with partial hookups, for tents or RVs up to 30 feet long and two group sites for up to 50 and 100 people, respectively. Picnic tables and fire grills are provided. Flush toilets, garbage bins, and drinking water are available. A boat ramp is nearby. Leashed pets are permitted.

Reservations, fees: Reservations are accepted at 877/444-6777 or www.recreation.gov ($10 reservation fee). Sites are $20–22 per night and $50–75 per night for group sites. Open May–December.

Directions: From Eugene, drive west on Highway 126 for 61 miles to Florence and U.S. 101. Turn north on U.S. 101 and drive six miles to Sutton Beach Road (Forest Road 794). Turn left (northwest) and drive 1.5 miles to the campground entrance.

Contact: Siuslaw National Forest, Reedsport Ranger District, 541/271-6000, fax 541/271-1563, www.fs.fed.us.

58 MAPLE LANE RV PARK AND MARINA
🏃 🛶 🚤 🐕 🚗 ⛺

Scenic rating: 5

on the Siuslaw River

Map 1.3, page 83

This park along the shore of the Siuslaw River in Mapleton is close to hiking trails. The general area is surrounded by Siuslaw National Forest land. A U.S. Forest Service map details nearby backcountry side-trip options. Fall is the most popular time of the year here, as it's prime time for salmon fishing on the Siuslaw. Most sites are taken by monthly renters.

Campsites, facilities: There are five tent sites and 39 sites with full hookups for RVs up to 35 feet long. Some sites are pull-through. Drinking water, restrooms with flush toilets and showers, and propane gas are available. A bait and tackle shop is open during the fishing season. Boat docks and launching facilities are on-site. A store, café, and ice are nearby. Small pets (under 15 pounds) are permitted.

Reservations, fees: Reservations are accepted. RV sites are $25–30 per night, tent sites are $18 per night, $1.50 per night for more than two people, and $2 per night per additional vehicle. Monthly rates are available. Open year-round.

Directions: From Eugene, drive west on Highway 126 for 47 miles to Mapleton. Continue on Highway 126 for 0.25 mile past the business district to the park entrance on the left.

Contact: Maple Lane RV Park and Marina, 541/268-4822.

59 ARCHIE KNOWLES
🎣 🐕 🚗 ⛺

Scenic rating: 6

on Knowles Creek in Siuslaw National Forest

Map 1.3, page 83

This little campground along Knowles Creek about three miles east of Mapleton is rustic, with a mix of forested and lawn areas, yet it offers easy proximity to the highway.

Campsites, facilities: There are nine sites for tents or RVs up to 16 feet long. Picnic tables and fire grills are provided. Flush toilets, garbage bins, and drinking water are available. Leashed pets are permitted.

Reservations, fees: Reservations are not accepted. Sites are $15 per night. Open May–early September, weather permitting.

Directions: From Eugene, drive west on Highway 126 for 44 miles to the campground entrance (three miles east of Mapleton).

Contact: Siuslaw National Forest, Reedsport Ranger District, 541/271-6000, fax 541/271-1563, www.fs.fed.us.

60 HARBOR VISTA COUNTY PARK
🏃 🛶 🚤 🐕 🏊 ♿ 🚗 ⛺

Scenic rating: 6

near Florence

Map 1.4, page 84

This county park out among the dunes near the entrance to the harbor offers a great lookout point from its observation deck. The park is perched above the North Jetty of the Siuslaw River and encompasses 15 acres. Beach access is one mile away. A number of side trips are available, including to the Sea Lion Caves, Darlington State Park, Jessie M. Honeyman Memorial State Park, and the Indian Forest, just four miles north. Florence also has displays of Native American dwellings and crafts.

Campsites, facilities: There are 38 sites with partial hookups for tents or RVs up to 60 feet long. Picnic tables, fire rings, and garbage bins are provided. Restrooms with flush toilets and coin showers, dump station, drinking water, pay phone, and a playground are available. A camp host is on-site. Some facilities are wheelchair accessible. Leashed pets are permitted.

Reservations, fees: Reservations are accepted at 541/682-2000 ($10 reservation fee). Sites are $20 per night, $6.50 per night per additional vehicle. Some credit cards are accepted. Open year-round.

Directions: From Florence and U.S. 101, drive north for four miles to 35th Street. Turn left and drive to where it dead-ends into Rhododendron Drive. Turn right and drive 1.4 miles to North Jetty Road. Turn left and drive half a block to Harbor Vista Road. Turn left and continue to the campground at 87658 Harbor Vista Road.

Note: Follow these exact directions. Previous visitors to this park taking a different route will discover that part of Harbor Vista Road is now gated.

Contact: Harbor Vista County Park, 541/997-5987, www.co.lane.or.us/.

61 B AND E WAYSIDE MOBILE HOME AND RV PARK

Scenic rating: 5

near Florence

Map 1.4, page 84

Adjacent to this landscaped RV park is a 28-unit mobile home park for ages 55 and up. Some sites at the RV park are taken by monthly rentals. Nearby recreation options include two golf courses and a riding stable, two miles away.

Campsites, facilities: There are 24 sites with full hookups for RVs of any length. Picnic tables are provided. Restrooms with flush toilets and showers, dump station, recreation room, modem access, and a coin laundry are available. Propane gas, a store, ice, a café, and a restaurant are within two miles. Boat-launching facilities are nearby. Small, leashed pets are permitted.

Reservations, fees: Reservations are accepted. Sites are $24 per night, $2 per person per night for more than two people. Weekly and monthly rates are available. Open year-round.

Directions: From Florence and U.S. 101, drive north for 1.8 miles to the park on the right.

Contact: B and E Wayside Mobile Home and RV Park, 541/997-6451.

62 PORT OF SIUSLAW RV PARK AND MARINA

Scenic rating: 8

on the Siuslaw River

Map 1.4, page 84　　　　　　　　**BEST (**

This public resort can be found along the Siuslaw River in a grassy, urban setting. Anglers with boats will find that the U.S. 101 bridge support pilings make good spots for crabbing, as well as fishing for perch and flounder. A new set of docks with drinking water, electricity, gasoline, security, and a fish-cleaning station are available. The Sea Lion Caves and estuary are a bonus for wildlife lovers, and nearby lakes make swimming and waterskiing a possibility. Golf is within driving distance, and horses can be rented about nine miles away.

Campsites, facilities: There are 10 tent sites and 92 sites with full or partial hookups for tents or RVs of any length. Drinking water, cable TV, and picnic tables are provided. Restrooms with flush toilets and showers, dump station, coin laundry, wireless Internet service, and boat docks are available. A café, grocery store, and ice are within one mile. Some facilities are wheelchair accessible. Leashed pets are permitted.

Reservations, fees: Reservations are accepted at 541/997-3040 or www.portofsiuslaw.com ($10 reservation fee). Sites are $22–30 per night, $2 per night per additional vehicle. Weekly rates available. Some credit cards are accepted. Open year-round.

Directions: From Florence and U.S. 101, drive south to Nopal Street. Turn left (east) and drive two blocks to 1st Street. Turn left and drive 0.25 mile to the park at the end of the road.

Contact: Port of Siuslaw RV Park and Marina, 541/997-3040, www.portofsiuslaw.com.

63 JESSIE M. HONEYMAN MEMORIAL STATE PARK

🚶 🚴 🏊 ⛵ 🚗 🏕 🎣 ♿ 🚐 ⛰

Scenic rating: 7

near Cleowax Lake

Map 1.4, page 84

This popular state park is within walking distance of the shore of Cleawox Lake and adjacent to the dunes of the Oregon Dunes National Recreation Area. Dunes stretch for two miles between the park and the ocean. The dunes here are quite impressive, with some reaching to 500 feet. In the winter, the area is open to OHV use. For thrill-seekers, sandboard rentals (for sand-boarding on the dunes) are available in nearby Florence. The two lakes in the park offer facilities for boating, fishing, and swimming. A one-mile hiking trail with access to the dunes is available in the park, and off-road-vehicle trails are nearby in the sand dunes.

Campsites, facilities: There are 187 sites for tents or RVs (no hookups) up to 60 feet long, 168 sites with full or partial hookups for RVs, a camping area for hikers and bicyclists, six group tent areas for up to 25 people and 10 vehicles each, and 10 yurts. Picnic tables, garbage bins, and fire grills are provided. Drinking water, restrooms with flush toilets and showers, a dump station, seasonal interpretive programs, a playground, an amphitheater, and firewood are available. A meeting hall and picnic shelters can be reserved. Boat docks and launching facilities are nearby. Some facilities are wheelchair accessible. Leashed pets are permitted.

Reservations, fees: Reservations are accepted at 800/452-5687 or www.oregonstateparks.org ($8 reservation fee). RV sites are $17–26 per night, tent sites are $13–21 per night, $5 per night per additional vehicle, $4–5 per person per night for hikers/bicyclists, $29–39 per night for yurts, and $43–76 per night for group sites. Some credit cards are accepted. Open year-round.

Directions: From Florence and U.S. 101, drive south for three miles to the park entrance on the west side of the road.

Contact: Jessie M. Honeyman Memorial State Park, 541/997-3641 or 800/551-6949, www.oregonstateparks.org.

64 LAKESHORE RV PARK

🏊 ⛵ 🚐 🏕 🚗

Scenic rating: 5

on Woahink Lake

Map 1.4, page 84

Here's a prime area for vacationers. This park is set along the shore of Woahink Lake, a popular spot to fish for bass, bluegill, catfish, crappie, perch, and trout. It's adjacent to Jessie M. Honeyman Memorial State Park and the Oregon Dunes National Recreation Area. Off-road-vehicle access to the dunes is four miles northeast and three miles south of the park. Hiking trails through the dunes can be found at Honeyman Memorial State Park. Some sites are filled with monthly rentals.

Campsites, facilities: There are 20 sites with full hookups for RVs of any length; some are pull-through sites. Picnic tables and cable TV are provided. Drinking water, restrooms with flush toilets and showers, modem access, wireless Internet service, and a coin laundry are available. A café is within three miles. Boat docks are nearby. Leashed pets are permitted.

Reservations, fees: Reservations are accepted at 866/240-4269. Sites are $29 per night, $2 per person per night for more than two people. Monthly rentals are available. Open year-round.

Directions: From Florence and U.S. 101, drive south for four miles to Milepost 195. The park is on the left (east side of road).

Contact: Lakeshore RV Park, 541/997-2741, www.lakeshorerv.com.

65 MERCER LAKE RESORT

Scenic rating: 7

on Mercer Lake

Map 1.4, page 84

This resort is in a forested setting situated above the shore of Mercer Lake, one of a number of lakes that have formed among the ancient dunes in this area. The 375-acre lake has 11 miles of shoreline and numerous coves. Fishing for rainbow trout and largemouth bass in the stocked lake is the most popular activity. A sandy swimming beach is also available, and the ocean is four miles away.

Campsites, facilities: There are 10 sites with full or partial hookups for RVs up to 40 feet long and 10 cabins. Some sites are pull-through. No open fires are allowed. Drinking water, cable TV, and picnic tables are provided. Restrooms with flush toilets and showers, dump station, convenience store, coin laundry, and ice are available. Boat docks, launching facilities, and fishing boat rentals are on-site. Leashed pets are permitted.

Reservations, fees: Reservations are accepted at 800/355-3633. Sites are $22–35 per night, $2 per night per additional vehicle, $5 per night per pet. Some credit cards are accepted. Open year-round.

Directions: From Florence and U.S. 101, drive north for five miles to Mercer Lake Road. Turn east and drive just under one mile to Bay Berry Lane. Turn left and drive to the resort.

Contact: Mercer Lake Resort, 541/997-3633, www.mlroregon.com.

66 CARTER LAKE

Scenic rating: 9

on Carter Lake in
Oregon Dunes National Recreation Area

Map 1.4, page 84   BEST (

This campground sits on the north shore of Carter Lake, and you can fish almost right from your campsite. Boating and fishing are permitted on this long, narrow lake, which is set among dunes overgrown with vegetation. The nearby Taylor Dunes Trail is a half-mile, wheelchair-accessible trail to the dunes past Taylor Lake. Hiking is allowed in the dunes, but there is no off-road-vehicle access here. If you want off-road access, head north one mile to Siltcoos Road, turn west, and drive 1.3 miles to Driftwood II.

Campsites, facilities: There are 22 sites for tents or RVs up to 30 feet long. Picnic tables, garbage service, and fire grills are provided. Drinking water, flush toilets, and firewood are available. A camp host is on-site. Leashed pets are permitted.

Reservations, fees: Reservations are accepted at 877/444-6777 or www.recreation.gov ($10 reservation fee). Sites are $17–20 per night, $5 per night per additional vehicle. Open May–September.

Directions: From Florence and U.S. 101, drive south for 8.5 miles to Forest Road 1084. Turn right on Forest Road 1084 and drive west 200 yards to the camp.

Contact: Oregon Dunes National Recreation Area, Visitors Center, 541/271-3611, fax 541/750-7244.

67 DRIFTWOOD II

Scenic rating: 6

near Siltcoos Lake in
Oregon Dunes National Recreation Area

Map 1.4, page 84

Primarily a campground for off-road vehicles, Driftwood II is set near the ocean, but without an ocean view, in the Oregon Dunes National Recreation Area. It has off-road-vehicle access. Several small lakes, the Siltcoos River, and Siltcoos Lake are nearby. Note that ATV use is prohibited between 10 P.M. and 6 A.M.

Campsites, facilities: There are 68 sites for tents or RVs up to 59 feet long, including 10 pull-through sites. Picnic tables, garbage service, and fire grills are provided at back-in sites but not at the 10 pull-through sites. Drinking water and restrooms with flush toilets and showers are available. A dump station is within five miles. Boat docks, launching facilities, and rentals can be found about four miles away on Siltcoos Lake. Some facilities are wheelchair accessible. Leashed pets are permitted.

Reservations, fees: Reservations are accepted at 877/444-6777 or www.recreation.gov ($10 reservation fee). Sites are $20 per night. Open year-round.

Directions: From Florence and U.S. 101, drive south for seven miles to Siltcoos Beach Road. Turn right and drive 1.5 miles west to the campground.

Contact: Oregon Dunes National Recreation Area, Visitors Center 541/271-6000 or 541/271-3611, fax 541/750-7244.

68 LAGOON
🚶 🏊 🛶 🏠 ♿ 🚐 ⛺

Scenic rating: 9

near Siltcoos Lake in
Oregon Dunes National Recreation Area

Map 1.4, page 84

One of several campgrounds in the area, this camp is located along the lagoon, about one mile from Siltcoos Lake and set 0.5 mile inland. The Lagoon Trail offers prime wildlife-viewing for marine birds and other aquatic species.

Campsites, facilities: There are 41 sites for tents or RVs of any length. Picnic tables, garbage service, and fire grills are provided. Drinking water and flush and vault toilets are available. A camp host is on-site. Boat docks, launching facilities, and rentals are nearby on Siltcoos Lake. A telephone and a dump station are within five miles. Some facilities are wheelchair accessible. Leashed pets are permitted.

Reservations, fees: Reservations are accepted

at 877/444-6777 or www.recreation.gov ($10 reservation fee). Sites are $20 per night. Open year-round.

Directions: From Florence and U.S. 101, drive south for seven miles to Siltcoos Beach Road. Turn right on Siltcoos Beach Road and drive west for 1.2 miles to the campground.

Contact: Oregon Dunes National Recreation Area, Visitors Center 541/271-6000 or 541/271-3611, fax 541/750-7244.

69 DARLINGS RESORT AND MARINA
🚶 🛶 🚐 🦌 🚙

Scenic rating: 7

on Siltcoos Lake

Map 1.4, page 84

This park, in a rural area along the north shore of Siltcoos Lake, is adjacent to the extensive Oregon Dunes National Recreation Area. Sites are right on the lake; fish from your picnic table. An access point to the dunes for hikers and off-road vehicles is just across the highway. The lake has a full-service marina. About half the sites are taken by monthly rentals.

Campsites, facilities: There are 14 sites with partial hookups for RVs up to 38 feet long. Cable TV, drinking water, fire pits, and picnic tables are provided. Restrooms with flush toilets and coin showers, firewood, convenience store, tavern, deli, boat docks, boat rentals, launching facilities, and a coin laundry are available. Leashed pets are permitted.

Reservations, fees: Reservations are accepted. Sites are $29.96 per night, $5 per night per additional vehicle. Some credit cards are accepted. Open year-round.

Directions: From Florence and U.S. 101, drive south for five miles to North Beach Road. Turn left (east) and drive 0.25 mile to Darlings Loop Road. Turn right and drive 0.25 mile to the resort.

Contact: Darlings Resort and Marina, 541/997-2841, www.darlingsresortrv.com.

70 TYEE

Scenic rating: 6

on the Siltcoos River in
Oregon Dunes National Recreation Area

Map 1.4, page 84

This wooded campground along the shore of the Siltcoos River provides an alternative to Driftwood II and Lagoon. Fishing is permitted at the nearby lake, where there is a canoe portage trail and a boat ramp. Off-road-vehicle access to the dunes is available from Driftwood II, and there are hiking trails in the area.

Campsites, facilities: There are 16 sites for tents or RVs up to 30 feet long. Picnic tables, garbage service, and fire grills are provided. Drinking water, vault toilets, firewood, and a day-use area with horseshoe pits are available. A camp host is on-site. A store, boat docks, launching facilities, and rentals are nearby. Some facilities are wheelchair accessible. Leashed pets are permitted.

Reservations, fees: Reservations are accepted at 877/444-6777 or www.recreation.gov ($10 reservation fee). Sites are $17–18.35 per night, $5 per night per each additional vehicle. Open May–September.

Directions: From Florence and U.S. 101, drive south for six miles to the Westlake turnoff. Take that exit and continue a short distance to the campground.

Contact: Oregon Dunes National Recreation Area, Visitors Center 541/271-6000 or 541/271-3611, fax 541/750-7244; campground management 541/997-4479.

71 WAXMYRTLE

Scenic rating: 7

near Siltcoos Lake in
Oregon Dunes National Recreation Area

Map 1.4, page 84

One of three camps in the immediate vicinity, Waxmyrtle is adjacent to Lagoon and less than a mile from Driftwood II. The camp is near the Siltcoos River and a couple of miles from Siltcoos Lake, a good-sized lake with boating facilities where you can fish. A pleasant hiking trail here meanders through the dunes and along the estuary.

Campsites, facilities: There are 57 sites for tents or RVs of any length. Picnic tables, garbage service, and fire grills are provided. Drinking water and flush toilets are available. A camp host is on-site. Boat docks, launching facilities, and rentals are nearby on Siltcoos Lake. Leashed pets are permitted.

Reservations, fees: Reservations are accepted at 877/444-6777 or www.recreation.gov ($10 reservation fee). Sites are $20 per night. Open year-round.

Directions: From Florence and U.S. 101, drive south for seven miles to Siltcoos Beach Road. Turn right and drive 1.3 miles west to the campground.

Contact: Oregon Dunes National Recreation Area, Visitors Center 541/271-6000 or 541/271-3611, fax 541/750-7244.

72 TAHKENITCH LANDING

Scenic rating: 6

near Tahkenitch Lake in
Oregon Dunes National Recreation Area

Map 1.4, page 84

This camp overlooking Tahkenitch Lake (Lake of Many Fingers) has easy access to excellent fishing.

Campsites, facilities: There are 29 sites for tents or RVs up to 40 feet long. Picnic tables and garbage service are provided. Vault toilets, boat-launching facilities, and a floating dock are available, but there is no drinking water. A camp host is on-site. Leashed pets are permitted.

Reservations, fees: Reservations are accepted at 877/444-6777 or www.recreation.gov ($10 reservation fee). Sites are $17–19 per night, $5 per night per additional vehicle. Open year-round.

Directions: From Florence and U.S. 101, drive south for 14 miles to the campground on the east side of the road.

Contact: Oregon Dunes National Recreation Area, Visitors Center 541/271-6000 or 541/271-3611, fax 541/750-7244; campground management 541/997-4479.

73 TAHKENITCH

Scenic rating: 7

near Tahkenitch Lake in
Oregon Dunes National Recreation Area

Map 1.4, page 84

This very pretty campground with dense vegetation is set in a wooded area across the highway from Tahkenitch Lake, which has numerous coves and backwater areas for fishing. A hiking trail close to the camp goes through the dunes out to the beach, as well as to Threemile Lake. If this camp is full, Tahkenitch Landing provides space nearby.

Campsites, facilities: There are 26 sites for tents or RVs up to 30 feet long. Picnic tables, garbage service, and fire grills are provided. Drinking water, firewood, and flush toilets are available. A camp host is on-site. Boat docks and launching facilities are on the lake across the highway. Some facilities are wheelchair accessible. Leashed pets are permitted.

Reservations, fees: Reservations are accepted at 877/444-6777 or www.recreation.gov ($10 reservation fee). Sites are $16.83–19.80 per night, $5 per night per additional vehicle. Open mid-May–September.

Directions: From Florence and U.S. 101, drive south for 14 miles. The campground entrance is on the right.

Contact: Oregon Dunes National Recreation Area, Visitors Center 541/271-6000 or 541/271-3611, fax 541/750-7244; campground management 541/997-4479.

74 DISCOVERY POINT RESORT & RV PARK

Scenic rating: 7

on Winchester Bay

Map 1.4, page 84

This resort sits on the shore of Winchester Bay, adjacent to sandy dunes, in a fishing village near the mouth of the Umpqua River. The park was designed around motor sports, and ATVs are available for rent. It is somewhat noisy, but that's what most people come for.

Campsites, facilities: There are five tent sites, 60 sites with full hookups for RVs of any length, 13 cabins, and two condos. Some sites are pull-through. Picnic tables and fire pits are provided at most sites. Restrooms with flush toilets and showers, drinking water, cable TV, convenience store, coin laundry, a weekend snack bar, and ice are available. A dump station and propane gas are within one mile. Boat docks and launching facilities are nearby. Leashed pets are permitted.

Reservations, fees: Reservations are accepted. RV sites are $28–33 per night, tent sites are $14–16 per night, condos are $260–275 per night, $7 per night per each additional vehicle. Call for cabin rates. Some credit cards are accepted. Open year-round.

Directions: From Reedsport and U.S. 101, drive south for two miles to Winchester Bay and Salmon Harbor Drive. Turn right at Salmon Harbor Drive and proceed west for one mile to the resort on the left.

Contact: Discovery Point Resort & RV Park, 541/271-3443, www.discoverypointresort. com; ATV rentals, 541/271-9357.

7 5 WINDY COVE COUNTY PARK

🏃 🏊 🚣 🛥 🐎 ♿ 🚐 ⛺

Scenic rating: 7

adjacent to Salmon Harbor at Winchester Bay

Map 1.4, page 84

This Douglas County park actually comprises two campgrounds, Windy Cove A and B. Set near ocean beaches and sand dunes, both offer a variety of additional recreational opportunities, including an 18-hole golf course, hiking trails, and a lighthouse.

Campsites, facilities: There are 33 tent sites and 64 sites with full or partial hookups for RVs up to 60 feet long. Drinking water and picnic tables are provided. Fire pits are provided at some Windy A sites, but not at Windy B sites. Restrooms with flush toilets and showers and cable TV are available. Propane gas, dump station, a store, café, coin laundry, and ice are within one mile. Boat docks, launching facilities, boat charters, and rentals are nearby. Some facilities are wheelchair accessible. Leashed pets are permitted.

Reservations, fees: Reservations are accepted for selected Windy B sites only at 541/957-7001. Sites are $15–20 per night, $3 per night per additional vehicle. Some credit cards are accepted. Open year-round.

Directions: From Reedsport and U.S. 101, drive south for three miles to the Windy Cove exit near Winchester Bay. Take that exit and drive west to the park on the left.

Contact: Windy Cove County Park, Windy B, 541/271-5634; Windy A, 541/271-4138, www.co.douglas.or.us/parks.

7 6 UMPQUA LIGHTHOUSE STATE PARK

🏃 🏊 🚣 🚐 🐎 🚐 ⛺

Scenic rating: 7

on the Umpqua River

Map 1.4, page 84

This park is located near Lake Marie and less than a mile from Salmon Harbor on Winchester Bay. A one-mile trail circles Lake Marie, and swimming and non-motorized boating are allowed. Near the mouth of the Umpqua River, this unusual area features dunes as high as 500 feet. Hiking trails lead out of the park and into the Oregon Dunes National Recreation Area. The park offers more than two miles of beach access on the ocean and 0.5 mile along the Umpqua River. The adjacent lighthouse is still in operation, and tours are available during the summer season.

Campsites, facilities: There are 24 sites for tents or RVs up to 45 feet long (no hookups), 20 sites with full hookups for RVs up to 45 feet long, a hiker/bicyclist camp, two cabins, two rustic yurts, and six deluxe yurts. Picnic tables and fire pits are provided. Drinking water, garbage bins, restrooms with flush toilets and showers, and firewood are available. Boat docks and launching facilities are on the Umpqua River. Leashed pets are permitted.

Reservations, fees: Reservations are accepted at 800/452-5687 or www.oregonstateparks.org ($8 reservation fee). RV sites are $16–24 per night, tent sites are $12–19 per night, $5 per night for an additional vehicle, $4–5 per person per night for hikers/bikers, $35–39 per night for cabins, $27–36 per night for rustic yurts, and $45–76 for deluxe yurts. Some credit cards are accepted. Open year-round.

Directions: From Reedsport and U.S. 101, drive south for six miles to Umpqua Lighthouse Road. Turn right (west) and drive one mile to the park.

Contact: Umpqua Lighthouse State Park, 541/271-4118 or 800/551-6949, www.oregonstateparks.org.

77 WILLIAM M. TUGMAN STATE PARK

🚶 🚲 🛶 🛥 🚐 🦌 🏕 ♿ 🚙 ⛺

Scenic rating: 7

on Eel Lake

Map 1.4, page 84

This campground is set along the shore of Eel Lake, which offers almost five miles of shoreline for boating, fishing, sailing, and swimming. It's perfect for bass fishing. A boat ramp is available, but there is a 10-mph speed limit for boats. Oregon Dunes National Recreation Area is across the highway. Hiking is available just a few miles north at Umpqua Lighthouse State Park. A developed, 2.5-mile trail along the south end of the lake allows hikers to get away from the developed areas of the park and explore the lake's many outlets.

Campsites, facilities: There are 94 sites with partial hookups for tents or RVs up to 50 feet long, a camping area for hikers and bicyclists, and 16 yurts. Drinking water, fire rings, and picnic tables are provided. Restrooms with flush toilets and showers, dump station, firewood, and a picnic shelter are available. Boat docks and launching facilities are nearby. Some facilities are wheelchair accessible. Leashed pets are permitted.

Reservations, fees: Reservations are accepted at 800/452-5687 or www.oregonstateparks.org ($8 reservation fee). Sites are $12–20 per night, $5 per night per additional vehicle, $4–5 per person per night for hikers/bicyclists, and $27–39 per night for yurts. Some credit cards are accepted. Open year-round.

Directions: From Reedsport and U.S. 101, drive south for eight miles to the park entrance on the left (east side of the road).

Contact: Sunset Bay State Park, 541/759-3604 or 800/551-6949, www.oregonstateparks.org.

78 NORTH LAKE RESORT AND MARINA

🛶 🛥 🚐 🦌 🚙 ⛺

Scenic rating: 8

on Tenmile Lake

Map 1.4, page 84

This 40-acre resort along the shore of Tenmile Lake is wooded and secluded, has a private beach, and makes the perfect layover spot for U.S. 101 travelers. The lake has a full-service marina, and bass fishing can be good here. About 25 percent of the sites are taken by summer season rentals.

Campsites, facilities: There are 20 tent sites and 75 sites with full or partial hookups for RVs of any length. Picnic tables are provided and there are fire pits at most sites. Restrooms with flush toilets and coin showers, dump station, firewood, convenience store, ice, phone/modem hookups, cable TV, drinking water, coin laundry, horseshoe pits, and a volleyball court are available. Boat docks, launching facilities, and a marina are also available. A café and boat rentals are nearby. Leashed pets are permitted.

Reservations, fees: Reservations are accepted. Tent sites are $20 per night; RV sites are $25 per night. Some credit cards are accepted. Open April–October.

Directions: From Reedsport and U.S. 101, drive south on U.S. 101 for 11 miles to the Lakeside exit. Take that exit east into town for 0.75 mile (across the railroad tracks) to North Lake Road. Turn left (north) and drive 0.5 mile to the resort on the left.

Contact: North Lake Resort and Marina, 541/759-3515, fax 541/759-3326, www.north-lakeresort.com.

79 OSPREY POINT RV RESORT

🚶 ≋ 🛶 �331 🐴 🚐 ⛺

Scenic rating: 7

on Tenmile Lake

Map 1.4, page 84

Tenmile is one of Oregon's premier bass fishing lakes and yet is located only three miles from the ocean. The resort is situated in a large, open area adjacent to Tenmile Lake and 0.5 mile from North Lake. A navigable canal connects the lakes. The Oregon Dunes National Recreation Area provides nearby hiking trails, and Elliot State Forest offers wooded trails. With weekend barbecues and occasional live entertainment, Osprey Point is more a destination resort than an overnight stop.

Campsites, facilities: There are 132 sites for tents or RVs of any size (full hookups), a grassy area for tents, and five park-model cabins. Drinking water, picnic tables, and fire pits are provided. Cable TV, modem access, restrooms with flush toilets and showers, dump station, coin laundry, restaurant, cocktail lounge, convenience store, full-service marina with boat docks, launch, fishing pier, fish-cleaning station, horseshoe pits, volleyball, tetherball, recreation hall, video arcade, and a pizza parlor are available. Leashed pets are permitted.

Reservations, fees: Reservations are accepted. RV sites are $25–36 per night, tent sites are $18 per night, $3.50 per person per night for more than two people. Monthly rates are available. Some credit cards are accepted. Open year-round.

Directions: From Reedport, drive north on U.S. 101 for 11 miles to the Lakeside exit. Take that exit east into town for 0.75 mile (across the railroad tracks) to North Lake Road. Turn left (north) on North Lake Road and drive 0.5 mile to the resort on the right.

Contact: Osprey Point RV Resort, 541/759-2801, fax 541/759-3198, www.ospreypoint.net.

80 EEL CREEK

🚶 ≋ 🛶 �331 🐴 🚐 ⛺

Scenic rating: 8

near Eel Lake in Oregon Dunes National Recreation Area

Map 1.4, page 84

This campground along Eel Creek is located near both Eel and Tenmile Lakes. Although Tenmile Lake allows waterskiing, Eel Lake does not. Nearby trails offer access to the Umpqua Dunes Scenic Area, where you'll find spectacular scenery in an area closed to off-road vehicles. Off-road access is available at Spinreel.

Campsites, facilities: There are 38 sites for tents or RVs up to 50 feet long. Picnic tables, garbage service, and fire grills are provided. Drinking water, flush toilets, and firewood are available. A camp host is on-site. Boat docks, launching facilities, and rentals are nearby. Leashed pets are permitted.

Reservations, fees: Reservations are accepted at 877/444-6777 or www.recreation.gov ($10 reservation fee). Sites are $20 per night, $5 per night per additional vehicle. Open mid-May–September.

Directions: From Reedsport and U.S. 101, drive south for 10.5 miles to the park entrance.

Contact: Oregon Dunes National Recreation Area, Visitors Center 541/271-6000 or 541/271-3611, fax 541/750-7244.

81 SPINREEL

🚶 🛶 🚐 🐴 ♿ 🚐 ⛺

Scenic rating: 6

on Tenmile Creek in Oregon Dunes National Recreation Area

Map 1.4, page 84

Spinreel campground is set several miles inland at the outlet of Tenmile Lake in the Oregon Dunes National Recreation Area. A boat launch (for drift boats and canoes) is near the camp. Primarily for off-road-vehicle enthusiasts, Spinreel's other recreational opportunities include hiking trails and off-road-vehicle access to the dunes. Off-road-vehicle rentals are available adjacent to the camp.

Campsites, facilities: There are 37 sites for tents or RVs up to 61 feet long. Drinking water, garbage service, and flush toilets are available. Picnic tables and fire grills are provided. Firewood, store, and a coin laundry are nearby. Boat docks, launching facilities, and rentals are on Tenmile Lake. Some facilities are wheelchair accessible. Leashed pets are permitted.

Reservations, fees: Reservations are accepted at 877/444-6777 or www.recreation.gov ($10 reservation fee). Sites are $20 per night. Open year-round.

Directions: From Coos Bay, drive north on U.S. 101 for 10 miles to the campground entrance road (well signed). Turn northwest and drive one mile to the campground.

Contact: Oregon Dunes National Recreation Area, Visitors Center 541/271-6000 or 541/271-3611, fax 541/750-7244.

82 LOON LAKE RECREATION AREA

🧍‍♀️🏊‍♂️🚣‍♂️🛶🐕🏕️🎣♿🚐🏕️

Scenic rating: 8

on Loon Lake

Map 1.4, page 84   BEST (

Loon Lake was created 1,400 years ago when a nearby mountain crumbled and slid downhill, damming a creek with house-sized boulders. Today, the lake is half a mile wide and nearly two miles long, covers 260 acres, and is more than 100 feet deep in places. Its ideal location provides a warm, wind-sheltered summer climate for various water activities. A nature trail leads to a waterfall about half a mile away. Evening interpretive programs are held during summer weekends.

Campsites, facilities: There are 57 sites for tents or RVs of any length; some sites can be combined into a group site for up to 12

people. Picnic tables and fire pits are provided. Drinking water, restrooms with flush toilets and showers, garbage bins, dump station, basketball court, firewood, playground, horseshoe pits, volleyball, fish-cleaning station, a sand beach, and a boat ramp and moorings are available. Some facilities are wheelchair accessible, including the fishing pier. Leashed pets are permitted in the campground, but not on the beach or in the day-use area.

Reservations, fees: Reservations are accepted at 877/444-6777 or www.recreation.gov ($10 reservation fee). Sites are $18 per night, $7 per night per additional vehicle, and $36 per night for group sites. Open late May–November, weather permitting.

Directions: From Eugene, drive south on I-5 to Exit 162 and Highway 38. Turn west on Highway 38 and drive 43 miles to Milepost 13.5 and the County Road 3 exit. Turn left (south) and drive 7.5 miles to the campground on the right.

Contact: Bureau of Land Management, Coos Bay District Office, 541/756-0100, fax 541/751-4303, www.blm.gov.

83 LOON LAKE LODGE AND RV

🧍‍♀️🚴‍♂️🏊‍♂️🛶🚣‍♂️🚐🏕️

Scenic rating: 8

on Loon Lake

Map 1.4, page 84

This resort boasts one mile of lake frontage and nestles among the tall trees on pretty Loon Lake. It's not a long drive from either U.S. 101 or I-5, making it an ideal layover spot for travelers eager to get off the highway. The lake offers good bass fishing, boating, swimming, and waterskiing.

Campsites, facilities: There are 25 tent sites, 40 sites with full or partial hookups for tents or RVs up to 40 feet long, four group sites for up to 20–30 people each, eight cabins, and a six-unit motel. Some RV sites are pull-through. Picnic tables and fire rings are provided. Pit toilets and drinking water are available. A restaurant, general store, wireless Internet service, ice, gas, a beach, boat ramp, dock, marina, and boat rentals are also available. Leashed pets are permitted, with certain restrictions.

Reservations, fees: Reservations are accepted. Tent sites are $19 per night, RV sites are $35 per night, $7 per person per night for more than five, $5 per night per additional vehicle. Some credit cards are accepted. Open year-round.

Directions: From Eugene, drive south on I-5 to Exit 162 and Highway 38. Turn west on Highway 38 and drive 20 miles through the town of Elkton. Continue on Highway 38 for another 22 miles until you cross a large bridge and reach Loon Lake Road. Turn left at Loon Lake Road and drive nine miles to the resort.

Contact: Loon Lake Lodge and RV Resort, 541/599-2244, fax 541/599-2274, www.loon-lakerv.com.

84 OREGON DUNES KOA

Scenic rating: 5

north of North Bend, next to the
Oregon Dunes National Recreation Area

Map 1.4, page 84

This ATV-friendly park has direct access to Oregon Dunes National Recreation Area, which offers miles of ATV trails. The fairly open campground features a landscape of grass, young trees, and a small lake. The ocean is a 15-minute drive away. Mill Casino is about six miles south on U.S. 101. Freshwater and ocean fishing are nearby. A golf course is about five miles away.

Campsites, facilities: There are 51 sites for tents or RVs of any size (full hookups), six tent sites, and nine cabins. Most sites are pull-through, and 30- and 50-amp service is available. RV sites have drinking water, picnic tables, fire pits, and cable TV provided. Drinking water, restrooms with flush toilets

and showers, wireless Internet service, modem access, coin laundry, convenience store, game room, playground, seasonal organized activities, a snack bar, firewood, propane gas, horseshoe pits, volleyball, and a picnic shelter are available. ATV rentals are nearby. Some facilities are wheelchair accessible. Leashed pets are permitted, except in cabins.

Reservations, fees: Reservations are accepted at 800/562-4236. Tent sites are $18–32 per night, RV sites are $25–55 per night, and it costs $3.25–5 per person per night for more than two people and $4.50 per night per additional vehicle. Some credit cards are accepted. Open year-round.

Directions: From Coos Bay, drive north on U.S. 101 past North Bend for nine miles to Milepost 229. The campground entrance road is on the left.

Contact: Oregon Dunes KOA, 541/756-4851, fax 541/756-8838, www.koa.com.

85 TYEE

Scenic rating: 7

on the Umpqua River

Map 1.4, page 84

Here's a classic spot along the Umpqua River with great salmon, smallmouth bass, and steelhead fishing in season. Boat launches are available a few miles upstream and downstream of the campground. Eagleview Group camp, a BLM campground, is one mile away.

Campsites, facilities: There are 15 sites for tents or RVs up to 70 feet long. Drinking water, garbage service, fire grills, and picnic tables are provided. Vault toilets, a day-use area with horseshoe pits, and a pavilion are available. A camp host is on-site. A store is within one mile. Some facilities are wheelchair accessible. Leashed pets are permitted.

Reservations, fees: Reservations are not accepted. Sites are $10 per night, $4 per night for each additional vehicle. Open mid-March–November.

Directions: From Roseburg, drive north on I-5 to Exit 136 and Highway 138. Take that exit and drive west on Highway 138 for 12 miles. Cross Bullock Bridge and continue to County Road 57. Turn right and drive 0.5 mile to the campground entrance.

Contact: Bureau of Land Management, Roseburg District, 541/440-4930, fax 541/440-4948, www.blm.gov.

86 WILD MARE HORSE CAMP

Scenic rating: 7

in Oregon Dunes National Recreation Area

Map 1.4, page 84

This horse camp has paved parking, with single and double corrals. No off-road vehicles are allowed within the campground. Horses can be ridden straight out into the dunes and to the ocean; they cannot be ridden on developed trails, such as Bluebill Lake Trail. The heavily treed shoreline gives rise to treed sites with some bushes.

Campsites, facilities: There are 11 horse campsites for tents or RVs up to 61 feet long. There is a maximum of two vehicles per site. Picnic tables and fire pits are provided. Drinking water, vault toilets, and garbage bins are available. Leashed pets are permitted.

Reservations, fees: Reservations are accepted at 877/444-6777 or www.recreation.gov ($10 reservation fee). Sites are $20 per night. Some credit cards are accepted. Open year-round.

Directions: From Coos Bay, drive north on U.S. 101 for 1.5 miles to Horsfall Dunes and Beach Access Road. Turn left and drive west for one mile to the campground access road. Turn right and drive 0.75 mile to the campground on the left.

Contact: Oregon Dunes National Recreation Area, Visitors Center 541/271-6000 or 541/271-3611, fax 541/750-7244.

87 BLUEBILL

Scenic rating: 6

on Bluebill Lake in Oregon Dunes National Recreation Area

Map 1.4, page 84

This campground gets very little camping pressure, although there are some good hiking trails available. It's located next to little Bluebill Lake, which sometimes dries up during the summer. A one-mile trail goes around the lake bed. The camp is a short distance from Horsfall Lake, which is surrounded by private property. If you continue west on the forest road, you'll come to a picnicking and parking area near the beach. This spot provides off-road-vehicle access to the dunes at the Horsfall day-use area and Horsfall Beach.

Campsites, facilities: There are 19 sites for tents or RVs of any length. Picnic tables, garbage service, and fire grills are provided. Flush toilets and drinking water are available. Leashed pets are permitted.

Reservations, fees: Reservations are accepted at 877/444-6777 or www.recreation.gov ($10 reservation fee). Sites are $20 per night. Open May–September.

Directions: From Coos Bay, drive north on U.S. 101 for 1.5 miles north to Horsfall Dunes and Beach Access Road. Turn west and drive one mile to Horsfall Road. Turn northwest and drive two miles to the campground entrance.

Contact: Oregon Dunes National Recreation Area, Visitors Center 541/271-6000 or 541/271-3611, fax 541/750-7244.

88 HORSFALL

Scenic rating: 4

in Oregon Dunes National Recreation Area

Map 1.4, page 84

Horsfall campground is actually a nice, large paved area for parking RVs; it's the staging area for off-road-vehicle access into the southern section of Oregon Dunes National Recreation Area. If Horsfall is full, try nearby Horsfall Beach, an overflow area with 34 tent and RV sites.

Campsites, facilities: There are 69 sites for RVs up to 52 feet in length. Picnic tables and fire rings are provided. Drinking water, garbage service, restrooms with flush toilets and coin showers, and a pay phone are available. Some facilities are wheelchair accessible. Leashed pets are permitted.

Reservations, fees: Reservations are accepted at 877/444-6777 or www.recreation.gov ($10 reservation fee). Sites are $20 per night. Open year-round.

Directions: From Coos Bay, drive north on U.S. 101 for 1.5 miles to Horsfall Road. Turn west on Horsfall Road and drive about one mile to the campground access road. Turn on the campground access road (well signed) and drive 0.5 mile to the campground.

Contact: Oregon Dunes National Recreation Area, Visitors Center 541/271-6000541/271-3611, fax 541/750-7244.

89 SUNSET BAY STATE PARK
🚶 🚴 ⛴ 🎣 🦌 🏕 ♿ 🚐 ⛺

Scenic rating: 8

near Sunset Bay

Map 1.4, page 84

Scenic Sunset Bay sits on the beautiful Oregon Coast, amid coastal forest and headlands. The sandy beach is secluded, protected by cliffs and confiers, and tidepooling is a popular activity. A series of hiking trails leads to Shore Acres and Cape Arago Parks. Clamming and fishing is available in nearby Charleston. Golfing and swimming are some of the recreation options here.

Campsites, facilities: There are 66 sites for tents or self-contained RVs, 63 sites with full or partial hookups for tents or RVs up to 47 feet long, a separate area for hikers and bicyclists, eight yurts, and two group camps

for up to 25 and 250 people, respectively. Drinking water, picnic tables, garbage bins, and fire grills are provided. Restrooms with flush toilets and showers, a fish-cleaning station, boat ramp, and firewood are available. A camp host is on-site. A gazebo and meeting hall can be reserved at nearby Shore Acres. A restaurant is within three miles. Some facilities are wheelchair accessible. Leashed pets are permitted, except in yurts.

Reservations, fees: Reservations are accepted at 800/452-5687 or www.oregonstateparks.org ($8 reservation fee). RV sites are $16–24 per night, tent sites are $12–19 per night, $5 per night per additional vehicle, $4–5 per person per night for hikers/bicyclists, $27–36 per night for yurts, $40–71 per night for group camps, and $2.40 per person per night for more than 25 people. Some credit cards are accepted. Open year-round.

Directions: In Coos Bay, take the Charleston/State Parks exit to Empire Coos Bay Highway. Drive west to Newmark Avenue. Bear left and continue to Cape Arago Highway. Turn left and drive about five miles south to Charleston and cross the South Slough Bridge. Continue on Cape Arago Highway about three miles to the park entrance on the left.

Contact: Sunset Bay State Park, 541/888-4902 or 800/551-6949, www.oregonstateparks.org.

90 BASTENDORFF BEACH PARK
🚶 🚴 ⛴ 🎣 🛶 🦌 🏇 ♿ 🚐 ⛺

Scenic rating: 8

near Cape Arago State Park

Map 1.4, page 84

This campground is surrounded by large trees and provides access to the ocean and a small lake. Nearby activities include boating, clamming, crabbing, dune buggy riding, fishing, golfing, swimming, and whale-watching. Swimmers should be aware of undertows and sneaker waves. Horses may be rented near Bandon. A nice side trip is to Shore Acres State Park and Botanical Gardens, about 2.5 miles away.

Campsites, facilities: There are 35 tent sites, 56 sites with partial hookups for tents or RVs (of any length), and two cabins. Group camping is available. Picnic tables and fire pits are provided. Drinking water, restrooms with flush toilets and coin showers, and a dump station are available. A fish-cleaning station, horseshoe pits, playground, basketball courts, and a picnic area are also available. Some facilities are wheelchair accessible. Leashed pets are permitted.

Reservations, fees: Reservations are accepted for groups, cabins, and the picnic area only at 541/396-3121, ext. 354 ($10 reservation fee). Sites are $15–20 per night, $5 per night per additional vehicle, and cabins are $30 per night. Some credit cards are accepted. Open year-round.

Directions: In Coos Bay, take the Charleston/State Parks exit to Empire Coos Bay Highway. Drive west to Newmark Avenue. Bear left and continue to Cape Arago Highway. Turn left and drive about five miles south to Charleston and cross the South Slough Bridge. Continue on Cape Arago Highway for 1.25 miles to the park entrance.

Contact: Bastendorff Beach Park, 541/888-5353, www.co.coos.co.or.us/ccpark.

91 CHARLESTON MARINA RV PARK

🧗 🚣 🏊 �t 🐕 🤸 ♿ 🚐 ⛺

Scenic rating: 7

on Coos Bay

Map 1.4, page 84

This large, developed public park and marina is located near Charleston on the Pacific Ocean. Recreational activities in and near the campground include boating, clamming, crabbing, fishing (halibut, salmon, and tuna), hiking, huckleberry and blackberry picking, and swimming.

Campsites, facilities: There are 100 sites for tents or RVs up to 50 feet long (full hookups), six tent sites, and two yurts. Picnic tables are provided. No open fires are allowed. Drinking water, satellite TV, modem access, restrooms with showers, dump station, public phone, coin laundry, playground, fish-cleaning station, crab-cooking facilities, and propane gas are available. A marina with a boarding dock and launch ramp are on-site. Some facilities are wheelchair accessible. Leashed pets are permitted.

Reservations, fees: Reservations are accepted at 541/888-9512 or rvpark@charlestonmarina. com. RV sites are $22–25 per night, tent sites are $13 per night, and yurts are $31 per night. Weekly and monthly rates are available. Some credit cards are accepted. Open year-round.

Directions: In Coos Bay, take the Charleston/State Parks exit to Empire Coos Bay Highway. Drive west to Newmark Avenue. Bear left and continue to Cape Arago Highway. Turn left and drive about five miles south to Charleston and cross the South Slough Bridge. Continue to Boat Basin Drive. Turn right and drive 0.2 mile to Kingfisher Drive. Turn right and drive 200 feet to the campground on the left.

Contact: Charleston Marina RV Park, 541/888-9512, fax 541/888-6111, www. charlestonmarina.com.

92 BULLARDS BEACH STATE PARK

🧗 🚴 🚣 �t 🐕 🤸 ♿ 🚐 ⛺

Scenic rating: 7

on the Coquille River

Map 1.4, page 84

The Coquille River, which has good fishing in season for both boaters and crabbers, is the centerpiece of this park with four miles of shore access. If fishing is not your thing, the park also has several hiking trails. The Coquille River Lighthouse is at the end of the road that wanders through the park; during the summer, there are tours to the tower. Equestrians can explore the seven-mile horse trail.

Campsites, facilities: There are 185 sites with full or partial hookups for tents or RVs up to 64 feet long, a hiker/bicyclist camping area, a primitive horse camp with eight sites and three corrals, and 13 yurts. Drinking water, garbage bins, picnic tables, and fire grills are provided. Restrooms with flush toilets and showers, dump station, playground, firewood, a yurt meeting hall, and picnic shelters are available. Boat docks and launching facilities are in the park on the Coquille River. Some facilities are wheelchair accessible. Leashed pets are permitted.

Reservations, fees: Reservations are accepted at 800/452-5687 or www.oregonstateparks.org ($8 reservation fee). Sites are $16–24 per night, $5 per vehicle per night, $4–5 per person per night for hikers/bicyclists, and yurts are $27–36 per night. Horse camping is $12–19 per night. Some credit cards are accepted. Open year-round.

Directions: In Coos Bay, drive south on U.S. 101 for about 22 miles to the park on the right (west side of road), two miles north of Bandon.

Contact: Bullards Beach State Park, 541/347-3501 or 800/551-6949, www.oregonstateparks.org.

93 BANDON RV PARK
🚶 🚲 🎣 🚐 🐕 📷

Scenic rating: 6

near Bullards Beach State Park

Map 1.4, page 84

This in-town RV park is a good base for many adventures. Some sites are filled with renters, primarily anglers, for the summer season. Rock hounds will enjoy combing for agates and other semiprecious stones hidden along the beaches, while kids can explore the West Coast Game Park Walk-Through Safari petting zoo seven miles south of town. Bandon State Park, four miles south of town, has a nice wading spot in the creek at the north end of the park. Nearby recreation opportunities include two

18-hole golf courses, a riding stable, and tennis courts. Bullards Beach is about 2.5 miles north. Nice folks run this place.

Campsites, facilities: There are 44 sites with full hookups for RVs of any length; some are pull-through sites. Picnic tables are provided at most sites. No open fires are allowed. Restrooms with flush toilets and showers, dump station, cable TV, modem access, and a coin laundry are available. Propane gas and a store are within two blocks. Boat docks and launching facilities are nearby. Leashed pets are permitted.

Reservations, fees: Reservations are accepted at 800/393-4122. Sites are $22–24 per night, $2 per person per night for more than two people. Some credit cards are accepted. Open year-round.

Directions: From Coos Bay, drive south on U.S. 101 for 26 miles to Bandon and the Highway 42S junction. Continue south on U.S. 101 for one block to the park (located on the right at 935 2nd Street Southeast).

Contact: Bandon RV Park, 541/347-4122.

94 LAVERNE AND WEST LAVERNE GROUP CAMP
🚶 🚲 🏊 🛶 🚗 🏕 🐕 ♿ 🚐 ⛺

Scenic rating: 9

in Fairview on the north fork of the Coquille River

Map 1.4, page 84

This beautiful, 350-acre park sits on a river with a small waterfall and many trees, including a myrtle grove and old-growth Douglas fir. Mountain bikers can take an old wagon road, and golfers can enjoy any of several courses. There are a few hiking trails and a very popular swimming hole. You can fish for salmon, steelhead, and trout, and the wildlife includes bears, cougars, deer, elk, and raccoons. You can take a side trip to the museums at Myrtle Point and Coos Bay, which display local indigenous items, or an old stagecoach house in Dora.

Campsites, facilities: There are 30 tent sites

and 46 RV sites with partial hookups for RVs of any length. There is also a large group site at West Laverne B that includes 22 RV sites with partial hookups. One cabin is also available. Drinking water, picnic tables, and fire pits are provided. Restrooms with flush toilets and coin showers, garbage bins, dump station, ice, playground, a picnic area that can be reserved, swimming hole (unsupervised), horseshoe pits, and volleyball and softball areas are available. A restaurant is within 1.5 miles. Propane gas, a store, and gasoline are within five miles. Some facilities are wheelchair accessible. Leashed pets are permitted.

Reservations, fees: Reservations are not accepted for family sites but are accepted for the group site and cabin ($10 reservation fee) at 541/396-3121, ext. 354. RV sites are $12–16 per night, tent sites are $10–11 per night, $5 per night per each additional vehicle. The group site is $140 per night for the first six camping units, plus $16 per night for each additional unit. The cabin is $30 per night. Some credit cards are accepted. Open year-round.

Directions: From Coos Bay, drive south on U.S. 101 for six miles to the junction with Highway 42. Turn east and drive 11 miles to Coquille and West Central. Turn left and drive 0.5 mile to Fairview McKinley Road. Turn right and drive eight miles to the Fairview Store. Continue east another five miles (past the store) to the park on the right.

Contact: Laverne County Park, Coos County, 541/396-2344, www.co.coos.or.us/ccpark.

95 PARK CREEK
🐕 🚐 🏕️

Scenic rating: 7

near Coquille

Map 1.4, page 84

Want to be by yourself? You came to the right place. This pretty little campground offers peaceful, shady campsites under an old-growth canopy of Douglas fir, myrtle, red cedar, and western hemlock. Relax and enjoy nearby Park Creek and Middle Creek.

Campsites, facilities: There are 15 sites for tents or small RVs. Picnic tables and fire grills are provided. Vault toilets and garbage bins are available. There is no drinking water. Leashed pets are permitted.

Reservations, fees: Reservations are not accepted. There is no fee, but the stay limit is 14 days. Open year-round.

Directions: From Coos Bay, drive south on U.S. 101 for six miles to the junction with Highway 42. Turn east and drive 11 miles to Coquille and Coquille Fairview Road. Turn left (east) on Coquille Fairview Road and drive 7.5 miles to Fairview and Coos Bay Wagon Road. Turn right and drive four miles to Middle Creek Access Road. Turn left (east) and drive nine miles to the campground on the right.

Contact: Bureau of Land Management, Coos Bay District, 541/756-0100, fax 541/751-4303, www.or.blm.gov/coosbay.

96 KOA BANDON/ PORT ORFORD
🧍 🏊 🐕 🚵 🚐 🏕️

Scenic rating: 7

near the Elk River

Map 1.5, page 85

This spot is considered just a layover camp, but it offers large, secluded sites nestled among big trees and coastal ferns. A pool and spa are available. During the summer season, a daily pancake breakfast and ice cream social are held. The Elk and Sixes Rivers, where the fishing can be good, are minutes away, and Cape Blanco State Park is just a few miles down the road.

Campsites, facilities: There are 46 tent sites and 26 pull-through sites with full hookups (20-, 30-, and 50-amp) for RVs of any length. Six cabins are also available. Picnic tables and fire rings are provided. Restrooms with flush toilets and showers, cable TV, modem access, snack bar, propane gas, dump station, firewood, recreation hall, convenience store, coin laundry, seasonal heated swimming pool, hot tub, horseshoe pits, basketball court, ice, and a playground are available. Leashed pets are permitted.

Reservations, fees: Reservations are accepted at 800/562-3298. Sites are $24–32 per night, $3 per person per night for more than two people, and $5 per night per additional vehicle. Some credit cards are accepted. Open March–November.

Directions: From Bandon, drive south on U.S. 101 for 16 miles to the campground at Milepost 286 near Langlois, on the west side of the highway.

Contact: KOA Bandon/Port Orford, 541/348-2358, www.koa.com.

97 CAPE BLANCO STATE PARK

Scenic rating: 8

between the Sixes and Elk Rivers

Map 1.5, page 85   **BEST (**

This large park is named for the white *(blanco)* chalk appearance of the sea cliffs here, which rise 200 feet above the ocean. Sea lions inhabit the offshore rocks, and trails and a road lead to the black sand beach below the cliffs. The park offers good fishing access to the Sixes River, which runs for more than two miles through meadows and forests. There are seven miles of trails for horseback riding available and more than eight miles of hiking trails, some with ocean views. Tours of the lighthouse and historic Hughes House are available.

Campsites, facilities: There are 53 sites with partial hookups for tents or RVs up to 65 feet long. Other options include an equestrian camp with eight sites, a hiker/bicyclist camping area, four cabins, and four primitive group sites for tents or RVs for up to 25 people. Garbage bins, picnic tables, drinking water, and fire grills are provided. Firewood and restrooms with flush toilets and showers

are available. Some facilities are wheelchair accessible. Leashed pets are permitted.

Reservations, fees: Reservations are not accepted for single sites, but are accepted for cabins, the group site, and the horse camp at 800/452-5687 or www.oregonstateparks.org ($8 reservation fee). Single sites are $12–20 per night, $5 per night per additional vehicle. The horse camp is $10–17 per night; the hiker/biker sites are $4–5 per person per night. The group site is $40–71 per night for the first 25 people, then $2.40–3 per additional person per night. Some credit cards are accepted. Open year-round.

Directions: From Coos Bay, turn south on U.S. 101 and drive approximately 46 miles (south of Sixes, five miles north of Port Orford) to Cape Blanco Road. Turn right (northwest) and drive five miles to the campground on the left.

Contact: Humbug Mountain State Park, 541/332-6774 or 800/551-6949, www.oregonstateparks.org. (This park is under the same management as Humbug Mountain State Park.)

98 EDSON

Scenic rating: 6

on the Sixes River

Map 1.5, page 85

This is a popular campground along the banks of the Sixes River. Edson is similar to Sixes River Campground, except it has less tree cover and Sixes River has the benefit of a boat ramp.

Campsites, facilities: There are 25 sites for tents or RVs up to 30 feet long, and four group sites for up to 50 people. Picnic tables and fire grills are provided. Drinking water, vault toilets, garbage service, a boat launch, and a camp host are available. Some facilities are wheelchair accessible. Leashed pets are permitted.

Reservations, fees: Reservations are not accepted for single sites but are required for group sites at 541/332-8027. Sites are $8 per night and $4 per night for each additional vehicle, with a 14-day stay limit. Open May–November, weather permitting.

Directions: From Coos Bay, drive south on U.S. 101 for 40 miles to Sixes and Sixes River Road/County Road 184. Turn left (east) on Sixes River Road and drive four miles to the campground entrance on the left. It's located before the Edson Creek Bridge.

Contact: Bureau of Land Management, Coos Bay District, 541/756-0100 or 541/332-8027, fax 541/751-4303, www.blm.gov.

99 SIXES RIVER

Scenic rating: 6

on the Sixes River

Map 1.5, page 85

Set along the banks of the Sixes River at an elevation of 4,303 feet, this camp is a favorite of anglers, miners, and nature lovers. There are opportunities to pan or sluice for gold year-round or through a special limited permit. Dredging is permitted from July 15 through September. The camp roads are paved.

Campsites, facilities: There are 19 sites for tents or RVs up to 30 feet long. Picnic tables, garbage service, and fire grills are provided. Drinking water and vault toilets are available. Some facilities are wheelchair accessible. Leashed pets are permitted.

Reservations, fees: Reservations are not accepted. Sites are $8 per night, $4 per night for an additional vehicle, with a 14-day stay limit. Open May–November, weather permitting.

Directions: From Coos Bay, drive south on U.S. 101 for 40 miles to Sixes and Sixes River Road/County Road 184. Turn left (east) on Sixes River Road and drive 11 miles to the campground on the right. The last 0.5 mile is an unpaved road.

Contact: Bureau of Land Management, Coos Bay District, 541/756-0100, fax 541/751-4303, www.blm.gov.

100 POWERS COUNTY PARK

Scenic rating: 9

near the south fork of the Coquille River

Map 1.5, page 85

This private and secluded public park in a wooded, mountainous area is a great stop for travelers going between I-5 and the coast. A 30-acre lake at the park provides a spot for visitors to boat and fish for trout. The lake is stocked with bass, catfish, crappie, and trout. Only electric boat motors are allowed. Swimming is not recommended because of the algae in the lake. A bike trail is available. On display at the park are an old steam donkey and a hand-carved totem pole. The biggest cedar tree in Oregon is reputed to be about 12 miles away.

Campsites, facilities: There are 30 sites for tents or RVs up to 54 feet long and 40 sites with partial hookups (20- and 30-amp). One cabin is also available. Picnic tables, fire pits, drinking water, restrooms with flush toilets and showers, a dump station, fish-cleaning station, picnic shelters, and a public phone are provided. Recreational facilities include a boat ramp, horseshoe pits, playground, basketball and volleyball courts, tennis courts, and a softball field. Supplies are available within one mile. Some facilities are wheelchair accessible. Leashed pets are permitted.

Reservations, fees: Reservations ($10 reservation fee) are accepted for the cabin only at 541/396-3121, ext. 354. RV sites are $12–16 per night, tent sites are $10–11 per night, and cabins are $30 per night. Some credit cards are accepted. Open year-round.

Directions: From Coos Bay, drive south on U.S. 101 for six miles to the junction with Highway 42. Turn east and drive 20 miles to Myrtle Point. Continue on Highway 42 to the Powers Highway (Highway 242) exit. Turn right (southwest) and drive 19 miles to the park on the right.

Contact: Powers County Park, Coos County, 541/439-2791, www.co.coos.or.us/ccpark/.

101 ELK RIVER CAMPGROUND

Scenic rating: 7

near the Elk River

Map 1.5, page 85

This quiet and restful camp makes an excellent base for fall and winter fishing on the Elk River, which is known for its premier salmon fishing. A one-mile private access road goes to the river, so guests get their personal fishing holes. About half of the sites are taken by monthly rentals.

Campsites, facilities: There are 50 sites with full hookups for RVs up to 40 feet long; some sites are pull-through. Picnic tables are provided. No open fires are allowed. Drinking water, restrooms with showers, dump station, public phone, modem hookups, cable TV, and a coin laundry are available. Recreational facilities include a sports field, horseshoe pits, recreation hall, and a boat ramp. Some facilities are wheelchair accessible. Leashed pets are permitted.

Reservations, fees: Reservations are recommended. Sites are $20.20 per night. Weekly and monthly rates are available. Open year-round.

Directions: From Port Orford, drive north on U.S. 101 for 1.5 miles to Elk River Road (Milepost 297). Turn right (east) on Elk River Road and drive 1.8 miles to the campground on the left.

Contact: Elk River Campground, 541/332-2255.

102 LAIRD LAKE

Scenic rating: 8

on Laird Lake in Siskiyou National Forest

Map 1.5, page 85   BEST (

This secluded campground is set at 1,600 feet elevation, along the shore of pretty Laird Lake (six feet at its deepest point). Some old-growth cedar logs are in the lake. Most campers have no idea such a place exists in the area. This very private and scenic spot can be just what you're looking for if you're tired of fighting the crowds at the more developed camps along U.S. 101.

Campsites, facilities: There are four sites for tents or RVs up to 25 feet long. There is no drinking water, and garbage must be packed out. Leashed pets are permitted.

Reservations, fees: Reservations are not accepted. There is no fee for camping. Open year-round.

Directions: From Port Orford, drive north on U.S. 101 for three miles to County Road 208. Turn right and drive 7.5 miles southeast (the road becomes Forest Road 5325). Continue for 15.5 miles (the road bears to the right when you reach the gravel) to the campground. The road is paved for 11 miles and is gravel for the last 4.5 miles to the campground.

Contact: Siskiyou National Forest, Powers Ranger District, 541/439-6200, fax 541/439-6217, www.fs.fed.us.

103 BUTLER BAR

Scenic rating: 6

on the Elk River in Siskiyou National Forest

Map 1.5, page 85

This campground, at an elevation of 800 feet, is set back from the shore of the Elk River and surrounded by old-growth and hardwood forest, with some reforested areas nearby. Across the river is the Grassy Knob Wilderness, which has no trails and is generally too rugged to hike. Check fishing regulations before fishing.

Campsites, facilities: There are seven sites for tents. Picnic tables and fire grills are provided. Vault toilets are available. There is no drinking water, and garbage must be packed out. Leashed pets are permitted.

Reservations, fees: Reservations are not accepted. There is no fee for camping. Open year-round, weather permitting.

Directions: From Port Orford, drive north on U.S. 101 for three miles to County Road 208. Turn right and drive 7.5 miles southeast (the road becomes Forest Road 5325). Continue for 7.5 miles to the campground. The road is paved.

Contact: Siskiyou National Forest, Powers Ranger District, 541/439-6200, fax 541/439-6217, www.fs.fed.us.

104 PORT ORFORD RV VILLAGE

Scenic rating: 5

near the Elk and Sixes Rivers

Map 1.5, page 85

Each evening, an informal group campfire and happy hour enliven this campground. Other nice touches include a small gazebo where you can get free coffee each morning and a patio where you can sit. Fishing is good during the fall and winter on the nearby Elk and Sixes Rivers, and the campground has a smokehouse, freezer, and fish-cleaning station. Some sites here are taken by summer season rentals or permanent residents.

Campsites, facilities: There are 47 sites with full or partial hookups for RVs of any length. Some sites are pull-through. Picnic tables are provided, and fire pits are available on request. Restrooms with flush toilets and showers, propane gas, dump station, horseshoe pits, recreation hall, and a coin laundry are available. Boat docks and launching facilities are nearby. Lake, river, and ocean are all within 1.5 miles. Leashed pets are permitted.

Reservations, fees: Reservations are accepted. Sites are $26 per night, plus $2 per person per night for more than two people. Open year-round.

Directions: In Port Orford on U.S. 101, drive to Madrona Avenue. Turn east and drive one block to Port Orford Loop. Turn left (north) and drive 0.5 mile to the camp on the left side.

Contact: Port Orford RV Village, 541/332-1041, www.portorfordrv.com.

105 HUMBUG MOUNTAIN STATE PARK

Scenic rating: 7

near Port Orford

Map 1.5, page 85

Humbug Mountain, at 1,756 feet elevation, looms over its namesake state park. Fortunately, this natural guardian affords the campground some of the warmest weather on the coast by blocking cold winds from the ocean. Windsurfing and scuba diving are popular, as is hiking the three-mile trail to Humbug Peak. Both ocean and freshwater fishing are accessible nearby.

Campsites, facilities: There are 62 sites for tents or RVs (no hookups), 32 sites with partial hookups for RVs up to 55 feet long, and a hiker/bicyclist camp. Some sites are pull-through. Fire grills, picnic tables, garbage bins, and drinking water are provided. Firewood and restrooms with flush toilets and showers are available. A camp host is on-site. Some facilities are wheelchair accessible. Leashed pets are permitted.

Reservations, fees: Reservations are not accepted. RV sites are $12–20 per night, tent sites are $10–17 per night, $5 per night per additional vehicle, and $4–5 per person per night for hikers/bicyclists. The group camp is $60 per night for up to 25 people, plus $2.40 per person per night for additional persons. Some credit cards are accepted. Open year-round.

Directions: From Port Orford, drive south on U.S. 101 for six miles to the park entrance on the left.

Contact: Humbug Mountain State Park, 541/332-6774 or 800/551-6949, www.oregonstateparks.org.

106 MYRTLE GROVE

🚶 🐕 ⛺

Scenic rating: 6

on the south fork of the Coquille River in
Siskiyou National Forest

Map 1.5, page 85

This U.S. Forest Service campground is located along the south fork of the Coquille River, a little downstream from Daphne Grove, at an elevation of 500 feet. No fishing is allowed. Campsites are set under a canopy of big leaf maple and Douglas fir in a narrow, steep canyon. The Big Tree Observation Site, home to a huge Port Orford cedar, is a few miles away. The trail that runs adjacent to Elk Creek provides a prime hike. (The road to Big Tree may be closed because of slides, so be sure to check with the ranger district in advance.)

Campsites, facilities: There are five tent sites. Picnic tables and fire grills are provided. Vault toilets and garbage bins are available. There is no drinking water. Leashed pets are permitted.

Reservations, fees: Reservations are not accepted. There is no fee for camping. Open year-round.

Directions: From Coos Bay, drive south on U.S. 101 for six miles to the junction with Highway 42. Turn east and drive 20 miles to Myrtle Point. Continue on Highway 42 to Powers Highway (Highway 242). Turn right (southwest) and drive 18 miles (the road becomes County Road 90) to Powers. Continue for 4.3 miles (the road becomes Forest Road 33). Turn south and drive to the camp. The road is paved all the way to the camp.

Contact: Siskiyou National Forest, Powers Ranger District, 541/439-6200 or 541/439-6217, www.fs.fed.us.

107 DAPHNE GROVE

🐕 ♿ 🚗 ⛺

Scenic rating: 7

on the south fork of the Coquille River in
Siskiyou National Forest

Map 1.5, page 85

This prime spot is far enough out of the way to attract little attention. At 1,000 feet elevation, it sits along the south fork of the Coquille River and is surrounded by old-growth cedar, Douglas fir, and maple. No fishing is allowed. The road is paved all the way to, and in, the campground, a plus for RVs and "city cars."

Campsites, facilities: There are 15 sites for tents or RVs up to 35 feet long. Picnic tables, garbage bins, and fire grills are provided. Vault toilets are available. There is no drinking water. Some facilities are wheelchair accessible. Leashed pets are permitted.

Reservations, fees: Reservations are not accepted. Sites are $6 per night, $3 per night per additional vehicle. Open year-round.

Directions: From Coos Bay, drive south on U.S. 101 for six miles to the junction with Highway 42. Turn east and drive 20 miles to Myrtle Point. Continue on Highway 42 to Powers Highway (Highway 242). Turn right (southwest) and drive 18 miles (the road becomes County Road 90) to Powers. Continue for 4.3 miles (the road becomes Forest Road 33). Continue for 10.5 miles to the campground entrance.

Contact: Siskiyou National Forest, Powers Ranger District, 541/439-6200, fax 541/439-6217, www.fs.fed.us.

108 ISLAND

🚶 🏊 🐕 🚗 ⛺

Scenic rating: 7

near Coquille River Falls

Map 1.5, page 85

Island Camp is an excellent base camp for hikers with many trailheads nearby. It is located along the south fork of the Coquille River at 1,000-foot elevation in Siskiyou National Forest. Nearby hiking opportunities include the Azalea Lake Trail, Panther Ridge Trail, Coquille River Falls Trail, and Sucker Creek Trail. Note: Do not confuse this Island Campground with the Island Campground in Umpqua National Forest.

Campsites, facilities: There are five sites for tents or RVs to 16 feet. Picnic tables and fire rings are provided. Vault toilets and garbage bins are available, but there is no drinking water. Leashed pets are permitted.

Reservations, fees: Reservations are not accepted. Sites are $6 per night. Open year-round.

Directions: From Coos Bay, drive south on U.S. 101 for six miles to the junction with Highway 42. Turn east and drive 20 miles to Myrtle Point. Continue on Highway 42 to Powers Highway (Highway 242). Turn right (southwest) and drive 18 miles (the road becomes County Road 90) to Powers. Drive south 17 miles on Forest Service Road 3300 to the campground.

Contact: Siskiyou National Forest, Powers Ranger District, 541/439-6200, fax 541/439-6217, www.fs.fed.us.

109 SRU LAKE
🚶🏊🐕🚐🏕

Scenic rating: 8

on Squaw Lake in Siskiyou National Forest

Map 1.5, page 85

Sru (pronounced "Shrew") campground is set along the shore of one-acre Sru Lake at 2,200 feet elevation in rich, old-growth forest. Sru is more of a pond than a lake, but it is stocked with trout in the spring. Get there early—the fish are generally gone by midsummer. The trailheads for the Panther Ridge Trail and Coquille River Falls Trail are a 10-minute drive from the campground. It's strongly advised that you obtain a U.S. Forest Service map detailing the backcountry roads and trails.

Campsites, facilities: There are seven sites

for tents or RVs up to 21 feet long. Picnic tables and fire rings are provided. Vault toilets are available. There is no drinking water, and garbage must be packed out. Leashed pets are permitted.

Reservations, fees: Reservations are not accepted. There is no fee for camping. Open year-round.

Directions: From Coos Bay, drive south on U.S. 101 for six miles to the junction with Highway 42. Turn east and drive 20 miles to Myrtle Point. Continue on Highway 42 to Powers Highway (Highway 242). Turn right (southwest) and drive 18 miles (the road becomes County Road 90) to Powers. Continue for 4.3 miles (the road becomes Forest Road 33). Continue on Forest Road 33 for 15 miles to the South Fork Coquille River Bridge. Continue on Forest Road 33 for 0.5 mile to Forest Road 3347 (paved road). Turn right and drive one mile to the camp.

Contact: Siskiyou National Forest, Powers Ranger District, 541/439-6200, fax 541/439-6217, www.fs.fed.us.

110 TUCKER FLAT
🚶🏊🐕♿🏕

Scenic rating: 7

on the Rogue River

Map 1.5, page 85

Above the clear waters of Mule Creek, this campground borders the Wild Rogue Wilderness. Tucker Flat offers a trailhead into the Wild Rogue Wilderness and lots of evidence of historic mining. Mosquitoes can be a problem, and bears occasionally wander through. The historic Rogue River Ranch is just 0.25 mile away, and the museum and other buildings are open during the summer. The Rogue River Ranch is on the National Register of Historic Places. There are also scenic bridges along Mule Creek. Tucker Flat campground can also be reached by hiking the Rogue River Trail or by floating the Rogue River and hiking up past the Rogue River Ranch. Campers and hikers are advised to stop by the Medford BLM office for maps.

Campsites, facilities: There are six primitive tent sites. Picnic tables and fire grills are provided. Vault toilets and bear-proof trash cans are available. There is no drinking water. Some facilities are wheelchair accessible. Leashed pets are permitted.

Reservations, fees: Reservations are not accepted. There is no fee for camping. Open May–October, weather permitting.

Directions: From Grants Pass, drive one mile north on I-5 to Exit 61. Take that exit and drive west on Merlin-Galice Access Road for 20 miles to the Grave Creek Bridge (the second bridge over the Rogue River). Cross the bridge and drive a short distance to BLM Road 34-8-1. Turn left and drive 16 miles to BLM Road 32-8-31. Turn left and drive seven miles to BLM Road 32-9-14.2. Turn left and drive 15 miles to the campground (around the bend from the Rogue River Ranch).

Contact: Bureau of Land Management, Medford District, 541/618-2200, fax 541/618-2400, www.blm.gov.

111 HONEY BEAR CAMPGROUND & RV RESORT

Scenic rating: 10

near Gold Beach

Map 1.5, page 85 **BEST**

This campground offers wooded sites with ocean views. The owners have built a huge, authentic chalet, which contains a German deli, recreation area, and a big dance floor. On summer nights, they hold dances with live music. A restaurant is available on-site with authentic German food. A fishing pond is stocked with trout.

Campsites, facilities: There are 20 sites for tents or RVs (no hookups) and 65 sites with full hookups for RVs of any length. Thirty are pull-through sites with full hookups and 15 have patios. Picnic tables and fire rings are provided. Restrooms with flush toilets and showers, drinking water, cable TV, modem access, dump station, firewood, recreation hall, restaurant, convenience store, coin laundry, ice, and a playground are available. Leashed pets are permitted.

Reservations, fees: Reservations are accepted at 800/822-4444. Sites are $21.95 per night, $3 per person per night for more than two people, and $1 per night per additional vehicle. Open year-round, weather permitting.

Directions: From Gold Beach, drive north on U.S. 101 for eight miles to Ophir Road near Milepost 321. Turn right and drive two miles to the campground on the right side of the road.

Contact: Honey Bear Campground & RV Resort, 541/247-2765, www.honeybearrv.com.

112 ROCK CREEK

Scenic rating: 6

near the south fork of the Coquille River in Siskiyou National Forest

Map 1.5, page 85

This little-known camp (elevation 1,400 feet) in a tree-shaded canyon is surrounded by old-growth forest and some reforested areas. It is set near Rock Creek, just upstream from its confluence with the south fork of the Coquille River. No fishing is allowed. For a good side trip, take the one-mile climb to Azalea Lake, a small, shallow lake where there are some hike-in campsites. In July, the azaleas are spectacular.

Campsites, facilities: There are seven sites for tents or RVs up to 16 feet long. Picnic tables and fire grills are provided. Vault toilets, garbage bins, and firewood are available. There is no drinking water. Leashed pets are permitted.

Reservations, fees: Reservations are not accepted. Sites are $6 per night, $3 per night per additional vehicle. Open year-round, with limited winter facilities.

Directions: From Coos Bay, drive south on U.S. 101 for six miles to the junction with Highway 42. Turn east and drive 20 miles to Myrtle Point. Continue on Highway 42 to Powers Highway (Highway 242). Turn right (southwest) and drive 18 miles (the road becomes County Road 90) to Powers. Continue for 4.3 miles (the road becomes Forest Road 33). Continue on Forest Road 33 for 15 miles to the South Fork Coquille River Bridge. Continue on Forest Road 33 for 0.5 mile to Forest Road 3347 (paved road). Turn right and drive 0.5 mile to the camp.

Contact: Siskiyou National Forest, Powers Ranger District, 541/439-6200, fax 541/439-6217, www.fs.fed.us.

113 FOSTER BAR

Scenic rating: 5

on the Rogue River in Siskiyou National Forest

Map 1.5, page 85

This camping area is set near the banks of the Rogue River. There's a take-out point for rafters. Hiking opportunities are good nearby, and you can also fish from the river bar. Agness RV Park provides a nearby camping alternative.

Campsites, facilities: There are eight sites for tents. Drinking water, flush toilets, garbage bins, and boat-launching facilities are available. A camp host is on-site. Leashed pets are permitted.

Reservations, fees: Reservations are not accepted. Sites are $5 per night, $3 per night per additional vehicle. Open year-round.

Directions: From Gold Beach on U.S. 101, turn east on County Road 595 and drive 35 miles (it becomes Forest Road 33) to the junction for Illahe and Foster Bar. Turn right on County Road 375 and drive five miles to the campground.

Contact: Rogue River, Siskiyou National Forest, Gold Beach Ranger District, 541/247-3600, fax 541/247-3617, www.fs.fed.us.

114 ALMEDA PARK

Scenic rating: 6

on the Rogue River

Map 1.5, page 85

This rustic park, located along the Rogue River and featuring a grassy area, is popular for rafting and swimming. One of the main put-in points for floating the lower section of the river can be found right here. Fishing is also available. The Rogue River Trail is four miles west.

Campsites, facilities: There are 34 sites for tents or RVs of any length (no hookups), two group sites for tents or RVs for up to 30 people, and one yurt. Some sites are pull-through. Picnic tables and fire pits are provided. Drinking water, vault toilets, garbage bins, and a boat ramp are available. A seasonal camp host is on-site. Leashed pets are permitted.

Reservations, fees: Reservations are accepted. Sites are $19 per night, $5 per night per additional vehicle, and the yurt is $30 per night. The group site is $32 per night for up to 12 people, and $3 per person per night for more than 12 people. Open year-round.

Directions: From Grants Pass, drive north on I-5 for 3.5 miles to Exit 61 (Merlin-Galice Road). Take that exit and drive on Merlin-Galice Road for 19 miles to the park on the right. The park is approximately 16 miles west of Merlin.

Contact: Josephine County Parks, 541/474-5285, fax 541/474-5288, www.co.josephine.or.us/parks/index.htm.

115 NESIKA BEACH RV PARK

Scenic rating: 7

near Gold Beach

Map 1.5, page 85

This RV park next to Nesika Beach is a good layover spot for U.S. 101 cruisers. An 18-hole golf course is close by. There are many long-term rentals here.

Campsites, facilities: There are six tent sites and 32 sites with full or partial hookups for RVs of any length; some sites are pull-through. Drinking water, cable TV, and picnic tables are provided; some tent sites have fire rings. Restrooms with flush toilets and showers, a dump station, convenience store, coin laundry, and ice are available. Leashed pets are permitted.

Reservations, fees: Reservations are accepted. RV sites are $20–24 per night, tent sites are $15 per night, $1 per person per night for more than two people. Monthly rates are available. Open year-round.

Directions: From Gold Beach, drive north on U.S. 101 for six miles to Nesika Road. Turn left and drive 0.75 mile west to the park on the right.

Contact: Nesika Beach RV Park, 541/247-6077, www.nesikarv.com.

116 INDIAN CREEK RESORT

Scenic rating: 7

on the Rogue River

Map 1.5, page 85

This campground is set along the Rogue River on the outskirts of the town of Gold Beach. A few sites have river views. Nearby recreation options include boat trips on the Rogue.

Campsites, facilities: There are 26 tent sites and 90 sites with full hookups for RVs of any length; some sites are pull-through. Five park-model cabins are also available. Drinking water, cable TV hookups, and picnic tables are provided. Fire pits are provided at some sites. Restrooms with flush toilets and showers, modem access, firewood, recreation hall, convenience store, sauna, café, coin laundry, ice, and a playground are available. Propane gas is within two miles. Boat docks, launching facilities, and rentals are nearby. Leashed pets are permitted.

Reservations, fees: Reservations are accepted at 877/537-7704. RV sites are $27 per night, tent sites are $18 per night, $2 per person per

night for more than two people. Some credit cards are accepted. Open year-round, with limited winter facilities.

Directions: On U.S. 101, drive to the northern end of Gold Beach to Jerry's Flat Road (just south of the Patterson Bridge). Turn left (east) on Jerry's Flat Road and drive 0.5 mile to the resort.

Contact: Indian Creek Resort, 541/247-7704, www.indiancreekrv.com.

117 LUCKY LODGE RV PARK

Scenic rating: 6

on the Rogue River

Map 1.5, page 85

Lucky Lodge is a good layover spot for U.S. 101 travelers who want to get off the highway circuit. Set on the shore of the Rogue River, it offers opportunities for boating, fishing, and swimming. Most sites have a view of the river. Nearby recreation options include hiking trails. About one-third of the sites are occupied by monthly renters.

Campsites, facilities: There are 31 sites with full hookups for RVs of any length, three tent sites, and two cabins. Most sites are pull-through. Drinking water and picnic tables are provided. Restrooms with flush toilets and showers, propane gas, a recreation hall, and coin laundry are available. Boat docks and rentals are within eight miles. Leashed pets are permitted.

Reservations, fees: Reservations are accepted. RV sites are $27–30 per night, tent sites are $20 per night, $4 per person per night for more than two people. Open year-round.

Directions: From Gold Beach, drive north on U.S. 101 for four miles (on the north side of the Rogue River) to Rogue River Road. Turn right (east) and drive 3.5 miles to North Bank River Road. Turn right and drive 4.5 miles to the park on the right.

Contact: Lucky Lodge RV Park, 541/247-7618.

118 KIMBALL CREEK BEND RV RESORT

🏃 �"🐕 🚣 🚐 ⛺

Scenic rating: 6

on the Rogue River

Map 1.5, page 85

Kimball Creek campground on the scenic Rogue River is just far enough from the coast to provide quiet and its own distinct character. The resort offers guided fishing trips and sells tickets for jet boat tours. Nearby recreation options include an 18-hole golf course, hiking trails, and boating facilities. Note that about one-third of the sites are monthly rentals.

Campsites, facilities: There are 62 sites with full hookups for RVs of any length, 13 tent sites, one park-model cabin, and three motel rooms. Drinking water and picnic tables are provided, and fire rings are at some sites. Restrooms with flush toilets and showers, modem access, propane gas, dump station, recreation hall, store, coin laundry, ice, and a playground are available. Boat docks are on-site, and launching facilities are nearby. Leashed pets are permitted.

Reservations, fees: Reservations are accepted at 888/814-0633. RV sites are $27–39 per night, tent sites are $25 per night, $3 per person per night for more than two people. Some credit cards are accepted. Open year-round.

Directions: From Gold Beach, drive north on U.S. 101 for one mile (on the north side of the Rogue River) to Rogue River Road. Turn right (east) and drive about eight miles to the resort on the right.

Contact: Kimball Creek Bend RV Resort, 541/247-7580, www.kimballcreek.com.

119 QUOSATANA

🏃 🚴 🚣 🚤 🐕 ♿ 🚐 ⛺

Scenic rating: 6

on the Rogue River in Siskiyou National Forest

Map 1.5, page 85

This campground is set along the banks of the Rogue River, upstream from the much smaller Lobster Creek Campground. The campground features a large, grassy area and a barrier-free trail around the campground. Ocean access is just a short drive away, and the quaint town of Gold Beach offers a decent side trip. Nearby Otter Point State Park (day-use only) has further recreation options. The Shrader Old-Growth Trail, Lower Rogue River Trail, and Myrtle Tree Trail provide nearby hiking opportunities. Quosatana makes a good base camp for a hiking or fishing trip.

Campsites, facilities: There are 42 sites for tents or RVs up to 32 feet long. Drinking water, fire grills, garbage bins, and picnic tables are provided. Flush toilets, dump station, fish-cleaning station, and a boat ramp are available. A camp host is on-site. Some facilities are wheelchair accessible. Leashed pets are permitted.

Reservations, fees: Reservations are not accepted. Sites are $10 per night, $3 per night per additional vehicle. Open year-round.

Directions: From Gold Beach on U.S. 101, turn east on County Road 595 and drive 14.5 miles (it becomes Forest Road 33) to the campground on the left.

Contact: Rogue River Siskiyou National Forest, Gold Beach Ranger District, 541/247-3600, fax 541/247-3617, www.fs.fed.us.

120 LOBSTER CREEK

🏃 🚣 🚐 🐕 🚐 ⛺

Scenic rating: 6

on the Rogue River in Siskiyou National Forest

Map 1.5, page 85

This small campground on a river bar along the Rogue River is about a 15-minute drive from Gold Beach, and it makes a good base for a fishing or hiking trip. The area is heavily forested with myrtle and Douglas fir, and the Shrader Old-Growth Trail and Myrtle Tree Trail are nearby.

Campsites, facilities: There are six sites for tents or RVs up to 21 feet long. Fire rings and picnic tables are provided. Drinking water, flush toilets, and garbage bins are available, as is a boat launch. A camp host is on-site. Leashed pets are permitted.

Reservations, fees: Reservations are not accepted. Sites are $6 per night, $3 per night per additional vehicle. Camping is also permitted on a gravel bar area for $5 per night. Open year-round, weather permitting.

Directions: From Gold Beach on U.S. 101, turn east on County Road 595 and drive 10 miles (it becomes Forest Road 33) to the campground on the left.

Contact: Rogue River Siskiyou National Forest, Gold Beach Ranger District, 541/247-3600, fax 541/247-3617, www.fs.fed.us.

121 BIG PINE

Scenic rating: 4

on Myers Creek in Siskiyou National Forest

Map 1.5, page 85

This little campground (elevation 2,400 feet) is set near the banks of Myers Creek in a valley of large pine and Douglas fir. Many sites are right on the creek, and all are shaded. One of the world's tallest ponderosa pine trees grows near the campground. A 1.1-mile barrier-free interpretive trail starts at the campground, and a day-use area is available.

Campsites, facilities: There are 14 tent sites. Picnic tables and fire grills are provided. Vault toilets, drinking water, and garbage bins are available. Some facilities are wheelchair accessible. Leashed pets are permitted.

Reservations, fees: Reservations are not accepted. Sites are $5 per night, $2 per night per additional vehicle. Open late May–mid-October, weather permitting.

Directions: From Grants Pass, drive north on I-5 for 3.5 miles to Exit 61 (Merlin-Galice Road). Take that exit and drive northwest for 12.5 miles to Forest Road 25. Turn left on Forest Road 25 and head southwest for 12.8 miles to the campground on the right.

Contact: Siskiyou National Forest, Galice Ranger District, 541/471-6500, fax 541/471-6514, www.fs.fed.us.

122 SAM BROWN

Scenic rating: 4

near Grants Pass in Siskiyou National Forest

Map 1.5, page 85

This campground is located in an isolated area near Grants Pass along Briggs Creek in a valley of pine and Douglas fir. It is set at an elevation of 2,500 feet. Many sites lie in the shade of trees, and a creek runs along one side of the campground. Briggs Creek Trail, Dutchy Creek Trail, and Taylor Creek Trail are nearby and are popular for hiking and horseback riding. An amphitheater is available for small group presentations. Although the campground was spared, the Biscuit Fire of 2002 did burn nearby areas.

Campsites, facilities: There are 27 sites for tents or RVs of any length at Sam Brown and seven equestrian tent sites with small corrals across the road at Sam Brown Horse Camp. Picnic tables and fire rings or grills are provided. Drinking water and vault toilets are available. A picnic shelter, solar shower, and an amphitheater are available. Some facilities are wheelchair accessible. Leashed pets are permitted.

Reservations, fees: Reservations are not accepted. Sites are $5 per night, $2 per night per additional vehicle. Open late May–mid-October, weather permitting.

Directions: From Grants Pass, drive north on I-5 for 3.5 miles to Exit 61 (Merlin-Galice Road). Take that exit and drive northwest for 12.5 miles to Forest Road 25. Turn left on Forest Road 25 and head southwest for 14 miles to the campground.

Contact: Siskiyou National Forest, Galice Ranger District, 541/471-6500, fax 541/471-6514, www.fs.fed.us.

123 IRELAND'S OCEAN VIEW RV PARK

Scenic rating: 8

in Gold Beach

Map 1.5, page 85

This spot is situated on the beach in the quaint little town of Gold Beach, only one mile from the famous Rogue River. The park is very clean and features blacktop roads and grass beside each site. Recreation options include beachcombing, boating, and fishing. Great ocean views are possible from the observatory/lighthouse.

Campsites, facilities: There are 33 sites with full hookups (20-, 30-, and 50-amp) for RVs up to 40 feet long; some sites are pull-through. Picnic tables are provided. No open fires are allowed. Cable TV, restrooms with showers, coin laundry, recreation room, horseshoe pits, and modem access are available. Leashed pets are permitted.

Reservations, fees: Reservations are recommended. Sites are $24 per night, $1 per person per night for more than two people. Monthly rates are available. Open year-round.

Directions: On U.S. 101, drive to the southern end of Gold Beach (U.S. 101 becomes Ellensburg Avenue). The park is located at 20272 Ellensburg Avenue, across from the U.S. Forest Service office.

Contact: Ireland's Ocean View RV Park, 541/247-0148, www.irelandsrvpark.com.

124 OCEANSIDE RV PARK

Scenic rating: 5

in Gold Beach

Map 1.5, page 85

Set 100 yards from the ocean, this park is close to beachcombing terrain, marked bike trails, and boating facilities. The park is also adjacent to the mouth of the Rogue River, in the Port of Gold Beach.

Campsites, facilities: There are 80 sites with full or partial hookups for RVs up to 40 feet long and two yurts; some sites are pull-through. Drinking water and picnic tables are provided. Restrooms with flush toilets and showers, coin laundry, cable TV, a convenience store, picnic area, and ice are available. Propane gas, a store, and a café are within two miles. Boat docks, launching facilities, and rentals are nearby. Leashed pets are permitted.

Reservations, fees: Reservations are recommended. Sites are $25 –29, $1 per person per night for more than two people; yurts are $35 per night. Some credit cards are accepted. Open year-round.

Directions: On U.S. 101, drive to central Gold Beach and the intersection with Moore Street. Turn west and drive two blocks to Airport Way. Turn right and drive three blocks to South Jetty Road. Turn left and look for the park on the left.

Contact: Oceanside RV Park, 541/247-2301, www.oceansidervl.com.

125 WHALESHEAD BEACH RESORT

Scenic rating: 7

near Brookings

Map 1.5, page 85

This resort, about 0.25 mile from the beach, is set in a forested area with a small stream nearby. Activities at and around the camp include ocean and river fishing, jet boat trips, whale-watching excursions, and a golf course (13 miles away). Each campsite has a deck, and many cabins have an ocean view. One unique feature, a tunnel connects the campground to a trail to the beach.

Campsites, facilities: There are 45 sites with full hookups for RVs up to 60 feet long and 36 cabins. Picnic tables are provided and fire rings are available on request. Cable TV, restrooms with showers, coin laundry, modem access, limited groceries, ice, snacks, RV supplies, propane gas, and a restaurant are available. A dump station is six miles away. Some facilities are wheelchair accessible. Leashed pets are permitted.

Reservations, fees: Reservations are recommended. Sites are $25 per night, $2 per person per night for more than two people; cable TV is $1.50 per night. Some credit cards are accepted. Open year-round.

Directions: From Brookings, drive seven miles north on U.S. 101 until you pass Harris Beach. Look for the resort on the right.

Contact: Whalehead Beach Resort, 541/469-7446, fax 541/469-7447, www.whalehead-resort.com.

126 ALFRED A. LOEB STATE PARK

Scenic rating: 8

near the Chetco River

Map 1.5, page 85

This park is set in a canyon formed by the Chetco River. The campsites are set in a beautiful old myrtle grove. The 0.75-mile River View Trail follows the Chetco River to a redwood grove. Swimming, fishing, and rafting are popular activities. Nature programs and interpretive tours are available by request.

Campsites, facilities: There are 48 sites with partial hookups for tents or RVs up to 50 feet long and three log cabins. Picnic tables, drinking water, garbage bins, and fire grills are provided. Restrooms with flush toilets and showers and firewood are available. A camp host is on-site. Some facilities are wheelchair accessible. Leashed pets are permitted.

Reservations, fees: Reservations are accepted for cabins only at 800/452-5687 or www.oregonstateparks.org ($8 reservation fee). Sites are $12–20 per night, $5 per night per additional vehicle; cabins are $35–39 per night. Some credit cards are accepted. Open year-round.

Directions: On U.S. 101, drive south to

Brookings and County Road 784 (North Bank Chetco River Road). Turn northeast and drive eight miles northeast on North Bank Road to the park entrance on the right.

Contact: Harris Beach State Park, 541/469-2021 or 800/551-6949, www.oregonstateparks.org.

127 HARRIS BEACH STATE PARK

Scenic rating: 8

near Brookings

Map 1.5, page 85   BEST

This park is prime with wildlife-watching opportunities. Not only is it home to Bird Island, a breeding site for the tufted puffin and other rare birds, but gray whales, harbor seals, and sea lions can be spotted here as well. Tidepooling is also popular. Sites are shaded and well-spaced with plenty of beach and nature trails leading from the campground. In the fall and winter, the nearby Chetco River attracts good runs of salmon and steelhead, respectively.

Campsites, facilities: There are 63 sites for tents or RVs up to 50 feet (no hookups), 86 sites with full or partial hookups for RVs up to 60 feet long, a hiker/biker camp, and six yurts. Picnic tables, garbage bins, and fire grills are provided. Drinking water, cable TV, Wi-Fi, restrooms with flush toilets and showers, a dump station, coin laundry, and firewood are available. A camp host is on-site. Some facilities are wheelchair accessible. Leashed pets are permitted.

Reservations, fees: Reservations are accepted at 800/452-5687 or www.oregonstateparks.org ($8 reservation fee). RV sites are $17–26 per night, tent sites are $13–20 per night, $5 per night per additional vehicle, $4–5 per night per person for hikers/bikers, $17 per night for group tent sites, and $29–39 per night for yurts. Some credit cards are accepted. Open year-round.

Directions: From Brookings, drive north on U.S. 101 for two miles to the park entrance on the left (west side of road).
Contact: Harris Beach State Park, 541/469-2021, www.oregonstateparks.org.

128 BEACHFRONT RV PARK

near Brookings

Map 1.5, page 85

Scenic rating: 8

Beachfront RV, located just this side of the Oregon/California border on the Pacific Ocean, makes a great layover spot. Oceanfront sites are available, and recreational activities include boating, fishing, and swimming. Beach access is available from the park. Plan your trip early, as sites usually book up for the entire summer season. Nearby Harris Beach State Park, with its beach access and hiking trails, makes a good side trip.

Campsites, facilities: There are 25 tent sites and 138 sites with full or partial hookups for RVs of any length; some sites are pull-through. Picnic tables and fire rings are provided. Restrooms with showers, dump station, public phone, modem access, coin laundry, restaurant, ice, and a marina with a boat ramp, boat dock, and snacks are available. Supplies are available nearby. Some facilities are wheelchair accessible. Leashed pets are permitted.

Reservations, fees: Reservations are accepted at 800/441-0856. Tent sites are $14 per night and RV sites are $22–28.28 per night. Some credit cards are accepted. Open year-round.

Directions: From Brookings, drive south on U.S. 101 for 2.5 miles to Benham Lane. Turn west on Benham Lane and drive 1.5 miles (it becomes Lower Harbor Road) to Boat Basin Road. Turn left and drive two blocks to the park on the right.

Contact: Beachfront RV Park, 541/469-5867 or 800/441-0856; Port of Brookings Harbor, 541/469-2218, www.port-brookings-harbor.org.

129 ATRIVERS EDGE RV RESORT

Scenic rating: 7

on the Chetco River

Map 1.5, page 85

This resort lies along the banks of the Chetco River, just upstream from Brookings Harbor. A favorite spot for anglers, it features salmon and steelhead trips on the Chetco in the fall and winter. Deep-sea trips for salmon or rockfish are available nearby in the summer. This resort looks like the Rhine Valley in Germany, a pretty canyon between the trees and the river. A golf course is nearby.

Campsites, facilities: There are 110 sites with full hookups for RVs of any length; some are pull-through. Nine cabins are also available. Picnic tables are provided and fire rings are at most sites. Restrooms with flush toilets and showers, wireless Internet service, modem access, propane gas, dump station, recreation hall with exercise equipment, coin laundry, recycling station, small boat launch, and cable TV are available. Leashed pets are permitted.

Reservations, fees: Reservations are recommended at 888/295-1441. Sites are $30–33 per night, $2 per person per night for more than two people. Some credit cards are accepted. Open year-round.

Directions: On U.S. 101, drive to the southern end of Brookings (harbor side) and to South Bank Chetco River Road (a cloverleaf exit). Turn east on South Bank Chetco River Road and drive 1.5 miles to the resort entrance on the left (a slanted left turn, through the pillars, well signed).

Contact: AtRivers Edge RV Resort, 541/469-3356, www.atriversedge.com.

130 SEA BIRD RV PARK

Scenic rating: 5

near Brookings

Map 1.5, page 85

Sea Bird is one of several parks in the area. Nearby recreation options include marked bike trails, a full-service marina, and tennis courts. A nice, neat park, it features paved roads and gravel/granite sites. There is also a beach for surfing near the park. In summer, most of the sites are reserved for the season. An 18-hole golf course is within 2.5 miles.

Campsites, facilities: There are 60 sites with full or partial hookups for RVs of any length; some are pull-through sites. Picnic tables are provided. No open fires are allowed. Restrooms with flush toilets and showers, dump station, high-speed modem access, recreation hall, and a coin laundry are available. Boat docks, launching facilities, and rentals are nearby. Leashed pets are permitted.

Reservations, fees: Reservations are accepted. Sites are $18 per night, $2 per person per night for more than two people. Open year-round.

Directions: In Brookings, drive south on U.S. 101 to the Chetco River Bridge. Continue 0.25 mile south on U.S. 101 to the park entrance on the left.

Contact: Sea Bird RV Park, 541/469-3512, www.seabirdrv.com.

PORTLAND AND THE WILLAMETTE VALLEY

BEST CAMPGROUNDS

◖ **Most Scenic**
Long Bow Group, **page 157.**

Most visitors to the Willamette Valley only see a stretch of I-5 from Portland to Cottage Grove. Although there are some interesting things about this particular part of the state — it's Oregon's business center and most of my relatives and pals live there — the glimpse provided from I-5 doesn't capture its beauty. Residents, however, know the secret: Not only can you earn a good living here, it's also a great jumping-off point to adventure.

To discover what the locals know, venture east to west on the slow two-lane highways that border the streams. Among the most notable are Highway 26 along the Nacanticum River, little Highway 6 along the Wilson, little Highway 22 along Three Rivers, tiny Highway 15 on the Little Nestucca, Highway 18 on the Salmon River, Highway 34 on the Alsea, Highway 126 on the Siuslaw, and Highway 38 on the Umpqua (my favorite). These roads provide routes to reach the coast and can be used to create beautiful loop trips, with many hidden campgrounds to choose from while en route.

There are also parks and a number of lakes set in the foothills along dammed rivers. The highlight is Silver Falls State Park, Oregon's largest state park, with a seven-mile hike that is routed past 10 awesome waterfalls, some falling more than 100 feet from their brinks. Lakes are plentiful, too, including Cottage Grove Reservoir, Dorena Lake, Fall Creek Reservoir, and Green Peter Reservoir on the Santiam River.

Portland is a great hub for finding recreation in the region. To the east is the Columbia River corridor and Mount Hood, with its surrounding wilderness and national forest. To the south is Eugene, which leads to the McKenzie and Willamette Rivers and offers a good launch station to the Three Sisters in the east.

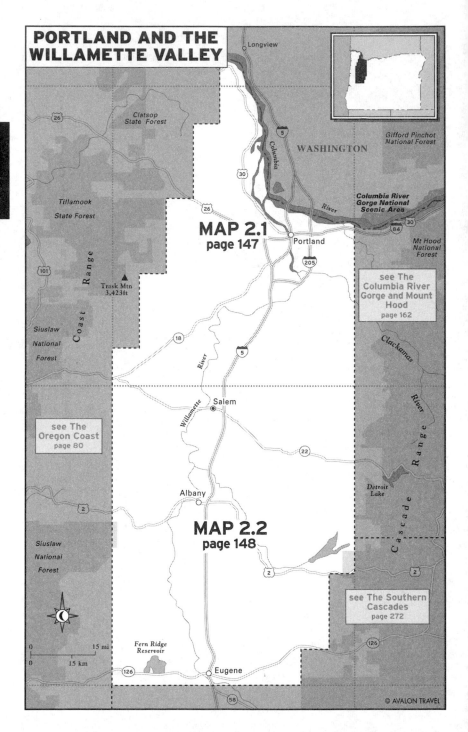

PORTLAND AND THE WILLAMETTE VALLEY

Longview

WASHINGTON

Clatsop State Forest

Columbia

Columbia River Gorge National Scenic Area

Gifford Pinchot National Forest

MAP 2.1
page 147

Portland

Tillamook State Forest

Coast Range

▲ Trask Mtn 3,423ft

Siuslaw National Forest

Mt Hood National Forest

see The Columbia River Gorge and Mount Hood
page 162

River

Willamette

Salem

Detroit Lake

Clackamas River

Cascade Range

see The Oregon Coast
page 80

Albany

MAP 2.2
page 148

see The Southern Cascades
page 272

Siuslaw National Forest

0   15 mi
0   15 km

Fern Ridge Reservoir

Eugene

© AVALON TRAVEL

Map 2.1

Campgrounds 1-8
Pages 149-152

Map 2.2

Campgrounds 9-22
Pages 152-158

1 SCAPPOOSE RV PARK

Scenic rating: 6

in Scappoose

Map 2.1, page 147

This county-operated RV park neighbors the rural Scappoose airport, making it a convenient spot for private pilots. The sites are partially shaded with maple, oak, and spruce trees. Set on the edge of a dike, it is less than a mile from the Columbia River and about a 30-minute drive from Portland.

Campsites, facilities: There are four tent sites in dispersed areas and seven sites for RVs up to 41 feet long, six with full hookups. Picnic tables and fire grills are provided. Drinking water, a restroom with flush toilets and showers, a dump station, firewood, a playground, and horseshoe pits are available. Some facilities are wheelchair accessible. Leashed pets are permitted.

Reservations, fees: Reservations are accepted at 503/366-3984. RV sites are $17–20 per night, tent sites are $12–15 per night, $5–7 per night for an additional vehicle. Open year-round.

Directions: From Portland, turn west on U.S. 30 and drive to Scappoose. Continue one mile north on U.S. 30 to West Lane Road. Turn right (east) and drive 0.75 mile to Honeyman Road. Turn left and drive one block to the park on the right.

Contact: Columbia County, Parks and Recreation, 503/397-2353; Scappoose RV Park, 503/543-3225.

2 PORTLAND FAIRVIEW RV PARK

Scenic rating: 7

east of Portland

Map 2.1, page 147

This is a massive yet pretty RV park located eight miles east of downtown Portland. The setting is peaceful, with the entire park landscaped, edged by tall conifers. A small brook runs nearby. Many I-5 ramblers have a chance to unwind for a spell here.

Campsites, facilities: There are 407 sites with full hookups for RVs of any length; most sites are pull-through. Picnic tables are provided. Drinking water and restrooms with flush toilets and coin showers, a barbecue and picnic area, horseshoe pits, seasonal swimming pool, basketball, recreation and fitness centers, Wi-Fi, satellite TV, coin laundry, a playground, and parking for boats and tow vehicles are available. Some facilities are wheelchair accessible. Leashed pets are permitted, with some breed restrictions.

Reservations, fees: Reservations are accepted online at www.portlandfairviewrv.com. Sites are $40 per night. Open year-round.

Directions: From I-84/Highway 30 in Portland, take Exit 14 and turn north on NE 207th Avenue. Drive on NE 207th Avenue to NE Sandy Boulevard. Turn right on NE Sandy Boulevard and drive a short distance to the park.

Contact: Portland Fairview RV Park, 877/777-1047, www.portlandfairviewrv.com.

3 RV PARK OF PORTLAND

Scenic rating: 6

in Tualatin

Map 2.1, page 147

This park, just south of Portland in a wooded setting, has spacious sites, all with access to lawn areas. More than half of the sites are taken by monthly rentals.

Campsites, facilities: There are 112 sites, most with full hookups and pull-throughs for RVs of any length. Cable TV and picnic tables are provided. Restrooms with flush toilets and showers, a dump station, coin laundry, modem access, and wireless Internet service are available. A store, café, and ice are within one mile. Leashed pets are permitted.

Reservations, fees: Reservations are accepted at 800/856-2066. Sites are $39.75 per night, plus $2.50 per person per night for more than two people. Some credit cards are accepted. Open year-round.

Directions: From Portland, drive south on I-5 to Tualatin and Exit 289. Take Exit 289 and turn left (east) on Nyberg Road. Drive 0.25 mile to Nyberg Lane. Turn left and drive a short distance to the park on the left.

Contact: RV Park of Portland, 503/692-0225 or 800/856-2066, www.rvparkofportland.com.

◼ BARTON PARK

Scenic rating: 6

near the Clackamas River
Map 2.1, page 147

Getting here may seem a bit of a maze, but the trip is well worth it. This camp is set on the Clackamas River and is surrounded by woods and tall trees. The river can provide good salmon and steelhead fishing.

Campsites, facilities: There are 98 sites for tents or RVs up to 40 feet; sites have partial hookups, and some sites are pull-through. Picnic tables and fire rings are provided. Restrooms with showers, a dump station, picnic area, and picnic shelters are available. Recreational facilities include horseshoe pits, a playground, volleyball court, softball field, and boat ramp. Supplies are available within one mile. A camp host is on-site. Some facilities are wheelchair accessible. Leashed pets are permitted.

Reservations, fees: Reservations are recommended. Sites are $16–19 per night, $5 per night per additional vehicle. Some credit cards are accepted for reservations. Open May–September.

Directions: From Portland, drive south on I-5 to I-205. Turn east and drive about 20 miles to Exit 12, the Clackamas/Estacada exit (Highway 212). Turn east on Highway 212/224 and drive 3.2 miles to the Carver exit/Rock Creek junction. Turn right on Highway 224 and

drive about 6.5 miles to the town of Barton and Baker's Ferry Road. Turn right and drive 0.2 mile to Barton Park Road. Turn left and drive to the park on the left.

Contact: Clackamas County Parks Department, 503/742-4414, fax 503/742-4420, www.co.clackamas.or.us.

◼ METZLER PARK

Scenic rating: 8

on Clear Creek
Map 2.1, page 147

This county campground on a small stream not far from the Clackamas River is a hot spot for fishing, picnicking, and swimming. Be sure to make your reservation early at this very popular park.

Campsites, facilities: There are 75 sites with partial hookups for tents or RVs up to 40 feet long. Picnic tables and fire pits are provided. Restrooms with flush toilets and showers, a dump station, playground, picnic areas, and a recreation field with baseball, basketball, and volleyball are available. Propane and ice are within five miles. Some facilities are wheelchair accessible. Leashed pets are permitted.

Reservations, fees: Reservations are recommended. Sites are $12–19 per night. Some credit cards are accepted with reservations. Open May–September.

Directions: From Portland, drive south on I-5 to I-205. Turn east and drive about 20 miles to Exit 12, the Clackamas/Estacada exit (Highway 212). Turn east on Highway 212/224 and drive 3.2 miles to the Carver exit/Rock Creek junction. Turn right on Highway 224 and drive approximately 15 miles to Estacada and Highway 211. Turn right, crossing a bridge, and drive four miles to Tucker Road. Turn right and drive 0.5 mile to Metzler Park Road. Turn left and drive 1.6 miles to the park entrance.

Contact: Clackamas County Parks Department, 503/742-4414, fax 503/742-4420, www.co.clackamas.or.us.

6 MULKEY RV PARK

Scenic rating: 7

near the South Yamhill River

Map 2.1, page 147

This wooded park sits near the South Yamhill River. Nearby recreation options include an 18-hole golf course, tennis courts, and the Western Deer Park and Arboretum, which has a playground. Note that most sites are taken by monthly renters.

Campsites, facilities: There are 70 sites with full hookups for RVs of any length; some sites are pull-through. Drinking water and picnic tables are provided. Restrooms with flush toilets and showers, a grocery store, propane gas, ice, and coin laundry are available. Some facilities are wheelchair accessible. Leashed pets are permitted.

Reservations, fees: Reservations are advised at 877/472-2475. RV sites are $28 per night, $5 per person per night for more than two people. Monthly rates are available. Some credit cards are accepted. Open year-round.

Directions: From Portland, turn south on Highway 99 and drive about 31 miles to McMinnville and Highway 18. Turn southwest on Highway 18 and drive 3.5 miles to the park entrance.

Contact: Mulkey RV Park, 503/472-2475, fax 503/472-0718.

7 CHAMPOEG STATE HERITAGE AREA

Scenic rating: 7

on the Willamette River

Map 2.1, page 147

Champoeg State Heritage Area lies on the south bank of the Willamette River and features an interpretive center, a botanical garden with native plants, and hiking and bike trails. A junior ranger program is available during the summer. The log cabin museum, the historic Newell House, and the visitors center are also worth a tour. Some of the best sturgeon fishing in North America is on the Willamette River below Oregon City Falls (also called Willamette Falls). I caught my biggest fish here in 2009, a nine-foot sturgeon that weighed 400 pounds. The best fishing guide to the area is Charlie Foster.

Campsites, facilities: There are 79 sites with full or partial hookups for tents or RVs up to 50 feet long. There are also three group tent areas that accommodate a maximum of 25 people each, six walk-in sites, six cabins, six yurts, a hiker/biker camp, and a 10-site tent and RV group area with electric hookups only. Picnic tables and fire grills are provided. Restrooms with flush toilets and showers, drinking water, garbage bins, a dump station, meeting hall, picnic area, off-leash dog park, disc golf, ice, and firewood are available. Boat docking facilities are nearby. Some facilities are wheelchair accessible. Leashed pets are permitted.

Reservations, fees: Reservations are accepted at 800/452-5687 or www.oregonstateparks.org ($8 reservation fee). Sites are $16–24 per night, $4–5 per person per night for hiker/biker sites, the group tent camps are $40–71 per night, the group RV/tent camp is $81–101 per night and $8–10 per RV after the first 10 units; yurts are $27–36 per night, and cabins are $35–39 per night. It costs $5 per night for an additional vehicle. Some credit cards are accepted. Open year-round.

Directions: From Portland, drive south on I-5 to Exit 278, the Donald/Aurora exit. Take that exit and turn right (west) on Ehlen Road and drive three miles to Case Road. Turn right (north) and drive 4.5 miles (the road becomes Champoeg Road) to the park on the right.

Contact: Champoeg State Heritage Area, 503/678-1251 or 800/551-6949, www.oregonstateparks.org; Charlie Foster's NW Sturgeon Adventures, 503/820-1189, www.nwsturgeonadventures.com.

8 FEYRER MEMORIAL PARK

Scenic rating: 5

on the Molalla River

Map 2.1, page 147

On the scenic Molalla River, this county park offers swimming and excellent salmon fishing. A superb option for weary I-5 cruisers, the park is only 30 minutes off the highway and provides a peaceful, serene environment.

Campsites, facilities: There are 20 sites with partial hookups for tents or RVs up to 40 feet long. Picnic tables and fire rings are provided. Drinking water, restrooms with showers, a dump station, and picnic areas are available. There are also a playground, horseshoe pits, volleyball, and softball. A boat ramp is nearby. Supplies are available within three miles. Some facilities are wheelchair accessible. Leashed pets are permitted.

Reservations, fees: Reservations are recommended. Sites are $16–19 per night. Some credit cards are accepted with reservations. Open May–September.

Directions: From Portland, drive south on I-5 to Woodburn. Take Exit 271 and drive east on Highway 214; continue (the road changes to Highway 211 at the crossing with Highway 99E) to Molalla and Mathias Road. Turn right and drive 0.25 mile to Feyrer Park Road. Turn right and drive three miles to the park on the left.

Contact: Clackamas County Parks Department, 503/742-4414, fax 503/742-4420, www.co.clackamas.or.us.

9 SALEM CAMPGROUND & RVS

Scenic rating: 5

in Salem

Map 2.2, page 148

This park with shaded sites is located next to I-5 in Salem; expect to hear traffic noise. A picnic area and a lake for swimming are within walking distance, and a nine-hole golf course, hiking trails, riding stable, and tennis courts are nearby. This is a good overnight campground, but not a destination place.

Campsites, facilities: There are 144 sites with full hookups (20-, 30-, and 50-amp) for RVs of any length; most sites are pull-through. There are also 25 tent sites. Picnic tables are provided, and there are fire pits at the tent sites; barbecues are available upon request. Restrooms with flush toilets and showers, propane gas, a dump station, recreation hall with a game room, convenience store, coin laundry, ice, a playground, cable TV, modem hookups, and drinking water are available. A café is within one mile. Some facilities are wheelchair accessible. Leashed pets are permitted; no pit bulls or rottweilers are allowed.

Reservations, fees: Reservations are accepted at 800/826-9605. Sites are $16–25 per night, $2 per person per night for more than two people. Weekly, monthly, and group rates are available. Some credit cards are accepted. Open year-round.

Directions: From Salem on I-5, take Exit 253 to Highway 22. Turn east and drive 0.25 mile to Lancaster Drive. Turn right on Lancaster Drive and continue 0.1 mile to Hagers Grove Road. Turn right on Hagers Grove Road and drive a short distance to the campground at the end of the road.

Contact: Salem Campground & RVs, 503/581-6736 or 800/826-9605, fax 503/581-9945, www.salemrv.com.

10 SILVER FALLS STATE PARK

Scenic rating: 8

near Salem

Map 2.2, page 148

Oregon's largest state park, Silver Falls covers more than 8,700 acres. Numerous trails crisscross the area, one of which is a seven-mile jaunt that meanders past 10 majestic waterfalls (some more than 100 feet high) in the rainforest of Silver Creek Canyon. Four of these falls have an amphitheater-like surrounding where you can walk behind the falls and feel the misty spray. A horse camp and a 14-mile equestrian trail are available in the park. Fitness-conscious campers can check out the three-mile jogging trail or the four-mile bike trail. There are also a rustic nature lodge and group lodging facilities. Pets are not allowed on the Canyon Trail.

Campsites, facilities: There are 45 sites for tents or self-contained RVs (no hookups), 52 sites with partial hookups for tents or RVs up to 60 feet long, three group tent sites for up to 50–75 people each, two group RV areas, five horse sites, a group horse camp, and 14 cabins. Picnic tables and fire grills are provided. Drinking water, garbage bins, restrooms with flush toilets and showers, a dump station, an amphitheater, firewood, ice, and a playground are available. Some facilities are wheelchair accessible. Leashed pets are permitted in the campground.

Reservations, fees: Reservations are accepted at 800/452-5687 or www.oregonstateparks. org ($8 reservation fee). Sites are $12–24 per night, $5 per night for an additional vehicle. The group tent site is $40–71 per night; the group RV sites are $60–101 per night for the first 10 units and then $10 per additional unit. Horse campsites are $12–19 per night, the group horse camp is $36–58 per night. Cabins are $35–39 per night. Some credit cards are accepted. RV sites are open year-round, tent sites April–October.

Directions: From Salem on I-5, take Exit 253 to Highway 22. Turn east and drive five miles to Highway 214. Turn left (east) and drive 15 miles to the park.

Contact: Silver Falls State Park, 503/873-8681, 503/873-4395, or 800/551-6949, 503/873-3890 (trail rides), www.oregonstateparks.org.

11 JOHN NEAL MEMORIAL PARK

Scenic rating: 6

on the North Santiam River

Map 2.2, page 148

This camp is set on the banks of the North Santiam River, offering good boating and trout fishing possibilities. The park covers about 27 acres, and there are hiking trails. Other recreation options include exploring lakes and trails in the adjacent national forest land or visiting Silver Falls State Park.

Campsites, facilities: There are 23 sites for tents or self-contained RVs up to 30 feet long, and 12 group sites for up to 100 people. Picnic tables and fire pits are provided. Restrooms with flush toilets and showers, garbage bins, and drinking water are available. Recreational facilities include a boat ramp, playground, horseshoe pits, picnic area, and a recreation field. Ice and a grocery store are within one mile. Some facilities are wheelchair accessible. Leashed pets are permitted.

Reservations, fees: Reservations are accepted. Sites are $11 per night for tent sites, $20 per night for RV sites, $5 per night per additional vehicle, and $200 per night for group sites plus a $50 reservation fee. Some credit cards are accepted for reservations. Open mid-April–mid-September, weather permitting.

Directions: From Salem, drive east on Highway 22 for about 20 miles to Highway 226. Turn right and drive south for two miles to Lyons and John Neal Park Road. Turn left (east) and drive a short distance to the campground on the left.

Contact: Linn County Parks Department, 541/967-3917, fax 541/924-6915, www.co.linn.or.us.

12 FISHERMEN'S BEND

🚶‍♂️ 🚴 🛶 🚐 🏠 🎣 ♿ 🏕️ ⛺

Scenic rating: 7

on the North Santiam River

Map 2.2, page 148

Fishermen's Bend is a popular spot for anglers of all ages, and the sites are spacious. The campground was renovated in 2005. A barrier-free fishing and river viewing area and a network of trails provide access to more than a mile of river. There's a one-mile, self-guided nature trail, and the nature center has a variety of displays. The amphitheater has films and activities on weekends. The front gate closes at 10 P.M.

Campsites, facilities: There are 51 sites for tents and RVs up to 38 feet long; some sites are pull-through, some have full hookups. There are also three group sites (for up to 60 people each) and two cabins. Drinking water, picnic tables, and fire pits are provided. Restrooms with flush toilets and showers, a dump station, and garbage containers are available. A boat ramp, fishing pier, day-use area with playgrounds, baseball fields, volleyball and basketball courts, horseshoe pits, firewood, and a picnic shelter are also available. Some facilities are wheelchair accessible. Leashed pets are permitted.

Reservations, fees: Reservations are accepted for cabins and the group site at 888/444-6777 or www.recreation.gov ($10 reservation fee). Sites are $12–22 per night, $5 per night per each additional vehicle. Group sites are $65–85 per night. Cabins are $40 per night. Open April–October.

Directions: From Salem on I-5, take Exit 253 to Highway 22. Turn east and drive 30 miles to the campground on the right.

Contact: Bureau of Land Management, Salem District Office, 503/897-2406, fax 503/375-5622, www.blm.gov/or/resources/recreation.

13 ELKHORN VALLEY

🚶‍♂️ 🏊 🛶 🏠 🎣 🏕️

Scenic rating: 7

on the Little North Santiam River

Map 2.2, page 148

This pretty campground along the Little North Santiam River, not far from the north fork of the Santiam River, has easy access and on-site hosts and is only a short drive away from a major metropolitan area. Swimming is good here during the summer, and the campground is popular with families. The front gate is locked 10 P.M.–7 A.M. daily. This site offers an alternative to Shady Cove, which is about 10 miles to the east.

Campsites, facilities: There are 24 sites for tents or RVs up to 24 feet long. Picnic tables, garbage bins, fire grills, vault toilets, and drinking water are available. Firewood is available for purchase. Leashed pets are permitted.

Reservations, fees: Reservations are not accepted. Sites are $10 per night, $5 per night per additional vehicle. There is a 14-day stay limit. Open late May–early September.

Directions: From Salem on I-5, take Exit 253 to Highway 22. Turn east and drive 25 miles to Elkhorn Road (Little North Fork Road). Turn left (northeast) and drive nine miles to the campground on the left.

Contact: Bureau of Land Management, Salem District Office, 503/375-5646, fax 503/375-5622, www.blm.gov/or/resources/recreation.

14 WATERLOO COUNTY PARK

🚶‍♂️ 🏊 🛶 🚐 🏠 🐎 ♿ 🏕️ ⛺

Scenic rating: 8

on the South Santiam River

Map 2.2, page 148

This campground features more than a mile of South Santiam River frontage. Field sports, fishing, picnicking, and swimming are options here. Small boats with trolling motors are the only boats allowed here.

Campsites, facilities: There are 120 sites for tents or RVs of any length; most have partial hookups. Drinking water, fire pits, and picnic tables are provided. Restrooms with showers, a dump station, boat ramps, a playground, day-use area, off-leash dog park, and picnic shelters are available. Some facilities are wheelchair accessible. Leashed pets are permitted.

Reservations, fees: Reservations are accepted at 541/967-3917 or www.co.linn.or.us ($11 reservation fee). Sites are $20–24 per night, $6 per night for an additional vehicle. Some credit cards are accepted for reservations. Open year-round.

Directions: From Albany, drive east on U.S. 20 for about 20 miles through Lebanon to the Waterloo exit. Turn left (north) at the Waterloo exit and drive approximately two miles to the camp on the right. The camp is on the south side of the South Santiam River, five miles east of Lebanon.

Contact: Linn County Parks Department, 541/967-3917, fax 541/924-6915, www. co.linn.or.us.

15 WHITCOMB CREEK COUNTY PARK

🏃 🏊 🎣 ⛵ 🏕 🐕 ♿ 🚐 ⛺

Scenic rating: 8

on Green Peter Reservoir

Map 2.2, page 148

This camp, located on the north shore of Green Peter Reservoir, is in a wooded area with lots of ferns, which gives it a rainforest feel. Recreation options include hiking, picnicking, sailing, swimming, and waterskiing. Two boat ramps are on the reservoir about a mile from camp.

Campsites, facilities: There are 39 sites for tents or RVs up to 30 feet long (no hookups) and one group tent and RV area for up to 100 people. Picnic tables and fire pits are provided. Drinking water is available to haul; vault toilets, garbage bins, and a boat ramp are also available. Supplies are within 15 miles. Leashed pets are permitted.

Reservations, fees: Reservations are accepted at 541/967-3917 or www.co.linn.or.us ($11 reservation fee). Sites are $18 per night, $6 per night per additional vehicle; the group site is $200 per night, plus a $50 reservation fee. Some credit cards are accepted. Open mid-April–mid-September.

Directions: From Albany, drive east on U.S. 20 for about 35 miles (through Lebanon and Sweet Home) to the Quartzville Road exit (near Foster Reservoir). Turn left (north) on Quartzville Road and drive 15 miles to the park.

Contact: Linn County Parks Department, 541/967-3917, fax 541/924-6915, www. co.linn.or.us.

16 YELLOWBOTTOM

🏃 🏊 🎣 🦌 ♿ 🚐 ⛺

Scenic rating: 7

on Quartzville Creek

Map 2.2, page 148

Out-of-town visitors always miss this campground across the road from Quartzville Creek. It's nestled under a canopy of old-growth forest. The Rhododendron Trail, which is just under a mile, provides a challenging hike through forest and patches of rhododendrons. Some folks pan for gold here, and swimming is popular in the creek. Though primitive, the camp is ideal for a quiet getaway weekend.

Campsites, facilities: There are 28 sites for tents or RVs up to 28 feet long, including 22 pull-through sites. Picnic tables, garbage bins, and fire grills are provided. Drinking water, vault toilets, and firewood are available. A camp host is on-site seasonally. Some facilities are wheelchair accessible. Leashed pets are permitted.

Reservations, fees: Reservations are not accepted. Sites are $8 per night, with a 14-day stay limit, and $5 per night for an additional vehicle. Open late May–early September.

Directions: From Albany, drive east on U.S.

20 for about 35 miles (through Sweet Home) to Quartzville Road. Turn left (northeast) on Quartzville Road and drive 24 miles to the campground, on the left.

Contact: Bureau of Land Management, Salem District, 503/375-5646, fax 503/375-5622, www.blm.gov/or/resources/recreation.

17 RIVER BEND COUNTY PARK

Scenic rating: 8

on the South Santiam River

Map 2.2, page 148

When River Bend opened in 2005, it was an instant hit. The park has plenty of hiking trails, the river current is calm in summer, and there are swimming beaches. The campground is in a woodsy setting of firs and ferns. Additional water activities include fishing and inner tubing, a favorite.

Campsites, facilities: There are 20 sites for tents and self-contained RVs (no hookups) and 60 sites with partial hookups for tents and RVs of any length. Picnic tables and fire pits are provided. Drinking water, restrooms with flush toilets and showers, a dump station, picnic area, athletic field, interpretive display, fishing area, and swimming and tubing area are available. An enclosed group shelter is also available. Some facilities are wheelchair accessible. Leashed pets are permitted.

Reservations, fees: Reservations are accepted at 541/967-3917 or www.co.linn.or.us ($11 reservation fee). Sites are $20–24 per night, $6 per night per additional vehicle. Some credit cards are accepted for reservations. Open year-round.

Directions: From Albany, drive east on U.S. 20 to Sweet Home. Continue east on U.S. 20 for five miles to the park on the left.

Contact: Linn County Parks Department, 541/967-3917, fax 541/924-6915, www. co.linn.or.us.

18 SUNNYSIDE COUNTY PARK

Scenic rating: 8

on Foster Reservoir

Map 2.2, page 148

Sunnyside is Linn County's most popular park. Recreation options at this 98-acre park include boating, fishing, swimming, and waterskiing. A golf course is within 15 miles.

Campsites, facilities: There are 165 sites for tents or RVs of any length; most sites have partial hookups. There are also three group sites for up to 80 people each. Picnic tables and fire rings are provided; there is also a community fire ring. Drinking water, restrooms with flush toilets and showers, a dump station, playground, dog park, stocked fishing ponds, fish-cleaning station, picnic shelter (available by reservation), volleyball courts, firewood, a boat ramp, and moorage are available. Supplies are available within three miles. Some facilities are wheelchair accessible. Leashed pets are permitted.

Reservations, fees: Reservations are accepted at 541/967-3917 or www.co.linn.or.us ($11 reservation fee, $50 reservation fee for group site). Sites are $20–24 per night, $6 per night for an additional vehicle. Open mid-March–early November.

Directions: From Albany, drive east on U.S. 20 for about 35 miles (through Lebanon and Sweet Home) to the Quartzville Road exit (near Foster Reservoir). Turn left (north) on Quartzville Road and drive one mile to the campground on the right. The camp is on the south side of Foster Reservoir.

Contact: Linn County Parks Department, 541/967-3917, fax 541/924-6915, www. co.linn.or.us.

19 CASCADIA STATE PARK

Scenic rating: 7

on the Santiam River
Map 2.2, page 148

Cascadia State Park is set along the banks of the Santiam River. The highlight of this 258-acre park is Soda Creek Falls, with a fun 0.75-mile hike to reach it. Another riverside trail leads through groves of Douglas fir and provides good fishing access. This is a choice spot for a less crowded getaway, and also for reunions and meetings for families, Boy Scouts, and other groups.

Campsites, facilities: There are 25 primitive sites for tents or self-contained RVs up to 35 feet long, and two group tent areas for up to 100 people each. Picnic tables, garbage bins, and fire grills are provided. Drinking water, flush and vault toilets, and firewood are available. A camp host is on-site. Some facilities are wheelchair accessible. Leashed pets are permitted.

Reservations, fees: Reservations are accepted for group tent areas only at 800/452-5687. Sites are $17 per night, $5 per night for an additional vehicle. Group sites are $71 per night for up to 25 people and $3 per night for each additional person. Some credit cards are accepted. Open May–September, weather permitting.

Directions: From Albany, drive east on U.S. 20 for 40 miles to the park on the left (14 miles east of the town of Sweet Home).

Contact: Cascadia State Park, 541/367-6021 or 800/551-6949, www.oregonstateparks.org.

20 LONG BOW GROUP

Scenic rating: 10

on the South Santiam River
Map 2.2, page 148   BEST (

Long Bow campground is located at 1,200 feet in elevation on the South Santiam River.

It's a pretty spot with fishing, hiking, and swimming options and a natural amphitheater on-site.

Note: No tents or trailers are allowed at the campground. Instead, your group will camp at one of six shelters.

Campsites, facilities: There are six sites with shelters for up to 48 people. Picnic tables and fire grills are provided. Drinking water, vault toilets, and a sheltered cooking and dining area are available. Leashed pets are permitted.

Reservations, fees: Reservations are accepted at 877/444-6777 or www.recreation.gov ($10 reservation fee). Sites are $100 per night. Open May–September, weather permitting.

Directions: From Albany, drive east on U.S. 20 for 43 miles (17 miles past Sweet Home) to Forest Road 2032. Turn right and drive 0.5 mile to the camp on the left.

Contact: Willamette National Forest, Sweet Home Ranger District, 541/367-5168, fax 541/367-9221, www.fs.fed.us.

21 ARMITAGE PARK

Scenic rating: 7

north of Eugene
Map 2.2, page 148

This 57-acre county park sits along on the banks of the McKenzie River outside Eugene. Hiking opportunities include the 0.5-mile Crilly Nature Trail through deciduous forest common around this river. Over the years, my brother Rambob, cousins Andy and Neil, and I have caught a lot of trout on the McKenzie in this area. Hopefully you will too.

Campsites, facilities: There are 37 sites for tents or RVs and two group sites for up to 40 people each. Picnic tables and fire rings are provided. Drinking water and restrooms with flush toilets are available. A boat ramp, volleyball courts, horseshoe pits, Wi-Fi, and a two-acre dog park are available. Some facilities are wheelchair accessible. Leashed pets are permitted.

Reservations, fees: Reservations are accepted ($10 reservation fee) for the group sites at 541/682-2000. Single sites are $25 per night, group sites are $100–150 per night, $6.50 for each additional vehicle, $3 parking fee. Open year-round.

Directions: From Portland, take I-5 to the Eugene area. Take Exit 195A-B and drive 0.7 mile toward Florence/Junction City. Merge onto Belt Line Highway and drive one mile to the Coburg exit. Take that exit and drive 0.2 mile to N. Coburg Road. Turn right on N. Coburg Road and drive 1.8 miles to the campground at 90064 Coburg Road.

Contact: Lane County Parks, 541/682-2000, http://ecomm.lanecounty.org/parks.

22 RICHARDSON PARK

🏃 🚴 ⚓ 🎣 ⛴ 🐕 🚣 ♿ 🚐 ⛰

Scenic rating: 7

on Fern Ridge Reservoir

Map 2.2, page 148

This pretty Lane County park is a favorite for sailing and sailboarding, as the wind is consistent. Boating and waterskiing are also popular. There is a walking trail that doubles as a bike trail. A kiosk display in the park features the historic Applegate Trail. Additional activities include fishing, swimming (unsupervised), and wildlife-viewing. The Corps of Engineers has wildlife areas nearby.

Campsites, facilities: There are 88 sites with partial hookups for tents or RVs of any length; some sites are pull-through. Group sites are double campsites. Drinking water, picnic tables, and fire pits are provided. A dump station, picnic areas, sand volleyball area, swimming area, playground, amphitheater, and restrooms with flush toilets, garbage bins, and coin showers are available. A seasonally attended marina offers minimal supplies including ice, a boat launch, and transient boat docks. There is a small town within five miles. Some facilities are wheelchair accessible. Leashed pets are permitted.

Reservations, fees: Reservations are accepted at 541/682-2000 or www.lanecounty.org/parks, ($10 reservation fee). Sites are $20 per night, plus $6.50 per night per additional vehicle. Maximum stay is 14 days within a 30-day period. Some credit cards are accepted. Open mid-April–mid-October.

Directions: In Eugene on I-5, drive to Exit 195B and Belt Line Road. Turn west on Belt Line Road and drive 6.5 miles to the Junction City Airport exit and Highway 99. Take that exit, turn left on Highway 99, and drive north for 0.5 mile to Clear Lake Road (the first stoplight). Turn left and drive 8.25 miles to the campground on the left.

Contact: Richardson Park, 541/935-2005 or 541/682-2000, www.co.lane.or.us/parks.

THE COLUMBIA RIVER GORGE AND MOUNT HOOD

© OSCAR WILLIAMS/123rf.com

BEST CAMPGROUNDS

◖ Most Scenic
Piety Island Boat-In, page 201.
Cove Creek, page 202.
Paul Dennis, page 205.

◖ Families
Cascade Locks Marine Park, page 177.
Hoover Group Camp, page 202.

◖ Fishing
Trillium Lake, page 186.
Gone Creek, page 192.
Pelton, page 209.

◖ Hiking
Eagle Creek, page 176.
Toll Gate, page 183.

◖ Waterfalls
Ainsworth State Park, page 169.

◖ Waterfront Campgrounds
Lost Lake, page 180.
Trillium Lake, page 186.
Meditation Point, page 194.

◖ Wildlife-Viewing
Pelton, page 209.

The Columbia River area is a living history lesson, a geological wonder, and a recreation paradise. The waterway is probably best known as the route the Lewis and Clark expedition followed two centuries ago. It's also famous for carving out a deep gorge through the Cascade Range that divides Oregon. Nearby Mount Hood and its surrounding national forest and many lakes provide almost unlimited opportunities for camping, fishing, and hiking.

The Columbia spans hundreds of square miles and is linked to a watershed that in turn is connected to the Snake River, which covers thousands of square miles. I-84 provides a major route along the southern shore of the Columbia, but the river view is not what you will remember. After you depart the traffic of the Portland area, driving west to east, you will pass along the wooded foothills of the Cascade Range to your south. When you pass Hood River, the world suddenly changes. The trees disappear.

In their place are rolling grasslands that seem to extend for as far as you can see. It is often hot and dry here, with strong winds blowing straight down the river.

However, the entire time you are within the realm of Mount Hood. At 11,239 feet, Hood is a beautiful mountain, shaped like a diamond, its flanks supporting many stellar destinations with campsites and small lakes set in forest. Snowmelt feeds many major rivers as well as numerous smaller streams, which roll down Mount Hood in every direction.

The transformation of the Gorge-area landscape from forest to grasslands to high desert is quick and striking. Particularly remarkable is how the Deschutes River has cut a path through the desert bluffs. And while the Deschutes is one of Oregon's better steelhead streams, unless you're fishing, you are more likely to encounter a desert chukar on a rock perch than anything water-bound.

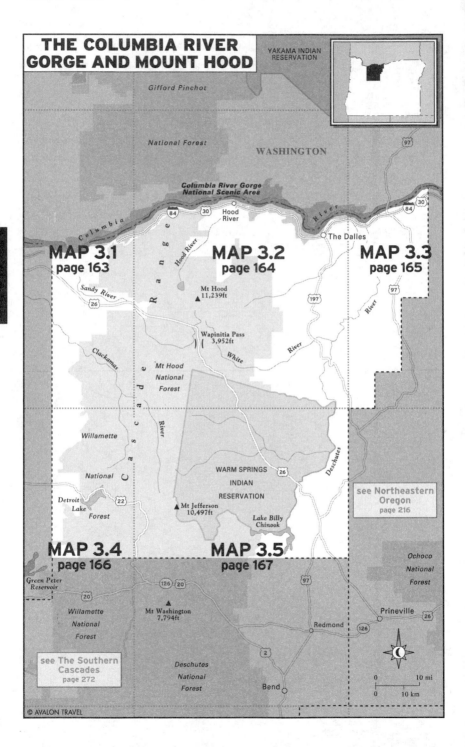

THE COLUMBIA RIVER GORGE AND MOUNT HOOD

YAKAMA INDIAN RESERVATION

Gifford Pinchot

National Forest

WASHINGTON

Columbia River Gorge
National Scenic Area

Columbia

Hood River

MAP 3.1
page 163

MAP 3.2
page 164

The Dalles

MAP 3.3
page 165

Sandy River

Mt Hood
11,239ft

Clackamas

Wapinitia Pass
3,952ft

White

River

Mt Hood
National
Forest

Willamette

River

National

WARM SPRINGS

INDIAN

RESERVATION

Deschutes

see Northeastern
Oregon
page 216

Detroit
Lake

Forest

Mt Jefferson
10,497ft

Lake Billy
Chinook

MAP 3.4
page 166

MAP 3.5
page 167

Ochoco

National

Forest

Green Peter
Reservoir

Willamette

National

Forest

Mt Washington
7,794ft

Redmond

Prineville

see The Southern
Cascades
page 272

Deschutes

National

Forest

Bend

0   10 mi

0   10 km

© AVALON TRAVEL

Map 3.1

Campgrounds 1-19
Pages 168-176

Map 3.2

Campgrounds 20-70

Pages 176-197

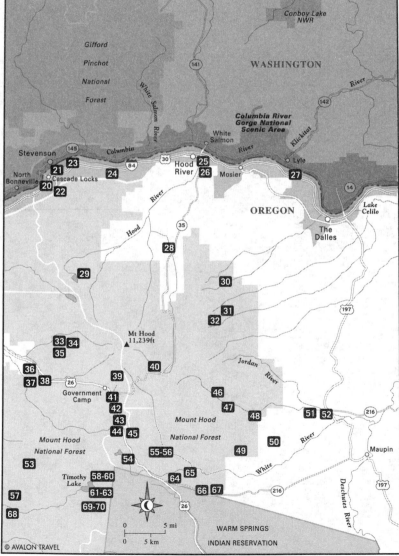

© AVALON TRAVEL

Map 3.3

Campgrounds 71-73
Pages 198-199

Map 3.4

Campgrounds 74-82
Pages 199-202

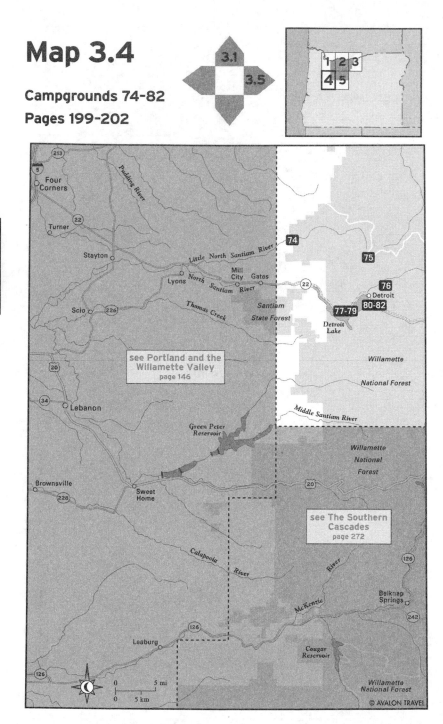

Map 3.5

Campgrounds 83-102

Pages 203-211

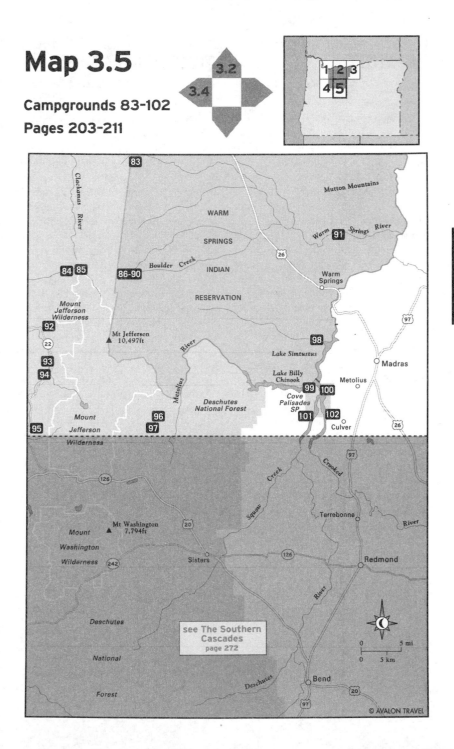

1 CROWN POINT RV PARK

Scenic rating: 6

near the Columbia River

Map 3.1, page 163

This little park is located near the Columbia River along scenic U.S. 30. Nearby Crown Point State Park is open during the day and offers views of the Columbia River Gorge and the historic Vista House, a memorial built in 1918 to honor Oregon's pioneers. Multnomah Falls offers another possible side trip.

Campsites, facilities: There are 22 sites with full or partial hookups for RVs of any length; some sites are pull-through. Drinking water and picnic tables are provided. Restrooms with flush toilets and coin showers, modem access, horseshoe pits, a hair salon, and a coin laundry are available. A store and ice are within walking distance. Leashed pets are permitted.

Reservations, fees: Reservations are accepted. Sites are $30 per night. Open year-round.

Directions: From Portland on I-84 eastbound, drive 16 miles to Exit 22 and Corbett. Take that exit and turn right on Corbett Hill Road. Drive 1.5 miles to a Y intersection with East Historic Columbia River Highway. Bear left and drive 0.25 mile to the park on the right.

Note: The recommended route has a 10 percent grade for 1.5 miles. An alternate route: From Portland on I-84 eastbound, drive to Exit 18/Lewis and Clark State Park. Take that exit and drive to East Historic Columbia River Highway and continue seven miles to the park on the right.

Contact: Crown Point RV Park, 503/695-5207, fax 503/695-3217.

2 OXBOW REGIONAL PARK

Scenic rating: 7

on the Sandy River

Map 3.1, page 163

This 1,200-acre park along the Sandy River, a short distance from the Columbia River Gorge, is a designated national scenic waterway. Fishing, non-motorized boating, and swimming are permitted here. The water is usually calm, and canoes, kayaks, and rafts are allowed. About 200 acres of the park are old-growth Douglas fir forest. There are several miles of hiking trails.

Campsites, facilities: There are 67 sites for tents or RVs up to 35 feet long; some sites are pull-through. Picnic tables, fire pits, and barbecues are provided. Drinking water, flush and vault toilets, coin showers, firewood, and a playground are available. Boat-launching facilities are nearby. Gates lock at sunset and open at 6:30 A.M. Services are approximately 10 miles away. Some facilities are wheelchair accessible. No pets are permitted.

Reservations, fees: Reservations are not accepted. Sites are $15 per night, $4 per night per additional vehicle. There is a park entrance fee of $4 per vehicle for the first day only. Open year-round.

Directions: From Portland on I-84, drive to Exit 17/Troutdale. Take that exit and drive on the frontage road for 0.5 mile to 257th Street. Turn right (south) on 257th Street and drive three miles to Division Street. Turn left and drive seven miles to the park entrance on the left.

Contact: Metro Regional Parks and Greenspaces, Oxbow Regional Park, 503/663-4708, www.oregonmetro.gov.

3 AINSWORTH STATE PARK

🏃 🏕 🚴 ♿ 🚐 ⛺

Scenic rating: 8

along the Columbia River Gorge

Map 3.1, page 163   **BEST (**

Set along the scenic Columbia River Gorge, Ainsworth State Park is waterfall central, with famous Multnomah Falls a highlight. A 1.3-mile trail leads from the campground to Horsetail Falls and the Nesmith Point Trail shares a great view of St. Peter's Dome. Anglers should check out the Bonneville Fish Hatchery about five miles away.

Campsites, facilities: There are 45 sites with full hookups for RVs up to 60 feet long and four walk-in tent sites. Picnic tables and fire grills are provided. Drinking water, restrooms with flush toilets and showers, garbage bins, a dump station, playground, camp host, amphitheater with occasional interpretive programs, and firewood are available. Some facilities are wheelchair accessible. Leashed pets are permitted.

Reservations, fees: Reservations are not accepted. Sites are $12–20 per night, $10–17 per night for walk-in tent sites, and $5 per night per additional vehicle. Some credit cards are accepted. Open mid-March–late October, weather permitting.

Directions: From Portland on I-84 eastbound, drive 35 miles to Exit 35. Turn southwest on the Columbia River Scenic Highway and continue a short distance to the park; the park is 17 miles east of Troutdale. An alternate route is to take the historic Columbia River Highway, a designated scenic highway, all the way from Portland (37 miles).

Contact: Ainsworth State Park, 503/695-2301 or 800/551-6949, www.oregonstateparks.org.

4 MILO McIVER STATE PARK

🏃 🛶 🚤 🏕 🐴 ♿ 🚐 ⛺

Scenic rating: 7

on the Clackamas River

Map 3.1, page 163

Though only 45 minutes from Portland, this park is far enough off the beaten track to provide a feeling of separation from the metropolitan area. It sits along the banks of the Clackamas River and has a boat ramp. There is fishing for salmon and steelhead in season; check current regulations. Trails for hiking are available, and a 4.5-mile equestrian trail is also accessible; bicycles are not allowed on trails. A fish hatchery is a nearby point of interest. Every September, actors participate in a Civil War reenactment here.

Campsites, facilities: There are 44 sites with partial hookups for RVs up to 50 feet long, nine primitive tent sites, one hiker/bicyclist site, and three group tent areas for up to 50 people each. Picnic tables and fire grills are provided. Drinking water, garbage bins, restrooms with flush toilets and showers, a dump station, picnic shelters, and firewood are available. Boat-launching facilities (canoes, inflatables, and kayaks), a model airplane field, and a 27-hole disc golf course are nearby. Group facilities are available. Some facilities are wheelchair accessible. Leashed pets are permitted, and there is a designated area for off-leash dog runs.

Reservations, fees: Reservations are accepted at 800/452-5687 or www.oregonstateparks.org ($8 reservation fee). Tent sites are $11–18 per night, RV sites are $13–27 per night, $5 per night per each additional vehicle. Hiker/biker sites are $4 per person per night, and group sites are $64–128.25 per night in summer, $43–103 the rest of the year. Some credit cards are accepted. Open mid-March–October.

Directions: From Portland, drive east on U.S. 26 to Gresham. Continue 11 miles to Sandy and Highway 211. Turn right (south) and drive six miles to a junction. Turn south (still Highway 211) and drive one mile to Hayden Road.

Turn right and drive one mile to Springwater Road. Turn right and drive one mile to the park on the right.

Contact: Milo McIver State Park, 503/630-6147, 503/630-7150, or 800/551-6949, www.oregonstateparks.org.

5 PROMONTORY

Scenic rating: 7

on North Fork Reservoir

Map 3.1, page 163

This Portland General Electric camp on North Fork Reservoir is part of a large recreation area and park. The reservoir, actually a dammed-up overflow of the Clackamas River, encompasses 350 acres. The water is calm and ideal for boating, and the trout fishing is excellent. A trail connects the campground to the marina. A one-acre lake is available for children's fishing.

Campsites, facilities: There are 35 sites for tents or RVs up to 35 feet long and 14 yomes (which are a cross between a yurt and a dome). There is also a group area for up to 35 people for tents or small self-contained RVs. There are no RV hookups. Picnic tables and fire rings are provided. Restrooms with flush toilets and showers, garbage bins, limited groceries, ice, a playground, horseshoes, covered picnic shelters, and snacks are available. A fish-cleaning station, a fishing pier, a children's fishing pond, boat ramp, dock, and boat rentals are also on-site. Some facilities, including the boat ramp and fishing pier, are wheelchair accessible. Leashed pets are permitted.

Reservations, fees: Reservations are accepted at 503/630-7229 or www.portlandgeneral.com. Sites are $16 per night, $25 per night for a yome. Some credit cards are accepted. Open mid-May–September.

Directions: From Portland, drive east on U.S. 26 to Gresham. Continue 11 miles to Sandy and Highway 211. Turn right (south) and drive six miles to a junction. Turn south (still Highway 211) and drive six miles to Estacada. Continue south on Highway 224 and drive seven miles to the campground on the right. The route is well signed.

Contact: Portland General Electric, 503/464-8515, fax 503/464-2944, www.portlandgeneral.com; store and marina, 503/630-5152; campground, 503/630-7229.

6 LAZY BEND

Scenic rating: 8

on the Clackamas River in
Mount Hood National Forest

Map 3.1, page 163

This campground is situated at 800 feet elevation along the banks of the Clackamas River near the large North Fork Reservoir. It's far enough off the highway to provide a secluded, primitive feeling, though it fills quickly on weekends and holidays. There's only catch-and-release fishing in the Clackamas.

Campsites, facilities: There are 23 sites for tents or RVs up to 52 feet long. Picnic tables, garbage service, and fireplaces are provided. Drinking water and flush toilets are available. Leashed pets are permitted.

Reservations, fees: Reservations are accepted at 877/444-6777 or www.recreation.gov ($10 reservation fee). Sites are $17 per night, $8 per night per additional vehicle. Open late early May–late September, weather permitting.

Directions: From Portland, drive south on U.S. 205 to the junction with Highway 24. Take the Highway 224/Estacada exit and turn left (south) onto Highway 224. Drive approximately 13 miles to Estacada. Continue south on Highway 224 for 10.5 miles to the campground on the right.

Contact: Mount Hood National Forest, Clackamas River Ranger District, 503/630-6861, fax 503/630-2299, www.fs.fed.us.

▐7▌ ARMSTRONG

Scenic rating: 5

on the Clackamas River in
Mount Hood National Forest

Map 3.1, page 163

Armstrong campground is set at an elevation of 900 feet along the banks of the Clackamas River and offers good fishing access. Fishing is catch-and-release only.

Campsites, facilities: There are 11 sites for tents or RVs up to 40 feet long. Picnic tables and fire rings are provided. Vault toilets and drinking water are available. Garbage service is available in the summer only. Some facilities are wheelchair accessible. Leashed pets are permitted.

Reservations, fees: Reservations are accepted at 877/444-6777 or www.recreation.gov ($10 reservation fee). Sites are $16 per night, $8 per night per additional vehicle. Open year-round, with limited winter services.

Directions: From Portland, drive south on U.S. 205 to the junction with Highway 24. Take the Highway 224/Estacada exit and turn left (south) onto Highway 224. Drive approximately 13 miles to Estacada. Continue south on Highway 224 for 15 miles to the campground on the right.

Contact: Mount Hood National Forest, Clackamas River Ranger District, 503/630-6861, fax 503/630-2299, www.fs.fed.us.

▐8▌ CARTER BRIDGE

Scenic rating: 5

on the Clackamas River in
Mount Hood National Forest

Map 3.1, page 163

This small, flat campground is popular with anglers. The Clackamas River flows along one end, and the other end borders the highway, with peripheral traffic noise.

Campsites, facilities: There are 15 sites for tents or RVs up to 28 feet long. Picnic tables and fire pits are provided. Vault toilets and garbage bins are available. There is no drinking water. Some facilities are wheelchair accessible. Leashed pets are permitted.

Reservations, fees: Reservations are not accepted. Sites are $14 per night, $7 per night per additional vehicle. Open late May–early September, weather permitting.

Directions: From Portland, drive south on U.S. 205 to the junction with Highway 24. Take the Highway 224/Estacada exit and turn left (south) onto Highway 224. Drive approximately 13 miles to Estacada. Continue south on Highway 224 for 15.2 miles to the campground on the left.

Contact: Mount Hood National Forest, Clackamas River Ranger District, 503/630-6861, fax 503/630-2299, www.fs.fed.us.

▐9▌ LOCKABY

Scenic rating: 6

on the Clackamas River in
Mount Hood National Forest

Map 3.1, page 163

This campground sits at an elevation of 900 feet along the banks of the Clackamas River, next to Armstrong. Fishing in the Clackamas River is catch-and-release only.

Campsites, facilities: There are 30 sites for tents or RVs up to 15 feet long. Picnic tables, fireplaces, drinking water, garbage service, vault toilets, and firewood are available. A camp host is on-site. Leashed pets are permitted.

Reservations, fees: Reservations are accepted at 877/444-6777 or www.recreation.gov ($10 reservation fee). Sites are $16 per night, $8 per night per additional vehicle. Open late May–early September.

Directions: From Portland, drive south on U.S. 205 to the junction with Highway 24. Take the Highway 224/Estacada exit and turn left (south) onto Highway 224. Drive approximately 13 miles to Estacada. Continue south on Highway 224 for 15.3 miles to the campground on the left.

Contact: Mount Hood National Forest, Clackamas River Ranger District, Estacada Ranger Station, 503/630-6861, fax 503/630-2299, www.fs.fed.us.

10 ROARING RIVER

Scenic rating: 8

on the Roaring River in
Mount Hood National Forest

Map 3.1, page 163

Set among old-growth cedars at the confluence of the Roaring and Clackamas Rivers at an elevation of 1,000 feet, this campground has access to the Dry Ridge Trail. The trail starts in camp, and it's a butt-kicker of an uphill climb. Several other trails into the adjacent roadless area are accessible from camp.

Campsites, facilities: There are 14 sites for tents or RVs up to 16 feet long. Picnic tables and fireplaces are provided. Garbage service, drinking water, and vault toilets are available. Leashed pets are permitted.

Reservations, fees: Reservations are accepted at 877/444-6777 or www.recreation.gov ($10 reservation fee). Sites are $16 per night, $8 per night per additional vehicle. Open mid-May–mid-September, weather permitting.

Directions: From Portland, drive south on U.S. 205 to the junction with Highway 24. Take the Highway 224/Estacada exit and turn left (south) onto Highway 224. Drive approximately 13 miles to Estacada. Continue south on Highway 224 for 18 miles to the campground on the left.

Contact: Mount Hood National Forest, Clackamas River Ranger District, 503/630-6861, fax 503/630-2299, www.fs.fed.us.

11 SUNSTRIP

Scenic rating: 3

on the Clackamas River in
Mount Hood National Forest

Map 3.1, page 163

This campground on the banks of the Clackamas River offers fishing and rafting access. One of several camps along the Highway 224 corridor, Sunstrip is a favorite with rafting and kayaking enthusiasts and can fill up quickly on weekends. The elevation is 1,000 feet. Note: This campground, squeezed between the river and the highway and traversed by power lines, may be a turnoff for those wanting another kind of experience.

Campsites, facilities: There are nine sites for tents or RVs up to 60 feet long. Picnic tables and fireplaces are provided. Garbage service, drinking water, firewood, and vault toilets are available. A camp host is on-site. Leashed pets are permitted.

Reservations, fees: Reservations are accepted at 877/444-6777 or www.recreation.gov ($10 reservation fee). Sites are $16 per night, $8 per night per additional vehicle. Open year-round, with limited winter services.

Directions: From Portland, drive south on U.S. 205 to the junction with Highway 24. Take the Highway 224/Estacada exit and turn left (south) onto Highway 224. Drive approximately 13 miles to Estacada. Continue south on Highway 224 for 19 miles to the campground.

Contact: Mount Hood National Forest, Clackamas River Ranger District, 503/630-6861, fax 503/630-2299, www.fs.fed.us.

12 RAINBOW

Scenic rating: 6

on the Oak Grove Fork of the Clackamas River
in Mount Hood National Forest

Map 3.1, page 163

Rainbow campground sits at an elevation of 1,400 feet along the banks of the Oak Grove Fork of the Clackamas River, not far from where it empties into the Clackamas River. The camp is less than a quarter mile from Ripplebrook Campground.

Campsites, facilities: There are 17 sites for tents or RVs up to 62 feet long. Picnic tables and fire grills are provided. Vault toilets are available. Garbage service is available during the summer. There is no drinking water. Leashed pets are permitted.

Reservations, fees: Reservations are accepted at 877/444-6777 or www.recreation.gov ($10 reservation fee). Sites are $14 per night, $8 per night per additional vehicle. Open year-round, with limited winter services.

Directions: From Portland, drive south on U.S. 205 to the junction with Highway 24. Take the Highway 224/Estacada exit and turn left (south) onto Highway 224. Drive approximately 13 miles to Estacada. Continue south on Highway 224 and drive 27 miles in national forest (the road becomes Forest Road 46). Continue south and drive about 100 yards to the campground on the right.

Contact: Mount Hood National Forest, Clackamas River Ranger District, 595 N.W. Industrial Way, Estacada, OR 97023, 503/630-6861, fax 503/630-2299, www.fs.fed.us.

13 INDIAN HENRY

Scenic rating: 8

on the Clackamas River in
Mount Hood National Forest

Map 3.1, page 163

One of the most popular campgrounds in the Clackamas River Ranger District, Indian Henry hugs the banks of the Clackamas River at an elevation of 1,250 feet and has a wheelchair-accessible trail. Group campsites and an amphitheater are available. The nearby Clackamas River Trail has fishing access.

Campsites, facilities: There are 84 sites for tents or RVs up to 40 feet long and eight group tent sites for up to 30 people. Picnic tables, garbage service, and fire grills are provided. Flush toilets, firewood, and drinking water are available. A camp host is on-site. Some facilities are wheelchair accessible. Leashed pets are permitted.

Reservations, fees: Reservations are accepted at 877/444-6777 or www.recreation.gov ($10 reservation fee). Sites are $17 per night, $8 per night per additional vehicle; group sites are $46–50 per night. Open late May–early September, weather permitting.

Directions: From Portland, drive south on U.S. 205 to the junction with Highway 24. Take the Highway 224/Estacada exit and turn left (south) onto Highway 224. Drive approximately 13 miles to Estacada. Continue south on Highway 224 for 23 miles to Forest Road 4620. Turn right and drive 0.5 mile southeast to the campground on the left.

Contact: Mount Hood National Forest, Clackamas River Ranger District, 503/630-6861, fax 503/630-2299, www.fs.fed.us.

14 RIPPLEBROOK

Scenic rating: 7

on the Oak Grove Fork of the Clackamas River
in Mount Hood National Forest

Map 3.1, page 163

Shaded sites with river views are a highlight at
this campground along the banks of the Oak
Grove Fork of the Clackamas River, where
anglers are limited to artificial lures and catch-
and-release only. Note: The road to this camp
experiences slides and washouts; check current
status before making a trip.

Campsites, facilities: There are 14 sites for
RVs up to 45 feet long. Picnic tables, garbage
service, and fire grills are provided. Vault
toilets are available, but there is no drinking
water. Leashed pets are permitted.

Reservations, fees: Reservations are accepted
at 877/444-6777 or www.recreation.gov ($10
reservation fee). Sites are $14 per night, $8 per
night per additional vehicle. Open late April–
late September, weather permitting.

Directions: From Portland, drive south on
U.S. 205 to the junction with Highway 24.
Take the Highway 224/Estacada exit and
turn left (south) onto Highway 224. Drive
approximately 13 miles to Estacada. Continue
south on Highway 224 for 26.5 miles to the
campground entrance on the left.

Contact: Mount Hood National Forest,
Clackamas River Ranger District, 503/630-
6861, fax 503/630-2299, www.fs.fed.us.

15 ALDER FLAT HIKE-IN

Scenic rating: 9

on the Clackamas River in
Mount Hood National Forest

Map 3.1, page 163

This secluded hike-in campground is set
along the banks of the Clackamas River in
old-growth forest. If you want peace and quiet
and don't mind a short walk to get there, this

is the spot. Be sure to pack out whatever you
bring in, and remember that fishing in the
Clackamas River is catch-and-release only.

Campsites, facilities: There are six tent sites
at this hike-in campground. Picnic tables and
fire grills are provided. There is no drinking
water and no toilet. Garbage must be packed
out. Leashed pets are permitted.

Reservations, fees: Reservations are not accepted. There is no fee for camping. Open
year-round.

Directions: From Portland, drive south on U.S.
205 to the junction with Highway 24. Take
the Highway 224/Estacada exit and turn left
(south) onto Highway 224. Drive approximately
13 miles to Estacada. Continue south on Highway 224 for 26 miles to the Ripplebrook Ranger
Station. Parking for the camp is about half a
mile west of the ranger station at the Alder Flat
Trailhead. Hike one mile to the campground.

Contact: Mount Hood National Forest,
Clackamas River Ranger District, 503/630-
6861, fax 503/630-2299, www.fs.fed.us.

16 RIVERSIDE

Scenic rating: 8

on the Clackamas River in
Mount Hood National Forest

Map 3.1, page 163

The banks of the Clackamas River are home to
this campground (elevation 1,400 feet). A worthwhile trail leaves the camp and follows the river
for four miles north. Fishing is another option
here, and several old forest roads in the vicinity
make excellent mountain-biking trails.

Campsites, facilities: There are 16 sites for
tents or RVs up to 40 feet long. Picnic tables,
garbage service, and fire grills are provided.
Vault toilets and drinking water are available. Some facilities are wheelchair accessible.
Leashed pets are permitted; no horses are allowed in the campground.

Reservations, fees: Reservations are accepted
at 877/444-6777 or www.recreation.gov ($10

reservation fee). Sites are $16 per night, $8 per night per additional vehicle. Open mid-May–late September, weather permitting.

Directions: From Portland, drive south on U.S. 205 to the junction with Highway 24. Take the Highway 224/Estacada exit and turn left (south) onto Highway 224. Drive approximately 13 miles to Estacada. Continue south on Highway 224 for 27 miles and into national forest (Highway 224 becomes Forest Road 46). Continue 2.5 miles south on Forest Road 46 to the campground on the right.

Contact: Mount Hood National Forest, Clackamas River Ranger District, 503/630-6861, fax 503/630-2299, www.fs.fed.us.

17 RIVERFORD

Scenic rating: 4

on the Clackamas and Collawash Rivers in Mount Hood National Forest

Map 3.1, page 163

This campground, just a two-minute walk from the confluence of the Clackamas and Collawash Rivers, offers access to good fishing. Otherwise, it's small, and the sites provide little privacy. It is set at an elevation of 1,500 feet. Although there is no drinking water at this camp, drinking water is available 0.75 mile away at Riverside Campground.

Campsites, facilities: There are eight sites for tents and two sites for RVs up to 20 feet long. Picnic tables and fire grills are provided. Vault toilets are available. Garbage service is provided in the summer. There is no drinking water. Leashed pets are permitted.

Reservations, fees: Reservations are not accepted. Sites are $16 per night, $7 per night per additional vehicle. Open year-round, with limited winter services.

Directions: From Portland, drive south on U.S. 205 to the junction with Highway 24. Take the Highway 224/Estacada exit and turn left (south) onto Highway 224. Drive approximately 13 miles to Estacada. Continue south

on Highway 224 for 27 miles in national forest (the road becomes Forest Road 46). Continue south on Forest Road 46 for 3.5 miles to the campground on the right.

Contact: Mount Hood National Forest, Clackamas River Ranger District, 503/630-6861, fax 503/630-2299, www.fs.fed.us.

18 RAAB GROUP

Scenic rating: 7

on the Collawash River in Mount Hood National Forest

Map 3.1, page 163

Raab Group camp (1,500 feet elevation) is located along the banks of the Collawash River, about a mile from its confluence with the Clackamas River. Raab gets moderate use, but it's usually quiet and has a nice, secluded atmosphere with lots of privacy among the sites.

Campsites, facilities: There are 27 sites for tents or RVs up to 16 feet long. Picnic tables, garbage service, and fire grills are provided. Vault toilets are available. There is no drinking water in the campground; water is available one mile away at Two Rivers Picnic Area. Leashed pets are permitted.

Reservations, fees: Reservations are accepted at 877/444-6777 or www.recreation.gov ($10 reservation fee). Sites are $35–42 per night. Open late May–early September, weather permitting.

Directions: From Portland, drive south on U.S. 205 to the junction with Highway 24. Take the Highway 224/Estacada exit and turn left (south) onto Highway 224. Drive approximately 13 miles to Estacada. Continue south on Highway 224 for 27 miles in national forest (the road becomes Forest Road 46). Continue south on Forest Road 46 for 2.5 miles to Forest Road 63. Turn right and drive 1.5 miles to the campground on the right.

Contact: Mount Hood National Forest, Clackamas River Ranger District, 503/630-6861, fax 503/630-2299, www.fs.fed.us; park concessionaire, 503/668-1700.

19 KINGFISHER
♜ ⛴ ⅏ 🐾 🏕 ⛺ 🛖

$21.00/night Scenic rating: 7

on the Hot Springs Fork of the Collawash River in Mount Hood National Forest

Map 3.1, page 163

This pretty campground, surrounded by old-growth forest, sits on the banks of the Hot Springs Fork of the Collawash River and provides fishing access. It's about three miles from Bagby Hot Springs, a U.S. Forest Service day-use area. The hot springs are an easy 1.5-mile hike from the day-use area. The camp sits at 1,250 feet elevation.

Campsites, facilities: There are 23 sites for tents or RVs up to 66 feet long. Picnic tables and fireplaces are provided. Garbage service is provided during the summer. Vault toilets and drinking water are available. Leashed pets are permitted.

Reservations, fees: Reservations are accepted at 877/444-6777 or www.recreation.gov ($10 reservation fee). Sites are $16 per night, $8 per night per additional vehicle. Open year-round, weather permitting, with limited winter facilities.

Directions: From Portland, drive south on U.S. 205 to the junction with Highway 24. Take the Highway 224/Estacada exit and turn left (south) onto Highway 224. Drive approximately 13 miles to Estacada. Continue south on Highway 224 for 27 miles in national forest (the road becomes Forest Road 46). Continue south on Forest Road 46 for 3.5 miles to Forest Road 63. Turn right and drive three miles to Forest Road 70. Turn right again and drive one mile to the campground on the left.

Contact: Mount Hood National Forest, Clackamas River Ranger District, 503/630-6861, fax 503/630-2299, www.fs.fed.us.

20 EAGLE CREEK
♜ ⛴ 🐾 ♿ 🏕 ⛺

Scenic rating: 8   **BEST (**

near the Columbia Wilderness in Mount Hood National Forest

Map 3.2, page 164

Eagle Creek is the oldest Forest Service Camp in America. Set at 400 feet elevation among old-growth Douglas fir and hemlock, it makes a good base camp for a hiking trip. The Eagle Creek Trail leaves the campground and travels 13 miles to Wahtum Lake, where it intersects with the Pacific Crest Trail. A primitive campground sits at the 7.5-mile point. The upper seven miles of the trail pass through the Hatfield Wilderness.

Campsites, facilities: There are 20 sites for tents or RVs up to 20 feet long and one group site for up to 90 people. Picnic tables and fire grills are provided. Drinking water, garbage bins, and flush toilets are available. A camp host is on-site. Boat docks and launching facilities are nearby on the Columbia River. Some facilities are wheelchair accessible. Leashed pets are permitted.

Reservations, fees: Reservations are not accepted for single sites, but are required for the group site at 877/444-6777 or www.recreation.gov ($10 reservation fee). Sites are $10 per night, $5 per night per additional vehicle; the group site is $75–125. Open May–September.

Directions: From Portland, drive east on I-84 for 41 miles to Bonneville. Continue east for two miles to the campground.

Contact: Columbia River Gorge National Scenic Area, 541/308-1700, fax 541/386-1916, www.fs.fed.us/r6/columbia.

21 CASCADE LOCKS MARINE PARK

Scenic rating: 8

in Cascade Locks

Map 3.2, page 164 **BEST (**

This public riverfront park covers 23 acres and offers a museum and boat rides. The salmon fishing is excellent here. Stern-wheeler dinner cruises are available. Hiking trails and tennis courts are nearby; the Pacific Crest Trail is within one mile.

Campsites, facilities: There are 16 sites for tents or RVs of any length; some sites have partial hookups. Picnic tables are provided. Drinking water, restrooms with flush toilets and showers, a dump station, boat docks, launching facilities, a picnic area, and a playground are available. A camp host is on-site. Propane gas, gasoline, a store, café, coin laundry, and ice are within one mile. Some facilities are wheelchair accessible. Leashed pets are permitted.

Reservations, fees: Reservations are accepted at 541/374-8619. Sites are $15–25 per night. Some credit cards are accepted. Open year-round, with limited winter facilities.

Directions: From Portland, drive east on I-84 for 44 miles to Cascade Locks. Take Exit 44/Cascade Locks to Wanapa Street. Turn left and drive 0.5 mile to the sign for the park on the left (well signed).

Contact: Port of Cascade Locks, Cascade Locks Marine Park, 541/374-8619, fax 541/374-8428, www.portofcascadelocks.org.

22 KOA CASCADE LOCKS

Scenic rating: 5

near the Columbia River

Map 3.2, page 164

This KOA is a good layover spot for RVers touring the Columbia River corridor. The campground offers level, shaded RV sites and grassy tent sites. A pancake breakfast is available on weekends during the summer season. Nearby recreation options include bike trails, hiking trails, and tennis courts. The 200-acre Cascade Locks Marine Park is close by and offers everything from museums to boat trips.

Campsites, facilities: There are 33 sites for tents, 78 sites with full or partial hookups for RVs of any length, nine cabins, and two cottages. Most RV sites are pull-through. Picnic tables and fire pits are provided. Restrooms with flush toilets and showers, drinking water, propane gas, a dump station, firewood, a spa, cable TV, wireless Internet service, a recreation hall, convenience store, coin laundry, ice, a playground, bicycle rentals, and a heated seasonal swimming pool are available. A café is within one mile. Some facilities are wheelchair accessible. Leashed pets are permitted.

Reservations, fees: Reservations are accepted at 800/562-8698. Sites are $27–36 per night, $5 per person per night for more than two people. Cabins are $45–55 per night; cottages are $55–89 per night. Some credit cards are accepted. Open February–November.

Directions: From Portland, drive east on I-84 for 44 miles to Cascade Locks and Exit 44. Take that exit to Forest Lane. Turn east on Forest Lane and drive one mile to the campground on the left.

Contact: KOA Cascade Locks, 541/374-8668, www.koa.com.

23 HERMAN CREEK HORSE CAMP

Scenic rating: 9

near the Pacific Crest Trail in Mount Hood National Forest

Map 3.2, page 164

This rustic campground sits at 300 feet elevation and is about half a mile from Herman Creek, not far from the Pacific Crest Trail. This area, separated from Washington by the Columbia River, is particularly beautiful. The campsites are spacious, and the many recreation options include biking, boating, fishing, and hiking. Note that new rules regarding stock feed require certified weed-free hay, feed, and crop products on national forest land.

Campsites, facilities: There are seven sites for tents or RVs up to 20 feet long. Drinking water, garbage bins, fire grills, and picnic tables are provided. Restrooms with flush toilets and showers, stock-handling facilities, a store, a café, a coin laundry, and ice are available. Leashed pets are permitted.

Reservations, fees: Reservations are not accepted. Sites are $10 per night, $5 per night per additional vehicle. Open May–September.

Directions: From Portland, drive east on I-84 for 44 miles to Cascade Locks and Exit 44. Take that exit and drive straight ahead (east) onto Wanapa Street and drive back under the highway. Continue 1.5 miles (the road becomes Herman Creek Road) to the campground on the right.

Contact: Columbia River Gorge National Scenic Area, 541/308-1700, fax 541/386-1916, www.fs.fed.us/r6/columbia.

24 WYETH

Scenic rating: 5

on Gordon Creek in
Mount Hood National Forest

Map 3.2, page 164

Wyeth makes a good layover spot for Columbia River corridor cruisers. The camp (100 feet elevation) borders Gordon Creek, near the Columbia River. Recreation options include biking, boating, fishing, and hiking.

Campsites, facilities: There are 16 sites for tents or RVs up to 30 feet long and three group sites. Fire grills and picnic tables are provided. Drinking water and flush toilets are available. A camp host is on-site. Leashed pets are permitted.

Reservations, fees: Reservations are not accepted. Sites are $15 per night, $5 per night

per additional vehicle, group sites are $30 per night. Open April–mid-October.

Directions: From Portland, drive east on I-84 for 44 miles to Cascade Locks. Continue east on I-84 for seven miles to Wyeth and Exit 51. Turn right and drive 0.25 mile to the campground entrance.

Contact: Columbia River Gorge National Scenic Area, 541/308-1700, fax 541/386-1916, www.fs.fed.us/r6/columbia.

25 VIENTO STATE PARK

Scenic rating: 8

along the Columbia River Gorge

Map 3.2, page 164

This park along the Columbia River Gorge offers scenic hiking trails and some of the best windsurfing in the Gorge. Just 12 miles to the east, old U.S. 30 skirts the Columbia River, offering a picturesque drive. Viento has a day-use picnic area right next to a babbling creek. Look for weekend interpretive programs during the summer. There are several other day-use state parks along I-84 just west of Viento, including Seneca Fouts, Vinzenz Lausmann, and Wygant. All offer quality hiking trails and scenic views.

Campsites, facilities: There are 56 sites with partial hookups for RVs up to 30 feet long (with some up to 40 feet long) and 18 tent sites. Picnic tables and fire grills are provided. Drinking water, garbage bins, restrooms with flush toilets and showers, firewood, and a playground are available. Some facilities are wheelchair accessible. Leashed pets are permitted.

Reservations, fees: Reservations are not accepted. RV sites are $12–20 per night, tent sites are $10–17 per night, $5 per night per additional vehicle. Some credit cards are accepted. Open mid-March–October, weather permitting.

Directions: From Portland, drive east on I-84 for 56 miles to Exit 56 (eight miles west of

Hood River). Take Exit 56 and drive to the park entrance. The park is set on both sides of I-84.

Contact: Viento State Park, 541/374-8811 or 800/551-6949, www.oregonstateparks.org.

26 TUCKER COUNTY PARK

🏕 🚲 🏠 🦌 🚐 ⛰

Scenic rating: 6

on the Hood River

Map 3.2, page 164

This county park along the banks of the Hood River is just far enough out of the way to be missed by most of the tourist traffic. Many people who choose this county park come for the windsurfing. Other recreation opportunities include rafting and kayaking. Fishing is not allowed at the park.

Campsites, facilities: There are 84 tent sites and 14 sites with partial hookups for tents or RVs up to 30 feet long. Picnic tables and fire rings are provided. Drinking water, restrooms with flush toilets and showers, and a playground are available. A store, café, gasoline, and ice are within two miles. Leashed pets are permitted.

Reservations, fees: Reservations are not accepted. Sites are $18–20 per night, and it costs $8 per night per additional tent and $5 per night per additional vehicle. Open April–October.

Directions: From Portland, turn east on I-84 and drive about 65 miles to the town of Hood River and Exit 62. Take the exit and drive east on Cascade Street, continuing to 13th Street (first light). Turn right (south) and drive through and out of town; 13th Street becomes Tucker Road and then Dee Highway (Highway 281). Follow the signs to Parkdale. The park is four miles out of town on the right.

Contact: Hood River County Parks, 541/387-6889 or 541/386-4477, fax 541/386-6325, www.co.hood-river.or.us.

27 MEMALOOSE STATE PARK

🐕 🚲 🚐 ⛰

Scenic rating: 7

in the Columbia River Gorge

Map 3.2, page 164

This park borrows its name from nearby Memaloose Island, which Native Americans used as a sacred burial ground. Situated along the hottest part of the scenic Columbia River Gorge, the campground makes a prime layover spot for campers cruising the Oregon/Washington border. Nature programs and interpretive events are held here. This popular camp receives a good deal of traffic, so plan on arriving early to claim a spot, even if you have a reservation.

Campsites, facilities: There are 66 tent sites and 44 sites with full hookups for RVs up to 60 feet long. Picnic tables and fire grills are provided. Drinking water, garbage bins, restrooms with flush toilets and showers, a dump station, playground, and firewood are available. Leashed pets are permitted.

Reservations, fees: Reservations are accepted at 800/452-5687 or www.oregonstateparks.org ($8 reservation fee). RV sites are $16–20 per night, tent sites are $12–24 per night, $5 per night per additional vehicle. Some credit cards are accepted. Open mid-March–October.

Directions: Memaloose State Park is accessible only to westbound traffic on I-84. From The Dalles, drive west on I-84 for 11 miles to the signed turnoff. (The park is about 75 miles east of Portland.)

If eastbound on I-84, take Exit 76. Drive under the freeway to the I-84 west on-ramp. Once on I-84 west, drive 2.5 miles to the sign for Rest Area/Memaloose State Park. Drive into the rest area and take an immediate right into the campground.

Contact: Memaloose State Park, 541/478-3008 or 800/551-6949, www.oregonstateparks.org.

28 KINNICKKINNICK

🚶 🚲 ⛵ 🛶 🏊 🐕 ♿ 🚐 ⛺

Scenic rating: 5

on Laurence Lake in
Mount Hood National Forest

Map 3.2, page 164

Kinnickkinnick campground sits on a peninsula that juts into Laurence Lake; only non-motorized boats are allowed on the lake. Campsite privacy varies because of the fairly sparse tree cover, and more than half of the sites are a short walk from your vehicle.

Campsites, facilities: There are 20 sites for tents or RVs up to 16 feet long. Picnic tables and fire rings with fire grills are provided. There is no drinking water. Vault toilets, garbage bins, and a boat ramp are available. Some facilities are wheelchair accessible. Leashed pets are permitted.

Reservations, fees: Reservations are not accepted. Sites are $12 per night, $7 per night per additional vehicle. Open May–September, weather permitting.

Directions: From Portland, drive 62 miles west on I-84 to the city of Hood River. Take Exit 64 and drive about 14 miles south on Highway 35 to the town of Mount Hood and Cooper Spur Road. Turn right and drive three miles to Parkdale and Clear Creek Road. Turn left (south) and drive three miles to the Laurence Lake turnoff. Turn right on Forest Road 2840 (Laurence Lake Road) and drive four miles to the campground on the right.

Contact: Mount Hood National Forest, Hood River Ranger District, 541/352-6002, fax 541/352-7365, www.fs.fed.us.

29 LOST LAKE

🚶 🚲 ⛵ 🛶 🚐 🐕 ♿ 🚐 ⛺

Scenic rating: 9

on Lost Lake in Mount Hood National Forest

Map 3.2, page 164   BEST (

Only non-motorized boats are allowed on this clear, 240-acre lake set against the Cascade Range. The campground is nestled in an old-growth forest of cedar, Douglas fir, and hemlock trees at 3,200 feet elevation. Many sites have a lake view, and the campground affords a great view of Mount Hood.

Campsites, facilities: There are 125 sites for tents or RVs up to 32 feet long and several group sites. A horse camp with a corral is also available. Picnic tables and fire rings with grills are provided. Drinking water, vault toilets, garbage containers, a dump station, and a covered picnic shelter are available. Cabins, a grocery store, showers, beach picnic areas, a boat launch, and boat rentals are nearby. Some facilities are wheelchair accessible, including a barrier-free boat launch and fishing pier, as well as 3.5 miles of barrier-free trails. Leashed pets are permitted.

Reservations, fees: Reservations are not accepted for single sites but are required for the group sites at 541/386-6366. Single sites are $25 per night, $7 per night per additional vehicle. There are three group sites that can accommodate up to 15 people and five vehicles each. The group sites are $75–125 per night. Some credit cards are accepted. Open mid-May–mid-October, weather permitting.

Directions: From Portland, drive 62 miles east on I-84 to the city of Hood River. Take Exit 62/Westcliff to Cascade Street. Drive east on Cascade Street to 13th Street. Turn right on 13th Street and drive through Hood River Heights. The road turns into Dee Highway. Continue seven miles to Lost Lake Road/Forest Road 13. Turn right and drive seven miles to the campground.

Contact: Mount Hood National Forest, Hood River Ranger District, 541/352-6002, fax 541/352-7365; Lost Lake Resort, 541/6366, www.fs.fed.us.

30 KNEBAL SPRINGS

🏃 🚴 🐎 🚐 ⛺

Scenic rating: 6

near Knebal Springs in
Mount Hood National Forest

Map 3.2, page 164

This spot (4,000 feet elevation) is in a semi-primitive area near Knebal Springs, an ephemeral water source. The Knebal Springs Trail begins at the campground. A nice, level family bike trail is available here. Another trail from the camp provides access to a network of trails in the area. A U.S. Forest Service map is advised.

Campsites, facilities: There are eight sites for tents or RVs up to 22 feet long. Picnic tables and fire grills are provided. There is no drinking water. Vault toilets and horse-loading and -tending facilities are available. Garbage must be packed out. Leashed pets are permitted.

Reservations, fees: Reservations are not accepted. Sites are $10 per night. Open mid-May–October, weather permitting.

Directions: From Portland, turn east on I-84 and drive about 90 miles to Exit 87. Take Exit 87 and turn south on U.S. 197; drive 13 miles to Dufur and Dufur Valley Road. Turn right on Dufur Valley Road and drive west for 12 miles to Forest Road 44. Continue west on Forest Road 44 for four miles to Forest Road 4430. Turn right and drive four miles to Forest Road 1720. Turn left (southwest) and drive one mile to the campground.

Contact: Mount Hood National Forest, Barlow Ranger District, 541/467-2291, fax 541/467-2271, www.fs.fed.us.

31 EIGHTMILE CROSSING

🏃 🚴 🛶 🐎 ♿ 🚐 ⛺

Scenic rating: 7

on Eightmile Creek in
Mount Hood National Forest

Map 3.2, page 164

This campground sits at an elevation of 4,200 feet along Eightmile Creek. Although pretty and shaded, with sites scattered along the banks of the creek, it gets relatively little camping pressure. From the day-use area, you have access to a nice hiking trail that runs along Eightmile Creek. In addition, a 0.75-mile wheelchair-accessible trail links Eightmile Campground to Lower Crossing Campground. The fishing can be good here, so bring your gear.

Campsites, facilities: There are 21 sites for tents or RVs up to 30 feet long. Picnic tables and fire grills are provided. Vault toilets are available. No drinking water is available, and garbage must be packed out. Some facilities are wheelchair accessible. Leashed pets are permitted.

Reservations, fees: Reservations are not accepted. Sites are $10 per night. Open June–mid-October, weather permitting.

Directions: From Portland, turn east on I-84 and drive about 90 miles to Exit 87. Take Exit 87 and turn south on U.S. 197; drive 13 miles to Dufur and Dufur Valley Road. Turn right on Dufur Valley Road and drive west for 12 miles to Forest Road 44. Continue west on Forest Road 44 for four miles to Forest Road 4430. Turn right and drive 0.5 mile to the campground.

Contact: Mount Hood National Forest, Barlow Ranger District, 541/467-2291, fax 541/467-2271, www.fs.fed.us.

32 PEBBLE FORD

🏃 🚴 🐎 🚐 ⛺

Scenic rating: 6

in Mount Hood National Forest

Map 3.2, page 164

This is just a little camping spot by the side of a gravel forest road. Primitive and quiet, it's an alternative to the better-known Eightmile Crossing. There are some quality hiking trails in the area if you're willing to drive two or three miles. The elevation is 4,200 feet.

Campsites, facilities: There are three sites for tents or RVs up to 16 feet long. Picnic tables and fire grills are provided. Vault toilets are available. There is no drinking water. Leashed pets are permitted.

Reservations, fees: Reservations are not accepted. Sites are $10 per night. Open June–early October, weather permitting.

Directions: From Portland, turn east on I-84 and drive about 90 miles to Exit 87. Take Exit 87 and turn south on U.S. 197; drive 13 miles to Dufur and Dufur Valley Road. Turn right on Dufur Valley Road and drive west for 12 miles to Forest Road 44. Continue west on Forest Road 44 for five miles to Forest Road 130. Turn left (south) and drive a short distance to the campground on the left.

Contact: Mount Hood National Forest, Barlow Ranger District, 541/467-2291, fax 541/467-2271, www.fs.fed.us.

33 McNEIL

Scenic rating: 5

on the Clear Fork of the Sandy River in Mount Hood National Forest

Map 3.2, page 164

McNeil campground (2,040 feet elevation) is located in Old Maid Flat, a special geological area along the Clear Fork of the Sandy River. There's a good view of Mount Hood from the campground entrance. Several trails nearby provide access to the wilderness backcountry.

Campsites, facilities: There are 34 sites for tents or RVs up to 22 feet long. Picnic tables and vault toilets are provided. There is no drinking water. Leashed pets are permitted.

Reservations, fees: Reservations are not accepted. Sites are $12 per night, $6 per night per additional vehicle. Open May–October, weather permitting.

Directions: From Portland, drive 40 miles east on U.S. 26 to Zigzag. Turn left on County Road 18/East Lolo Pass Road and drive 4.5

miles to Forest Road 1825. Turn right on Forest Road 1825, drive less than one mile, bear right onto a bridge to stay on Forest Road 1825, and drive 0.25 mile to the campground on the left.

Contact: Mount Hood National Forest, Zigzag Ranger District, 503/622-3191, fax 503/622-5622, www.fs.fed.us.

34 RILEY HORSE CAMP

Scenic rating: 6

near the Clear Fork of the Sandy River in Mount Hood National Forest

Map 3.2, page 164

Riley Horse Camp is close to McNeil and offers the same opportunities, except Riley provides stock facilities and is reserved for horse camping only on holidays. Secluded in an area of Douglas fir and lodgepole pine at 2,100 feet elevation, Riley is a popular base camp for horse-packing trips.

Campsites, facilities: There are 14 sites for tents or RVs up to 45 feet long. Picnic tables and fire grills are provided. Drinking water, vault toilets, garbage bins, and firewood are available. Corrals and hitching posts for horses are available. Leashed pets are permitted.

Reservations, fees: Reservations are accepted at 877/444-6777 or www.recreation.gov ($10 reservation fee). Sites are $16 per night, $8 per night per additional vehicle. Open May–September, weather permitting.

Directions: From Portland, drive 40 miles east on U.S. 26 to Zigzag. Turn left (northeast) on County Road 18/East Lolo Pass Road and drive 4.5 miles to Forest Road 1825. Turn right and drive 0.5 mile to Forest Road 380. Turn right and drive 100 yards to the camp.

Contact: Mount Hood National Forest, Zigzag Ranger District, 503/622-3191, fax 503/622-5622, www.fs.fed.us.

35 LOST CREEK

Scenic rating: 8

on Lost Creek in Mount Hood National Forest

Map 3.2, page 164

This campground near McNeil and Riley has some of the same opportunities. Set in a cool, lush area on a creek at 2,600 feet elevation, it's barrier-free and offers an interpretive nature trail about one mile long, as well as a wheelchair-accessible fishing pier.

Campsites, facilities: There are 14 sites for tents or RVs up to 40 feet long, including some pull-through sites and some walk-in sites. Picnic tables and fire grills are provided. Drinking water, garbage service, and vault toilets are available. Some facilities are wheelchair accessible. Leashed pets are permitted.

Reservations, fees: Reservations are accepted at 877/444-6777 or www.recreation. gov ($10 reservation fee). Sites are $16 for a single site, $32 for a double site, and $8–9 per night per additional vehicle. Open May–late September.

Directions: From Portland, drive 40 miles east on U.S. 26 to Zigzag. Turn left (northeast) on County Road 18/East Lolo Pass Road and drive 4.5 miles to Forest Road 1825. Turn right and drive two miles to a fork. Bear right and drive 0.25 mile to the campground on the right.

Contact: Mount Hood National Forest, Zigzag Ranger District, 503/622-3191, fax 503/622-5622, www.fs.fed.us.

36 TOLL GATE

Scenic rating: 8

on the Zigzag River in
Mount Hood National Forest

Map 3.2, page 164   BEST (

This shady campground along the banks of the Zigzag River near Rhododendron is extremely popular, and finding a site on a summer weekend can be next to impossible.

Luckily, you can make a reservation. There are numerous hiking trails in the area. The nearest one leads east for several miles along the river. The campground features a historic Civilian Conservation Corps shelter from the 1930s, which can be used by campers for day use.

Campsites, facilities: There are 15 sites for tents or RVs up to 40 feet long. Picnic tables and fire grills are provided. Drinking water, garbage service, firewood, a group picnic area (available by reservation), and vault toilets are available. A camp host is on-site. Leashed pets are permitted.

Reservations, fees: Reservations are accepted at 877/444-6777 or www.recreation.gov ($10 reservation fee). Sites are $16 per night, $8 per night per additional vehicle. Open late May–early September, weather permitting.

Directions: From Portland, drive east on U.S. 26 for 40 miles to Zigzag. Continue 2.5 miles southeast on U.S. 26 to the campground entrance.

Contact: Mount Hood National Forest, Zigzag Ranger District, 503/622-3191, fax 503/622-5622, www.fs.fed.us.

37 GREEN CANYON

Scenic rating: 8

on the Salmon River in
Mount Hood National Forest

Map 3.2, page 164

Few out-of-towners know about this winner. But the locals do, and they keep the place hopping in the summer. The camp sits at 1,600 feet elevation along the banks of the Salmon River. A long trail cuts through the area and parallels the river, passing through a magnificent old-growth forest.

Campsites, facilities: There are 15 sites for tents or RVs up to 22 feet long. Picnic tables and fire grills are provided. Drinking water, garbage bins, and vault toilets are available. A store, café, and ice are within five miles. Leashed pets are permitted.

Reservations, fees: Reservations are not accepted. Sites are $16–18 per night, $8–9 per night per additional vehicle. Open May–October, weather permitting.

Directions: From Portland, drive east on U.S. 26 for 39 miles to Forest Road 2618 (Salmon River Road) near Zigzag. Turn right and drive 4.5 miles to the campground on the right.

Contact: Mount Hood National Forest, Zigzag Ranger District, 503/622-3191, fax 503/622-5622, www.fs.fed.us.

38 CAMP CREEK

Scenic rating: 8

near the Zigzag River in Mount Hood National Forest

Map 3.2, page 164

This campground (2,200 feet elevation) sits along Camp Creek, not far from the Zigzag River. It looks similar to Toll Gate, but larger and farther from the road. A hiking trail runs through camp and along the river; another one leads south to Still Creek. This campground, along with Toll Gate to the west, is very popular—you'll probably need a reservation.

Campsites, facilities: There are 25 sites for tents or RVs up to 45 feet long. Picnic tables and fire grills are provided. Drinking water, vault toilets, and garbage bins are available. A camp host is on-site. Some facilities are wheelchair accessible. Leashed pets are permitted.

Reservations, fees: Reservations are accepted at 877/444-6777 or www.recreation.gov ($10 reservation fee). Sites are $16 per night, $32 for a double site, and $8 per night per additional vehicle. Open May–September, weather permitting.

Directions: From Portland, drive east on U.S. 26 for 40 miles to Zigzag. Continue southeast on U.S. 26 for about four miles to the camp on the right.

Contact: Mount Hood National Forest, Zigzag Ranger District, 503/622-3191, fax 503/622-5622, www.fs.fed.us.

39 ALPINE

Scenic rating: 8

near the Pacific Crest Trail in Mount Hood National Forest

Map 3.2, page 164

The small Alpine campground is set on the south slope of Mount Hood at 5,400 feet elevation, one mile from the Timberline Ski Area lodge. If you can bear some traffic noise, you'll be rewarded with big trees, a mountain feel, and year-round skiing and snowboarding less than one mile away. The Pacific Crest Trail is accessible from the Timberline Lodge. It can get quite crowded here on weekends. In the shoulder seasons, come prepared for cold nights.

Campsites, facilities: There are 16 sites for tents or RVs up to 16 feet long. Picnic tables and fire grills are provided. Drinking water, a portable toilet, and garbage service are available. Some facilities are wheelchair accessible. Leashed pets are permitted.

Reservations, fees: Reservations are not accepted. Sites are $16 per night, $8 per night per additional vehicle. Open mid-July–September, weather permitting.

Directions: From Portland, drive east on U.S. 26 for 55 miles to the small town of Government Camp. Continue east for one mile to Timberline Road (Forest Road 173). Turn left and drive 4.5 miles to the campground on the left.

Contact: Mount Hood National Forest, Zigzag Ranger District, 503/622-3191, fax 503/622-5622, www.fs.fed.us.

40 NOTTINGHAM

Scenic rating: 7

near the East Fork of the Hood River

Map 3.2, page 164

Nottingham campground, situated at 3,300 feet in elevation on the East Fork of the Hood River, has a variety of shady and sunny spots.

The primary tree cover is Douglas fir and ponderosa pine. The Tamanawas Falls Trail (near Sherwood Camp) is three miles away, and the Gumjuwac Trail is 1.5 miles north. Fishing is only fair because of the swift water and lack of pools.

Campsites, facilities: There are 23 sites for tents or RVs up to 32 feet long. Picnic tables and fire rings are provided. Vault toilets and garbage bins are available. There is no drinking water. Some facilities are wheelchair accessible. Leashed pets are permitted.

Reservations, fees: Reservations are not accepted. Sites are $12 per night, $7 per night per additional vehicle. Open May–October, weather permitting.

Directions: From Mount Hood, drive south on Highway 35 for 13 miles to the camp on the right.

Contact: Mount Hood National Forest, Hood River Ranger District, 541/352-6002, fax 541/352-7365, www.fs.fed.us.

41 STILL CREEK

Scenic rating: 6

on Still Creek in Mount Hood National Forest

Map 3.2, page 164

This primitive camp, shaded primarily by fir and hemlock, sits along Still Creek where the creek pours off Mount Hood's south slope. Adjacent to Summit Meadows and the site of a pioneer gravesite from the Oregon Trail days, it's a great place for mountain views, sunsets, and wildlife. Anglers should bring along their rods: The fishing in Still Creek can be excellent. The camp sits at 3,600 feet elevation.

Campsites, facilities: There are 27 sites for tents or RVs up to 40 feet long. Picnic tables and fire grills are provided. Vault toilets, drinking water, and garbage service are available. Leashed pets are permitted.

Reservations, fees: Reservations are accepted at 877/444-6777 or www.recreation.

gov ($10 reservation fee). Sites are $16–18 per night, $8–9 per night per additional vehicle. Open mid-June–mid-September, weather permitting.

Directions: From Portland, drive 55 miles east on U.S. 26 to Government Camp. Continue east on U.S. 26 for one mile to Forest Road 2650. Turn right and drive south for 500 yards to the campground.

Contact: Mount Hood National Forest, Zigzag Ranger District, 503/622-3191, fax 503/622-5622, www.fs.fed.us.

42 GRINDSTONE

Scenic rating: 7

near Barlow Creek in
Mount Hood National Forest

Map 3.2, page 164

This tiny campground, located at 3,400 feet elevation in a meadow along Barlow Creek, is a little-known and little-used spot. You won't find much out here but wind, water, and trees—but sometimes that's all you need. High-clearance vehicles are recommended. This camp was a site first used by the pioneers.

Campsites, facilities: There are three primitive sites for tents. Picnic tables and fire grills are provided. Vault toilets are available. There is no drinking water, and garbage must be packed out. Leashed pets are permitted.

Reservations, fees: Reservations are not accepted. There is no fee for camping. Open May–September, weather permitting.

Directions: From Portland, turn east on U.S. 26 and drive 57 miles (just past the town of Government Camp) to the junction with Highway 35. Take that exit, bear right onto Highway 35, and drive 4.5 miles to Forest Road 3530. Turn right and drive two miles to the campground on the right.

Contact: Mount Hood National Forest, Hood River Ranger District, 541/352-6002, fax 541/352-7365, www.fs.fed.us.

43 DEVIL'S HALF ACRE MEADOW

Scenic rating: 8

on Barlow Creek in
Mount Hood National Forest

Map 3.2, page 164

On a site used by the pioneers, this campground is situated a few miles upstream from Grindstone Campground on Barlow Creek. Several hiking trails close to camp, including the Pacific Crest Trail, provide access to small lakes in the area. There are many historic points of interest in the vicinity. High-clearance vehicles are recommended. The camp is at 3,600 feet elevation.

Campsites, facilities: There are two sites for tents or RVs up to 16 feet long. Picnic tables and fire grills are provided. Vault toilets are available. There is no drinking water, and garbage must be packed out. Leashed pets are permitted.

Reservations, fees: Reservations are not accepted. There is no fee. Open May–October, weather permitting.

Directions: From Portland, drive east on U.S. 26 for 57 miles (just past the town of Government Camp) to the junction with Highway 35. Take that exit, bear right on Highway 35, and drive 4.5 miles to Forest Road 3530. Turn southeast and drive one mile to the campground.

Contact: Mount Hood National Forest, Hood River Ranger District, 541/352-6002, fax 541/352-7365, www.fs.fed.us

44 TRILLIUM LAKE

Scenic rating: 9

on Trillium Lake in
Mount Hood National Forest

Map 3.2, page 164   BEST (

This campground (3,600 feet elevation) hugs the shores of Trillium Lake, which is about half a mile long and a quarter mile wide. Fishing is good in the evening here, and the nearby boat ramp makes this an ideal camp for anglers. The lake is great for canoes, rafts, and small rowboats. Trillium Lake is an extremely popular vacation destination, so expect plenty of company. Reservations are highly recommended.

Campsites, facilities: There are 57 sites for tents or RVs of any length. Picnic tables and fire grills are provided. Vault toilets and drinking water are available. Boat docks and launching facilities are available on the lake, but no motors are allowed. Some facilities are wheelchair accessible. Leashed pets are permitted.

Reservations, fees: Reservations are accepted at 877/444-6777 or www.recreation.gov ($10 reservation fee). Sites are $17 per night; double sites are $34 per night, $8–9 per night per additional vehicle. Open late May–late September, weather permitting.

Directions: From Portland, drive east on U.S. 26 for 55 miles to the small town of Government Camp. Continue east on U.S. 26 for 1.5 miles to Forest Road 2656. Turn right and drive 1.3 miles to the campground on the right.

Contact: Mount Hood National Forest, Zigzag Ranger District, 503/622-3191, fax 503/622-5622, www.fs.fed.us.

45 FROG LAKE

Scenic rating: 6

near the Pacific Crest Trail in
Mount Hood National Forest

Map 3.2, page 164

This classic spot in the Cascade Range is situated on the shore of little Frog Lake (more of a pond than a lake), at an elevation of 3,800 feet and a short distance from the Pacific Crest Trail. Several other trails lead to nearby lakes. Clear Lake, to the south, provides a possible day trip and offers more recreation options.

Campsites, facilities: There are 33 sites for

tents or RVs up to 35 feet long. Picnic tables and fire rings are provided. Drinking water, vault toilets, garbage bins, and firewood are available. A camp host is on-site. Boat-launching facilities are nearby; no motorized boats are allowed. Some facilities are wheelchair accessible. Leashed pets are permitted.

Reservations, fees: Reservations are accepted at 877/444-6777 or www.recreation. gov ($10 reservation fee). Sites are $15–18 per night, $8–9 per night per additional vehicle. Open mid-May–mid-September, weather permitting.

Directions: From Portland, drive east on U.S. 26 for 57 miles to the junction with Highway 35 (two miles past Government Camp). Take that exit, bear right onto Highway 35, and drive seven miles to Forest Road 2610. Turn left and drive 0.5 mile to the campground.

Contact: Mount Hood National Forest, Hood River Ranger District, 541/352-6002, fax 541/352-7365, www.fs.fed.us; park phone, 503/622-3191.

46 BADGER LAKE

Scenic rating: 8

on Badger Lake in Mount Hood National Forest

Map 3.2, page 164

This campground (4,400 feet elevation) sits along the shore of Badger Lake. Nonmotorized boating is permitted if you can manage to get a boat in here over the rough roads. No trailers are allowed on the campground road. The camp is adjacent to the Badger Creek Wilderness, and numerous trails provide access to the backcountry. Badger Creek Trail heads out of camp, northeast along Badger Creek for several miles.

Campsites, facilities: There are four sites for tents only, accessible only by high-clearance vehicles. Picnic tables and fire grills are provided. Vault toilets are available. There is no drinking water, and garbage must be packed out. Leashed pets are permitted.

Reservations, fees: Reservations are not accepted. Some designated sites are $10 per night; others require a Northwest Forest Pass. Open June–September, weather permitting.

Directions: From Portland, drive east on I-84 for 65 miles to Hood River, Exit 64 and Highway 35. Turn right (south) on Highway 35 and drive 37 miles to Forest Road 48. Turn left and drive 16 miles to Forest Road 4860. Turn left (north) and drive eight miles to Forest Road 140. Bear right and drive four miles to the lake. The last two miles on this primitive road require a high-clearance vehicle.

Contact: Mount Hood National Forest, Barlow Ranger District, 541/467-2291, fax 541/467-2271, www.fs.fed.us.

47 BONNEY MEADOW

Scenic rating: 9

in Mount Hood National Forest

Map 3.2, page 164

This primitive campground is on the east side of the Cascade Range at an elevation of 4,800 feet. As a result, there is little water in the area, and also very few people, so you're liable to have the place all to yourself. Bonney Meadow Trail leaves from the campground and travels 1.5 miles up to a group of small lakes. This trail provides great mountain views.

Campsites, facilities: There are six sites for tents or RVs up to 16 feet long. Picnic tables and fire grills are provided. Vault toilets are available. There is no drinking water and garbage must be packed out. Leashed pets are permitted.

Reservations, fees: Reservations are not accepted. Sites are $10 per night. Open June–early October, weather permitting.

Directions: From Portland, turn east on I-84 and drive 65 miles to the town of Hood River, Exit 64 and Highway 35. Turn right (south) on Highway 35 and drive 37 miles to Forest Road 48. Turn left and drive 14 miles to Forest Road 4890. Turn left and drive four miles north to

Forest Road 4891. Turn right and drive a short distance to the campground.

Contact: Mount Hood National Forest, Barlow Ranger District, 541/467-2291, fax 541/467-2271, www.fs.fed.us.

48 BONNEY CROSSING

Scenic rating: 7

on Badger Creek in
Mount Hood National Forest

Map 3.2, page 164

Bonney Crossing campground at 2,200 feet elevation along Badger Creek is the trailhead for the Badger Creek Trail, which provides access to the Badger Creek Wilderness. The camp gets fairly light use and is usually very quiet. Fishing is available in the creek and is usually pretty good. Horse campers are welcome here.

Campsites, facilities: There are eight sites for tents or RVs up to 16 feet long. Picnic tables and fire grills are provided. Vault toilets are available. There is no drinking water, and garbage must be packed out. Stock facilities include horse corrals. Leashed pets are permitted.

Reservations, fees: Reservations are not accepted. Sites are $10 per night. Open mid-April–mid-October, weather permitting.

Directions: From The Dalles, drive south on U.S. 197 for 32 miles to Tygh Valley. Take the Tygh Valley exit to Tygh Valley Road. Turn west and drive 0.25 mile to Wamic Market Road (County Road 226). Turn right (west) and drive eight miles to Wamic. Continue through Wamic and drive seven miles to Forest Road 4810. Bear right and drive three miles to Forest Road 4811. Turn right and drive two miles to a junction with Forest Road 2710. Turn right and drive three miles to the campground on the right.

Contact: Mount Hood National Forest, Barlow Ranger District, 541/467-2291, fax 541/467-2271, www.fs.fed.us.

49 FOREST CREEK

Scenic rating: 6

on Forest Creek in
Mount Hood National Forest

Map 3.2, page 164

This is a very old camp that borders Forest Creek on the original Barlow Trail, once used by early settlers. Shaded by an old-growth Douglas fir and ponderosa pine forest, you'll camp amid solitude. The elevation here is 3,000 feet. See a U.S. Forest Service map for specific roads and trails.

Campsites, facilities: There are eight sites for tents or RVs up to 16 feet long. Picnic tables and fire grills are provided. No drinking water is available. Vault toilets are available. Garbage must be packed out. Leashed pets are permitted.

Reservations, fees: Reservations are not accepted. Sites are $10 per night. Open June–early October, weather permitting.

Directions: From Portland, turn east on I-84 and drive 91 miles to The Dalles/Exit 87/Highway 197. Turn south and drive 31 miles to Tygh Valley and Wamic Market Road. Turn right and drive west for six miles to Forest Road 48. Continue west and drive 12.5 miles southwest to Forest Road 4885. Turn left and drive one mile to Forest Road 3530. Turn left and drive a short distance to the campground.

Contact: Mount Hood National Forest, Barlow Ranger District, 541/467-2291, fax 541/467-2271, www.fs.fed.us.

50 ROCK CREEK RESERVOIR

Scenic rating: 7

on Rock Creek Reservoir in
Mount Hood National Forest

Map 3.2, page 164

Fishing is excellent, and the environment is perfect for canoes or rafts at this campground along the shore of Rock Creek Reservoir. Enjoy views of Mount Hood from the day-use area (Northwest Forest Pass required). No hiking trails are in the immediate vicinity, but there are many old forest roads that are ideal for walking or mountain biking. The camp sits at 2,200 feet elevation.

Campsites, facilities: There are 33 sites for tents or RVs up to 18 feet long. Picnic tables, garbage service, and fire grills are provided. Vault toilets, drinking water, and firewood are available. There are boat docks nearby, but no motorboats are allowed on the reservoir. Some facilities are wheelchair accessible. Leashed pets are permitted.

Reservations, fees: Reservations are accepted at 877/444-6777 or www.recreation.gov ($10 reservation fee). Sites are $14–16 per night, $7–8 per night per additional vehicle. Open late May–early October.

Directions: From Portland, turn east on I-84 and drive 91 miles to The Dalles/Exit 87/ Highway 197. Turn south and drive 31 miles to Tygh Valley and Wamic Market Road. Turn right and drive west for six miles to Forest Road 48. Turn west and drive one mile to Forest Road 4820. Turn west and drive a short distance to the campground.

Contact: Mount Hood National Forest, Barlow Ranger District, 541/467-2291, fax 541/467-2271, www.fs.fed.us.

51 PINE HOLLOW LAKESIDE RESORT

Scenic rating: 8

on Pine Hollow Reservoir

Map 3.2, page 164

This resort on the shore of Pine Hollow Reservoir is the best game in town for RV campers, with some shaded lakefront sites and scenic views. Year-round boating, fishing, swimming, and waterskiing are some recreation options here.

Campsites, facilities: There are 35 tent sites,

78 sites with partial hookups for RVs of any length, and 10 cabins. Picnic tables and fire pits are provided. Drinking water, restrooms with flush toilets and coin showers, propane gas, a dump station, firewood, a convenience store, café, coin laundry, and ice are available. Boat docks, launching facilities, and boat and personal watercraft rentals are nearby. Leashed pets are permitted.

Reservations, fees: Reservations are accepted. Sites are $25 per night, $2 per person per night for more than two people, $2 per night per additional vehicle, and $2 per pet per night. Some credit cards are accepted. Open mid-March–October.

Directions: From Portland, turn east on I-84 and drive 91 miles to The Dalles/Exit 87/ Highway 197. Turn south on Highway 197 and drive 31 miles to Tygh Valley and Wamic Market Road. Turn right (west) and drive four miles to Ross Road. Turn right (north) and drive 3.5 miles to the resort on the right.

Contact: Pine Hollow Lakeside Resort, 541/544-2271, www.pinehollowlakeside. com.

52 HUNT PARK

Scenic rating: 6

near Badger Creek

Map 3.2, page 164

This Wasco County campground is set near the confluence of Badger and Tygh Creeks. Hiking trails, marked bike trails, and tennis courts are nearby, and fishing and rafting are available on the Deschutes River.

Campsites, facilities: There are 150 tent sites, 120 pull-through sites with partial hookups for RVs of any length, and a group site for tents only. Picnic tables are provided. Drinking water, restrooms with flush toilets and coin showers, a dump station, garbage bins, a basketball court, wireless Internet, and picnic shelters (which can be reserved) are available. Horse facilities, including stalls and an arena, are also available. A camp host is on-site. A store, café, and ice are within one mile. Some facilities are wheelchair accessible. Leashed pets are permitted.

Reservations, fees: Reservations are accepted at 541/483-2288. Sites are $12–15 per night, $3 per night per additional vehicle. The group site is $5 per person per night for up to 100 people, $3 per person thereafter. Open May–October.

Directions: From Portland, turn east on I-84 and drive 91 miles to The Dalles/Exit 87/Highway 197. Turn south on Highway 197 and drive 31 miles to Tygh Valley and Main Street. Turn right on Main Street and drive two blocks to Fairgrounds Road. Turn right and drive one mile to the fairgrounds on the right.

Contact: Wasco County, 541/483-2288, http://co.wasco.or.us.

53 HIDEAWAY LAKE

Scenic rating: 9

near the Rock Lakes Basin in Mount Hood National Forest

Map 3.2, page 164

This jewel of a spot features a small, deep lake where non-motorized boats are allowed, but they must be carried about 100 yards to the lake. The campsites are separate and scattered around the shore. At the north end of the lake, an 8.5-mile loop trail passes a number of lakes in the Rock Lakes Basin, all of which support populations of rainbow and brook trout. If you don't want to make the whole trip in a day, you can camp overnight at Serene Lake. See a U.S. Forest Service map for information.

Campsites, facilities: There are nine sites for tents or small RVs up to 16 feet long. Picnic tables and fire grills are provided. Vault toilets are available. There is no drinking water. Leashed pets are permitted.

Reservations, fees: Reservations are not accepted. Sites are $14 per night, $7 per night per additional vehicle. Open mid-June–late September, weather permitting.

Directions: From Portland, drive south on U.S. 205 to the junction with Highway 224/Estacada. Take the exit and turn left onto Highway 224, heading south. Drive approximately 13 miles to Estacada. Continue south on Highway 224 and drive 27 miles to Forest Road 57. Turn left (east) and drive 7.5 miles to Forest Road 58. Turn left (north) and drive three miles to Forest Road 5830. Turn left (northwest) and drive 5.5 miles to the campground on the left.

Contact: Mount Hood National Forest, Clackamas River Ranger District, 503/630-6861, fax 503/630-2299, www.fs.fed.us.

54 CLEAR LAKE

Scenic rating: 4

near the Pacific Crest Trail in Mount Hood National Forest

Map 3.2, page 164

This campground is located along the shore of Clear Lake, a spot favored by anglers, swimmers, and windsurfers, but as a reservoir, it is subject to water-level fluctuations. The boating speed limit is 10 mph. This wooded camp features shady sites and is set at 3,600 feet elevation. The camp sometimes gets noisy from the revels of the party set. If you want quiet, this spot is probably not for you. A nearby trail heads north from the lake and provides access to the Pacific Crest Trail and Frog Lake, both good recreation options.

Campsites, facilities: There are 28 sites for tents or RVs up to 30 feet long and one lookout cabin. Picnic tables and fire grills are provided. Drinking water, garbage bins, firewood, and vault toilets are available. Some facilities are wheelchair accessible. Boat-launching facilities are nearby. Leashed pets are permitted.

Reservations, fees: Reservations are accepted at 877/444-6777 or www.recreation.gov ($10 reservation fee). Sites are $16–18 per night, $8–9 per night per additional vehicle. The lookout cabin is $30 per night. Open mid-May–late September, weather permitting.

Directions: From Portland, drive east on U.S. 26 for 57 miles to the junction with Highway 35 (two miles past Government Camp). Bear right (southeast) on U.S. 26 and drive nine miles to Forest Road 2630. Turn right (south) and drive one mile to the campground on the right.

Contact: Mount Hood National Forest, Hood River Ranger District, 541/352-6002, fax 541/352-7365, www.fs.fed.us.

55 BARLOW CREEK

Scenic rating: 7

on Barlow Creek in
Mount Hood National Forest

Map 3.2, page 164

One of several primitive U.S. Forest Service camps in the immediate vicinity, this campground is set along Barlow Creek at an elevation of 3,100 feet. It is on Old Barlow Road, which was the wagon trail for early settlers in this area. If this campground is full, Barlow Crossing Campground is one mile southeast on Forest Road 3530.

Campsites, facilities: There are three sites for tents. Picnic tables and fire grills are provided. Vault toilets are available. There is no drinking water, and garbage must be packed out. Leashed pets are permitted.

Reservations, fees: Reservations are not accepted. Sites are $10 per night. Open May–September, weather permitting.

Directions: From Portland, drive east on U.S. 26 for 57 miles to the junction with Highway 35 (two miles past Government Camp). Stay on U.S. 26 and continue 12 miles to Forest Road 43. Turn left and drive five miles to Forest Road 3530. Turn left (north) and drive 1.5 miles to the campground on the left.

Contact: Mount Hood National Forest, Hood River Ranger District, 541/352-6002, fax 541/352-7365, www.fs.fed.us.

56 WHITE RIVER STATION

Scenic rating: 9

on the White River in
Mount Hood National Forest

Map 3.2, page 164

This tiny campground is set along the White River at an elevation of 3,000 feet. It is on Old Barlow Road, an original wagon trail used by early settlers. One of several small, secluded camps in the area, White River Station is quiet and private, but with poor fishing prospects.

Campsites, facilities: There are five sites for tents or RVs up to 32 feet long. Picnic tables and fire grills are provided. Vault toilets are available. There is no drinking water, and garbage must be packed out. Leashed pets are permitted.

Reservations, fees: Reservations are not accepted. Sites are $10 per night, $5 per night per additional vehicle. Open May–September, weather permitting.

Directions: From Portland, drive east on U.S. 26 for 57 miles to the junction with Highway 35 (two miles past Government Camp). Stay on U.S. 26 and continue 12 miles to Forest Road 43. Turn left and drive five miles to Forest Road 3530. Turn right and drive approximately 1.5 miles to the campground on the left. (White River is less than one mile away from Barlow Creek.)

Contact: Mount Hood National Forest, Barlow Ranger District, 541/467-2291, fax 541/467-2271, www.fs.fed.us.

57 LAKE HARRIET

Scenic rating: 5

on Lake Harriet in Mount Hood National Forest

Map 3.2, page 164

Formed by a dam on the Oak Grove Fork of the Clackamas River, this little lake is a popular spot during the summer. Rowboats and boats with small motors are permitted, but only non-motorized boats are encouraged. The lake is stocked regularly and can provide good fishing for a variety of trout, including brook, brown, cutthroat, and rainbow. Anglers often stand shoulder to shoulder in summer.

Campsites, facilities: There are 11 sites for tents or RVs up to 40 feet long. Picnic tables and fire grills are provided. Drinking water and vault toilets are available. Garbage service is provided in the summer. A fishing pier and boat-launching facilities are on the lake. Some facilities are wheelchair accessible. Leashed pets are permitted.

Reservations, fees: Reservations are accepted at 877/444-6777 or www.recreation.gov ($10 reservation fee). Sites are $16 per night, $8 per night per additional vehicle. Open year-round, weather permitting, with limited winter services.

Directions: From Portland, drive south on U.S. 205 to the junction with Highway 224/Estacada. Take the exit and turn left onto Highway 224, heading south. Drive approximately 13 miles to Estacada. Continue south on Highway 224 and drive 27 miles to Forest Road 57. Turn east and drive 7.5 miles to Forest Road 4630. Turn left and drive two miles to the campground on the left.

Contact: Mount Hood National Forest, Clackamas River Ranger District, 503/630-6861, fax 503/630-2299, www.fs.fed.us.

58 GONE CREEK
🏃 🛶 🚐 🐕 🚍 ⛺

Scenic rating: 8

on Timothy Lake in
Mount Hood National Forest

Map 3.2, page 164 · **BEST (**

This campground, set along the south shore of Timothy Lake at 3,200 feet elevation, is one of five camps at the lake. Timothy Lake provides good fishing for brook trout, cutthroat trout, kokanee salmon, and rainbow trout. Boats with motors are allowed, but a 10-mph speed limit keeps it quiet. Several

trails in the area—including the Pacific Crest Trail—provide access to a number of small mountain lakes.

Campsites, facilities: There are 49 sites for tents or RVs up to 45 feet long. Picnic tables and fire grills are provided. Drinking water, garbage service, vault toilets, and firewood are available. A boat ramp is nearby. Leashed pets are permitted.

Reservations, fees: Reservations are accepted at 877/444-6777 or www.recreation.gov ($10 reservation fee). Sites are $17–18 per night, $8–9 per night per additional vehicle. Open mid-May–early September, weather permitting.

Directions: From Portland, drive on U.S. 26 for 55 miles (just past the town of Government Camp) to the junction with Highway 35. Bear southeast, staying on U.S. 26, and drive 15 miles to Forest Road 42 (Skyline Road). Turn right and drive eight miles to Forest Road 57. Turn right and drive one mile west to the campground on the right.

Contact: Mount Hood National Forest, Zigzag Ranger District, 503/622-3191, fax 503/622-5622, www.fs.fed.us.

59 OAK FORK
🏃 🚲 🛶 🚐 🛥 🐕 🚍 ⛺

Scenic rating: 8

on Timothy Lake in
Mount Hood National Forest

Map 3.2, page 164

Heavy timber and bear grass surround this forested camp along the south shore of Timothy Lake, where fishing is good for brook trout, cutthroat trout, kokanee salmon, and rainbow trout. Boats with motors are allowed, but a 10-mph speed limit is enforced. Oak Fork is located just east of Hoodview and Gone Creek campgrounds, at an elevation of 3,200 feet. Several area trails—including the Pacific Crest—provide access to various small mountain lakes.

Campsites, facilities: There are 46 sites for

tents or RVs up to 45 feet long. Picnic tables and fire grills are provided. Drinking water, firewood, and vault toilets are available. A boat ramp and launching facilities are nearby; the speed limit on the lake is 10 mph. Leashed pets are permitted.

Reservations, fees: Reservations are accepted at 877/444-6777 or www.recreation.gov ($10 reservation fee). Sites are $17–18 per night, $8–9 per night per additional vehicle. Open May–early October, weather permitting.

Directions: From Portland, turn east on U.S. 26 and drive 57 miles (just past the town of Government Camp) to the junction with Highway 35. Bear southeast, staying on U.S. 26, and drive 15 miles to Forest Road 42 (Skyline Road). Turn right and drive eight miles to Forest Road 57. Turn right and drive three miles to the camp on the right.

Contact: Mount Hood National Forest, Zigzag Ranger District, 503/622-3191, fax 503/622-5622, www.fs.fed.us.

60 PINE POINT

Scenic rating: 8

on Timothy Lake in
Mount Hood National Forest

Map 3.2, page 164

One of five camps on Timothy Lake, Pine Point spot sits at an elevation of 3,400 feet on the southwest shore. This camp has lake access and more open vegetation than the other Timothy Lake campgrounds. There's good fishing for brook trout, cutthroat trout, kokanee salmon, and rainbow trout, and a 10-mph speed limit keeps it pleasant for everyone. The trail that leads around the lake and to the Pacific Crest Trail passes along this campground.

Campsites, facilities: There are 25 sites for tents or RVs up to 45 feet long, including 12 single sites, eight double sites, and five group sites for up to 25 people each. Picnic tables, garbage service, and fire grills are provided. Drinking water and vault toilets are available.

A boat ramp, launching facilities, and fishing pier are nearby; the speed limit on the lake is 10 mph. Leashed pets are permitted.

Reservations, fees: Reservations are accepted at 877/444-6777 or www.recreation.gov ($10 reservation fee). Single sites are $17 per night, $34 per night for a double site, and $8–9 per night per additional vehicle. Group sites are $50 per night. Open late May–mid-September, weather permitting.

Directions: From Portland, turn east on U.S. 26 and drive 57 miles (just past the town of Government Camp) to the junction with Highway 35. Bear southeast, staying on U.S. 26, and drive 15 miles to Forest Road 42 (Skyline Road). Turn right and drive eight miles to Forest Road 57. Turn right and drive four miles to the park on the right.

Contact: Mount Hood National Forest, Zigzag Ranger District, 503/622-3191, fax 503/622-5622, www.fs.fed.us.

61 HOODVIEW

Scenic rating: 9

on Timothy Lake in
Mount Hood National Forest

Map 3.2, page 164

Here's another camp along the south shore of Timothy Lake; this one is set at 3,200 feet elevation. Timothy Lake provides good fishing for brook trout, cutthroat trout, kokanee salmon, and rainbow trout. Motorized boats are allowed, and the speed limit is 10 mph. A trail out of camp branches south for a few miles and, if followed to the east, eventually leads to the Pacific Crest Trail.

Campsites, facilities: There are 41 sites for tents or RVs up to 45 feet long. Picnic tables and fire grills are provided. Vault toilets, drinking water, garbage service, and firewood are available. A boat ramp is nearby. Leashed pets are permitted.

Reservations, fees: Reservations are accepted at 877/444-6777 or www.recreation.gov ($10 reservation fee). Sites are $17–18 per night, $8–9 per night per additional vehicle. Open mid-May–mid-September, weather permitting.

Directions: From Portland, turn east on U.S. 26 and drive 57 miles (just past the town of Government Camp) to the junction with Highway 35. Bear southeast, staying on U.S. 26, and drive 15 miles to Forest Road 42 (Skyline Road). Turn right and drive eight miles to Forest Road 57. Turn right and drive three miles to the campground on the right.

Contact: Mount Hood National Forest, Zigzag Ranger District, 503/622-3191, fax 503/622-5622, www.fs.fed.us.

62 MEDITATION POINT

Scenic rating: 9

on Timothy Lake in
Mount Hood National Forest

Map 3.2, page 164   **BEST (**

Accessible only by foot or boat, this remote and rustic camp sits at 3,200 feet elevation and offers the most secluded location along Timothy Lake. It's one of two campgrounds on the north shore of the lake, which means you'll get a quieter, less crowded environment, though you'll have to bring your own water. The lake has a 10-mph speed limit for boaters. Timothy Lake Trail makes a 14-mile loop around the lake.

Campsites, facilities: There are five boat-in or walk-in tent sites. Picnic tables and fire grills are provided. Vault toilets are available. There is no drinking water, and garbage must be packed out. Boat docks and launching facilities are nearby. Leashed pets are permitted.

Reservations, fees: Reservations are not accepted. Access from PGE Day Use Area requires a $5 fee or a Northwest Forest Pass. There is no fee for camping. Open late May–mid-September, weather permitting.

Directions: From Portland, drive east on U.S. 26 and drive 57 miles to the junction with Highway 35 (two miles past Government Camp). Bear right (southeast), staying on U.S.

26, and continue for 15 miles to Forest Road 42/Skyline Road. Turn right and drive eight miles south to Forest Road 57. Turn right and drive five miles, passing Pine Point Campground and crossing the Timothy Lake Dam. Park in the day-use area and hike one mile or take a boat to the north shore of the lake.

Contact: Mount Hood National Forest, Zigzag Ranger District, 503/622-3191, fax 503/622-5622, www.fs.fed.us.

63 LITTLE CRATER LAKE

Scenic rating: 7

on Clear Creek in Mount Hood National Forest

Map 3.2, page 164

Little Crater campground (3,200 feet elevation) nestles against Crater Creek and scenic Little Crater Lake. This camp is popular with hunters in the fall. Both the drinking water and the lake water are spring fed, and the water is numbingly cold. The Pacific Crest Trail is located near camp, providing hiking trail access. Fishing is poor at Little Crater Lake. Little Timothy Lake lies about 10 miles away; note the 10-mph speed limit for boats. Bring your mosquito repellent—you'll need it.

Campsites, facilities: There are 16 sites for tents or RVs up to 35 feet long. Picnic tables, garbage bins, and fire grills are provided. Vault toilets, firewood, and drinking water are available. Leashed pets are permitted.

Reservations, fees: Reservations are accepted at 877/444-6777 or www.recreation.gov ($10 reservation fee). Sites are $16 per night, $8 per night per additional vehicle. Open May–mid-September, weather permitting.

Directions: From Portland, drive east on U.S. 26 for 57 miles to the junction with Highway 35 (two miles past Government Camp). Bear right (southeast), staying on U.S. 26, and drive 15 miles to Forest Road 42 (Skyline Road). Turn right and drive about six miles to Forest Road 58. Turn right and drive about 2.5 miles to the campground on the left.

Contact: Mount Hood National Forest, Zigzag Ranger District, 503/622-3191, fax 503/622-5622, www.fs.fed.us.

64 CLEAR CREEK CROSSING

Scenic rating: 7

on Clear Creek in Mount Hood National Forest

Map 3.2, page 164

This secluded, little-known spot hugs the banks of Clear Creek at an elevation of 3,600 feet. Clear Creek Trail, a very pretty walk, begins at the campground. Fishing and hiking are two recreation options here.

Campsites, facilities: There are seven sites for tents or RVs up to 16 feet long. Picnic tables and fire grills are provided. Vault toilets are available. There is no drinking water, and garbage must be packed out. Leashed pets are permitted.

Reservations, fees: Reservations are not accepted. Sites are $10 per night. Open May–September, weather permitting.

Directions: From Portland, drive east on U.S. 26 for 55 miles to Government Camp. Continue three miles to a junction and bear right, staying on U.S. 26, and drive south for 12 miles to Highway 216. Turn left (east) on Highway 216 and drive two miles to Forest Road 2130. Turn left (north) on Forest Road 2130 and drive three miles to the campground.

Contact: Mount Hood National Forest, Barlow Ranger District, 541/467-2291, fax 541/467-2271, www.fs.fed.us.

65 KEEPS MILL

Scenic rating: 9

on Clear Creek in Mount Hood National Forest

Map 3.2, page 164

This small, pretty campground is situated at the confluence of Clear Creek and the White River. No RVs are permitted. The elevation is 2,600 feet. Many hiking trails, some with awesome views of the White River Canyon, crisscross the area, but be warned: These are butt-kicking canyon climbs.

Campsites, facilities: There are five sites for tents only. The road to the campground is not good for trailers. Picnic tables and fire grills are provided. Vault toilets are available. There is no drinking water, and garbage must be packed out. Leashed pets are permitted.

Reservations, fees: Reservations are not accepted. Sites are $10 per night. Open May–September, weather permitting.

Directions: From Portland, drive east on U.S. 26 for 55 miles to Government Camp. Continue three miles to a junction, turn right on U.S. 26, and drive south for 12 miles to Highway 216. Turn left (east) on Highway 216 and drive three miles to Forest Road 2120. Turn left (north) on Forest Road 2120 and drive three miles to the campground.

Contact: Mount Hood National Forest, Barlow Ranger District, 541/467-2291, fax 541/467-2271, www.fs.fed.us.

66 BEAR SPRINGS

Scenic rating: 6

on Indian Creek in Mount Hood National Forest

Map 3.2, page 164

This campground is set along the banks of Indian Creek on the border of the Warm Springs Indian Reservation and features both secluded and open sites set in old-growth forest. The elevation is 3,000 feet.

Campsites, facilities: There are 21 sites for tents or RVs up to 32 feet long. Picnic tables and fire grills are provided. Drinking water, garbage bins, vault toilets, and firewood are available. Leashed pets are permitted.

Reservations, fees: Reservations are not accepted. Sites are $12 per night and $6 per night for each additional vehicle. Open June–September, weather permitting.

Directions: From Portland, drive east on U.S. 26 for 55 miles to Government Camp. Continue three miles to a junction and bear right, staying on U.S. 26, and drive south for 12 miles to Highway 216. Turn left (east) on Highway 216 and drive four miles to Reservation Road. Turn right (east) on Reservation Road and look for the campground on the right.

Contact: Mount Hood National Forest, Barlow Ranger District, 541/467-2291, fax 541/467-2271, www.fs.fed.us.

67 McCUBBINS GULCH

Scenic rating: 5

in Mount Hood National Forest

Map 3.2, page 164

This small, primitive camp sits alongside a small creek at 3,000 feet in elevation and offers decent fishing and OHV (off-highway vehicle) recreation. A 40-mile network of OHV trails runs through the surrounding forest, with access right from camp. So, though out of the way, this camp gets heavy use; claim a spot early in the day. To the south is the Warm Springs Indian Reservation; do not trespass, as large fines are assessed to those prosecuted. Bear Springs provides a nearby camping alternative.

Campsites, facilities: There are 15 sites for tents and RVs up to 25 feet long. Picnic tables and fire grills are provided. Vault toilets are available. There is no drinking water, and garbage must be packed out. Leashed pets are permitted.

Reservations, fees: Reservations are not accepted. Sites are $10 per night. Open May–September, weather permitting.

Directions: From Portland, drive east on U.S. 26 for 55 miles to Government Camp. Continue three miles to a junction and bear right, staying on U.S. 26, and drive south for 12 miles to Highway 216. Turn left (east) on Highway 216 and drive six miles to Forest Road 2110. Take a sharp left and drive 1.5 miles to the campground entrance on the right.

Contact: Mount Hood National Forest, Barlow Ranger District, 541/467-2291, fax 541/467-2271, www.fs.fed.us.

68 SHELLROCK CREEK

Scenic rating: 6

on Shellrock Creek in Mount Hood National Forest

Map 3.2, page 164

This quiet little campground (2,200 feet elevation) occupies a nice spot on Shellrock Creek and has been used primarily as an overflow area for Lake Harriet campground. Small trout can be caught here, but remember that on the Clackamas River it's catch-and-release only. Obtain a U.S. Forest Service map for details on the backcountry roads and trails.

Campsites, facilities: There are eight sites for tents or RVs up to 16 feet long. Picnic tables and fire grills are provided. Vault toilets are available. There is no drinking water and garbage must be packed out. Leashed pets are permitted.

Note: In 2010, the Forest Service plans some changes to several campgrounds in the Estacada Ranger District.

Reservations, fees: Reservations are not accepted. Sites are $14 per night, $7 per night per additional vehicle. Open year-round, with limited winter services.

Directions: From Portland, drive south on U.S. 205 to the junction with Highway 224. Take the Highway 224/Estacada exit and turn left (south) onto Highway 224. Drive approximately 13 miles to Estacada. Continue south on Highway 224 for 27 miles in national forest (the road becomes Forest Road 46) to Forest Road 57. Turn left (east) and drive 7.5 miles to Forest Road 58. Turn left and drive north one mile to the campground on the left.

Contact: Mount Hood National Forest, Clackamas River Ranger District, Estacada Ranger Station, 503/630-6861, fax 503/630-2299, www.fs.fed.us.

69 JOE GRAHAM HORSE CAMP

Scenic rating: 8

near Clackamas Lake in
Mount Hood National Forest

Map 3.2, page 164

Named for a forest ranger, this campground sits at 3,250 feet elevation among majestic Douglas fir and hemlock, just north of tiny Clackamas Lake. It's one of two campgrounds in the area that allow horses. Timothy Lake (the setting for the Gone Creek, Hoodview, Meditation Point, Oak Fork, and Pine Point camps) provides a nearby alternative to the northwest. The Pacific Crest Trail is just east of camp.

Campsites, facilities: There are 15 sites for tents, horse trailers, or RVs up to 45 feet long; 11 have corrals, and two have hitching rails. Picnic tables, hitching posts, garbage service, and fire grills are provided. Drinking water and vault toilets are available. Leashed pets are permitted.

Reservations, fees: Reservations are accepted at 877/444-6777 or www.recreation.gov ($10 reservation fee). Sites are $17 per night, $8.50 per night per additional vehicle. Open mid-May–mid-October, weather permitting.

Directions: From Portland, turn east on U.S. 26 and drive 57 miles (just past the town of Government Camp) to the junction with Highway 35. Bear right, continuing southeast on U.S. 26, and drive 15 miles to Forest Road 42 (Skyline Road). Turn right and drive eight miles to the campground on the left.

Contact: Mount Hood National Forest, Zigzag Ranger District, 503/622-3191, fax 503/622-5622, www.fs.fed.us.

70 CLACKAMAS LAKE

Scenic rating: 7

near the Clackamas River in
Mount Hood National Forest

Map 3.2, page 164

This camp, set at 3,400 feet elevation, is a good place to go to escape the hordes of people at the lakeside sites in neighboring camps. The Pacific Crest Trail passes nearby, and Timothy Lake requires little more than a one-mile hike from camp. The Clackamas Lake Historic Ranger Station, a visitors center, is worth a visit and is still using the old, hand crank–style phones once used in lookout towers and guard stations. This is a popular spot for campers with horses, although the facilities could use some updating and repairs.

Campsites, facilities: There are 46 sites for tents, trailers, horse trailers, or RVs up to 45 feet long. Some sites have hitch rails, and horses are permitted at the first 19 sites. Drinking water, garbage service, fire grills, and picnic tables are provided. Vault toilets are available. Boat docks and launching facilities are nearby at Timothy Lake, but only non-motorized boats are allowed. Leashed pets are permitted.

Reservations, fees: Reservations are accepted at 877/444-6777 or www.recreation.gov ($10 reservation fee). Sites are $16 per night, $8 per night per additional vehicle. Open May–mid-September, weather permitting.

Directions: From Portland, turn east on U.S. 26 and drive 57 miles (just past the town of Government Camp) to the junction with Highway 35. Bear southeast, staying on U.S. 26, and drive 15 miles to Forest Road 42 (Skyline Road). Turn right and drive eight miles to Forest Road 57. Continue 500 feet (on Forest Road 42) past the Clackamas Lake Historic Ranger Station to Forest Road 4270. Turn left and drive 0.5 mile to the campground on the left.

Contact: Mount Hood National Forest, Zigzag Ranger District, 503/622-3191, fax 503/622-5622, www.fs.fed.us.

7.1 DESCHUTES RIVER STATE RECREATION AREA

Scenic rating: 7

on the Deschutes River

Map 3.3, page 165

This tree-shaded park along the Deschutes River in the Deschutes Canyon offers bicycling and hiking trails and good steelhead fishing in season. The river-level Atiyeh Deschutes River Trail is a favorite jaunt for hikers. A small day-use state park called Heritage Landing, which has a boat ramp and restroom facilities, is located across the river. The U.S. Army Corps of Engineers offers a free train ride and tour of the dam at The Dalles during the summer. Good rafting is a bonus here. For 25 miles upstream, the river is mostly inaccessible by car. Many anglers launch boats here and then go upstream to steelhead fishing grounds. Note that boat fishing is not allowed here; you must wade into the river or fish from shore.

Campsites, facilities: There are 34 sites with partial hookups for tents or RVs up to 50 feet, 25 primitive sites for tents or self-contained RVs up to 30 feet, and four group areas for RVs and tents, which can hold up to 25 people and five RVs each. Picnic tables and fire grills are provided, but campfires are prohibited July 1–September 30. Drinking water, garbage bins, and flush toilets are available. Leashed pets are permitted.

Reservations, fees: Reservations are accepted at 800/452-5687 or www.oregonstateparks.org ($8 reservation fee). Sites with partial-hookup are $12–20 per night, primitive sites are $5–9 per night, $5 per night per additional vehicle. Group sites are $40–71 per night. Some credit cards are accepted. Open year-round, with limited services November–March.

Directions: From Portland, turn east on I-84 and drive about 90 miles to The Dalles. Continue east on I-84 for 12 miles to Exit 97/ Deschutes State Recreation Area, turn right, and drive 50 feet to Biggs-Rufus Highway. Turn left and drive about three miles, cross the Deschutes River, and turn right to the campground entrance.

Contact: Deschutes River State Recreation Area, 541/739-2322 or 800/452-5687, www.oregonstateparks.org.

7.2 LePAGE PARK

Scenic rating: 6

on the John Day River

Map 3.3, page 165

Half of the campsites are adjacent to the John Day River and the other half are on the opposite side of the road at this partially shaded campground. The John Day River feeds into the Columbia just 0.12 mile north of the campground. Rattlesnakes are occasionally seen in the area but are not abundant. Anglers come for the smallmouth bass and catfish during the summer. The day-use area has a swimming beach, lawn, boat launch, and boat docks. There are several other campgrounds nearby.

Campsites, facilities: There is a grassy area with 20 walk-in sites for tents and 22 sites with partial hookups for tents or RVs up to 56 feet long; some sites are pull-through. Picnic tables and fire pits are provided. Drinking water, restrooms with flush toilets and showers, and pit toilets are available. A boat ramp, docks, dump station, fish-cleaning station, and garbage containers are also available. Food, gasoline, and coin laundry are available five miles away in the town of Rufus. Leashed pets are permitted.

Reservations, fees: Reservations are accepted at 877/444-6777 or www.recreation.gov ($10 reservation fee). RV sites are $18–20 per night, and tent sites are $12–14 per night. Some credit cards are accepted. Open April–October.

Directions: From Portland on I-84, drive east 120 miles (30 miles past The Dalles) to Exit 114, the John Day River Recreation Area. The campground is just off I-84.

Contact: Army Corps of Engineers, Portland

District, 503/808-5150, fax 503/808-4515; LePage Park, 541/739-2713.

Prineville District, 541/416-6700, fax 541/416-6798, www.blm.gov.

7.3 BEAVERTAIL

Scenic rating: 6

on the Deschutes River

Map 3.3, page 165

This isolated campground is set at an elevation of 2,900 feet along the banks of the Deschutes River, one of the classic steelhead streams in the Pacific Northwest. The camp provides fishing and rafting options. The open landscape affords canyon views. This is my favorite put-in spot for a drift boat for fishing float trips on the Deschutes. I've made the trip from Beavertail to the mouth of the Deschutes, ideal in four days, camping at BLM boat-in sites along the river and fly-fishing for steelhead. A boating pass is required to float the river. There are 12 other BLM campgrounds along upper and lower Deschutes River Road. The hardest part is getting used to the freight trains that rumble through the canyon at night.

Campsites, facilities: There are 17 sites for tents or RVs up to 30 feet long and two group sites for up to 16 people. Picnic tables, garbage bins, and fire grills are provided. No campfires are allowed June 1–October 15. Drinking water and vault toilets are available. Boat-launching facilities are nearby. Some facilities are wheelchair accessible. Leashed pets are permitted.

Reservations, fees: Reservations are not accepted. Sites are $8–12 per night, with a 14-day stay limit. Group sites are $25–35 per night. Open year-round.

Directions: From Portland, drive east on U.S. 84 to The Dalles and Highway 197. Turn south and drive to Maupin. Continue through Maupin, cross the bridge, and within a mile look for Deschutes River Road on your left. Turn left on Deschutes River Road and drive 21 miles northeast to the campground.

Contact: Bureau of Land Management,

7.4 SHADY COVE

Scenic rating: 7

on the Little North Santiam River in Willamette National Forest

Map 3.4, page 166

Shady Cove campground is on the Little North Santiam River in the recently designated Opal Creek Scenic Recreation Area. The Little North Santiam Trail runs adjacent to the campground.

Campsites, facilities: There are 12 sites for tents or RVs up to 16 feet long. Picnic tables, garbage service (summer only), fire grills, and vault toilets are available. There is no drinking water. Leashed pets are permitted.

Reservations, fees: Reservations are not accepted. Sites are $8–10 per night, $5 per night per additional vehicle. Open year-round, weather permitting.

Directions: From Salem on I-5, take Exit 253 to Highway 22. Turn east and drive 23 miles to Mehama and North Fork Road (Marion County Road). Turn left and drive 17 miles northeast to the fork. Bear right on Forest Road 2207 and continue for two miles to the campground on the right.

Contact: Willamette National Forest, Detroit Ranger District, 503/854-3366, fax 503/854-4239, www.fs.fed.us.

7.5 ELK LAKE

Scenic rating: 9

near Bull of the Woods Wilderness

Map 3.4, page 166

This remote and primitive campground (3,700 feet elevation) borders the shore of Elk Lake, where boating, fishing, and swimming can be quite good in the summer. Wildflower blooms can be beautiful in the nearby meadows. Several trails in the area provide access to the Bull of the Woods Wilderness (operated by Mount Hood National Forest) and the newly designated Opal Creek Wilderness. The campground also offers beautiful views of Battle Ax Mountain.

Campsites, facilities: There are 12 primitive tent sites. Pit toilets are available. There is no drinking water, and garbage must be packed out. Primitive boat-launching facilities are available. Leashed pets are permitted.

Reservations, fees: Reservations are not accepted. There is no fee for camping. Open June–October, weather permitting.

Directions: From Salem on I-5, take Exit 253, turn east on Highway 22, and drive 52 miles to Detroit. Turn left on Forest Road 46/Breitenbush Road and drive 4.5 miles to Forest Road 4696/Elk Lake Road. Turn left and drive less than one mile to Forest Road 4697. Turn left and drive 9.5 miles to the campground on the left. The road is extremely rough for the last five miles; high-clearance vehicles are recommended.

Contact: Willamette National Forest, Detroit Ranger District, 503/854-3366, fax 503/854-4239, www.fs.fed.us.

76 HUMBUG

Scenic rating: 9

on the Breitenbush River in
Willamette National Forest

Map 3.4, page 166

Fishing and hiking are popular at this campground along the banks of the Breitenbush River, about four miles from where it empties into Detroit Lake. The lake offers many other recreation opportunities. The Humbug Flat Trailhead is behind Sites 9 and 10, and a scenic stroll through an old-growth forest follows the Breitenbush River. The rhododendrons put on a spectacular show May–July.

Campsites, facilities: There are 22 sites for tents or RVs up to 30 feet long. Picnic tables and fire grills are provided. Garbage service (summer only), drinking water, firewood, and vault toilets are available. Leashed pets are permitted.

Reservations, fees: Reservations are not accepted. Sites are $12 per night, $5 per night per additional vehicle. Open year-round, weather permitting, with limited winter facilities.

Directions: From Salem on I-5, take Exit 253, turn east on Highway 22, and drive 52 miles to Detroit. Turn left on Forest Road 46/Breitenbush Road and drive five miles northeast to the campground on the right.

Contact: Willamette National Forest, Detroit Ranger District, 503/854-3366, fax 503/854-4239, www.fs.fed.us.

77 DETROIT LAKE STATE RECREATION AREA

Scenic rating: 7

on Detroit Lake

Map 3.4, page 166

This campground is set at 1,600 feet elevation along the shore of Detroit Lake, which is 400 feet deep, nine miles long, and has more than 32 miles of shoreline. The park offers a fishing dock and a moorage area, and a boat ramp and bathhouse are available nearby at the Mongold Day Use Area. The heavily stocked lake is crowded on the opening day of trout season in late April.

Campsites, facilities: There are 178 sites with full or partial hookups for RVs up to 60 feet long, 133 tent sites, and 82 boat slips. Drinking water, garbage bins, fire grills, and picnic tables are provided. Firewood and restrooms with flush toilets and showers are available. Recreation facilities include two playgrounds, swimming areas, horseshoe pits, basketball and volleyball courts, an amphitheater, a gift shop, and a visitors center. A camp host is on-site. Two boat docks and launching facilities are nearby. Some facilities are wheelchair accessible. Leashed pets are permitted.

Reservations, fees: Reservations are accepted at 800/452-5687 or www.oregonstateparks.org ($8 reservation fee). RV sites are $16–24 per night, tent sites are $12–19 per night, $5 per night per additional vehicle. Boating moorage is $7 per night. Some credit cards are accepted. Open mid-March–September, weather permitting.

Directions: From Salem, drive east on Highway 22 for 50 miles to the park entrance on the right (located two miles west of Detroit).

Contact: Detroit Lake State Recreation Area, 503/854-3406 or 503/854-3346, www.oregonstateparks.org.

78 PIETY ISLAND BOAT-IN

Scenic rating: 10

on Detroit Lake in Willamette National Forest

Map 3.4, page 166   BEST (

This island gets crowded and has a reputation for sometimes attracting rowdy groups. Other campgrounds along the shore have drinking water. Piety Island Trail climbs 1.5 miles to the top of the island. You'll find great vistas on this island, which sits at 1,600 feet in elevation.

Campsites, facilities: This is an island campground with 22 tent sites accessible only by boat. Picnic tables and fire grills are provided. Pit toilets are available. There is no drinking water. Boat docks, launching facilities, and rentals are nearby. Leashed pets are permitted.

Reservations, fees: Reservations are not accepted. Single sites are $10 per night; double sites are $20 per night. Open year-round, weather permitting.

Directions: From Salem, drive east on Highway 22 for 45 miles to Detroit Lake. Continue east on Highway 22 along the north side of the lake to the boat ramp (three miles west of the town of Detroit). Launch your boat and

head southeast to the island in the middle of the lake. The campground is on the east side of the island.

Contact: Willamette National Forest, Detroit Ranger District, 503/854-3366, fax 503/854-4239, www.fs.fed.us.

79 SOUTHSHORE

Scenic rating: 9

on Detroit Lake in Willamette National Forest

Map 3.4, page 166

This popular camp hugs the south shore of Detroit Lake, where fishing, swimming, and waterskiing are some of the recreation options. The Stahlman Point Trailhead is about half a mile from camp. There's a day-use area for picnicking and swimming. The views of the lake and surrounding mountains are outstanding.

Campsites, facilities: There are eight walk-in tent sites and 22 sites for tents or RVs up to 30 feet long. Fire grills, garbage service, and picnic tables are provided. Vault toilets, drinking water, and firewood are available. Boat-launching facilities are nearby at a day-use area. Some facilities are wheelchair accessible. Leashed pets are permitted.

Reservations, fees: Reservations are not accepted. Sites are $16 for a single site, $32 for double site, and $5 per night per additional vehicle. Open May–late September, with a gate preventing access during the off-season.

Directions: From Salem, drive east on Highway 22 for 52 miles to Detroit. Continue southeast on Highway 22 for 2.5 miles to Forest Road 10 (Blowout Road). Turn right and drive four miles to the campground on the right.

Contact: Willamette National Forest, Detroit Ranger District, 503/854-3366, fax 503/854-4239, www.fs.fed.us.

80 COVE CREEK

🚶 🏊 🛶 ⛴ 🚐 🏠 ♿ 🚃 ⛺

Scenic rating: 10

on Detroit Lake in Willamette National Forest

Map 3.4, page 166   BEST (

Cove Creek is a popular campground, and it gets high use in the summer. Situated in a forest, the campground is located on the south side of the lake, about one mile from both Hoover and Southshore campgrounds. Water sports are popular, and both waterskiing and personal watercraft are allowed.

Campsites, facilities: There are 63 sites for tents or RVs of any length and one group site for up to 70 people. Picnic tables and fire rings are provided. Drinking water, restrooms with flush toilets and coin showers, garbage bins, firewood, and a boat ramp are available. Some facilities are wheelchair accessible. Leashed pets are permitted.

Reservations, fees: Reservations are accepted only for the group site at 877/444-6777 or www.recreation.gov ($10 reservation fee). Single sites are $18 per night, double sites are $36 per night, $5 per night per additional vehicle. Group sites are $150 per night and require a two-night minimum stay on weekends. Open May–September, with a gate preventing access in the off-season.

Directions: From Salem, drive east on Highway 22 for 52 miles to Detroit. Continue southeast on Highway 22 for 2.5 miles to Forest Road 10 (Blowout Road). Turn right and drive three miles to the campground on the right.

Contact: Willamette National Forest, Detroit Ranger District, 503/854-3366, fax 503/854-4239, www.fs.fed.us; park information, 503/854-3251.

81 HOOVER

🚶 🏊 🛶 ⛴ 🚐 🏠 ♿ 🚃 ⛺

Scenic rating: 9

on Detroit Lake in Willamette National Forest

Map 3.4, page 166

Hoover campground is located along the eastern arm of Detroit Lake at an elevation of 1,600 feet, near the mouth of the Santiam River. The camp features a wheelchair-accessible fishing area and interpretive trail; fishing, swimming, and waterskiing are some of the recreation options. You're likely to see osprey fishing during the day, a truly special sight.

Campsites, facilities: There are 37 sites for tents or RVs up to 30 feet long. Picnic tables, garbage service, and fire grills are provided. Flush toilets and drinking water are available. Boat docks and launching facilities are nearby. Some facilities are wheelchair accessible. Leashed pets are permitted.

Reservations, fees: Reservations are not accepted. Single sites are $16 per night, double sites are $32 per night, $5 per night per additional vehicle. Open mid-May–mid-September; a gate prevents access in the off-season.

Directions: From Salem, drive east on Highway 22 for 52 miles to Detroit. Continue southeast on Highway 22 for 2.5 miles to Forest Road 10 (Blowout Road). Turn right and drive one mile to the campground on the right.

Contact: Willamette National Forest, Detroit Ranger District, 503/854-3366, fax 503/854-4239, www.fs.fed.us.

82 HOOVER GROUP CAMP

🚶 🏊 🛶 🚐 🏠 ♿ 🚃 ⛺

Scenic rating: 9

on Detroit Lake in Willamette National Forest

Map 3.4, page 166   BEST (

This is a perfect spot for a family reunion or club trip. Detroit Lake offers a myriad of activities, including boating, fishing, hiking, and swimming, just to name a few. The campground has nice, open sites and direct access to the lake.

Campsites, facilities: There is one group camp for tents or RVs up to 30 feet long, for up to 70 people and 20 vehicles. Drinking water, fire rings, and picnic tables are provided. Flush toilets, garbage bins, firewood, and a group picnic shelter are available. Boat docks, launching facilities, and rentals are nearby. Some facilities are wheelchair accessible. Leashed pets are permitted.

Reservations, fees: Reservations are accepted at 877/444-6777 or www.recreation.gov ($10 reservation fee). The site is $150 per night, with a two-night minimum for weekend reservations. Open mid-April–late September; a gate prevents access during the off-season.

Directions: From Salem, drive east on Highway 22 for 52 miles to Detroit. Continue southeast on Highway 22 for 2.5 miles to Forest Road 10 (Blowout Road). Turn right and drive 0.5 mile to the campground on the right.

Contact: Willamette National Forest, Detroit Ranger District, 503/854-3366, fax 503/854-4239, www.fs.fed.us; park information, 503/854-3251.

83 SUMMIT LAKE

Scenic rating: 6

on Summit Lake in
Mount Hood National Forest

Map 3.5, page 167

This idyllic camp is set in a remote area along the western slopes of the Cascade Range at an elevation of 4,200 feet. On the shore of little Summit Lake, the camp is primitive but a jewel. It's a perfect alternative to the more crowded camps at Timothy Lake, and you have access to all the same recreation options by driving just a short distance north. Non-motorized boats are allowed.

Campsites, facilities: There are five tent sites. Fire grills, garbage service, and picnic tables are provided. Vault toilets are available. There is no drinking water. Leashed pets are permitted.

Reservations, fees: Reservations are not accepted. Sites are $12 per night. Open mid-July–September, weather permitting.

Directions: From Portland, turn east on U.S. 26 and drive 57 miles (just past the town of Government Camp) to the junction with Highway 35. Bear southeast, staying on U.S. 26, and drive 15 miles to Forest Road 42 (Skyline Road). Turn right and drive 12 miles south to Forest Road 141 (a dirt road). Turn right and drive west two miles to the campground on the left.

Contact: Mount Hood National Forest, Zigzag Ranger District, 503/622-3191, fax 503/622-5622, www.fs.fed.us.

84 CLEATER BEND

Scenic rating: 8

near the Breitenbush River in
Willamette National Forest

Map 3.5, page 167

Creek views and pretty, shaded sites are the highlights of Cleater Bend, situated on the banks of the Breitenbush River at 2,200 feet elevation. This camp is 0.25 mile from Breitenbush and is a good option if that campground is full. Nearby recreation options include fishing access along the Breitenbush River, the South Breitenbush Gorge National Recreation Trail (three miles away), and Breitenbush Hot Springs (just over a mile away).

Campsites, facilities: There are nine sites for tents or RVs up to 24 feet long. Picnic tables and fire grills are provided. Garbage service, drinking water, vault toilets, and firewood are available. Some facilities are wheelchair accessible. Leashed pets are permitted.

Reservations, fees: Reservations are not accepted. Sites are $12 per night, $5 per night per additional vehicle. Open May–September, with a gate preventing access during the off-season.

Directions: From Salem on I-5, take Exit 253, turn east on Highway 22, and drive 50 miles to Detroit. Turn left on Forest Road 46/Breitenbush Road and drive nine miles to the campground on the right.

Contact: Willamette National Forest, Detroit Ranger District, 503/854-3366, fax 503/854-4239, www.fs.fed.us.

85 BREITENBUSH

Scenic rating: 8

on the Breitenbush River in
Willamette National Forest

Map 3.5, page 167

There is fishing access at this campground along the Breitenbush River. Nearby recreation options include the South Breitenbush Gorge National Recreation Trail, three miles away, and Breitenbush Hot Springs, just over a mile away. If this campground is crowded, try nearby Cleater Bend.

Campsites, facilities: There are 30 sites for tents or RVs up to 24 feet long (longer trailers may be difficult to park and turn). Picnic tables and fire grills are provided. Drinking water, vault toilets, garbage service, and firewood are available. Some facilities are wheelchair accessible. Leashed pets are permitted.

Reservations, fees: Reservations are not accepted. Sites are $12 per night for a single site, $24 per night for a double site, and $5 per night per additional vehicle. Open May–September; a gate prevents access during the off-season.

Directions: From Salem on I-5, take Exit 253, turn east on Highway 22, and drive 50 miles to Detroit. Turn left (north) on Forest Road 46/Breitenbush Road and drive 10 miles to the campground on the right.

Contact: Willamette National Forest, Detroit Ranger District, 503/854-3366, fax 503/854-4239, www.fs.fed.us.

86 LOWER LAKE

Scenic rating: 7

near Olallie Lake in
Mount Hood National Forest

Map 3.5, page 167

This sunny, open campground is set at an elevation of 4,600 feet, about 0.75 mile from Lower Lake, a small but deep lake that's perfect for fishing and swimming. It's also less than a mile from Olallie Lake and near a network of trails that provide access to other nearby lakes. It's advisable to obtain a U.S. Forest Service map that details the backcountry roads and trails.

Note: This camp will likely be upgraded in 2010.

Campsites, facilities: There are eight sites for tents or RVs up to 16 feet long. Picnic tables and fire grills are provided. Vault toilets and garbage service are available. There is no drinking water. Leashed pets are permitted.

Reservations, fees: Reservations are not accepted. Sites are $12 per night. Open July–October.

Directions: From Portland, drive south on U.S. 205 to the junction with Highway 24. Take the Highway 224/Estacada exit and turn left (south) onto Highway 224. Drive approximately 13 miles to Estacada. Continue south on Highway 224 and drive 27 miles in national forest (the road becomes Forest Road 46). Continue south on Forest Road 46 for 20 miles to Forest Road 4690. Turn left on Forest Road 4690 and drive southeast for 8.2 miles to Forest Road 4220. Turn right (south) and drive about 4.5 miles of rough road to the campground on the right.

Contact: Mount Hood National Forest, Clackamas River Ranger District, 503/630-6861, fax 503/630-2299, www.fs.fed.us.

87 CAMP TEN

Scenic rating: 9

on Olallie Lake in Mount Hood National Forest

Map 3.5, page 167

Here's a camp along the shore of Olallie Lake, a popular area. Camp Ten sits at an elevation of 5,000 feet, on the lake's western shore in the midst of the Olallie Lake Scenic Area, which is home to a number of pristine mountain lakes and a network of hiking trails. (See a U.S. Forest Service map for trail locations.) Boats without motors—including canoes, kayaks, and rafts—are permitted on the lake.

Campsites, facilities: There are 10 sites for tents or RVs up to 16 feet long. Picnic tables, garbage service, and fire grills are provided. Vault toilets are available. There is no drinking water. Leashed pets are permitted.

Reservations, fees: Reservations are not accepted. Sites are $12 per night. Open July–October, weather permitting.

Directions: From Portland, drive south on U.S. 205 to the junction with Highway 24. Take the Highway 224/Estacada exit and turn left (south) onto Highway 224. Drive approximately 13 miles to Estacada. Continue south on Highway 224 and drive 27 miles in national forest (the road becomes Forest Road 46). Continue south on Forest Road 46 for 20 miles to Forest Road 4690. Turn left on Forest Road 4690 and drive southeast for 8.2 miles to Forest Road 4220. Turn right (south) and drive about six miles of rough road to the campground.

Contact: Mount Hood National Forest, Clackamas River Ranger District, 503/630-6861, fax 503/630-2299, www.fs.fed.us.

88 PAUL DENNIS

Scenic rating: 10

on Olallie Lake in Mount Hood National Forest

Map 3.5, page 167   BEST (

This campground, set at an elevation of 5,000 feet, borders the north shore of Olallie Lake. From here, you can see the reflection of Mount Jefferson (10,497 feet). Boats with motors are not permitted on the lake. A trail from camp leads to Long Lake (just east of the border of the Warm Springs Indian Reservation), Monon Lake, and Nep-Te-Pa Lake. It's advisable to obtain a U.S. Forest Service map.

Campsites, facilities: There are 17 sites for tents or RVs up to 16 feet long (trailers not recommended) and three hike-in tent sites. Picnic tables, garbage service, and fire grills are provided. Pit toilets are available. There is no drinking water. A store and ice are nearby. Leashed pets are permitted.

Reservations, fees: Reservations are not accepted. Sites are $12 per night. Open July–October, weather permitting.

Directions: From Portland, drive south on U.S. 205 to the junction with Highway 24. Take the Highway 224/Estacada exit and turn left (south) onto Highway 224. Drive approximately 13 miles to Estacada. Continue south on Highway 224 and drive 27 miles in national forest (the road becomes Forest Road 46). Continue south on Forest Road 46 for 20 miles to Forest Road 4690. Turn left and drive southeast for 8.2 miles to Forest Road 4220. Turn right (south) and drive 6.2 miles to Forest Road 4220-170. Turn left and drive 0.12 mile to the campground.

Contact: Mount Hood National Forest, Clackamas River Ranger District, 503/630-6861, fax 503/630-2299, www.fs.fed.us.

89 PENINSULA

Scenic rating: 10

on Olallie Lake in Mount Hood National Forest

Map 3.5, page 167

Peninsula, the largest of several campgrounds along Olallie Lake, is set at an elevation of 5,000 feet on the south shore. An amphitheater is located near the campground, and rangers present campfire programs during the summer. Nonmotorized boats are permitted on the lake, and nearby trails lead to a number of smaller lakes in the area, such as Long Lake, Monon Lake, and Nep-Te-Pa Lake.

Campsites, facilities: There are 35 sites for tents or RVs up to 24 feet long and six walk-in tent sites. Picnic tables, garbage service, and fire grills are provided. Vault toilets are available. There is no drinking water. Leashed pets are permitted.

Reservations, fees: Reservations are not accepted. Sites are $12 per night, $6 per night per additional vehicle, and $6 per night for walk-in sites. Open July–October, weather permitting.

Directions: From Portland, drive south on U.S. 205 to the junction with Highway 24. Take the Highway 224/Estacada exit and turn left (south) onto Highway 224. Drive approximately 13 miles to Estacada. Continue south on Highway 224 and drive 27 miles in national forest (the road becomes Forest Road 46). Continue south on Forest Road 46 for 20 miles to Forest Road 4690. Turn left and drive southeast for 8.2 miles to Forest Road 4220. Turn right (south) and drive 6.5 miles of rough road to the campground on the left.

Contact: Mount Hood National Forest, Clackamas River Ranger District, 503/630-6861, fax 503/630-2299, www.fs.fed.us.

90 OLALLIE MEADOWS

Scenic rating: 8

near Olallie Lake in
Mount Hood National Forest

Map 3.5, page 167

Olallie Meadows is set at 4,500 feet elevation along a large and peaceful alpine meadow about three miles from Olallie Lake. Nonmotorized boats are allowed on Olallie Lake. The Pacific Crest Trail passes very close to the campground.

Campsites, facilities: There are seven sites for tents or RVs up to 16 feet long. Picnic tables, garbage service, and fire grills are provided. Vault toilets are available. There is no drinking water. Leashed pets are permitted.

Reservations, fees: Reservations are not accepted. Sites are $12 per night. Open July–October, weather permitting.

Directions: From Portland, drive south on U.S. 205 to the junction with Highway 24. Take the Highway 224/Estacada exit and turn left (south) onto Highway 224. Drive approximately 13 miles to Estacada. Continue south on Highway 224 and drive 27 miles in national forest (the road becomes Forest Road 46). Continue south on Forest Road 46 for 20 miles to Forest Road 4690. Turn left and drive southeast for 8.2 miles to Forest Road 4220. Turn right (south) and drive 1.5 miles to the campground on the left.

Contact: Mount Hood National Forest, Clackamas River Ranger District, 503/630-6861, fax 503/630-2299, www.fs.fed.us.

91 KAH-NEE-TA RESORT

Scenic rating: 7

on the Warm Springs Indian Reservation

Map 3.5, page 167

This resort features a stellar-rated, full-concept spa, with the bonus of a nearby casino. It is also the only public camp on the east side of the Warm Springs Indian Reservation; there are no other camps within 30 miles. The Warm Springs River runs nearby. Recreation options in the area include an 18-hole golf course, miniature golf, biking and hiking trails, a riding stable, and tennis courts.

Campsites, facilities: There are 55 pull-through sites with full hookups for RVs of any length. A motel and cottage are also available. Cable TV, restrooms with flush toilets and coin showers, propane gas, a dump station, concession stand, coin laundry, ice, a play-ground, a spa, mineral baths, and an Olympic-sized, spring-fed swimming pool with a 140-foot water slide are available. Some facilities are wheelchair accessible. Leashed pets are permitted, but some areas are restricted.

Reservations, fees: Reservations are accepted at 800/554-4786. Sites are $45 per night for three people. There is a two-night minimum on weekends, and a three-night minimum on holiday weekends. Some credit cards are accepted. Open year-round.

Directions: From Portland, turn east on U.S. 26 and drive about 105 miles to Warm Springs and Agency Hot Springs Road on the left. Turn left and drive 11 miles northeast to Kah-Nee-Ta and the resort on the right.

Contact: Kah-Nee-Ta Resort, 541/553-1112, http://kahneetaresort.com.

92 WHISPERING FALLS
🥾 🏊 🏕 🚐 ⛺

Scenic rating: 10

on the North Santiam River near Detroit Lake in Willamette National Forest

Map 3.5, page 167

This popular campground sits on the banks of the North Santiam River, where you can fish. If the campsites at Detroit Lake are crowded, this camp provides a more secluded option, and it's only about a 10-minute drive from the lake. Ospreys sometimes nest near the campground.

Campsites, facilities: There are 16 sites for tents or RVs up to 30 feet long. Picnic tables, garbage

service, and fire grills are provided. Drinking water and flush toilets are available. Bring your own firewood. Leashed pets are permitted.

Reservations, fees: Reservations are not accepted. Sites are $12 per night, $5 per night per additional vehicle. Open late April–mid-September; a gate prevents access in the off-season.

Directions: From Salem, drive east on Highway 22 for 50 miles to Detroit. Continue east on Highway 22 for eight miles to the campground on the right.

Contact: Willamette National Forest, Detroit Ranger District, 503/854-3366, fax 503/854-4239, www.fs.fed.us.

93 RIVERSIDE
🏊 🏕 🚐 ⛺

Scenic rating: 7

on the North Santiam River in Willamette National Forest

Map 3.5, page 167

This campground is set at an elevation of 2,400 feet along the banks of the North Santiam River, where the fishing can be good. A point of interest, the Marion Forks Fish Hatchery and interpretive site lies just 2.5 miles south. Other day-trip options include the Mount Jefferson Wilderness, directly to the east in Willamette National Forest, and Minto Mountain Trail, three miles east.

Campsites, facilities: There are 37 sites for tents or RVs up to 24 feet long. Picnic tables and fire grills are provided. Drinking water and vault toilets are available. Leashed pets are permitted.

Reservations, fees: Reservations are not accepted. Sites are $12 per night, $5 per night per additional vehicle. Open late May–September; a gate prevents access during the off-season.

Directions: From Salem, drive east on Highway 22 for 50 miles to Detroit. Continue southeast on Highway 22 for 14 miles to the campground on the right.

Contact: Willamette National Forest, Detroit

Ranger District, 503/854-3366, fax 503/854-4239, www.fs.fed.us.

94 MARION FORKS

Scenic rating: 8

on the Santiam River in
Willamette National Forest

Map 3.5, page 167

Situated along Marion Creek at 2,500 feet in elevation, this campground is adjacent to the Marion Forks Fish Hatchery. A U.S. Forest Service guard station and a restaurant are across Highway 22. The area boasts some quality hiking trails; the nearest is Independence Rock Trail, 0.25 mile north of the campground.

Campsites, facilities: There are 15 sites for tents or RVs up to 24 feet long. Picnic tables, fire grills, and garbage containers are provided. Vault toilets are available. There is no drinking water. Leashed pets are permitted.

Reservations, fees: Reservations are not accepted. Sites are $10 per night, $5 per night per additional vehicle. Open year-round, weather permitting, with no winter services.

Directions: From Salem, drive east on Highway 22 for 50 miles to Detroit. Continue southeast on Highway 22 for 16 miles to the campground on the left.

Contact: Willamette National Forest, Detroit Ranger District, 503/854-3366, fax 503/854-4239, www.fs.fed.us.

95 BIG MEADOWS HORSE CAMP

Scenic rating: 10

near Mount Jefferson Wilderness in
Willamette National Forest

Map 3.5, page 167

Built by the U.S. Forest Service with the support of a horse club, this camp is used heavily by equestrians riding into the Big Meadows area and the adjacent Mount Jefferson Wilderness. If you're not a horse lover, you may want to stick with Riverside or Marion Forks.

Campsites, facilities: There are nine sites for tents or RVs up to 36 feet long. Picnic tables, garbage service, fire grills, and enclosed four-horse corrals are provided at each site. Drinking water, vault toilets, firewood, and stock water troughs are available. Some facilities are wheelchair accessible. Leashed pets are permitted.

Reservations, fees: Reservations are not accepted. Sites are $14 per night, $5 per night per additional vehicle. Open June–October, weather permitting.

Directions: From Salem, drive east on Highway 22 for 50 miles to Detroit. Continue southeast on Highway 22 for 27 miles to Big Meadows Road (Forest Road 2267). Turn left and drive one mile to Forest Road 2257. Turn left and drive 0.5 mile to the campground on the left.

Contact: Willamette National Forest, Detroit Ranger District, 503/854-3366, fax 503/854-4239, www.fs.fed.us.

96 SHEEP SPRINGS HORSE CAMP

Scenic rating: 7

near the Mount Jefferson Wilderness in
Deschutes National Forest

Map 3.5, page 167

This well-shaded equestrian camp with privacy screening between sites is near the trailhead for the Metolius-Windigo Horse Trail, which heads northeast into the Mount Jefferson Wilderness and south to Black Butte. Contact the U.S. Forest Service for details and maps of the backcountry. The camp is set at an elevation of 3,200 feet.

Campsites, facilities: There are 11 sites for tents or RVs up to 45 feet long. Fire grills are provided. Drinking water, vault toilets, garbage bins, and corrals and box stalls for horses are available.

Reservations, fees: Reservations are accepted at 877/444-6777 or www.recreation.gov ($10 reservation fee). Sites are $14–16 per night, $8 per night per additional vehicle. Open early May–mid-September, weather permitting.

Directions: From Albany, drive east on U.S. 20 for 87 miles to the sign for Jack Lake (located one mile east of Suttle Lake) and Suttle-Sherman Road. Turn left on Forest Road 12 and drive eight miles to Forest Road 1260. Turn left and drive 1.5 miles to Forest Road 1260-200. Turn right and drive 1.5 miles to the campground on the right.

Contact: Deschutes National Forest, Sisters Ranger District, 541/549-7700, fax 541/549-7746; Hoodoo District, 541/822-3799, www.fs.fed.us.

97 JACK CREEK

Scenic rating: 5

near Mount Jefferson Wilderness in Deschutes National Forest

Map 3.5, page 167

A more primitive alternative to the other camps in the area, this campground sits along the banks of Jack Creek in an open setting among ponderosa pine. The elevation is 3,100 feet. To protect the bull trout habitat, no fishing is permitted here.

Campsites, facilities: There are 20 sites for tents or RVs up to 40 feet long. Picnic tables and fire grills are provided. Vault toilets and garbage bins are available. There is no drinking water. Leashed pets are permitted.

Reservations, fees: Reservations are not accepted. Sites are $12 per night, $6 per night per additional vehicle. Open mid-April–mid-October.

Directions: From Albany, drive east on U.S. 20 for 87 miles to the sign for Jack Lake (located one mile east of Suttle Lake) and Suttle-Sherman Road. Turn left on Forest Road 12 and

drive five miles to Forest Road 1230. Turn left and drive 0.75 mile to Forest Road 1232. Turn left and drive 0.25 mile to the campground on the left.

Contact: Deschutes National Forest, Sisters Ranger District, 541/549-7700, fax 541/549-7746, www.fs.fed.us.

98 PELTON

Scenic rating: 8

on Lake Simtustus in Deschutes National Forest

Map 3.5, page 167   BEST (

This campground claims 0.5 mile of shoreline along the north side of Lake Simtustus. Campsites here are shaded with juniper in an area of rolling hills and sagebrush. One section of the lake is accessible for water skis and personal watercraft. Simtustus is a trophy fishing lake for kokanee and brown, bull, and rainbow trout. Just north of the park is the Pelton Wildlife Overlook, where you can view a variety of waterfowl, such as great blue herons, ducks, geese, and shorebirds, as well as eagles and other raptors. Cove Palisades State Park, about 15 miles south, provides additional recreational opportunities.

Campsites, facilities: There are 69 sites, some with partial hookups, for tents or RVs up to 56 feet long, three group sites for up to 12–35 people, and 10 yomes (which are a cross between a yurt and a dome). Drinking water, picnic tables, garbage service, and fire grills are provided. Restrooms with flush toilets and showers, a restaurant, snack bar, general store, ice, fishing supplies, gasoline, and a picnic shelter are available. Also, a full-service marina with boat rentals, marine fuel, a boat launch, boat dock, fishing pier, moorage, swimming beach, volleyball courts, horseshoe pits, and a playground are available. Some facilities are wheelchair accessible. Leashed pets are permitted, and a dog run area is available.

Reservations, fees: Reservations are accepted at 541/475-0517 or www.portlandgeneral. com. Sites are $16–21 per night; the group site is $42–65 per night; yomes are $25 per night. Some credit cards are accepted. Open mid-April–September.

Directions: From Portland, drive south on U.S. 26 for 108 miles to the town of Warm Springs. Continue south two miles to Pelton Dam Road. Turn right and drive three miles to the campground on the right.

Contact: Portland General Electric, 503/464-8515 or 541/475-0516 (store and marina), fax 503/464-2944, www.portlandgeneral.com/parks; campground, 541/475-0517.

99 PERRY SOUTH

🏊 🎣 🛶 🏕️ ♿ 🚐 ⛺

Scenic rating: 6

on Lake Billy Chinook in
Deschutes National Forest

Map 3.5, page 167

Perry South campground is located near the shore of the Metolius arm of Lake Billy Chinook. The lake borders the Warm Springs Indian Reservation and can get very crowded and noisy, as it attracts powerboat/water-ski enthusiasts. Recreation options include waterskiing and fishing for bass and panfish, and one of Oregon's nicest golf courses is nearby.

Campsites, facilities: There are 63 sites for tents or RVs up to 95 feet long. Picnic tables, garbage service, and fire grills are provided. Drinking water, vault toilets, firewood, a fish-cleaning station, boat docks, and launching facilities are available. A camp host is on-site. Some facilities are wheelchair accessible. Leashed pets are permitted.

Reservations, fees: Reservations are accepted at 877/444-6777 or www.recreation.gov ($10 reservation fee). Sites are $16–18 per night, $8 per night per additional vehicle. Open May–September, weather permitting.

Directions: From Bend, drive north on U.S. 97 to Redmond, then continue north for 15 miles to the Culver Highway. Take the Culver Highway north to Culver, and continue two miles to Gem Lane. Turn left and drive two miles to Frazier Drive. Turn left and drive a short distance to Peck Road. Turn right and drive through Cove Palisades State Park to Jordan Road at the shore of Lake Billy Chinook. Turn left on Jordan Road and drive about 10 miles (over the bridge) to County Road 64. Continue (bearing left) and drive about eight miles to the campground entrance on the left (on the upper end of the Metolius Fork of Lake Billy Chinook).

Contact: Deschutes National Forest, Sisters Ranger District, 541/549-7700, fax 541/549-7746, www.fs.fed.us.

100 MONTY

🚶 🎣 🏕️ 🚐 ⛺

Scenic rating: 5

on the Metolius River in
Deschutes National Forest

Map 3.5, page 167

Remote Monty campground is set at 2,000 feet elevation and gets light use. Trout fishing can be good along the banks of the Metolius River, near where it empties into Lake Billy Chinook. Warm Springs Indian Reservation is across the river.

Campsites, facilities: There are 20 sites for tents or RVs up to 20 feet long. Picnic tables, garbage service, and fire grills are provided. Firewood and pit toilets are available. There is no drinking water. Boat docks and launching facilities are nearby at Perry South. Leashed pets are permitted.

Reservations, fees: Reservations are not accepted. Sites are $14 per night, $7 per night per additional vehicle. Open June–mid-September, weather permitting.

Directions: From Bend, drive north on U.S. 97 to Redmond and continue north for 15 miles to the Culver Highway. Take the Culver Highway north to Culver and continue two miles to Gem Lane. Turn left and drive two miles to Frazier Drive. Turn left and drive a short distance to Peck Road. Turn right and drive through Cove Palisades State Park to Jordan Road at the shore of Lake Billy Chinook. Turn left on Jordan Road and drive about 10 miles (over the bridge) to County Road 64. Turn left and drive about 13 miles to the campground entrance (on the Metolius River above the headwaters of Lake Billy Chinook). The last five miles are very rough.

Contact: Deschutes National Forest, Sisters Ranger District, 541/549-7700, fax 541/549-7746, www.fs.fed.us.

101 COVE PALISADES STATE PARK

Scenic rating: 7

on Lake Billy Chinook

Map 3.5, page 167

This park is a mile away from the shore of Lake Billy Chinook, where some lakeshore cabins are available. Here in Oregon's high-desert region, summers are warm and sunny with fairly mild but cold winters. Lofty cliffs surround the lake, and about 10 miles of hiking trails crisscross the area. Two popular special events are held here annually: Lake Billy Chinook Day in September and the Eagle Watch in February.

Campsites, facilities: There are two campgrounds: Crooked River Campground offers 91 sites with partial hookups for tents or RVs and three deluxe cabins; Deschutes Campground has 92 tent sites, 82 sites with full hookups for RVs up to 60 feet long, and three group tent areas for up to 25 people each. Picnic tables and fire grills are provided. Drinking water, garbage bins, restrooms with flush toilets and showers, a dump station, firewood, a convenience store, amphitheater, horseshoe pit, playground, and ice are available. Boat

docks, launching facilities, a marina, boat rentals, fish-cleaning station, and a restaurant are nearby. Some facilities are wheelchair accessible. Leashed pets are permitted, and there is a designated pet exercise area.

Reservations, fees: Reservations are accepted at 800/452-5687 or www.oregonstateparks.org ($8 reservation fee). RV sites are $17–26 per night, tent sites are $13–20 per night, cabins are $48–80 per night, the group areas are $43–75 per night, $5 per night per additional vehicle. Some credit cards are accepted. Crooked River Campground is open year-round; Deschutes Campground is open May–mid-September.

Directions: From Bend, drive north on U.S. 97 for 13 miles to Redmond and continue north for 15 miles to the Culver Highway. Take the Culver Highway north to Culver and continue two miles to Gem Lane. Turn left and drive two miles to Frazier Drive. Turn left and drive a short distance to Peck Road. Turn right and drive to the park entrance.

Contact: Cove Palisades State Park, 541/546-3412 or 800/551-6949, www.oregonstateparks.org.

102 KOA MADRAS/CULVER

Scenic rating: 6

near Lake Billy Chinook

Map 3.5, page 167

This KOA has a relaxing atmosphere, with some mountain views. It is set about three miles from Lake Billy Chinook, a steep-sided reservoir formed where the Crooked River, Deschutes River, Metolius River, and Squaw Creek all merge. Like much of the country east of the Cascades, this is a high-desert area.

Campsites, facilities: There are 22 tent sites and 58 pull-through sites with full or partial hookups for RVs of any length; most sites are pull-through. There are also three cabins. Drinking water, fire pits, and picnic tables are provided. Restrooms with flush toilets and showers, propane gas, a dump station, firewood, a convenience store, coin laundry, ice, and a playground are available. Recreational activities include a recreation hall, seasonal heated pool, bicycle rentals, volleyball, horseshoe pits, and tetherball. Boat docks and launching facilities are nearby. Leashed pets are permitted.

Reservations, fees: Reservations are accepted at 800/562-1992. Sites are $21–30 per night, $2–4 per person per night for more than two people. Some credit cards are accepted. Open year-round.

Directions: From Madras, drive south on U.S. 97 for nine miles to Jericho Lane. Turn left (east) and drive 0.5 mile to the campground on the right.

Contact: KOA Madras/Culver, 541/546-3046, fax 541/546-7972, www.koa.com.

NORTHEASTERN OREGON

© LEAH McDANIEL/123rf.com

BEST CAMPGROUNDS

◖ Most Scenic
Anthony Lakes, page 252.

It might be difficult to believe that there are many places left in America that are little known and little traveled. Yet that is how it is in northeastern Oregon. Even longtime residents often overlook this area of Oregon (the same is true with the southeastern portion of the state, detailed in Chapter 6). With its high desert abutting craggy Blue Mountains, it just doesn't look like the archetypal Oregon.

In this corner of the state, you'll find Wallowa-Whitman National Forest and little-known sections of Malheur, Ochoco, and Umatilla National Forests. The Hells Canyon National Recreation Area, Idaho, and the Snake River border this region to the east. My favorite destinations are the

Wallowa Mountains and the Eagle Cap Wilderness, a wildlife paradise with bears, bighorn sheep, deer, elk, and mountain lions.

This region covers a huge swatch of land, most of it explored by few. But those few have learned to love it for its unique qualities. Among the highlights are the John Day River and its headwaters, the Strawberry Mountain Wilderness in Malheur National Forest, and various sections of the linked John Day Fossil Beds National Monument. One of the prettiest spots in northeastern Oregon is Wallowa Lake State Park, where 9,000-foot snowcapped mountains surround a pristine lake on three sides.

NORTHEASTERN OREGON

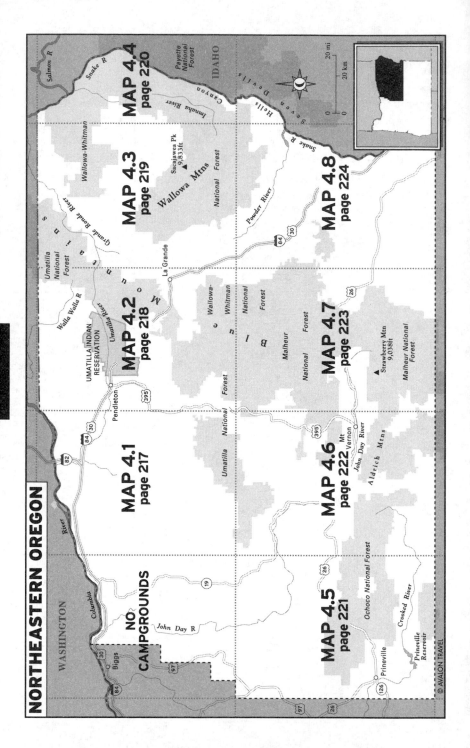

MAP 4.1 page 217

MAP 4.2 page 218

MAP 4.3 page 219

MAP 4.4 page 220

MAP 4.5 page 221

MAP 4.6 page 222

MAP 4.7 page 223

MAP 4.8 page 224

WASHINGTON

IDAHO

Payette National Forest

Salmon R

Snake R

Imnaha River

Hells Canyon

Seven Devils

Snake R

Wallowa-Whitman

Sacajawea Pk 9,833ft

Wallowa Mtns

National Forest

Grande Ronde River

Umatilla National Forest

Walla Walla R

Umatilla River

UMATILLA INDIAN RESERVATION

La Grande

Wallowa-Whitman National Forest

Pendleton

Powder River

Blue Mountains

Malheur National Forest

Strawberry Mtn 9,038ft

Malheur National Forest

Umatilla National Forest

Mt Vernon

John Day River

Aldrich Mtns

Columbia River

Biggs

NO CAMPGROUNDS

John Day R

Ochoco National Forest

Prineville

Prineville Reservoir

Crooked River

20 mi
20 km

© AVALON TRAVEL

Map 4.1

Campgrounds 1-8
Pages 225-228

Map 4.2

Campgrounds 9-25
Pages 228-235

Map 4.3

Campgrounds 26-41
Pages 235-241

Map 4.4

Campgrounds 42-45
Pages 241-243

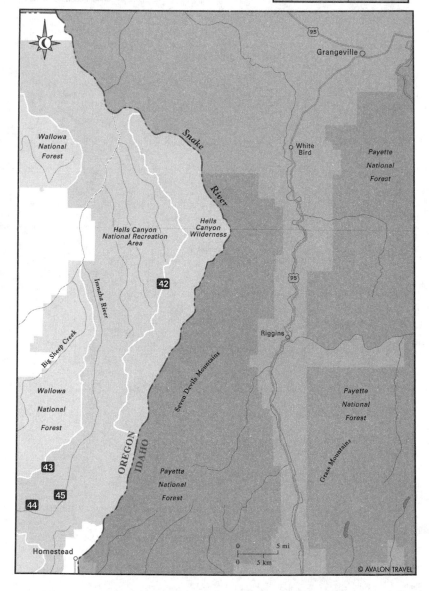

Map 4.5

Campgrounds 46-59
Pages 243-248

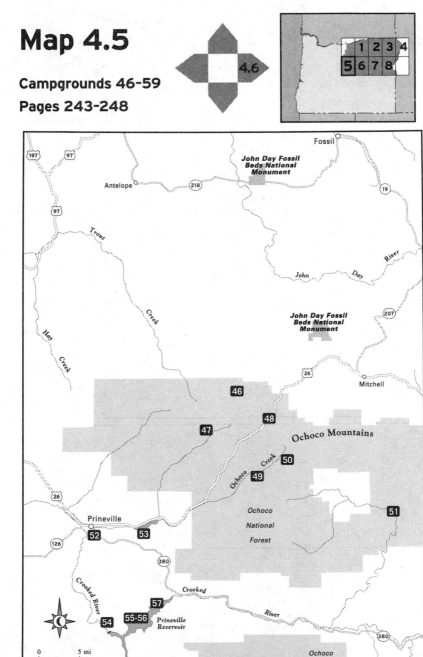

Map 4.6

Campgrounds 60-66
Pages 248-251

Map 4.7

Campgrounds 67-100
Pages 251-264

Map 4.8

Campgrounds 101-108

Pages 265-268

◻1 BOARDMAN MARINA AND RV PARK

🚲 🌊 ⛱ 🚤 🐕 🚐 ⛺

Scenic rating: 7

on the Columbia River

Map 4.1, page 217

This public campground is set on the Columbia River among linden, maple, and sycamore trees. Some sites are located along the riverbank. In addition to fishing for bass, crappie, and walleye, nearby recreation options include a marina and golf course (five miles away).

Campsites, facilities: There are four tent sites and 63 sites for tents or RVs of any length; most sites have full hookups, some are pull-through. Drinking water, picnic tables, and fire pits are provided. Restrooms with flush toilets and showers, fire pits, a dump station, garbage bins, coin laundry, a day-use area with picnic shelters, a pay phone, Wi-Fi, seasonal firewood and ice for sale, and a boat dock and launch are available. Recreational facilities include a basketball court, horseshoe pits, sand volleyball, and a hiking/biking path along the river. A boat marina and grocery store are available within one mile. Leashed pets are permitted.

Reservations, fees: Reservations are accepted at 888/481-7217. Tent sites are $15.90 per night; RV sites are $26.50 per night. Some credit cards are accepted. Discounts are sometimes available. Open year-round, with limited winter facilities.

Directions: From Portland on I-84 eastbound, drive 164 miles to Boardman and Exit 164. Take that exit and turn left (north) on Main Street. Drive 0.25 mile over the railroad bridge, bear left, and continue 0.2 mile to the Y intersection and the park on the right.

Contact: Boardman Marina Park, Boardman Park and Recreation District, 541/481-7217, fax 541/481-2828, www.boardmanmarina-park.com.

◻2 HAT ROCK CAMPGROUND

🚶 🚲 ⛱ 🏊 🚤 🚣 🐕 🦽 🚐 ⛺

Scenic rating: 7

near the Columbia River

Map 4.1, page 217

Hat Rock State Park is a day-use area with a boat launch along the banks of the Columbia River. The campground itself is very pretty, with lots of trees, and offers close access to the river and fishing.

Campsites, facilities: There are eight tent sites and 60 sites with full or partial hookups for RVs of any length. Drinking water and picnic tables are provided. Fire pits are provided at some sites. Restrooms with flush toilets and showers, a dump station, convenience store, café, coin laundry, seasonal swimming pool, and ice are available. Boat docks and launching facilities are nearby. Some facilities are wheelchair accessible. Leashed pets are permitted.

Reservations, fees: Reservations are accepted at 541/567-4188 or 541/567-0917. Sites are $18–22 per night, $2 per person per night for more than two people. Some credit cards are accepted. Open year-round.

Directions: From Portland, drive east on U.S. 84 for roughly 170 miles past Boardman to the junction of U.S. 84 and U.S. 730. Turn northeast on U.S. 730 and drive 18 miles to the junction with I-82. Continue east on U.S. 730 for seven miles to the state park access road. Turn left (north) and drive 0.5 mile to the park on the left.

Contact: Hat Rock Campground, 541/567-4188 or 541/567-0917 (Hat Rock Store).

◻3 FORT HENRIETTA RV PARK

🚶 🚲 ⛱ ⚓ 🐕 🦽 🚐 ⛺

Scenic rating: 7

on the Umatilla River

Map 4.1, page 217

This park, located in the historic community of Echo, sits along the Umatilla River.

It provides a quiet, pleasant layover spot for travelers cruising I-84. The river has some good trout fishing.

Campsites, facilities: There are seven sites with full or partial hookups for RVs of any length, two pull-through sites with partial hookups, and an area for dispersed tent camping. Picnic tables are provided, and cable TV is available at some sites. Drinking water, restrooms with showers, and a dump station are available. The camp is within walking distance of two restaurants. Some facilities are wheelchair accessible. Leashed pets are permitted.

Reservations, fees: Reservations available at 541/571-3597. Sites are $16–19 per night, $2 per person per night for more than two people. Open year-round.

Directions: From Pendleton, drive west on I-84 to Exit 188 and the Echo Highway. Take the exit, turn left (southeast), and drive one mile; cross the railroad tracks and continue 0.5 mile to Dupont Street. Turn right (south) and drive 0.3 mile to Main Street. Turn left (west) and drive one block to the park on the left.

Contact: Echo City Hall, 541/571-3597, fax 541/376-8218.

4 CUTSFORTH PARK
🏃 🚴 ♿ 🐕 🛶 👣 ♿ 🚐 ⛺

Scenic rating: 8

on Willow Creek
Map 4.1, page 217

Cutsforth is a secluded and private county park set beside a small, wheelchair-accessible pond in a quiet, wooded area. Unfortunately, the pond was closed to fishing in 2009 and it is unknown if it will reopen. In winter, the park serves as a staging area for snowmobilers, and in spring mushroom hunting is an attraction.

Campsites, facilities: There are 52 sites, most with full or partial hookups for tents or RVs up to 36 feet long. Three of the campsites have horse pens available for rent. A large building

with kitchen facilities is available for rent by groups. Picnic tables and fire rings are provided. Restrooms with coin showers, a dump station, horseshoe pits, firewood, ice, and a playground are available. Supplies are available in Heppner (22 miles away). Some facilities are wheelchair accessible. Leashed pets are permitted.

Reservations, fees: Reservations are accepted at 541/989-8214. Sites are $10–15 per night, $2 per night per additional vehicle, and $3 per night per horse. Weekly rates are available. Open mid-May–November, weather permitting.

Directions: From Pendleton on I-84, drive west for 27 miles to Exit 182 and Highway 207 (Heppner Highway). Turn south and drive 32 miles to Lexington and Highway 74. Turn left (southeast) on Highway 74 (becomes Highway 207) and drive 10 miles to Heppner. Continue south on Highway 207 for 0.5 mile to Willow Creek Road. Turn left on Willow Creek Road and drive 23 miles to the park.

Contact: Morrow County Public Works, 541/989-8214, fax 541/989-8352, www.morrowcountyparks.org.

5 ANSON WRIGHT MEMORIAL PARK
🏃 🚴 ♿ 🐕 🛶 👣 ♿ 🚐 ⛺

Scenic rating: 7

on Rock Creek
Map 4.1, page 217

Set among wooded hills along a small stream, this county park offers visitors prime trout fishing in several stocked ponds, as well as hiking opportunities. One of the fishing ponds is wheelchair accessible. Attractions in the area include Emigrant Springs State Park, Hardman Ghost Town (10 miles away), and the Pendleton Mills. There's also a nearby opal mine.

Campsites, facilities: There are 44 sites for tents or RVs up to 42 feet long and one cabin. Some sites have full hookups and/or are pull-through. Picnic tables and fire rings are provided. Restrooms with coin showers, a picnic area, dump station, firewood, ice, and a playground are provided. Some facilities are wheelchair accessible. Leashed pets are permitted.

Reservations, fees: Reservations are accepted at 541/989-8214. Sites are $10–15 per night, $2 per night per additional vehicle. Open mid-May–mid-November, weather permitting.

Directions: From Pendleton, drive west on I-84 for 27 miles to Exit 182 and Highway 207 (Heppner Highway). Turn south and drive 32 miles to Lexington and Highway 74. Turn left (south) on Highway 74 (becomes Highway 20) and drive 10 miles to Heppner. Continue south on Highway 207 for 11 miles to Ruggs and a fork. Bear left at the fork (still Highway 207) and drive 12 miles to the park on the right.

Contact: Morrow County Public Works, 541/989-8214, fax 541/989-8352, www.morrowcountyparks.org.

6 OHV PARK

Scenic rating: 5

in Morrow County Park

Map 4.1, page 217

This 6,200-acre park is very popular. It is designed primarily for OHV use and has more than 150 miles of trails specifically for off-highway vehicles. There is a day-use area, and the campground itself is wooded. Campers are allowed to use the showers at Anson Wright campground, 10 miles away.

Campsites, facilities: There are 67 sites for tents or RVs up to 42 feet long, three group sites, and six cabins. Picnic tables and fire rings are provided at some sites. Drinking water, portable toilets, dump station, firewood, coin wash rack, helmet rental, propane, a seasonal snack bar, and a day-use area are available. Some facilities are wheelchair accessible. Leashed pets are permitted.

Reservations, fees: Reservations accepted at 541/989-8214. Sites are $10–15 per night; it's $35 per night for the group site, and $2 per night per additional vehicle. Open year-round, weather permitting; call ahead December–February.

Directions: From Pendleton, drive west on I-84 for 27 miles to Exit 182 and Highway 207 (Heppner Highway). Turn south and drive 32 miles to Lexington and Highway 74. Turn left (south) on Highway 74 (becomes Highway 20) and drive 10 miles to Heppner. Continue south on Highway 207 for 11 miles to Ruggs and a fork. Bear left at the fork (still Highway 207) and drive 22 miles to the park on the right.

Contact: Morrow County Public Works, 541/989-8214, fax 541/989-8352, www.morrowcountyparks.org

7 PENLAND LAKE

Scenic rating: 10

near Penland Lake in the
Umatilla National Forest

Map 4.1, page 217　　　　　　　**BEST (**

This campground (4,950 feet elevation) has partial tree cover, so there are many open spaces. The lake is small, and electric-motor boats are allowed. The fishing can be good at times, with rainbow trout and bluegill the primary fish species. Hiking and bicycling are popular on the nearby trails. The wildlife viewing can be outstanding; species include bear, deer, and elk, as well as grouse and other birds.

Campsites, facilities: There are eight sites for tents or RVs up to 50 feet long. Picnic tables and fire rings are provided. Vault toilets are available. There is no drinking water. Garbage must be packed out. A boat ramp is nearby. Leashed pets are permitted.

Reservations, fees: Reservations are not accepted. There is no fee. Open May–October, weather permitting. A 14-day stay limit is enforced.

Directions: From Heppner, drive south on Highway 207 to Willow Creek Road (Forest

Road 54/County Road 678). Turn left (east) and drive 23 miles to Forest Road 21. Turn right (gravel road) and drive three miles to Forest Road 2103. Turn left and drive two miles to the lake and campground.

Contact: Umatilla National Forest, Heppner Ranger District, 541/676-9187, fax 541/676-2105, www.fs.fed.us.

8 DIVIDE WELLS

Scenic rating: 5

in Umatilla National Forest

Map 4.1, page 217

Divide Wells is a primitive campground, but it is busy in the summer, and even occasionally used for reunions. Set at 4,700 feet elevation, it can serve as a good base camp for a hunting trip. Mule deer and Rocky Mountain elk can be spotted in the surrounding ponderosa pine and fir forest. Potamus Point Scenic Overlook, offering a spectacular view of the John Day River drainage, is 11 miles south of the camp on Forest Road 5316 and provides a good opportunity to see bighorn sheep.

Campsites, facilities: There are eight sites for tents or RVs up to 20 feet long and three group sites. A vault toilet is provided. There is no drinking water, and garbage must be packed out. Leashed pets are permitted.

Reservations, fees: Reservations are not accepted. Sites are $8 per night, $5 per night per additional vehicle. Open late May–November, weather permitting. A 14-day stay limit is enforced.

Directions: From Pendleton, drive south on U.S. 395 for 48 miles to Ukiah and Highway 244. Turn right (the road becomes Forest Road 53) and drive west on Forest Road 53 for about 14 miles to Forest Road 5327. Turn left (south) and drive seven miles to the campground on the right. A U.S. Forest Service map is recommended.

Contact: Umatilla National Forest, North Fork John Day Ranger District, 541/427-3231, fax 541/427-3018, www.fs.fed.us.

9 WOODWARD

Scenic rating: 7

near Langdon Lake in Umatilla National Forest

Map 4.2, page 218

Nestled among the trees at an elevation of 4,950 feet, this popular campground has a view of Langdon Lake (though campers do not have access to the private lake). A flat trail encircles the campground, and there is some privacy screening between the sites.

Campsites, facilities: There are 18 sites for tents or RVs up to 28 feet long. Picnic tables, garbage bins, fire grills, and vault toilets are provided. There is no drinking water. Leashed pets are permitted.

Reservations, fees: Reservations are not accepted. Sites are $12 per night. Open late June–September, weather permitting. A 14-day stay limit is enforced.

Directions: From Pendleton on I-84, turn north on Highway 11 and drive approximately 27 miles to Weston and Highway 204. Turn right (southeast) on Highway 204 and drive 17 miles to the campground on the right (near Langdon Lake).

Contact: Umatilla National Forest, Walla Walla Ranger District, 509/522-6290, fax 509/522-6000, www.fs.fed.us.

10 TARGET MEADOWS

Scenic rating: 6

near the south fork of the Walla Walla River in Umatilla National Forest

Map 4.2, page 218

This quiet campground with shady sites and a sunny meadow is situated at 4,800 feet elevation. The camp is adjacent to the Burnt Cabin Trailhead, which leads to the south fork of the Walla Walla River Trail and an old military site.

Campsites, facilities: There are 16 sites for tents or RVs up to 28 feet long. Picnic tables and fire grills are provided. Garbage bins and vault toilets are available. There is no drinking water. Leashed pets are permitted.

Reservations, fees: Reservations are not accepted. Sites are $12 per night. Open late June–mid-November, weather permitting. A 14-day stay limit is enforced.

Directions: From Pendleton, drive north on Highway 11 for 16 miles to Highway 204 near Weston. Turn right (southeast) on Highway 204 and drive 17.5 miles to Forest Road 64. Turn left and drive 0.5 mile to Forest Road 6401. Turn left (north) and drive two miles to Road 6401-050. Turn right (north) and drive 0.5 mile to the camp.

Contact: Umatilla National Forest, Walla Walla Ranger District, 509/522-6290, fax 509/522-6000, www.fs.fed.us.

11 UMATILLA FORKS

Scenic rating: 3

along the Umatilla River in
Umatilla National Forest

Map 4.2, page 218

Umatilla Forks campground lies in a canyon between the South and North Forks of the Umatilla River at an elevation of 2,400 feet. Expect warm temperatures in mid- to late summer; tree cover provides some relief. Fishing on the Umatilla River is catch-and-release only, and hiking is possible in the North Fork Umatilla Wilderness.

Campsites, facilities: There are 15 sites for tents or RVs up to 28 feet long. Picnic tables and fire grills are provided. Vault toilets are available. There is no drinking water. Garbage must be packed out. Leashed pets are permitted.

Reservations, fees: Reservations are not accepted. Sites are $10 per night. Open May–October, weather permitting. A 14-day stay limit is enforced.

Directions: From Pendleton, drive north on Highway 11 for about 25 miles to Athena and Pambrun Road. Turn right on Pambrun

Road and drive five miles to Spring Hollow Road. Turn left on Spring Hollow Road (it becomes Thorn Hollow Road) and drive about 6.5 miles to Bingham Road (River Road). Turn left on Bingham Road (River Road), cross the railroad tracks, and follow signs for about five miles to Gibbon. Cross the railroad tracks at Gibbon and continue on Bingham Road (it becomes Forest Road 32) about 11 miles to the campground on the right.

Contact: Umatilla National Forest, Walla Walla Ranger District, 509/522-6290, fax 509/522-6000, www.fs.fed.us.

12 WOODLAND

Scenic rating: 4

in Umatilla National Forest

Map 4.2, page 218

Primitive Woodland campground is set at 5,200 feet elevation with easy highway access—and related road noise. The camp has both shaded and sunny sites and can be a perfect spot for I-84 cruisers looking for a short detour. During fall, the area is popular with hunters; hikers and mountain bikers will enjoy the area the rest of the year.

Campsites, facilities: There are seven sites for tents or RVs up to 28 feet long. Picnic tables, fire grills, and vault toilets are provided. There is no drinking water. Garbage must be packed out. Leashed pets are permitted.

Reservations, fees: Reservations are not accepted. Sites are $8 per night. Open mid-June–mid-November, weather permitting. A 14-day stay limit is enforced.

Directions: From Pendleton, drive north on Highway 11 for 16 miles to Highway 204 near Weston. Turn right (southeast) on Highway 204 and drive 23 miles. The campground is just off the highway on the left.

Contact: Umatilla National Forest, Walla Walla Ranger District, 509/522-6290, fax 509/522-6000, www.fs.fed.us.

13 EMIGRANT SPRINGS STATE HERITAGE AREA

Scenic rating: 7

near the Umatilla Indian Reservation

Map 4.2, page 218

Emigrant Springs sits in old-growth forest at the summit of the Blue Mountains. The campground is popular with horse campers and offers wildlife-watching opportunities. The nearby Oregon Trail and Pendleton Woolen Mills provide interesting side-trips.

Campsites, facilities: There are 32 tent sites, 19 sites with full hookups for RVs of any length, a designated horse camp (closed in winter), group tent site, and eight cabins. Picnic tables, fire grills, and horse corrals are provided. Drinking water, garbage bins, restrooms with flush toilets and showers, firewood, some horse facilities, a community building with kitchen, basketball court, amphitheater, and baseball field are available. Some facilities are wheelchair accessible. Leashed pets are permitted.

Reservations, fees: Reservations are accepted at 800/452-5687 or www.reserveamerica.com ($8 reservation fee). Tent sites are $10–17 per night, RV sites are $12–20 per night, cabins are $35–39 per night, equestrian sites are $10–17 per night, and the group site is $71 for up to 25 people. Additional vehicles cost $5 per night. Some credit cards are accepted. Open year-round (water is off mid-Oct.–mid-April).

Directions: From Pendleton, drive southeast on I-84 for 26 miles to Exit 234. Take that exit to Old Oregon Trail Road (frontage road) and drive 0.5 mile to the park on the right.

Contact: Emigrant Springs State Heritage Area, 541/983-2277 or 800/551-6949, www.oregonstateparks.org.

14 LANE CREEK

Scenic rating: 4

on Camas Creek in Umatilla National Forest

Map 4.2, page 218

This primitive campground (3,850 feet elevation) borders Camas Creek and Lane Creek, just inside the forest boundary, and provides easy access to all the amenities of town. It's a popular stop for overnighters passing through the area. Some of the sites close to the highway get traffic noise. Highlights in the area include hot springs (privately owned) and good hunting and fishing. A U.S. Forest Service map details the back roads.

Campsites, facilities: There are six sites for tents or RVs up to 28 feet long and one group site. Picnic tables and fire grills are provided. Vault toilets are available. There is no drinking water, and garbage must be packed out. Leashed pets are permitted.

Reservations, fees: Reservations are not accepted. Sites are $8 per night, $25 per night for the group site. Open April–November, weather permitting. A 14-day stay limit is enforced.

Directions: From Pendleton, drive south on U.S. 395 for 50 miles to Ukiah and Highway 244. Turn east on Highway 244 and drive nine miles to the campground on the left.

Contact: Umatilla National Forest, North Fork John Day Ranger District, 541/427-3231, fax 541/427-3018, www.fs.fed.us.

15 BEAR WALLOW CREEK

Scenic rating: 5

on Bear Wallow Creek in Umatilla National Forest

Map 4.2, page 218

Situated near the confluence of Bear Wallow and Camus Creeks at an elevation of 3,900 feet, Bear Wallow is one of three off Highway 244 (the others are Lane Creek and Frazier).

Quiet and primitive, the camp is used primarily in the summer. A 0.5-mile, wheelchair-accessible, interpretive trail meanders next to Bear Wallow Creek, highlighting the steelhead habitat.

Campsites, facilities: There are seven sites for tents or RVs up to 28 feet long and one group site. Picnic tables and fire grills are provided. Vault toilets are available. No drinking water is available, and garbage must be packed out. Some facilities are wheelchair accessible. Leashed pets are permitted.

Reservations, fees: Reservations are not accepted. Sites are $8 per night, and the group site is $25 per night. Open April–November, weather permitting. A 14-day stay limit is enforced.

Directions: From Pendleton, drive south on U.S. 395 for 50 miles to Ukiah and Highway 244. Turn east on Highway 244 and drive 10 miles to the camp on the left.

Contact: Umatilla National Forest, North Fork John Day Ranger District, 541/427-3231, fax 541/427-3018, www.fs.fed.us.

16 FRAZIER

Scenic rating: 5

on Frazier Creek in Umatilla National Forest

Map 4.2, page 218

With nearly 130 miles of OHV and motorcycle trails at the Winom-Frazier Off-Highway-Vehicle Complex, this camp is popular in the summer with the OHV crowd. The campground is set at 4,300 feet elevation along the banks of Frazier Creek. It is a popular hunting area in the fall, and some fishing is available in the area. It's advisable to obtain a map of Umatilla National Forest. On weekends, it's not a good spot for the traditional camper looking for quiet and solitude. Lehman Hot Springs, one mile away, provides a side-trip option.

Campsites, facilities: There are 14 sites for tents or RVs up to 28 feet long and four group

sites. Picnic tables and fire grills are provided. An OHV loading ramp and vault toilets are available. There is no drinking water, and garbage must be packed out. Some facilities are wheelchair accessible. Leashed pets are permitted. A 14-day stay limit is enforced.

Reservations, fees: Reservations are not accepted. Sites are $8 per night; group sites are $25 per night. Open April–November, weather permitting.

Directions: From Pendleton, drive south on U.S. 395 for 50 miles to Ukiah and Highway 244. Turn left (east) on Highway 244 and drive 18 miles to Forest Road 5226. Turn right (south) and drive 0.5 mile to the campground.

Contact: Umatilla National Forest, North Fork John Day Ranger District, 541/427-3231, fax 541/427-3018, www.fs.fed.us.

17 SPOOL CART

Scenic rating: 6

on the Grande Ronde River in Wallowa-Whitman National Forest

Map 4.2, page 218

Spool Cart gets its name from the large cable spools that were left on a cart here for some years. The wooded campground sits at 3,500 feet elevation on the banks of the Grande Ronde River; sites offer privacy. The camp is popular with hunters in the fall, and the gurgling Grande Ronde offers fishing for bull trout. Hilgard Junction State Park to the north provides numerous recreation options, and the Oregon Interpretive Trail Park at Blue Crossing is nearby.

Campsites, facilities: There are nine sites for tents or RVs up to 22 feet long. Picnic tables and fire grills are provided. Vault toilets are available. There is no drinking water, and garbage must be packed out. Some facilities are wheelchair accessible. Leashed pets are permitted.

Reservations, fees: Reservations are not

accepted. Sites are $5 per night per vehicle. Open late May–late November.

Directions: From Pendleton, drive southeast on U.S. 84 for 42 miles to Highway 244. Turn southwest on Highway 244 and drive 13 miles to Forest Road 51. Turn left (south) and drive five miles to the campground on the right.

Contact: Wallowa-Whitman National Forest, LaGrande Ranger District, 541/963-7186, fax 541/962-8580, www.fs.fed.us.

18 BIRD TRACK SPRINGS

Scenic rating: 7

near the Grande Ronde River in Wallowa-Whitman National Forest

Map 4.2, page 218

Bird Track Springs is located at 3,100 feet elevation and is about a five-minute walk from the Grande Ronde River. The spacious campsites are right off the highway in surrounding woods of primarily ponderosa pine and white fir. The Bird Track Springs Interpretive Trail, across the campground, offers a hiking and bird-watching opportunity.

Campsites, facilities: There are 21 sites for tents or RVs up to 22 feet long. Picnic tables and fire rings are provided. Vault toilets are available. There is no drinking water, and garbage must be packed out. A camp host is on-site in the summer. Some facilities are wheelchair accessible. Leashed pets are permitted.

Reservations, fees: Reservations are not accepted. Sites are $5 per night per vehicle. Open mid-May–November, weather permitting.

Directions: From Pendleton, drive southeast on U.S. 84 for 42 miles to Highway 244. Turn right (southwest) and drive seven miles to the campground on the left.

Contact: Wallowa-Whitman National Forest, LaGrande Ranger District, 541/963-7186, fax 541/962-8580, www.fs.fed.us.

19 DRIFT FENCE

Scenic rating: 5

near Ross Springs in Umatilla National Forest

Map 4.2, page 218

Get this: Drift Fence is not marked on the Umatilla National Forest Map. The camp, set at 4,250 feet elevation, is adjacent to Blue Mountain National Forest Scenic Byway. With some elk and deer in the area, hunting is a highlight here. The Bridge Creek Interpretive Trail, three miles northwest of the campground off Forest Road 52, leads to a beautiful view of open meadow with various wildflowers and wildlife. Elk may be seen roaming in the Bridge Creek area.

Campsites, facilities: There are four sites for tents or RVs up to 30 feet long and one group site. Picnic tables are provided. A pit toilet is available. There is no drinking water, and garbage must be packed out. Leashed pets are permitted.

Reservations, fees: Reservations are not accepted. There is no fee for camping. Open May–November, weather permitting. A 14-day stay limit is enforced.

Directions: From Pendleton, drive south on U.S. 395 for 50 miles to Highway 244. Turn east on Highway 244 and drive one mile to Ukiah and Forest Road 52. Turn right (south) on Forest Road 52 and drive eight miles to the campground on the right.

Contact: Umatilla National Forest, North Fork John Day Ranger District, 541/427-3231, fax 541/427-3018, www.fs.fed.us.

20 UKIAH-DALE FOREST STATE SCENIC CORRIDOR

Scenic rating: 7

near the North Fork of the John Day River

Map 4.2, page 218

Fishing is a prime activity at this Camas Creek campground, nestled near the banks of the north fork of the John Day River at an elevation of 3,140 feet. It's a good layover for visitors cruising U.S. 395 looking for a shady spot for the night. Emigrant Springs State Park near Pendleton is a possible side trip.

Campsites, facilities: There are 27 sites for tents or self-contained RVs of any length. Picnic tables and fire pits are provided. Drinking water, firewood, and restrooms with flush toilets are available. Leashed pets are permitted.

Reservations, fees: Reservations are not accepted. Sites are $5–9 per night, $5 per night per additional vehicle. Open May–late October.

Directions: From Pendleton, drive south on U.S. 395 for 50 miles to Highway 244 (near Ukiah). Continue south on U.S. 395 for three miles to the park.

Contact: Emigrant Springs State Heritage Park, 541/983-2277 or 800/551-6949, www.oregonstateparks.org.

21 TOLLBRIDGE
🏊 🐕 🚐 ⛺

Scenic rating: 4

on the north fork of the John Day River in Umatilla National Forest

Map 4.2, page 218

This small, secluded campground (elevation 3,800 feet) lies at the confluence of Desolation Creek and the north fork of the John Day River and is adjacent to the Bridge Creek Wildlife Area. It can be beautiful or ugly, depending upon which direction you look. It's dusty in the summer, and there's sparse tree cover. Hunting and fishing are two options here, or explore the geological interpretive sign in the camp.

Campsites, facilities: There are seven sites for tents or RVs up to 26 feet long. Picnic tables and fire grills are provided. A vault toilet is available. There is no drinking water, and garbage must be packed out. Leashed pets are permitted.

Reservations, fees: Reservations are not accepted. Sites are $8 per night, with a 14-day stay limit. Open April–November, weather permitting. A 14-day stay limit is enforced.

Directions: From Pendleton, drive south on U.S. 395 for 50 miles to the intersection with Highway 244. Continue south on U.S. 395 for 18 miles to Forest Road 55 (one mile north of Dale). Turn left and drive 0.5 mile southeast to Forest Road 10 and the campground access road. Drive a short distance to the campground.

Contact: Umatilla National Forest, North Fork John Day Ranger District, 541/427-3231, fax 541/427-3018, www.fs.fed.us.

22 GOLD DREDGE CAMP
🏊 🐕 🚐 ⛺

Scenic rating: 7

on the north fork of the John Day River in Umatilla National Forest

Map 4.2, page 218

Gold Dredge lies along the banks of the north fork of the John Day River, a federally designated Wild and Scenic River. This camp is an excellent launch point for recreation: swimming, fishing, rafting (spring only), float-tubing, and hunting (fall) are among the many activities. Dredge tailings from old mining activity are visible from the camp. At the end of Forest Road 5506, you can access a trailhead that heads into the adjacent North Fork John Day Wilderness. Special fishing regulations are in effect for the North Fork John Day River; check Oregon fishing regulations before heading out.

Parking is provided at Big Creek Bridge for the North Fork John Day Wilderness Trailhead and the OHV trail that leads to the Winom-Frazier OHV Complex. Those driving to the end of Forest Road 5506 will need a high-clearance vehicle.

Campsites, facilities: There are six sites for tents or RVs up to 28 feet long. Picnic tables are provided. Vault toilets are available. There is no drinking water, and garbage must be packed out. Leashed pets are permitted.

Reservations, fees: Reservations are not accepted. There is no fee for camping. Open May–November, weather permitting. A 14-day stay limit is enforced.

Directions: From Pendleton, drive south on U.S. 395 for 62 miles to Forest Road 55 (one mile north of Dale). Turn left and drive six miles to the crossroads. Continue straight onto Forest Road 5506 and drive 2.5 miles to the campground on the right. Note: The last two miles of road are very rough.

Contact: Umatilla National Forest, North Fork John Day Ranger District, 541/427-3231, fax 541/427-3018, www.fs.fed.us.

23 DRIFTWOOD

Scenic rating: 6

on the north fork of the John Day River in Umatilla National Forest

Map 4.2, page 218

This tiny campground with ponderosa pine and Douglas fir cover sits on the banks of the north fork of the John Day River at an elevation of 2,500 feet. Recreational opportunities at this remote spot include fishing, float tubing, hunting, rafting, and swimming.

Campsites, facilities: There are five sites for tents or RVs up to 28 feet long. Fire grills and picnic tables are provided. A vault toilet is available. No drinking water is available. Garbage must be packed out. Leashed pets are permitted. A 14-day stay limit is enforced.

Reservations, fees: Reservations are not accepted. Sites are $8 per night. Open April–November, weather permitting.

Directions: From Pendleton, drive south on U.S. 395 for 62 miles to Forest Road 55 (one mile north of Dale; it's easier to find if you know the marker, Texas Bar Road). Turn left and drive six miles to the crossroads. Continue straight ahead onto Forest Road 5506 and drive one mile to the campground on the right. Note: The last two miles of road are very rough.

Contact: Umatilla National Forest, North Fork John Day Ranger District, 541/427-3231, fax 541/427-3018, www.fs.fed.us.

24 ORIENTAL CREEK

Scenic rating: 4

on the north fork of the John Day River in Umatilla National Forest

Map 4.2, page 218

Oriental Creek nestles in a stand of mixed conifer at 3,500 feet elevation along the banks of the north fork of the John Day River. Evidence of old mining activity is visible here. The campground is popular with horse campers, motorcyclists, and off-roaders alike. Hunting and fishing are two possible activities, and nearby trails provide access to the North Fork John Day Wilderness. (No mountain bikes or motorcycles are permitted in the wilderness area.) Be advised that the road into this campground is rough and narrow in places.

Campsites, facilities: There are seven primitive tent sites. Pit toilets and picnic tables are available. There is no drinking water, and garbage must be packed out. Leashed pets are permitted.

Reservations, fees: Reservations are not accepted. There is no fee for camping. Open April–November, weather permitting. A 14-day stay limit is enforced.

Directions: From Pendleton, drive south on U.S. 395 for 62 miles to Forest Road 55 (one mile north of Dale; it's easier to find if you know the marker, Texas Bar Road). Turn left and drive six miles to the crossroads. Continue straight ahead onto Forest Road 5506 and drive six miles to the campground on the right. This road is rough and not recommended for trailers.

Contact: Umatilla National Forest, North Fork John Day Ranger District, 541/427-3231, fax 541/427-3018, www.fs.fed.us.

25 WINOM CREEK

Scenic rating: 2

on Winom Creek in Umatilla National Forest

Map 4.2, page 218

Winom Creek campground is set at 5,000 feet elevation and provides access to the Winom-Frazier Off-Highway Vehicle Complex, with 130 miles of OHV trails of varying difficulty. The complex was developed in the late 1980s for OHV enthusiasts and has worn in well. The camp is also near the North Fork John Day Wilderness, perfect for hikers. (Check the campground bulletin boards for detailed maps of the terrain.)

Campsites, facilities: There are five sites for tents or RVs up to 28 feet long and three group sites. Picnic tables and fire rings are provided. Vault toilets and an OHV loading ramp are available. There is no drinking water, and garbage must be packed out. Two of the group sites have picnic shelters. Leashed pets are permitted.

Reservations, fees: Reservations are not accepted. Sites are $8 per night, $25 per night for group sites. Open May–early November, weather permitting. A 14-day stay limit is enforced.

Directions: From Pendleton, drive south on U.S. 395 for 50 miles to Highway 244. Turn east on Highway 244 and drive one mile to Ukiah and Forest Road 52. Turn right (south) on Forest Road 52 and drive 20 miles to Forest Road 440. Turn right and drive one mile to the campground on the right. The last mile of the access road is narrow and steep.

Contact: Umatilla National Forest, North Fork John Day Ranger District, 541/427-3231, fax 541/427-3018, www.fs.fed.us.

26 MOTTET

Scenic rating: 6

near the south fork of the Walla Walla River in Umatilla National Forest

Map 4.3, page 219

Mottet sits perched at 5,200 feet elevation along a ridge top, surrounded by a heavily timbered forest. Far from the beaten path, it's quite primitive and relatively unknown, so you're almost guaranteed privacy. A trailhead across the road leads down to the south fork of the Walla Walla River.

Campsites, facilities: There are seven sites for tents or RVs up to 22 feet. Picnic tables and fire grills are provided. Spring water and vault toilets are available. Garbage must be packed out. Leashed pets are permitted.

Reservations, fees: Reservations are not accepted. Sites are $8 per night. Open early July–November, weather permitting. A 14-day stay limit is enforced.

Directions: From Pendleton, drive north on Highway 11 for 16 miles to Highway 204 near Weston. Turn right (southeast) on Highway 204 and drive 17.5 miles to Forest Road 64. Turn left and drive about 15 miles to Forest Road 6403. Turn left and drive about two miles to the campground on the left. The road is rough for the last two miles.

Contact: Umatilla National Forest, Walla Walla Ranger District, 509/522-6290, fax 509/522-6000, www.fs.fed.us.

27 JUBILEE LAKE

Scenic rating: 8

on Jubilee Lake in Umatilla National Forest

Map 4.3, page 219　　　　　**BEST (**

Jubilee Lake is the largest and most popular campground in Umatilla National Forest, and it fills up on weekends and holidays. Located along the shore of 90-acre Jubilee Lake (elevation 4,800 feet), this spot offers good fishing, hiking, and swimming. Electric boat motors are permitted on the lake, but gas-powered motors are prohibited. A 2.8-mile trail loops around the lake and provides different levels of accessibility for those in wheelchairs; fishing access is available along the trail.

Campsites, facilities: There are 50 sites for tents and RVs up to 28 feet long. Picnic tables and fire grills are provided. Drinking water, firewood, picnic areas, and restrooms with flush toilets are available. Boat docks and launching facilities are nearby. Garbage bins are available during the summer. Some facilities are wheelchair accessible. Leashed pets are permitted.

Reservations, fees: Reservations are not accepted. Sites are $17 per night, $5 per night for each additional vehicle. Open late June–mid-October, weather permitting. A 14-day stay limit is enforced.

Directions: From Pendleton, drive north on Highway 11 for 16 miles to Highway 204 near Weston. Turn right (southeast) on Highway 204 and drive 17.5 miles to Forest Road 64. Turn left and drive 12 miles northeast to Forest Road 6400-250. Turn right (south) and drive 0.5 mile to the camp.

Contact: Umatilla National Forest, Walla Walla Ranger District, 509/522-6290, fax 509/522-6000, www.fs.fed.us.

28 DOUGHERTY SPRINGS

Scenic rating: 5

near Dougherty Springs in
Wallowa-Whitman National Forest

Map 4.3, page 219

This wooded, primitive campground (elevation 5,100 feet) adjacent to Dougherty Springs is one in a series of remote camps set near natural springs. The camp is in an open area with sparse Douglas and white fir. Birds, deer, elk, and small mammals can be seen in the area. Hells Canyon National Recreation Area to the east provides many recreation options.

Campsites, facilities: There are 12 sites for tents or RVs up to 22 feet long. Picnic tables and fire rings are provided. Vault toilets are available. There is no drinking water, and garbage must be packed out. Leashed pets are permitted.

Reservations, fees: Reservations are not accepted. There is no fee for camping. Open June–late November, weather permitting.

Directions: From LaGrande, drive northeast on Highway 82 for 64 miles to Enterprise and Highway 3. Turn north on Highway 3 and drive 15 miles to Forest Road 46. Turn right (northeast) and drive 30 miles to the campground on the left.

Contact: Hells Canyon National Recreation Area, Wallowa Mountains Visitors Center, 541/426-5546, fax 541/426-5522, www.fs.fed.us/r6/w-w.

29 COYOTE

Scenic rating: 4

near Coyote Springs in
Wallowa-Whitman National Forest

Map 4.3, page 219

Coyote campground is set at 4,800 feet elevation and adjacent to Coyote Springs. This is the largest of the three primitive camps in the vicinity, offering open sites and privacy.

Campsites, facilities: There are 30 sites for tents or RVs up to 22 feet long. Picnic tables and fire rings are provided. Vault toilets are available. There is no drinking water, and garbage must be packed out. Leashed pets are permitted.

Reservations, fees: Reservations are not accepted. There is no fee for camping. Open May–November, weather permitting.

Directions: From LaGrande, drive northeast on Highway 82 for 64 miles to Enterprise and Highway 3. Turn north on Highway 3 and drive 15 miles to Forest Road 46. Turn right (northeast) and drive 25 miles to the campground on the left.

Contact: Wallowa-Whitman National Forest, Wallowa Valley Ranger District, Wallowa Mountains Visitors Center, 541/426-5546, fax 541/426-5522, www.fs.fed.us.

30 VIGNE

Scenic rating: 5

on Chesnimnus Creek in
Wallowa-Whitman National Forest

Map 4.3, page 219

Vigne campground sits at 3,500 feet elevation on the banks of Chesnimnus Creek. The campground has pretty riverside sites shaded by Douglas and white fir. Recreation opportunities include fishing and exploring a few of the many hiking trails in the area.

Campsites, facilities: There are seven sites for tents or RVs up to 22 feet long. Picnic tables and fire rings are provided. Drinking water and vault toilets are available. Garbage must be packed out. Leashed pets are permitted.

Reservations, fees: Reservations are not accepted. Sites are $6 per night. Open May–November, weather permitting.

Directions: From LaGrande, drive northeast on Highway 82 for 64 miles to Enterprise and Highway 3. Turn north on Highway 3 and drive 15 miles to Forest Road 46. Turn right (northeast) and drive 10 miles to Forest Road 4625. Turn right (east) and drive 10 miles to the campground. The last 10 miles are potholed and rough.

Contact: Wallowa-Whitman National Forest, Wallowa Valley Ranger District, Wallowa Mountains Visitors Center, 541/426-5546, fax 541/426-5522, www.fs.fed.us.

31 MINAM STATE PARK

Scenic rating: 7

near the Grande Ronde River

Map 4.3, page 219

This small and pretty park is well worth the detour off I-84 necessary to get there. Once you do, you'll be greeted by large pines towering above the sharp valley, cut through by the Wallowa River. Rafting and fishing for steelhead are popular activities, and the area is teeming with wildlife, including bears, cougars, deer, elk, and the occasional mountain sheep downriver.

Campsites, facilities: There are 12 primitive sites for tents or self-contained RVs up to 71 feet. Picnic tables and fire grills are provided. Drinking water is available May–mid-October. Garbage bins and vault toilets are available. Raft rentals are available nearby. Leashed pets are permitted.

Reservations, fees: Reservations are not accepted. Sites are $5–9 per night, $5 per night for an additional vehicle. Open April–October.

Directions: From LaGrande, drive northeast on Highway 82 for 18 miles to Elgin, then continue 14 miles to the park entrance road. Turn left (north) and drive two miles to the park.

Contact: Wallowa Lake State Park, 541/432-8855 or 800/551-6949, www.oregonstateparks.org.

32 BOUNDARY

Scenic rating: 6

near the Eagle Cap Wilderness in
Wallowa-Whitman National Forest

Map 4.3, page 219

This pretty and primitive campground is set 100 yards from the banks of Bear Creek at 3,600 feet elevation and is heavily wooded with Douglas, red, tamarack, and white fir. Recreation options here include hiking, fishing, and horseback riding. Nearby trails provide access to the Eagle Cap Wilderness. This is another in a series of little-known, primitive sites in the area.

Campsites, facilities: There are eight primitive tent sites. Picnic tables and fire rings are provided. Vault toilets are available. There is no drinking water, and garbage must be packed out. Leashed pets are permitted.

Reservations, fees: Reservations are not accepted. There is no fee for camping. Open mid-June–November, weather permitting.

Directions: From LaGrande, drive north on Highway 82 for 46 miles to Wallowa and Forest Road 8250. Turn south and drive eight miles to Forest Road 8250-040. Bear right (south) and drive 0.75 mile to the camp.

Contact: Wallowa-Whitman National Forest, Eagle Cap Ranger District, Wallowa Mountains Visitors Center, 541/426-5546, www.fs.fed.us.

33 MOSS SPRINGS

Scenic rating: 7

near the Eagle Cap Wilderness in
Wallowa-Whitman National Forest

Map 4.3, page 219

At 6,000 feet elevation, Moss Springs campground is heavily forested with spruce and fir and has good views of the Grande Ronde Valley in some locations. The camp is popular with horse packers, and there is a loading ramp on-site. A trailhead provides access to the Eagle Cap Wilderness, a good jumping-off point for a multi-day backpacking trip. (Obtain a map of Wallowa-Whitman National Forest for detailed trail information.) The Breshears OHV Trail and the Mount Fanny Mountain bike trails are just north of the camp.

Campsites, facilities: There are seven sites for tents and RVs up to 16 feet long. Picnic tables and fire grills are provided. No drinking water is provided, but water is available for stock. Horse facilities and vault toilets are available. Garbage must be packed out. Some facilities are wheelchair accessible. Leashed pets are permitted.

Reservations, fees: Reservations are not accepted. Sites are $5 per night per vehicle. Open June–mid-October, weather permitting.

Directions: From LaGrande, drive east on Highway 237 for 15 miles to Cove and County Road 65 (signed for Moss Springs). Turn right (southeast) and drive 1.5 miles to Forest Road 6220. Turn left (east) and drive eight miles to the camp entrance. Note: The last five miles are on a steep gravel road.

Contact: Wallowa-Whitman National Forest, LaGrande Ranger District, 541/963-7186, fax 541/962-8580, www.fs.fed.us.

34 SHADY

Scenic rating: 6

on the Lostine River in
Wallowa-Whitman National Forest

Map 4.3, page 219

Shady campground sits along the banks of the Lostine River at an elevation of 5,400 feet. The camp has wooded as well as meadow areas. It is close to trails that provide access to the Eagle Cap Wilderness, a beautiful and pristine area that's perfect for an extended backpacking trip. You can sometimes spot mountain sheep in the area.

Campsites, facilities: There are 12 sites for tents or RVs up to 16 feet long. Picnic tables and fire grills are provided. Vault toilets are available. There is no drinking water, and garbage must be packed out. Leashed pets are permitted.

Reservations, fees: Reservations are not accepted. Sites are $6 per night. Open mid-June–November, weather permitting.

Directions: From LaGrande, turn north on Highway 82 and drive 52 miles to Lostine and Forest Road 8210. Turn right (south) and drive 15 miles to the campground.

Contact: Wallowa-Whitman National Forest, Eagle Cap Ranger District, 541/426-5546, www.fs.fed.us.

35 TWO PAN

Scenic rating: 6

on the Lostine River in
Wallowa-Whitman National Forest

Map 4.3, page 219

Two Pan lies at the end of a forest road on the banks of the Lostine River. At 5,600 feet elevation, this camp is a prime jumping-off spot for a multi-day wilderness adventure. Adjacent trails provide access to numerous lakes and streams in the Eagle Cap Wilderness. If full, another campground option is Williamson, seven miles north on Forest Road 8210.

Campsites, facilities: There are nine sites for tents or RVs up to 16 feet. Picnic tables and fire grills are provided. Vault toilets are available. There is no drinking water, and garbage must be packed out. Leashed pets are permitted.

Reservations, fees: Reservations are not accepted. A Northwest Forest Pass is required, but there is no camping fee. Open mid-June–November, weather permitting.

Directions: From LaGrande, turn north on Highway 82 and drive 52 miles to Lostine and Forest Road 8210. Turn right (south) and drive 17 miles to the campground.

Contact: Wallowa-Whitman National Forest, Eagle Cap Ranger District, Wallowa Mountains Visitors Center, 541/426-5546, www.fs.fed.us.

36 HURRICANE CREEK

Scenic rating: 5

near the Eagle Cap Wilderness in
Wallowa-Whitman National Forest

Map 4.3, page 219

Set along Hurricane Creek at an elevation of 5,000 feet, this campground is on the edge of the Eagle Cap Wilderness and provides a good place to begin a backcountry backpacking trip. Sites are wooded, and some sit close to the creek—perfect for fishing. There is no access for medium to large RVs, which gives the camp more of a wilderness environment. Obtaining maps of the area from the ranger district is essential.

Campsites, facilities: There are 12 sites for tents or RVs up to 16 feet long. Picnic tables and fire grills are provided. Vault toilets are available. There is no drinking water, and garbage must be packed out. Leashed pets are permitted.

Reservations, fees: Reservations are not accepted. Sites are $6 per night. Open mid-June–November, weather permitting.

Directions: From LaGrande, turn north on Highway 82 and drive 62 miles to Enterprise and Hurricane Creek Road. Turn right (south) on Hurricane Creek Road and drive five miles to Hurricane Grange Hall and Forest Road 8205; bear right (off the paved road) and drive two miles to the campground on the left.

Contact: Wallowa-Whitman National Forest, Eagle Cap Ranger District, 541/426-5546, www.fs.fed.us.

37 MOUNTAIN VIEW MOTEL AND RV PARK

Scenic rating: 3

near Wallowa Lake

Map 4.3, page 219

Mountain View is centrally located for exploring the greater Wallowa Lake area. Fishing and jet boating are available only a mile away at Wallowa Lake, and nearby recreational facilities include bike paths, a golf course, hiking trails, and a riding stable. The park has a fish pond and creek and offers views of the Seven Devils Mountains and of the Eagle Cap Wilderness.

Campsites, facilities: There are 30 sites with full hookups (some pull-through) for RVs of any length, a grassy area for tents, and nine cabins. Picnic tables and fire pits are provided. Restrooms with flush toilets and showers, a dump station, Wi-Fi, firewood, and coin laundry are available. Propane gas, a store, and café are within two miles. Leashed pets are permitted, but pit bulls and rottweilers are not allowed.

Reservations, fees: Reservations are accepted. RV sites are $24.95 per night, tent sites are $19.95 per night, $3.50 per person per night for more than two people. Some credit cards are accepted. Open year-round.

Directions: From LaGrande, turn north on Highway 82 and drive 62 miles to Enterprise and the junction with Highway 3. Continue north on Highway 82 for four miles to the campground on the right (1.5 miles north of Joseph).

Contact: Mountain View Motel and RV Park, 866/262-9891 (toll free) or 541/432-2982 (phone or fax), www.rvmotel.com.

38 WALLOWA LAKE STATE PARK

Scenic rating: 8

on Wallowa Lake

Map 4.3, page 219   BEST (

Surrounded by snowy peaks, Wallowa Lake is a large lake with plenty of fishing and boating, including waterskiing and parasailing. Recreational activities include canoeing, horseback riding, and hiking. Bumper boats, miniature golf, and an artist community provide other diversions. Other highlights include a pretty one-mile nature trail and trailheads that provide access into the Eagle Cap Wilderness and Hells Canyon gorge. A marina is nearby for boaters and anglers. Picnicking, swimming, and wildlife-viewing are a few of the other activities available to visitors.

Campsites, facilities: There are 121 sites with full hookups for RVs of any length, 89 tent sites, three group tent areas for up to 25 people each, two yurts, and one cabin. Picnic tables and fire rings are provided. Garbage bins, drinking water, restrooms with flush toilets

and showers, a dump station, and firewood are available. A store, café, and ice are within one mile. Boat docks, launching facilities, and rentals are nearby. Some facilities are wheelchair accessible. Leashed pets are permitted.

Reservations, fees: Reservations are accepted at 800/452-5687 or www.reserveamerica.com ($8 reservation fee). RV sites are $17–25 per night, tent sites are $13–20 per night, hiker/biker sites are $4–5 per person per night, group areas are $42–74 per night, yurts are $29–38 per night, the cabin is $58–90 per night, and $5 per night per additional vehicle. Some credit cards are accepted. Open year-round, with limited availability in winter (no water).

Directions: From LaGrande, turn north on Highway 82 and drive 62 miles to Enterprise and the junction with Highway 3. Continue south on Highway 82 to Joseph. Continue for six miles to the south shore of the lake and the campground.

Contact: Wallowa Lake State Park, 541/432-4185, www.oregonstateparks.org.

39 LICK CREEK

Scenic rating: 7

on Lick Creek in
Wallowa-Whitman National Forest

Map 4.3, page 219

Located along the banks of Lick Creek in Hells Canyon National Recreation Area, this secluded and pretty campground sits in park-like surroundings at an elevation of 5,400 feet. Interspersed throughout the campground, tall Douglas fir, lodgepole pine, tamarack, and white fir provide a wildlife habitat for the area's birds and small animals.

Campsites, facilities: There are seven tent sites and five sites for RVs up to 30 feet long. Picnic tables and fire rings are provided. Vault toilets are available. There is no drinking water, and garbage must be packed out. Leashed pets are permitted.

Reservations, fees: Reservations are not accepted. Sites are $6 per night. Open mid-June–late November, weather permitting.
Directions: From LaGrande, turn north on Highway 82 and drive 64 miles to Enterprise. Continue south on Highway 82 to Joseph and Highway 350. Turn left (east) and drive 7.5 miles to Forest Road 39. Turn right (south) and drive 15 miles to the campground.
Contact: Hells Canyon National Recreation Area, Wallowa Mountains Visitors Center, 541/426-5546, fax 541/426-5522, www.fs.fed.us/r6/w-w.

40 COVERDALE

Scenic rating: 7

near the Imnaha River
Map 4.3, page 219

Located at 4,300 feet in elevation along the Imnaha River, this campground is in a lushly forested drainage area. Wildflower viewing can be spectacular and fishing can be good. Hiking trails are nearby.
Campsites, facilities: There are four sites for tents and two sites for RVs up to 24 feet long. Picnic tables and fire rings are provided. There is no drinking water. Garbage must be packed out. Some facilities are wheelchair accessible. Leashed pets are permitted.
Reservations, fees: Reservations are not accepted. Sites are $6 per night. Open June–October, weather permitting.
Directions: From Joseph, drive east on Highway 350 for eight miles to Wallowa Mountain Loop Road (Forest Road 39). Turn right and drive approximately 38 miles to Forest Road 3960. Turn right and drive four miles to the campground on the left.
Contact: Hells Canyon National Recreation Area, Wallowa Mountains Visitors Center, 541/426-5546, fax 541/426-5522.

41 OLLOKOT

Scenic rating: 5

on the Imnaha River in
Wallowa-Whitman National Forest
Map 4.3, page 219

This campground sits on the banks of the Imnaha River in Hells Canyon National Recreation Area at an elevation of 4,000 feet. It's named for Chief Joseph's brother, a member of the Nez Perce tribe. For those seeking a little more solitude, this could be the spot.
Campsites, facilities: There are 12 sites for tents or RVs up to 30 feet long. Picnic tables and fire rings are provided. Vault toilets are available. There is no drinking water, and garbage must be packed out. Leashed pets are permitted.
Reservations, fees: Reservations are not accepted. Sites are $8 per night. Open June–late November, weather permitting.
Directions: From I-84 at LaGrande, turn north on Highway 82 and drive 64 miles to Enterprise. Continue six miles south to Joseph and Highway 350. Turn left (east) on Highway 350 and drive eight miles to Forest Road 39. Turn right (south) on Forest Road 39 and drive 30 miles to the campground on the left.
Contact: Hells Canyon National Recreation Area, Wallowa Mountains Visitors Center, 541/426-5546, fax 541/426-5522, www.fs.fed.us/r6/w-w.

42 SADDLE CREEK

Scenic rating: 8

near the Hells Canyon Wilderness in
Wallowa-Whitman National Forest
Map 4.4, page 220

Saddle Creek campground is set at 6,800 feet, nestled in a wooded environment on a ridge between two canyons. It provides excellent views of the Seven Devils Mountains. Nearby trails provide access to Saddle Creek and Hells Canyon National Recreation Area.

Campsites, facilities: There are four sites for tents. Picnic tables and fire rings are provided. Vault toilets are available. There is no drinking water, and garbage must be packed out. Leashed pets are permitted. Note: RVs and trailers are not recommended on the access road.

Reservations, fees: Reservations are not accepted. There is no fee for camping. Open July–mid-November, weather permitting.

Directions: From LaGrande, turn north on Highway 82 and drive 64 miles to Enterprise. Continue south on Highway 82 and drive six miles to Joseph and Highway 350. Turn left (east) on Highway 350 and drive 30 miles to the small town of Imnaha and Forest Road 4240. Drive straight up the hill on Forest Road 4240 and continue 19 miles (on a gravel road) to the campground.

Contact: Hells Canyon National Recreation Area, Wallowa Mountains Visitors Center, 541/426-5546 or 541/426-5522, www.fs.fed. us/r6/w-w.

43 BLACKHORSE
🚶 🎣 🛶 🐕 🚐 ⛺

Scenic rating: 7

on the Imnaha River in
Wallowa-Whitman National Forest

Map 4.4, page 220

This campground along the banks of the Imnaha River in Hells Canyon National Recreation Area is located in a secluded section of Wallowa-Whitman National Forest at an elevation of 4,000 feet.

Campsites, facilities: There are 15 sites for tents or RVs up to 30 feet long. Picnic tables and fire rings are provided. Vault toilets are available. There is no drinking water, and garbage must be packed out. Leashed pets are permitted.

Reservations, fees: Reservations are not accepted. Sites are $8 per night. Open June–late November, weather permitting.

Directions: From I-84 at LaGrande, turn north on Highway 82 and drive 64 miles to Enterprise. Continue six miles south to Joseph and Highway 350. Turn left (east) and drive eight miles on Highway 350 to Forest Road 39. Turn right (south) on Forest Road 39 and drive 29 miles to the campground.

Contact: Hells Canyon National Recreation Area, Wallowa Mountains Visitors Center, 541/426-5546, fax 541/426-5522, www.fs.fed. us/r6/w-w.

44 HIDDEN
🚶 🚴 🛶 🐕 🚐 ⛺

Scenic rating: 6

on the Imnaha River in
Wallowa-Whitman National Forest

Map 4.4, page 220

River views and spacious sites can be found at this campground in a pretty spot along the banks of the Imnaha River in the Hells Canyon National Recreation Area. It's essential to obtain a map of Wallowa-Whitman National Forest that details back roads and hiking trails. If full, Coverdale Campground is an option, just four miles northeast on Forest Road 3960.

Campsites, facilities: There are 10 tent sites and three sites for tents or small, self-contained RVs. Picnic tables and fire rings are provided. Vault toilets are available. There is no drinking water, and garbage must be packed out. Leashed pets are permitted.

Reservations, fees: Reservations are not accepted. Sites are $6 per night. Open June–late November, weather permitting.

Directions: From LaGrande, drive east on Highway 82 for 64 miles to Enterprise. Continue six miles south to Joseph and Highway 350. Turn left (east) and drive eight miles to Wallowa Mountain Loop Road (Forest Road 39). Turn right (south) and drive 30 miles to Forest Road 3960. Turn right (southwest) and drive seven miles to the campground.

Contact: Hells Canyon National Recreation Area, Wallowa Mountains Visitors Center, 541/426-5546, fax 541/426-5522, www.fs.fed. us/r6/w-w.

45 INDIAN CROSSING

Scenic rating: 6

on the Imnaha River in
Wallowa-Whitman National Forest

Map 4.4, page 220

Indian Crossing is situated at an elevation of 4,500 feet and is more developed than nearby Hidden Campground. A trailhead for the Eagle Cap Wilderness is near; obtain a U.S. Forest Service map for trail options.

Campsites, facilities: There are 14 sites for tents or RVs up to 30 feet long. Picnic tables and fire rings are provided. Drinking water, vault toilets, and horse facilities are available. Garbage must be packed out. Leashed pets are permitted.

Reservations, fees: Reservations are not accepted. Sites are $8 per night. Open June–late November, weather permitting.

Directions: From LaGrande, turn north on Highway 82 and drive 62 miles to Enterprise. Continue on Highway 82 for six miles to Joseph and Highway 350. Turn left (east) on Highway 350 and drive eight miles to Forest Road 39. Turn right (south) and drive about 30 miles to Forest Road 3960. Turn right and drive 10 miles to the campground at the end of the road.

Contact: Hells Canyon National Recreation Area, Wallowa Mountains Visitors Center, 541/426-5546, fax 541/426-5522, www.fs.fed.us/r6/w-w.

46 WHISTLER

Scenic rating: 7

in Ochoco National Forest

Map 4.5, page 221

Whistler is a trailhead camp for the Wildcat Trail, which heads into the Mill Creek Wilderness. The area is extremely popular with rock hounds, who search for agates, jasper, and thunder eggs. (Digging and collecting are forbidden in wilderness areas, however.) Though primitive, this pretty camp in a conifer forest guarantees quiet and privacy.

Campsites, facilities: There are two group sites for dispersed tent camping. A picnic table and a vault toilet are provided. There is no drinking water, and garbage must be packed out. Horses are welcome. Leashed pets are permitted.

Reservations, fees: Reservations are not accepted. There is no fee for camping. Open late May–late October, weather permitting.

Directions: From Prineville, drive east on U.S. 26 for about 30 miles to Forest Road 27 (just east of Bandit Spring State Rest Area, near Ochoco Pass). Turn left on Forest Road 27 and drive nine miles to the campground entrance on the left. Note: Trailers are not recommended on this road.

Contact: Ochoco National Forest, Lookout Mountain Ranger District, 541/416-6500, fax 541/416-6695, www.fs.fed.us.

47 WILDCAT

Scenic rating: 4

on the east fork of Mill Creek in
Ochoco National Forest

Map 4.5, page 221

Surrounded by conifer forest, Wildcat campground sits at an elevation of 3,700 feet in a cool canyon. Situated along the east fork of Mill Creek, the quiet camp is near the Twin Pillars Trailhead, which provides access into the Mill Creek Wilderness. No climbing is allowed in the wilderness. Ochoco Lake and Ochoco Lake State Park to the south provide side-trip possibilities.

Campsites, facilities: There are 17 sites for tents or RVs up to 30 feet long. Picnic tables and fire grills are provided. Drinking water and vault toilets are available. Garbage must be packed out. Leashed pets are permitted.

Reservations, fees: Reservations are not accepted. Sites are $8 per night, $3 per night for each additional vehicle. Open mid-May–late October, weather permitting.

Directions: From Prineville, drive east on U.S. 26 for nine miles to Mill Creek Road (Forest Road 33). Turn left on Mill Creek Road and drive about 10 miles to the campground.

Contact: Ochoco National Forest, Lookout Mountain Ranger District, 541/416-6500, fax 541/416-6695, www.fs.fed.us.

48 OCHOCO DIVIDE

Scenic rating: 5

in Ochoco National Forest

Map 4.5, page 221

This quiet campground is set at an elevation of 4,700 feet in a ponderosa pine forest. Hiking is available along a forest road near the camp and at nearby Marks Creek and Bandit Springs. This is a quick jump off U.S. 26; campers tend to set up in the afternoon and leave early in the morning, so you may get the place to yourself.

Campsites, facilities: There are 28 sites for tents or RVs up to 30 feet long, with a separate area of walk-in and bike-in sites. Picnic tables and fire pits are provided. Vault toilets are available. There is no drinking water, and garbage must be packed out. Some facilities are wheelchair accessible. Leashed pets are permitted.

Reservations, fees: Reservations are not accepted. Sites are $13 per night, plus $6.50 per night for an additional vehicle. Hike-in/bike-in sites are $13 per person per night. Open late May–mid-October, weather permitting.

Directions: From Prineville, drive east on U.S. 26 for 30 miles to the campground at the summit of Ochoco Pass.

Contact: Ochoco National Forest, Lookout Mountain Ranger District, 541/416-6500, fax 541/416-6695, www.fs.fed.us.

49 OCHOCO CAMPGROUND

Scenic rating: 4

in Ochoco National Forest

Map 4.5, page 221

Ochoco Campground sits at an elevation of 4,000 feet along Ochoco Creek amid pine and aspen trees. There's fair fishing for rainbow trout, and hiking is nearby in the Lookout Mountain Recreation Area—that's 15,000 acres without roads. But hey, the truth is: don't expect privacy and solitude at this campground. The log shelter and picnic area are often reserved for weddings, family reunions, and other group events.

Campsites, facilities: There are six sites for tents or RVs up to 24 feet long and one group site. Picnic tables and fire rings are provided. Drinking water, garbage bins, vault toilets, and a picnic shelter (by reservation) are available. Some facilities are wheelchair accessible. Leashed pets are permitted.

Reservations, fees: Reservations are only accepted for the group site at 877/444-6777 or www.recreation.gov. Sites are $13 per night, the group site is $60 per night, $6.50 per night for an additional vehicle. Open mid-May–October, weather permitting.

Directions: From Prineville, drive east on U.S. 26 for 16.5 miles to County Road 23. Turn right on County Road 23 and drive nine miles (County Road 23 becomes Forest Road 42) to the campground, across from the Ochoco Ranger Station.

Contact: Ochoco National Forest, Lookout Mountain Ranger District, 541/416-6500, fax 541/416-6695, www.fs.fed.us.

50 WALTON LAKE

Scenic rating: 7

on Walton Lake in Ochoco National Forest

Map 4.5, page 221

This campground, surrounded by meadows and ponderosa pine, borders the shore of small Walton Lake. Fishing and swimming are popular; the lake is stocked with rainbow trout, and the fishing can range from middle-of-the-road right up to downright excellent. Only non-motorized boats or boats with electric motors are allowed on the lake. Hikers can explore a nearby trail that leads south to Round Mountain.

Campsites, facilities: There are 30 sites for tents or RVs up to 28 feet long and two group sites. Picnic tables, garbage bins, and fire grills are provided. Drinking water and vault toilets are available. Boat-launching facilities are nearby (only electric motors are allowed). Some facilities are wheelchair accessible. Leashed pets are permitted.

Reservations, fees: Reservations accepted only for the group sites at 877/444-6777 or www.recreation.gov ($10 reservation fee). Sites are $15 per night, $7.50 per night per additional vehicle. Group sites are $50 per night. Open mid-May–mid-September, weather permitting.

Directions: From Prineville, drive east on U.S. 26 for 16.5 miles to County Road 23. Turn right (northeast) and drive nine miles (County Road 23 becomes Forest Road 42) to the Ochoco Ranger Station and Forest Road 22. Turn left and drive north on Forest Road 22 for seven miles to the campground.

Contact: Ochoco National Forest, Lookout Mountain Ranger District, 541/416-6500, fax 541/416-6695, www.fs.fed.us.

51 DEEP CREEK

Scenic rating: 5

on the north fork of the Crooked River in Ochoco National Forest

Map 4.5, page 221

This small camp on the edge of high desert (4,200 feet elevation) gets little use, but it's in a nice spot. Located right at the confluence of Deep Creek and the north fork of the Crooked River, the pretty, shady sites allow for river access and fishing.

Campsites, facilities: There are six sites for tents or RVs up to 22 feet long. Picnic tables and fire grills are provided. Drinking water and vault toilets are available. Garbage must be packed out. Leashed pets are permitted.

Reservations, fees: Reservations are not accepted. Sites are $8 per night, $3 per night per additional vehicle. Open mid-May–mid-October, weather permitting.

Directions: From Prineville, drive east on U.S. 26 for 16.5 miles to County Route 23. Turn right (northeast) and drive 8.5 miles (it becomes Forest Road 42). Continue east on Forest Road 42 (paved road) for 23.5 miles to the campground on the right.

Contact: Ochoco National Forest, Lookout Mountain Ranger District, 541/416-6500, fax 541/416-6695, www.fs.fed.us.

52 CROOK COUNTY RV PARK

Scenic rating: 6

near the Crooked River

Map 4.5, page 221

This five-acre public campground sits in a landscaped, grassy area near the Crooked River, where fly-fishing is popular. The camp is located right next to the Crook County Fairgrounds, which offers seasonal expositions, horse races, and rodeos.

Campsites, facilities: There are 81 sites for tents or RVs up to 70 feet long (full hookups); most sites are pull-through. In addition, there are nine tent sites and two log cabins available. Picnic tables are provided. Fire pits are provided at the tent sites. Restrooms with flush toilets and showers, a dump station, cable TV, and modem access are available. A convenience store, restaurant, ice, gasoline, and propane are available within one mile. Some facilities are wheelchair accessible. Leashed pets are permitted with restrictions on some breeds.

Reservations, fees: Reservations are accepted at 800/609-2599. Tent sites are $10 per night, RV sites are $28–30 per night, $5 per night per additional vehicle. Weekly and monthly rates are available. Some credit cards are accepted. Open year-round.

Directions: From Redmond, drive east on Highway 126 for 18 miles to Prineville (Highway 126 becomes 3rd Street) and Main Street. Turn right on Main Street and drive about 0.5 mile south to the campground on the left, before the fairgrounds.

Contact: Crook County RV Park, 541/447-2599, fax 541/416-9022, www.ccprd.org/parks_rv.cfm.

53 OCHOCO LAKE

Scenic rating: 6

on Ochoco Lake

Map 4.5, page 221

This is one of the nicer camps along U.S. 26 in eastern Oregon. The campground is located on the shore of Ochoco Lake, where boating and fishing are popular pastimes. Some quality hiking trails can be found in the area.

Campsites, facilities: There are 21 primitive sites for tents or self-contained RVs up to 50 feet long and a special area for hikers and bicyclists. Picnic tables, garbage bins, and fire grills are provided. Drinking water, firewood, restrooms with showers and flush toilets, ice, a fish-cleaning station, and boat-launching facilities are available. Leashed pets are permitted.

Reservations, fees: Reservations are not accepted. Sites are $16 per night, $5 per person per night for hike-in/bike-in sites, and $7 per night per additional vehicle. Some credit cards are accepted. Open April–October, weather permitting.

Directions: From Prineville, drive east on U.S. 26 for seven miles to the park entrance on the right.

Contact: Crook County Parks and Recreation, 541/447-1209, fax 541/447-9894, www.ccprd.org/parks_ochoco.cfm.

54 CHIMNEY ROCK

Scenic rating: 6

on the Crooked River

Map 4.5, page 221

Chimney Rock Campground is one of eight BLM camps along a six-mile stretch of Highway 27. This well-spaced campground is a favorite for picnicking and wildlife-viewing. The Chimney Rock Trailhead, just across the highway, is the jumping-off point for the 1.7-mile, moderately difficult hike to Chimney Rock. There are numerous scenic overlooks along the trail, and wildlife sightings are common. The elevation here is 3,000 feet.

Campsites, facilities: There are 20 sites for tents or RVs of any length. Picnic tables are provided. Vault toilets, drinking water, and garbage bins are available. Some facilities are wheelchair accessible, including a fishing dock. Leashed pets are permitted.

Reservations, fees: Reservations are not accepted. Sites are $8 per night, $2 per night for an additional vehicle. Open year-round.

Directions: In Prineville, drive south on Highway 27 for 16.4 miles to the campground.

Contact: Bureau of Land Management, Prineville District, 541/416-6700, fax 541/416-6798, www.blm.gov.

55 PRINEVILLE RESERVOIR STATE PARK

Scenic rating: 7

on Prineville Reservoir

Map 4.5, page 221

This state park is set along the shore of Prineville Reservoir, which formed with the damming of the Crooked River. This is one of two campgrounds on the reservoir (the other is Prineville Reservoir Resort). Boating, fishing, swimming, and waterskiing are popular activities here; the nearby boat docks and ramp are a bonus. The reservoir supports rainbow and cutthroat trout, small and largemouth bass, catfish, and crappie; you can even ice fish in the winter.

Campsites, facilities: There are 44 sites with partial hookups for RVs up to 40 feet long, 23 tent sites, two rustic cabins, and three deluxe cabins. Picnic tables and fire pits are provided. Drinking water, garbage bins, restrooms with flush toilets and showers, ice, and firewood are available. Boat docks, launching facilities, and moorings that can be reserved are nearby. Some facilities are wheelchair accessible. Leashed pets are permitted.

Reservations, fees: Reservations are accepted at 800/452-5687 or www.reserveamerica.com ($8 reservation fee). RV sites are $18–26, tent sites are $13–21 per night, cabins are $38–82 per night, boat moorage is $7–10, and $5 per night per additional vehicle. Some credit cards are accepted. Open year-round.

Directions: From Prineville, drive east on U.S. 26 for one mile to Combs Flat Road. Turn right (south) and drive one mile to Juniper Canyon Road. Turn right (south) and drive 18 miles to the campground.

Contact: Prineville Reservoir State Park, 541/447-4363 or 800/551-6949, www.oregonstateparks.org.

56 PRINEVILLE RESERVOIR RESORT

🧍 🚴 🏊 ⛵ 🎣 🏕 🐕 ♿ 🚙 ⛰

Scenic rating: 6

on Prineville Reservoir

Map 4.5, page 221

This resort sits on the shore of Prineville Reservoir in the high desert, a good spot for water sports and fishing. The mostly shaded sites are a combination of dirt and gravel. The camp features easy access to the reservoir and some colorful rock formations to check out.

Campsites, facilities: There are 70 sites with partial hookups (including four pull-through sites) for tents or RVs of any length, seven motel rooms, and one primitive cabin.

Drinking water, fire pits, and picnic tables are provided. Restrooms with flush toilets and coin showers, propane gas, a dump station, firewood, a convenience store, a café, and ice are available. A full-service marina, boat ramp, boat rentals, fish-cleaning station, and fishing licenses are on-site. Some facilities are wheelchair accessible. Leashed pets are permitted.

Reservations, fees: Reservations are accepted at 541/447-7468 ($7 reservation fee). Sites are $16–24 per night. Some credit cards are accepted. Open May–mid-October, weather permitting.

Directions: From Prineville, drive east on U.S. 26 for one mile to Combs Flat Road. Turn right (south) and drive one mile to Juniper Canyon Road. Turn right (south) and drive 18 miles to the resort at the end of the road.

Contact: Prineville Reservoir Resort, tel./fax 541/447-7468, www.prinevillereservoirresort.com.

57 JASPER POINT STATE PARK

🧍 🏊 ⛵ 🎣 🐕 🚙 ⛰

Scenic rating: 7

on Prineville Reservoir

Map 4.5, page 221

Jasper Point is a quiet alternative to Prineville Reservoir State Park. The park is not as popular as Prineville; although it does fill up on summer weekends, it's used mainly by locals. Although the park is named Jasper Point, the setting is in a cove and the views are not as good as those at Prineville Reservoir State Park. A 1.75-mile trail connects the two campgrounds, and another 0.7-mile trail runs along the shoreline.

Campsites, facilities: There are 30 sites for tents or RVs of any length. Picnic tables and fire pits are provided. Drinking water, vault toilets, garbage containers, a day-use area, and a boat launch are available. Leashed pets are permitted.

Reservations, fees: Reservations are not

accepted. Sites are $22–26 per night, $5 per night per additional vehicle. Open May–September.

Directions: From Prineville, drive east on U.S. 26 for one mile to Combs Flat Road. Turn right (south) and drive one mile to Juniper Canyon Road. Turn right (south) and drive 21 miles to the campground.

Contact: Prineville Reservoir State Park, 541/447-4363 or 800/551-6949, www.oregonstateparks.org.

58 ANTELOPE FLAT RESERVOIR

Scenic rating: 6

on Antelope Flat Reservoir in Ochoco National Forest

Map 4.5, page 221

This pretty spot is situated along the west shore of Antelope Flat Reservoir amid ponderosa pine and juniper. The campground is on the edge of the high desert at an elevation of 4,600 feet. It features wide sites and easy access to the lake. Trout fishing can sometimes be good in the spring, and boating with motors is permitted. This is also a good lake for canoes.

Campsites, facilities: There are 25 sites for tents or RVs up to 30 feet long. Picnic tables and fire grills are provided. Drinking water and vault toilets are available. Garbage must be packed out. Boat-launching facilities are nearby. Leashed pets are permitted.

Reservations, fees: Reservations are not accepted. Sites are $8 per night, $3 per night for each additional vehicle. Open early May–late October, weather permitting.

Directions: From Prineville, drive southeast on Combs Flat Road (Paulina Highway) for 30 miles to Forest Road 17 (Antelope Reservoir Junction). Turn right on Forest Road 17 and drive about 10 miles to Forest Road 1700-600. Drive 0.25 mile on Forest Road 1700-600 to the campground.

Contact: Ochoco National Forest, Lookout Mountain Ranger District, 541/416-6500, fax 541/416-6695, www.fs.fed.us.

59 WILEY FLAT

Scenic rating: 3

on Wiley Creek in Ochoco National Forest

Map 4.5, page 221

Wiley Flat campground is set along Wiley Creek in a nice, hidden spot with minimal crowds. It is popular with horseback riders and seasonal hunters. Tower Point Lookout is one mile north of the camp. A map of Ochoco National Forest details nearby access roads.

Campsites, facilities: There are five sites for tents or RVs up to 30 feet long. Picnic tables and fire grills are provided. Vault toilets are available. There is no drinking water, and garbage must be packed out. Leashed pets are permitted.

Reservations, fees: Reservations are not accepted. There is no fee for camping. Open mid-June–late October, weather permitting.

Directions: From Prineville, drive southeast on the Paulina Highway (Combs Flat Road) for 34 miles to Forest Road 16. Turn right (southeast) and drive 10 miles to Forest Road 1600-400. Turn right (west) and drive one mile to the camp.

Contact: Ochoco National Forest, Lookout Mountain Ranger District, 541/416-6500, fax 541/416-6695, www.fs.fed.us.

60 BULL PRAIRIE LAKE

Scenic rating: 8

on Bull Prairie Lake in Umatilla National Forest

Map 4.6, page 222   **BEST (**

Set on the shore of Bull Prairie Lake, a 28-acre lake at 4,000 feet elevation, this spot attracts little attention from out-of-towners, yet it offers plenty of recreation opportunities, making it an ideal vacation destination. Boating (no motors permitted), fishing for blue gill and trout, hunting, and swimming are some of the attractions here. A hiking trail circles the lake.

Campsites, facilities: There are 28 sites for tents or RVs up to 31 feet long and one group site for up to 25 people. Picnic tables and fire grills are provided. Vault toilets are available. Drinking water and garbage bins are available late May–mid-October. Boat docks and a boat ramp are on-site. Some facilities are wheelchair accessible, including the boat ramp. Leashed pets are permitted.

Reservations, fees: Reservations are not accepted. Single sites are $14, double sites are $19, the group site is $28, $5–8 per night for an additional vehicle. Open year-round, weather permitting.

Directions: From Heppner, drive south on Highway 207 for roughly 35 miles to the national forest boundary and continue four miles to Forest Road 2039 (paved). Turn left and drive three miles northeast to the campground on the right.

Contact: Umatilla National Forest, Heppner Ranger District, 541/676-9187, fax 541/676-2105, www.fs.fed.us.

61 FAIRVIEW

Scenic rating: 5

near Bull Prairie Lake in
Umatilla National Forest

Map 4.6, page 222

This small, rugged campground is located in a remote area at 4,300 feet elevation near Mahogany Butte and adjacent to Fairview Springs. Known by very few people, it's very easy to miss and not even marked on Umatilla National Forest maps. Hunters use it primarily as a base camp. Bull Prairie Lake is only four miles away.

Campsites, facilities: There are five sites for tents or RVs up to 16 feet long. Picnic tables and fire grills are provided. Vault toilets are available. Drinking water is available May–October. Garbage must be packed out. Boat docks and launching facilities are nearby at Bull Prairie Lake. Leashed pets are permitted.

Reservations, fees: Reservations are not accepted. There is no fee for camping. Open May–October, weather permitting.

Directions: From Heppner, drive south on Highway 207 for roughly 35 miles to the national forest boundary. Continue four miles to Forest Road 2039 (the turnoff for Bull Prairie Lake). Continue on Highway 207 for one mile to Forest Road 400 (if you pass through an immediate series of hairpin turns, you have gone too far). Turn west and drive 500 yards to the campground.

Contact: Umatilla National Forest, Heppner Ranger District, 541/676-9187, fax 541/676-2105, www.fs.fed.us.

62 WOLF CREEK

Scenic rating: 5

on Wolf Creek in Ochoco National Forest

Map 4.6, page 222

This campground, at 4,000 feet elevation, is set along the banks of Wolf Creek, a nice trout stream that runs through Ochoco National Forest.

Campsites, facilities: There are 10 sites for tents or RVs up to 20 feet long. Picnic tables and fire grills are provided. Vault toilets are available. There is no drinking water, and garbage must be packed out. Leashed pets are permitted.

Reservations, fees: Reservations are not accepted. Sites are $6 per night, with a 14-day stay limit, and $3 per night for an additional vehicle. Open May–November, weather permitting.

Directions: From Prineville, drive southeast on Combs Flat Road (Paulina Highway) for 55 miles to Paulina. Continue east for 3.5 miles to County Road 112. Turn left (north) and drive 6.5 miles to Forest Road 42. Turn left (north) and drive 1.5 miles to the campground on the right.

Contact: Ochoco National Forest, Paulina Ranger District, 541/477-6900, fax 541/477-6949, www.fs.fed.us.

63 SUGAR CREEK
👣 🏕 ♿ 🚙 ⛺

Scenic rating: 6

on Sugar Creek in Ochoco National Forest
Map 4.6, page 222

This small, quiet, and remote campground sits along the banks of Sugar Creek at an elevation of 4,000 feet in a forest of ponderosa pine. A 0.5-mile trail loops along the creek. The camp also offers a covered group shelter in the day-use area and a wheelchair-accessible trail. Bald eagles occasionally nest in the area.

Campsites, facilities: There are 17 sites for tents or RVs up to 22 feet long. Picnic tables and fire grills are provided. Drinking water, a picnic shelter, and vault toilets are available. Garbage must be packed out. Some facilities are wheelchair accessible. Leashed pets are permitted.

Reservations, fees: Reservations are not accepted. Sites are $8 per night, with a 14-day stay limit, and $3 per night for an additional vehicle. Open May–November.

Directions: From Prineville, drive southeast on Combs Flat Road (Paulina Highway) for 55 miles to Paulina. Continue east and drive 3.5 miles to a fork with County Road 112. Bear left at the fork onto County Road 112 and drive 7.5 miles to Forest Road 58. Bear right on Forest Road 58 and continue for 1.3 miles to the campground on the right.

Contact: Ochoco National Forest, Paulina Ranger District, 541/477-6900, fax 541/477-6949, www.fs.fed.us.

64 FRAZIER
👣 🚴 🐎 🚙 ⛺

Scenic rating: 4

on Frazier Creek in Ochoco National Forest
Map 4.6, page 222

Frazier is a small, remote, and little-used campground located at an elevation of 4,600 feet. The landscape is open, grassy, and sprinkled with a few large pine trees. Some dirt roads adjacent to the camp are good for mountain biking in summer, and the camp's meadow setting is occasionally the site of family reunions during summer holidays.

Campsites, facilities: There are seven sites for tents or RVs up to 22 feet long. Picnic tables and fire grills are provided. Vault toilets are available. There is no drinking water, and garbage must be packed out. Leashed pets are permitted.

Reservations, fees: Reservations are not accepted. There is no fee for camping. The stay limit is 14 days. Open May–November, weather permitting.

Directions: From Prineville, drive southeast on Combs Flat Road (Paulina Highway) for 55 miles to Paulina. Continue east and drive 3.5 miles to a fork with County Road 112. Bear left at the fork onto County Road 112 and drive 2.5 miles to County Road 135/Puett Road. Turn right (east) and drive 10 miles to Forest Road 58. Turn right and drive six miles to Forest Road 58-500. Turn left and drive two miles (bearing to the left) to the campground.

Contact: Ochoco National Forest, Paulina Ranger District, 541/477-6900, fax 541/477-6949, www.fs.fed.us.

65 CLYDE HOLLIDAY STATE RECREATION SITE
👣 🚴 🏊 🏕 🚙 ⛺

Scenic rating: 7

near the John Day River
Map 4.6, page 222

Clyde Holliday campground borders the John Day River, a spawning site for steelhead. Sites are private and shaded with cottonwood trees. Wildlife is prevalent in the area; watch for mule deer and elk near the campsites.

Campsites, facilities: There are 31 sites with partial hookups for tents or RVs up to 60 feet long, a hiker/biker tent area, and two tepees. Picnic tables and fire grills are provided. Drinking water, firewood, a dump station, and restrooms with showers and flush toilets are available. Leashed pets are permitted.

Reservations, fees: Reservations are not accepted for campsites but are advised for the tepees at 541/932-4453 or 800/932-4953. Sites are $13–22 per night, $4–5 per person per night for hike-in/bike-in sites, $29–39 per night for tepees, $5 per night for an additional vehicle. Open March–November, weather permitting.

Directions: From John Day, drive west on U.S. 26 for six miles to the park on the left.

Contact: Clyde Holliday State Recreation Site, 541/932-4453 or 800/551-6949, www. oregonstateparks.org.

66 STARR

Scenic rating: 4

on Starr Ridge in Malheur National Forest

Map 4.6, page 222

A good layover spot for travelers on U.S. 395, Starr happens to be adjacent to Starr Ridge, a snow play area popular in winter for skiing and sledding. The camp itself doesn't offer much in the way of recreation, but to the northeast is the Strawberry Mountain Wilderness, which has a number of lakes, streams, and trails. The camp sits at an elevation of 5,100 feet.

Campsites, facilities: There are eight sites for tents or RVs up to 22 feet long. Picnic tables and fire rings are provided. Vault toilets are available. There is no drinking water, and garbage must be packed out. Some facilities are wheelchair accessible. Leashed pets are permitted.

Reservations, fees: Reservations are not

accepted. Sites are $6 per night, $3 per night for an additional vehicle. Open late May–November, weather permitting.

Directions: From John Day, drive south on U.S. 395 for 15 miles to the campground on the right.

Contact: Malheur National Forest, Blue Mountain Ranger District, 541/575-3000, fax 541/575-3319, www.fs.fed.us.

67 WELCH CREEK

Scenic rating: 4

on Desolation Creek in Umatilla National Forest

Map 4.7, page 223

Welch Creek is a primitive camp set on the banks of Desolation Creek. Road noise and dust may be a problem for some, and there's little privacy among sites. The camp features trail access to the Desolation Area, both for non-motorized and motorized traffic. Hunting and fishing are popular here.

Campsites, facilities: There are five sites for tents or RVs up to 30 feet long and one group site. Picnic tables and fire rings are provided. A vault toilet is available. There is no drinking water. Garbage must be packed out. Leashed pets are permitted.

Reservations, fees: Reservations are not accepted. Sites are $8 per night, $25 for the group site, $5 per night for an additional vehicle. Open late May–early November, weather permitting. A 14-day stay limit is enforced.

Directions: From Pendleton, drive south on U.S. 395 for 62 miles to Forest Road 55 (one mile north of Dale; it's easier to find if you know the marker, Texas Bar Road). Turn left and drive one mile to Forest Road 10. Turn right and drive 13 miles to the campground on the right.

Contact: Umatilla National Forest, North Fork John Day Ranger District, 541/427-3231, fax 541/276-5026, www.fs.fed.us.

68 NORTH FORK JOHN DAY

🏃 🚣 🐕 🚙 ⛺

Scenic rating: 6

on the north fork of the John Day River in
Umatilla National Forest

Map 4.7, page 223

Set along the banks of the north fork of the
John Day River at an elevation of 5,200 feet,
this campground sits in a stand of lodgepole
pine at the intersection of Elkhorn and Blue
Mountain National Forest Scenic Byways.
The campground has a great view of salmon
spawning in the river in spring and fall and
also makes an ideal launch point for a wilderness backpacking trip. Trails from camp lead
into the North Fork John Day Wilderness. A
horse-handling area is also available for wilderness users. No mountain bikes or motorcycles
are permitted in the wilderness.

Campsites, facilities: There are 12 sites for
tents or RVs up to 28 feet long, five sites for
tents only, and one group site. Picnic tables
and fire rings are provided. Vault toilets are
available. There is no drinking water. Garbage must be packed out. Leashed pets are
permitted.

Reservations, fees: Reservations are not accepted. Sites are $8 per night, $25 for the
group site, $5 per night for an additional ve-
hicle. Open June–November, weather permitting. A 14-day stay limit is enforced.

For trailhead use, a Northwest Forest Pass
is required ($5 daily fee or $30 annual fee per
parked vehicle).

Directions: From Pendleton, drive south on
U.S. 395 for 50 miles to Highway 244. Turn
east on Highway 244 and drive one mile to
Ukiah and Forest Road 52. Turn right (south)
on Forest Road 52 and drive 36 miles to the
campground on the right.

Contact: Umatilla National Forest, North
Fork John Day Ranger District, 541/427-3231,
fax 541/427-3018, www.fs.fed.us.

69 ANTHONY LAKES

🏃 🚴 🚣 🛶 ⛵ 🎣 🐕 ♿ 🚙 ⛺

Scenic rating: 10

on Anthony Lake in
Wallowa-Whitman National Forest

Map 4.7, page 223   **BEST (**

This campground (7,100 feet elevation) is adjacent to Anthony Lake, where non-motorized
boating is permitted. Sites are wooded, providing good screening between them. Alas,
mosquitoes are often in particular abundance.
Several smaller lakes within two miles by car
or trail are ideal for trout fishing from a canoe,
float tube, or raft. Sometimes mountain goats
can be seen from the Elkhorn Crest Trail,
which begins near here. Weekends and holidays the campground tends to fill up.

Campsites, facilities: There are 10 sites for
tents, 32 sites for RVs up to 22 feet long, and
one group site for up to 75 people. Drinking
water, fire grills, garbage bins (summer only),
and picnic tables are provided. Vault toilets
are available. Garbage must be packed out the
rest of the year. Boat-launching facilities are
nearby. Some facilities are wheelchair accessible. Leashed pets are permitted.

Reservations, fees: Reservations are not accepted for tent or RV sites but are required
for the group site at 541/894-2404. Sites
are $8–12 per night, $50 per night for the
group site, and $6 per night per additional
vehicle. Open June–late September, weather
permitting.

Directions: From Baker City on I-84, turn
north on U.S. 30. Drive north for 10 miles
to Haines and County Road 1146 (signed
for Anthony Lakes Ski Resort). Turn left on
County Road 1146 and drive 20 miles (the
road becomes Forest Road 73) to the campground on the left.

Contact: Wallowa-Whitman National Forest,
Whitman Ranger District, 541/523-4476,
fax 541/523-1965, www.fs.fed.us; Aud & Di
Campground Services, 541/894-2404.

70 GRANDE RONDE LAKE

Scenic rating: 8

on Grande Ronde Lake in
Wallowa-Whitman National Forest

Map 4.7, page 223

Grande Ronde campground sits amid Douglas and white fir at an elevation of 6,800 feet along the shore of Grande Ronde Lake. Trout fishing can be good at this small lake, and mountain goats are sometimes seen in the area. Several trails lie to the south, near Anthony Lake.

Campsites, facilities: There are eight sites for tents or RVs up to 16 feet long. Picnic tables and fire grills are provided. Drinking water and vault toilets are available. Garbage must be packed out. Boat launching facilities are nearby. Some facilities are wheelchair accessible. Leashed pets are permitted.

Reservations, fees: Reservations are not accepted. Sites are $8 per night, $4 per night per additional vehicle. Open late June–September, weather permitting.

Directions: Drive on I-84 to Baker City and U.S. 30. From Baker City, drive north on U.S. 30 for 10 miles to Haines and County Road 1146 (signed for Anthony Lakes Ski Resort). Turn left on County Road 1146 and drive 20 miles (the road becomes Forest Road 73) to the campground on the right.

Contact: Wallowa-Whitman National Forest, Whitman Ranger District, 541/523-4476, www.fs.fed.us; Aud & Di Campground Services, 541/894-2404.

71 MUD LAKE

Scenic rating: 7

on Mud Lake in
Wallowa-Whitman National Forest

Map 4.7, page 223

Set at an elevation of 7,100 feet, tiny yet pleasant Mud Lake campground is filled with lots of vegetation and sees relatively little use. The campground is situated in fir forest on the shore of small Mud Lake, where the trout fishing can be fairly good. Mud Lake is shallow and more marshy than muddy. Bring your mosquito repellent.

Campsites, facilities: There are eight sites for tents or RVs up to 16 feet long. Picnic tables and fire grills are provided. Drinking water and vault toilets are available. Garbage must be packed out. Boat launching facilities are nearby at Anthony Lake. Leashed pets are permitted.

Reservations, fees: Reservations are not accepted. Sites are $8 per night, $4 per night per additional vehicle. Open June–late September, weather permitting.

Directions: Drive on I-84 to Baker City and U.S. 30. From Baker City, drive north on U.S. 30 for 10 miles to Haines and County Road 1146 (signed for Anthony Lakes Ski Resort). Turn left on County Road 1146 and drive 21 miles (the road becomes Forest Road 73) to the campground on the right.

Contact: Wallowa-Whitman National Forest, Whitman Ranger District, 541/523-4476, www.fs.fed.us; Aud & Di Campground Services, 541/894-2404.

72 OLIVE LAKE

Scenic rating: 9

on Olive Lake in Umatilla National Forest

Map 4.7, page 223

This campground (6,100 feet elevation) is nestled along the shore of Olive Lake, between two sections of the North Fork John Day Wilderness. Dammed to hold an increased volume of water, the glacial lake is a beautiful tint of blue. Motorized boats are allowed, but waterskiing is prohibited. Fishing is fair for kokanee salmon and brook, cutthroat, and rainbow trout. A 2.5-mile trail circles the lake. Nearby trails provide access to the wilderness; motorbikes and mountain bikes are not permitted in the wilderness. Sections of the old wooden pipeline for the historic Fremont Powerhouse can still be seen. The old mining town of Granite is 12 miles east of camp.

Campsites, facilities: There are 22 sites for tents or RVs up to 28 feet long, four sites for tents only, and two group sites. Picnic tables and fire grills are provided. Vault toilets are available. There is no drinking water, and garbage must be packed out. Two boat docks, launching facilities, and picnic areas are available. A camp host is on-site. Some facilities are wheelchair accessible. Leashed pets are permitted.

Reservations, fees: Reservations are not accepted. Sites are $12 per night, $25 per night for the group camp, $5 per night per additional vehicle. Open June–early October, weather permitting. A 14-day stay limit is enforced.

Directions: From Pendleton, drive south on U.S. 395 for 62 miles to Forest Road 55 (one mile north of Dale). Turn right and drive 0.5 mile to Forest Road 10. Turn right on Forest Road 10 and drive 26 miles to Forest Road 480. Turn right and drive 0.5 mile to the campground.

Contact: Umatilla National Forest, North Fork John Day Ranger District, 541/427-3231, fax 541/427-3018, www.fs.fed.us.

7.3 McCULLY FORKS

Scenic rating: 5

on McCully Creek in
Wallowa-Whitman National Forest

Map 4.7, page 223

Here's an easy-access campground that's tiny and primitive. Set at 4,600 feet elevation along the banks of McCully Creek, McCully Forks gets moderately heavy use and is often full on weekends. Wedged between highway and mountains, sites are wooded with alder and cottonwood; highway noise can be audible.

Campsites, facilities: There are eight sites for tents. Picnic tables and fire grills are provided.

Vault toilets are available. There is no drinking water, and garbage must be packed out. Some facilities are wheelchair accessible. Leashed pets are permitted.

Reservations, fees: Reservations are not accepted. Sites are $6 per night. Open late May–late October, weather permitting.

Directions: From Baker City, drive southwest on Highway 7 for 29 miles (bear west at Salisbury) to Sumpter. Continue three miles past Sumpter (the road becomes Forest Road 24) to the campground on the right.

Contact: Wallowa-Whitman National Forest, Baker-Whitman Ranger District, 541/523-4476, fax 541/523-1965, www.fs.fed.us.

7.4 UNION CREEK

Scenic rating: 8

on Phillips Lake in
Wallowa-Whitman National Forest

Map 4.7, page 223

Union Creek campground along the north shore of Phillips Lake is easy to reach, yet missed by most I-84 travelers. It's the largest of three camps on the lake and the only one with drinking water. An old narrow-gauge railroad has been restored and runs up the valley from McEwen Depot (six miles from the campground) to Sumpter (10 miles away). Visit Sumpter to see an old dredge.

Campsites, facilities: There are 70 sites for tents or RVs up to 32 feet long and one group site; some sites have full hookups. Drinking water, garbage bins (summer only), and picnic tables are provided. Flush toilets, a dump station, firewood, and ice are available. There is a seasonal concession stand for packaged goods and fishing tackle. Boat docks and launching facilities are adjacent to the campground. Some facilities are wheelchair accessible. Leashed pets are permitted.

Reservations, fees: Reservations are not accepted for tent or RV sites but are required for the group site at 541/894-2404. Sites are

$12–20 per night, additional fee for hookups, $50 per night for group sites, $6 per night per additional vehicle. Open May–September, weather permitting.

Directions: From Baker City, drive southwest on Highway 7 for 20 miles to the campground on the left.

Contact: Wallowa-Whitman National Forest, Whitman Ranger District, 541/523-4476 or 541/894-2505, www.fs.fed.us; Aud & Di Campground Services, 541/894-2404.

75 SOUTHWEST SHORE
🏃 ≈ 🛶 ⛴ 🐕 🚙 ⛺

Scenic rating: 7

on Phillips Lake in
Wallowa-Whitman National Forest

Map 4.7, page 223

Southwest Shore is one of two primitive campgrounds on Philips Lake, a four-mile-long reservoir created by the Mason Dam on the Powder River. Set at 4,120 feet elevation, the camp borders the south shore of the lake; the boat ramp here is usable only when water is high in the reservoir. An old narrow-gauge railroad runs out of McEwen Depot (six miles from the campground) to Sumpter (10 miles away) for an interesting side-trip.

Campsites, facilities: There are 17 sites for tents or RVs up to 24 feet long. Fire grills and vault toilets are available. There is no drinking water, and garbage must be packed out. A boat ramp is adjacent to the campground. Leashed pets are permitted.

Reservations, fees: Reservations are not accepted. Sites are $8 per night, $4 per night per additional vehicle. Open May–October, weather permitting.

Directions: From Baker City, drive southwest on Highway 7 for 24 miles (just past Phillips Lake) to Hudspeth Lane (County Road 667). Turn left (south) on Hudspeth Lane and drive two miles to Forest Road 2220. Turn left (southeast) and drive 2.5 miles to the campground on the left.

Contact: Wallowa-Whitman National Forest, Whitman Ranger District, 541/523-4476, www.fs.fed.us; Aud & Di Campground Services, 541/894-2404.

76 MILLERS LANE
🏃 ≈ 🛶 ⛴ 🐕 🚙 ⛺

Scenic rating: 7

on Phillips Lake in
Wallowa-Whitman National Forest

Map 4.7, page 223

Millers Lane is one of two primitive camps on Philips Lake (the other is Southwest Shore). Phillips Lake is a long, narrow reservoir (and the largest in the region), and this small campground is situated along the south shore at an elevation of 4,120 feet. The camp is also near an old narrow-gauge railroad that runs out of McEwen Depot.

Campsites, facilities: There are seven sites for tents or RVs up to 20 feet long. Picnic tables and fire grills are provided. Vault toilets are available. There is no drinking water, and garbage must be packed out. A boat ramp is at Southwest Shore. Leashed pets are permitted.

Reservations, fees: Reservations are not accepted. Sites are $8 per night, $4 per night per additional vehicle. Open May–October, weather permitting.

Directions: From Baker City, drive southwest on Highway 7 for 24 miles (just past Phillips Lake) to Hudspeth Lane (County Road 667). Turn left (south) on Hudspeth Lane and drive two miles to Forest Road 2220. Turn left (southeast) and drive 3.5 miles to the campground on the left.

Contact: Wallowa-Whitman National Forest, Whitman Ranger District, 541/523-4476, www.fs.fed.us; Aud & Di Campground Services, 541/894-2404.

7.7 MAGONE LAKE
Scenic rating: 8

on Magone Lake in Malheur National Forest

Map 4.7, page 223

This campground is set along the shore of little Magone Lake at an elevation of 5,500 feet. A 1.8-mile trail rings the lake, and the section extending from the beach area to the campground (about 0.25 mile) is wheelchair accessible. A 0.5-mile trail leads to Magone Slide, an unusual geological formation. Canoeing, fishing, sailing, and swimming are some of the popular activities at this lake. Easy-access bike trails can be found within 0.25 mile of the campground. Just so you know, Magone is pronounced "Ma-Goon." Got it?

Campsites, facilities: There are 22 sites for tents or RVs up to 40 feet long (some pull-through), eight tent sites, and a separate group camp designed for 10 families and a picnic shelter. Picnic tables and fire grills are provided. Drinking water, flush toilets, a boat ramp, and a beach area are available. A camp host is on-site. Boat docks are nearby. Some facilities, including a fishing pier, are wheelchair accessible. Leashed pets are permitted.

Reservations, fees: Reservations are required for the group site and group picnic shelter at 877/444-6777 or www.recreation.gov ($10 reservation fee). Sites are $13 per night, $60 per night for the group site, $6.50 per night per additional vehicle. Open late May–November, weather permitting.

Directions: From John Day, drive east on U.S. 26 for eight miles to County Road 18. Turn north and drive 10 miles to Forest Road 3620. Turn left (west) on Forest Road 3620 and drive 1.5 miles to Forest Road 3618. Turn right (northwest) and drive 1.5 miles to the campground. Note: The road is paved all the way.

Contact: Malheur National Forest, Blue Mountain Ranger District, 541/575-3000, fax 541/575-3319, www.fs.fed.us.

7.8 LOWER CAMP CREEK
Scenic rating: 5

in Malheur National Forest

Map 4.7, page 223

Lower Camp Creek is set at 5,026 feet elevation on the edge of a remote national forest. The camp is small and primitive, with a creek nearby, and is often overlooked, so you may have the place to yourself. In fall, a few hunters will often hunker down here and use it as their base camp.

Campsites, facilities: There are six sites for tents or RVs up to 40 feet long. Picnic tables, fire rings, and vault toilets are provided. There is no drinking water. Garbage must be packed out. Some facilities are wheelchair accessible. Leashed pets are permitted.

Reservations, fees: Reservations are not accepted. Sites are $6 per night for single sites, $3 per night per additional vehicle. Open late May–November, weather permitting.

Directions: From John Day, drive east on U.S. 26 for eight miles to County Road 18. Turn north and drive eight miles to Four Corners. Turn right on Forest Road 36 and drive 12 miles to the campground on the left.

Contact: Malheur National Forest, Blue Mountain Ranger District, 541/573-4300, fax 541/573-4398, www.fs.fed.us.

7.9 MIDDLE FORK
Scenic rating: 6

on the Middle Fork of the John Day River in Malheur National Forest

Map 4.7, page 223   **BEST (**

Scattered along the banks of the Middle Fork of the John Day River at 4,100 feet elevation, these rustic campsites are easy to reach off a paved road. Besides wildlife-viewing and berry picking, the main activity at this camp is fishing, so bring along your fly rod and pinch down your barbs for catch-and-release. The John Day is a state scenic waterway.

Campsites, facilities: There are 12 sites for tents or RVs up to 22 feet long. Picnic tables and fire rings are provided. Vault toilets are available. There is no drinking water, and garbage must be packed out. Some facilities are wheelchair accessible. Leashed pets are permitted.

Reservations, fees: Reservations are not accepted. Sites are $8 per night, $4 per night per additional vehicle. Open late May–November, weather permitting.

Directions: From John Day, drive northeast on U.S. 26 for 28 miles to Highway 7. Turn left (north) and drive one mile to County Road 20. Turn left and drive five miles to the campground on the left.

Contact: Malheur National Forest, Blue Mountain Ranger District, 541/575-3000, fax 541/575-3319, www.fs.fed.us.

80 DIXIE
🏕️🐕♿🚐⛺

Scenic rating: 5

near Dixie Summit in Malheur National Forest

Map 4.7, page 223

Perched at Dixie Summit (elevation 5,000 feet), this camp, just off U.S. 26, is close enough to provide easy access to nearby Bridge Creek, where you can toss in a fishing line. Dixie draws overnighters but otherwise gets light use. The Sumpter Valley Railroad interpretive site is one mile west on U.S. 26.

Campsites, facilities: There are 11 sites for tents or RVs up to 22 feet long. Picnic tables, vault toilets, and fire rings are provided. No drinking water is available, and garbage must be packed out. A store, café, gas, and ice are available within nine miles. Some facilities are wheelchair accessible. Leashed pets are permitted.

Reservations, fees: Reservations are not accepted. Sites are $8 per night, $4 per

night for an additional vehicle. Open late May–November, weather permitting.

Directions: From John Day, drive northeast on U.S. 26 for 24 miles to Forest Road 365. Turn left and drive 0.25 mile to the campground on the left.

Contact: Malheur National Forest, Blue Mountain Ranger District, 541/575-3000, fax 541/575-3319, www.fs.fed.us.

81 WETMORE
🚶🛶🏕️♿🚐⛺

Scenic rating: 7

on the Middle Fork of the Burnt River in Wallowa-Whitman National Forest

Map 4.7, page 223

This campground, set at an elevation of 4,320 feet near the Middle Fork of the Burnt River, makes a nice base camp for a fishing or hiking trip. The stream can provide good trout fishing. (Trails are detailed on maps of Wallowa-Whitman National Forest.) An excellent 0.5-mile, wheelchair-accessible trail passes through old-growth forest—watch for bald eagles.

Campsites, facilities: There are 10 sites for tents or RVs up to 16 feet long. Picnic tables and fire grills are provided. Vault toilets and drinking water (seasonal) are available. Garbage must be packed out. Some facilities are wheelchair accessible. Leashed pets are permitted.

Reservations, fees: Reservations are not accepted. Sites are $6 per night, $5 per night per additional vehicle. Open mid-May–mid-October, weather permitting.

Directions: From John Day, drive east on U.S. 26 for 29 miles to Austin Junction. Continue east on U.S. 26 for 10 miles to the campground on the left.

Contact: Wallowa-Whitman National Forest, Whitman Ranger District, 541/523-4476, fax 541/523-1965, www.fs.fed.us.

82 OREGON

🏃 🐕 🚐 ⛺

Scenic rating: 6

near Austin Junction in
Wallowa-Whitman National Forest

Map 4.7, page 223

Oregon campground sits at 4,880 feet elevation just off U.S. 26 surrounded by hillside as well as Douglas fir, tamarack, and white fir. It is the staging area for ATV enthusiasts, and the popular Blue Mountain OHV Trailhead is here; several trails crisscross the area. Bald eagles nest in the area.

Campsites, facilities: There are eight sites for tents or RVs up to 28 feet long. Picnic tables and fire grills are provided. Vault toilets are available. There is no drinking water, and garbage must be packed out. Leashed pets are permitted.

Reservations, fees: Reservations are not accepted. Sites are $6 per night, $5 per night per additional vehicle. Open mid-May–mid-October, weather permitting.

Directions: From John Day, drive east on U.S. 26 for 29 miles to Austin Junction. Continue east for 20 miles to the campground.

Contact: Wallowa-Whitman National Forest, Whitman Ranger District, 541/523-4476, fax 541/523-1965, www.fs.fed.us.

83 YELLOW PINE

🏃 🐕 ♿ 🚐 ⛺

Scenic rating: 7

near Middle Fork Burnt River

Map 4.7, page 223

Yellow Pine is similar to Oregon Campground, but larger; highlights include easy access and good recreation potential. The camp offers a number of hiking trails, including a 0.5-mile-long, wheelchair-accessible trail that connects to the Wetmore Campground. Keep an eye out for bald eagles in this area.

Campsites, facilities: There are 21 sites for tents or RVs up to 28 feet long. Picnic tables

and fire grills are provided. Vault toilets and drinking water (seasonal) are available. Garbage must be packed out. Some facilities are wheelchair accessible. Leashed pets are permitted.

Reservations, fees: Reservations are not accepted. Sites are $6 per night. Open late mid-May–mid-October, weather permitting.

Directions: From John Day, drive east on U.S. 26 for 29 miles to Austin Junction. Continue east for 21 miles to the campground.

Contact: Wallowa-Whitman National Forest, Whitman Ranger District, 541/523-4476, fax 541/523-1965, www.fs.fed.us.

84 UNITY LAKE
STATE RECREATION SITE

🏃 🚴 🏊 🛶 🎣 🐕 ♿ 🚐 ⛺

Scenic rating: 7

on Unity Reservoir

Map 4.7, page 223

The grassy setting of Unity Lake contrasts nicely with the bordering sagebrush and cheatgrass of the high desert. This camp, set along the east shore of Unity Reservoir, is a popular spot in good weather. Campers can choose from boating, fishing, hiking, picnicking, swimming, or enjoying the scenic views.

Campsites, facilities: There are 35 sites with partial hookups for tents or RVs up to 40 feet long, a separate area for hikers and bicyclists, and two rustic cabins. Picnic tables, garbage bins, and fire rings are provided. Drinking water, restrooms with flush toilets and showers, a dump station, horseshoe pits, and firewood are available. Boat docks and launching facilities are nearby. Some facilities are wheelchair accessible. Leashed pets are permitted.

Reservations, fees: Reservations are not accepted. Sites are $13–22 per night, $4 per person per night for hike-in/bike-in sites, $38–42 per night for rustic cabins, and $5 per night for an additional vehicle. Open April–late October.

Directions: From John Day, drive east on U.S.

26 for 50 miles to Highway 245. Turn left (north) on Highway 245 and drive three miles to the park on the left.

Contact: Clyde Holliday State Recreation Site, 541/932-4453 or 800/551-6949, www.oregonstateparks.org.

85 DEPOT PARK

Scenic rating: 6

on the John Day River

Map 4.7, page 223

Depot Park is a more developed alternative to the many U.S. Forest Service campgrounds in the area. This urban park sits on grassy flatlands and provides access to the John Day River, a good trout fishing spot. The camp features a historic rail depot on the premises, as well as a related museum. A nearby attraction, the Strawberry Mountain Wilderness, has prime hiking trails.

Campsites, facilities: There are 20 sites for tents or RVs up to 35 feet long (full hookups); some sites are pull-through. There is also a grassy area for hikers/bikers. Picnic tables and fire rings are provided. Restrooms with showers, a dump station, gazebo, playground, and picnic area are provided. A camp host is on-site seasonally. Some facilities are wheelchair accessible. Leashed pets are permitted.

Reservations, fees: Reservations are not accepted. Sites are $12–16 per night, $6 night for the hike-in/bike-in area. Open May–November, weather permitting.

Directions: From John Day, drive east on U.S. 26 for 13 miles to Prairie City and the junction of U.S. 26 and Main Street. Turn right (south) on Main Street and drive 0.5 mile to the park (well signed).

Contact: Prairie City Hall, 541/620-2790 or 541/820-3605, www.prairiecityoregon.com.

86 ELK CREEK CAMPGROUND

Scenic rating: 5

in Wallowa-Whitman National Forest

Map 4.7, page 223

Elk Creek campground is small, primitive, and remote. It has no designated campsites, but rather an area for dispersed-style tent camping. Its primary use is for OHV riders, with nearby OHV trail access.

Campsites, facilities: There are no specific sites, only dispersed camping areas for tents or small RVs. Picnic tables and fire rings are provided. Vault toilets are available. There is no drinking water. Garbage must be packed out. Leashed pets are permitted.

Reservations, fees: Reservations are not accepted. Sites are $6 per night. Open mid-May–mid-October, weather permitting.

Directions: From John Day, drive east on U.S. 26 for 49 miles to Unity and County Road 600. Turn right on County Road 600 and drive west for six miles (the road becomes Forest Road 6005/South Fork Road). Continue past the forest boundary for three miles to the campground on the right.

Contact: Wallowa-Whitman National Forest, Whitman Ranger District, 541/523-4476, fax 541/523-1965, www.fs.fed.us.

87 STEVENS CREEK

Scenic rating: 5

on the south fork of the Burnt River in Wallowa-Whitman National Forest

Map 4.7, page 223

This campground sits at an elevation of 4,480 feet along the banks of the south fork of the Burnt River and provides an alternative to the other small camps along the river. The trout fishing is often good here.

Campsites, facilities: There are seven sites for tents or RVs up to 30 feet. Picnic tables and fire grills are provided. There is no drinking water, and garbage must be packed out. Vault toilets are available. Leashed pets are permitted.

Reservations, fees: Reservations are not accepted. Sites are $6 per night, $5 per night per additional vehicle. Open mid-May–mid-October, weather permitting.

Directions: From John Day, drive east on U.S. 26 for 49 miles to Unity and County Road 600. Turn right on County Road 600 and drive west for six miles (the road becomes Forest Road 6005/South Fork Road). Continue past the forest boundary for two miles to the campground on the right.

Contact: Wallowa-Whitman National Forest, Whitman Ranger District, 541/523-4476, fax 541/523-1965, www.fs.fed.us.

88 SOUTH FORK

Scenic rating: 5

on the south fork of the Burnt River in
Wallowa-Whitman National Forest

Map 4.7, page 223

A gem of a spot, South Fork offers drinking water, privacy, and scenery. The campground (4,400 feet elevation) is set on the banks of the south fork of the Burnt River, a nice trout creek with good evening bites for anglers who know how to sneak-fish. An OHV staging area with trail access is across the road from the campground.

Campsites, facilities: There are 12 sites for tents or RVs up to 28 feet long; most sites are pull-through. Picnic tables and fire grills are provided. There are vault toilets, and drinking water is available seasonally. Garbage must be packed out. Some facilities are wheelchair accessible. Leashed pets are permitted.

Reservations, fees: Reservations are not accepted. Sites are $6 per night, $5 per night per additional vehicle. Open mid-May–mid-October, weather permitting.

Directions: From John Day, drive east on U.S.

26 for 49 miles to Unity and County Road 600. Turn right on County Road 600 and drive west for six miles (the road becomes Forest Road 6005/South Fork Road). Continue past the forest boundary for one mile to the campground on the left.

Contact: Wallowa-Whitman National Forest, Whitman Ranger District, 541/523-4476, fax 541/523-1965, www.fs.fed.us.

89 STRAWBERRY

Scenic rating: 7

on Strawberry Creek in
Malheur National Forest

Map 4.7, page 223

At 5,700 feet elevation, this campground hugs the banks of Strawberry Creek. Nearby trails provide access to the Strawberry Mountain Wilderness, Strawberry Lake, and Strawberry Falls. This pretty area features a variety of hiking and hunting options, as well as fishing in Strawberry Creek.

Campsites, facilities: There are 11 sites for tents. Picnic tables and fire rings are provided. Drinking water and vault toilets are available. Garbage must be packed out. Some facilities are wheelchair accessible. Leashed pets are permitted.

Reservations, fees: Reservations are not accepted. Sites are $8 per night, $4 per night for an additional vehicle. Open late May–November, weather permitting.

Directions: From John Day, drive east on U.S. 26 for 13 miles to Prairie City and County Road 62. Turn right (southeast) and drive 0.5 mile to County Road 60. Turn right and drive south on County Road 60 for 8.5 miles (County Road 60 becomes Forest Road 6001). Continue 2.5 miles to the campground on the left.

Contact: Malheur National Forest, Prairie City Ranger District, 541/820-3311, fax 541/820-3838, www.fs.fed.us.

90 SLIDE CREEK

Scenic rating: 5

in Malheur National Forest

Map 4.7, page 223

Slide Creek has tiny, overlooked sites known by a handful of backcountry horsemen. It is set at 4,900 feet in Malheur National Forest with a nearby creek to provide water for horses.

Campsites, facilities: There are three sites for tents or RVs up to 40 feet long. Picnic tables and fire rings are provided. Vault toilets, corrals, and hitching posts are available. There is no drinking water, and garbage must be packed out. Some facilities are wheelchair accessible. Leashed pets are permitted.

Reservations, fees: Reservations are not accepted. Sites are $8 per night, $4 per night for an additional vehicle. Open late May–November, weather permitting.

Directions: From John Day, drive east on U.S. 26 for 13 miles to Prairie City and County Road 62. Turn right (southeast) and drive 0.5 mile to County Road 60. Turn right and drive south on County Road 60 for 8.5 miles (County Road 60 becomes Forest Road 6001). Continue on Forest Road 6001 to the campground on the right.

Contact: Malheur National Forest, Prairie City Ranger District, 541/820-3311, fax 541/820-3838, www.fs.fed.us.

91 WICKIUP

Scenic rating: 5

on Wickiup Creek in Malheur National Forest

Map 4.7, page 223

This campground sits at an elevation of 4,300 feet along the forks of Wickiup Creek and Canyon Creek at a historic site; many of its original Civilian Conservation Corps structures are still in place. There is limited fishing in the creek. To the north are numerous trails that lead into the Strawberry Mountain Wilderness.

Campsites, facilities: There are four sites for tents or RVs up to 22 feet long. Picnic tables and fire rings are provided. A vault toilet is available. There is no drinking water, and garbage must be packed out. Some facilities are wheelchair accessible. Leashed pets are permitted.

Reservations, fees: Reservations are not accepted. Sites are $6 per night, $3 per night per additional vehicle. Open late May–November, weather permitting.

Directions: From John Day, drive south on U.S. 395 for 10 miles to Forest Road 15. Turn left (southeast) and drive eight miles to the campground on the right.

Contact: Malheur National Forest, Blue Mountain Ranger District, 541/575-3000, fax 541/575-3319, www.fs.fed.us.

92 PARISH CABIN

Scenic rating: 6

on Little Bear Creek in Malheur National Forest

Map 4.7, page 223

Parish Cabin campground sits along the banks of Little Bear Creek at an elevation of 4,900 feet. This is a pretty spot that's not heavily used, and the road is paved all the way to the campground. The creek offers limited fishing. The place is popular with groups of families and hunters in season.

Campsites, facilities: There are 19 sites for tents or RVs up to 22 feet long and one group site for up to 50 people. Picnic tables and fire rings are provided. Drinking water and vault toilets are available. Garbage must be packed out. Some facilities are wheelchair accessible. Leashed pets are permitted.

Reservations, fees: Reservations are not accepted. Sites are $8 per night, $4 per night per additional vehicle. Open late May–November, weather permitting.

Directions: From John Day, drive south on U.S. 395 for 10 miles to Forest Road 15. Turn left and drive 16 miles southeast to Forest Road 16. Turn right onto Forest Road 16 and drive a short distance to the campground on the right.

Contact: Malheur National Forest, Blue Mountain Ranger District, 541/575-3000, fax 541/575-3319, www.fs.fed.us.

93 CANYON MEADOWS

Scenic rating: 5

on Canyon Meadows Reservoir in Malheur National Forest

Map 4.7, page 223

Canyon Meadows campground sits on the shore of Canyon Meadows Reservoir, where non-motorized boating, fishing, hiking, sailing, and swimming are recreation options. However, this reservoir dries up by the Fourth of July because of a leak in the dam. Several hiking trails nearby lead north into the Strawberry Mountain Wilderness.

Campsites, facilities: There are five sites for tents or RVs up to 25 feet long. Picnic tables and fire grills are provided. A vault toilet is available. There is no drinking water, and garbage must be packed out. Some facilities are wheelchair accessible. Leashed pets are permitted.

Reservations, fees: Reservations are not accepted. There is no fee. Open late May–November, weather permitting.

Directions: From John Day, drive south on U.S. 395 for 10 miles to Forest Road 15. Turn left and drive nine miles southeast to Forest Road 1520. Turn left and drive five miles to the campground on the left.

Contact: Malheur National Forest, Blue Mountain Ranger District, 541/575-3000, fax 541/575-3319, www.fs.fed.us.

94 MURRAY CAMPGROUND

Scenic rating: 7

in Malheur National Forest

Map 4.7, page 223

Murray Elk Creek is set at an elevation of 5,200 feet with nearby Forest Service roads that provide access to the Strawberry Mountain Wilderness. The camp is used primarily as a layover for those heading into the wilderness to fish or hunt. Note that fishing is restricted to the use of artificial lures with a single, barbless hook.

Campsites, facilities: There are six sites for tents or RVs up to 40 feet long. Picnic tables and fire rings are provided. Vault toilets are available. There is no drinking water, and garbage must be packed out. Some facilities are wheelchair accessible. Leashed pets are permitted.

Reservations, fees: Reservations are not accepted. Sites are $8 per night, $4 per night for an additional vehicle. Open late May–November, weather permitting.

Directions: From John Day, drive east on U.S. 26 for 13 miles to Prairie City and County Road 62. Turn right and drive 24 miles to Forest Road 16. Turn right and follow signs to the campground on the right.

Contact: Malheur National Forest, Prairie City Ranger District, 541/820-3311, fax 541/820-3838, www.fs.fed.us.

95 BIG CREEK

Scenic rating: 6

near the Strawberry Mountain Wilderness in Malheur National Forest

Map 4.7, page 223

At 5,100 feet elevation, this campground hugs the banks of Big Creek. Nearby forest roads provide access to the Strawberry Mountain Wilderness. Other recreation options include fishing and mountain biking.

Note that fishing is restricted to the use of artificial lures with a single, barbless hook. In the appropriate seasons, bear, coyote, deer, and elk are hunted here.

Campsites, facilities: There are 15 sites for tents or RVs up to 40 feet long. Picnic tables and fire rings are provided. Drinking water and vault toilets are available. Garbage must be packed out. Some facilities are wheelchair accessible. Leashed pets are permitted.

Reservations, fees: Reservations are not accepted. Sites are $8 per night, $4 per night for an additional vehicle. Open late May–November, weather permitting.

Directions: From John Day, take U.S. 395 south for 10 miles to Forest Road 15. Turn left and on Forest Road 15 drive 16 miles to Forest Road 16. Turn right on Forest Road 16 and drive six miles to Forest Road 815. Turn right and drive 0.5 mile to the campground on the right.

Contact: Malheur National Forest, Prairie City Ranger District, 541/820-3311, fax 541/820-3838, www.fs.fed.us.

96 TROUT FARM

Scenic rating: 6

near Prairie City in Malheur National Forest
Map 4.7, page 223

Trout Farm campground (4,900 feet elevation) is situated on the Upper John Day River, which provides good trout fishing with easy access for people who don't wish to travel off paved roads. A picnic shelter is available for family picnics, and a small pond at the campground has a wheelchair-accessible trail.

Campsites, facilities: There are six sites for tents or RVs up to 21 feet long. Picnic tables and fire rings are provided. Drinking water and vault toilets are available. Garbage must be packed out. Some facilities are wheelchair accessible. Leashed pets are permitted.

Reservations, fees: Reservations are not accepted. Sites are $8 per night, $4 per night per additional vehicle. Open June–mid-October, weather permitting.

Directions: From John Day, drive east on U.S. 26 for 13 miles to Prairie City and Front Street. Turn right on Front Street and drive 0.5 mile to County Road 62. Turn left on County Road 62 and drive 15 miles to the campground entrance on the right.

Contact: Malheur National Forest, Prairie City Ranger District, 541/820-3311, fax 541/820-3838, www.fs.fed.us.

97 ELK CREEK

Scenic rating: 8

on Elk Creek in Malheur National Forest
Map 4.7, page 223

This tiny, pretty camp at the confluence of the north and south forks of Elk Creek (elevation 5,000 feet) has lots of hunting and fishing opportunities. The camp gets light use, except during the hunting season. If full, North Fork Malheur is an alternate camp in the area.

Campsites, facilities: There are five tent sites. Picnic tables and fire rings are provided. Vault toilets are available. There is no drinking water, and garbage must be packed out. Leashed pets are permitted.

Reservations, fees: Reservations are not accepted. There is no fee for camping. Open late May–November, weather permitting.

Directions: From John Day, drive east on U.S. 26 for 13 miles to Prairie City and County Road 62. Turn right (southeast) on County Road 62 and drive 8.5 miles to Forest Road 13. Turn left and drive 16 miles to Forest Road 16. Turn right and drive 1.5 miles south to the campground on the right.

Contact: Malheur National Forest, Prairie City Ranger District, 541/820-3311, fax 541/820-3838, www.fs.fed.us.

98 LITTLE CRANE

Scenic rating: 5

on Little Crane Creek in
Malheur National Forest

Map 4.7, page 223

Quiet, primitive, private, and small: all these words describe this camp along the banks of Little Crane Creek at an elevation of 5,500 feet. The creek provides good trout fishing (only artificial bait and artificial lures are allowed). There are also some nice hiking trails in the area, the closest one at the north fork of the Malheur River, about 10 miles away.

Campsites, facilities: There are four sites for tents or RVs up to 20 feet long. Picnic tables and fire rings are provided. Vault toilets are available. There is no drinking water, and garbage must be packed out. Leashed pets are permitted.

Reservations, fees: Reservations are not accepted. There is no fee for camping. Open late May–November, weather permitting.

Directions: From John Day, drive east on U.S. 26 for 13 miles to Prairie City and County Road 62. Turn right and drive 8.5 miles to Forest Road 13. Turn left and drive 16 miles to Forest Road 16. Turn right and drive 5.5 miles south to the campground on the left.

Contact: Malheur National Forest, Prairie City Ranger District, 541/820-3311, fax 541/820-3838, www.fs.fed.us.

99 NORTH FORK MALHEUR

Scenic rating: 7

on the north fork of the Malheur River in
Malheur National Forest

Map 4.7, page 223

The secluded North Fork Malheur campground sits at an elevation of 4,700 feet along the banks of the north fork of the Malheur River, a designated Wild and Scenic River. Hiking trails and dirt roads provide additional access to the river and backcountry streams.

(It's essential to obtain a U.S. Forest Service map.) Good fishing, hunting, and mountain biking opportunities abound in the area. Fishing is restricted to the use of artificial lures with a single, barbless hook.

Campsites, facilities: There are five sites for tents or RVs up to 21 feet long. Picnic tables and fire rings are provided. Vault toilets are available. There is no drinking water, and garbage must be packed out. Leashed pets are permitted.

Reservations, fees: Reservations are not accepted. There is no fee for camping. Open late May–November, weather permitting.

Directions: From John Day, drive east on U.S. 26 for 13 miles to Prairie City and County Road 62. Turn right and drive 8.5 miles to Forest Road 13. Turn left and drive 16 miles to Forest Road 16. Turn right and drive two miles south to a fork with Forest Road 1675. Take the left fork to Forest Road 1675 and drive two miles to the camp on the right.

Contact: Malheur National Forest, Prairie City Ranger District, 541/820-3311, fax 541/820-3838, www.fs.fed.us.

100 ROCK SPRINGS FOREST CAMP

Scenic rating: 5

at Rock Springs in Malheur National Forest

Map 4.7, page 223

If you want to camp in a big forest filled with the scent of ponderosa pines, Rock Springs Forest Camp is for you. This primitive camp has a sprinkling of pretty aspens and several little springs—in fact, it's located right on Rock Springs, with Cave Spring, House Creek Spring, and Sunshine Spring within a few miles. Do not count on the springs for drinking water, however, without a water filter. The elevation is 4,800 feet.

Campsites, facilities: There are 12 sites for tents or RVs up to 40 feet long. Picnic tables and fire grills are provided. Vault toilets are available. Drinking water is available from a spring (you must filter it first). Garbage must be packed out. Leashed pets are permitted.

Reservations, fees: Reservations are not accepted for single sites, but a permit is required for groups. Sites are $6 per night for first two vehicles, $3 per night for each additional vehicle. Open late May–mid-October, weather permitting.

Directions: From Burns, drive north on U.S. 395 for 30 miles to Van-Silvies Highway (County Road 73). Turn right on Van-Silvies Highway (which turns into Forest Road 17) and drive four miles to Forest Road 054. Turn right (south) and drive 0.75 mile to the camp on the left.

Contact: Malheur National Forest, Emigrant Creek Ranger District, 541/573-4300, fax 541/573-4398, www.fs.fed.us.

101 WEST EAGLE MEADOW
Scenic rating: 7

near West Eagle Creek in
Wallowa-Whitman National Forest

Map 4.8, page 224

West Eagle campground sits in a big, open meadow (5,200 feet elevation) about a five-minute walk from West Eagle Creek. The West Eagle Trail starts at the camp, providing access to the Eagle Cap Wilderness and offering a good opportunity to observe wildlife. The adjacent meadow fills with wildflowers in the summer. For campers with horses, there are new stock facilities with water available in a separate, adjacent campground.

Campsites, facilities: There are 24 sites for tents or RVs up to 30 feet long and an adjacent campground with six sites for campers with horses. Picnic tables and fire rings are provided. Vault toilets are available. There is no drinking water, and garbage must be packed out. Stock facilities include corrals and hitching rails. Some facilities are wheelchair accessible. Leashed pets are permitted.

Reservations, fees: Reservations are not accepted. Sites are $5 per night per vehicle. Open mid-June–late October, weather permitting.

Directions: From Baker City, drive north on I-84 for six miles to Highway 203. Turn east and drive 17 miles to the town of Medical Springs and County Road 71. Turn right (south) and drive two miles to Forest Road 67. Turn left and drive 12 miles to Forest Road 77. Turn left (north) and drive five miles to the camp on the right. Note: Segments of the road are narrow and steep.

Contact: Wallowa-Whitman National Forest, LaGrande Ranger District, 541/963-7186, fax 541/962-8580, www.fs.fed.us.

102 EAGLE FORKS
Scenic rating: 6

on Eagle Creek in
Wallowa-Whitman National Forest

Map 4.8, page 224

This campground (3,000 feet elevation) is located at the confluence of Little Eagle Creek and Eagle Creek. A trail follows the creek northwest for several miles, making for a prime day hike, yet the spot attracts few people. It's quite pretty and perfect for a weekend getaway or an extended layover.

Campsites, facilities: There are seven sites for tents or RVs up to 21 feet long. Picnic tables and fire rings are provided. Drinking water and vault toilets are available. Garbage must be packed out. Leashed pets are permitted.

Reservations, fees: Reservations are not accepted. Sites are $6 per night. Open May–late October, weather permitting.

Directions: From Baker City, drive east on Highway 86 for 42 miles to Richland and Newbridge. Turn north on Newbridge (after two miles on paved roads, it becomes Eagle Creek Rd.); then continue on Forest Road 7735 for seven miles to the campground entrance on the left.

Contact: Wallowa-Whitman National Forest, Pine Ranger District, 541/742-7511, fax 541/742-6705, www.fs.fed.us.

103 TWO COLOR

Scenic rating: 6

on Eagle Creek in
Wallowa-Whitman National Forest

Map 4.8, page 224

Two Color campground (4,800 feet elevation) sits on the banks of Eagle Creek, about a mile north of Tamarack. Evergreens shade the spacious campsites, and the creek is stocked with rainbow trout. If full, another option for campers is nearby Boulder Park campground, three miles northeast on Forest Road 7755.

Campsites, facilities: There are 14 sites for tents or RVs up to 16 feet long. Picnic tables and fire grills are provided. Vault toilets are available. There is no drinking water, and garbage must be packed out. Leashed pets are permitted.

Reservations, fees: Reservations are not accepted. Sites are $5 per night per vehicle. Open mid-June–late October, weather permitting.

Directions: From Baker City, drive north on I-84 for six miles to Highway 203. Turn east on Highway 203 and drive 17 miles to Medical Springs and County Road 71. Turn right (south) and drive two miles to Forest Road 67. Turn left and drive 12 miles to Forest Road 77. Turn left and drive one mile to Forest Road 7755. Turn right and drive one mile north to the camp.

Contact: Wallowa-Whitman National Forest, LaGrande Ranger District, 541/963-7186, fax 541/962-8580, www.fs.fed.us.

104 TAMARACK

Scenic rating: 5

on Eagle Creek in
Wallowa-Whitman National Forest

Map 4.8, page 224

On the banks of Eagle Creek in a beautiful area with lush vegetation and abundant wildlife sits Tamarack campground at 4,600 feet elevation. This is a good spot for fishing and hiking in a remote setting.

Campsites, facilities: There are 12 sites for tents or RVs up to 25 feet long. Picnic tables and fire rings are provided. Drinking water and vault toilets are available. Garbage must be packed out. Some facilities are wheelchair accessible. Leashed pets are permitted.

Reservations, fees: Reservations are not accepted. Sites are $6 per night. Open June–late October, weather permitting.

Directions: From Baker City, drive east on Highway 86 for 42 miles to Richland and Newbridge. Turn north on Newbridge (after two miles on paved roads, it becomes Eagle Creek Road); then continue on Forest Road 7735 for 20 miles to the campground entrance.

Contact: Wallowa-Whitman National Forest, Pine Ranger District, 541/742-7511, fax 541/742-6705, www.fs.fed.us.

105 FISH LAKE

Scenic rating: 6

on Fish Lake in
Wallowa-Whitman National Forest

Map 4.8, page 224

This is a pretty, well-forested camp with comfortable sites along the shore of 20-acre Fish Lake at an elevation of 6,600 feet. Fish Lake makes a good base for a fishing trip; side-trip options include hiking on nearby trails that lead to mountain streams. Sites on the upper loop accommodate longer RVs.

Campsites, facilities: There are 21 sites for tents or RVs up to 20 feet long. Picnic tables and fire rings are provided. Drinking water and vault toilets are available. Garbage must be packed out. Boat-launching facilities (for small boats only) are nearby. Leashed pets are permitted.

Reservations, fees: Reservations are not accepted. Sites are $6 per night. Open July–late October, weather permitting.

Directions: From Baker City, take I-84 north for four miles to Highway 86. Turn east on Highway 86 and drive 52 miles to Halfway and Main Street. Turn left (north) on Main Street and drive to Fish Lake Road. Turn right on Fish Lake Road, then drive five miles to Forest Road 66. Continue north on Forest Road 66 for 18.5 miles to the campground on the left.

Contact: Wallowa-Whitman National Forest, Pine Ranger District, 541/742-7511, fax 541/742-6705, www.fs.fed.us.

106 SPRING RECREATION SITE

🏊 🚤 🏕 🚻 🔥 ⛺

Scenic rating: 5

on the Snake River

Map 4.8, page 224

One of two camps in or near Huntington, this campground hugs the banks of the Brownlee Reservoir. Fishing is popular at this reservoir; it's known for large channel catfish. A more developed alternative, Farewell Bend State Recreation Area offers showers and all the other luxuries a camper could want.

Campsites, facilities: There are 35 sites for tents or RVs of any length. Picnic tables, garbage service, and fire grills are provided. Drinking water (summer only), a dump station, and vault toilets are available. Boat-launching facilities and a fish-cleaning station are on-site. A seasonal camp host is on-site. Leashed pets are permitted.

Reservations, fees: Reservations are not accepted. Sites are $5 per night per vehicle, with a 14-day stay limit. Open year-round, weather permitting.

Directions: From Ontario (near the Oregon/Idaho border), drive northwest on I-84 for 28 miles to Huntington and Snake River Road. Turn right (northeast) on Snake River Road and drive three miles (paved road) to the campground.

Contact: Bureau of Land Management, Baker City Office, 541/523-1256, fax 541/523-1965, www.blm.gov.

107 FAREWELL BEND STATE RECREATION AREA

🏊 🚤 🏕 🐾 🚻 ♿ 🔥 ⛺

Scenic rating: 7

on the Snake River

Map 4.8, page 224

Farewell Bend campground offers a green desert experience on the banks of the Snake River's Brownlee Reservoir. Situated along the Oregon Trail, the camp has historic interpretive displays and an evening interpretive program at the amphitheater during the summer. The lake provides good numbers of catfish.

Campsites, facilities: There are 101 sites with partial hookups for RVs up to 56 feet long, 30 tent sites, a hiker-biker camp, two cabins, and one group site for up to 25 people. Drinking water, garbage bins, fire rings, and picnic tables are provided. Restrooms with flush toilets and showers, a dump station, firewood, a fish-cleaning station, basketball hoops, horseshoe pits, sand volleyball court, and boat-launching facilities are available. Some facilities are wheelchair accessible. Leashed pets are permitted.

Reservations, fees: Reservations are accepted at 800/452-5687 or www.reserveamerica.com ($8 reservation fee). Tent sites are $11–18 per night, RV sites are $13–22, $4–5 per person per night for the hiker/biker camp, $43–76 per night for group sites, $38–42 per night for cabins, and $5 per night per extra vehicle. Some credit cards are accepted. Open year-round, with limited winter facilities.

Directions: From Ontario (near the Oregon/Idaho border), drive northwest on I-84 for 21 miles to Exit 353. Take that exit and drive one mile to the park.

Contact: Farewell Bend State Recreation Area, 541/869-2365 or 800/551-6949, www.oregonstateparks.org.

108 BULLY CREEK PARK

🚴 🏊 🎣 🛶 🏕 🐎 ♿ 🚐 ⛺

Scenic rating: 7

on Bully Creek Reservoir

Map 4.8, page 224

Bully Creek reservoir is located in a kind of high desert area with sagebrush and poplar trees for shade. It's beautiful if you like the desert, and the sunsets are worth the trip. People come here to boat, fish (mostly for warm-water fish, such as crappie and large and smallmouth bass), swim, and water ski, and there is biking on the gravel roads. At 2,300 feet elevation, the primitive setting is home to deer, jackrabbits, squirrels, and many birds. No monthly rentals are permitted here—a big plus for overnighters.

Campsites, facilities: There are 40 double sites with partial hookups for tents or RVs up to 40 feet in length; some sites are pull-through. There are also three group sites. Picnic tables and fire pits are provided. Drinking water, restrooms with flush toilets and showers, ice, garbage bins, a dump station, picnic area, and boat ramp and dock are available. A camp host is on-site. A restaurant, café, convenience store, gasoline, propane gas, charcoal, and coin laundry are within 10 miles. Bring your own firewood. Some facilities are wheelchair accessible. Leashed pets are permitted.

Reservations, fees: Reservations are accepted at 541/473-2969 ($15 deposit). Sites are $15 per night. Open mid-April–mid-November, weather permitting.

Directions: From Ontario (near the Oregon/Idaho border), drive west on U.S. 20/26 for 12 miles to Vale and Graham Boulevard. Turn right (northwest) on Graham Boulevard and drive five miles to Bully Creek Road. Turn right (west) and drive three miles to the park on the left.

Contact: Bully Creek Park, 541/473-2969, fax 541/473-9462; Malheur County Parks Department, 541/473-5191, fax 541/473-3701, www.malheurco.org.

THE SOUTHERN CASCADES

© PAT KULLBERG/123rf.com

BEST CAMPGROUNDS

◖ Most Scenic
Scott Lake Walk-In, **page 297.**
North Waldo, **page 312.**
Lava Lake, **page 334.**
Squaw Lake Hike-In, **page 387.**

◖ Families
Twin Lakes Resort, **page 340.**
Indian Mary Park, **page 358.**
Abbott Creek, **page 367.**
Lake of the Woods Resort, **page 377.**

◖ Fishing
Belknap Hot Springs Resort, **page 286.**
Mallard Marsh, **page 334.**
Trapper Creek, **page 350.**

◖ Hiking
Belknap Hot Springs Resort, **page 286.**
Boulder Flat, **page 321.**
Natural Bridge, **page 367.**
Aspen Point, **page 378.**

◖ Waterfalls
Salmon Creek Falls, **page 312.**
Susan Creek, **page 318.**
Steamboat Falls, **page 319.**
Hemlock Lake, **page 326.**

◖ Waterfront Campgrounds
Driftwood, **page 299.**
Hemlock Lake, **page 326.**
Gold Lake, **page 347.**
Bolan Lake, **page 366.**

◖ Wildlife-Viewing
Crooked River Ranch RV Park, **page 296.**
Bolan Lake, **page 366.**
Mount Ashland, **page 388.**

This region of Oregon is famous for one of its

lakes, but it holds many fantastic recreation secrets. The crown jewel is Crater Lake, of course, and visitors come from all over the world to see its vast cobalt-blue waters within cliff-like walls. The lake's Rim Drive is one of those trips that everybody should have on their life's to-do list.

Beyond the lake, though, you'll find stellar camping, fishing, and hiking spots. The best among them are neighboring Mount Washington Wilderness and Three Sisters Wilderness in Willamette National Forest, accessible via a beautiful drive on the McKenzie River Highway (Highway 126) east from Eugene and Springfield. Many ideal trailhead camps are detailed in this chapter for these areas.

But wait, there's more: Crane Prairie, Waldo Lake, and Wickiup Reservoir provide boating, camping, and good fishing. Wickiup, in turn, feeds into the headwaters of the Deschutes River, a prime steelhead locale. The Umpqua and Rogue National Forests offer some great water-sport destinations, including Diamond Lake, the headwaters of the Rogue River, and the headwaters of the North Umpqua, one of the prettiest rivers in North America. Upper Klamath Lake and the Klamath Basin are the number-one wintering areas in America for bald eagles. Klamath Lake also provides a chance to catch huge but elusive trout, as does the nearby Williamson River out of Chiloquin. All of this is but a small sampling of one of Oregon's best regions for adventure.

This region is all the more special for me because it evokes powerful personal memories. One of these is of a time at Hills Creek Reservoir southeast of Eugene. My canoe flipped on a cold winter day and I almost drowned after 20 minutes in the icy water. After I'd gone down for the count twice, my brother Bob jumped in, swam out, grabbed the front of the flipped canoe, and towed me to shore. Then, once ashore, he kept me awake, preventing me from lapsing into a coma from hypothermia.

Thanks, Bob.

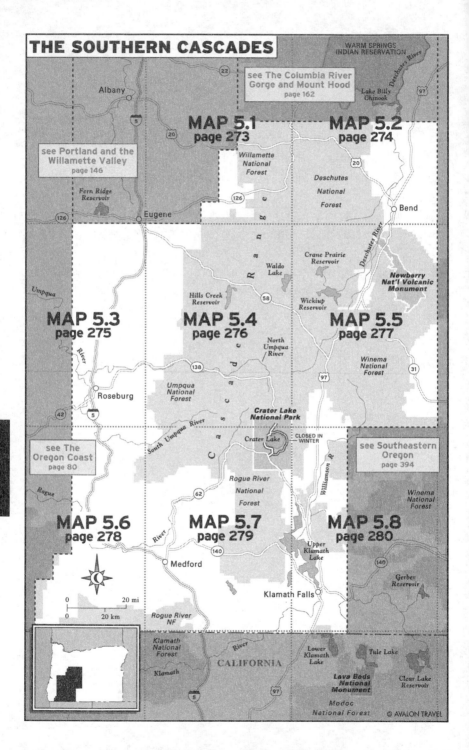

THE SOUTHERN CASCADES

WARM SPRINGS
INDIAN RESERVATION

see The Columbia River
Gorge and Mount Hood
page 162

Albany

MAP 5.1
page 273

MAP 5.2
page 274

see Portland and the
Willamette Valley
page 146

Willamette
National
Forest

Deschutes

National

Forest

Bend

Fern Ridge
Reservoir

Eugene

Crane Prairie
Reservoir

Deschutes River

Newberry
Nat'l Volcanic
Monument

Waldo
Lake

MAP 5.3
page 275

Hills Creek
Reservoir

MAP 5.4
page 276

Wickiup
Reservoir

MAP 5.5
page 277

Umpqua

North
Umpqua
River

Winema
National
Forest

River

Roseburg

Umpqua
National
Forest

South Umpqua River

Crater Lake
National Park

CLOSED IN
WINTER

Crater Lake

see The
Oregon Coast
page 80

see Southeastern
Oregon
page 394

Rogue

Rogue River

National

Winema
National
Forest

MAP 5.6
page 278

River

MAP 5.7
page 279

Forest

Williamson R

MAP 5.8
page 280

Medford

Upper
Klamath
Lake

Gerber
Reservoir

0   20 mi
0   20 km

Klamath Falls

Rogue River
NF

Klamath
National
Forest

River

CALIFORNIA

Klamath

Lower
Klamath
Lake

Tule Lake

Lava Beds
National
Monument

Clear Lake
Reservoir

Modoc
National Forest

© AVALON TRAVEL

Map 5.1

Campgrounds 1-17
Pages 281-287

Map 5.2

Campgrounds 18-51
Pages 288-301

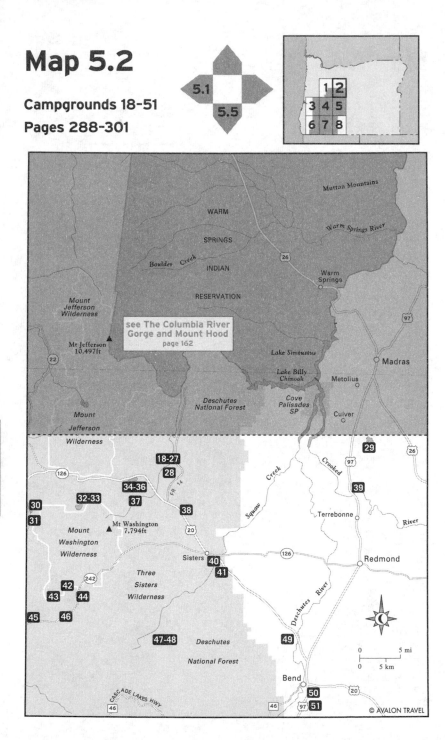

Map 5.3

Campgrounds 52-61
Pages 301-305

Map 5.4

Campgrounds 62-121
Pages 305-330

Map 5.5

Campgrounds 122-188
Pages 331-356

© AVALON TRAVEL

Map 5.6

Campgrounds 189-210

Pages 357-366

5.3

5.7

1 2
3 4 5
6 7 8

Riddle

Creek

Canyonville 189

South Umpqua River

227

42

Cow

190

5

Rogue

River

191

Glendale

192

see The
Oregon Coast
page 80

5

194

Siskiyou

193

Grants Pass 199-200

195

197 198

201

Rogue River

Gold Hill

234

202-203

196

199

National

Forest

Klamath Mountains

238

Chetco River

204-205

Kalmiopsis
Wilderness

Cave
Junction

207

206 46

208

209

Rogue River
National Forest

210

199

Siskiyou
National
Forest

Oregon Caves
Nat'l Monument

0   5 mi
0   5 km

© AVALON TRAVEL

OREGON

Map 5.7

Campgrounds 211-262

Pages 366-388

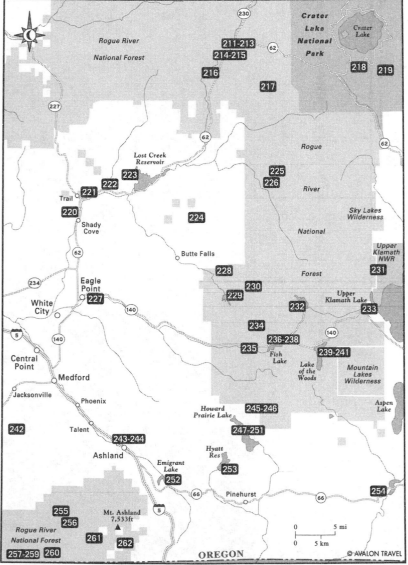

Map 5.8

Campgrounds 263-269

Pages 388-390

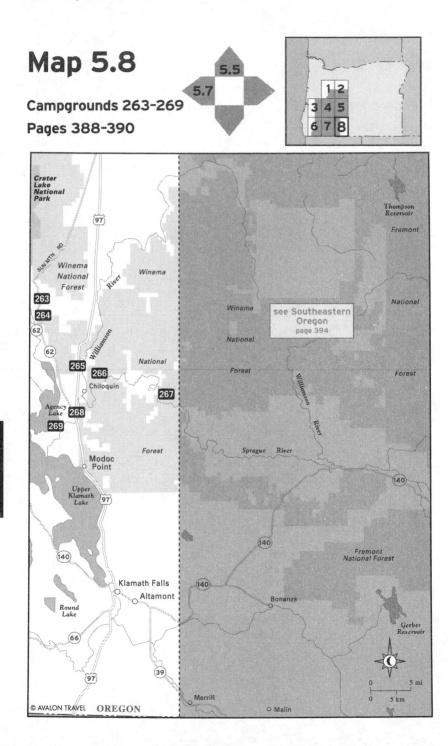

1 TROUT CREEK

🚶 🏊 🚣 🐕 ♿ 🚐 ⛺

Scenic rating: 8

on the South Santiam River in
Willamette National Forest

Map 5.1, page 273

Trout Creek campground is set along the banks
of the South Santiam River at 1,200 feet in elevation, about seven miles east of Cascadia. Fishing
and swimming are some of the recreation possibilities here. There is a historic shelter and the
remains of stonework from the era of the Civilian
Conservation Corps. The Trout Creek Trail, just
across the highway, leads into the Menagerie
Wilderness. The Long Ranch Elk Viewing Area
is immediately west of the campground, and,
at the Trout Creek Trailhead, you'll also find a
short trail leading to an elk-viewing platform.
Nearby is the Old Santiam Wagon Road.

Campsites, facilities: There are 24 sites for
tents or RVs up to 32 feet long. Picnic tables,
garbage bins, and fire rings are provided.
Drinking water and vault toilets are available. Some facilities are wheelchair accessible.
Leashed pets are permitted.

Reservations, fees: Reservations are not accepted. Sites are $12 per night, $5 per night
per additional vehicle. Open May–October,
weather permitting.

Directions: From Albany, drive east on U.S.
20 for 45 miles (19 miles past Sweet Home) to
the campground entrance on the right.

Contact: Willamette National Forest, Sweet
Home Ranger District, 541/367-5168, fax
541/367-2367, www.fs.fed.us.

2 YUKWAH

🚶 🏊 🚣 🐕 ♿ 🚐 ⛺

Scenic rating: 7

on the Santiam River in
Willamette National Forest

Map 5.1, page 273

Yukwah campground is nestled in a second-
growth Douglas fir forest on the banks of the
Santiam River. The camp is 0.25 mile east of
Trout Creek Campground and offers the same
recreation possibilities, including a 0.5-mile,
compacted-surface interpretive trail that's
barrier-free.

Campsites, facilities: There are 20 sites for
tents or RVs up to 32 feet long, including a
deluxe group site for up to 20 people. Picnic
tables, garbage bins, and fire grills are provided. Drinking water, vault toilets, a picnic
area, and a fishing platform are available.
Some facilities, including the fishing platform, are wheelchair accessible. Leashed pets
are permitted.

Reservations, fees: Reservations are not accepted. Sites are $12 per night, $5 per night
per additional vehicle. The deluxe site is $24
per night. Open May–October, weather
permitting.

Directions: From Albany, drive east on U.S.
20 for 45 miles (19 miles past Sweet Home)
to the campground.

Contact: Willamette National Forest, Sweet
Home Ranger District, 541/367-5168, fax
541/367-2367, www.fs.fed.us.

3 FERNVIEW

🚶 🏊 🚣 🐕 ♿ 🚐 ⛺

Scenic rating: 7

on the Santiam River in
Willamette National Forest

Map 5.1, page 273

This campground is perched high above the
confluence of Boulder Creek and the Santiam
River, just south of the Menagerie Wilderness.
A stepped walkway leads down to the river.
Just across U.S. 20 lies the Rooster Rock Trail,
which leads to—where else?—Rooster Rock,
the site of an old lookout tower. The Old
Santiam Wagon Road runs through the back
of the campground. The camp is best suited
for tent and small RV camping: The sites are
small. The elevation is 1,400 feet.

Campsites, facilities: There are nine sites for
tents or RVs up to 22 feet long and two tent-

only sites. Picnic tables, garbage bins, and fire grills are provided. Drinking water and vault toilets are available. Some facilities are wheelchair accessible. Leashed pets are permitted.

Reservations, fees: Reservations are not accepted. Sites are $12 per night, $5 per night per additional vehicle. Open mid-May–mid-September, weather permitting.

Directions: From Albany drive east on U.S. 20 for 49 miles (23 miles past Sweet Home) to the campground entrance on the right.

Contact: Willamette National Forest, Sweet Home Ranger District, 541/367-5168, fax 541/367-2367, www.fs.fed.us.

◢ HOUSE ROCK

Scenic rating: 8

on the Santiam River in
Willamette National Forest

Map 5.1, page 273

House Rock campground is situated at the confluence of Sheep Creek and the South Santiam River. The camp is set in the midst of an old-growth forest and is surrounded by huge, majestic Douglas fir. Trout fishing can be good, particularly during summer evenings. Botany students come here from long distances to see firsthand many uncommon and spectacular specimens of plantlife. History buffs should explore the short loop trail out of camp, which passes by House Rock, a historic rock shelter for Native Americans, and continues to the historic Old Santiam Wagon Road.

Campsites, facilities: There are 12 sites for tents or RVs up to 22 feet long and five tent-only sites. Picnic tables, garbage bins, and fire grills are provided. Vault toilets and drinking water are available. Some facilities are wheelchair accessible. Leashed pets are permitted.

Reservations, fees: Reservations are not accepted. Sites are $12 per night, $5 per night

per additional vehicle. Open May–October, weather permitting.

Directions: From Albany drive east on U.S. 20 for 52.5 miles (26 miles past Sweet Home) to Latiwi Road (Forest Road 2044). Turn right and drive a short distance to the campground.

Contact: Willamette National Forest, Sweet Home Ranger District, 541/367-5168, fax 541/367-2367, www.fs.fed.us.

◢ LOST PRAIRIE

Scenic rating: 7

on Hackleman Creek in
Willamette National Forest

Map 5.1, page 273

Lost Prairie campground hugs the banks of Hackleman Creek at 3,200 feet elevation in an area of Douglas fir and spruce. Three excellent hiking trails can be found within five miles of the camp: Hackleman Old-Growth Grove, Cone Peak, and Iron Mountain. The last two offer spectacular wildflower-viewing in the late spring and early summer. This camp provides an alternative to nearby Fish Lake.

Campsites, facilities: There are 10 sites for tents or RVs up to 28 feet long (eight are walk-in sites). Picnic tables, garbage bins, and fire grills are provided. Drinking water and vault toilets are available. Some facilities are wheelchair accessible. Leashed pets are permitted.

Reservations, fees: Reservations are not accepted. Sites are $14 per night, $7 per night per additional vehicle. Open May–October, weather permitting.

Directions: From Albany, drive east on U.S. 20 for 63 miles (approximately 38 miles past Sweet Home) to the camp on the right.

Contact: Willamette National Forest, Sweet Home Ranger District, 541/367-5168, fax 541/367-2367, www.fs.fed.us; Hoodoo Recreation, 541/822-3799.

6 LAKES END BOAT-IN

Scenic rating: 9

on Smith Reservoir in
Willamette National Forest

Map 5.1, page 273

This secluded boat-in campground is set along the shore of the headwaters of Smith Reservoir, a long narrow lake. You'll find no cars and no traffic. The trout fishing in this reservoir can be exceptional; note the 10-mph speed limit. The campground is split into two areas, providing camping opportunities on Smith Creek and on the reservoir.

Campsites, facilities: There are 17 boat-in tent sites. Picnic tables and fire grills are provided. Pit toilets are available. There is no drinking water, and garbage must be packed out. Boat docks are nearby. Leashed pets are permitted.

Reservations, fees: Reservations are not accepted. There is no fee for camping. Open May–September, weather permitting.

Directions: From Eugene, drive east on Highway 126 for 47 miles to the town of McKenzie Bridge. Continue on Highway 126 for 13 miles to the signed turnoff for Lakes End at the north end of Trail Bridge Reservoir. Turn left on Forest Road 1477 and drive a short distance; then bear left and continue (past Trail Bridge Campground) for 0.5 mile to Forest Road 730 (Smith Reservoir Road). Continue three miles to the boat launch.

Contact: Willamette National Forest, McKenzie River Ranger District, 541/822-3381, fax 541/822-7254, www.fs.fed.us.

7 TRAIL BRIDGE

Scenic rating: 6

on Trail Bridge Reservoir in
Willamette National Forest

Map 5.1, page 273

Set along the shore of Trail Bridge Reservoir (2,000 feet elevation), this campground offers boating, fishing, and hiking among its recreation options. From the camp, there is access to the McKenzie River National Recreation Trail. Highway 126 east of McKenzie Bridge is a designated scenic route, providing a pleasant trip to the camp and making Trail Bridge an exceptional spot for car campers. For a good side trip, take the beautiful 40-minute drive east to the little town of Sisters.

Campsites, facilities: There are 46 sites for tents or RVs up to 45 feet long and a large camping area at Trail Bridge Flats. Picnic tables, garbage service, and fire grills are provided. Drinking water and vault and flush toilets are available. Boat ramps are nearby. Some facilities are wheelchair accessible. Leashed pets are permitted.

Reservations, fees: Reservations are not accepted. Sites are $10 per night, $5 per night per additional vehicle. Open late April–September, weather permitting.

Directions: From Eugene, drive east on Highway 126 for 47 miles to the town of McKenzie Bridge. Continue on Highway 126 for 13 miles to Forest Road 1477. Turn left on Forest Road 1477 and drive a short distance; then bear left and continue 0.25 mile to the campground on the left.

Contact: Willamette National Forest, McKenzie River Ranger District, 541/822-3381, fax 541/822-7254, www.fs.fed.us.

8 OLALLIE

Scenic rating: 7

on the McKenzie River in
Willamette National Forest

Map 5.1, page 273

Olallie campground sits at an elevation of 2,000 feet elevation along the banks of the McKenzie River. Boating, fishing, and hiking are among its recreational opportunities, and fishing for rainbow trout usually is good. Other bonuses include easy access from Highway 126. The campground is two miles southwest of Trail Bridge Reservoir off Highway 126.

Campsites, facilities: There are 16 sites for tents or RVs up to 35 feet long. Picnic tables and fire grills are provided. Vault toilets, drinking water, and garbage service are available. A boat launch is nearby (non-motorized boats only). Leashed pets are permitted.

Reservations, fees: Reservations are accepted at 877/444-6777 or www.recreation.gov ($10 reservation fee). Sites are $12–14 per night, $7 per night per additional vehicle. Open late April–October, weather permitting.

Directions: From Eugene, drive east on Highway 126 for 47 miles to the town of McKenzie Bridge. Continue on Highway 126 for 11 miles to the campground on the left.

Contact: Willamette National Forest, McKenzie River Ranger District, 541/822-3381, fax 541/822-7254, www.fs.fed.us; Hoodoo Recreation, 541/822-3799.

9 MONA

Scenic rating: 8

near Blue River Reservoir in Willamette National Forest

Map 5.1, page 273

This forested campground (1,360 feet elevation) is set along the shore of Blue River Reservoir, close to where the Blue River joins it. A boat ramp is located across the river from the campground (at Lookout Campground); another boat ramp is situated at the south end of the reservoir. After launching a boat, campers can ground it near their campsite. Note that this camp is extremely popular when the reservoir is full.

Campsites, facilities: There are 23 sites for tents or RVs up to 36 feet long. Picnic tables, garbage bins, and fire grills are provided. Drinking water and flush toilets are available. Some facilities are wheelchair accessible. Leashed pets are permitted.

Reservations, fees: Reservations are not accepted. Single sites are $16 per night, $30 per

night for double sites, $8 per night per additional vehicle. Open May–mid-September, weather permitting.

Directions: From Eugene, drive east on Highway 126 for 41 miles to Blue River. Continue east on Highway 126 for three miles to Forest Road 15. Turn left (north) and drive three miles to the campground on the left.

Contact: Willamette National Forest, McKenzie River Ranger District, 541/822-3381, fax 541/822-7254, www.fs.fed.us; Hoodoo Recreation, 541/822-3799.

10 PATIO RV PARK

Scenic rating: 7

near the South Fork of the McKenzie River

Map 5.1, page 273

This RV park is situated near the banks of the South Fork of the McKenzie River, not far from Cougar Lake, which offers opportunities for fishing, swimming, and waterskiing. Nearby recreation options include a golf course, hiking trails, and bike paths. The Hoodoo Ski Area is approximately 30 miles away.

Campsites, facilities: There are 60 sites with full hookups for RVs of any length and a grassy area for tents. Picnic tables are provided. Restrooms with flush toilets and coin showers, ice, firewood, a recreation hall, video rentals, group kitchen facilities, cable TV, modem access, a community fire pit, horseshoe pits, and a coin laundry are available. A store, gasoline, propane, and a café are within two miles. Leashed pets are permitted.

Reservations, fees: Reservations are accepted at 800/650-0290 or via email at reservations@patiorv.com. RV sites are $26–31 per night, tent sites are $20 per night, $2 per person per night for more than two people, and $8 per night per additional vehicle. Some credit cards are accepted. Open year-round, weather permitting.

Directions: From Eugene, drive east on Highway 126 for 37 miles to the town of Blue River.

Continue east on Highway 126 for six miles to McKenzie River Drive. Turn right and drive two miles to the park on the right.
Contact: Patio RV Park, 541/822-3596, fax 541/822-8392, www.patiorv.com.

1.1 DELTA

Scenic rating: 8

on the McKenzie River in
Willamette National Forest
Map 5.1, page 273

This popular campground sits along the banks of the McKenzie River in a spot heavily forested primarily with old-growth Douglas fir. The Delta Old Growth Nature Trail, a 0.5-mile wheelchair-accessible interpretive trail, is adjacent to the campground. The camp also features an amphitheater. Nearby are Blue River and Cougar Reservoirs (seven and five miles away, respectively), both of which offer swimming, trout fishing, and waterskiing.
Campsites, facilities: There are 38 sites for tents or RVs up to 36 feet long. Picnic tables, garbage bins, and fire grills are provided. Drinking water and vault toilets are available. Some facilities are wheelchair accessible. Leashed pets are permitted.
Reservations, fees: Reservations are not accepted. Single sites are $14 per night, $26 per night for double sites, and $7 per night per additional vehicle. Open late April–October, weather permitting.
Directions: From Eugene, drive east on Highway 126 for 37 miles to the town of Blue River. Continue east on Highway 126 for five miles to Forest Road 19 (Aufderheide Scenic Byway). Turn right (south) and drive 0.25 mile to Forest Road 400. Turn right and drive one mile to the campground.
Contact: Willamette National Forest, McKenzie River Ranger District, 541/822-3381, fax 541/822-7254, www.fs.fed.us; Hoodoo Recreation, 541/822-3799.

1.2 McKENZIE BRIDGE

Scenic rating: 8

on the McKenzie River in
Willamette National Forest
Map 5.1, page 273

McKenzie campground is set at 1,400 feet elevation along the banks of the McKenzie River, one mile from the town of McKenzie Bridge. During the summer, this stretch of river provides good evening fly-fishing for trout; only non-motorized boats are permitted on the river.
Campsites, facilities: There are 20 sites for tents or RVs up to 40 feet long. Picnic tables, garbage service, and fire rings are provided. Flush toilets and drinking water are available. A grocery store and restaurants are available within one mile. Some facilities are wheelchair accessible. Leashed pets are permitted.
Reservations, fees: Reservations are accepted at 877/444-6777 or www.recreation.gov ($10 reservation fee). Sites are $14 per night, $7 per night per additional vehicle. Open April–September, weather permitting.
Directions: From Eugene, drive east on Highway 126 for 46 miles to the campground entrance on the right (one mile west of the town of McKenzie Bridge).
Contact: Willamette National Forest, McKenzie River Ranger District, 541/822-3381, fax 541/822-7254, www.fs.fed.us; Hoodoo Recreation, 541/822-3799.

1.3 HORSE CREEK GROUP CAMP

Scenic rating: 9

on Horse Creek in Willamette National Forest
Map 5.1, page 273

This campground reserved for groups borders Horse Creek near the town of McKenzie Bridge. In spite of the name, no horse camping is permitted. Fishing is catch-and-release only;

check current regulations. The camp sits at 1,400 feet elevation.

Campsites, facilities: This is a group camp with 21 sites for tents or RVs up to 27 feet long. Picnic tables and fire grills are provided. Vault toilets, drinking water, and garbage service are available. Leashed pets are permitted.

Reservations, fees: Reservations are accepted at 877/444-6777 or www.recreation.gov ($10 reservation fee). The fees are $40 per night for up to 49 people and $60 per night for 50–100 people. Open May–September, weather permitting.

Directions: From Eugene, drive east on Highway 126 for 47 miles to the town of McKenzie Bridge and Horse Creek Road. Turn right (south) on Horse Creek Road and drive one mile to the campground on the left.

Contact: Willamette National Forest, McKenzie River Ranger District, 541/822-3381, fax 541/822-7254, www.fs.fed.us.

14 PARADISE

Scenic rating: 9

on the McKenzie River in
Willamette National Forest

Map 5.1, page 273

Paradise campground (1,600 feet elevation), along the banks of the McKenzie River, may be right off the highway, but it offers a rustic, streamside setting with access to the McKenzie River National Recreation Trail. Trout fishing can be good here.

Campsites, facilities: There are 64 sites for tents or RVs of any length. Picnic tables, garbage service, and fire rings are provided. Flush and vault toilets, drinking water, a boat ramp, and firewood are available. Some facilities are wheelchair accessible. Leashed pets are permitted.

Reservations, fees: Reservations are accepted at 877/444-6777 or www.recreation.gov ($10 reservation fee). Single sites are $18 per night, double sites are $32 per night, $9 per night

per additional vehicle. Open May–September, weather permitting.

Directions: From Eugene, drive east on Highway 126 for 47 miles to the town of McKenzie Bridge. Continue east on Highway 126 for 3.5 miles to the campground on the left.

Contact: Willamette National Forest, McKenzie River Ranger District, 541/822-3381, fax 541/822-7254, www.fs.fed.us; Hoodoo Recreation, 541/822-3799.

15 BELKNAP HOT SPRINGS RESORT

Scenic rating: 9

on the McKenzie River

Map 5.1, page 273   **BEST (**

This beautiful park, with 60 acres of developed and landscaped gardens, has been featured on at least one magazine cover. It's in a wooded, mountainous area on the McKenzie River. Trout fishing can be excellent here. If you're looking for hiking opportunities, the McKenzie River Trail can be accessed from camp. Other hiking opportunities include the Three Sisters and Mount Washington Wilderness Areas, both accessible by driving west of Sisters on Highway 242. Exceptionally scenic and pristine expanses of forest, they are well worth exploring. The Pacific Crest Trail runs north and south through both wilderness areas.

Campsites, facilities: There are 62 sites with full or partial hookups for RVs of any length, 15 sites for tents, a lodge with 18 rooms, and six cabins. Picnic tables and fire pits are provided. Drinking water, restrooms with showers, and a dump station are available. Recreational facilities include two hot-spring fed swimming pools, massage therapy on weekends, and a recreation field. Some facilities are wheelchair accessible. Leashed pets are permitted at the campground and in some of the cabins; pets are not permitted in the other cabins and lodge rooms.

Reservations, fees: Reservations are accepted

at 541/822-3512. Tent sites are $25–30 per night, RV sites are $35 per night, cabins are $65–400, $10 pet fee, lodge rooms are $100–185, $8 per person per night for more than two people. All fees include access to the hot springs. Some credit cards are accepted. Open year-round.

Directions: From Eugene, drive east on Highway 126 for 56 miles to Belknap Springs Road. Turn left and drive 0.5 mile until the road dead-ends at the lodge.

Contact: Belknap Hot Springs Resort, 541/822-3512, fax 541/822-3327, www. belknaphotsprings.com.

16 SLIDE CREEK

Scenic rating: 6

on Cougar Reservoir in
Willamette National Forest

Map 5.1, page 273

Slide Creek campground sits on a hillside overlooking Cougar Reservoir, which covers about 1,300 acres, has a paved boat landing and offers opportunities for fishing, swimming, and waterskiing. This pretty lakeside camp at 1,700 feet in elevation is quite popular, so plan to arrive early on weekends. If the camp is full, Cougar Crossing (off Road 19) and Sunnyside (off Road 500) are nearby alternatives.

Campsites, facilities: There are 16 sites for tents or RVs up to 50 feet long. Picnic tables and fire grills are provided. Drinking water, garbage bins, and vault toilets are available. A boat ramp is also available. Leashed pets are permitted.

Reservations, fees: Reservations are not accepted. Single sites are $16 per night, $30 per night for double sites, $8 per night per additional vehicle. Open May–September, weather permitting.

Directions: From Eugene, drive east on Highway 126 for 41 miles to the town of Blue River. Continue east on Highway 126 for five miles

to Aufderheide Scenic Byway. Turn right (south) and drive 11 miles (along the west shore of Cougar Reservoir, crossing the reservoir bridge) to Eastside Road (Forest Road 500). Turn left and drive 1.5 miles northeast to the campground set on the southeast shore of the lake.

Contact: Willamette National Forest, McKenzie River Ranger District, 541/822-3381, fax 541/822-7254, www.fs.fed.us; Hoodoo Recreation, 541/822-3799.

17 FRENCH PETE

Scenic rating: 8

on the South Fork of the McKenzie River in
Willamette National Forest

Map 5.1, page 273

This quiet, wooded campground is set on the banks of the south fork of the McKenzie River and French Pete Creek at 1,800 feet in elevation. Fishing is catch-and-release only. A trail across the road from the campground provides access to the Three Sisters Wilderness (permit required; contact district office). French Pete is only two miles from Cougar Reservoir, and the camp attracts campers wanting to use Cougar Reservoir facilities. Two more primitive camps (Homestead and Frissell Crossing) are located a few miles southeast on the same road.

Campsites, facilities: There are 17 sites for tents or RVs up to 40 feet long. Picnic tables, garbage containers, and fire grills are provided. Drinking water and vault toilets are available. Leashed pets are permitted.

Reservations, fees: Reservations are not accepted. Sites are $14 per night, $5 per night per additional vehicle. Open May–September, weather permitting.

Directions: From Eugene, drive east on Highway 126 for 41 miles to the town of Blue River. Continue east on Highway 126 for five miles to Forest Road 19 (Aufderheide Scenic Byway). Turn right (south) and drive 12 miles to the campground on the right.

Contact: Willamette National Forest, McKenzie River Ranger District, 541/822-3381, fax 541/822-7254, www.fs.fed.us.

18 CAMP SHERMAN

Scenic rating: 6

on the Metolius River in
Deschutes National Forest

Map 5.2, page 274

Camp Sherman is set at an elevation of 2,950 feet along the banks of the Metolius River, where you can fish for wild trout. This place is for expert fly anglers seeking a quality fishing experience. Camp Sherman is one of five camps in the immediate area. It's advisable to obtain a map of the Deschutes National Forest that details back roads, streams, and trails.

A personal note: My late pal, John Korb, named his dog Sherman after this camp.

Campsites, facilities: There are 14 sites for tents or RVs up to 40 feet long. Picnic tables and fire grills are provided. Drinking water and garbage service is available mid-April–mid-October. Vault toilets and a picnic shelter are available. Leashed pets are permitted.

Reservations, fees: Reservations are accepted at 877/444-6777 or www.recreation.gov ($10 reservation fee). Sites are $12–16 per night, $6–8 per night per additional vehicle. Open year-round, weather permitting.

Directions: From Albany, drive east on U.S. 20 for 87 miles (near Black Butte) to the sign for Camp Sherman and Forest Road 14. Turn left on Forest Road 14 and drive five miles to Camp Sherman, the store, and Forest Road 900. Turn left on Forest Road 900 and drive 0.5 mile to the campground on the left.

Contact: Deschutes National Forest, Sisters Ranger District, 541/549-7700, fax 541/549-7746, www.fs.fed.us.

19 ALLINGHAM

Scenic rating: 5

on the Metolius River in
Deschutes National Forest

Map 5.2, page 274

One of five camps in the immediate area, Allingham sits along the banks of the Metolius River. The river is perfect for trout fishing, and fly anglers will find a quality fishing experience.

Campsites, facilities: There are 10 sites for tents or RVs up to 40 feet long. Picnic tables and fire grills are provided. Vault toilets, drinking water, and garbage service are available. A dump station is nearby. Leashed pets are permitted.

Reservations, fees: Reservations are not accepted. Sites are $16 per night, $8 per night per additional vehicle. Open May–September, weather permitting.

Directions: From Albany, drive east on U.S. 20 for 87 miles (near Black Butte) to the sign for Camp Sherman and Forest Road 14. Turn left on Forest Road 14 and drive five miles to Camp Sherman, the store, and Forest Road 900. Turn left on Forest Road 900 and drive one mile to the campground on the left.

Contact: Deschutes National Forest, Sisters Ranger District, 541/549-7700, fax 541/549-7746, www.fs.fed.us.

20 BLACK BUTTE RESORT

Scenic rating: 6

near the Metolius River

Map 5.2, page 274

Black Butte offers a choice of graveled or grassy sites in a clean, scenic environment. Located near the Camp Sherman area, this is a nice spot for bird-watching, fishing, and hiking.

Campsites, facilities: There are 30 sites with

full or partial hookups for RVs of any length and six motel rooms. Picnic tables and barbecues are provided. Restrooms with flush toilets and showers, a dump station, recreation room, firewood, and a coin laundry are available. Propane gas, an additional dump station, a store, café, and ice are within one block. Leashed pets are permitted.

Reservations, fees: Reservations are accepted. Sites are $26–28 per night, $3 per person per night for more than two people, $7 per additional vehicle (unless towed). Some credit cards are accepted. Open year-round.

Directions: From Albany, drive east on U.S. 20 for 87 miles (near Black Butte) to the sign for Camp Sherman. Turn left (north) on Forest Road 1419 and drive four miles to a stop sign and the resort access road. Turn right and drive 0.25 mile to the park on the right.

Contact: Black Butte Resort, 541/595-6514, fax 541/595-5971, http://blackbutterv.com.

21 PINE REST

Scenic rating: 5

on the Metolius River in
Deschutes National Forest

Map 5.2, page 274

Pine Rest campground is set at an elevation of 2,900 feet along the banks of the Metolius River. Fly-fishing and hiking are recreation options.

Campsites, facilities: There are eight tent sites. Picnic tables and fire grills are provided. Vault toilets, a picnic shelter, and drinking water are available. Garbage service is available in season. Leashed pets are permitted.

Reservations, fees: Reservations are not accepted. Sites are $16–30 per night, $6–8 per night per additional vehicle. Open year-round, weather permitting.

Directions: From Albany, drive east on U.S. 20 for 87 miles (near Black Butte) to the sign

for Camp Sherman and Forest Road 14. Turn left on Forest Road 14 and drive five miles to Camp Sherman, the store, and Forest Road 900. Turn left on Forest Road 900 and drive two miles to the campground on the left.

Contact: Deschutes National Forest, Sisters Ranger District, 541/549-7700, fax 541/549-7746, www.fs.fed.us.

22 GORGE

Scenic rating: 5

on the Metolius River in
Deschutes National Forest

Map 5.2, page 274

Here is another of the camps set along the banks of the Metolius River near Camp Sherman. Gorge campground is located at an elevation of 2,900 feet and is more open, with less vegetation than many of the others. Fly-fishing and hiking trails provide recreation opportunities.

Campsites, facilities: There are 18 sites for tents or RVs up to 40 feet long. Picnic tables and fire grills are provided. Vault toilets, drinking water, and garbage service are available. Leashed pets are permitted.

Reservations, fees: Reservations are not accepted. Sites are $16 per night, $8 per night per additional vehicle. Open May–September, weather permitting.

Directions: From Albany, drive east on U.S. 20 for 87 miles (near Black Butte) to the sign for Camp Sherman and Forest Road 14. Turn left on Forest Road 14 and drive five miles to Camp Sherman, the store, and Forest Road 900. Turn left on Forest Road 900 and drive 2.5 miles to the campground on the left.

Contact: Deschutes National Forest, Sisters Ranger District, 541/549-7700, fax 541/549-7746, www.fs.fed.us.

23 SMILING RIVER
🚶 🛶 🏕 🚐 ⛺

Scenic rating: 5

on the Metolius River in
Deschutes National Forest

Map 5.2, page 274

Smiling River sits along the banks of the
Metolius River at an elevation of 2,900 feet.
Another campground in the popular Camp
Sherman area, Smiling River has access to fly-
fishing and nearby hiking trails.

Campsites, facilities: There are 35 sites for
tents or RVs up to 50 feet long. Picnic tables
and fire grills are provided. Vault toilets,
drinking water, and garbage service are available. Leashed pets are permitted.

Reservations, fees: Reservations are accepted
at 877/444-6777 or www.recreation.gov ($10
reservation fee). Sites are $16 per night, $8
per night per additional vehicle. Open May–
October, weather permitting.

Directions: From Albany, drive east on U.S.
20 for 87 miles (near Black Butte) to the sign
for Camp Sherman and Forest Road 14. Turn
left on Forest Road 14 and drive five miles to
Camp Sherman, the store, and Forest Road
900. Turn left on Forest Road 900 and drive
one mile to the campground on the left.

Contact: Deschutes National Forest, Sisters
Ranger District, 541/549-7700, fax 541/549-
7746, www.fs.fed.us.

24 ALLEN SPRINGS
🚶 🛶 🏕 🚐 ⛺

Scenic rating: 7

on the Metolius River in
Deschutes National Forest

Map 5.2, page 274

Shady Allen Springs campground is nestled in
a conifer forest along the banks of the Metolius
River, where fishing and hiking can be good.
For an interesting side trip, head to the Wizard
Falls Fish Hatchery about a mile away.

Campsites, facilities: There are 16 sites for

tents or RVs up to 36 feet long. Picnic tables
and fire grills are provided. Vault toilets, drinking water, and garbage service are available.
A store, café, and ice are within five miles.
Leashed pets are permitted.

Reservations, fees: Reservations are not accepted. Single sites are $14 per night, double
sites are $30 per night, $7 per night per additional vehicle. Open April–October, weather
permitting.

Directions: From Albany, drive east on U.S.
20 for 87 miles (near Black Butte) to the sign
for Camp Sherman and Forest Road 14. Turn
left on Forest Road 14 and drive about nine
miles to the campground on the left.

Contact: Deschutes National Forest, Sisters
Ranger District, 541/549-7700, fax 541/549-
7746, www.fs.fed.us.

25 LOWER BRIDGE
🚶 🛶 🏕 🚐 ⛺

Scenic rating: 6

on the Metolius River in
Deschutes National Forest

Map 5.2, page 274

Lower Bridge campground is set along the
banks of the Metolius River at an elevation of
2,700 feet. The setting is similar to Pioneer
Ford, but with less vegetation. A picnic area
is located across the bridge.

Campsites, facilities: There are 12 sites for
tents or RVs up to 30 feet long. Picnic tables
and fire grills are provided. Vault toilets,
drinking water, and garbage service are available. Leashed pets are permitted.

Reservations, fees: Reservations are not accepted. Sites are $16 per night, $8 per night
per additional vehicle. Open May–October,
weather permitting.

Directions: From Albany, drive east on U.S.
20 for 87 miles (near Black Butte) to the sign
for Camp Sherman and Forest Road 14. Turn
left on Forest Road 14 and drive 12 miles to
the campground on the right.

Contact: Deschutes National Forest, Sisters

Ranger District, 541/549-7700, fax 541/549-7746, www.fs.fed.us.

26 PIONEER FORD

🏃 ♨ 🛏 ♿ 🚐 ⛺

Scenic rating: 7

on the Metolius River in
Deschutes National Forest

Map 5.2, page 274

Quiet and serene Pioneer Ford campground is set along the banks of the Metolius River at an elevation of 2,750 feet. The wooded campground features grassy sites north of the Camp Sherman area. Hiking and fly-fishing are activities here.

Campsites, facilities: There are 20 sites for tents or RVs up to 50 feet long. Picnic tables and fire grills are provided. Drinking water and garbage service are provided. Vault toilets are available. Some facilities are wheelchair accessible. Leashed pets are permitted.

Reservations, fees: Reservations are not accepted. Sites are $16 per night, $8 per night per additional vehicle. Open May–September, weather permitting.

Directions: From Albany, drive east on U.S. 20 for 87 miles (near Black Butte) to the sign for Camp Sherman and Forest Road 14. Turn left on Forest Road 14 and drive 11 miles to the campground on the left.

Contact: Deschutes National Forest, Sisters Ranger District, 541/549-7700, fax 541/549-7746, www.fs.fed.us.

27 COLD SPRINGS RESORT & RV PARK

🏃 🚲 ♨ 🛶 🚣 🎣 🛏 🚐 ⛺

Scenic rating: 7

on the Metolius River

Map 5.2, page 274

This pretty, wooded RV park on the Metolius River is world-famous for its fly-fishing and features an acre of riverfront lawn. Bird-watching is also popular. Recreation options in the area include boating, swimming, waterskiing, and windsurfing. In addition, nearby facilities include a golf course, hiking and biking trails, a riding stable, and tennis courts. Winter activities vary from alpine and Nordic skiing to sledding, snowmobiling, and winter camping. A private footbridge leads from the resort to Camp Sherman; the towns of Sisters and Bend are nearby (15 miles and 35 miles, respectively).

Campsites, facilities: There are 45 sites with full hookups for RVs of any length, a grassy area for tents, and five cabins on the river. Fire pits, picnic tables, and patios are provided. Restrooms with showers, coin laundry, wireless Internet service, firewood, and a riverfront picnic facility are available. Propane gas, a convenience store, fishing and sport supplies, a café, a post office, and ice are within 0.25 mile. Leashed pets are permitted.

Reservations, fees: Reservations are accepted. Sites are $30 per night, $2 per person per night for more than two people, and $2 per pet per night. Some credit cards are accepted. Open year-round.

Directions: From Albany, drive east on U.S. 20 for 87 miles (near Black Butte) to the sign for Camp Sherman/Metolius River. Turn left (north) on Forest Road 14 and drive 4.5 miles to a stop sign. Turn right (still Forest Road 14) and drive about 300 feet to Cold Springs Resort Lane. Turn right and drive through the forest and the meadow, crossing Cold Springs Creek, to the resort.

Contact: Cold Springs Resort & RV Park, 541/595-6271, fax 541/595-1400, www.coldsprings-resort.com.

28 RIVERSIDE WALK-IN

🏃 🚲 ♨ 🛏 ⛺

Scenic rating: 7

on the Metolius River in
Deschutes National Forest

Map 5.2, page 274

Riverside Walk-In is set 100 yards back from the banks of the Metolius River, less than a mile from Metolius Springs at the base of Black Butte. Because this is a tent-only campground, and just far enough off the highway to be missed by most other people, it stays very quiet. You'll find plenty of solitude here. After parking along the road, you must walk to the campsites, carrying any gear in the process.

Campsites, facilities: There are 16 tent sites. Picnic tables and fire grills are provided. Vault toilets, garbage service, and drinking water are available. Leashed pets are permitted.

Reservations, fees: Reservations are not accepted. Sites are $12 per night, $6 per night per additional vehicle. Open May–September, weather permitting.

Directions: From Albany, drive east on U.S. 20 for 87 miles to the sign for Camp Sherman and Forest Road 14. Turn left and drive five miles to Forest Road 800. Turn left and drive a short distance to the campground.

Contact: Deschutes National Forest, Sisters Ranger District, 541/549-7700, fax 541/549-7746, www.fs.fed.us.

29 HAYSTACK RESERVOIR

Scenic rating: 5

on Haystack Reservoir in
Crooked River National Grassland

Map 5.2, page 274

This campground can be found in the high desert along the shore of Haystack Reservoir, a bright spot in an expansive desert landscape. The camps feature a moderate amount of privacy, as well as views of nearby Mount Jefferson. Haystack Reservoir receives moderate numbers of people who boat, camp, fish, swim, and water ski.

Campsites, facilities: There are 24 sites for tents or RVs up to 32 feet long; some sites are pull-through. Picnic tables and fire grills are provided. Flush toilets, drinking water, and covered picnic shelters are available. A store, café, and ice are within five miles. Boat docks

and launching facilities are nearby. Leashed pets are permitted.

Reservations, fees: Reservations are not accepted. Sites are $8 per night, $3 per night per additional vehicle. Open mid-May–mid-September.

Directions: From Madras, drive south on U.S. 97 for nine miles to Jericho Lane. Turn left and drive one mile to County Road 100. Turn right and drive two miles to Forest Road 96. Turn left (north) and drive 0.5 mile to the campground.

Contact: Crooked River National Grassland, 541/475-9272 or 541/416-6640, www.fs.fed. us.

30 COLD WATER COVE

Scenic rating: 10

on Clear Lake in Willamette National Forest

Map 5.2, page 274

Cold Water campground sits at 3,000 feet elevation on the south shore of Clear Lake, a spring-fed lake formed by a natural lava dam and the source of the McKenzie River. No motors are permitted on the lake, making it ideal for anglers in rowboats or canoes. The northern section of the McKenzie River National Recreation Trail passes by the camp.

Campsites, facilities: There are 35 sites for tents or RVs up to 40 feet long. Picnic tables and fire grills are provided. Vault toilets, drinking water, and garbage service are available. Boat docks, launching facilities, rowboats, a store, a café, and cabin rentals are available nearby at Clear Lake Resort. Some facilities are wheelchair accessible. Leashed pets are permitted.

Reservations, fees: Reservations are accepted at 877/444-6777 or www.recreation.gov ($10 reservation fee). Sites are $16 per night, $30 per night for double sites, $8 per night per additional vehicle. Open mid-May–mid-October, weather permitting.

Directions: From Eugene, drive east on

Highway 126 for 47 miles to the town of McKenzie Bridge. Continue on Highway 126 for 14 miles to Forest Road 770. Turn right (east) and drive to the campground.
Contact: Willamette National Forest, McKenzie River Ranger District, 541/822-3381, fax 541/822-7254, www.fs.fed.us; Hoodoo Recreation, 541/822-3799.

31 ICE CAP

Scenic rating: 9

on Carmen Reservoir in Willamette National Forest

Map 5.2, page 274

Ice Cap campground is perched at 3,000 feet elevation on a hill above Carmen Reservoir, created by a dam on the McKenzie River. The McKenzie River National Recreation Trail passes by the camp, and Koosah Falls and Sahalie Falls are nearby. Clear Lake, a popular local vacation destination, is two miles away.

Campsites, facilities: There are 13 sites for tents or RVs up to 50 feet long, and nine walk-in sites. Picnic tables and fire grills are provided. Vault toilets, drinking water, and garbage service are available. Boat-launching facilities and boat rentals are about two miles away at Clear Lake Resort (541/967-5030). Only non-motorized boats are allowed on Carmen Reservoir. Leashed pets are permitted.

Reservations, fees: Reservations are not accepted. Sites are $16 per night, $8 per night per additional vehicle. Open mid-May–September, weather permitting.

Directions: From Eugene, drive east on Highway 126 for 47 miles to the town of McKenzie Bridge. Continue on Highway 126 for 19 miles to the campground entrance road on the left. Turn left and drive 200 yards to the campground.

Contact: Willamette National Forest, McKenzie River Ranger District, 541/822-3381,

fax 541/822-7254, www.fs.fed.us; Hoodoo Recreation, 541/822-3799.

32 BIG LAKE

Scenic rating: 9

on Big Lake in Willamette National Forest

Map 5.2, page 274

This jewel of a spot on the north shore of Big Lake at 4,650 feet elevation offers a host of activities, including fishing, hiking, swimming, and waterskiing. Big Lake has heavy motorized boat use. One of the better hikes is the five-mile wilderness loop trail (Patjens Lakes Trail) that heads out from the south shore of the lake and cuts past a few small lakes before returning. There's a great view of Mount Washington from the lake. The Pacific Crest Trail is only 0.5 mile away.

Campsites, facilities: There are 49 sites for tents or RVs up to 35 feet long. Picnic tables and fire grills are provided. Drinking water, vault and flush toilets, and garbage service are available. Boat ramps are nearby. Some facilities are wheelchair accessible. Leashed pets are permitted.

Reservations, fees: Reservations are accepted at 877/444-6777 or www.recreation.gov ($10 reservation fee). Single sites are $18 per night, $32 for double sites, $9 per night per additional vehicle. Open late May–mid-October, weather permitting.

Directions: From Eugene, drive east on Highway 126 for 47 miles to the town of McKenzie Bridge. Continue northeast on Highway 126 for 40 miles to Big Lake Road (Forest Road 2690). Turn right and drive three miles to the campground on the left.

Contact: Willamette National Forest, McKenzie River Ranger District, 541/822-3381, fax 541/822-7254, www.fs.fed.us; Hoodoo Recreation, 541/822-3799.

33 BIG LAKE WEST WALK-IN
🚶 🏊 🚣 🚤 🏠 ⛺

Scenic rating: 9

on Big Lake in Willamette National Forest

Map 5.2, page 274

This spot, located west of the Big Lake Campground at an elevation of 4,650 feet, has many of the same attractions, but the walk-in sites offer some seclusion and quiet. The Mount Washington Wilderness and Patjens Lake access trails can be reached from here.

Campsites, facilities: There are 11 walk-in sites (only 200 feet from the road). Fire pits and picnic tables are provided. Vault toilets and garbage service are available. There is no drinking water. Leashed pets are permitted.

Reservations, fees: Reservations are not accepted. Single sites are $22 per night, $35 per night for double sites, $10 per night per additional vehicle. Open late May–early October, weather permitting.

Directions: From Eugene, drive east on Highway 126 for 47 miles to the town of McKenzie Bridge. Continue northeast on Highway 126 for 40 miles to Big Lake Road (Forest Road 2690). Turn right and drive four miles to the campground entrance on the left.

Contact: Willamette National Forest, McKenzie River Ranger District, 541/822-3381, fax 541/822-7254, www.fs.fed.us; Hoodoo Recreation, 541/822-3799.

34 SOUTH SHORE
🚶 🚴 🏊 🚣 🚤 🏠 🚐 ⛺

Scenic rating: 6

on Suttle Lake in Deschutes National Forest

Map 5.2, page 274

This campground is at 3,500 feet elevation on the south shore of Suttle Lake, where waterskiing is permitted. A hiking trail winds around the lake and other popular activities include fishing and windsurfing. The camp often fills up on weekends and holidays, so reserve early.

Campsites, facilities: There are 38 sites for tents or RVs up to 40 feet long. Picnic tables and fire grills are provided. Vault toilets, drinking water, and garbage service are available. A fish-cleaning station, boat docks, launching facilities, and rentals are nearby. Leashed pets are permitted.

Reservations, fees: Reservations are accepted at 877/444-6777 or www.recreation.gov ($10 reservation fee). Sites are $16 per night, $8 per night per additional vehicle. Open May–September, weather permitting.

Directions: From Albany, drive east on U.S. 20 to the junction with Highway 126. Continue east on Highway 126 for 12 miles to Forest Road 2070 (Suttle Lake). Turn right and proceed a short distance to the campground.

Contact: Deschutes National Forest, Sisters Ranger District, 541/549-7700, fax 541/549-7746, www.fs.fed.us.

35 LINK CREEK
🚶 🏊 🚣 🚤 🏠 🚐 ⛺

Scenic rating: 6

on Suttle Lake in Deschutes National Forest

Map 5.2, page 274

Link Creek campground is set at the west end of Suttle Lake at an elevation of 3,450 feet. The high-speed boating area is located on this end of the lake, making it a popular spot with water-skiers. Other activities include fishing, swimming, and windsurfing.

Campsites, facilities: There are 33 sites for tents or RVs up to 50 feet long. Picnic tables and fire grills are provided. Vault toilets, drinking water, and garbage service are available. Boat docks, launching facilities, and rentals are nearby. Leashed pets are permitted.

Reservations, fees: Reservations are accepted at 877/444-6777 or www.recreation.gov ($10 reservation fee). Sites are $16–30 per night, $8 per night per additional vehicle. Open April–mid-October, weather permitting.

Directions: From Albany, drive east on U.S. 20 for 74 miles to the junction of U.S. 20 and

Highway 126. Continue east on Highway 126 for 12 miles to Forest Road 2070 (Suttle Lake). Turn right and drive a short distance to the campground.

Contact: Deschutes National Forest, Sisters Ranger District, 541/549-7700, fax 541/549-7746, www.fs.fed.us.

36 BLUE BAY

Scenic rating: 7

on Suttle Lake in Deschutes National Forest

Map 5.2, page 274

Blue Bay campground is situated along the south shore of Suttle Lake at an elevation of 3,450 feet. It's a quieter campground at the low-speed end of the lake, and with more tree cover than South Shore or Link Creek. Recreation activities include fishing, boating, and hiking.

Campsites, facilities: There are 21 single sites and three double sites for tents or RVs up to 50 feet long. Picnic tables and fire grills are provided. Vault toilets, drinking water, and garbage service are available. A fish-cleaning station, boat docks, launching facilities, and rentals are nearby. Leashed pets are permitted.

Reservations, fees: Reservations are accepted at 877/444-6777 or www.recreation.gov ($10 reservation fee). Sites are $16–30 per night, $8 per night per additional vehicle. Open May–mid-September, weather permitting.

Directions: From Albany, drive east on U.S. 20 for 74 miles to the junction of U.S. 20 and Highway 126. Continue east on Highway 126 for 12 miles to Forest Road 2070 (Suttle Lake). Turn right and drive a short distance to the campground.

Contact: Deschutes National Forest, Sisters Ranger District, 541/549-7700, fax 541/549-7746, www.fs.fed.us.

37 SCOUT LAKE GROUP

Scenic rating: 5

on Scout Lake in Deschutes National Forest

Map 5.2, page 274

Scout Lake is a group campground, with a mix of sunny and shady sites, at an elevation of 3,700 feet. The camp lies about 0.5 mile from Suttle Lake and is a good spot for swimming and hiking.

Campsites, facilities: There are nine sites—singles, doubles and triple sites—for tents or RVs up to 40 feet long. The triple group site can accommodate up to 100 people. Picnic tables and fire grills are provided. Vault toilets, drinking water, garbage service, a picnic shelter, a volleyball court, and horseshoe pits are available. Leashed pets are permitted in the campground only (not in the day-use area).

Reservations, fees: Reservations are accepted at 877/444-6777 or www.recreation.gov ($10 reservation fee). Single sites are $16 per night, double sites are $30 per night, triple group site is $40 per night, $8 per night per additional vehicle. Open May–September, weather permitting.

Directions: From Eugene, drive east on Highway 126 for 74 miles to the junction of U.S. 20 and Highway 126. Continue east on Highway 126 for 12 miles to Forest Road 2070 (Suttle Lake). Turn right and drive to Forest Road 2066. Turn left and drive less than one mile to the campground.

Contact: Deschutes National Forest, Sisters Ranger District, 541/549-7700, fax 541/549-7746, www.fs.fed.us.

38 KOA SISTERS/BEND

Scenic rating: 7

on Branchwater Lake

Map 5.2, page 274

This park is located amid wooded mountains outside of Sisters at an elevation of 3,200 feet.

Branchwater Lake, a three-acre lake at the camp-ground, offers good trout fishing. (For hiking opportunities, explore the McKenzie River Trail or the Three Sisters and Mount Washington Wilderness Areas (west of Sisters on Hwy. 242). The Pacific Crest Trail runs north and south through both wilderness areas.

Campsites, facilities: There are 100 sites for tents or RVs of any length (full hookups); many sites are pull-through. There are also three cabins. Picnic tables and fire pits are provided. Drinking water, air-conditioning, cable TV, modem access, restrooms with showers, a dump station, coin laundry, convenience store, ice, RV supplies, and propane gas are available. Recreational facilities include a playground, game room, horseshoes, table tennis, a spa, and a seasonal heated swimming pool. Leashed pets are permitted.

Reservations, fees: Reservations are accepted at 800/562-0363. Sites are $48–65 per night, $2–9 per person per night for more than two people, and $2 per night per additional vehicle. Some credit cards are accepted. Open late March–November, weather permitting.

Directions: From Eugene, drive east on Highway 126 to its junction with U.S. 20. Turn east on U.S. 20 and drive 26 miles to Sisters. Continue southeast on U.S. 20 for three miles to the park on the right side of the highway.

Contact: KOA Sisters/Bend, 541/549-3021, fax 541/549-8144, www.koa.com.

39 CROOKED RIVER RANCH RV PARK
🚲 🏊 🛶 🚐 🐎 👫 🚙 ⛺

Scenic rating: 6

near Smith Rock State Park

| Map 5.2, page 274 | BEST (|

Crooked River Ranch is a short distance from Smith Rock State Park, which contains unusual, colorful volcanic formations overlooking the Crooked River Canyon. Spectacular wildlife abounds in this area. Lake

Billy Chinook to the north is a good spot for waterskiing and fishing for bass and panfish. The park has a basketball court and a softball field, and seasonal horseback riding is available. Nearby recreation options include fishing, golf, and tennis; one of Oregon's nicest golf courses is nearby.

Campsites, facilities: There are 90 sites with full or partial hookups for RVs of any length (some pull-through) and 20 tent sites. Picnic tables are provided. No open fires are allowed; propane is permitted. Restrooms with flush toilets and coin showers, a dump station, cable TV, Wi-Fi, a convenience store, coin laundry, ice, a covered picnic shelter, playground, horseshoe pits, a tennis court, and a seasonal swimming pool are available. A café is nearby. Leashed pets are permitted, with certain restrictions.

Reservations, fees: Reservations are accepted at 800/841-0563. RV sites are $25–34 per night; tent sites are $20–24 per night. Some credit cards are accepted. Open mid-March–October, weather permitting.

Directions: From Redmond, drive north on U.S. 97 for six miles to Terrebonne and Lower Bridge Road. Turn left (west) on Lower Bridge Road and drive approximately two miles to 43rd Street. Turn right and drive two miles to a T-intersection with Chinook. Turn left on Chinook and drive approximately 4.5 miles (becomes Clubhouse Road, then Hays Road) to the ranch on the right.

Contact: Crooked River Ranch RV Park, 541/923-1441 or 800/841-0563, www.crookedriverranch.com.

40 INDIAN FORD
🐕 🚙 ⛺

Scenic rating: 4

on Indian Ford Creek in
Deschutes National Forest

| Map 5.2, page 274 |

This campground sits on the banks of Indian Ford Creek at an elevation of 3,250 feet. Used primarily by overnighters on their way to the town of Sisters, the camp is subject to a lot of traffic noise from U.S. 20. The grounds are sprinkled with aspen trees and great bird-watching opportunities are available.

Campsites, facilities: There are 25 sites for tents or RVs up to 50 feet long. Picnic tables, garbage service, and fire grills are provided. Vault toilets are available. There is no drinking water. Leashed pets are permitted.

Reservations, fees: Reservations are not accepted. Sites are $12 per night, $6 per night per additional vehicle. Open May–mid-October, weather permitting.

Directions: From Albany, drive east on U.S. 20 to the junction with Highway 126. Continue east on Highway 126 and drive 21 miles to the campground on the left.

Contact: Deschutes National Forest, Sisters Ranger District, 541/549-7700, fax 541/549-7746, www.fs.fed.us.

41 COLD SPRINGS
🦌 🚐 ⛰️

Scenic rating: 7

in Deschutes National Forest

Map 5.2, page 274

Wooded Cold Springs campground is set at 3,400 feet elevation at the source of a small seasonal creek. It's just far enough off the main drag to be missed by many campers. Spring and early summer are the times to come for great bird-watching in the area's abundant aspen trees.

Campsites, facilities: There are 22 sites for tents or RVs up to 50 feet long. Picnic tables, fire grills, and garbage service are provided. Vault toilets and drinking water are available. Leashed pets are permitted.

Reservations, fees: Reservations are not accepted. Sites are $14 per night, $7 per night per additional vehicle. Open May–October, weather permitting.

Directions: From Albany, drive east on U.S. 20 to the junction with Highway 126. Continue

east on Highway 126 and drive 26 miles to Sisters and Highway 242. Turn right and drive 4.2 miles to the campground on the right.

Contact: Deschutes National Forest, Sisters Ranger District, 541/549-7700, fax 541/549-7746, www.fs.fed.us.

42 SCOTT LAKE WALK-IN
🚶 ≈ 🛶 ⛵ 🦌 ⛰️

Scenic rating: 10

on Scott Lake in Willamette National Forest

Map 5.2, page 274 **BEST (**

Scott Lake Walk-In offers hike-in sites just over 0.1 mile from the road. The campground borders Scott Lake at an elevation of 4,680 feet; only non-motorized boats are allowed on the lake. Trails leading out of the camp provide access to several small lakes in the Mount Washington Wilderness, and there are great views of the Three Sisters Mountains. Be forewarned: Mosquitoes are heavy during the spring and early summer.

Campsites, facilities: There are 20 walk-in tent sites. Picnic tables and fire rings are provided. Vault toilets are available. There is no drinking water, and garbage must be packed out. Leashed pets are permitted.

Reservations, fees: Reservations are not accepted. Sites are $5 per night. Open July–October, weather permitting.

Directions: From Eugene, drive east on Highway 126 for 54 miles to the junction with Highway 242 (part of the Santiam Scenic Byway). Turn right (east) on Highway 242 and drive 14.5 miles to Forest Road 260. Turn left and drive to the campground.

Note: Highway 242 is spectacularly scenic, but it's also very narrow, winding, and steep; it is not recommended for RVs or trailers. The maximum vehicle length is 35 feet.

Contact: Willamette National Forest, McKenzie River Ranger District, 541/822-3381, fax 541/822-7254, www.fs.fed.us.

43 LAVA CAMP LAKE

🏃 🛶 🐕 🚐 ⛺

Scenic rating: 4

near the Pacific Crest Trail in
Deschutes National Forest

Map 5.2, page 274

Lava campground sits at an elevation of 5,300 feet among subalpine fir in the McKenzie Pass. It's not far from the Pacific Crest Trail, and a number of other trails provide additional hiking possibilities. Fishing is allowed, but don't expect to catch anything—perhaps that is why this campground gets such light use!

Campsites, facilities: There are 10 sites for tents or RVs up to 20 feet long. Picnic tables and fire grills are provided. Vault toilets are available. There is no drinking water, and garbage must be packed out. Leashed pets are permitted.

Reservations, fees: Reservations are not accepted. There is no fee for camping. Open June–October, weather permitting.

Directions: From Eugene, drive east on Highway 126 for 47 miles to the town of McKenzie Bridge. Continue east on Highway 126 for five miles to Highway 242. Turn right (east) and drive 14.6 miles on Highway 242 to the campground entrance on the right. Note: Highway 242 is spectacularly scenic, but also very narrow, winding, and steep. RVs and trailers are strictly held to a 35-foot length limit.

Contact: Deschutes National Forest, Sisters Ranger District, 541/549-7700, fax 541/549-7746, www.fs.fed.us.

44 WHISPERING PINE HORSE CAMP

🏃 🐎 🚐 ⛺

Scenic rating: 5

near the Trout Creek Swamp in
Deschutes National Forest

Map 5.2, page 274

This wooded campground (elevation 4,400 feet) near Trout Creek Swamp is pretty, isolated, and private. Although generally not crowded, it's set up as a horse camp with corrals and is gaining in popularity; groups of horse users occasionally fill it up. Hikers, beware: You'll be sharing the trails with horses.

Campsites, facilities: There are nine primitive sites for tents or RVs up to 30 feet long. Picnic tables and fire grills are provided. Vault toilets and garbage service are available. There is no drinking water. Leashed pets are permitted.

Reservations, fees: Reservations are not accepted. Sites are $16 per night, $8 per night per additional vehicle. Open May–October, weather permitting.

Directions: From Albany, drive east on U.S. 20 to the junction with U.S. 126. Turn east on U.S. 126 and drive for 26 miles to Sisters and Highway 142. Turn right (east) and drive six miles on Highway 242 to Forest Road 1018. Turn left and drive four miles to the campground entrance. Note: Highway 242 is spectacularly scenic, but also very narrow, winding, and steep. RVs and trailers are discouraged (a 35-foot length limit is in effect).

Contact: Deschutes National Forest, Sisters Ranger District, 541/549-7700, fax 541/549-7746, www.fs.fed.us or www.hoodoo.com.

45 LIMBERLOST

🛶 🐎 ♿ 🚐 ⛺

Scenic rating: 9

on Lost Creek in Willamette National Forest

Map 5.2, page 274

Limberlost is a secluded campground set at 1,800 feet elevation along Lost Creek, about two miles from where it empties into the McKenzie River. Relatively unknown, the camp gets light use; it makes a good base camp for a trout-fishing trip.

Campsites, facilities: There are 12 sites for tents or RVs up to 16 feet long. Picnic tables, garbage service, and fire grills are provided. Vault toilets are available, but there is no drinking water. Some facilities are wheelchair accessible. Leashed pets are permitted.

Reservations, fees: Reservations are not accepted. Sites are $12 per night, $6 per night per additional vehicle. Open May–September, weather permitting.

Directions: From Eugene, drive east on Highway 126 for 47 miles to the town of McKenzie Bridge. Continue east on Highway 126 for five miles to Highway 242. Turn right (east) and drive 1.5 miles on Highway 242 to the camp. Note: Highway 242 is spectacularly scenic, but also very narrow, winding, and steep. RVs and trailers are discouraged (a 35-foot length limit is in effect).

Contact: Willamette National Forest, McKenzie River Ranger District, 541/822-3381, fax 541/822-7254, www.fs.fed.us.

46 ALDER SPRINGS

Scenic rating: 7

in Willamette National Forest

Map 5.2, page 274

Remote Alder Springs campground sits at 3,600 feet elevation in the Willamette Forest. The camp features good hiking possibilities, including access to the Linton Lake Trail, a three-mile hike that leads to Linton Lake… and fishing. The Three Sisters Wilderness is just south of the highway.

Campsites, facilities: There are six tent sites. Picnic tables and fire grills are provided. Vault toilets are available. No drinking water is available, and garbage must be packed out. Some facilities are wheelchair accessible. Leashed pets are permitted.

Reservations, fees: Reservations are not accepted. There is no fee for camping. Open June–September, weather permitting.

Directions: From Eugene, drive east on Highway 126 for 47 miles to the town of McKenzie Bridge. Continue east on Highway 126 for five miles to Highway 242. Turn right (east) and drive 10 miles on Highway 242 to the campground on the left. Note: Highway 242 is spectacularly scenic, but also very narrow,

winding, and steep. RVs and trailers are discouraged (a 35-foot length limit is in effect).

Contact: Willamette National Forest, McKenzie River Ranger District, 541/822-3381, fax 541/822-7254, www.fs.fed.us.

47 DRIFTWOOD

Scenic rating: 9

on Three Creek Lake in
Deschutes National Forest

Map 5.2, page 274   BEST (

This wooded campground, at 6,600 feet elevation, is often blocked by snowdrifts until early July. At this high elevation, the views of Tam McArthur Rim are spectacular. Although located on the lakeshore and hidden from outsiders, the area can get very crowded, and the campground is full most weekends from the Fourth of July through Labor Day. Some recreation options include boating (non-motorized only), fishing, hiking, and swimming.

Campsites, facilities: There are 18 sites for tents or RVs up to 40 feet long. Picnic tables and fire grills are provided. Vault toilets and garbage service are available. There is no drinking water. Boats with motors are not allowed. Leashed pets are permitted.

Reservations, fees: Reservations are not accepted. Sites are $14 per night, $7 per night per additional vehicle. Open June–October, weather permitting.

Directions: From Eugene, drive east on Highway 126 to its junction with U.S. 20. Turn east and drive 26 miles to Sisters and Forest Road 16. Turn right and drive 16.4 miles to the campground.

Contact: Deschutes National Forest, Sisters Ranger District, 541/549-7700, fax 541/549-7746, www.fs.fed.us.

48 THREE CREEK LAKE

Scenic rating: 8

on Three Creek Lake in
Deschutes National Forest

Map 5.2, page 274

Three Creek Lake is in a pretty spot at 6,600
feet elevation; this forested campground lies
along the south shore of its namesake lake.
Boating (non-motorized only), fishing, hiking,
and swimming are the highlights.

Campsites, facilities: There are 11 sites for
tents or RVs up to 40 feet long. Picnic tables
and fire grills are provided. Vault toilets and
garbage service are available. There is no
drinking water. Boats with motors are not
allowed. Leashed pets are permitted.

Reservations, fees: Reservations are not accepted. Sites are $14 per night, $7 per night
per additional vehicle. Open June–October,
weather permitting.

Directions: From Eugene, drive east on Highway 126 to its junction with Highway 20.
Turn east and drive 26 miles to Sisters and
Forest Road 16. Turn right and drive 17 miles
to the campground.

Contact: Deschutes National Forest, Sisters
Ranger District, 541/549-7700, fax 541/549-
7746, www.fs.fed.us.

49 TUMALO STATE PARK

Scenic rating: 7

on the Deschutes River

Map 5.2, page 274

Tumalo State Park sits along the banks of the
Deschutes River, just four miles from Bend.
Trout fishing can be good, and bird-watching
is popular. The swimming area is generally
safe and a good spot for children. Rafting is
also an option here. Mount Bachelor is just up
the road and provides plenty of winter recreation opportunities.

Campsites, facilities: There are 54 sites for

tents or self-contained RVs, 23 sites with full
hookups for RVs up to 44 feet long, a hiker/
bicyclist area, seven yurts, and two group
tent areas for up to 25 people each. Drinking
water, fire grills, and picnic tables are provided. Restrooms with flush toilets and showers,
firewood, and a playground are available. A
store, café, and ice are within one mile. Some
facilities are wheelchair accessible. Leashed
pets are permitted.

Reservations, fees: Reservations are accepted
at 800/452-5687 or www.reserveamerica.com
($8 reservation fee). RV sites are $17–26 per
night, tent sites are $13–21, $4–5 per person
per night for hikers/bikers, $29–39 per night
for yurts, $43–76 per night for the group areas,
and $5 per night per additional vehicle. Some
credit cards are accepted. Open year-round.

Directions: From Bend, drive north on U.S. 97
for two miles to U.S. 20 West. Turn west and
drive five miles to Tumalo Junction. Turn left
at Tumalo Junction onto Cook Avenue (the
road becomes O. B. Riley), and drive one mile
to the campground.

Contact: High Desert Management Unit, Oregon State Parks, 541/388-6055 or 800/551-
6949, www.oregonstateparks.org.

50 SCANDIA RV AND MOBILE PARK

Scenic rating: 5

near the Deschutes River

Map 5.2, page 274

This in-town park near the Deschutes River
is close to bike paths, a golf course, a stable,
and tennis courts.

Campsites, facilities: There are 97 sites for
tents or RVs of any length (full hookups); some
are pull-through sites. Picnic tables and cable
TV are provided. Restrooms with flush toilets
and showers, modem access, a picnic area, and
a coin laundry are available. Propane gas, a
dump station, store, café, and ice are within
one mile. Leashed pets are permitted.

Reservations, fees: Reservations are accepted. Sites are $28–32 per night, plus $2.50 per person per night for more than two people. Some credit cards are accepted. Open year-round.

Directions: In Bend, drive south on Business U.S. 97 (3rd Street) for 0.5 mile to the park entrance on the right.

Contact: Scandia RV and Mobile Park, 541/382-6206, fax 541/382-4087.

51 CROWN VILLA RV RESORT

Scenic rating: 6

near Bend

Map 5.2, page 274

This RV park offers large and landscaped grassy sites. Nearby recreation options include horseback riding and golf.

Campsites, facilities: There are 116 sites with full or partial hookups for RVs of any length; some sites are pull-through. Picnic tables are provided. Restrooms with flush toilets and showers, cable TV, wireless Internet service, a coin laundry, a bistro, propane gas, and ice are available. A store and a café are within one mile. Some facilities are wheelchair accessible. Leashed pets are permitted.

Reservations, fees: Reservations are accepted. Sites are $35–70 per night, $3 per person per night for more than four people. Some credit cards are accepted. Open year-round.

Directions: From Bend, drive south on Business U.S. 97 (3rd Street) for two miles to Brosterhous Road. Turn left (east) and drive approximately one mile to a T intersection. Bear right to stay on Brosterhous Road. Continue about one mile to the park on the right.

Contact: Crown Villa RV Resort, 541/388-1131, www.crownvillarvresort.com.

52 WHITTAKER CREEK

Scenic rating: 7

near the Siuslaw River

Map 5.3, page 275

Whittaker Creek campground is home to one of the area's premier salmon spawning grounds, where annual runs of chinook, coho salmon, and steelhead can be viewed. The (Whitaker Creek) Old Growth Ridge Trail, a national recreation trail, is accessible from the campground. This moderately difficult trail ascends 1,000 feet above the Siuslaw River through a stand of old-growth Douglas fir.

Campsites, facilities: There are 31 sites for tents or RVs up to 35 feet long. Picnic tables and fire pits are provided. Drinking water, vault toilets, garbage bins, a boat ramp, swimming beach, playground, and picnic shelter are available. A camp host is on-site. Some facilities are wheelchair accessible. Leashed pets are permitted.

Reservations, fees: Reservations are not accepted. Sites are $10 per night, $5 per night for each additional vehicle. Open mid-May–September, weather permitting.

Directions: From Eugene, drive west on Highway 126 for 33 miles to Siuslaw River Road. Turn left (south) and drive two miles to the first junction. Turn right and drive a short distance across Siuslaw River to the campground on the right.

Contact: Bureau of Land Management, Eugene District Office, 541/683-6600 or 888/442-3061, fax 541/683-6981, www.blm.gov.

53 CLAY CREEK

Scenic rating: 7

near the Siuslaw River

Map 5.3, page 275

This campground gets a medium amount of use. Sites are situated in a forest of cedar, Douglas fir, and maple trees. Clay Creek Trail, a two-mile loop, takes you to a ridge overlooking the river valley and is well worth the walk. Fishing for trout and crayfish is popular.

Campsites, facilities: There are 21 sites for tents or RVs up to 35 feet long. Picnic tables and fire pits are provided. Drinking water, vault toilets, garbage bins, a swimming beach with changing rooms, a softball field, horseshoe pits, and two group picnic shelters with fireplaces are available. There is a camp host. Some facilities are wheelchair accessible. Leashed pets are permitted.

Reservations, fees: Reservations are not accepted. Sites are $10 per night, $5 per night for each additional vehicle. Open mid-May–September, weather permitting.

Directions: From Eugene, drive west on Highway 126 for 33 miles to Siuslaw River Road. Turn left (south) and drive 16 miles to BLM Road 19-7-2001 (signed for Clay Creek). Turn right and drive a short distance to the campground on the right.

Contact: Bureau of Land Management, Eugene District Office, 541/683-6600 or 888/442-3061, fax 541/683-6981, www.blm.gov.

54 PASS CREEK COUNTY PARK

Scenic rating: 7

near Cottage Grove

Map 5.3, page 275

Pass Creek provides a decent layover spot for travelers on I-5. Situated in a wooded, hilly area, the camp features many shaded sites, and mountain views give the park scenic value. There is a covered pavilion and gazebo with barbecue grills for get-togethers. A bonus is the fishing pond with bluegill, crappie, and largemouth bass. There are no other campgrounds in the immediate area, so if it's late and you need a place to stay, grab this one.

Campsites, facilities: There is a grassy area for

tents and 30 sites with full hookups (50-amp) for RVs up to 45 feet long. Picnic tables and fire rings or barbecues are provided. Drinking water, restrooms with flush toilets and showers, a coin laundry, and a playground are available. A store and ice are within one mile. Some facilities are wheelchair accessible. Leashed pets are permitted.

Reservations, fees: Reservations are not accepted. Sites are $15–20 per night, $3 per night for an additional vehicle unless towed. Open year-round.

Directions: On I-5, drive to Exit 163 (between Roseburg and Eugene). Take Exit 163 and turn west on Curtin Park Road. Drive west (under the freeway) for a very short distance to the park entrance.

Contact: Pass Creek County Park, 541/942-3281, www.co.douglas.or.us.

55 PINE MEADOWS

Scenic rating: 6

on Cottage Grove Reservoir

Map 5.3, page 275

Pine Meadows campground is surrounded by a varied landscape of forest, grassland, and marsh near the banks of Cottage Grove Reservoir. Campsites are within 200 feet of the water. Boating, fishing, swimming, and waterskiing are among the recreation options. It's an easy hop from I-5.

Campsites, facilities: There are 93 sites for tents or RVs of any length, with some pull-through sites. Drinking water, picnic tables, garbage bins, and fire rings are provided. Restrooms with flush toilets and showers, a dump station, a children's play area, an amphitheater, interpretive displays, and a swimming area are available. A boat dock, launching facilities, and a small store are nearby. Leashed pets are permitted.

Reservations, fees: Reservations are accepted at 877/444-6777 or www.recreation.gov ($10 reservation fee). Sites are $15 per night, $5 per night for an additional vehicle. Open mid-May–mid-September.

Directions: From Eugene, drive south on I-5 past Cottage Grove to Exit 172. Take that exit to London Road and drive south for 4.5 miles to Reservoir Road. Turn left and drive three miles to the camp entrance on the right.

Contact: U.S. Army Corps of Engineers, Recreation Information, Cottage Grove, 541/942-8657 or 541/942-5631, fax 541/942-1305, www.nwp.usace.army.mil.

56 PINE MEADOWS PRIMITIVE SITES

Scenic rating: 6

on Cottage Grove Reservoir

Map 5.3, page 275

Located adjacent to Pine Meadows, this primitive campground offers the same boating, fishing, swimming, and waterskiing activities on Cottage Grove Reservoir.

Campsites, facilities: There are 15 primitive sites for tents or small, self-contained RVs. Picnic tables, vault toilets, drinking water, garbage bins, and fire rings are provided. Boat docks, launching facilities, and a mini-market are nearby. Leashed pets are permitted.

Reservations, fees: Reservations are accepted at 877/444-6777 or www.recreation.gov ($10 reservation fee). Sites are $10 per night, $5 per night for an additional vehicle. Campers must have a permit, obtained at the entrance booth. Open late May–early September.

Directions: From Eugene, drive south on I-5 past Cottage Grove to Exit 172. Take that exit to London Road and drive south for 4.5 miles to Reservoir Road. Turn left and drive three miles to the camp entrance.

Contact: U.S. Army Corps of Engineers, Recreation Information, Cottage Grove, 541/942-8657 or 541/942-5631, fax 541/942-1305, www.nwp.usace.army.mil.

57 WHISTLER'S BEND PARK

Scenic rating: 7

on the North Umpqua River

Map 5.3, page 275

This 175-acre county park along the banks of the North Umpqua River is an idyllic spot because it gets little pressure from outsiders, yet it is just a 20-minute drive from I-5. Two boat ramps accommodate boaters, and fishing is a plus. A wildlife reserve provides habitat for deer.

Campsites, facilities: There are 23 sites for tents or RVs up to 35 feet long (no hookups) and two yurts. Two group camps are available. Picnic tables and fire grills are provided. Drinking water, restrooms with flush toilets and showers, a playground, disc golf, and launching facilities are available. Some facilities are wheelchair accessible. Leashed pets are permitted.

Reservations, fees: Reservations are accepted for yurts and group camps at 541/957-7001 ($10 reservation fee) but not for tent or RV sites. Single sites are $15 per night, $3 per night per additional vehicle, $32 per night for yurts, $50 per night for the group camp for up to 50 people, $100 per night for the group camp for up to 100 people. Some credit cards are accepted. Individual sites are open April–November; group sites are open year-round.

Directions: From Roseburg, drive east on Highway 138 for 12 miles to Whistler's Bend Park Road (well signed). Turn left and drive two miles to the end of the road and the park entrance.

Contact: Whistler's Bend Park, 541/673-4863, www.co.douglas.or.us.

58 AMACHER PARK

Scenic rating: 5

on the Umpqua River

Map 5.3, page 275

A wooded Douglas County park set along the banks of the North Umpqua River, Amacher is a prime layover spot for I-5 RV cruisers. This park has one of the few Myrtlewood groves in the country. Tent sites are located underneath the freeway next to the railroad tracks; trains come by intermittently. An 18-hole golf course and tennis courts are close by, riding stables are within a 20-minute drive, and Winchester Dam is within 0.25 mile.

Campsites, facilities: There are 10 sites for tents or self-contained RVs and 20 sites with full or partial hookups (20-amp service only) for RVs up to 30 feet long. Picnic tables are provided; some sites have fire rings. Drinking water, restrooms with flush toilets and showers, a gazebo, and picnic area are available. Propane gas, a store, café, coin laundry, and ice are within one mile. Boat-launching facilities are available. Some facilities are wheelchair accessible. Leashed pets are permitted.

Reservations, fees: Reservations are not accepted. Sites are $15–20 per night, $3 per night per additional vehicle. Cash only. Open March–October (closed in winter).

Directions: From Roseburg, drive five miles north on I-5 to Exit 129. Take that exit and drive south on Old Highway 99 for 0.25 mile to the park on the right (just across Winchester Bridge).

Contact: Amacher Park, 541/672-4901; Douglas County, 541/672-4901, www.co.douglas.or.us.

59 TWIN RIVERS VACATION PARK

Scenic rating: 6

near the Umpqua River

Map 5.3, page 275

This wooded campground is near the Umpqua River. It features large shaded pull-through sites and more than 100 kinds of trees on the property. Groups are welcome and clubhouses are available for group use. Nearby recreation options include bike paths, a county park, and a golf course.

Campsites, facilities: There are 82 sites with full or partial hookups for RVs of any length; many are pull-through sites. Cable TV, fire pits, and picnic tables are provided. Restrooms with flush toilets and showers, modem access, propane gas, firewood, a convenience store, a coin laundry, ice, and a playground are available. Boat-launching facilities are nearby. Leashed pets are permitted.

Reservations, fees: Reservations are accepted. Sites are $22–33 per night, $3 per person per night for more than two people. Some credit cards are accepted. Open year-round.

Directions: In Roseburg on I-5, take Exit 125 to Garden Valley Road. Drive west for five miles (over the river) to Old Garden Valley Road. Turn left and drive 1.5 miles to River Forks Road. Turn left and drive a short distance to the park entrance on the left.

Contact: Twin Rivers Vacation Park, 541/673-3811, www.twinriversrvpark.com.

60 DOUGLAS COUNTY FAIRGROUNDS RV PARK

Scenic rating: 8

on the South Umpqua River

Map 5.3, page 275

This 74-acre county park is very easily accessible off the highway. Nearby Umpqua River, one of Oregon's prettiest rivers, often has good fishing in season. Bike paths, a golf course, and tennis courts are nearby. Horse stalls and a boat ramp are available at the nearby fairgrounds. The campground fills up the third weekend in March, during the annual fiddlers' convention.

Campsites, facilities: There are 50 sites with partial hookups for tents or RVs of any length. Drinking water and picnic tables are provided. Restrooms with flush toilets and showers and a dump station are available. A store, café, coin laundry, and ice are within one mile. Some facilities are wheelchair accessible. Leashed pets are permitted.

Reservations, fees: Reservations are not accepted. Sites are $15–20 per night, with a 14-day stay limit. Tent camping is limited to two nights. Open year-round, except one week in August during the county fair. Phone ahead to confirm current status.

Directions: Heading south on I-5 in Roseburg, take Exit 123 and drive south under the freeway to Frear Street. Turn right and enter the park.

Contact: Douglas County Fairgrounds & Speedway, 541/957-7010, fax 541/440-6023, www.co.douglas.or.us/dcfair.

61 CAVITT CREEK FALLS

Scenic rating: 8

west of Roseburg

Map 5.3, page 275

The locals might try to hunt me down for revealing this spot, but here it is. This campground is located near a sensational swimming hole at the base of a 10-foot waterfall on Cavitt Creek. The elevation is 1,040 feet, and an abundant forest of fir, maple, and oak trees surrounds the campground. It is overlooked because it is set on land run by the Bureau of Land Management, not the Park Service or Forest Service. Fishing is closed on Cavitt Creek by the Oregon Department of Fish and Wildlife.

Campsites, facilities: There are 10 sites for tents or RVs up to 20 feet long. Picnic tables, garbage bins, and fire rings are provided. Drinking water and vault toilets are available. A camp host is on-site. Some facilities are wheelchair accessible. Leashed pets are permitted.

Reservations, fees: Reservations are not accepted. Sites are $8 per night, $4 per night for an additional vehicle. Open mid-May–mid-October, weather permitting.

Directions: From Roseburg, drive east on Highway 138 for 16.5 miles to Little River Road. Turn right (south) on Little River Road and drive 6.7 miles to the covered bridge. Turn right onto Cavitt Creek Road and drive 3.2 miles to Cavitt Creek Falls Recreation Site.

Contact: Bureau of Land Management, Roseburg District, 541/440-4930, fax 541/440-4948, www.or.blm.gov/or/resources/recreation.

62 DEXTER SHORES RV PARK

Scenic rating: 7

near Dexter Reservoir

Map 5.4, page 276

If you're traveling on I-5, this RV park is well worth the 15-minute drive out of Springfield. It's across the street from Dexter Reservoir, where fishing and boating are permitted year-round. Speedboat races are held at Dexter in the summer. There is seasonal fishing for salmon and steelhead below Dexter dam. The local area is good for bird-watching. Nearby Lookout and Fall Creek Lakes offer sailing, swimming, waterskiing, and windsurfing. There are three authentic Sioux tepees on the property in the summer and two cabins. Many of the campsites have a lake view.

Campsites, facilities: There are 56 sites with full or partial hookups for RVs up to 40 feet long; 12 sites are pull-through. There are also eight tent sites, three tepees, and two one-bedroom cabins. Drinking water, cable TV and telephone hookups, picnic tables, and fire pits are provided. Restrooms with flush toilets and showers, a dump station, modem access, a clubhouse, lending library, video rentals, firewood, horseshoe pits, and a coin laundry are available. Propane gas, a café, restaurant, and ice are within one mile. Boat docks and launching facilities are nearby. Leashed pets are permitted in the campground, but not in the cabins or tepees.

Reservations, fees: Reservations are accepted at 866/558-9777. RV sites are $30–45 per night, tent sites are $20 per night, tepees are $25–35 per night, $3 per person per night for more than four people, and $1 per pet per night. Some credit cards are accepted. Open year-round.

Directions: From south Eugene on I-5, drive to Exit 188A and Highway 58. Take Highway 58 east and drive 11.5 miles to Lost Creek Road. Turn right (south) and drive several hundred feet to Dexter Road. Turn left (in front of the café) and drive east for half a block to the park on the right.

Contact: Dexter Shores RV Park, 866/558-9777 or 541/937-3711, fax 541/937-1724, www.dextershoresrv.com.

63 FALL CREEK STATE RECREATION AREA

Scenic rating: 7

in Fall Creek State Recreation Area

Map 5.4, page 276

There are two campgrounds here: Cascara and the group camp area, Fisherman's Park. Most of these spacious sites have Douglas fir and white fir tree cover. Water recreation is the primary activity here; boating and water skis are allowed. The lake level drops in August, and water temperatures are ideal for summer swimming.

Campsites, facilities: There are 42 primitive sites for tents or RVs up to 45 feet, five walk-in sites for tents, and a group area for RVs of any length up to 16 vehicles; there are no pull-through sites. Picnic tables and fire rings are provided. Drinking water, vault toilets, garbage service, and firewood are available. A camp host is on-site. A boat launch, dock, and swimming area are also available. Leashed pets are permitted.

Reservations, fees: Reservations are accepted for the RV group area only at 800/452-5687. Sites are $19 per night, $10 per night for primitive sites, $5 per night for an additional vehicle. The group RV area is $109 per night for up to 10 RVs. Some credit cards are accepted. Open May–September.

Directions: From south Eugene on I-5, take Exit 188 to Highway 58. Drive 11 miles south to Lowell and Pioneer Street (at the covered bridge). Turn left on Pioneer Street and drive less than 0.25 mile to West Boundary Road. Turn left and drive one block to Lowell Jasper Road. Turn right and drive 1.5 miles to Unity and Place Road. Turn right and drive about one mile to a fork with North Shore Road (Big Fall Creek Road). Bear left onto Big Fall Creek Road and drive about eight miles to the head of Fall Creek Reservoir and Peninsula Road (Forest Road 6250). Turn right and drive 0.5 mile to the campground. The park is approximately 27 miles southeast of Eugene.

Contact: Fall Creek State Recreation Area, 541/937-1173 or 800/551-6949, www.oregonstateparks.org.

64 DOLLY VARDEN

Scenic rating: 6

on Fall Creek in Willamette National Forest

Map 5.4, page 276

This pretty campground is adjacent to Fall Creek and is at the lower trailhead for the scenic, 13.7-mile Fall Creek National Recreation Trail, which follows the creek and varies between 960 and 1,385 feet in elevation. This small campground gets moderate-heavy use. It is set on the inlet stream for Fall Creek Reservoir.

Campsites, facilities: There are five sites for tents or RVs up to 30 feet. Picnic tables and fire grills are provided. Vault toilets and garbage service are available. There is no drinking water. Leashed pets are permitted.

Reservations, fees: Reservations are not accepted. Sites are $12 per night, $6 per night per additional vehicle. Open May–September, weather permitting.

Directions: From south Eugene on I-5, take Exit 188 to Highway 58. Drive 11 miles south to Lowell and Pioneer Street (at the covered bridge). Turn left and drive 0.2 mile to West Boundary Road. Turn left and drive one block to Lowell Jasper Road. Turn right and drive 1.5 miles to Unity and Place Road. Turn right and drive about one mile to a fork with North Shore Road. Bear left onto North Shore Road (Big Fall Creek Road) and drive about 10 miles (the road becomes Forest Road 18) to the campground on the left.

Contact: Willamette National Forest, Middle Fork Ranger District, 541/782-2283, fax 541/782-5306, www.fs.fed.us; Hoodoo Recreation, 541/822-3799.

65 BIG POOL

Scenic rating: 6

on Fall Creek in Willamette National Forest

Map 5.4, page 276

Big Pool campground is quiet, secluded, and primitive. The camp sits along Fall Creek at about 1,000 feet elevation, and the scenic Fall Creek National Recreation Trail passes the camp on the other side of the creek, providing hiking opportunities.

Campsites, facilities: There are three tent sites and two sites for tents or RVs up to 24 feet long. Picnic tables, garbage containers, and fire grills are provided. Vault toilets and drinking water are available. Leashed pets are permitted.

Reservations, fees: Reservations are not accepted. Sites are $12 per night, $6 per night

per additional vehicle. Open late May–September, weather permitting.

Directions: From south Eugene on I-5, take Exit 188 to Highway 58. Drive 11 miles south to Lowell and Pioneer Street (at the covered bridge). Turn left and drive 0.2 mile to West Boundary Road. Turn left and drive one block to Lowell Jasper Road. Turn right and drive 1.5 miles to Unity and Place Road. Turn right and drive about one mile to a fork with North Shore Road. Bear left onto North Shore Road (Big Fall Creek Road) and drive about 12 miles (the road becomes Forest Road 18) to the campground on the right.

Contact: Willamette National Forest, Middle Fork Ranger District, 541/782-2283, fax 541/782-5306, www.fs.fed.us; Hoodoo Recreation, 541/822-3799.

66 BEDROCK

Scenic rating: 6

on Fall Creek in Willamette National Forest

Map 5.4, page 276

Bedrock lies along the banks of Fall Creek amid Douglas firs and cedars. This is one of the access points for the scenic Fall Creek National Recreation Trail, which in turn offers access to Jones Trail, a six-mile uphill climb. Swimming holes offer relief in summer. Note that the campground suffered previous fire damage, but it is recovering.

Campsites, facilities: There are 18 single sites and one multiple site for tents or RVs up to 36 feet long. Picnic tables and fire grills are provided. Vault toilets and garbage service are available. There is no drinking water. Some facilities are wheelchair accessible. Leashed pets are permitted.

Reservations, fees: Reservations are not accepted. Single sites are $14 per night, $22 per night for double sites, and $7 per night per additional vehicle. Open May–mid-September, weather permitting.

Directions: From south Eugene on I-5, take

Exit 188 to Highway 58. Drive 11 miles south to Lowell and Pioneer Street (at the covered bridge). Turn left and drive 0.2 mile to West Boundary Road. Turn left and drive one block to Lowell Jasper Road. Turn right and drive 1.5 miles to Unity and Place Road. Turn right and drive about one mile to a fork with North Shore Road. Bear left onto North Shore Road (Big Fall Creek Road) and drive about 14 miles (the road becomes Forest Road 18) to the campground on the left.

Contact: Willamette National Forest, Middle Fork Ranger District, 541/782-2283, fax 541/782-5306, www.fs.fed.us; Hoodoo Recreation, 541/822-3799.

67 PUMA

Scenic rating: 6

on Fall Creek in Willamette National Forest

Map 5.4, page 276

Puma campground hugs the banks of Fall Creek at an elevation of 1,100 feet. This is one of four camps in the immediate area, located across from the popular Fall Creek National Recreation Trail. The trail offers hiking opportunities, while Fall Creek provides a nice spot to cool off in summer.

Campsites, facilities: There are 11 sites for tents or RVs up to 36 feet long. Picnic tables and fire grills are provided. Vault toilets, drinking water, and garbage bins are available. Leashed pets are permitted.

Reservations, fees: Reservations are not accepted. Sites are $14 per night, $7 per night per additional vehicle. Open late May–September, weather permitting.

Directions: From I-5 south of Eugene, take Exit 188 to Highway 58. Drive about 11 miles to Lowell. Turn left at Pioneer Street (at the covered bridge), drive 0.2 mile, and turn left on West Boundary Road. Drive one block and turn right at Lowell Jasper

Road. Drive 1.5 miles to Place Road and turn right. Drive about one mile to a fork and bear left onto North Shore Road (Big Fall Creek Road). Drive about 16 miles (the road becomes Forest Road 18) to the campground on the left.

Contact: Willamette National Forest, Middle Fork Ranger District, 541/782-2283, fax 541/782-5306, www.fs.fed.us.

68 FRISSELL CROSSING

Scenic rating: 8

near the Three Sisters Wilderness in Willamette National Forest

Map 5.4, page 276

If you're looking for solitude, this place should be heaven to you. Frissell campground (elevation 2,600 feet) sits on the banks of the South Fork of the McKenzie River, adjacent to a trailhead that provides access to the backcountry of the Three Sisters Wilderness. Note that Frissell Crossing is the only camp in the immediate area that has drinking water.

Campsites, facilities: There are 12 sites for tents or RVs up to 36 feet long. Picnic tables, garbage bins, and fire grills are provided. Drinking water and vault toilets are available. Leashed pets are permitted.

Reservations, fees: Reservations are not accepted. Sites are $12 per night, $6 per night per additional vehicle. Open mid-May–mid-September, weather permitting.

Directions: From Eugene, drive east on Highway 126 for 37 miles to Blue River. Continue east on Highway 126 for five miles to Forest Road 19 (Aufderheide Scenic Byway). Turn right (south) and drive 21.5 miles to the camp on the left.

Contact: Willamette National Forest, McKenzie River Ranger District, 541/822-3381, fax 541/822-7254, www.fs.fed.us; Hoodoo Recreation, 541/822-3799.

69 WINBERRY

Scenic rating: 6

on Winberry Creek in
Willamette National Forest

Map 5.4, page 276

This campground is on Winberry Creek in a tree-shaded area at 1,900 feet elevation. The closest hiking option is Station Butte Trail, just downstream from the campground on Forest Road 1802-150. Be cautious: Poison oak grows at the top of the butte.

Campsites, facilities: There are six sites for tents or RVs up to 14 feet long. Picnic tables and fire grills are provided. Drinking water, vault toilets, garbage service, and two A-frame shelters are available. Some facilities are wheelchair accessible. Leashed pets are permitted.

Reservations, fees: Reservations are not accepted. Sites are $5 per night, $2 per night per additional vehicle. Open late May–early September, weather permitting.

Directions: From south Eugene on I-5, take Exit 188 to Highway 58. Drive 11 miles south to Lowell and Pioneer Street (at the covered bridge). Turn left and drive 0.2 mile to West Boundary Road. Turn left and drive one block to Lowell Jasper Road. Turn right and drive 1.5 miles to Unity and Place Road. Turn right and drive about one mile to a fork with Winberry Road. Bear right and drive six miles (the road becomes Forest Road 1802). Continue 3.5 miles to the campground.

Contact: Willamette National Forest, Middle Fork Ranger District, 541/782-2283, fax 541/782-5306, www.fs.fed.us.

70 BLAIR LAKE WALK-IN

Scenic rating: 6

on Blair Lake in Willamette National Forest

Map 5.4, page 276

If you're looking for a pristine, alpine lakeside setting, you'll find it here. The lake, set at 4,800 feet elevation, is small (only 35 acres) and shallow (20 feet). It supports a population of brook and rainbow trout and is stocked in the summer. The surrounding meadows and woods are well known for their wide range of wildflowers and huckleberries.

Campsites, facilities: There are seven walk-in tent sites. Picnic tables and fire rings are provided. Drinking water, a vault toilet, and garbage bins are available. Some facilities are wheelchair accessible. Leashed pets are permitted.

Reservations, fees: Reservations are not accepted. Sites are $8 per night, $4 per night per additional vehicle. Open mid-June–October, weather permitting.

Directions: From south Eugene on I-5, take Exit 188 to Highway 58. Drive 35 miles southeast on Highway 58 to Oakridge. Turn left at the signal to downtown and Salmon Creek Road. Turn east and drive nine miles (it becomes Forest Road 24) to Forest Road 1934. Turn left and drive eight miles to Forest Road 733. Turn right and continue for 1.25 miles to the campground.

Contact: Willamette National Forest, Middle Fork Ranger District, 541/782-2283, fax 541/782-5306, www.fs.fed.us.

71 KIAHANIE

Scenic rating: 5

on the North Fork of the Willamette River in
Willamette National Forest

Map 5.4, page 276

This is one heck of a spot for fly-fishing (and the only kind of fishing allowed). Kiahanie is a remote campground that sits at 2,200 feet elevation along the North Fork of the Willamette River, a designated Wild and Scenic River. If you want beauty and quiet among enormous Douglas fir trees, you came to the right place. An even more remote campground, Box Canyon Horse Camp, is farther north on Forest Road 19.

Campsites, facilities: There are 19 sites for tents or RVs up to 24 feet long. Picnic tables and fire rings are provided. Drinking water, vault toilets, garbage bins, and a recycling center are available. Some facilities are wheelchair accessible. Leashed pets are permitted.

Reservations, fees: Reservations are not accepted. Sites are $10 per night, $5 per night per additional vehicle. Open late May–late October, weather permitting.

Directions: From south Eugene on I-5, take Exit 188 to Highway 58. Drive 31 miles southeast on Highway 58 to Westfir. Take the Westfir exit and drive two miles to Westfir and the junction with Aufderheide Scenic Byway (Forest Road 19). Bear left (northeast) and drive 19 miles to the campground.

Contact: Willamette National Forest, Middle Fork Ranger District, 541/782-2283, fax 541/782-5306, www.fs.fed.us.

72 BOX CANYON HORSE CAMP

Scenic rating: 4

near Chucksney Mountain in Willamette National Forest

Map 5.4, page 276

Only 80 miles from Eugene, this secluded campground with sparse tree cover offers wilderness trails, including the Chucksney Mountain Trail, Crossing-Way Trail, and Grasshopper Trail. It's a good base camp for a backpacking trip and is at 3,600 feet in elevation.

Campsites, facilities: There are 13 sites for tents or RVs up to 30 feet long that allow horse and rider to camp close together. Picnic tables, fire grills, stock water, and corrals are provided. Vault toilets are available. There is no drinking water, and garbage must be packed out. Leashed pets are permitted.

Reservations, fees: Reservations are not accepted. There is no fee for camping. Open June–November, weather permitting.

Directions: From Eugene, drive east on

Highway 126 for 41 miles to Blue River. Continue east on Highway 126 for five miles to Forest Road 19 (Aufderheide Scenic Byway). Turn right (south) and drive 33 miles to the camp on the right.

Contact: Willamette National Forest, McKenzie River Ranger District, 541/822-3381, fax 541/822-7254, www.fs.fed.us.

73 BLACK CANYON

Scenic rating: 7

on the Middle Fork of the Willamette River in Willamette National Forest

Map 5.4, page 276

Black Canyon campground is set along the banks of the Middle Fork of the Willamette River, not far above Lookout Point Reservoir, where fishing and boating are available. The elevation is 1,000 feet. The camp is pretty and wooded and has comfortable sites. Within the camp is a one-mile-long nature trail with interpretive signs. You will hear train noise from the other side of the river.

Campsites, facilities: There are 70 sites for tents or RVs up to 40 feet long, and one group site is available. Picnic tables, garbage service, and fire grills are provided. Drinking water, vault toilets, and firewood are available. A dump station, café, and coin laundry are within six miles. Launching facilities are nearby at the south end of Lookout Point Reservoir. Some facilities are wheelchair accessible. Leashed pets are permitted.

Reservations, fees: Reservations are accepted at 877/444-6777 or www.recreation.gov ($10 reservation fee). Single sites are $16 per night, $30 per night for double site, $8 per night per additional vehicle, $75 for the group site. Open late April–early October, weather permitting.

Directions: From south Eugene on I-5, take Exit 188 to Highway 58. Drive southeast on Highway 58 for 27 miles to the camp on the left (six miles west of Oakridge).

Contact: Willamette National Forest, Middle Fork Ranger District, 541/782-2283, fax 541/782-5306, www.fs.fed.us.

74 BAKER BAY COUNTY PARK

Scenic rating: 6

on Dorena Lake

Map 5.4, page 276

Baker Bay is set along the shore of Dorena Lake, where boating, canoeing, fishing, sailing, swimming, and waterskiing are among the recreation options. Row River Trail follows part of the lake for a hike or bike ride, and there are covered bridges in the area. For golf, head to Cottage Grove.

Campsites, facilities: There are 49 sites for tents or self-contained RVs up to 35 feet, plus two group sites for up to 25 people each. Picnic tables and fire grills are provided. Drinking water, restrooms with flush toilets and coin showers, firewood, garbage bins, and a dump station are available. A concession stand with ice is in the park, and a store is within two miles. Boat docks, launching, and rentals are nearby, with seasonal onshore facilities for catamarans. Some facilities are wheelchair accessible. Leashed pets are permitted.

Reservations, fees: Reservations are accepted for group sites only at 541/682-2000 ($10 reservation fee). Single sites are $16 per night, $6.50 for an additional vehicle. Group sites are $50 per night. Open April–October.

Directions: From Eugene, drive south on I-5 for 22 miles to Cottage Grove and Exit 174 (Dorena Lake exit). Take that exit to Row River Road and drive east for 4.4 miles (the road becomes Shore View Drive). Bear right on Shore View Drive and continue 2.8 miles to the campground entrance on the left.

Contact: Baker Bay Park, 541/942-7669, www.co.lane.or.us/parks.

75 SCHWARZ PARK

Scenic rating: 7

on Dorena Lake

Map 5.4, page 276

This large campground sits below Dorena Lake on the Row River, where boating, fishing, swimming, and waterskiing are among the recreation options at the lake. Note that chances of rain are high May to mid-June and that there is a posted warning against consumption of fish from Dorena Lake. The Row River Trail, a paved trail for biking, walking, and shoreline access, parallels Dorena Lake's north shoreline and then extends 12 miles.

Campsites, facilities: There are 69 sites for tents or RVs of any length and six group sites for up to 15–50 people. Drinking water, garbage bins, picnic tables, and fire rings are provided. Restrooms with flush toilets and showers and a dump station are available. Boat-launching facilities are on the lake about two miles upstream. Some facilities are wheelchair accessible. Leashed pets are permitted.

Reservations, fees: Reservations are accepted at 877/444-6777 or www.recreation.gov ($10 reservation fee). Sites are $13 per night, group sites are $130 per night, and an additional vehicle is $5 per night. Open late April–late September.

Directions: From Eugene, drive south on I-5 for 22 miles to Cottage Grove and Exit 174. Take that exit to Shoreview Drive and drive one mile to Row River Road. Turn left and drive four miles east to the campground entrance.

Contact: U.S. Army Corps of Engineers, Recreation Information, Cottage Grove, 541/942-1418 or 541/942-5631, fax 541/942-1305, http://corpslakes.usace.army.mil.

76 SALMON CREEK FALLS

🚶 🚴 🛶 🎣 🏕 🚙 ⛺

Scenic rating: 8

on Salmon Creek in Willamette National Forest

Map 5.4, page 276   **BEST (**

This pretty campground sits in a lush, old-growth forest, right along Salmon Creek at 1,500 feet in elevation. The rocky gorge area creates two small but beautiful waterfalls and several deep pools in the clear, blue-green waters. Springtime brings a full range of wildflowers and wild thimbleberries; hazelnuts abound in the summer. This area is a popular recreation spot.

Campsites, facilities: There are 14 sites for tents or RVs up to 40 feet long. Picnic tables, garbage bins, and fire grills are provided. Drinking water and vault toilets are available. A store, café, coin laundry, and ice are available within five miles. Leashed pets are permitted.

Reservations, fees: Reservations are not accepted. Sites are $14 per night, $7 per night per additional vehicle. Open late April–mid-September, weather permitting.

Directions: From south Eugene on I-5, take Exit 188 to Highway 58. Drive southeast on Highway 58 for 35 miles to Oakridge and the signal light for downtown. Turn left on Crestview Street and drive 0.25 mile to 1st Street. Turn right and drive five miles (the road becomes Forest Road 24, then Salmon Creek Road) to the campground entrance on the right.

Contact: Willamette National Forest, Middle Fork Ranger District, 541/782-2283, fax 541/782-5306, www.fs.fed.us; Hoodoo Recreation, 541/822-3799.

77 SKOOKUM CREEK

🚶 🛶 🐕 ♿ ⛺

Scenic rating: 7

near the Three Sisters Wilderness in Willamette National Forest

Map 5.4, page 276

Skookum Creek, at 4,500 feet elevation, is a popular starting point for backcountry fishing, hiking, and horseback riding. The Erma Bell Lakes Trail, a portal into the Three Sisters Wilderness, begins here. This trail is maintained for wheelchair accessibility, though it is challenging.

Campsites, facilities: There are nine walk-in tent sites. Picnic tables and fire rings are provided. Drinking water, hitching rails, garbage service, and vault toilets are available. Some facilities are wheelchair accessible. Leashed pets are permitted.

Reservations, fees: Reservations are not accepted. Sites are $8 per night, $4 per night per additional vehicle. Open mid-June–mid-October, weather permitting.

Directions: From Eugene, drive east on Highway 126 for 37 miles to Blue River. Continue east for five miles to Forest Road 19 (Aufderheide Scenic Byway). Turn right and drive 35 miles south to Forest Road 1957. Turn right (south) and drive four miles to the campground.

Contact: Willamette National Forest, Middle Fork Ranger District, 541/782-2283, fax 541/782-5306.

78 NORTH WALDO

🚶 🚴 🛶 🎣 🛶 🐕 🚙 ⛺

Scenic rating: 10

on Waldo Lake in Willamette National Forest

Map 5.4, page 276   **BEST (**

North Waldo is the most popular of the Waldo Lake campgrounds. Set at an elevation of 5,400 feet, Waldo Lake has the special distinction of being one of the three purest lakes in the world. The boat launch here is deeper than the others on the lake, which makes it more accommodating for large sailboats (gas motors are not allowed on the lake). Amphitheater programs are presented here on weekends late July–Labor Day. North Waldo is also a popular starting point to many wilderness trails and lakes, most notably Rigdon, Torrey, and Wahanna lakes. The drier environment supports fewer mosquitoes, but they can still be plentiful in season.

Campsites, facilities: There are 56 sites for tents or RVs up to 40 feet long. Picnic tables and fire rings are provided. Drinking water, composting toilets, garbage bins, recycling center, swimming area, and amphitheater are available. Boat-launching facilities are available. Leashed pets are permitted.

Reservations, fees: Reservations are not accepted. Single sites are $18 per night, double sites $20 per night, $9 per night per additional vehicle. A Northwest Forest Pass ($5 daily fee or $30 annual fee per vehicle) is required at the nearby boat launch and trailheads. Open early June–early October, weather permitting.

Directions: From Eugene, drive south on I-5 for four miles to Exit 188 and Highway 58. Turn southeast and drive about 60 miles to Waldo Lake Road (Forest Road 5897). Turn left and drive north on Waldo Lake Road for 14 miles to Forest Road 5898. Turn left and drive about two miles to the campground at the northeast end of Waldo Lake.

Contact: Willamette National Forest, Middle Fork Ranger District, 541/782-2283, fax 541/782-5306, www.fs.fed.us; Hoodoo Recreation, 541/822-3799.

79 ISLET

Scenic rating: 10

on Waldo Lake in Willamette National Forest

Map 5.4, page 276

You'll find sandy beaches and an interpretive sign at this campground at the north end of Waldo Lake. The winds blow consistently every afternoon, great for sailing. A picnic table placed strategically on the rock jetty provides a great spot to enjoy a sunset. A one-mile shoreline trail stretches between Islet and North Waldo Campground. Bring your mosquito repellent June–August—you'll need it.

Campsites, facilities: There are 55 sites, including four multiple sites, for tents or RVs up to 40 feet long. Picnic tables, garbage bins, a recycling center, and fire rings are provided. Drinking water and composting toilets are available. Boat-launching facilities are available nearby. Leashed pets are permitted.

Reservations, fees: Reservations are not accepted. Single sites are $18 per night, $9 per night per additional vehicle. Double sites are $25 per night. A Northwest Forest Pass ($5 daily fee or $30 annual fee per parked vehicle) is required at the nearby boat launch and trailheads. Open July–October, weather permitting.

Directions: From Eugene, drive south on I-5 for four miles to Exit 188 and Highway 58. Turn southeast and drive about 60 miles to Waldo Lake Road (Forest Road 5897). Turn left and drive north on Waldo Lake Road for 14 miles to Forest Road 5898. Turn left and continue 1.5 miles to the campground at the northeast end of Waldo Lake.

Contact: Willamette National Forest, Middle Fork Ranger District, 541/782-2283, fax 541/782-5306, www.fs.fed.us; Hoodoo Recreation, 541/822-3799.

80 SHADOW BAY

Scenic rating: 10

on Waldo Lake in Willamette National Forest

Map 5.4, page 276

Shadow Bay campground, at 5,400 in elevation, is situated on a large bay at the south end of Waldo Lake. It has a considerably wetter environment than either North Waldo or Islet, supporting a more diverse and prolific ground cover—as well as more mosquitoes. The camp receives considerably lighter use than North Waldo. You have access to the Shore Line Trail and then the Waldo Lake Trail from here. Note that gas motors are not permitted on Waldo Lake.

Campsites, facilities: There are 92 sites, including several multiple sites, for tents or RVs up to 44 feet long. Picnic tables, garbage bins, a recycling center, and fire grills are provided. Drinking water and vault and composting toilets are available. A camp host is on-site in season. Boat-launching facilities and a swimming area are nearby. Leashed pets are permitted.

Reservations, fees: Reservations are accepted at 877/444-6777 or www.recreation.gov ($10 reservation fee). Single sites are $18 per night, $32 per night for double sites, $9 per night per additional vehicle. A Northwest Forest Pass ($5 daily fee or $30 annual fee per vehicle) is required at the nearby boat launch and trailheads. Open July–October, weather permitting.

Directions: From Eugene, drive south on I-5 for four miles to Exit 188 and Highway 58. Turn southeast and drive about 60 miles to Waldo Lake Road (Forest Road 5897). Turn left on Waldo Lake Road and drive north for 6.5 miles to the Shadow Bay turnoff. Turn left and drive on Forest Road 5896 to the campground at the south end of Waldo Lake.

Contact: Willamette National Forest, Middle Fork Ranger District, 541/782-2283, fax 541/782-5306, www.fs.fed.us; Hoodoo Recreation, 541/822-3799.

81 BLUE POOL

Scenic rating: 4

on Salt Creek in Willamette National Forest

Map 5.4, page 276

This campground is situated in an old-growth forest alongside Salt Creek at 1,900 feet elevation. The camp features a large picnic area along the creek with picnic tables, a large grassy area, and fire stoves built in the 1930s by the Civilian Conservation Corps. One-half mile east of the campground on Highway 58 is McCredie Hot Springs. This spot is undeveloped, without any facilities. Exercise caution when using the hot springs; they can be very hot.

Campsites, facilities: There are 24 sites for tents or RVs up to 36 feet long. Picnic tables,

garbage bins, a recycling center, and fire rings are provided. Drinking water and vault and flush toilets are available. Leashed pets are permitted.

Reservations, fees: Reservations are not accepted. Sites are $14 per night, $7 per night per additional vehicle. Open mid-May–September, weather permitting.

Directions: From Eugene, drive south on I-5 for four miles to Exit 188 and Highway 58. Turn southeast and drive 35 miles to Oakridge. Continue east on Highway 58 for eight miles to the campground on the right.

Contact: Willamette National Forest, Middle Fork Ranger District, 541/782-2283, fax 541/782-5306, www.fs.fed.us; Hoodoo Recreation, 541/822-3799.

82 SHARPS CREEK

Scenic rating: 5

on Sharps Creek

Map 5.4, page 276

Like nearby Rujada, this camp on the banks of Sharps Creek is just far enough off the beaten path to be missed by most campers. It's quiet, primitive, and remote, and fishing, gold-panning, and swimming are popular activities in the day-use area.

Campsites, facilities: There are 10 sites for tents or RVs up to 30 feet long. Picnic tables and fire pits are provided. Drinking water and vault toilets are available. A camp host is here in summer. Some facilities are wheelchair accessible. Leashed pets are permitted.

Reservations, fees: Reservations are not accepted. Sites are $8 per night, with a 14-day stay limit, and $3 per night per additional vehicle. Open mid-May–September, weather permitting.

Directions: From Eugene, drive south on I-5 to Cottage Grove and Exit 174. Take that exit and drive east on Row River Road for 18 miles to Sharps Creek Road. Turn right (south) and drive four miles to the campground.

Contact: Bureau of Land Management, Eugene District, 541/683-6600 or 888/442-3061, fax 541/683-6981, www.blm.gov.

83 RUJADA

🚶 🚴 🏊 ⛵ 🐕 ♿ 🚐 ⛺

Scenic rating: 7

on Layng Creek in Umpqua National Forest

Map 5.4, page 276

Rujada campground is nestled on a river terrace on the banks of Layng Creek, right at the national forest border. The Swordfern Trail follows Layng Creek through a beautiful forest within a lush fern grotto. There is a fair swimming hole near the campground. Those with patience and persistence can fish in the creek. By continuing east on Forest Road 17, you reach a trailhead that leads 0.5 mile to beautiful Spirit Falls, a spectacular 60-foot waterfall. A bit farther east is another easy trail, which leads to Moon Falls, even more awe-inspiring at 125 feet. Another campground option is Cedar Creek, about six miles southeast on Brice Creek Road (County Road 2470).

Campsites, facilities: There are 15 sites for tents or RVs up to 22 feet long. Picnic tables, garbage bins, and fire pits are provided. Flush and vault toilets, drinking water, and a softball field are available. Some facilities are wheelchair accessible. Leashed pets are permitted.

Reservations, fees: Reservations are not accepted. Sites are $8 per night, $3 per night per additional vehicle. Open late May–late September, weather permitting.

Directions: From Eugene, drive south on I-5 to Cottage Grove and Exit 174. Take that exit and drive east on Row River Road for 19 miles to Layng Creek Road (Forest Road 17). Turn left and drive two miles to the campground on the right.

Contact: Umpqua National Forest, Cottage Grove Ranger District, 541/767-5000, fax 541/767-5075, www.fs.fed.us.

84 PACKARD CREEK

🚶 🏊 ⛵ 🛶 🐕 ♿ 🚐 ⛺

Scenic rating: 6

on Hills Creek Reservoir in
Willamette National Forest

Map 5.4, page 276

Packard Creek campground is located on a large flat beside Hills Creek Reservoir. This camp is extremely popular with families and fills up on weekends and holidays. The mix of vegetation in the campground unfortunately includes an abundance of poison oak. The speed limit around the swimming area and boat ramp is 5 mph. The elevation is 1,600 feet.

Campsites, facilities: There are 37 sites, including two multiple sites, for tents or RVs up to 40 feet long, and a group area for up to 75 people. Picnic tables and fire rings are provided. Drinking water, vault toilets, garbage bins, a recycling center, and firewood are available. Fishing and boat docks, boat-launching facilities, a roped swimming area, picnic shelter, and an amphitheater are available. Some sites have their own docks. Some facilities are wheelchair accessible. Leashed pets are permitted.

Reservations, fees: Reservations are accepted at 877/444-6777 or www.recreation.gov ($10 reservation fee). Single sites are $16 per night, $30 per night for double sites, $8 per night per additional vehicle, $125 for the group site. Open mid-April–mid-September, weather permitting.

Directions: From Eugene, drive south on I-5 for four miles to Exit 188 and Highway 58. Turn southeast and drive 35 miles to Oakridge. Continue east on Highway 58 for two miles to Kitson Springs Road. Turn right and drive 0.5 mile to Forest Road 21. Turn right and continue six miles to the campground on the left.

Contact: Willamette National Forest, Middle Fork Ranger District, 541/782-2283, fax 541/782-5306, www.fs.fed.us; Hoodoo Recreation, 541/822-3799.

85 SAND PRAIRIE

Scenic rating: 6

on the Willamette River in
Willamette National Forest

Map 5.4, page 276

Situated at 1,600 feet elevation in a mixed stand of cedar, dogwood, Douglas fir, hazelnut, and western hemlock, this campground provides easy access to the Middle Fork of the Willamette River. An access road leads to the south (upstream) end of the Hills Creek Reservoir. The 27-mile Middle Fork Trail begins at the south end of the campground. Fishing is good here; you can expect to catch large cutthroat trout, rainbow trout, and suckers in the Middle Fork.

Campsites, facilities: There are 21 sites for tents or RVs up to 40 feet long. Picnic tables, garbage bins, and fire rings are provided. Vault and flush toilets, a group picnic area, and drinking water are available. A camp host is on-site. A boat launch is nearby on Hills Creek Reservoir. Some facilities are wheelchair accessible. Leashed pets are permitted.

Reservations, fees: Reservations are not accepted. Sites are $12 per night, $6 per night per additional vehicle. Open late May–early September, weather permitting.

Directions: From Eugene, drive south on I-5 for four miles to Exit 188 and Highway 58. Turn southeast and drive 35 miles to Oakridge. Continue east on Highway 58 for two miles to Kitson Springs Road. Turn right and drive 0.5 mile to Forest Road 21. Turn right and continue 11 miles to the campground on the right.

Contact: Willamette National Forest, Middle Fork Ranger District, 541/782-2283, fax 541/782-5306, www.fs.fed.us.

86 SACANDAGA

Scenic rating: 5

on the Willamette River in
Willamette National Forest

Map 5.4, page 276

Sacandaga campground sits along the middle fork of the Willamette River, where a segment of the historic Oregon Central Military Wagon Road is visible. Two trails from the campground access the Willamette River, and the Middle Fork Trail is in close proximity. Also, a short trail leads to a viewpoint with a bench, great for a short break. This campground gets low use, and the sites are well separated by vegetation. Count on solitude here. The elevation is 2,400 feet.

Campsites, facilities: There are 17 sites for tents or RVs up to 24 feet long. Picnic tables and fire rings are provided. Drinking water, vault toilets, and firewood are available. Leashed pets are permitted.

Reservations, fees: Reservations are not accepted. Sites are $8 per night, $4 per night per additional vehicle. Open mid-May–mid-November, weather permitting.

Directions: From Eugene, drive south on I-5 for four miles to Exit 188 and Highway 58. Turn southeast and drive 35 miles to Oakridge. Continue east on Highway 58 for two miles to Kitson Springs Road. Turn right and drive 0.5 mile to Forest Road 21. Turn right and drive 24 miles to the campground on the right.

Contact: Willamette National Forest, Middle Fork Ranger District, 541/782-2283, fax 541/782-5306, www.fs.fed.us.

87 CAMPERS FLAT

Scenic rating: 5

on the Willamette River in
Willamette National Forest

Map 5.4, page 276

Small, pretty Campers Flat campground sits adjacent to the Middle Fork Willamette River, near Deadhorse Creek. Though the camp is right next to Forest Road 21, you're likely to hear more river than road. Fishing is a popular activity here, with good river access. For mountain bikers, the Young's Rock Trailhead awaits on the other side of the road. While at camp, be sure to check out the interpretive sign detailing the history of the Oregon Central Military Wagon Road.

Campsites, facilities: There are five sites for tents or RVs up to 40 feet long. Picnic tables, garbage bins, and fire grills are provided. Vault toilets and firewood are available. Well water may be available for drinking, but bring your own just in case. Leashed pets are permitted.

Reservations, fees: Reservations are not accepted. Sites are $12 per night, $6 per night per additional vehicle. Open late May–September.

Directions: From Eugene, drive south on I-5 for five miles to Exit 188 and Highway 58. Turn east and drive 35 miles to the town of Oakridge. From Oakridge, continue east on Highway 58 about two miles to Kitson Springs Road. Turn right and drive 0.5 mile to Forest Road 21. Turn right and drive 19 miles to the campground on the right.

Contact: Willamette National Forest, Middle Fork Ranger District, 541/782-2283, fax 541/782-5306, www.fs.fed.us.

88 SECRET

Scenic rating: 5

on the Willamette River in
Willamette National Forest

Map 5.4, page 276

This small campground, set on the middle fork of the Willamette River, gets regular use from locals in the know. The tree cover is scant, but there is adequate vegetation to buffer the campsites from the nearby road noise. Fishing the Middle Fork Willamette is generally fair.

Campsites, facilities: There are six sites for tents or RVs up to 36 feet long. Picnic tables, garbage bins, and fire rings are provided. Pit toilets are available, but there is no drinking water. Leashed pets are permitted.

Reservations, fees: Reservations are not accepted. Sites are $12 per night, $6 per night per additional vehicle. Open May–late September, weather permitting.

Directions: From Eugene, drive south on I-5 for five miles to Exit 188 and Highway 58. Turn east and drive 35 miles to the town of Oakridge. From Oakridge, continue east on Highway 58 about two miles to Kitson Springs Road. Turn right and drive 0.5 mile to Forest Road 21. Turn right and drive 18 miles to the campground.

Contact: Willamette National Forest, Middle Fork Ranger District, 541/782-2283, fax 541/782-5306, www.fs.fed.us; Hoodoo Recreation, 541/822-3799.

89 INDIGO SPRINGS

Scenic rating: 5

near the Willamette River in
Willamette National Forest

Map 5.4, page 276

This small, semi-open tent campground sits at 2,800 feet elevation in a stand of old-growth Douglas fir. A nearby 250-foot walk leads to the origin of this cold-water spring. A remnant of the historic Oregon Central Military Wagon Road passes near the campground, with an interpretive sign explaining it.

Campsites, facilities: There are three sites for tents. Picnic tables and fire grills are provided. Vault toilets and firewood are available. There is no drinking water. Leashed pets are permitted.

Reservations, fees: Reservations are not accepted. There is no fee for camping. Open May–October, weather permitting.

Directions: From Eugene, drive south on I-5 for five miles to Exit 188 and Highway 58. Turn east and drive 35 miles to the town of Oakridge. From Oakridge, continue east on Highway 58 about two miles to Kitson Springs

Road. Turn right and drive 0.5 mile to Forest Road 21. Turn right and drive 27 miles to the campground on the left.

Contact: Willamette National Forest, Middle Fork Ranger District, 541/782-2283, fax 541/782-5306, www.fs.fed.us.

90 ROCK CREEK

Scenic rating: 8

on Rock Creek

Map 5.4, page 276

Since I started roaming around the state 20 years ago, this campground on the banks of Rock Creek in a relatively obscure spot has been considerably improved by the BLM. It's not well known, either, so you're likely to have privacy as a bonus. No fishing is allowed in Rock Creek.

Campsites, facilities: There are 17 sites for tents or RVs up to 40 feet long. Picnic tables and fire grills are provided. A camp host is on-site, and vault toilets, drinking water, a pavilion, and firewood are available. Some facilities are wheelchair accessible. Leashed pets are permitted.

Reservations, fees: Reservations are not accepted. Sites are $10 per night, with a 14-day stay limit, and $4 per night per additional vehicle. Open mid-May–mid-September.

Directions: From Roseburg, drive east on Highway 138 for 22 miles to Rock Creek Road. Turn right (north) and drive seven miles to the campground on the right.

Contact: Bureau of Land Management, Roseburg District, 541/440-4930, fax 541/440-4948, www.blm.gov.

91 MILLPOND

Scenic rating: 8

on Rock Creek

Map 5.4, page 276

Rock Creek flows past Millpond and empties into the North Umpqua River five miles downstream. Just above this confluence is the Rock Creek Fish Hatchery, which is open year-round to visitors, with free access. This campground along the banks of Rock Creek is the first camp you'll see along Rock Creek Road, which accounts for its relative popularity in the area. Like Rock Creek Campground, it's primitive and remote. No fishing is allowed in Rock Creek.

Campsites, facilities: There are 12 sites for tents or RVs up to 45 feet long. Picnic tables, garbage service, and fire grills are provided. A camp host is on-site, and flush and vault toilets, drinking water, firewood, a ball field, playground, and pavilion are available. Some facilities are wheelchair accessible. Leashed pets are permitted.

Reservations, fees: Reservations are not accepted. Sites are $10 per night, with a 14-day stay limit, and $4 per night per additional vehicle. Open early May–early November.

Directions: From Roseburg, drive east on Highway 138 for 22 miles to Rock Creek Road. Turn right (north) and drive five miles to the campground on the right.

Contact: Bureau of Land Management, Roseburg District, 541/440-4930, fax 541/440-4948, www.blm.gov.

92 SUSAN CREEK

Scenic rating: 9

on the North Umpqua River

Map 5.4, page 276   **BEST (**

This popular and pretty campground borders the North Umpqua Wild and Scenic River. This lush setting features plenty of trees and river access. Highlights include two barrier-free trails, one traveling 0.5 mile to the day-use area. From there, a hike of about 0.75 mile leads to the 50-foot Susan Creek Falls. Another 0.4 mile up the trail are the Susan Creek Indian Mounds. These moss-covered rocks are believed to be a spiritual site and are visited by Native Americans in search of guardian spirit visions. This area also boasts an excellent osprey interpretive site with a viewing platform along the river.

Campsites, facilities: There are 29 sites for RVs up to 65 feet long. Picnic tables, garbage service, and fire grills are provided. Restrooms with flush toilets and showers, drinking water, and firewood are available, and there is a camp host. Some facilities and trails are wheelchair accessible. Leashed pets are permitted.

Reservations, fees: Reservations are not accepted. Sites are $14 per night, with a 14-day stay limit, and $4 per night per additional vehicle. Open late April–mid-November.

Directions: From Roseburg, drive east on Highway 138 for 29.5 miles to the campground (turnoff well signed).

Contact: Bureau of Land Management, Roseburg District, 541/440-4930, fax 541/440-4948, www.blm.gov.

93 STEAMBOAT FALLS

Scenic rating: 8

on Steamboat Creek in
Umpqua National Forest

Map 5.4, page 276   **BEST (**

This Steamboat Creek campground boasts some excellent scenery. Beautiful Steamboat Falls features a fish ladder that provides passage for steelhead and salmon on their upstream migration. No fishing is permitted in Steamboat Creek. Other nearby camping options are Island and Canton Creek.

Campsites, facilities: There are 10 sites for tents or RVs up to 24 feet long. Picnic tables, garbage bins, vault toilets, and fire grills are provided. There is no drinking water. Leashed pets are permitted.

Reservations, fees: Reservations are not accepted. Sites are $7 per night, $4 per night per additional vehicle. Open year-round, weather permitting.

Directions: From Roseburg on I-5, take Exit 120 to Highway 138. Drive east on Highway

138 to Steamboat and Forest Road 38. Turn left on Forest Road 38 (Steamboat Creek Road) and drive six miles to a fork with Forest Road 3810. Turn right and drive one mile on a paved road to the campground.

Contact: Umpqua National Forest, North Umpqua Ranger District, 541/496-3532, fax 541/496-3534, www.fs.fed.us.

94 SCAREDMAN

Scenic rating: 6

on Canton Creek

Map 5.4, page 276

Scaredman is a small campground along the banks of Canton Creek, virtually unknown to out-of-towners. Set in an old-growth forest, this private and secluded camp offers a chance to swim in the creek. Scaredman gets its name from an old legend that says some early settlers camped here, heard a pack of hungry wolves, and then ran off, scared to death. This is one of the few free camps left in the region. Although fishing is closed on Canton Creek and all Steamboat drainages, the North Umpqua River 3.5 miles downstream offers fly-fishing for steelhead or salmon.

Campsites, facilities: There are nine sites for tents or RVs up to 25 feet long. Picnic tables, garbage service, and fire grills are provided. Vault toilets and drinking water are available. A camp host is on-site in season. Leashed pets are permitted.

Reservations, fees: Reservations are not accepted. There is no fee for camping. The stay limit is 14 days. Open year-round.

Directions: From Roseburg, drive east on Highway 138 for 40 miles to Steamboat Creek Road. Turn left (north) and drive 0.5 mile to Canton Creek Road. Turn left (north) and drive three miles to the campground.

Contact: Bureau of Land Management, Roseburg District, 541/440-4930, fax 541/440-4948, www.blm.gov.

95 ISLAND

Scenic rating: 8

on the Umpqua River in
Umpqua National Forest

Map 5.4, page 276

The North Umpqua is one of Oregon's most beautiful rivers, and this scenic campground borders its banks at a spot popular for both rafting and steelhead fishing. Note: Only fly-fishing is allowed here. A hiking trail that leads east and west along the river is accessible a short drive to the west.

Campsites, facilities: There are seven sites for tents or RVs up to 24 feet long. Picnic tables, garbage bins, and fire grills are provided. There is no drinking water. Some facilities are wheelchair accessible. Leashed pets are permitted.

Reservations, fees: Reservations are not accepted. Sites are $8 per night, $4 per night per additional vehicle. Open year-round, weather permitting.

Directions: From Roseburg, drive east on Highway 138 for 40 miles (just past Steamboat) to the camp on the right. The campground is along the highway.

Contact: Umpqua National Forest, North Umpqua Ranger District, 541/496-3532, fax 541/496-3534, www.fs.fed.us.

96 CANTON CREEK

Scenic rating: 8

near the North Umpqua River in
Umpqua National Forest

Map 5.4, page 276

Set at an elevation of 1,195 feet at the confluence of Canton and Steamboat Creeks, this camp is less than a mile from the North Umpqua River and gets little overnight use—but lots of day swimmers come here in July and August. No fishing is permitted on Steamboat or Canton Creeks because they are spawning areas for steelhead and salmon. Steamboat Falls is six miles north on Forest Road 38.

Campsites, facilities: There are five sites for tents or RVs up to 22 feet long. Picnic tables, garbage bins, and fire grills are provided. Drinking water, a covered picnic gazebo, and flush toilets are available. Leashed pets are permitted.

Reservations, fees: Reservations are not accepted. Sites are $8 per night, $4 per night per additional vehicle. Open mid-May–mid-October, weather permitting.

Directions: From Roseburg, drive east on Highway 138 for 39 miles to Steamboat and Forest Road 38 (Steamboat Creek Road). Turn left and drive 0.25 mile to the campground on the right.

Contact: Umpqua National Forest, North Umpqua Ranger District, 541/496-3532, fax 541/496-3534, www.fs.fed.us.

97 HORSESHOE BEND/ DEER FLAT GROUP

Scenic rating: 8

on the Umpqua River in
Umpqua National Forest

Map 5.4, page 276

This campground, set at an elevation of 1,300 feet, is in the middle of a big bend in the North Umpqua River. This spot is a major launching point for white-water rafting. Fly-fishing is popular here.

Campsites, facilities: There are 24 sites for tents or RVs up to 35 feet long and one group site, Deer Flat, for up to 70 people. Picnic tables, fire grills, garbage bins, drinking water, and flush toilets are provided. A store, gas, and propane are available one mile east. Raft-launching facilities are nearby. Some facilities are wheelchair accessible. Leashed pets are permitted.

Reservations, fees: Reservations are accepted for the group site (Deer Flat, not Horseshoe Bend) at 877/444-6777 or www.recreation.

gov ($10 reservation fee) but are not accepted for family sites. Sites are $12 per night, $4 per night per additional vehicle, and $85 per night for group sites. Open mid-May–late September, weather permitting.

Directions: From Roseburg on I-5, take Exit 120. Drive east on Highway 138 for 47 miles to Forest Road 4750. Turn right and drive south a short distance to the campground entrance road on the right.

Contact: Umpqua National Forest, North Umpqua Ranger District, 541/496-3532, fax 541/496-3534, www.fs.fed.us.

98 EAGLE ROCK

Scenic rating: 9

on the North Umpqua River in
Umpqua National Forest

Map 5.4, page 276

Eagle Rock camp sits next to the North Umpqua River and adjacent to the Boulder Creek Wilderness. It is named after Eagle Rock, which, along with Rattlesnake Rock, towers above the campground. The camp offers outstanding views of these unusual rock formations. It gets moderate use, heavy on weekends. The camp sits at 1,676 feet elevation near Boulder Flat, a major launch point for rafting. Fishing here is restricted to the use of artificial lures with a single barbless hook.

Campsites, facilities: There are 25 sites for tents or RVs up to 30 feet long. Picnic tables and fire grills are provided. Vault toilets and garbage bins are available. There is no drinking water. A store, propane, and ice are within five miles. Some facilities are wheelchair accessible. Leashed pets are permitted.

Reservations, fees: Reservations are not accepted. Sites are $10 per night, $4 per night per additional vehicle. Open mid-May–October, weather permitting.

Directions: From Roseburg, drive east on Highway 138 for 53 miles to the campground on the left.

Contact: Umpqua National Forest, North Umpqua Ranger District, 541/496-3532, fax 541/496-3534, www.fs.fed.us.

99 BOULDER FLAT

Scenic rating: 8

on the North Umpqua River in
Umpqua National Forest

Map 5.4, page 276   **BEST (**

Boulder Flat campground is nestled along the banks of the North Umpqua River at the confluence with Boulder Creek. There's good trout fishing here (fly-fishing only) and outstanding scenery. The camp sits at a major launching point for white-water rafting. Across the river from the campground, a trail follows Boulder Creek north for 10.5 miles through the Boulder Creek Wilderness, a climb in elevation from 2,000 to 5,400 feet. It's a good thumper for backpackers. Access to the trail is at Soda Springs Dam, two miles east of the camp. A little over a mile to the east you can see some huge, dramatic pillars of volcanic rock, colored with lichen.

Campsites, facilities: There are nine sites for tents or RVs up to 24 feet long. Picnic tables, garbage bins, and fire grills are provided. Vault toilets are available. There is no drinking water. A store, propane, and ice are within five miles. A raft launch is on-site. Leashed pets are permitted.

Reservations, fees: Reservations are not accepted. Sites are $8 per night, $4 per night per additional vehicle. Open year-round.

Directions: From Roseburg, drive east on Highway 138 for 54 miles to the campground on the left.

Contact: Umpqua National Forest, North Umpqua Ranger District, 541/496-3532, fax 541/496-3534, www.fs.fed.us.

100 TOKETEE LAKE

🚶 🏊 🚤 🛶 🎿 🐎 🚐 ⛺

Scenic rating: 7

on Toketee Lake in Umpqua National Forest

Map 5.4, page 276

Located just north of Toketee Lake, this camp-ground sits at an elevation of 2,200 feet. The North Umpqua River Trail passes near camp and continues east along the river for many miles. Die-hard hikers can also take the trail west toward the Boulder Creek Wilderness. Toketee Lake, a 97-acre reservoir, offers a good population of brown and rainbow trout and many recreation options. A worthwhile point of interest is Toketee Falls, just west of the lake turnoff. Another is Umpqua Hot Springs, a few miles northeast of the camp. The area sustains a wide variety of wildlife; you might see bald eagles, beavers, a variety of ducks and geese, great blue herons, kingfishers, and otters in fall and winter.

Campsites, facilities: There are 33 sites for tents or RVs up to 22 feet long and one group site for up to 30 people. Picnic tables, garbage bins, and fire grills are provided. Vault toilets are available, but there is no drinking water. Boat docks and launching facilities are nearby. Leashed pets are permitted.

Reservations, fees: Reservations are accepted only for the group site at 541/498-2531. Sites are $7 per night, $3 per night per additional vehicle, and $25 per night for the group site. Open year-round.

Directions: From Roseburg, drive east on Highway 138 for 59 miles to Forest Road 34. Turn left (north) and drive 1.5 miles to the campground on the right.

Contact: Umpqua National Forest, Diamond Lake Ranger District, 541/498-2531, fax 541/498-2515, www.fs.fed.us.

101 EAST LEMOLO

🚶 🚴 🏊 🚤 🛶 🐎 🚐 ⛺

Scenic rating: 8

on Lemolo Lake in Umpqua National Forest

Map 5.4, page 276

This campground is on the southeastern shore of Lemolo Lake, where boating and fishing are some of the recreation possibilities. Boats with motors and personal watercraft are allowed. The North Umpqua River and its adjacent trail lie just beyond the north shore of the lake. If you hike for two miles northwest of the lake, you can reach spectacular Lemolo Falls. Large German brown trout, a wild, native fish, can be taken on troll and fly. Lemolo Lake also provides fishing for brook trout, kokanee, and a sprinkling of rainbow trout.

Campsites, facilities: There are 14 sites for tents or small RVs up to 22 feet long. No drinking water is available. Picnic tables, gar-bage bins, and fire rings are provided. Vault toilets are available. Boat docks, launching facilities, boat rentals, dump station, restau-rants, a store, coin laundry, and showers are nearby. Leashed pets are permitted.

Reservations, fees: Reservations are not ac-cepted. Sites are $7 per night, $3 per night per additional vehicle. Open mid-May–late October, weather permitting.

Directions: From Roseburg, drive east on Highway 138 for 73 miles to Forest Road 2610 (three miles east of Clearwater Falls). Turn left (north) and drive three miles to Forest Road 2614. Turn right and drive two miles to Forest Road 2614-430. Turn left and drive a short distance to the campground at the end of the road.

Contact: Umpqua National Forest, Diamond Lake Ranger District, 541/498-2531, fax 541/498-2515, www.fs.fed.us.

102 POOLE CREEK

Scenic rating: 8

on Lemolo Lake in Umpqua National Forest

Map 5.4, page 276

Poole Creek campground on the western shore of Lemolo Lake isn't far from Lemolo Lake Resort, which is open for recreation year-round. The camp is just south of the mouth of Poole Creek in a lodgepole pine, mountain hemlock, and Shasta red fir forest. This is by far the most popular U.S. Forest Service camp at the lake, especially with water-skiers, who are allowed to ski in designated areas of the lake.

Campsites, facilities: There are 60 sites for tents or RVs up to 35 feet long and a group site for up to 60 people. Picnic tables and fire grills are provided. Drinking water and vault toilets are available. A grocery store, a restaurant, boat docks, launching facilities, and rentals are nearby. Leashed pets are permitted.

Reservations, fees: Reservations are not accepted for single sites but are required for the group camp at 877/444-6777 or www.recreation.gov ($10 reservation fee). Single sites are $11–14 per night, $4 per night per additional vehicle, and $72 per night for the group camp. Open late April–late October, weather permitting.

Directions: From Roseburg, drive east on Highway 138 for 73 miles to Forest Road 2610 (Bird's Point Road). Turn left (north) and drive four miles to the signed turnoff for the campground entrance on the right.

Contact: Umpqua National Forest, Diamond Lake Ranger District, 541/498-2531, fax 541/498-2515, www.fs.fed.us.

103 INLET

Scenic rating: 5

on Lemolo Lake in Umpqua National Forest

Map 5.4, page 276

Inlet campground sits on the eastern inlet of Lemolo Lake, hidden in the deep, green, and quiet forest where the North Umpqua River rushes into Lemolo Reservoir. The camp is just across the road from the North Umpqua River Trail, which is routed east into the Oregon Cascades Recreation Area and the Mount Thielsen Wilderness. Lemolo Lake exceeds 100 feet in depth in some spots; boating and fishing for brook trout, kokanee, and rainbow trout are some recreation possibilities. (Boats with motors and personal watercraft are allowed.) Two miles northwest of the lake lies spectacular Lemolo Falls, a good hike.

Campsites, facilities: There are 14 sites for tents or RVs up to 22 feet long. Vault toilets are available, but there is no drinking water. Picnic tables, garbage bins, and fire grills are provided. Boat docks, launching facilities, rentals, a restaurant, groceries, and a gas station are available nearby. Leashed pets are permitted.

Reservations, fees: Reservations are not accepted. Sites are $7 per night, $3 per night per additional vehicle. Open mid-May–late October, weather permitting.

Directions: From Roseburg, drive east on Highway 138 for 73 miles to Forest Road 2610. Turn left (north) and drive three miles to Forest Road 2614. Turn right (east) and drive three miles to the campground.

Contact: Umpqua National Forest, Diamond Lake Ranger District, 541/498-2531, fax 541/498-2515, www.fs.fed.us.

104 BUNKER HILL

Scenic rating: 7

on Crescent Lake in Umpqua National Forest

Map 5.4, page 276

Bunker Hill campground, on the northwest shore of Lemolo Reservoir, is in a heavily wooded area of lodgepole pine. Fishing is excellent for kokanee as well as brook, rainbow, and large native brown trout. Nearby hiking trails lead to Lemolo Falls, the North Umpqua River, and the Pacific Crest Trail.

Campsites, facilities: There are five sites for

tents or RVs up to 22 feet long. Picnic tables and fire rings are provided. Vault toilets and garbage bins are available. There is no drinking water. A boat ramp, boat rentals, a dump station, a restaurant, coin laundry, and coin showers are available 1.5 miles away at Lemolo Lake Resort (541/643-0750). Leashed pets are permitted.

Reservations, fees: Reservations are not accepted. Sites are $7 per night, $3 per night per additional vehicle. Open May–October, weather permitting.

Directions: From Roseburg, drive east on Highway 138 for 73 miles to Bird's Point Road/Forest Road 2610. Turn left and drive 5.5 miles (crossing the dam) to Forest Road 2612. Turn right and drive to the camp at the north end of the lake.

Contact: Umpqua National Forest, Diamond Lake Ranger District, 541/498-2531, fax 541/498-2515, www.fs.fed.us.

105 LEMOLO LAKE RV PARK

🏃‍♂️ 🚴 🏊 🎣 🛶 🎿 🚐 ⛺

Scenic rating: 7

in Umpqua National Forest

Map 5.4, page 276

Lemolo Lake is situated high in the Cascade Mountains at just over 4,000 feet elevation. This RV park is set up for folks to bring their own boats and enjoy the lake. Boating, waterskiing, wakeboarding, and Jet Skis are all popular, along, of course, with fishing and swimming, on the lake (40-mph speed limit). Each campground reservation includes free boat launch. There are also miles of hiking trails in the vicinity, plus Crater Lake National Park and Diamond Lake are a quick drive away. In winter, cross-country skiing is popular, and an extensive snowmobile loop runs through the property.

Campsites, facilities: There are 26 sites for tents or RVs; full hookups are available. Picnic tables and fire rings are provided. Drinking water, flush toilets, coin showers, and coin laundry are available. A restaurant and store are on the premises. Boat and ATV rentals are available.

Reservations, fees: Reservations are accepted at 541/643-0750. RV sites with full hookups are $25, tent sites are $12–16. Open year-round.

Directions: From Roseburg, drive east on Highway 138 (Diamond Lake Highway) for about 73 miles to Birds Point Road. Turn left on Birds Point Road and drive five miles to the resort.

Contact: Lemolo Lake RV Park, 541/643-0750, www.lemololakeresort.com.

106 TIMPANOGAS

🏃‍♂️ 🏊 🎣 🛶 🏕 🐕 ♿ 🚐 ⛺

Scenic rating: 8

on Timpanogas Lake in
Willamette National Forest

Map 5.4, page 276

Timpanogas Lake is the headwaters of the Middle Fork Willamette River. This campground, at 5,200 feet elevation, is situated in a stand of grand, noble, and silver fir. Fishing for brook trout and cutthroat is good; only non-motorized boating is permitted. Nearby activities include 23 miles of hiking trails in the Timpanogas Basin trails, with views of the Cowhorn Mountains, Diamond Peak, and Sawtooth. Warning: Time it wrong (July–Aug.) and the mosquitoes will eat you alive if you forget insect repellent.

Campsites, facilities: There are 10 sites for tents or RVs up to 24 feet long. Picnic tables, garbage bins, and fire rings are provided. Drinking water, vault toilets, and firewood are available. A primitive boat ramp is nearby, but no boats with motors are allowed. Some facilities are wheelchair accessible. Leashed pets are permitted.

Reservations, fees: Reservations are not accepted. Sites are $8 per night, $4 per night per additional vehicle. Open June–October, weather permitting.

Directions: From Eugene, drive south on I-5 for five miles to Exit 188 and Highway 58. Turn east and drive 35 miles to the town of Oakridge. Continue east on Highway 58 for two miles to Kitson Springs Road. Turn right and drive 0.5 mile to Forest Road 21. Turn right and drive 32 miles to Forest Road 2154. Turn left and drive about 10 miles to the campground on the left.

Contact: Willamette National Forest, Middle Fork Ranger District, 541/782-2283, fax 541/782-5306, www.fs.fed.us.

107 WOLF CREEK

Scenic rating: 6

on the Little River in Umpqua National Forest

Map 5.4, page 276

This pretty Little River camp is located at the entrance to the national forest, near the Wolf Creek Civilian Conservation Center. It is set at an elevation of 1,100 feet, with easy access to civilization. The campground has abundant wildflowers in the spring. If you want to get deeper into the Cascades, Hemlock Lake and Lake of the Woods are about 21 and 15 miles east, respectively.

Campsites, facilities: There are eight sites for tents or RVs up to 30 feet long and one group site for up to 130 people. Picnic tables and fire grills are provided. Flush toilets, drinking water, a covered pavilion for groups, garbage bins, horseshoe pits, a softball field, and a volleyball court are available. Note that if the group site is taken, some recreation facilities may not be available to single-site campers. Some facilities are wheelchair accessible. Leashed pets are permitted.

Reservations, fees: Reservations are accepted only for the group site at 877/444-6777 or www.recreation.gov ($10 reservation fee). Sites are $10 per night, $4 per night per additional vehicle, and $95 per night for the group site. Open mid-May–September, weather permitting.

Directions: From Roseburg on I-5, take Exit 120. Drive east on Highway 138 for 18 miles to Glide and County Road 17. Turn right (southeast) and drive 12 miles (the road becomes Little River Road) to the campground on the right.

Contact: Umpqua National Forest, North Umpqua Ranger District, 541/496-3532, fax 541/496-3534, www.fs.fed.us.

108 COOLWATER

Scenic rating: 6

on the Little River in Umpqua National Forest

Map 5.4, page 276

Coolwater campground (1,300 feet elevation) along the banks of the Little River gets moderate use. It features a pretty forest setting with some scenic hiking trails nearby. Overhang Trail is within 0.5 mile of the campground. Fishing and swimming are also options here. Scenic Grotto Falls can be reached by traveling north on Forest Road 2703 (across the road from the camp). Near the falls, you'll find Emile Grove, home of a thicket of old-growth Douglas firs and the huge "Bill Taft Tree," named after the former president.

Campsites, facilities: There are seven sites for tents or RVs up to 24 feet long. Picnic tables and fire grills are provided. Vault toilets are available. There is no drinking water. Leashed pets are permitted.

Reservations, fees: Reservations are not accepted. Sites are $6 per night, $4 per night per additional vehicle. Open year-round, weather permitting.

Directions: From Roseburg on I-5, take Exit 120. Drive east on Highway 138 for 18 miles to Glide and County Road 17. Turn right (southeast) and drive 17 miles (the road becomes Little River Road) to the campground on the right.

Contact: Umpqua National Forest, North Umpqua Ranger District, 541/496-3532, fax 541/496-3534, www.fs.fed.us.

109 WHITE CREEK

Scenic rating: 6

on the Little River in Umpqua National Forest

Map 5.4, page 276

Hiking and fishing are two of the recreation options at this campground set at the confluence of White Creek and the Little River. There is a sandy beach on shallow Little River, and waterfalls are in the area.

Campsites, facilities: There is an open parking area for tents or RVs up to 16 feet long. Picnic tables, fire grills, and garbage bins are provided. Vault toilets are available. There is no drinking water. Leashed pets are permitted.

Reservations, fees: Reservations are not accepted. Sites are $6 per night, $4 per night per additional vehicle. Open year-round, weather permitting.

Directions: From Roseburg on I-5, take Exit 120. Drive east on Highway 138 for 18 miles to Glide and County Road 17. Turn right (southeast) and drive 18 miles (the road becomes Little River Road) to Forest Road 2792 (Red Butte Road). Bear right and drive 0.25 mile to the campground on the left.

Contact: Umpqua National Forest, North Umpqua Ranger District, 541/496-3532, fax 541/496-3534, www.fs.fed.us.

110 LAKE IN THE WOODS

Scenic rating: 7

on Lake in the Woods in
Umpqua National Forest

Map 5.4, page 276

The shore of little Lake in the Woods is the setting of this camp, which makes a nice home base for several good hikes. One of them leaves the camp and heads south for about three miles to the Hemlock Lake Campground. Two other nearby trails provide short, scenic hikes to either Hemlock Falls or Yakso Falls. The campground sits at 3,200 feet elevation. This is a man-made,

four-acre lake, eight feet at its deepest point. Boats without motors are allowed.

Campsites, facilities: There are 11 sites for tents or RVs up to 35 feet long. Picnic tables, fire grills, and garbage bins are provided. Vault toilets are available. There is no drinking water. Leashed pets are permitted.

Reservations, fees: Reservations are not accepted. Sites are $10 per night, $4 per night per additional vehicle. Open late May–late October, weather permitting.

Directions: From Roseburg on I-5, take Exit 120. Drive east on Highway 138 for 18 miles to Glide and County Road 17. Turn right (southeast) and drive 18 miles (the road becomes Little River Road) to Forest Road 27. Continue 11 miles to the campground. The last seven miles are gravel.

Contact: Umpqua National Forest, North Umpqua Ranger District, 541/496-3532, fax 541/496-3534, www.fs.fed.us.

111 HEMLOCK LAKE

Scenic rating: 8

on Hemlock Lake in Umpqua National Forest

Map 5.4, page 276   BEST (

This is a little-known jewel of a spot. For starters, it's set along the shore of Hemlock Lake at 4,400 feet elevation. This is a 28-acre, manufactured reservoir that is 33 feet at its deepest point. An eight-mile loop trail called the Yellow Jacket Loop is just south of the campground. Another trail leaves camp and heads north for about three miles to the Lake in the Woods campground. From there, it's just a short hike to either Hemlock Falls or Yakso Falls, both spectacularly scenic.

Campsites, facilities: There are 13 sites for tents or RVs up to 35 feet long. Picnic tables, fire grills, and garbage bins are provided. Vault toilets are available, but there is no drinking water. Boat docks and launching facilities are nearby. No motors are allowed on the lake. Leashed pets are permitted.

Reservations, fees: Reservations are not accepted. Sites are $8 per night, $4 per night per additional vehicle. Open year-round, weather permitting.

Directions: From Roseburg on I-5, take Exit 120. Drive east on Highway 138 for 18 miles to Glide and County Road 17. Turn right (southeast) and drive 32 miles to the campground on the right.

Contact: Umpqua National Forest, North Umpqua Ranger District, 541/496-3532, fax 541/496-3534, www.fs.fed.us.

112 WHITEHORSE FALLS
🚶 🏊 🛶 🐕 ⛺

Scenic rating: 8

on the Clearwater River in
Umpqua National Forest

Map 5.4, page 276

Whitehorse Falls campground sits along the Clearwater River, one of the coldest streams in Umpqua National Forest. Even though the camp is adjacent to the highway, the setting is primitive. It is shaded by old-growth Douglas fir and is located at an elevation of 3,790 feet. Pretty Clearwater Falls, a few miles east, makes for a good side trip. Other recreation options include fishing and hiking.

Campsites, facilities: There are five sites for tents or RVs up to 22 feet long. Picnic tables, fire grills, and garbage bins are provided. Vault toilets are available, but there is no drinking water. Leashed pets are permitted.

Reservations, fees: Reservations are not accepted. Sites are $7 per night, $3 per night per additional vehicle. Open June–late October, weather permitting.

Directions: From Roseburg, drive east on Highway 138 for 66 miles to the campground on the left.

Contact: Umpqua National Forest, Diamond Lake Ranger District, 541/498-2531, fax 541/498-2515, www.fs.fed.us.

113 CLEARWATER FALLS
🚶 🛶 🏕 �0 ⛺

Scenic rating: 8

on the Clearwater River in
Umpqua National Forest

Map 5.4, page 276

The main attraction at this campground along the banks of the Clearwater River is the nearby cascading section of stream called Clearwater Falls. Hiking and fishing opportunities abound. The camp sits at an elevation of 4,100 feet.

Campsites, facilities: There are nine sites for tents or RVs up to 30 feet long. Picnic tables, fire grills, and garbage bins are provided. Vault toilets are available. There is no drinking water. Leashed pets are permitted.

Reservations, fees: Reservations are not accepted. Sites are $7 per night, $3 per night per additional vehicle. Open mid-May–October, weather permitting.

Directions: From Roseburg, drive east on Highway 138 for 70 miles to a signed turn for Clearwater Falls. Turn right and drive to the campground.

Contact: Umpqua National Forest, Diamond Lake Ranger District, 541/498-2531, fax 541/498-2515, www.fs.fed.us.

114 BROKEN ARROW
🚶 🚴 🏊 🛶 🚣 🏕 ♿ 🚐 ⛺

Scenic rating: 6

on Diamond Lake in Umpqua National Forest

Map 5.4, page 276

Broken Arrow campground sits at 5,190 feet elevation near the south shore of Diamond Lake, the largest natural lake in Umpqua National Forest. Set back from the lake, it is surrounded by lodgepole pine and features views of Mount Bailey and Mount Thielsen. Bicycling, boating, fishing, hiking, and swimming keep visitors busy here. Diamond Lake is adjacent to Crater Lake National Park, Mount Bailey, and the Mount Thielsen Wilderness, all of which offer a variety of recreation opportunities year-round. Diamond Lake is quite popular with anglers because of its good trout trolling, particularly in early summer.

Campsites, facilities: There are 117 sites for tents or RVs up to 40 feet long and group sites for 40–104 people. Picnic tables, fire grills, and garbage bins are provided. Restrooms with flush toilets and showers, a dump station, and drinking water are available. Boat docks, launching facilities, and rentals are nearby. Some facilities are wheelchair accessible. Leashed pets are permitted.

Reservations, fees: Reservations are accepted only for group sites at 877/444-6777 or www.recreation.gov ($10 reservation fee). Sites are $11–14 per night, $4 per night per additional vehicle, and $54–132 per night for group sites. Open June–mid-September.

Directions: From Roseburg, drive east on Highway 138 for 78.5 miles to Diamond Lake Loop (Forest Road 4795). Turn right (south) and drive four miles (along the east shore) to the campground turnoff road. Turn right and continue one mile to the camp on the left at the southern end of the lake.

Contact: Umpqua National Forest, Diamond Lake Ranger District, 541/498-2531, fax 541/498-2515, www.fs.fed.us.

115 THIELSEN VIEW

Scenic rating: 7

on Diamond Lake in Umpqua National Forest
Map 5.4, page 276

This campground sits along the west shore of Diamond Lake in the shadow of majestic Mount Bailey. There is a beautiful view of Mount Thielsen from here.

Diamond Lake is popular with anglers, and bicycling, boating, fishing, hiking, and swimming keep everyone else busy. Nearby Crater Lake National Park, Mount Bailey, and the Mount Thielsen Wilderness offer recreation opportunities year-round.

Campsites, facilities: There are 60 sites for tents or RVs up to 30 feet long. Picnic tables, fire grills, and garbage bins are provided. Drinking water and vault toilets are available. Boat docks and launching facilities are located adjacent to the campground, and boats can be rented at a resort five miles away. Some facilities are wheelchair accessible. Leashed pets are permitted.

Reservations, fees: Reservations are not accepted. Sites are $11–14 per night, $4 per night per additional vehicle. Open mid-May–mid-September, weather permitting.

Directions: From Roseburg, drive east on Highway 138 for 78.5 miles to Diamond Lake Loop (Forest Road 4795). Turn right and drive a short distance to the junction with the loop road. Continue on the loop road and drive four miles to the campground on the left.

Contact: Umpqua National Forest, Diamond Lake Ranger District, 541/498-2531, fax 541/498-2515, www.fs.fed.us.

116 DIAMOND LAKE

Scenic rating: 9

on Diamond Lake in Umpqua National Forest
Map 5.4, page 276

Diamond Lake is a true gem of the Cascades, and there's finally hope the trout fishing will return to its once famous status. This extremely popular camp along the east shore of Diamond Lake has all the luxuries: flush toilets, showers, and drinking water. There are campfire programs every Friday and Saturday night in the summer. Jet Skis and other motorized watercraft are not allowed.

Campsites, facilities: There are 238 sites for tents or RVs up to 45 feet long. Picnic tables, garbage bins, and fire grills are provided. Restrooms with flush toilets and showers, drinking water, a dump station, and an amphitheater are available. Boat docks, launching facilities, and a fish-cleaning station are available. Boat rentals are nearby. Leashed pets are permitted.

Reservations, fees: Reservations are accepted at 877/444-6777 or www.recreation.gov ($10 reservation fee). Sites are $12–24 per night, $6 per night per additional vehicle. Open late April–late October, weather permitting.

Directions: From Roseburg, drive east on Highway 138 for 78.5 miles to Diamond Lake Loop (Forest Road 4795). Turn right and drive a short distance to the junction with a loop road. Turn right (south) and drive two miles (along the east shore) to the campground on the right.

Contact: Umpqua National Forest, Diamond Lake Ranger District, 541/498-2531, fax 541/498-2515, www.fs.fed.us.

117 CAMP COMFORT

Scenic rating: 6

on the South Umpqua River in
Umpqua National Forest

Map 5.4, page 276

Camp Comfort is located near the upper South Umpqua River, deep in the Umpqua National Forest, at an elevation of 2,000 feet. Large old-growth cedars shade the campsites. No fishing is permitted. South Umpqua Falls (you will pass the access point while driving to this camp) makes a good side trip. Nearby trailheads provide access to Rogue-Umpqua Divide Wilderness (a map of Umpqua National Forest will be helpful in locating them).

Campsites, facilities: There are five sites for tents or RVs up to 22 feet long. Picnic tables and fire grills are provided. A vault toilet and garbage bins are available. There is no drinking water. Some facilities are wheelchair accessible. Leashed pets are permitted.

Reservations, fees: Reservations are not accepted. Sites are $6 per night, $3 per night per additional vehicle. Open May–October.

Directions: At Canyonville on I-5, take Exit 99 to County Road 1. Drive east on County Road 1 for 25 miles to Tiller and County Road 46. Turn left and drive six miles northeast (County Road 46 turns into South Umpqua Road/Forest Road 28). Continue northeast and drive 22 miles to the camp on the right.

Contact: Umpqua National Forest, Tiller Ranger District, 541/825-3100, fax 541/825-3110, www.fs.fed.us.

118 HAMAKER

Scenic rating: 8

near the Upper Rogue River in
Rogue River National Forest

Map 5.4, page 276

Set at 4,000 feet elevation near the Upper Rogue River, Hamaker is a beautiful little spot high in a mountain meadow. Wildflowers and wildlife abound in the spring and early summer. One of the least-used camps in the area, it's a prime camp for Crater Lake visitors.

Campsites, facilities: There are 10 sites for tents or RVs up to 30 feet long. Picnic tables, fire grills, garbage service, and stoves are provided. Drinking water and vault toilets are available. Firewood is available for purchase. Leashed pets are permitted.

Reservations, fees: Reservations are not accepted. Sites are $10 per night, $5 per night per additional vehicle. Open late May–late October, weather permitting.

Directions: From Medford, drive northeast on Highway 62 for 57 miles (just past Union Creek) to Highway 230. Turn left (north) and drive 11 miles to a junction with Forest Road 6530. Continue on Forest Road 6530 for 0.5 mile to Forest Road 6530-900. Turn right and drive 0.5 mile to the campground.

Contact: Rogue River National Forest, Prospect Ranger District, 541/560-3400, fax 541/560-3444; Rogue Recreation, 541/560-3900, www.fs.fed.us.

119 BOULDER CREEK

🚶 🐕 ♿ 🚐 ⛺

Scenic rating: 4

on the South Umpqua River in
Umpqua National Forest

Map 5.4, page 276

Set at 1,400 feet elevation, this campground
hugs the banks of the South Umpqua River
near Boulder Creek. Unfortunately, no fishing is allowed here, but pleasant side trips include the fishing ladder and waterfall at nearby
South Umpqua Falls.

Campsites, facilities: There are seven sites for
tents or RVs up to 22 feet long. Picnic tables,
fire grills, and garbage bins are provided. Vault
toilets and drinking water are available. Some
facilities are wheelchair accessible. Leashed
pets are permitted.

Reservations, fees: Reservations are not accepted. Sites are $6 per night, $3 per night
per additional vehicle. Open May–October,
weather permitting.

Directions: At Canyonville on I-5, take Exit
99 to County Road 1. Drive east on County
Road 1 for 25 miles to Tiller and County Road
46. Turn left, then drive six miles northeast
(County Road 46 turns into South Umpqua
Road/Forest Road 28). Continue northeast
and drive seven miles to the camp.

Contact: Umpqua National Forest, Tiller
Ranger District, 541/825-3100, fax 541/825-
3110, www.fs.fed.us.

120 DUMONT CREEK

🏊 🐕 ♿ ⛺

Scenic rating: 4

on the South Umpqua River in
Umpqua National Forest

Map 5.4, page 276

Dumont Creek is set at 1,300 feet elevation
along the banks of the South Umpqua River,
just above the mouth of Dumont Creek.
Quiet, primitive, and remote, it gets moderate to heavy use. A short trail leads to a small
beach on the river. No fishing is allowed at
this camp, and there is no trailer turnaround
here. Boulder Creek, just a few miles east, provides a camping alternative. A good side trip
is nearby South Umpqua Falls, a beautiful,
wide waterfall featuring a fish ladder and a
platform so you can watch the fish struggle
upstream.

Campsites, facilities: There are three sites for
tents. Picnic tables, fire grills, and garbage
bins are provided. Vault toilets are available,
but there is no drinking water. Some facilities are wheelchair accessible. Leashed pets
are permitted.

Reservations, fees: Reservations are not accepted. Sites are $6 per night, $3 per night
per additional vehicle. Open May–October,
weather permitting.

Directions: At Canyonville on I-5, take Exit
99 to County Road 1. Drive east on County
Road 1 for 25 miles to Tiller and County Road
46. Turn left and drive six miles northeast
(County Road 46 turns into South Umpqua
Road/Forest Road 28). Continue northeast
and drive 5.5 miles to the camp.

Contact: Umpqua National Forest, Tiller
Ranger District, 541/825-3100, fax 541/825-
3110, www.fs.fed.us.

121 COVER

🚶 🐕 ♿ 🚐 ⛺

Scenic rating: 4

on Jackson Creek in Umpqua National Forest

Map 5.4, page 276

If you want quiet, this camp set at 1,700 feet
elevation along the banks of Jackson Creek
is the right place, since hardly anyone knows
about it. Cover gets light use during the summer. During the fall hunting season, however,
it is known to fill. If you head east to Forest
Road 68 and follow the road south, you'll have
access to a major trail into the Rogue-Umpqua
Divide Wilderness. Be sure not to miss the
world's largest sugar pine tree, a few miles west
of camp. No fishing is allowed here.

Campsites, facilities: There are seven sites for tents or RVs up to 22 feet long. Picnic tables, fire grills, and garbage bins are provided. Drinking water and vault toilets are available. Some facilities are wheelchair accessible. Leashed pets are permitted.

Reservations, fees: Reservations are not accepted. Sites are $6 per night, $2 per night per additional vehicle. Open May–October, weather permitting.

Directions: At Canyonville on I-5, take Exit 99 to County Road 1. Drive east on County Road 1 for 25 miles to Tiller and County Road 46. Turn left and drive five miles to Forest Road 29 (Jackson Creek Road). Turn right and drive east for 12 miles to the campground on the right.

Contact: Umpqua National Forest, Tiller Ranger District, 541/825-3100, fax 541/825-3110, www.fs.fed.us.

122 QUINN MEADOW HORSE CAMP

Scenic rating: 8

near Quinn Creek in Deschutes National Forest

Map 5.5, page 277

This scenic campground (elevation 5,100 feet) is open only to horse camping and gets high use. The Elk-Devil's Trail and Wickiup Plains Trail offer access to the Three Sisters Wilderness. There's also a horse route to Devil's Lake via Katsuk Trail.

Campsites, facilities: There are 26 sites for tents or RVs up to 40 feet long. Picnic tables and fire rings are provided. Horse corrals, stalls, and a manure disposal site are available. Drinking water, vault toilets, and garbage bins are also available. Some facilities are wheelchair accessible. Leashed pets are permitted.

Reservations, fees: Reservations are accepted at 877/444-6777 or www.recreation.gov ($10 reservation fee). Two-horse corral sites are $14 and four-horse sites are $18; it's $7 per night

per additional vehicle. Open late June–September, weather permitting.

Directions: From Bend, drive southwest on Cascades Lakes Highway (also called Century Drive Highway and County Road 46) for 31.2 miles to the campground entrance on the left.

Contact: Deschutes National Forest, Bend-Fort Rock Ranger District, 541/383-4000, fax 541/383-4700, www.fs.fed.us.

123 DEVIL'S LAKE WALK-IN

Scenic rating: 8

on Devil's Lake in Deschutes National Forest

Map 5.5, page 277

This walk-in campground borders the shore of a scenic alpine lake with aqua-jade water and fishing access. Devil's Lake, set at 5,500 feet, is a popular rafting and canoeing spot, and several trailheads lead from the lake into the wilderness. The Elk-Devil's Trail and Wickiup Plains Trail offer access to the Three Sisters Wilderness. There's also a horse route to Quinn Meadow Horse Camp via Katsuk Trail.

Campsites, facilities: There are nine walk-in tent sites. Picnic tables and fire grills are provided. Vault toilets are available. There is no drinking water, and garbage must be packed out. Leashed pets are permitted.

Reservations, fees: Reservations are not accepted. There is no fee, but a Northwest Forest Pass ($5 daily fee or $30 annual fee per parked vehicle) is required. Open June–October, weather permitting.

Directions: From Bend, drive southwest on Cascades Lakes Highway (Century Drive Highway, which becomes County Road 46) for 28.7 miles to the parking area. Walk 200 yards to the campground.

Contact: Deschutes National Forest, Bend-Fort Rock Ranger District, 541/383-4000, fax 541/383-4700, www.fs.fed.us.

124 SODA CREEK

Scenic rating: 5

near Sparks Lake in Deschutes National Forest

Map 5.5, page 277

This campground, nestled between two meadows in a pastoral setting, is on the road to Sparks Lake. Boating—particularly canoeing—is ideal at Sparks Lake, about a two-mile drive away. Also at the lake, a loop trail hugs the shore; about 0.5 mile of it is paved and barrier-free. Only fly-fishing is permitted. The camp sits at 5,450 feet elevation.

Campsites, facilities: There are six sites for tents or RVs up to 30 feet long and one multiple site. Picnic tables and fire grills are provided. Vault toilets are available. There is no drinking water, and garbage must be packed out. Leashed pets are permitted.

Reservations, fees: Reservations are not accepted. Single sites are $10 per night, multiple sites are $20 per night, $5 per night per extra vehicle. Open June–October, weather permitting.

Directions: From Bend, drive southwest on Cascades Lakes Highway (also called Century Drive Highway and County Road 46) for 26.2 miles to Forest Road 400 (at sign for Sparks Lake). Turn left (east) and drive 25 yards to the campground.

Contact: Deschutes National Forest, Bend-Fort Rock Ranger District, 541/383-4000, fax 541/383-4700, www.fs.fed.us.

125 TODD LAKE HIKE-IN

Scenic rating: 8

near Todd Lake in Deschutes National Forest

Map 5.5, page 277

Todd Lake is a trailhead camp, with a trail access point here for hikers and horses to the Three Sisters Wilderness. One of numerous camps in the area that offer a pristine mountain experience yet can be reached by car, small Todd Lake campground sits 0.5 mile from the shore of an alpine lake at 6,200 feet elevation. It's popular for canoeing and offers great views. No bikes or horses are allowed on the trail around the lake.

Campsites, facilities: There are 11 hike-in tent sites. Picnic tables and fire grills are provided. Vault toilets are available. There is no drinking water, and garbage must be packed out. Leashed pets are permitted.

Reservations, fees: Reservations are not accepted. There no fee, but a Northwest Forest Pass ($5 daily fee or $30 annual fee per parked vehicle) is required. Open July–October, weather permitting.

Directions: From Bend, drive southwest on Cascades Lakes Highway (also called Century Drive Highway and County Road 46) for 24 miles to Forest Road 370. Turn right (north) and drive 0.5 mile to the parking area. Hike 0.5 mile to the campground.

Contact: Deschutes National Forest, Bend-Fort Rock Ranger District, 541/383-4000, fax 541/383-4700, www.fs.fed.us.

126 POINT

Scenic rating: 8

on Elk Lake in Deschutes National Forest

Map 5.5, page 277

Point campground is situated along the shore of Elk Lake at an elevation of 4,900 feet. Fishing for kokanee salmon and brook trout can be good; hiking is another option. Swimming and water sports are popular during warm weather.

Campsites, facilities: There are eight sites for tents or RVs up to 26 feet long, and one group site. Picnic tables and fire grills are provided. Vault toilets, drinking water, and garbage service are available. Boat docks and launching facilities are on-site. A store, restaurant, and propane are at Elk Lake Resort, one mile away. Leashed pets are permitted.

Reservations, fees: Reservations are not

accepted. Sites are $12 per night, $6 per night per additional vehicle; the group site is $22 for up to 15 people and four vehicles. Open late May–late September, weather permitting.

Directions: From Bend, drive southwest on Cascades Lakes Highway (Century Drive Highway, which becomes County Road 46) for 34 miles to the campground on the left.

Contact: Deschutes National Forest, Bend-Fort Rock Ranger District, 541/383-4000, fax 541/383-4700, www.fs.fed.us.

127 ELK LAKE

Scenic rating: 8

on Elk Lake in Deschutes National Forest

Map 5.5, page 277

This campground hugs the shore of Elk Lake at 4,900 feet elevation. It is adjacent to Elk Lake Resort, which has a store, a restaurant, and propane. Elk Lake is popular for windsurfing and sailing.

Campsites, facilities: There are 22 sites for tents or RVs up to 30 feet long. Picnic tables and fire grills are provided. Vault toilets, drinking water, and garbage service are available. Boat-launching facilities are on-site. Boat rentals can be obtained nearby. Leashed pets are permitted.

Reservations, fees: Reservations are not accepted. Sites are $14 per night, $7 per night per additional vehicle. Open mid-May–mid-September, weather permitting.

Directions: From Bend, drive southwest on Cascades Lakes Highway (Century Drive Highway, which becomes County Road 46) and drive 33.1 miles to the campground at the north end of Elk Lake.

Contact: Deschutes National Forest, Bend-Fort Rock Ranger District, 541/383-4000, fax 541/383-4700, www.fs.fed.us.

128 LITTLE FAWN

Scenic rating: 5

on Elk Lake in Deschutes National Forest

Map 5.5, page 277

Choose between sites on the water's edge or nestled in the forest at this campground along the eastern shore of Elk Lake. Afternoon winds are common here, making this a popular spot for sailing and windsurfing. Fishing for kokanee salmon and brook trout can be good; hiking is another option. Swimming and water sports are popular during warm weather. A play area for children can be found at one of the lake's inlets. The camp sits at 4,900 feet elevation, with Little Fawn Group Camp located just beyond Little Fawn campground.

Campsites, facilities: There are 20 sites for tents or RVs up to 36 feet long and one group site for up to 75 campers. Picnic tables and fire grills are provided. Vault toilets, drinking water, and garbage service are available. Boat-launching facilities and rentals are on-site. Leashed pets are permitted.

Reservations, fees: Reservations are accepted only for the group site at 877/444-6777 or www.recreation.gov ($10 reservation fee). Sites are $12 per night, $6 per night per additional vehicle, and $75 per night for the group site. Open late May–September, weather permitting.

Directions: From Bend, drive southwest on Cascades Lakes Highway (Century Drive Highway, which becomes County Road 46) and drive 35.5 miles to Forest Road 4625. Turn left (east) and drive 1.7 miles to the campground.

Contact: Deschutes National Forest, Bend-Fort Rock Ranger District, 541/383-4000, fax 541/383-4700, www.fs.fed.us.

129 MALLARD MARSH

🏕 🚴 🚤 🎣 🐕 🚐 ⛺

Scenic rating: 8

on Hosmer Lake in Deschutes National Forest

Map 5.5, page 277   BEST (

Quiet Mallard Marsh campground is located on the shore of Hosmer Lake, at an elevation of 5,000 feet. The lake is stocked with brook trout and Atlantic salmon and reserved for catch-and-release fly-fishing only. You'll get a pristine, quality fishing experience here. The lake is ideal for canoeing. Only non-motorized boats are allowed.

Campsites, facilities: There are 15 sites for tents or RVs up to 40 feet long. Picnic tables, garbage service, and vault toilets are provided. No drinking water is available. Boat-launching facilities are nearby. Leashed pets are permitted.

Reservations, fees: Reservations are not accepted. Sites are $10 per night, $5 per night per additional vehicle. Open May–October, weather permitting.

Directions: From Bend, drive southwest on Cascades Lakes Highway (Century Drive Highway, which becomes County Road 46) and drive 35.5 miles to Forest Road 4625. Turn left (southeast) and drive 1.3 miles to the camp.

Contact: Deschutes National Forest, Bend-Fort Rock Ranger District, 541/383-4000, fax 541/383-4700, www.fs.fed.us.

130 SOUTH

🏕 🚴 🚤 🎣 🐕 🚐 ⛺

Scenic rating: 8

on Hosmer Lake in Deschutes National Forest

Map 5.5, page 277

South campground is located along the shore of Hosmer Lake, adjacent to Mallard Marsh, and enjoys the same fishing experience. It's a good option if Mallard Marsh is full.

Campsites, facilities: There are 23 sites for tents or RVs up to 40 feet long. Picnic tables, garbage service, and fire grills are provided. Vault toilets and boat-launching facilities are available. No drinking water is provided. Leashed pets are permitted.

Reservations, fees: Reservations are not accepted. Sites are $10 per night, $5 per night per additional vehicle. Open late May–early October, weather permitting.

Directions: From Bend, drive southwest on Cascades Lakes Highway (Century Drive Highway, which becomes County Road 46) and drive 35.5 miles to Forest Road 4625. Turn left (east) and drive 1.2 miles to the campground on the right.

Contact: Deschutes National Forest, Bend-Fort Rock Ranger District, 541/383-4000, fax 541/383-4700, www.fs.fed.us.

131 LAVA LAKE

🏕 🚴 🚤 🎣 🐕 ♿ 🚐 ⛺

Scenic rating: 10

on Lava Lake in Deschutes National Forest

Map 5.5, page 277   BEST (

This well-designed campground sits on the shore of pretty Lava Lake at 4,750 feet elevation. Mount Bachelor and the Three Sisters are in the background, making a classic picture. Boating and fishing are popular here. A bonus is nearby Lava Lake Resort, which has showers, laundry facilities, an RV dump station, store, gasoline, and propane.

Campsites, facilities: There are 44 sites for tents or RVs up to 40 feet long. Picnic tables, garbage service, and fire grills are provided. Vault toilets, drinking water, and a fish-cleaning station are available. Boat docks and launching facilities are on-site. Boat rentals are nearby. Some facilities are wheelchair accessible. Leashed pets are permitted.

Reservations, fees: Reservations are not accepted. Sites are $14 per night, $7 per night per additional vehicle. Open mid-April–October, weather permitting.

Directions: From Bend, drive southwest on Cascades Lakes Highway (Century Drive

Highway, which becomes County Road 46) and drive 38.4 miles to Forest Road 4600-500. Turn left (east) and drive one mile to the campground.

Contact: Deschutes National Forest, Bend-Fort Rock Ranger District, 541/383-4000, fax 541/383-4700, www.fs.fed.us.

132 LITTLE LAVA LAKE

Scenic rating: 8

on Little Lava Lake in
Deschutes National Forest

Map 5.5, page 277

Little Lake feeds into the Deschutes River; boating, fishing, hiking, and swimming are some of the recreation options here. Choose from lakeside or riverside sites set at an elevation of 4,750 feet.

Campsites, facilities: There are 15 sites for tents or RVs up to 40 feet long and a group site for up to 30 people. Picnic tables and fire grills are provided. Vault toilets, drinking water, and garbage service are available. A boat launch, docks, and rentals are nearby. There are also launching facilities on-site. Leashed pets are permitted.

Reservations, fees: Reservations are not accepted for the single sites. The group site can be reserved at 877/444-6777 or www.recreation.gov ($10 reservation fee). Sites are $12 per night, $6 per night per additional vehicle. Open early May–late October, weather permitting.

Directions: From Bend, drive southwest on Cascades Lakes Highway (Century Drive Highway, which becomes County Road 46) and drive 38.4 miles to Forest Road 4600-500. Turn left (east) and drive 0.7 mile to Forest Road 4600-520. Continue east for 0.4 mile to the campground.

Contact: Deschutes National Forest, Bend-Fort Rock Ranger District, 541/383-4000, fax 541/383-4700, www.fs.fed.us.

133 SWAMP WELLS HORSE CAMP

Scenic rating: 3

near the Arnold Ice Caves in
Deschutes National Forest

Map 5.5, page 277

If you look at the map, this campground may appear to be quite remote, but it's actually in an area less than 30 minutes from Bend. Set at an elevation of 5,450 feet, this camp is a good place for horseback riding, but you don't need a horse to enjoy this spot. Trails heading south re-enter the forested areas. The system of lava tubes at the nearby Arnold Ice Caves is fun to explore; bring a bicycle helmet, a flashlight, and knee pads.

Campsites, facilities: There are five primitive sites for tents or RVs up to 16 feet long. Picnic tables and fire grills are provided. There are vault toilets, but no drinking water, and garbage must be packed out. Manure bins are available for horses. Leashed pets are permitted.

Reservations, fees: Reservations are not accepted. There is no fee for camping. Open April–late November, weather permitting.

Directions: From Bend, drive south on U.S. 97 for four miles to Forest Road 18/China Hat Road. Turn left (southeast) and drive 5.4 miles to Forest Road 1810. Turn right (south) and drive 5.8 miles to Forest Road 1816. Turn left (east) and drive three miles to the campground. The last mile is rough and primitive.

Contact: Deschutes National Forest, Bend-Fort Rock Ranger District, 541/383-4000, fax 541/383-4700, www.fs.fed.us.

134 WEST CULTUS LAKE

Scenic rating: 5

on Cultus Lake in Deschutes National Forest

Map 5.5, page 277

This campground, set at 4,700 feet elevation along the west shore of Cultus Lake, is accessible by boat or trail only. It's about three miles by trail from the parking area to the campground. The lake is a good spot for fishing, swimming, and waterskiing. Trails branch out from the campground and provide access to numerous small backcountry lakes. Drinking water and boat-launching facilities are available at Cultus Lake.

Campsites, facilities: There are 12 boat-in or hike-in tent sites. Picnic tables and fire pits are provided. Vault toilets are available. There is no drinking water, and garbage must be packed out. Boat docks are available on-site; boat rentals are at Cultus Lake Resort. Leashed pets are permitted.

Reservations, fees: Reservations are not accepted. Sites are $15 per night. A Northwest Forest Pass ($5 daily fee or $30 annual fee per parked vehicle) is required. Open May–late September, weather permitting.

Directions: From Bend, drive southwest on Cascades Lakes Highway (Century Drive Highway, which becomes County Road 46) and drive 46 miles to Forest Road 4635. Turn right (west) and drive two miles to the parking area. Boat or hike in about three miles to the west end of the lake.

Contact: Deschutes National Forest, Bend-Fort Rock Ranger District, 541/383-4000, fax 541/383-4700, www.fs.fed.us.

135 CULTUS LAKE
Scenic rating: 7

on Cultus Lake in Deschutes National Forest

Map 5.5, page 277

Located along the east shore of Cultus Lake at 4,700 feet elevation, this camp is a popular spot for fishing, hiking, swimming, waterskiing, and windsurfing. The sites fill up early on weekends and holidays.

Campsites, facilities: There are 55 sites for tents or RVs up to 36 feet long. Picnic tables and fire grills are provided. Vault toilets, drinking water, and garbage service are available.

Boat docks and launching facilities are on-site. Boat rentals are nearby. A restaurant, gasoline, and cabins are available nearby at Cultus Lake Resort. Leashed pets are permitted.

Reservations, fees: Reservations are not accepted. Sites are $16 per night, $8 per night per additional vehicle. Open mid-April–late September, weather permitting.

Directions: From Bend, drive southwest on Cascades Lakes Highway (Century Drive Highway, which becomes County Road 46) and drive 46 miles to Forest Road 4635. Turn right (west) and drive two miles to the campground.

Contact: Deschutes National Forest, Bend-Fort Rock Ranger District, 541/383-4000, fax 541/383-4700, www.fs.fed.us.

136 CULTUS CORRAL HORSE CAMP
Scenic rating: 3

near Cultus Lake in Deschutes National Forest

Map 5.5, page 277

Located at 4,450 feet elevation, about one mile from Cultus Lake, this camp sits in a stand of lodgepole pine. Several nearby trails provide access to backcountry lakes. This is a good overflow campground for Quinn Meadow Horse Camp.

Campsites, facilities: There are 11 sites for tents or RVs up to 40 feet long. Picnic tables, garbage service, fire grills, and four-horse corrals are provided. Drinking water and vault toilets are available. Leashed pets are permitted.

Reservations, fees: Reservations accepted at 877/444-6777 or www.recreation.gov ($10 reservation fee). Sites are $14 per night, $7 per night per additional vehicle. Open May–late September, weather permitting.

Directions: From Bend, drive southwest on Cascades Lakes Highway (Century Drive Highway, which becomes County Road 46) and drive 46 miles to Forest Road 4635. Turn right (west) and drive one mile to Forest Road

4630. Turn right and drive 0.75 mile to the campground on the right.

Contact: Deschutes National Forest, Bend-Fort Rock Ranger District, 541/383-4000, fax 541/383-4700, www.fs.fed.us.

137 DESCHUTES BRIDGE

Scenic rating: 5

on the Upper Deschutes River in
Deschutes National Forest

Map 5.5, page 277

Wooded Deschutes campground is set on the banks of the Deschutes River in a beautiful, green spot at 4,650 feet elevation. Fishing—the main activity—is often difficult and is restricted to artificial lures with a single barbless hook.

Campsites, facilities: There are 12 sites for tents or RVs up to 30 feet long. Picnic tables and fire grills are provided. Vault toilets, drinking water, and garbage service are available. Leashed pets are permitted.

Reservations, fees: Reservations are not accepted. Sites are $6 per night per vehicle. Open August–October.

Directions: From Bend, drive southwest on Cascades Lakes Highway (Century Drive Highway, which becomes County Road 46) and drive 41.1 miles to the campground on the left (just past the Deschutes River Bridge).

Contact: Deschutes National Forest, Bend-Fort Rock Ranger District, 541/383-4000, fax 541/383-4700, www.fs.fed.us.

138 LITTLE CULTUS LAKE

Scenic rating: 7

on Little Cultus Lake in
Deschutes National Forest

Map 5.5, page 277

This campground is set near the shore of Little Cultus Lake at an elevation of 4,800 feet. It's a popular spot for boating (10-mph speed limit), fishing, hiking, and swimming. Nearby trails offer access to numerous backcountry lakes, and the Pacific Crest Trail passes about six miles west of the camp.

Campsites, facilities: There are 31 sites for tents or RVs up to 40 feet long. Picnic tables, garbage service, and fire grills are provided. Drinking water, vault toilets, and a boat launch are available. Leashed pets are permitted.

Reservations, fees: Reservations are not accepted. Sites are $14 per night, $7 per night per additional vehicle. Open May–September, weather permitting.

Directions: From Bend, drive southwest on Cascades Lakes Highway (Century Drive Highway, which becomes County Road 46) and drive 46 miles to Forest Road 4635. Turn right (west) and drive two miles to Forest Road 4630. Turn left (south) and drive 1.7 miles to Forest Road 4636. Turn left (west) and drive one mile to the campground.

Contact: Deschutes National Forest, Bend-Fort Rock Ranger District, 541/383-4000, fax 541/383-4700, www.fs.fed.us.

139 IRISH AND TAYLOR

Scenic rating: 7

near Irish and Taylor Lakes in
Deschutes National Forest

Map 5.5, page 277

Little known and beautiful, this remote campground is situated between two small lakes about a mile from the Pacific Crest Trail. Other nearby trails provide access into the Three Sisters Wilderness. A four-wheel-drive vehicle with high clearance is recommended for access. The camp sits at 5,550 feet elevation.

Campsites, facilities: There are six tent sites. Picnic tables and fire grills are provided. Vault toilets are available. There is no drinking water. Leashed pets are permitted.

Reservations, fees: Reservations are not

accepted. There is no fee. Open June–early October, weather permitting.

Directions: From Bend, drive southwest on Cascades Lakes Highway (Century Drive Highway, which becomes County Road 46) and drive 46 miles to Forest Road 4635. Turn right (west) on Forest Road 4635 and drive a short distance to Forest Road 4630. Turn right (south) and drive 1.7 miles to Forest Road 4636. Turn left (west) and drive 6.4 miles to the campground. A high-clearance vehicle is needed for the last four miles.

Contact: Deschutes National Forest, Bend-Fort Rock Ranger District, 541/383-4000, fax 541/383-4700, www.fs.fed.us.

140 COW MEADOW

Scenic rating: 6

on Crane Prairie Reservoir in
Deschutes National Forest

Map 5.5, page 277

Cow Meadow campground is located near the north end of Crane Prairie Reservoir and near the Deschutes River. It's a pretty spot (elevation is 4,450 feet), great for fly-fishing and bird-watching.

Campsites, facilities: There are 18 sites for tents or RVs up to 30 feet long. Picnic tables, garbage service, and fire grills are provided. Vault toilets are available. There is no drinking water. A boat launch for small boats is nearby. Leashed pets are permitted.

Reservations, fees: Reservations are not accepted. Sites are $10 per night, $5 per night per additional vehicle. Open May–mid-October, weather permitting.

Directions: From Bend, drive southwest on Cascades Lakes Highway (Century Drive Highway, which becomes County Road 46) for 44.7 miles to Forest Road 40. Turn left (east) on Forest Road 40 and drive 0.4 mile to Forest Road 4000-970. Turn right (south) and drive two miles to the campground on the right.

Contact: Deschutes National Forest, Bend-Fort Rock Ranger District, 541/383-4000, fax 541/383-4700, www.fs.fed.us.

141 CRANE PRAIRIE

Scenic rating: 6

on Crane Prairie Reservoir in
Deschutes National Forest

Map 5.5, page 277

This campground along the north shore of Crane Prairie Reservoir is a good spot for anglers and boaters. World-renowned for rainbow trout fishing, this reservoir is also popular for bass fishing.

Campsites, facilities: There are 146 sites for tents or RVs of any length. There are also four group sites for up to 150 people each, depending on the site. Picnic tables and fire grills are provided. Vault toilets, drinking water, and garbage service are available. Boat docks, launching facilities, and a fish-cleaning station are available on-site. Boat rentals, showers, gas, and a coin laundry are nearby. Some facilities are wheelchair accessible. Leashed pets are permitted.

Reservations, fees: Reservations are accepted for group sites only at 877/444-6777 or www.recreation.gov ($10 reservation fee). Single sites are $16 per night, multiple sites are $30 per night, group sites are $200 per night, $8 per night per additional vehicle. Open April–October, weather permitting.

Directions: From Bend, drive south on U.S. 97 for 26.8 miles to Wickiup Junction and County Road 43. Turn right (west) on County Road 43 and drive 11 miles to Forest Road 42. Continue west on Forest Road 42 for 5.4 miles to Forest Road 4270. Turn right (north) and drive 4.2 miles to the campground on the left.

Contact: Deschutes National Forest, Bend-Fort Rock Ranger District, 541/383-4000, fax 541/383-4700, www.fs.fed.us.

142 QUINN RIVER

Scenic rating: 5

on Crane Prairie Reservoir in
Deschutes National Forest

Map 5.5, page 277

Set along the western shore of Crane Prairie
Reservoir, this campground is a popular spot
for anglers and a great spot for bird-watching.
A separate, large parking lot is available for
boats and trailers. Boat speed is limited to 10
mph here. The elevation is 4,450 feet.

Campsites, facilities: There are 41 sites for tents
or RVs up to 45 feet long. Picnic tables and fire
grills are provided. Vault toilets, drinking water,
and garbage service are available. Boat-launching
facilities are available. Some facilities are wheelchair accessible. Leashed pets are permitted.

Reservations, fees: Reservations are not accepted. Sites are $14 per night, $7 per night
per additional vehicle. Open late April–September, weather permitting.

Directions: From Bend, drive southwest on
Cascade Lakes Highway (Century Drive
Highway, which becomes County Road 46)
for 48 miles to the campground.

Contact: Deschutes National Forest, Bend-
Fort Rock Ranger District, 541/383-4000,
fax 541/383-4700, www.fs.fed.us.

143 ROCK CREEK

Scenic rating: 5

on Crane Prairie Reservoir in
Deschutes National Forest

Map 5.5, page 277

Rock Creek campground is set along the west
shore of Crane Prairie Reservoir at an elevation
of 4,450 feet. The setting is similar to Quinn
River campground, and provides another good
spot for anglers when that camp is full.

Campsites, facilities: There are 31 sites for tents
or RVs up to 40 feet long. Picnic tables, garbage
service, and fire grills are provided. Drinking

water, a fish-cleaning station, and vault toilets
are available. Boat docks and launching facilities are on-site. Some facilities are wheelchair
accessible. Leashed pets are permitted.

Reservations, fees: Reservations are not accepted. Sites are $14 per night, $7 per night
per additional vehicle. Open April–September,
weather permitting.

Directions: From Bend, drive southwest on
Cascade Lakes Highway (Century Drive
Highway, which becomes County Road 46)
for 48.8 miles to the campground.

Contact: Deschutes National Forest, Bend-
Fort Rock Ranger District, 541/383-4000,
fax 541/383-4700, www.fs.fed.us.

144 FALL RIVER

Scenic rating: 5

on the Fall River in Deschutes National Forest

Map 5.5, page 277

Fall River is beautiful, crystal clear, and cold,
and this campground is right on it at an elevation of 4,300 feet. Fishing is restricted to
fly-fishing only, and it's wise to check the
regulations for other restrictions. The Fall
River Trail meanders along the river for 3.5
miles and is open for bicycling.

Campsites, facilities: There are 12 sites for
tents or RVs up to 40 feet long. Picnic tables,
garbage service, and fire grills are provided.
Vault toilets are available. There is no drinking
water. Leashed pets are permitted.

Reservations, fees: Reservations are not accepted. Sites are $10 per night, $5 per night
per additional vehicle. Open early May–late
October, weather permitting.

Directions: From Bend, drive south on U.S. 97
for 17.3 miles to the Vandevert Road exit. Take
that exit and turn right on Vandevert Road.
Drive 1.5 miles to Forest Road 42. Turn left
and drive 12.2 miles to the campground.

Contact: Deschutes National Forest, Bend-
Fort Rock Ranger District, 541/383-4000,
fax 541/383-4700, www.fs.fed.us.

145 SHEEP BRIDGE

Scenic rating: 3

near Wickiup Reservoir in
Deschutes National Forest

Map 5.5, page 277

This campground is set along the north De-schutes River Channel of Wickiup Reservoir in an open, treeless area that has minimal privacy and is dusty in summer. Dispersed sites here are popular with group campers. The elevation is 4,350 feet.

Campsites, facilities: There are 20 sites and three group sites for tents or RVs up to 40 feet long. Picnic tables, garbage service, and fire grills are provided. Drinking water, vault toilets, boat-launching facilities, and a picnic area are available. Leashed pets are permitted.

Reservations, fees: Reservations are not ac-cepted for single sites; group sites can be re-served at 877/444-6777 or www.recreation. gov ($10 reservation fee). Single sites are $12 per night, $22 for multiple sites, $6 per night per additional vehicle. Open early May–Oc-tober, weather permitting.

Directions: From Bend, drive south on U.S. 97 for 26.8 miles to Wickiup Junction. Turn right (west) on County Road 43 and drive 11 miles to Forest Road 42. Continue 4.6 miles west on Forest Road 42 to Forest Road 4260. Turn left (south) and drive 0.75 mile to the campground on the right.

Contact: Deschutes National Forest, Bend-Fort Rock Ranger District, 541/383-4000, fax 541/383-4700, www.fs.fed.us.

146 NORTH TWIN LAKE

Scenic rating: 6

on North Twin Lake in
Deschutes National Forest

Map 5.5, page 277

Although small and fairly primitive, North Twin Lake has lake access and a pretty setting.

The campground is located on the shore of North Twin Lake and is a popular weekend spot for families. Only non-motorized boats are permitted. The elevation is 4,350 feet.

Campsites, facilities: There are 20 sites for tents or RVs up to 40 feet long. Picnic tables and fire grills are provided. Vault toilets are available. There is no drinking water. Boat-launching facilities are on-site. Leashed pets are permitted.

Reservations, fees: Reservations are not ac-cepted. Sites are $12 per night, $6 per night per additional vehicle. Open April–October, weather permitting.

Directions: From Bend, drive southwest on Cascade Lakes Highway (Century Drive High-way, which becomes County Road 46) for 52 miles and drive past Crane Prairie Reservoir to Forest Road 42. Turn east and drive four miles to Forest Road 4260. Turn right (south) and drive 0.25 mile to the campground.

Contact: Deschutes National Forest, Bend-Fort Rock Ranger District, 541/383-4000, fax 541/383-4700, www.fs.fed.us.

147 TWIN LAKES RESORT

Scenic rating: 8

on Twin Lakes

Map 5.5, page 277   BEST (

Twin Lakes Resort is a popular family vaca-tion destination with a full-service marina and all the amenities, including beach areas. Recreational activities vary from hiking to boating, fishing, and swimming on Wickiup Reservoir. Nearby South Twin Lake is popular with paddleboaters and kayakers; it's stocked with rainbow trout.

Campsites, facilities: There are 22 full-hook-up sites for RVs of any length. There are also 14 cabins. Picnic tables and fire rings are pro-vided. Restrooms with flush toilets and coin showers, a dump station, coin laundry, con-venience store, restaurant, ice, snacks, some RV supplies, propane gas, and gasoline are available. A boat ramp, rentals, and a dock are provided; no motors are permitted on South Twin Lake. Leashed pets are permitted.

Reservations, fees: Reservations are recommended. Sites are $30 per night, $10 per tent in addition to RV. There are no tent-only sites. Some credit cards are accepted. Open late April–mid-October, weather permitting.

Directions: From Bend, drive south on U.S. 97 for 26.8 miles to Wickiup Junction. Turn right (west) on County Road 43 and drive 11 miles to Forest Road 42. Turn left and continue 4.6 miles west on Forest Road 42 to Forest Road 4260. Turn left (south) and drive two miles to the resort.

Contact: Twin Lakes Resort, 541/382-6432, fax 541/410-4688, www.twinlakesresort oregon.com.

148 SOUTH TWIN LAKE

🏃 🚴 🏊 🛶 🚐 🦌 🛻 ♿ 🚗 ⛺

Scenic rating: 6

on South Twin Lake in
Deschutes National Forest

Map 5.5, page 277

This campground is on the shore of South Twin Lake, a popular spot for boating (non-motorized only), fishing, and swimming. The elevation is 4,350 feet.

Campsites, facilities: There are 21 sites for tents or RVs up to 40 feet long. Picnic tables, garbage service, and fire grills are provided. Drinking water, vault and flush toilets, and dump station are available. Boat-launching facilities (small boats only), boat rentals, showers, and laundry facilities are nearby. Some facilities are wheelchair accessible. Leashed pets are permitted.

Reservations, fees: Reservations are not accepted. Sites are $16 per night, $8 per night per additional vehicle. Open April–October, weather permitting.

Directions: From Bend, drive south on U.S. 97 for 26.8 miles to Wickiup Junction. Turn right (west) on County Road 43 and drive 11

miles to Forest Road 42. Continue west on Forest Road 42 for 4.6 miles to Forest Road 4260. Turn left (south) and drive two miles to the campground on the left.

Contact: Deschutes National Forest, Bend-Fort Rock Ranger District, 541/383-4000, fax 541/383-4700, www.fs.fed.us.

149 WEST SOUTH TWIN

🏃 🚴 🏊 🛶 🚐 🦌 🛻

Scenic rating: 4

on South Twin Lake in
Deschutes National Forest

Map 5.5, page 277

A major access point to the Wickiup Reservoir, this camp is situated on South Twin Lake adjacent to the reservoir. It's a popular angling spot with very good kokanee salmon fishing. Twin Lakes Resort is adjacent to West South Twin. The elevation is 4,350 feet.

Campsites, facilities: There are 24 sites for RVs up to 40 feet long. Picnic tables and fire grills are provided. Vault toilets, drinking water, garbage service, and a dump station are available. Boat-launching facilities are on-site, and boat rentals, a restaurant, showers, coin laundry, gas, propane, cabins, and a store are nearby. Leashed pets are permitted.

Reservations, fees: Reservations are not accepted. Sites are $14 per night, $7 per night per additional vehicle. Open April–mid-October, weather permitting.

Directions: From Bend, drive southwest on Cascade Lakes Highway (Century Drive Highway, which becomes County Road 46) for 40 miles (past Crane Prairie Reservoir) to Forest Road 42. Turn left (east) and drive four miles to Forest Road 4260. Turn right (south) and drive 0.25 mile to the campground.

Contact: Deschutes National Forest, Bend-Fort Rock Ranger District, 541/383-4000, fax 541/383-4700, www.fs.fed.us.

150 GULL POINT

Scenic rating: 5

on Wickiup Reservoir in
Deschutes National Forest

Map 5.5, page 277

Gull Point campground sits in an open ponderosa stand on the north shore of Wickiup
Reservoir. You'll find good fishing for kokanee salmon here. About two miles from
West South Twin Campground, Gull Point
is the most popular campground on Wickiup
Reservoir.

Campsites, facilities: There are 73 sites for
tents or RVs up to 40 feet long and two group
sites for up to 30 people each. Picnic tables,
garbage service, and fire grills are provided.
Drinking water, a dump station, and flush
and vault toilets are available. Boat-launching
facilities and fish-cleaning stations are on-site.
Coin showers and a small store are nearby.
Some facilities are wheelchair accessible.
Leashed pets are permitted.

Reservations, fees: Reservations are not accepted for single sites but can be made for the
group sites at 877/444-6777 or www.recre-
ation.gov ($10 reservation fee). Sites are $16
per night, $8 per night per additional vehicle,
and $75 per night for group sites. Open mid-
April–October, weather permitting.

Directions: From Bend, drive south on U.S. 97
for about 26.8 miles to County Road 43 (three
miles north of LaPine). Turn right (west) on
County Road 43 and drive 11 miles to Forest
Road 42. Turn west on Forest Road 42 and
drive 4.6 miles to Forest Road 4260. Turn
left (south) and drive three miles to the campground on the right.

Contact: Deschutes National Forest, Bend-
Fort Rock Ranger District, 541/383-4000,
fax 541/383-4700, www.fs.fed.us.

151 BULL BEND

Scenic rating: 5

on the Deschutes River in
Deschutes National Forest

Map 5.5, page 277

Bull Bend campground is located on the inside of a major bend in the Deschutes River at
4,300 feet elevation. For a mini-float trip, start
at the upstream end of camp, float around the
bend, and then take out at the downstream
end of camp. This is a low-use getaway spot.

Campsites, facilities: There are 12 sites for tents
or RVs up to 40 feet long. Picnic tables, garbage
service, fire grills, vault toilets, and boat-launching facilities are available. There is no drinking
water. Leashed pets are permitted.

Reservations, fees: Reservations are not accepted. Sites are $10 per night, $5 per night
per additional vehicle. Open early May–late
October, weather permitting.

Directions: From Bend, drive south on U.S. 97
for 26.8 miles to Wickiup Junction. Turn right
(west) on County Road 43 and drive eight
miles to Forest Road 4370. Turn left (south)
and drive 1.5 miles to the campground.

Contact: Deschutes National Forest, Bend-
Fort Rock Ranger District, 541/383-4000,
fax 541/383-4700, www.fs.fed.us.

152 PRINGLE FALLS

Scenic rating: 4

on the Deschutes River in
Deschutes National Forest

Map 5.5, page 277

This campground fringing the Deschutes River
is less than a mile from Pringle Falls. The camp
gets light use and is pretty and serene.

Campsites, facilities: There are seven sites for
tents or RVs up to 30 feet long. Picnic tables,
garbage service, and fire grills are provided.
Vault toilets are available. There is no drinking
water. Leashed pets are permitted.

Reservations, fees: Reservations are not accepted. Sites are $10 per night, $5 per night per additional vehicle. Open May–October, weather permitting.

Directions: From Bend, drive south on U.S. 97 for 26.8 miles to Wickiup Junction. Turn right (west) on County Road 43 and drive 7.4 miles to Forest Road 4330-500. Turn north (right) and drive one mile to the campground.

Contact: Deschutes National Forest, Bend-Fort Rock Ranger District, 541/383-4000, fax 541/383-4700, www.fs.fed.us.

153 BIG RIVER

Scenic rating: 4

on the Deschutes River in
Deschutes National Forest

Map 5.5, page 277

Big River is a good spot. Located between the banks of the Deschutes River and the road, it has easy access and is popular as an overnight camp. Fishing, motorized boating, and rafting are permitted.

Campsites, facilities: There are 10 sites for tents or RVs up to 40 feet long, and one group site for up to 40 people. Picnic tables, garbage service, and fire grills are provided. Vault toilets are available. There is no drinking water. Boat-launching facilities are on-site. Some facilities are wheelchair accessible. Leashed pets are permitted.

Reservations, fees: Reservations are not accepted. Sites are $10 per night, $5 per night per additional vehicle, and the group site is $30 per night. Open early May–late October, weather permitting.

Directions: From Bend, drive south on U.S. 97 for 17.3 miles to the Vandevert Road exit. Take that exit and turn right on Vandevert Road. Drive 1.5 miles to Forest Road 42. Turn left and drive 7.9 miles to the campground.

Contact: Deschutes National Forest, Bend-Fort Rock Ranger District, 541/383-4000, fax 541/383-4700, www.fs.fed.us.

154 PRAIRIE

Scenic rating: 4

on Paulina Creek in Deschutes National Forest

Map 5.5, page 277

Here's another good overnight campground that is quiet and private. Set along the banks of Paulina Creek, Prairie is located about 0.5 mile from the trailhead for the Peter Skene Ogden National Recreation Trail. The elevation is 4,300 feet.

Campsites, facilities: There are 16 sites for tents or RVs up to 40 feet long. Picnic tables, garbage service, and fire grills are provided. Drinking water, firewood, and vault toilets are available. Leashed pets are permitted.

Reservations, fees: Reservations are not accepted. Sites are $14 per night, $7 per night per additional vehicle. Open mid-May–late September, weather permitting.

Directions: From Bend, drive south on U.S. 97 for 23.5 miles to County Road 21 (Paulina/East Lake Road). Turn left (east) and drive 3.1 miles to the campground.

Contact: Deschutes National Forest, Bend-Fort Rock Ranger District, 541/383-4000, fax 541/383-4700, www.fs.fed.us.

155 PAULINA LAKE

Scenic rating: 8

on Paulina Lake in Deschutes National Forest

Map 5.5, page 277

This campground (6,350 feet elevation) is located along the south shore of Paulina Lake and within the Newberry National Volcanic Monument. The camp is adjacent to Paulina Lake Resort. The lake itself sits in a volcanic crater. Nearby trails provide access to the remains of volcanic activity, including craters and obsidian flows. My longtime friend, Guy Carl, caught the state's record brown trout here, right after I'd written a story about his unique method of using giant Rapala and

Rebel bass lures for giant browns. The recreation options here include boating, fishing, hiking, mountain biking, and sailing. The boat speed limit is 10 mph. Note that food-raiding bears are common at all the campgrounds in the Newberry Caldera area and that all food must be kept out of reach. Do not store food in vehicles.

Campsites, facilities: There are 69 sites for RVs up to 30 feet long. Picnic tables, garbage service, and fire grills are provided. Drinking water and flush and vault toilets are available. Boat docks, launching facilities, boat rentals, coin showers, coin laundry, a small store, restaurant, cabins, gas, and propane are within five miles. The Newberry RV dump station is nearby. Some facilities are wheelchair accessible. Leashed pets are permitted.

Reservations, fees: Reservations are accepted at 877/444-6777 or www.recreation.gov ($10 reservation fee). Sites are $16–18 per night, $8 per night per additional vehicle. Open May–late October, weather permitting.

Directions: From Bend, drive south on U.S. 97 for 23.5 miles to County Road 21 (Paulina/East Lake Road). Turn left (east) and drive 12.9 miles to the campground on the left.

Contact: Deschutes National Forest, Bend-Fort Rock Ranger District, 541/383-4000, fax 541/383-4700, www.fs.fed.us.

156 CHIEF PAULINA HORSE CAMP

Scenic rating: 4

on Paulina Lake in Deschutes National Forest

Map 5.5, page 277

Chief Paulina campground sits at an elevation of 6,400 feet, about 0.25 mile from the south shore of Paulina Lake, where fishing is good. Horse trails and a vista point are close by. Horse campers must use only certified weed-seed-free hay.

Campsites, facilities: There are 14 sites for tents or RVs up to 40 feet long. Picnic tables and fire grills are provided. A vault toilet, garbage service, and corrals are available. There is no drinking water. Boat docks and rentals are nearby. Leashed pets are permitted.

Reservations, fees: Reservations are accepted at 877/444-6777 or www.recreation.gov ($10 reservation fee). Sites are $14–18 per night, $7 per night per additional vehicle. Open May–late October, weather permitting.

Directions: From Bend, drive south on U.S. 97 for 23.5 miles to County Road 21 (Paulina/East Lake Road). Turn left (east) and drive 14 miles to the campground.

Contact: Deschutes National Forest, Bend-Fort Rock Ranger District, 541/383-4000, fax 541/383-4700, www.fs.fed.us.

157 LITTLE CRATER

Scenic rating: 8

near Paulina Lake in Deschutes National Forest

Map 5.5, page 277

Little Crater is a very popular campground (6,350 feet elevation) near the east shore of Paulina Lake in Newberry National Volcanic Monument, a caldera. Sites are situated on the scenic lake edge, perfect for fishing, and there are great hiking opportunities in the area. The place fills up most summer weekends.

Campsites, facilities: There are 50 sites for tents or RVs up to 40 feet long. Picnic tables and fire grills are provided. Vault toilets, drinking water, and garbage service are available. Boat docks and launching facilities are on-site, and boat rentals are nearby. Some facilities are wheelchair accessible. Leashed pets are permitted.

Reservations, fees: Reservations are not accepted. Sites are $16 per night, $8 per night for each additional vehicle. Parking at the nearby trailhead requires a Northwest Forest Pass ($5 daily fee or $30 annual fee per parked vehicle). Open early May–late October, weather permitting.

Directions: From Bend, drive south on U.S.

97 for 23.5 miles to County Road 21 (Paulina/East Lake Road). Turn left (east) and drive 14.5 miles to Forest Road 2100. Turn left (north) and drive 0.5 mile to the campground on the left.
Contact: Deschutes National Forest, 541/383-4000, fax 541/383-4700.

158 NEWBERRY GROUP CAMP

Scenic rating: 7

west of Roseburg

Map 5.5, page 277

Newberry Group has a great location on Paulina Lake and is the only area on Newberry Monument designed exclusively for group camping. The parking area and roads are paved, and the group sites are separated from one another, although group sites B and C can be joined to accommodate large groups. One site accommodates groups of up to 35 people, while the other two accommodate up to 50. The entire campground can be reserved as well. Cabins were renovated in 2009 for use starting 2010.

Campsites, facilities: There are three group sites for tents or RVs to 40 feet. Picnic tables and fire rings are provided. Drinking water and vault toilets are available. Leashed pets are permitted.

Reservations, fees: Reservations are accepted at 877/444-6777 or www.recreation.gov ($10 reservation fee). Sites are $75 per night for the smaller camp, $100 per night for the larger two camps. Open June–September, weather permitting.

Directions: From Bend, drive south on U.S. 97 for 23.5 miles to County Road 21 (Paulina/East Lake Road). Turn left (east) and drive 1.5 miles to the campground.

Contact: Deschutes National Forest, 541/383-4000, fax 541/383-4700.

159 CINDER HILL

Scenic rating: 7

on East Lake in Deschutes National Forest

Map 5.5, page 277

This campground hugs the northeast shore of East Lake at an elevation of 6,400 feet. Located within the Newberry National Volcanic Monument, Cinder Hill makes a good base camp for area activities. Boating, fishing, and hiking are among the recreation options here. Boat speed is limited to 10 mph.

Campsites, facilities: There are 110 sites, including pull-through sites, for tents or RVs of any length. Picnic tables and fire grills are provided. Drinking water, flush and vault toilets, and garbage service are available. A camp host is on-site. Boat docks and launching facilities are on-site, and boat rentals, a store, restaurant, coin showers, coin laundry, and cabins are nearby at East Lake Resort. Some facilities are wheelchair accessible. Leashed pets are permitted.

Reservations, fees: Reservations are accepted at 877/444-6777 or www.recreation.gov ($10 reservation fee). Sites are $16 per night, $8 per night per additional vehicle. Parking at the nearby trailhead requires a Northwest Forest Pass ($5 daily fee or $30 annual fee per parked vehicle). Open mid-May–September, weather permitting.

Directions: From Bend, drive south on U.S. 97 for 23.5 miles to County Road 21 (Paulina/East Lake Road). Turn left (east) and drive 17.6 miles to Forest Road 2100-700. Turn left (north) and drive 0.5 mile to the campground.

Contact: Deschutes National Forest, Bend-Fort Rock Ranger District, 541/383-4000, fax 541/383-4700, www.fs.fed.us.

160 EAST LAKE

🚶 🚴 🏊 🛶 🎣 🏕 ♿ 🚐 ⛺

Scenic rating: 8

on East Lake in Deschutes National Forest

Map 5.5, page 277

This campground is set along the south shore of East Lake at an elevation of 6,400 feet. Boating and fishing are popular here, and hiking trails provide access to signs of former volcanic activity in the area. East Lake Campground is similar to Cinder Hill, but smaller. Boat speed is limited to 10 mph.

Campsites, facilities: There are 29 sites for tents or RVs up to 40 feet long. Picnic tables and fire grills are provided. Drinking water, flush and vault toilets, and garbage service are available. A camp host is on-site. Boat docks, launching facilities, and rentals are nearby. Some facilities are wheelchair accessible. Leashed pets are permitted.

Reservations, fees: Reservations are not accepted. Sites are $16 per night, $8 per night per additional vehicle. Open early May–late October, weather permitting.

Directions: From Bend, drive south on U.S. 97 for 23.5 miles to County Road 21 (Paulina/East Lake Road). Turn left (east) and drive 16.6 miles to the campground on the left.

Contact: Deschutes National Forest, Bend-Fort Rock Ranger District, 541/383-4000, fax 541/383-4700, www.fs.fed.us.

161 HOT SPRINGS

🚶 🚴 🏊 🛶 🎣 🏕 🚐 ⛺

Scenic rating: 5

near East Lake in Deschutes National Forest

Map 5.5, page 277

Don't be fooled by the name: there are no hot springs at this campsite. It lies across the road from East Lake at 6,400 feet elevation, making it a good tent camping spot if you want to be near East Lake but farther away from RVs.

Campsites, facilities: There are 52 sites for tents or RVs up to 26 feet long. Picnic tables and fire grills are provided. Vault toilets, drinking water, and garbage service are available. Boat docks, launching facilities, and rentals are nearby. Leashed pets are permitted.

Reservations, fees: Reservations are not accepted. Sites are $10 per night and $5–7 per night per additional vehicle. Open July–late September, weather permitting.

Directions: From Bend, drive south on U.S. 97 for 23.5 miles to County Road 21 (Paulina/East Lake Road). Turn left (east) and drive 17.2 miles to the campground on the right.

Contact: Deschutes National Forest, Bend-Fort Rock Ranger District, 541/383-4000, fax 541/383-4700, www.fs.fed.us.

162 EAST LAKE RESORT AND RV PARK

🚶 🏊 🛶 🚐 🏕 🏨 🚐 ⛺

Scenic rating: 7

on East Lake

Map 5.5, page 277

This resort offers shaded sites in a wooded, mountainous setting on the east shore of East Lake. Opportunities for boating, fishing, and swimming abound.

Campsites, facilities: There are 40 sites with partial hookups for tents or RVs up to 40 feet long and 16 cabins. Some sites are pull-through. Drinking water, barbecues, and picnic tables are provided. Restrooms with flush toilets and coin showers, propane gas, firewood, a dump station, convenience store, café, coin laundry, ice, boat-launching facilities, boat rentals, moorage, and a playground are available. Leashed pets are permitted.

Reservations, fees: Reservations are accepted. Sites are $27 per night. Some credit cards are accepted. Open mid-May–September, weather permitting.

Directions: From Bend, drive south on U.S. 97 for 23.5 miles to County Road 21 (Paulina/East Lake Road). Turn left (east) and drive 18 miles to the park at the end of the road.

Contact: East Lake Resort and RV Park, 541/536-2230, www.eastlakeresort.com.

163 CHINA HAT

Scenic rating: 3

in Deschutes National Forest

Map 5.5, page 277

Remote China Hat campground is located at 5,100 feet elevation in a rugged, primitive area. There is direct trail access here to the East Fort Rock OHV Trail System. Hunters use China Hat as a base camp in the fall, but in summer it is a base camp for off-road motorcyclists.

Campsites, facilities: There are 14 sites for tents or RVs up to 30 feet long. Picnic tables and fire grills are provided. Vault toilets are available. There is no drinking water, and garbage must be packed out. Leashed pets are permitted.

Reservations, fees: Reservations are not accepted. There is no fee for camping. Open April–early November, weather permitting.

Directions: From Bend, drive south on U.S. 97 for 29.6 miles to Forest Road 22. Turn left (east) and drive 26.4 miles to Forest Road 18. Turn left (north) and drive 5.9 miles to the campground on the left.

Contact: Deschutes National Forest, Bend-Fort Rock Ranger District, 541/383-4000, fax 541/383-4700, www.fs.fed.us.

164 CABIN LAKE

Scenic rating: 3

in Deschutes National Forest

Map 5.5, page 277

This remote campground (4,550 feet elevation) is adjacent to a bird blind that's more than 80 years old—it's a great place to watch birds. Primitive and secluded with sparse tree cover, this spot receives little use even in the busy summer months.

Campsites, facilities: There are 14 sites for tents or RVs up to 30 feet long. Picnic tables and fire grills are available, but not at each site. There are no toilets or drinking water, and garbage must be packed out. Leashed pets are permitted.

Reservations, fees: Reservations are not accepted. There is no fee for camping. Open April–late October, weather permitting.

Directions: From Bend, drive south on U.S. 97 for 29.6 miles to Forest Road 22. Turn left (east) and drive 26.4 miles to Forest Road 18. Turn left (north) and drive six miles to the campground on the left.

Contact: Deschutes National Forest, Bend-Fort Rock Ranger District, 541/383-4000, fax 541/383-4700, www.fs.fed.us.

165 GOLD LAKE

Scenic rating: 8

on Gold Lake in Willamette National Forest

Map 5.5, page 277   BEST (

Gold Lake campground wins the popularity contest for high use. Although motors are not allowed on this small lake (100 acres, 25 feet deep), rafts and rowboats provide excellent fishing access. A primitive log shelter built in the early 1940s provides a dry picnic area. In the spring and summer, this area abounds with wildflowers and huckleberries. The Gold Lake Bog is another special attraction where one can often see deer, elk, and smaller wildlife.

Campsites, facilities: There are 21 sites for tents or RVs up to 32 feet long. Picnic tables, garbage bins, and fire grills are provided. Drinking water and vault toilets are available. Boat docks and launching facilities are nearby. Some facilities are wheelchair accessible. Leashed pets are permitted.

Reservations, fees: Reservations are not accepted. Sites are $16 per night, $8 per night per additional vehicle. Open mid-May–October, weather permitting.

Directions: From Eugene, drive south on I-5 for five miles to Exit 188 and Highway 58. Turn east and drive 35 miles to the town of Oakridge. From Oakridge, continue east on Highway 58 for 28 miles to Gold Lake Road (Forest Road 500). Turn left (north) and drive two miles to the campground on the right.

Contact: Willamette National Forest, Middle Fork Ranger District, 541/782-2283, fax 541/782-5306, www.fs.fed.us.

166 NORTH DAVIS CREEK

Scenic rating: 4

on North Davis Creek in Deschutes National Forest

Map 5.5, page 277

Set at an elevation of 4,350 feet, this remote, secluded campground is located along a western channel that feeds into Wickiup Reservoir. Fishing for brown and rainbow trout as well as kokanee salmon is good here. In late summer, the reservoir level tends to drop. The camp receives little use and makes a good overflow camp if campsites are filled at Wickiup.

Campsites, facilities: There are 14 sites for tents or RVs up to 40 feet long. Picnic tables and fire grills are provided. Vault toilets and garbage service are available. There is no drinking water. Boat-launching facilities are on-site. Leashed pets are permitted.

Reservations, fees: Reservations are not accepted. Sites are $10 per night, $5 per night per additional vehicle. Open April–early September.

Directions: From Bend, drive southwest on Cascade Lake Highway (Highway 46/Forest Road 46) for 56.2 miles to the campground on the left.

Contact: Deschutes National Forest, Bend-Fort Rock Ranger District, 541/383-4000, fax 541/383-4700, www.fs.fed.us.

167 RESERVOIR

Scenic rating: 4

on Wickiup Reservoir in Deschutes National Forest

Map 5.5, page 277

You'll find this campground along the south shore of Wickiup Reservoir, where the kokanee salmon fishing is good. The camp is best in early summer, before the lake level drops. This camp gets little use, so you won't find crowds here. The elevation is 4,350 feet.

Campsites, facilities: There are 28 sites for tents or RVs up to 24 feet long. Picnic tables, garbage service, and fire grills are provided. Boat-launching facilities and vault toilets are available, but there is no drinking water. Leashed pets are permitted.

Reservations, fees: Reservations are not accepted. Sites are $6 per night. Open April–September, weather permitting.

Directions: From Bend, drive southwest on Cascade Lakes Highway (Century Drive Highway, which becomes County Road 46) for 57.8 miles to Forest Road 44. Turn left (east) and drive 1.7 miles to the campground.

Contact: Deschutes National Forest, Bend-Fort Rock Ranger District, 541/383-4000, fax 541/383-4700, www.fs.fed.us.

168 WICKIUP BUTTE

Scenic rating: 4

on Wickiup Reservoir in Deschutes National Forest

Map 5.5, page 277

Wickiup Butte is more remote than the other campgrounds on Wickiup Reservoir, set at an elevation of 4,350 feet. This campground borders the southeast shore of Wickiup Reservoir, where kokanee salmon fishing is good during the early summer.

Campsites, facilities: There are eight sites for tents or RVs up to 22 feet long. Picnic tables, garbage service, and fire grills are provided. Vault toilets are available. There is no drinking water. Boat-launching facilities are nearby. Leashed pets are permitted.

Reservations, fees: Reservations are not accepted. Sites are $5 per night per vehicle. Open April–late September, weather permitting.

Directions: From Bend, drive south on U.S. 97 for 26.8 miles to Wickiup Junction. Turn right (west) on County Road 43 and drive 10.4 miles to Forest Road 4380. Turn left (south) and drive 3.6 miles to Forest Road 4260. Turn left (east) and drive three miles to the campground.

Contact: Deschutes National Forest, Bend-Fort Rock Ranger District, 541/383-4000, fax 541/383-4700, www.fs.fed.us.

169 LaPINE STATE PARK

Scenic rating: 7

on the Deschutes River

Map 5.5, page 277

This peaceful and clean campground sits next to the trout-filled Deschutes River (a legendary fly-fishing spot) with many more high-mountain lakes in proximity. The camp is set in a subalpine pine forest populated by eagles or red-tailed hawks. Trails surround the campground; be sure to check out Oregon's "Big Tree." Skiing is a popular wintertime option in the area.

Campsites, facilities: There are 128 sites with full or partial hookups for tents or RVs of any length; only 20-amp service is available. There are also 10 cabins. Picnic tables and fire grills are provided. Drinking water, restrooms with flush toilets and showers, garbage bins, a dump station, a seasonal store, a day-use area with a sandy beach, a meeting hall that can be reserved, ice, and firewood are available. A boat launch is nearby. Some facilities are wheelchair accessible. Leashed pets are permitted.

Reservations, fees: Reservations are accepted at 800/452-5687 or www.oregonstateparks.org

($8 reservation fee). Sites are $13–22 per night, $5 per night per additional vehicle. Cabins are $38–81 per night. Some credit cards are accepted. Open year-round, weather permitting.

Directions: From Bend, turn south on U.S. 97 and drive 23 miles to State Recreation Road. Turn right and drive four miles to the park.

Contact: LaPine State Park, 541/536-2071 or 800/551-6949, www.oregonstateparks.org.

170 HIDDEN PINES RV PARK

Scenic rating: 7

near the Little Deschutes River

Map 5.5, page 277

So you think you've come far enough, eh? If you want a spot in a privately run RV park two miles from the bank of the Little Deschutes River, you've found it. Within a 30-minute drive are two reservoirs, four lakes, and a golf course. The nearby town of LaPine is the gateway to the Newberry National Volcanic Monument.

Campsites, facilities: There is an area for tents, plus 25 sites with full or partial hookups for RVs of any length; most are pull-through sites. Drinking water, cable TV, and picnic tables are provided. Restrooms with flush toilets and showers, a dump station, coin laundry, RV supplies, propane gas, a community fire ring with firewood, and ice are available. The full-service community of LaPine is about five miles away. Leashed pets are allowed.

Reservations, fees: Reservations are accepted. Sites are $19.44–25.92 per night, plus $2.50 per person per night for more than two people. Some credit cards are accepted. Open year-round.

Directions: From Bend, drive south on U.S. 97 for 24 miles to Wickiup Junction, Milepost 165, and County Road 43/Burgess Road. Turn right (west) on Burgess Road and drive 2.4 miles to Pine Forest Road. Turn left and drive 0.7 mile to Wright Avenue. Turn left and drive one block to the park on the left.

Contact: Hidden Pines RV Park, 541/536-2265.

171 NORTH LAVA FLOW

Scenic rating: 8

on Davis Lake in Deschutes National Forest

Map 5.5, page 277

North Lava Flow campground is surrounded by old-growth forest along the northeast shore of Davis Lake, a very shallow lake formed by lava flow. The water level fluctuates here, and this campground can sometimes be closed in summer. There's good duck hunting during the fall. Fishing can be decent, but only fly-fishing is allowed. Boat speed is limited to 10 mph.

Campsites, facilities: There are 25 sites for tents or RVs up to 30 feet long. Picnic tables and fire grills are provided. Vault toilets and firewood (which can be gathered from the surrounding area) are available. There is no drinking water, and garbage must be packed out. A primitive boat ramp is nearby. Leashed pets are permitted.

Reservations, fees: Reservations are not accepted. Sites are $9–11 per night, $5 per night per additional vehicle. Open April–December, weather permitting.

Directions: From Eugene, drive south on I-5 for five miles to Exit 188 and Highway 58. Turn east on Highway 58 and drive 86 miles to County Road 61. Turn left and drive three miles to Forest Road 46. Turn left and drive 7.7 miles to Forest Road 850. Turn left and drive 1.8 miles to the campground.

Contact: Deschutes National Forest, Crescent Ranger District, 541/433-3200, fax 541/433-3224, www.fs.fed.us.

172 EAST DAVIS LAKE

Scenic rating: 9

on Davis Lake in Deschutes National Forest

Map 5.5, page 277

This campground is nestled in the lodgepole pines along the south shore of Davis Lake. Recreation options include boating (speed limit 10 mph), fly-fishing, and hiking. Leeches prevent swimming here. Bald eagles and sandhill cranes are frequently seen.

Campsites, facilities: There are 29 sites for tents or RVs up to 40 feet long. Picnic tables, garbage service, fire grills, drinking water, and vault toilets are provided. Firewood may be gathered from the surrounding area. Primitive boat-launching facilities are available on-site. Some facilities are wheelchair accessible. Leashed pets are permitted.

Reservations, fees: Reservations are not accepted. Sites are $12 per night, $6 per night per additional vehicle. Open mid-April–late September, weather permitting.

Directions: From Eugene, drive south on I-5 for five miles to Exit 188 and Highway 58. Turn east and drive 73 miles to County Road 61. Turn left (east) and drive three miles to Forest Road 46. Turn left and drive 7.7 miles to Forest Road 850. Turn left and drive 0.25 mile to the campground entrance road on the right.

Contact: Deschutes National Forest, Crescent Ranger District, 541/433-3200, fax 541/433-3224, www.fs.fed.us.

173 TRAPPER CREEK

Scenic rating: 8

on Odell Lake in Deschutes National Forest

Map 5.5, page 277   BEST (

The west end of Odell Lake is the setting for this camp. Boat docks and rentals are available nearby at the Shelter Cove Resort. One of Oregon's prime fisheries for kokanee salmon and mackinaw (lake trout), this lake also has some huge brown trout.

Campsites, facilities: There are 26 sites for tents or RVs up to 40 feet long and three group sites. Picnic tables and fire grills are provided. Drinking water, vault toilets, garbage service and a boat launch are available. Firewood may be gathered from the surrounding area.

A store, coin laundry, and ice are within one mile. Leashed pets are permitted.

Reservations, fees: Reservations are accepted at 877/444-6777 or www.recreation.gov ($10 reservation fee). Sites are $16–18 per night, $5 per night per additional vehicle; group sites are $30–34, $8 per night per additional vehicle. Open mid-May–October, weather permitting.

Directions: From Eugene, drive south on I-5 for five miles to Exit 188 and Highway 58. Turn east and drive 61 miles to the turnoff for Odell Lake and Forest Road 5810. Turn right on Forest Road 5810 and drive 1.9 miles to the campground on the left.

Contact: Deschutes National Forest, Crescent Ranger District, 541/433-3200, fax 541/433-3224, www.fs.fed.us.

174 SHELTER COVE RESORT
🥾 🚴 🏊 ⛵ 🎣 🐕 🚐 ⛺

Scenic rating: 9

on Odell Lake

Map 5.5, page 277

Shelter Cove is a private resort along the north shore of Odell Lake, set at the base of the Diamond Peak Wilderness. The area offers opportunities for fishing, hiking, and swimming. The cabins sit right on the lakefront, and a general store and tackle shop are available.

Campsites, facilities: There are 64 sites with partial or full hookups for RVs up to 40 feet long; some sites are pull-through. There are also 13 cabins. Picnic tables and fire rings are provided. Drinking water, restrooms with flush toilets and showers, a dump station, wireless Internet service, an ATM, convenience store, coin laundry, and ice are available. Boat docks, launching facilities, and boat rentals are onsite. Leashed pets are permitted.

Reservations, fees: Reservations are accepted at 800/647-2729. Sites are $16–27 per night. Some credit cards are accepted. Open year-round.

Directions: From Eugene, drive south on I-5 for five miles to Exit 188 and Highway 58. Turn east and drive 61 miles to the turnoff for Odell Lake and West Odell Lake Road. Turn right and drive south for 1.8 miles to the resort at the end of the road.

Contact: Shelter Cove Resort, 541/433-2548, www.sheltercoveresort.com.

175 ODELL CREEK
🥾 🏊 ⛵ 🎣 🐕 🚐 ⛺

Scenic rating: 9

on Odell Lake in Deschutes National Forest

Map 5.5, page 277

You can fish, hike, and swim at this campground (4,800 feet elevation) along the east shore of Odell Lake. A trail from the nearby Crater Buttes trailhead leads southwest into the Diamond Peak Wilderness and provides access to several small lakes in the backcountry. Another trail follows the north shore of the lake. Boat docks, launching facilities, and rentals are available at the Odell Lake Lodge and Resort, adjacent to the campground. Windy afternoons are common here.

Campsites, facilities: There are 26 sites for tents or RVs up to 50 feet long. Picnic tables and fire grills are provided. Vault toilets, drinking water, and garbage service are available. Firewood may be gathered from the surrounding area. Leashed pets are permitted.

Reservations, fees: Reservations are accepted at 541/433-2540. Sites are $13–15 per night, $5 per night per additional vehicle. Open May–late September, weather permitting.

Directions: From Eugene, drive south on I-5 for five miles to Exit 188 and Highway 58. Turn east and drive 68 miles to Odell Lake and Forest Road 680 (at the east end of the lake). Turn right on Forest Road 680 and drive 400 yards to the campground on the right.

Contact: Deschutes National Forest, Crescent Ranger District, 541/433-3200, fax 541/433-3224, www.fs.fed.us; Odell Lake Lodge, 541/433-2540.

176 SUNSET COVE

Scenic rating: 8

on Odell Lake in Deschutes National Forest

Map 5.5, page 277

Sunset Cove campground borders the northeast shore of Odell Lake. Boat docks and rentals are available nearby at Odell Lake Lodge and Resort. Campsites are surrounded by large Douglas fir and some white pine trees. The camp backs up to the highway; expect to hear the noise.

Campsites, facilities: There are 20 sites for tents or RVs up to 22 feet long. Picnic tables and fire grills are provided. Drinking water, vault toilets, garbage service, a boat launch and day-use area, and fish-cleaning facilities are available. Firewood may be gathered from the surrounding area. Some facilities are wheelchair accessible. Leashed pets are permitted.

Reservations, fees: Reservations are not accepted. Sites are $13 per night, $5 per night per additional vehicle. Open mid-May–mid-October, weather permitting.

Directions: From Eugene, drive south on I-5 for five miles to Exit 188 and Highway 58. Turn east and drive 67 miles to the campground on the right.

Contact: Deschutes National Forest, Crescent Ranger District, 541/433-3200, fax 541/433-3224, www.fs.fed.us.

177 PRINCESS CREEK

Scenic rating: 9

on Odell Lake in Deschutes National Forest

Map 5.5, page 277

This wooded campground is on the northeast shore of Odell Lake, but it backs up to the highway so expect traffic noise. Boat docks and rentals are available nearby at the Shelter Cove Resort. Fishing, hiking, and swimming are popular activities at the lake. A trail from the nearby Crater Buttes trailhead leads southwest into the Diamond Peak Wilderness and provides access to several small lakes in the backcountry.

Campsites, facilities: There are 44 sites for tents or RVs up to 30 feet long. Picnic tables and fire grills are provided. Vault toilets, garbage service, and boat-launching facilities are available. Drinking water is available at times, but not guaranteed. Firewood may be gathered from the surrounding area. Showers, a store, coin laundry, and ice are within five miles. Leashed pets are permitted.

Reservations, fees: Reservations are not accepted. Sites are $14 per night, $7 per night per additional vehicle. Open April–September, weather permitting.

Directions: From Eugene, drive south on I-5 for five miles to Exit 188 and Highway 58. Turn east and drive 64 miles to the campground on the right.

Contact: Deschutes National Forest, Crescent Ranger District, 541/433-3200, fax 541/433-3224, www.fs.fed.us.

178 CONTORTA FLAT

Scenic rating: 8

on Crescent Lake in Deschutes National Forest

Map 5.5, page 277

This campground on Crescent Lake was named for the particular species of lodgepole pine *(pinus contorta)* that grows here. The elevation is 4,850 feet.

Campsites, facilities: There are 19 sites for tents or RVs up to 40 feet long. Picnic tables and fire grills are provided. Vault toilets and garbage bins are available. There is no drinking water. Some facilities are wheelchair accessible. Leashed pets are permitted.

Reservations, fees: Reservations are not accepted. Sites are $12 per night, $6 per night per additional vehicle. Open June–October, weather permitting.

Directions: From Eugene, drive south on I-5 for five miles to Exit 188 and Highway 58. Turn east and drive 69 miles to County Road

60. Turn right (west) and drive 10 miles to the camp on the left.

Contact: Deschutes National Forest, Crescent Ranger District, 541/433-3200, fax 541/433-3224, www.fs.fed.us.

179 WINDY GROUP

Scenic rating: 8

on Crescent Lake in Deschutes National Forest

Map 5.5, page 277

Windy Group is located near the beaches on Crescent Lake. The lake warms up more easily than many high-mountain lakes, making swimming and waterskiing two popular options. Mountain biking and hiking are also available.

Campsites, facilities: There is one group site for tents or RVs up to 60 feet long and up to 40 people. Picnic tables and fire rings are provided. Vault toilets and garbage bins are available. There is no drinking water. Some facilities are wheelchair accessible. Leashed pets are permitted.

Reservations, fees: Reservations are accepted at 877/444-6777 or www.recreation.gov ($10 reservation fee). The site is $65 per night. Open May–September, weather permitting.

Directions: From Eugene, drive south on I-5 for five miles to Exit 188 and Highway 58. Turn east and drive 69 miles to County Road 60. Turn right (west) and drive 7.5 miles to the camp.

Contact: Deschutes National Forest, Crescent Ranger District, 541/433-3200, fax 541/433-3224, www.fs.fed.us.

180 SIMAX GROUP CAMP

Scenic rating: 8

on Crescent Lake in Deschutes National Forest

Map 5.5, page 277

This camp is set at an elevation of 4,850 feet on Crescent Lake and provides trails to day-use beaches. Fishing is variable year to year and is usually better earlier in the season. A boat launch is available at neighboring Crescent Lake, about two miles away. Nearby Diamond Peak Wilderness (free permit required) provides hiking options.

Campsites, facilities: There are three group campsites for 30–50 campers each. Drinking water, tent pads, restrooms with flush toilets and showers, picnic tables, garbage service, fireplaces, and a group shelter are available. Tents must be placed on tent pads. Some facilities are wheelchair accessible. Leashed pets are permitted.

Reservations, fees: Reservations are accepted at 877/444-6777 or www.recreation.gov ($10 reservation fee). Site A is $80–100 per night and Sites B and C are $100–120 per night. (Note that Site C is best for RVs.) The group shelter is $50 per day. Open mid-May–October, weather permitting.

Directions: From Eugene, drive south on I-5 for five miles to Exit 188 and Highway 58. Turn east and drive 70 miles to Crescent Lake Highway (Forest Road 60). Turn right and drive two miles to Forest Road 6005. Turn left and drive one mile to the campground on the right.

Contact: Deschutes National Forest, Crescent Ranger District, 541/433-3200, fax 541/433-3224, www.fs.fed.us.

181 CRESCENT LAKE

Scenic rating: 8

on Crescent Lake in Deschutes National Forest

Map 5.5, page 277

This campground is set along the north shore of Crescent Lake, and it is often windy here in the afternoon. Boat docks, launching facilities, and rentals are available at Crescent Lake Resort, adjacent to the campground. A trail from camp heads into the Diamond Peak Wilderness (free permit required; available on-site) and also branches north to Odell Lake.

Campsites, facilities: There are 46 sites for tents or RVs up to 36 feet long. Picnic tables and fire grills are provided. Drinking water, vault toilets, garbage service, and boat-launching facilities are available. Firewood may be gathered from the surrounding area. Leashed pets are permitted.

Reservations, fees: Reservations are not accepted. Sites are $16 per night, $8 per night per additional vehicle. Open April–late October, weather permitting.

Directions: From Eugene, drive south on I-5 for five miles to Exit 188 and Highway 58. Turn east and drive 70 miles to Crescent Lake Highway (Forest Road 60). Turn right (west) and drive 2.2 miles southwest. Bear right to remain on Forest Road 60, and drive another 0.25 mile to the campground on the left.

Contact: Deschutes National Forest, Crescent Ranger District, 541/433-3200, fax 541/433-3224, www.fs.fed.us.

182 SPRING
🚶 🚲 🏊 ⛴ 🛶 🎣 🐕 🚐 ⛺

Scenic rating: 8

on Crescent Lake in Deschutes National Forest

Map 5.5, page 277

Spring campground is nestled in a lodgepole pine forest on the southern shore of Crescent Lake. Sites are open, with some on the lake offering Diamond Peak views. Boating, swimming, and waterskiing are popular activities, and the Windy-Oldenburg Trailhead provides access to the Oregon Cascades Recreation Area. The camp is at an elevation of 4,850 feet.

Campsites, facilities: There are five sites for tents only, 64 sites for tents or RVs up to 40 feet long, four multiple sites, and 12 sites that can be reserved together as a group site. Picnic tables and fire grills are provided. Drinking water, vault toilets, garbage service, boat-launching facilities, and firewood (may be gathered from the surrounding area) are available. Leashed pets are permitted.

Reservations, fees: Reservations are not accepted for single sites. Reservations are accepted for group sites at 877/444-6777 or www.recreation.gov ($10 reservation fee). Sites are $16 per night, $8 per night per additional vehicle; multiple sites are $30 per night, and the group site is $125 per night. Open May–September, weather permitting.

Directions: From Eugene, drive south on I-5 for five miles to Exit 188 and Highway 58. Turn east and drive 70 miles to Crescent Lake Highway (Forest Road 60). Turn right and drive eight miles west to the campground entrance road on the left. Turn left and drive one mile to the campground.

Contact: Deschutes National Forest, Crescent Ranger District, 541/433-3200, fax 541/433-3224, www.fs.fed.us.

183 CONTORTA POINT GROUP CAMP
🚶 🚲 🏊 ⛴ 🛶 🎣 🐕 🚐 ⛺

Scenic rating: 8

on Crescent Lake in Deschutes National Forest

Map 5.5, page 277

This campground (4,850 feet elevation) sits on the southern shore of Crescent Lake, where boating, swimming, and waterskiing are among the summer pastimes. A number of trails from the nearby Windy-Oldenburg Trailhead provide access to lakes in the Oregon Cascades Recreation Area. Motorized vehicles are restricted to open roads only.

Campsites, facilities: There are two group sites for tents or RVs up to 30 feet long that can accommodate up to 40 people each. There is no drinking water. Picnic tables and fire rings are provided. Vault toilets and garbage bins are available. Firewood can be gathered in surrounding forest. Boat docks and launching facilities are three miles away at Spring Campground. Leashed pets are permitted.

Reservations, fees: Reservations are accepted at 877/444-6777 or www.recreation.gov ($10 reservation fee). Sites are $65 per night. Open May–September, weather permitting.

Directions: From Eugene, drive south on I-5 for five miles to Exit 188 and Highway 58. Turn east and drive 70 miles to Crescent Lake Highway (Forest Road 60). Turn right and drive 9.9 miles to Forest Road 280. Turn left and drive one mile to the campground.

Contact: Deschutes National Forest, Crescent Ranger District, 541/433-3200, fax 541/433-3224, www.fs.fed.us.

184 WHITEFISH HORSE CAMP

Scenic rating: 5

on Whitefish Creek in
Deschutes National Forest

Map 5.5, page 277

This just might be the best horse camp in the state. Only horse camping is allowed here, and manure removal is required. High lines are not allowed; horses must be kept in stalls. On Whitefish Creek at the west end of Crescent Lake, this campground is set in lodgepole pine and has shaded sites. Although located in a flat area across the road from the lake, the campground has no lake view. Moderately to heavily used, it has access to about 100 miles of trail, leading to Diamond Peak Wilderness, the Metolius-Windigo National Recreation Trail, the Oregon Cascades Recreation Area, and many high mountain lakes. The camp sits at 4,850 feet elevation.

Campsites, facilities: There are 19 sites for tents or RVs up to 40 feet long. Picnic tables and fire rings are provided. Drinking water, garbage bins, vault toilets, horse corrals, and manure disposal site are available are available. Firewood may be gathered from the surrounding area. Leashed pets are permitted.

Reservations, fees: Reservations are accepted at 877/444-6777 or www.recreation.gov ($10 reservation fee). Sites are $14 per night for two stalls, $18 per night for four stalls, and $7 per night per additional vehicle. Open May–September, weather permitting.

Directions: From Eugene, drive south on I-5 for five miles to Exit 188 and Highway 58. Turn east and drive 70 miles to Crescent Lake Highway (Forest Road 60). Turn right (west) and drive 2.2 miles southwest. Stay to the right to remain on Forest Road 60, and drive six miles to the campground on the right.

Contact: Deschutes National Forest, Crescent Ranger District, 541/433-3200, fax 541/433-3224, www.fs.fed.us.

185 CRESCENT CREEK

Scenic rating: 7

on Crescent Creek in
Deschutes National Forest

Map 5.5, page 277

One of the Cascade's classic hidden campgrounds, Crescent Creek camp sits along the banks of its namesake at 4,500 feet elevation. The buzzwords here are pretty, developed, and private. A registered bird-watching area is nearby. Hunters are the primary users of this campground, mainly in the fall. Otherwise, it gets light use. There's some highway noise here, and even if you can't hear it, traffic is visible from some sites.

Campsites, facilities: There are nine sites for tents or RVs up to 40 feet long. Picnic tables and fire grills are provided. Vault toilets, drinking water, and garbage service are available. Firewood may be gathered from the surrounding area. Leashed pets are permitted.

Reservations, fees: Reservations are not accepted. Sites are $14 per night, $7 per night per additional vehicle. Open May–late September, weather permitting.

Directions: From Eugene, drive south on I-5 for five miles to Exit 188 and Highway 58. Turn east and drive 73 miles to County Road 61. Turn left (east) and drive three miles to the campground on the right.

Contact: Deschutes National Forest, Crescent Ranger District, 541/433-3200, fax 541/433-3224, www.fs.fed.us.

186 CORRAL SPRING

Scenic rating: 4

in Winema National Forest

Map 5.5, page 277

This flat campground with no water source is located next to Corral Spring at 4,900 feet elevation. The main attraction is solitude; it's primitive, remote, and quiet. The landscape features stands of lodgepole pine, interspersed by several small meadows.

Campsites, facilities: There are six sites for tents or RVs up to 50 feet long. Picnic tables and fire grills are provided. Vault toilets are available. There is no drinking water, and garbage must be packed out. A store, café, coin laundry, and ice are within five miles. Leashed pets are permitted.

Reservations, fees: Reservations are not accepted. There is no fee for camping. Open mid-May–late October, weather permitting.

Directions: From Eugene, drive southeast on Highway 58 for 86 miles to U.S. 97. Turn south and drive five miles to Forest Road 9774 (2.5 miles north of Chemult). Turn right and drive two miles west to the campground.

Contact: Winema National Forest, Chemult Ranger District, 541/365-7001, fax 541/365-2206, www.fs.fed.us.

187 DIGIT POINT

Scenic rating: 7

on Miller Lake in Winema National Forest

Map 5.5, page 277

This campground is nestled in a lodgepole pine and mountain hemlock forest at 5,600 feet elevation on the shore of Miller Lake, a popular spot for boating, fishing, and swimming. Nearby trails provide access to the Mount Thielsen Wilderness and the Pacific Crest Trail.

Campsites, facilities: There are 64 sites for tents or RVs up to 30 feet long. Picnic tables and fire grills are provided. Drinking water, flush toilets, garbage service and a dump station are available. Boat docks and launching facilities are nearby. Some facilities are wheelchair accessible. Leashed pets are permitted.

Reservations, fees: Reservations are not accepted. Sites are $12 per night, $5 per night per additional vehicle. Open Memorial Day–mid-October, weather permitting.

Directions: From Eugene, drive southeast on Highway 58 for 86 miles to U.S. 97. Turn south and drive seven miles to Forest Road 9772 (one mile north of Chemult). Turn right and drive 12 miles west to the campground.

Contact: Winema National Forest, Chemult Ranger District, 541/365-7001, fax 541/365-2206, www.fs.fed.us.

188 WALT HARING SNO-PARK

Scenic rating: 6

in Winema National Forest near Chemult

Map 5.5, page 277

For eons, this has been a tiny, unknown, and free campground used as a staging area for snowmobiling and cross-country skiing in winter. In summer, it has primarily been a picnic site and layover spot. Note: In 2009, the Forest Service began improving the site and may start charging fees in 2010. The elevation is 4,700 feet.

Campsites, facilities: There are five sites for tents or RVs. Picnic tables and fire rings are provided. Drinking water, vault toilets, and an RV dump station are available. Some facilities are wheelchair accessible. Leashed pets are permitted.

Reservations, fees: No reservations are accepted. There is no fee, however, the Forest Service may start charging fees starting in 2010. If this is critical to your trip, call first. A sno-park permit is required. Open year-round.

Directions: From Eugene, drive southeast on

Highway 58 for 86 miles to U.S. 97. Turn south and drive seven miles to Forest Road 9772 (one mile north of Chemult). Turn right on Forest Road 9772 (Miller Lake Road) and drive 0.5 mile to the campground.

Contact: Winema National Forest, 541/365-7001, fax 541/365-2206.

189 CHARLES V. STANTON PARK

Scenic rating: 7

on the South Umpqua River

Map 5.6, page 278

Charles V. Stanton Park, along the banks of the South Umpqua River, is an all-season spot with a nice beach for swimming in the summer and good steelhead fishing in the winter.

Campsites, facilities: There are 20 sites for tents or self-contained RVs (no hookups), 20 sites with full hookups for RVs up to 60 feet long, and one group area for up to 13 camping units. Picnic tables and fire pits or barbecues are provided. Drinking water, restrooms with flush toilets and showers, a dump station, pavilion, picnic area, and playground are available. Propane gas, a store, café, coin laundry, and ice are within one mile. Some facilities are wheelchair accessible. Leashed pets are permitted.

Reservations, fees: No reservations are accepted for single sites; reservations are required for the group site ($10 reservation fee) at 541/957-7001. Sites are $15–20 per night for single sites, $200 per night for the group site. Some credit cards are accepted. Open year-round.

Directions: Depending on which direction you're heading on I-5, there are two routes to reach this campground. In Canyonville northbound on I-5, take Exit 99 and drive one mile north on the frontage road to the campground on the right. Otherwise: In Canyonville southbound on I-5, take Exit 101. Turn right at the first stop sign, and almost immediately turn

right again onto the frontage road. Drive one mile south on the frontage road to the campground on the left.

Contact: Charles V. Stanton Park, Douglas County Parks, 541/839-4483, fax 541/440-4500, www.co.douglas.or.us/parks.

190 CHIEF MIWALETA CAMPGROUND

Scenic rating: 7

on Galesville Reservoir, east of Azalea

Map 5.6, page 278

If location is everything, then this camp has got it. Wooded sites are set along the shore of beautiful Gales Reservoir, providing a base camp for a trip filled with fishing, boating, hiking, camping, and picnicking. A pavilion can be reserved in the day-use area.

Campsites, facilities: There are 20 sites with full hookups for RVs up to 60 feet long (some pull-through), dispersed sites for tents, and one cabin. Picnic tables and fire rings are provided. Drinking water, vault toilets, and a boat ramp are available. Some facilities are wheelchair accessible. Leashed pets are permitted.

Reservations, fees: Reservations are accepted only for the cabin ($10 reservation fee) at 541/957-7001. RV sites are $20 per night, $3 per night per additional vehicle, tent sites are $15 per night, and the cabin is $32 per night. Some credit cards are accepted for reservations only. Open year-round.

Directions: From Azalea, take I-5 north about 0.5 mile to Exit 88 east to Upper Cow Creek Road. Merge onto Upper Cow Creek and drive eight miles to the campground on the left.

Contact: Chief Miwaleta County Campground, 541/837-3302, www.co.douglas.or.us/parks/campgrounds.asp.

191 MEADOW WOOD RV PARK

🏃 🚴 ⛵ 🐴 👥 🚐 ⛺

Scenic rating: 6

in Glendale

Map 5.6, page 278

Meadow Wood is a good option for RVers looking for a camping spot along I-5. It features 80 wooded acres and all the amenities. Nearby attractions include a ghost town, gold panning, and Wolf Creek Tavern.

Campsites, facilities: There are 25 tent sites and 75 pull-through sites with full or partial hookups for RVs up to 40 feet long. Drinking water and picnic tables are provided. Restrooms with flush toilets and showers, propane gas, a dump station, modem access, firewood, a coin laundry, ice, a playground, and a seasonal heated swimming pool are available. Leashed pets are permitted.

Reservations, fees: Reservations are accepted at 800/606-1274. Sites are $12.50–25 per night. Monthly rentals are available. Open year-round.

Directions: From Grants Pass, drive north on I-5 to Exit 83 (near Glendale) and drive east for 0.25 mile to Autumn Lane. Turn right (south) on Autumn Lane and drive one mile to the park. Alternatively, if you are instead driving south from Roseburg, drive south on I-5 to Exit 86 (near Glendale). Take that exit and drive over the freeway and turn right onto the frontage road. Continue for three miles to Barton Road. Turn left (east) and drive one mile to Autumn Lane. Turn right (south) on Autumn Lane and drive 0.75 mile to the park.

Contact: Meadow Wood RV Park, 541/832-3114 or 800/606-1274, fax 541/832-2454.

192 WOLF CREEK PARK

🏃 🐴 ⛵ ♿ 🚐 ⛺

Scenic rating: 6

near the town of Wolf Creek

Map 5.6, page 278

This rustic campground is located on Wolf Creek near the historic Wolf Creek Inn. A hiking trail leads to the top of London Peak through old-growth forest. Although close to I-5 and the town of Wolf Creek, this spot gets low to average use.

Campsites, facilities: There are 19 sites for tents or RVs (no hookups) and 15 sites for tents or RVs up to 40 feet long (partial hookups). Picnic tables and fire pits are provided. Drinking water, vault toilets, a dump station, a softball field, playground, horseshoe pits, disc golf, and a picnic shelter are available. A camp host is on-site. Supplies are available nearby. Some facilities are wheelchair accessible. Leashed pets are permitted.

Reservations, fees: Reservations are accepted ($8 reservation fee) at 800/452-5687 or www.reserveamerica.com. Sites are $19–20 per night, $5 per night per additional vehicle. Open year-round, but with no water November–early April.

Directions: From Grants Pass, drive north on I-5 for approximately 18 miles to exit 76/Wolf Creek. Take that exit to Wolf Creek Road. Turn left and drive 0.5 mile to the town of Wolf Creek and Main Street. Turn left and drive 0.25 mile to the park.

Contact: Josephine County Parks, 541/474-5285, fax 541/474-5288, www.co.josephine.or.us/parks/index.htm.

193 INDIAN MARY PARK

🏃 ⛵ 🎣 🚐 🐴 ⛵ ♿ 🚐 ⛺

Scenic rating: 9

on the Rogue River

Map 5.6, page 278   BEST (

This park is the crown jewel of the Josephine County parks. Set right on the Rogue River at an elevation of 900–1,000 feet, the park offers disc golf (Frisbee golf), fishing, hiking trails, a historic mining town nearby, a picnic shelter, a swimming beach (unsupervised), and volleyball. Rogue River is famous for its rafting, which can be done with a commercial outfit or on your own.

Campsites, facilities: There are 34 sites for tents or self-contained RVs (no hookups), 58 sites for tents or RVs of up to 40 feet long (full or partial hookups), and two yurts. Picnic tables and fire pits are provided. Drinking water, restrooms with flush toilets and coin showers, garbage bins, a dump station, boat ramp, day-use area, a picnic shelter that can be reserved, playground, ice, and firewood are available. A camp host is on-site. A store and café are seven miles away, and a coin laundry is 16 miles away. Some facilities are wheelchair accessible. Leashed pets are permitted.

Reservations, fees: Reservations are accepted ($8 reservation fee) at 800/452-5687 or www.reserveamerica.com. Sites are $19–22 per night, $5 per night per additional vehicle; yurts are $30 per night. Open year-round.

Directions: From Grants Pass, drive north on I-5 for 3.5 miles to Exit 61 (Merlin-Galice Road). Take that exit and drive west on Merlin-Galice Road for 19 miles to Indian Mary Park on the right.

Contact: Josephine County Parks, 541/474-5285, fax 541/474-5288, www.co.josephine.or.us/parks/index.htm.

194 ELDERBERRY FLAT

Scenic rating: 7

on West Fork Evans Creek

Map 5.6, page 278

This camp is virtually unknown except to the OHV crowd. On weekends, this is usually not the place to find quiet and serenity. OHV and motorcycle activity is common here. It is located on the banks of Evans Creek, about a 30-minute drive from I-5. Small and primitive, it

has access to swimming holes along the creek. No fishing is allowed in the creek.

Campsites, facilities: There are nine primitive tent sites. Picnic tables and fire grills are provided. Vault toilets and garbage service are available, but there is no drinking water. Some facilities are wheelchair accessible. Leashed pets are permitted.

Reservations, fees: Reservations are not accepted. There is no fee for camping, but there is a 14-day stay limit. Open mid-April–mid-November.

Directions: From Grants Pass, drive south on I-5 for 10 miles to the Rogue River exit. Take that exit, turn right on Depot Street, and drive to Pine Street. Turn left and drive 18 miles (it becomes East Evans Creek Road) to West Fork Evans Creek Road. Turn left and drive nine miles to the campground.

Contact: Bureau of Land Management, Medford District, 541/618-2200, fax 541/618-2400, www.or.blm.gov/medford.

195 GRIFFIN PARK

Scenic rating: 7

on the Rogue River

Map 5.6, page 278

This high-use campground and 16-acre park has grassy sites situated 100–150 yards from the Rogue River. The river current is slow in this area, so it is good for swimming and water play. Fishing and rafting are also popular. Hiking and bicycling are available nearby on Bureau of Land Management property.

Campsites, facilities: There are four sites for tents or RVs (no hookups), 15 sites for tents or RVs up to 40 feet long (full hookups), and one yurt. Picnic tables and fire pits are provided. Drinking water, restrooms with flush toilets and showers, a dump station, recreation field, playground, and horseshoe pits are available. A camp host is on-site. A boat ramp, convenience store, swimming area, and playground are within one mile. Some facilities are wheelchair accessible. Leashed pets are permitted.

Reservations, fees: Reservations are accepted ($8 reservation fee) at 800/452-5687 or www.reserveamerica.com. Sites are $19–22 per night, $5 per night per additional vehicle; yurts are $30 per night. Open year-round, but with no water November–early April.

Directions: From Grants Pass on I-5, take the U.S. 199 exit. Turn south on U.S. 199 and drive 6.7 miles to Riverbanks Road. Turn right and drive 6.2 miles to Griffin Park Road. Turn right and drive 0.5 mile to the park.

Contact: Josephine County Parks, 541/474-5285, fax 541/474-5288, www.co.josephine. or.us/parks/index.htm.

196 GRANTS PASS/ REDWOOD HIGHWAY

Scenic rating: 8

near Grants Pass

Map 5.6, page 278

This KOA campground along a stream in the hills outside of Grants Pass attracts birdwatchers. It also makes a perfect layover spot for travelers who want to get away from the highway for a while. For an interesting side trip, drive south down scenic U.S. 199 to Cave Junction or Illinois River State Park.

Campsites, facilities: There are 40 sites for tents or RVs of any length (full hookups); some sites are pull-through. There is also one cabin. Picnic tables are provided, and tent sites have fire pits. Restrooms with showers, drinking water, a dump station, coin laundry, convenience store, ice, RV supplies, propane gas, and modem access are available. There are also a recreation hall, playground, and recreation field. Leashed pets are permitted with certain restrictions.

Reservations, fees: Reservations are accepted at 888/476-6508 and receive a 10 percent discount. Sites are $35–39 per night, plus $4 per person per night for more than two people. Some credit cards are accepted. Open year-round.

Directions: In Grants Pass on I-5, take the U.S. 199 exit. Turn southwest on U.S. 199 and drive 14.5 miles to the campground on the right (at Milepost 14.5).

Contact: Grants Pass/Redwood Highway KOA, 541/476-6508 or 888/476-6508.

197 SCHROEDER

Scenic rating: 9

on the Rogue River

Map 5.6, page 278

Steelhead and salmon fishing, swimming, and boating are among the possibilities at this popular camp along the Rogue River. Just a short jog off the highway, it makes an excellent layover for I-5 travelers. A bonus for RVers is 50-amp service. The park is set close to Hellgate Excursions, which provides jet boat trips on the Rogue River. Tennis courts are close by.

Campsites, facilities: There are 22 sites for tents and RVs (no hookups), 29 sites for tents or RVs of any length (full hookups), and two yurts. Picnic tables and fire pits are provided. Restrooms with flush toilets and coin showers and a picnic shelter that can be reserved are available. Recreational facilities include ball fields, tennis and basketball courts, horseshoe pits, volleyball court, a dog park, picnic area, playground, and boat ramp. A camp host is on-site. Some facilities, including a fishing pier, are wheelchair accessible. Leashed pets are permitted.

Reservations, fees: Reservations are accepted ($8 reservation fee) at 800/452-5687 or www.reserveamerica.com. Sites are $19–22 per night, $5 per night per additional vehicle; yurts are $30 per night. Open year-round.

Directions: In Grants Pass on I-5, take Exit 55 to U.S. 199. Drive west on U.S. 199 for 0.7 mile to Redwood Avenue. Turn right and drive 1.5 miles to Willow Lane. Turn right and drive 0.9 mile to Schroeder Lane and the park.

Contact: Josephine County Parks, 541/474-5285, fax 541/474-5288, www.co.josephine. or.us/parks/index.htm.

198 ROGUE VALLEY OVERNITERS

🚲 🏊 🎣 🚗 🐾 🚐 ⛺

Scenic rating: 5

near the Rogue River

Map 5.6, page 278

This park is just off the freeway in Grants Pass, the jumping-off point for trips down the Rogue River. The summer heat in this part of Oregon can surprise visitors in late June and early July. This is a nice, comfortable park with shade trees. About half of the sites are taken by monthly renters.

Campsites, facilities: There are 30 sites for tents or RVs of any length (full hookups); some are pull-through sites. Cable TV and picnic tables are provided. Restrooms with flush toilets and showers, modem access, a dump station, and coin laundry are available. Propane gas, a store, café, and ice are available within one mile. Leashed pets are permitted.

Reservations, fees: Reservations are accepted. Sites are $33.30 per night, plus $2 per person per night for more than two people. Weekly and monthly rates are available. Open year-round.

Directions: In Grants Pass on I-5, take Exit 58 to 6th Street. Drive south on 6th Street for 0.25 mile to the park on the right.

Contact: Rogue Valley Overniters, 541/479-2208.

199 WHITEHORSE

🚶 🎣 🚣 🐴 🐎 ♿ 🚐 ⛺

Scenic rating: 9

near the Rogue River

Map 5.6, page 278

This pleasant county park is set about a quarter mile from the banks of the Rogue River. It is one of several parks in the Grants Pass area that provide opportunities for salmon and steelhead fishing, hiking, and boating. This is a popular bird-watching area. Wildlife Images, a wildlife rehabilitation center,

is nearby. Possible side trips include Crater Lake National Park (two hours away), Kerby Museum, and Oregon Caves.

Campsites, facilities: There are 34 sites for tents or RVs of any length (no hookups), eight sites for RVs of any any length (full hookups), and one yurt. Picnic tables and fire pits are provided. Restrooms with flush toilets and coin showers, a boat ramp, horseshoe pits, volleyball, a picnic shelter, and a playground are available. A camp host is on-site. Some facilities are wheelchair accessible. Leashed pets are permitted.

Reservations, fees: Reservations are accepted ($8 reservation fee) at 800/452-5687 or www.reserveamerica.com. Sites are $19–22 per night, $5 per night per additional vehicle, and $30 per night for the yurt. The group site is $30 per night for up to 12 people and $3 per person per night for additional people. Open year-round, but only to self-contained RVs in the winter.

Reservation note: When making a reservation for this campground, note that ReserveAmerica.com mistakenly lists it as White Horse, not Whitehorse, and its computer system will not recognize it as one word.

Directions: In Grants Pass on I-5, take Exit 58 to 6th Street. Drive south on 6th Street to G Street. Turn right (west) and drive approximately seven miles (the road becomes Upper River Road, then Lower River Road). The park is on the left at 7600 Lower River Road.

Contact: Josephine County Parks, 541/474-5285, fax 541/474-5288, www.co.josephine.or.us/parks/index.htm.

200 RIVER PARK RV RESORT

🚶 🚲 🏊 🎣 🐾 🚐 ⛺

Scenic rating: 6

on the Rogue River

Map 5.6, page 278

This park has a quiet, serene riverfront setting, yet it is close to all the conveniences of a small city. Highlights here include 700 feet of Rogue River frontage for trout fishing and swimming. It's one of several parks in the immediate area.

Campsites, facilities: There are three tent sites and 47 sites with full or partial hookups for RVs up to 40 feet long. Picnic tables are provided. Cable TV, restrooms with showers, a dump station, public phone, coin laundry, and ice are available. Leashed pets are permitted.

Reservations, fees: Reservations are accepted at 800/677-8857. Sites are $31–38 per night, $3.50 per person per night for more than two people, and $2 per night for an additional vehicle if not towed. Some credit cards are accepted. Open year-round.

Directions: In Grants Pass on I-5, take Exit 55 west to Highway 199. Drive west on Highway 199 for two miles to Parkdale. Turn left on Parkdale and drive one block to Highway 99. Turn left on Highway 99 and drive two miles to the park on the left.

Contact: River Park RV Resort, 541/479-0046 or 800/677-8857.

201 CHINOOK WINDS RV PARK

🏃 🚴 🏊 ♨ 🚐 🐕 🚗

Scenic rating: 6

on the Rogue River

Map 5.6, page 278

This campground along the Rogue River is close to chartered boat trips down the Rogue and a golf course. Fishing and swimming access are available from the campground. (Note: This park was previously known as Circle W RV Park.)

Campsites, facilities: There are 25 sites with full or partial hookups for RVs of any length; some are pull-through sites. Picnic tables and cable TV are provided. Restrooms with flush toilets and showers, a dump station, coin laundry, and ice are available. A boat dock is nearby. Leashed pets are permitted.

Reservations, fees: Reservations are accepted. Sites are $27–40 per night, plus $1.50 per

person per night for more than two people. Some credit cards are accepted. Open year-round.

Directions: From Grants Pass, drive south on I-5 for 10 miles to Exit 48 at Rogue River. Take that exit west (over the bridge) to Highway 99. Turn right and drive west one mile to the park on the right.

Contact: Chinook Winds RV Park, 541/582-1686.

202 VALLEY OF THE ROGUE STATE PARK

🚴 🏊 🚐 🏕 🐕 ♿ 🚗 ⛺

Scenic rating: 7

on the Rogue River

Map 5.6, page 278

With easy highway access, this popular campground along the banks of the Rogue River often fills to near capacity during the summer. Recreation options include fishing and boating. This spot makes a good base camp for taking in the Rogue Valley and surrounding attractions: Ashland's Shakespeare Festival, the Britt Music Festival, Crater Lake National Park, historic Jacksonville, and Oregon Caves National Monument.

Campsites, facilities: There are 147 sites with full or partial hookups for tents or RVs up to 75 feet long, some with pull-through sites, and 21 sites for tents. Three group tent areas for up to 25 people each and six yurts are available. Picnic tables and fire grills are provided. Restrooms with flush toilets and showers, drinking water, garbage bins, a dump station, firewood, Wi-Fi, coin laundry, a meeting hall, amphitheater, and playgrounds are available. A restaurant is nearby. Boat-launching facilities are nearby. Some facilities are wheelchair accessible. Leashed pets are permitted.

Reservations, fees: Reservations are accepted at 800/452-5687 or www.oregonstateparks. org ($8 reservation fee). Tent sites are $12–19 per night, RV sites are $16–24 per night, $5 per night per extra vehicle. Group areas are

$40–71 per night; yurts are $27–36 per night. Some credit cards are accepted. Open year-round.

Directions: From Grants Pass, drive south on I-5 for 12 miles to Exit 45B/Valley of the Rogue State Park. Take that exit, turn right, and drive a short distance to the park on the right.

Contact: Valley of the Rogue State Park, 541/582-1118 or 800/551-6949, www.oregon-stateparks.org.

203 KOA GOLD N' ROGUE

Scenic rating: 6

on the Rogue River

Map 5.6, page 278

This campground is set 0.5 mile from the Rogue River, with bike paths, a golf course, and the Oregon Vortex (the house of mystery) in the vicinity. It's one of the many campgrounds between Gold Hill and Grants Pass.

Campsites, facilities: There are 64 sites with full hookups for RVs of any length, 12 tent sites, and four cabins. Some sites are pull-through. Picnic tables are provided, and tent sites have fire rings. Restrooms with flush toilets and showers, modem access, propane gas, a dump station, firewood, a convenience store, coin laundry, ice, a playground, and a seasonal swimming pool are available. A café is within one mile, and boat-launching facilities are within five miles. Leashed pets are permitted.

Reservations, fees: Reservations are accepted at 800/562-7608. Sites are $25–38 per night, plus $2 per person per night for more than two people. Some credit cards are accepted. Open year-round.

Directions: From Medford, drive north on I-5 for 10 miles to South Gold Hill and Exit 40. Take that exit, turn right, and drive 0.25 mile to Blackwell Road. Turn right (on a paved road) and drive 0.25 mile to the park.

Contact: KOA Gold n' Rogue, 541/855-7710, www.koa.com.

204 LAKE SELMAC

Scenic rating: 9

on Lake Selmac

Map 5.6, page 278

Nestled in a wooded, mountainous area, this 300-acre park offers boating, hiking, sailing, swimming, and good trophy bass fishing on beautiful, 160-acre Lake Selmac. Horse trails are also available. There are seasonal hosts and an assistant park ranger on-site.

Campsites, facilities: There are 94 sites for tents or RVs up to 40 feet long, some with full or partial hookups, and a group area for up to 50 people. There are also six horse camps with corrals and two yurts. Picnic tables and fire pits are provided. Drinking water, restrooms with coin showers, a dump station, convenience store, picnic area, horseshoe pits, playground, ball fields, two boat ramps, and a dock are available. Some facilities are wheelchair accessible. Leashed pets are permitted.

Reservations, fees: Reservations are accepted ($8 reservation fee) at 800/452-5687 or www.reserveamerica.com. Sites are $19–22 per night, $5 per night per additional vehicle, $19 per night for a horse site, $32 per night for a yurt, $32 per night for the first 12 people at the group site, and $3 per person per night for more than 12 people. Open year-round, with some facility limitations in winter.

Directions: In Grants Pass on I-5, take the U.S. 199 exit. Turn south on U.S. 199 and drive for 23 miles to Selma. Continue 0.5 mile to the Lake Selmac exit (Lakeshore Drive). Turn left (east) and drive 2.3 miles to the lake and the campground entrance.

Contact: Josephine County Parks, 541/474-5285, fax 541/474-5288, www.co.josephine.or.us/parks/index.htm.

205 LAKE SELMAC RESORT

🚶 🚵 🏊 🛶 🚣 🐴 ⛏ 🚐 ⛺

Scenic rating: 7

on Lake Selmac

Map 5.6, page 278

This resort borders the shore of Lake Selmac, a 160-acre lake. Fishing is great for largemouth bass (the state record has been set here three times). Bluegill, catfish, crappie, and trout are also catchable here. Fishing derbies are held during the summer. There is a 5-mph speed limit on the lake. Watch for waterfowl, including eagles, geese, osprey, and swans. A trail circles the lake, and bikers, hikers, and horses are welcome. A disc golf course is 1.5 miles away at the county park, and a golf course is about six miles away. Oregon Caves National Monument, about 30 miles away, makes a good side trip.

Campsites, facilities: There are 29 sites with partial hookups for tents or RVs of any length; most sites are pull-through. Drinking water, fire rings, and picnic tables are provided. Restrooms with flush toilets and showers, firewood, a general store, café, coin laundry, ice, propane, bait and tackle, miniature golf, and a playground are available. Boat docks and launching facilities are nearby, and rentals are on-site. Leashed pets are permitted.

Reservations, fees: Reservations are accepted. Sites are $30–35 per night, $3 per night per additional vehicle. Some credit cards are accepted. Open year-round, with limited winter facilities.

Directions: In Grants Pass on I-5, take the U.S. 199 exit. Turn southwest on U.S. 199 and drive 23 miles to Selma and the Lake Selmac exit (Lakeshore Drive). Turn left (east) and drive 2.5 miles to the lake and the resort on the left.

Contact: Lake Selmac Resort, 541/597-2277, www.lakeselmacresort.com.

206 MOUNTAIN MAN RV PARK

🏊 🚣 🐴 🚐 ⛺

Scenic rating: 7

on the Illinois River

Map 5.6, page 278

This park on the Illinois River provides good opportunities for swimming and boating (no motors are permitted). And yes, there is a mountain man here who often shows up in costume in the evening when camp groups build a fire. Great Cats World Park, a wildlife park, is 1.5 miles away. Other nearby side trips include Oregon Caves National Monument (21 miles) and Grants Pass (31 miles). Crescent City is 50 miles away. Note that a majority of the campground is taken by monthly rentals, with the remainder available for overnighters. This park was previously known as Town and Country RV Park.

Campsites, facilities: There are 51 sites for tents or RVs of any length (full hookups); some sites are pull-through. Picnic tables are provided, and some sites have fire rings. Cable TV, restrooms with showers, coin laundry, a community fire ring, and ice are available. Horseshoe pits and a clubhouse are also available. Leashed pets are permitted.

Reservations, fees: Reservations are accepted. Sites are $17–25 per night, plus $3 per person per night for more than two people. Monthly rates are available. Open year-round.

Directions: In Grants Pass on I-5, take the U.S. 199 exit. Go 30 miles west on U.S. 199 (past Cave Junction) to the park on the right.

Contact: Mountain Man RV Park, 541/592-2656 (phone or fax).

207 COUNTRY HILLS RESORT

Scenic rating: 7

near Oregon Caves National Monument

Map 5.6, page 278

Lots of sites at this wooded camp border Sucker Creek, a popular spot for swimming. Several wineries are located within two miles. Lake Selmac and Oregon Caves National Monument provide nearby side-trip options.

Campsites, facilities: There are 12 tent sites and 20 sites with partial or full hookups for RVs of any length; some are pull-through sites. There are also six cabins and a five-unit motel. Picnic tables and fire rings are provided. Restrooms with flush toilets and coin showers, a dump station, modem access, drinking water, firewood, a convenience store, coin laundry, motel, seasonal ice cream parlor, seasonal café, and ice are available. Leashed pets are permitted.

Reservations, fees: Reservations are accepted. Sites are $16–21 per night, $3 per night per additional vehicle. Some credit cards are accepted. Open year-round.

Directions: In Grants Pass on I-5, take the U.S. 199 exit. Go 28 miles on U.S. 199 to the junction of Cave Junction and Highway 46/ Oregon Caves. Turn left on Highway 46 and drive eight miles to the resort on the right.

Contact: Country Hills Resort, 541/592-3406 (phone or fax).

208 GRAYBACK

Scenic rating: 7

near Oregon Caves National Monument in Siskiyou National Forest

Map 5.6, page 278

This wooded campground (2,000 feet elevation) along the banks of Sucker Creek has sites with ample shade. It's a good choice if you're planning to visit Oregon Caves National Monument, about 10 miles away. The camp, set in a grove of old-growth firs, is also a prime place for bird-watching. A 0.5-mile trail cuts through the camp.

Campsites, facilities: There are 39 sites for tents and one RV site with partial hookups. Picnic tables, garbage bins, and fire grills are provided. Flush toilets and drinking water are available. Some facilities are wheelchair accessible, including a 0.5-mile trail. Leashed pets are permitted.

Reservations, fees: Reservations are not accepted. Sites are $16 per night, $5 per night per additional vehicle. Open May–September, weather permitting.

Directions: In Grants Pass on I-5, take Exit 55 for U.S. 199. Bear southwest on U.S. 199 for 30 miles to Cave Junction and Highway 46. Turn east on Highway 46 and drive 12 miles to the campground on the right.

Contact: Siskiyou National Forest, Wild Rivers Ranger District, 541/592-4000, fax 541/592-4010, www.fs.fed.us.

209 CAVE CREEK

Scenic rating: 7

near Oregon Caves National Monument In Siskiyou National Forest

Map 5.6, page 278

No campground is closer to Oregon Caves National Monument than this U.S. Forest Service camp, a mere four miles away. There is even a two-mile trail out of camp that leads directly to the caves. The camp, at an elevation of 2,500 feet, lies in a grove of old-growth timber along the banks of Cave Creek, a small stream with some trout fishing opportunities (catch-and-release only). The sites are shaded, and an abundance of wildlife can be spotted in the area. Hiking opportunities abound.

Campsites, facilities: There are 18 sites for tents or RVs up to 16 feet long. Picnic tables and fire rings are provided. Drinking water, garbage bins, and vault toilets are available.

Showers are within eight miles. Leashed pets are permitted.

Reservations, fees: Reservations are not accepted. Sites are $10 per night, $4 per night per additional vehicle. Open mid-May–mid-September, weather permitting.

Directions: In Grants Pass on I-5, take Exit 55 for U.S. 199. Bear southwest on U.S. 199 for 30 miles to Cave Junction and Highway 46. Turn east on Highway 46 and drive 16 miles to the campground on the right.

Contact: Siskiyou National Forest, Wild Rivers Ranger District, 541/592-4000, fax 541/592-4010, www.fs.fed.us.

210 BOLAN LAKE

Scenic rating: 9

on Bolan Lake in Siskiyou National Forest

Map 5.6, page 278   BEST (

Very few out-of-towners know about this camp, with pretty, shaded sites along the shore of 15-acre Bolan Lake. The lake is stocked with trout, and the fishing can be good. Only non-motorized boats are allowed. A trail from the lake leads up to a fire lookout and ties into miles of other trails, including the Bolan Lake Trail. This spot is truly a bird-watcher's paradise, with a variety of species to view. The camp is set at 5,500 feet elevation.

Campsites, facilities: There are 12 sites for tents or RVs up to 16 feet long. Picnic tables and fire grills are provided. Vault toilets and firewood are available. There is no drinking water. Leashed pets are permitted.

Reservations, fees: Reservations are not accepted. Sites are $5 per night per vehicle. Open June–early October, weather permitting.

Directions: From Grants Pass, drive south on U.S. 199 for 30 miles to Cave Junction and Rockydale Road (County Road 5560). Turn left (southeast) on Rockydale Road and drive eight miles to County Road 5828 (also called Waldo Road and Happy Camp Road). Turn

southeast and drive 14 miles to Forest Road 4812. Turn left (east) and drive four miles to Forest Road 4812-040. Turn left (south) and drive two miles to the campground. This access road is very narrow and rough. Large RVs are strongly discouraged.

Contact: Siskiyou National Forest, Wild Rivers Ranger District, 541/592-4000, fax 541/592-4010, www.fs.fed.us.

211 FAREWELL BEND

Scenic rating: 7

on the Upper Rogue River in Rogue River National Forest

Map 5.7, page 279

Extremely popular Farewell Bend campground is set at an elevation of 3,400 feet along the banks of the Upper Rogue River near the Rogue River Gorge. A 0.25-mile barrier-free trail leads from camp to the Rogue Gorge Viewpoint and is definitely worth the trip. The Upper Rogue River Trail passes near camp. This spot attracts a lot of the campers visiting Crater Lake.

Campsites, facilities: There are 61 sites for tents or RVs up to 40 feet long. Picnic tables, fire grills, and fire rings are provided. Drinking water, firewood, and flush toilets are available. Some facilities are wheelchair accessible. Leashed pets are permitted.

Reservations, fees: Reservations are not accepted. Sites are $16 per night, $8 per night per additional vehicle. Open mid-May–late October, weather permitting.

Directions: From Medford, drive northeast on Highway 62 for 57 miles (near Union Creek) to the campground on the left.

Contact: Rogue River National Forest, Prospect Ranger District, 541/560-3400, fax 541/560-3444; Rogue Recreation, 541/560-3900, www.fs.fed.us.

212 UNION CREEK

Scenic rating: 8

near the Upper Rogue River in
Rogue River National Forest

Map 5.7, page 279

One of the most popular camps in the district, this spot is more developed than the nearby camps of Mill Creek, Natural Bridge, and River Bridge. It sits at 3,200 feet elevation along the banks of Union Creek, where the creek joins the Upper Rogue River. The Upper Rogue River Trail passes near camp. Interpretive programs are offered in the summer, and a convenience store and restaurant are within walking distance.

Campsites, facilities: There are 78 sites for tents or RVs up to 30 feet long, and three RV sites with full hookups. Picnic tables and fire grills are provided. A restroom with flush toilets, vault toilets, drinking water, and garbage service are available. Firewood is available for purchase. An amphitheater is available for programs. A store and restaurant are within walking distance. Some facilities are wheelchair accessible. Leashed pets are permitted.

Reservations, fees: Reservations are not accepted. Sites are $12 per night, $6 per night per additional vehicle. Open mid-May–mid-October, weather permitting.

Directions: From Medford, drive northeast on Highway 62 for 56 miles (near Union Creek) to the campground on the left.

Contact: Rogue River National Forest, Prospect Ranger District, 541/560-3400, fax 541/560-3444; Rogue Recreation, 541/560-3900, www.fs.fed.us.

213 NATURAL BRIDGE

Scenic rating: 8

on the Upper Rogue River Trail in
Rogue River National Forest

Map 5.7, page 279   **BEST (**

Expect lots of company in midsummer at this popular camp, which sits at an elevation of 3,200 feet, where the Upper Rogue River runs underground. The Upper Rogue River Trail passes by the camp and follows the river for many miles to the Pacific Crest Trail in Crater Lake National Park. There is an interpretive area and a spectacular geological viewpoint adjacent to the camp. A 0.25-mile, barrier-free trail is also available.

Campsites, facilities: There are 17 sites for tents or RVs up to 30 feet long. Picnic tables, garbage service, and fire grills are provided. Vault toilets are available, but there is no drinking water. Some facilities are wheelchair accessible. Leashed pets are permitted.

Reservations, fees: Reservations are not accepted. Sites are $10 per night, $5 per night per additional vehicle. Open May–early November, weather permitting.

Directions: From Medford, drive northeast on Highway 62 for 55 miles (near Union Creek) to Forest Road 300. Turn left and drive one mile west to the campground on the right.

Contact: Rogue River National Forest, Prospect Ranger District, 541/560-3400, fax 541/560-3444; Rogue Recreation, 541/560-3900, www.fs.fed.us.

214 ABBOTT CREEK

Scenic rating: 8

on Abbott and Woodruff Creeks in
Rogue River National Forest

Map 5.7, page 279   **BEST (**

Situated at the confluence of Abbott and Woodruff Creeks about two miles from the Upper Rogue River, this camp is a better choice for visitors with children than some of the others along the Rogue River. Abbott Creek is small and tame compared to the roaring Rogue. The elevation here is 3,100 feet.

Campsites, facilities: There are 25 sites for tents or RVs up to 22 feet long. Picnic tables, garbage service, and fire grills are provided. Drinking water, vault toilets, and firewood are available. Leashed pets are permitted.

Reservations, fees: Reservations are not accepted. Sites are $10 per night, $6 per night per additional vehicle. Open mid-May–late October, weather permitting.

Directions: From Medford, drive northeast on Highway 62 for 50 miles (near Union Creek) to Forest Road 68. Turn left and drive 3.5 miles west to the campground on the left.

Contact: Rogue River National Forest, Prospect Ranger District, 541/560-3400, fax 541/560-3444; Rogue Recreation, 541/560-3900, www.fs.fed.us.

215 MILL CREEK

Scenic rating: 7

near the Upper Rogue River in
Rogue River National Forest

Map 5.7, page 279

This campground (elevation of 2,800 feet) along the banks of Mill Creek, about two miles from the Upper Rogue River, features beautiful, private sites and heavy vegetation. One in a series of remote, primitive camps near Highway 62 missed by out-of-towners, this camp is an excellent choice for tenters.

Campsites, facilities: There are 10 sites for tents. Picnic tables, garbage service, and fire grills are provided. Vault toilets are available. There is no drinking water. Leashed pets are permitted.

Reservations, fees: Reservations are not accepted. Sites are $8 per night, $4 per night per additional vehicle. Open early May–November, weather permitting.

Directions: From Medford, drive north on Highway 62 for 46 miles (near Union Creek) to Forest Road 6200-030. Turn right (southeast) and drive one mile to the campground on the left.

Contact: Rogue River National Forest, Prospect Ranger District, 541/560-3400, fax 541/560-3444; Rogue Recreation, 541/560-3900, www.fs.fed.us.

216 RIVER BRIDGE

Scenic rating: 7

on the Upper Rogue River in
Rogue River National Forest

Map 5.7, page 279

River Bridge campground, situated at 2,900 feet elevation along the banks of the Upper Rogue River, is particularly scenic, with secluded sites and river views. This is a calmer part of the Wild and Scenic Upper Rogue River, but swimming and rafting are not recommended. The Upper Rogue River Trail passes by the camp and follows the river for many miles to the Pacific Crest Trail in Crater Lake National Park.

Campsites, facilities: There are eight sites for tents or RVs up to 22 feet long. Picnic tables, garbage service, and fireplaces are provided. Vault toilets are available, but there is no drinking water. Leashed pets are permitted.

Reservations, fees: Reservations are not accepted. Sites are $8 per night, $4 per night per additional vehicle. Open early May–November, weather permitting.

Directions: From Medford, drive northeast on Highway 62 (Crater Lake Highway) for 42 miles (before reaching Union Creek) to Forest Road 6210. Turn left and drive one mile to the campground on the right.

Contact: Rogue River National Forest, Prospect Ranger District, 541/560-3400, fax 541/560-3444; Rogue Recreation, 541/560-3900, www.fs.fed.us.

217 HUCKLEBERRY MOUNTAIN

🚴 🐎 🚐 ⛺

Scenic rating: 6

near Crater Lake National Park in
Rogue River National Forest

Map 5.7, page 279

Here's a hideaway for Crater Lake visitors. The camp is located at the site of an old 1930s Civilian Conservation Corps camp, and an OHV trail runs through and next to the campground. Set at an elevation of 5,400 feet, this spot, about 15 miles from the entrance to Crater Lake National Park, really does get overlooked by highway travelers, so you have a good shot at privacy. About 10 miles of rough roads keep traffic down most of the time.

Campsites, facilities: There are 25 sites for tents or RVs up to 26 feet long. Picnic tables and fireplaces are provided. Drinking water and vault toilets are available. Garbage must be packed out. Leashed pets are permitted.

Reservations, fees: Reservations are not accepted. There is no fee for camping. Open June–late October, weather permitting.

Directions: From Medford, drive north on Highway 62 for 50 miles (near Union Creek) to Forest Road 60. Turn right and drive 12 miles to the campground.

Contact: Rogue River National Forest, Prospect Ranger District, 541/560-3400, fax 541/560-3444; Rogue Recreation, 541/560-3900, www.fs.fed.us.

218 MAZAMA

🚶 🚴 🏊 🐎 ♿ 🚐 ⛺

Scenic rating: 6

near the Pacific Crest Trail in
Crater Lake National Park

Map 5.7, page 279

One of two campgrounds at Crater Lake—the other being Lost Creek—this camp sits at 6,000 feet elevation and is known for cold nights, even in late June and early September.

I once got caught in a snowstorm here at the opening in mid-June. A nearby store is a great convenience. Seasonal boat tours and junior ranger programs are available. The Pacific Crest Trail passes through the park, but the only trail access down to Crater Lake is at Cleetwood Cove. Note that winter access to the park is from the west only on Highway 62 to Rim Village.

Campsites, facilities: There are 200 sites for tents or self-contained RVs up to 32 feet long; there are no hookups. Picnic tables, fire grills, bear-proof food lockers, and garbage bins are provided. Drinking water, restrooms with flush toilets and coin showers, a dump station, coin laundry, gasoline, mini-mart, firewood, and ice are available. Some facilities are wheelchair accessible. Leashed pets are permitted in the campground and on paved roads only.

Reservations, fees: Reservations are not accepted. Sites are $14.75 per night, RV space is $15.75 per night, plus a $10 park-entrance fee per vehicle and $3 per person per night for more than two people. Some credit cards are accepted. Open early June–mid October, weather permitting.

Directions: From I-5 at Medford, turn east on Highway 62 and drive 72 miles into Crater Lake National Park and to Annie Springs junction. Turn left and drive a short distance to the national park entrance kiosk. Just beyond the kiosk, turn right to the campground and Mazama store entrance.

Contact: Crater Lake National Park, 541/594-3000, www.nps.gov/crla.

219 LOST CREEK

🚶 🚴 🏊 🐎 ⛺

Scenic rating: 6

near the Crater Lake Pinnacles in
Crater Lake National Park

Map 5.7, page 279

In good weather, this is a prime spot in Crater Lake National Park; you avoid most of the crowd on Rim Drive. This campground is located near little Lost Creek and the Pinnacles, a series of spires. The only trail access down to Crater Lake is at Cleetwood Cove. Set in a lodgepole pine forest, the camp is more private than Mazama Campground. The roads in the campground are paved, and there is a possibility (hint, hint) that a black bear could visit your campsite. Be sure to follow bear precautions.

Campsites, facilities: There are 16 sites for tents. Picnic tables and fire grills are provided. Drinking water, flush toilets, and garbage bins are available. Leashed pets are permitted in the campground and on paved roads only.

Reservations, fees: Reservations are not accepted. Sites are $10 per night, plus a $10 park entrance fee per vehicle and $3 per person per night for more than two people. Open mid-July–mid-September, weather permitting.

Directions: From I-5 at Medford, turn east on Highway 62 and drive 72 miles into Crater Lake National Park and to Annie Springs junction. Turn left and drive less than one mile to the junction with Rim Drive. Turn right and drive east on Rim Drive for 8.5 miles to Pinnacles Road Junction. Turn right on Pinnacles Road and drive five miles to the campground.

Contact: Crater Lake National Park, 541/594-3000, fax 541/594-3010, www.nps.gov/crla.

220 FLY CASTERS RV PARK

Scenic rating: 6

on the Rogue River

Map 5.7, page 279

This spot along the banks of the Rogue River is a good base camp for RVers who want to fish or hike. The county park, located across the river in Shady Cove, offers picnic facilities and a boat ramp. Lost Creek Lake is about a 15-minute drive northeast. Note that about half of the sites are taken by long-term rentals.

Campsites, facilities: There are 47 sites with full hookups for RVs of any length; two are pull-through sites. Picnic tables are provided. Restrooms with flush toilets and showers, propane gas, cable TV, wireless Internet service, a clubhouse, barbecue area, and coin laundry are available. A store, café, and ice are within one mile. Boat-launching facilities are nearby. Leashed pets are permitted.

Reservations, fees: Reservations are accepted. Sites are $25–38 per night. Some credit cards are accepted. Monthly rates are available. Open year-round.

Directions: From Medford, drive northeast on Highway 62 for 21 miles to the park on the left.

Contact: Fly Casters RV Park, 541/878-2749, fax 541/878-2742.

221 BEAR MOUNTAIN RV PARK

Scenic rating: 7

on the Rogue River

Map 5.7, page 279

This campground is set in an open, grassy area on the Rogue River about six miles from Lost Creek Lake, where boat ramps and picnic areas are available for day use. The campsites are spacious and shaded.

Campsites, facilities: There is a grassy area for tent sites and 37 sites with full or partial hookups for RVs of any length. Drinking water and picnic tables are provided. Restrooms with flush toilets and showers, propane gas, coin laundry, ice, and a playground are available. A store and café are within one mile. Boat docks and launching facilities are nearby. Leashed pets are permitted.

Reservations, fees: Reservations are accepted at 541/878-2400 (from Oregon) or 800/586-2327 (from outside Oregon). Sites are $20–24 per night, plus $2 per person per night for more than two adults. Some credit cards are accepted. Open year-round.

Directions: From Medford, drive northeast on Highway 62 to the junction with Highway 227. Continue east on Highway 62 for 2.5 more miles to the park on the left.
Contact: Bear Mountain RV Park, 541/878-2400.

222 ROGUE ELK CAMPGROUND

Scenic rating: 8

on the Rogue River east of the city of Trail

Map 5.7, page 279

Right on the Rogue River at an elevation of 1,476 feet, the park has creek swimming (unsupervised), a Douglas fir forest, fishing, hiking trails, rafting, and wildlife. With 33 acres of space and 0.75 mile of river frontage, this is Jackson County's most popular park. The forest is very beautiful here. Lost Creek Lake on Highway 62 makes a good side trip.

Campsites, facilities: There are 15 sites for tents or RVs of up to 25 feet long; some have partial hookups. Picnic tables and fire pits are provided. Drinking water, restrooms with flush toilets and coin showers, garbage bins, a dump station, boat ramp, and playground are available. A café, mini-mart, ice, coin laundry, and firewood are available within three miles. Some facilities are wheelchair accessible. Leashed pets are permitted.

Reservations, fees: Reservations are not accepted. Family sites are $18–32 per night and $1 per pet per night. Open mid-April–mid-October.

Directions: From Medford, take Exit 30 for the Crater Lake Highway (Highway 62) and drive northeast on Highway 62 for 29 miles to the park entrance on the right.
Contact: Jackson County Parks, 541/774-8183, fax 541/774-6320, www.jacksoncountyparks.com.

223 JOSEPH H. STEWART STATE PARK

Scenic rating: 7

on Lost Creek Reservoir

Map 5.7, page 279

This state park is on the shore of Lost Creek Reservoir, about 40 miles from Crater Lake National Park, and is home to 11 miles of hiking and biking trails, a lake with a beach, boat rentals, and a marina. Grassy sites are spacious and sprinkled with conifers. The Cole River Hatchery is available for tours.

Note: At time of publication, a blue-green algae health advisory was in effect.

Campsites, facilities: There are 151 sites with partial hookups for tents or self-contained RVs, including some sites for RVs of any length, and 50 sites with water for tents or self-contained RVs. There are also two group areas for tents for up to 50 people each. Picnic tables and fire grills are provided. Restrooms with flush toilets and showers, garbage bins, drinking water, a dump station, firewood, and a playground with volleyball and horseshoes are available. Boat rentals, launching facilities, a swimming area, and a picnic area that can be reserved are nearby. Some facilities are wheelchair accessible. Leashed pets are permitted.

Reservations, fees: Reservations are accepted for the group sites at 800/452-5687 or www.oregonstateparks.org ($8 reservation fee) but are not accepted for single sites. Tent sites are $10–17 per night, sites for tents or RVs are $12–20 per night, $5 per night per additional vehicle. The group site is $40–71, plus $2.40–3 per person per night for more than 25 people. Some credit cards are accepted. Open year-round, weather permitting.

Directions: From Medford, drive northeast on Highway 62 for 34 miles to the Lost Creek Reservoir and the campground on the left.
Contact: Joseph H. Stewart State Park, 541/560-3334 or 800/551-6949, www.oregonstateparks.org.

224 WHISKEY SPRINGS

Scenic rating: 9

near Butte Falls in
Rogue River National Forest

Map 5.7, page 279

This campground at Whiskey Springs, near Fourbit Ford Campground, is one of the larger, more developed backwoods U.S. Forest Service camps in the area. A one-mile, wheelchair-accessible nature trail passes nearby. You can see beaver dams and woodpeckers here. The camp is set at 3,200 feet elevation.

Campsites, facilities: There are 36 sites for tents or RVs up to 30 feet long. Picnic tables, garbage service, and fire grills are provided. Drinking water and vault toilets are available. Some facilities are wheelchair accessible. Leashed pets are permitted.

Reservations, fees: Reservations are not accepted. Sites are $10 per night, $5 per night per additional vehicle. Open mid-May–September, weather permitting.

Directions: From Medford, drive northeast on Highway 62 for 14 miles to the Butte Falls Highway. Turn right and drive east for 16 miles to the town of Butte Falls. Continue southeast on Butte Falls Highway for nine miles to Forest Road 3065. Turn left on Forest Road 3065 and drive 300 yards to the campground on the left.

Contact: Rogue River National Forest, Butte Falls Ranger District, 541/865-2700, fax 541/865-2795, www.fs.fed.us.

225 IMNAHA

Scenic rating: 7

near the Sky Lakes Wilderness in
Rogue River National Forest

Map 5.7, page 279

Located along Imnaha Creek at an elevation of 3,800 feet, this campground makes a good base camp for a wilderness trip. Trailheads at the ends of the nearby forest roads lead east into the Sky Lakes Wilderness; there are also two shorter interpretive trails.

Campsites, facilities: There are four sites for tents or RVs up to 30 feet long. A cabin is also available. Picnic tables and fire grills are provided. Vault toilets, drinking water, and garbage service are available. Leashed pets are permitted.

Reservations, fees: Reservations are accepted only for the cabin at 877/444-6777 or www.recreation.gov ($10 reservation fee). Sites are $10 per night, $5 per night per additional vehicle, and $40 per night for the cabin. Open mid-May–October, weather permitting.

Directions: From Medford, drive northeast on Highway 62 for about 35 miles to Prospect and Mill Creek Drive. Turn right and drive one mile to County Road 992/Butte Falls Prospect Highway. Turn right and drive 2.5 miles to Forest Road 37. Turn left and drive 10 miles east to the campground.

Contact: Rogue River National Forest, Butte Falls Ranger District, 541/865-2700, fax 541/865-2795, www.fs.fed.us.

226 SOUTH FORK

Scenic rating: 7

on the South Rogue River in
Rogue River National Forest

Map 5.7, page 279

South Fork campground is set at an elevation of 4,000 feet along the South Rogue River. To the east, trails at the ends of the nearby forest roads provide access to the Sky Lakes Wilderness. The Southfork Trail, across the road from the campground, has a good biking trail in one direction and a hiking trail in the other. A map of Rogue River National Forest details all back roads, trails, and waters.

Campsites, facilities: There are two sites for tents and four sites for tents or RVs up to 16 feet long. Picnic tables, drinking water, garbage service, and fire grills are provided. Vault toilets are available. Leashed pets are permitted.

Reservations, fees: Reservations are not accepted. Sites are $10 per night, $5 per night per additional vehicle. Open early June–mid-November, weather permitting.

Directions: From Medford, drive northeast on Highway 62 for 14 miles to Butte Falls Highway. Turn right and drive 16 miles east to the town of Butte Falls. Continue one mile past Butte Falls to County Road 992 (Butte Falls Prospect Highway) and drive nine miles to Forest Road 34. Turn right and drive 8.5 miles to the campground on the right.

Contact: Rogue River National Forest, Butte Falls Ranger District, 541/865-2700, fax 541/865-2795, www.fs.fed.us.

227 MEDFORD OAKS RV PARK

Scenic rating: 6

near Eagle Point

Map 5.7, page 279

This park is in a quiet, rural setting among the trees. Just a short hop off I-5, it's an excellent choice for travelers heading to or from California. The campground is located along the shore of a pond that provides good fishing. Most sites are filled with monthly renters.

Campsites, facilities: There are six sites for tents and 55 sites with full or partial hookups for RVs of any length; most sites are pull-through. There are also three cabins. Restrooms with coin showers, a dump station, modem access, coin laundry, limited groceries, ice, RV supplies, and propane gas are available. Recreational facilities include a seasonal, heated swimming pool, movies, horseshoe pits, table tennis, a recreation field for baseball and volleyball, and a playground. Leashed pets are allowed with certain restrictions.

Reservations, fees: Reservations are recommended. Sites are $28–33 per night. Group rates are available. Some credit cards are accepted. Open year-round.

Directions: From Medford, drive northeast on Highway 62 for five miles to Exit 30 and Highway 140. Turn east on Highway 140 and drive 6.8 miles to the park on the left.

Contact: Medford Oaks RV Park, 541/826-5103, fax 541/826-5984, www.medfordoaks.com.

228 FOURBIT FORD

Scenic rating: 6

on Fourbit Creek in
Rogue River National Forest

Map 5.7, page 279

Fourbit Ford campground, situated at an elevation of 3,200 feet along Fourbit Creek, is one in a series of hidden spots tucked away near County Road 821.

Campsites, facilities: There are seven sites for tents. Picnic tables and fire grills are provided. Vault toilets, drinking water, and garbage service are available. Leashed pets are permitted.

Reservations, fees: Reservations are not accepted. Sites are $10 per night, $5 per extra vehicle per night. Open mid-May–late September, weather permitting.

Directions: From Medford, drive northeast on Highway 62 for 14 miles to Butte Falls Highway. Turn right and drive 16 miles east to the town of Butte Falls and County Road 821. Turn left and drive nine miles southeast to Forest Road 3065. Turn left and drive one mile to the campground on the left.

Contact: Rogue River National Forest, Butte Falls Ranger District, 541/865-2700, fax 541/865-2795, www.fs.fed.us.

229 WILLOW LAKE RESORT

Scenic rating: 9

on Willow Lake

Map 5.7, page 279

This campground sits on the shore of Willow Lake. Located at the base of Mount

McLoughlin at an elevation of 3,200 feet, it encompasses 927 wooded acres. The lake has fishing opportunities for bass, crappie, and trout. A hiking trail starts near camp. Waterskiing is allowed at the lake.

Campsites, facilities: There are 26 sites for tents or RVs (no hookups), 54 sites for tents or RVs (full or partial hookups), and a group area with 11 sites. There are also four cabins. Picnic tables and fire rings are provided. Restrooms with flush toilets and coin showers, a dump station, and firewood are available. A store, boat ramp, and boat rentals are on-site. Leashed pets are permitted.

Reservations, fees: Reservations are accepted for groups and cabins only at 541/560-3900. Sites are $15–25 per night, and it's $1 per pet per night. The group area is $175 per night. Open April–October.

Directions: From Medford, drive northeast on Highway 62 for 15 miles to Butte Falls Highway. Turn east and drive 25 miles to Willow Lake Road. Turn right (south) and drive two miles to the campground.

Contact: Rogue Recreation, 541/560-3900.

230 PARKER MEADOWS

Scenic rating: 7

on Parker Meadow in
Rogue River National Forest

Map 5.7, page 279

Fantastic views of nearby Mount McLoughlin are among the highlights of this rustic camp set at 5,000 feet elevation in a beautiful meadow. Trailheads at the ends of the forest roads lead into the Sky Lakes Wilderness. Parker Meadows is a nice spot, complete with water and lots of privacy between sites. Except during hunting season in the fall, this camp does not get much use.

Campsites, facilities: There are eight sites for tents or RVs up to 16 feet long. Picnic tables and fire grills are provided. Vault toilets, drinking water, and garbage service are available. Leashed pets are permitted.

Reservations, fees: Reservations are not accepted. Sites are $10 per night, $5 per night per additional vehicle. Open mid-June–late October, weather permitting.

Directions: From Medford, drive northeast on Highway 62 for 14 miles to Butte Falls Highway. Turn right and drive 16 miles east to the town of Butte Falls and County Road 821. Turn left and drive 10 miles southeast to Forest Road 37. Turn left and drive 11 miles to the campground on the left.

Contact: Rogue River National Forest, Butte Falls Ranger District, 541/865-2700, fax 541/865-2795, www.fs.fed.us.

231 ODESSA

Scenic rating: 4

near Klamath Lake in Winema National Forest

Map 5.7, page 279

This campground (4,100 feet elevation) borders Odessa Creek, near the shore of Upper Klamath Lake. The lake is the main attraction, with fishing the main activity. The lake can provide excellent fishing for rainbow trout on both flies and Rapalas. Boating is also popular. Campsites sit among scattered mixed conifers and native brush.

Campsites, facilities: There are five tent sites. Picnic tables, garbage bins, and fire grills are provided. Vault toilets are available, but there is no drinking water. Leashed pets are permitted.

Reservations, fees: Reservations are not accepted. There is no fee for camping. Open year-round, weather permitting.

Directions: From Klamath Falls, drive west on Highway 140 about 18 miles to Forest Road 3639. Turn right (northeast) and drive one mile to the campground.

Contact: Fremont-Winema National Forests, Klamath Ranger District, 541/885-3400, fax 541/885-3452, www.fs.fed.us.

232 FOURMILE LAKE

🥾 🏊 🛶 �站 🏕 🚐 ⛺

Scenic rating: 8

at Fourmile Lake in Winema National Forest

Map 5.7, page 279

This beautiful spot is the only camp on the shore of Fourmile Lake. Several nearby trails provide access to the Sky Lakes Wilderness. The Pacific Crest Trail passes about two miles from camp. Primitive and with lots of solitude, it attracts a calm and quiet crowd. Afternoon winds can be a problem, and in the evening, if the wind isn't blowing, the mosquitoes often arrive. Although this campground is near the foot of Mount McLoughlin (9,495 feet), there is no view of the mountain from here. Go to the east side of the lake for a good view.

Campsites, facilities: There are 25 sites for tents or RVs up to 22 feet long. Picnic tables, garbage bins, and fire grills are provided. Drinking water and vault toilets are available. Leashed pets are permitted.

Reservations, fees: Reservations are not accepted. Sites are $11 per night, $5.50 per night per additional vehicle. Open June–late September, weather permitting.

Directions: From Medford, drive northeast on Highway 62 for five miles to Exit 30 and Highway 140. Turn east on Highway 140 and drive approximately 40 miles to Forest Road 3661. Turn left (north) and drive six miles to the campground.

Contact: Fremont-Winema National Forests, Klamath Ranger District, 541/885-3400, fax 541/885-3452, www.fs.fed.us.

233 ROCKY POINT RESORT

🛥 🚣 🛶 🐕 🚐 ⛺

Scenic rating: 7

on Upper Klamath Lake

Map 5.7, page 279

Rocky Point Resort, at the Upper Klamath Wildlife Refuge, boasts 10 miles of canoe trails, along with opportunities for motorized boating and fishing. Ponderosa pines and Douglas firs create a quite picturesque setting for stellar sunsets and a peaceful retreat.

Campsites, facilities: There are 29 sites with partial or full hookups for RVs of any length, four tent sites, four cabins, and five motel rooms. Some sites are pull-through. Picnic tables and fire rings are provided. Restrooms with flush toilets and showers, drinking water, firewood, a convenience store, modem access, coin laundry, ice, a marina with boat gas, and boat and canoe rentals are available. There is a free boat launch and game area. A restaurant and lounge overlook the lake. Leashed pets are permitted.

Reservations, fees: Reservations are accepted. Sites are $28–30 per night, $4 per person per night for more than two people, $2 per pet per night, and $5 per night per additional vehicle. Some credit cards are accepted. Open April–November.

Directions: From Klamath Falls, drive northeast on Highway 140 for 25 miles to Rocky Point Road. Turn right and drive three miles to the resort on the right.

Contact: Rocky Point Resort, 541/356-2287, fax 541/356-2222, www.rockypointoregon.com.

234 WILLOW PRAIRIE

🚣 🐕 🚐 ⛺

Scenic rating: 7

near Fish Lake in Rogue River National Forest

Map 5.7, page 279

There are two campgrounds here, including one for equestrian campers. This spot is located near the origin of the west branch of Willow Creek and next to a beaver swamp and several large ponds that attract deer, ducks, elk, geese, and sandhill cranes. A number of riding trails pass nearby. A map of Rogue River National Forest details the back roads and can help you get here. Fish Lake is four miles south.

Campsites, facilities: There are 10 sites for tents or RVs up to 16 feet long, one primitive cabin with cots, and 10 equestrian sites. Picnic tables and fire grills are provided. Drinking water, vault toilets, and garbage service are available. The equestrian camp has 10 sites for tents or small RVs, two stock water troughs, and horse corrals. A store, café, ice, boat docks, launching facilities, and rentals are nearby. A camp host is on-site. Leashed pets are permitted.

Reservations, fees: Reservations are accepted only for the horse camp and cabin at 877/444-6777 or www.recreation.gov ($10 reservation fee). Sites are $10 per night, $5 per night per additional vehicle. Open late May–late October, weather permitting.

Directions: From Medford, drive northeast on Highway 62 for five miles to Exit 30 and Highway 140. Turn east on Highway 140 and drive 31.5 miles to Forest Road 37. Turn left and drive north 1.5 miles to Forest Road 3738. Turn left and drive one mile west to Forest Road 3735. Turn left and drive 100 yards to the campground. For the equestrian camp, continue for 0.25 mile to the campground entrance.

Contact: Rogue River National Forest, Butte Falls Ranger District, 541/865-2700, fax 541/865-2795, www.fs.fed.us.

235 NORTH FORK

Scenic rating: 7

near Fish Lake in Rogue River National Forest

Map 5.7, page 279

Here is a small, pretty campground with easy access from the highway and proximity to Fish Lake. Situated on the north fork of Little Butte Creek at an elevation of 4,500 feet, it's fairly popular, so grab your spot early. Excellent fly-fishing can be found along the Fish Lake Trail, which leads directly out of camp.

Campsites, facilities: There are nine sites for tents or RVs up to 24 feet long. Picnic tables and fire grills are provided. Vault toilets and drinking water are available. Garbage must be packed out. A camp host is on-site. Boat docks, launching facilities, and rentals are nearby. Some facilities are wheelchair accessible. Leashed pets are permitted.

Reservations, fees: Reservations are not accepted. Sites are $8 per night, $4 per night per additional vehicle. Open May–mid-November, weather permitting.

Directions: From Medford, drive northeast on Highway 62 for five miles to Exit 30 and Highway 140. Turn east on Highway 140 and drive 31.5 miles to Forest Road 37. Turn right (south) and drive 0.5 mile to the campground.

Contact: Rogue River National Forest, Butte Falls District, 541/865-2700, fax 541/865-2795; Rogue Recreation, 541/560-3900, www.fs.fed.us.

236 FISH LAKE

Scenic rating: 8

on Fish Lake in Rogue River National Forest

Map 5.7, page 279

Bicycling, boating, fishing, and hiking are among the recreation options at this campground on the north shore of Fish Lake. Easy, one-mile access to the Pacific Crest Trail is also available. If this campground is full, Doe Point and Fish Lake Resort are nearby.

Campsites, facilities: There are 19 sites for tents or RVs up to 40 feet long and two walk-in tent sites. Picnic tables, fire grills, and garbage bins are provided. Drinking water, flush toilets, a picnic shelter that can be reserved, a store, café, firewood, and ice are available. A camp host is on-site. Boat docks, launching facilities, boat rentals, coin laundry, dump station, and coin showers are nearby. Some facilities are wheelchair accessible. Leashed pets are permitted.

Reservations, fees: Reservations are accepted only for the picnic shelter at 541/560-3900. Sites are $16 per night, $8 per night per additional vehicle. Open mid-May–mid-October, weather permitting.

Directions: From Medford, drive northeast on Highway 62 for five miles to Exit 30 and Highway 140. Turn east on Highway 140 and drive 30 miles to the campground on the right.

Contact: Rogue River National Forest, Butte Falls District, 541/865-2700, fax 541/865-2795; Rogue Recreation, 541/560-3900, www.fs.fed.us.

237 DOE POINT

Scenic rating: 8

on Fish Lake in Rogue River National Forest

Map 5.7, page 279

This campground (at 4,600 feet elevation) sits along the north shore of Fish Lake, nearly adjacent to Fish Lake Campground. Doe Point is slightly preferable because of its dense vegetation, offering shaded, quiet, well-screened sites. Privacy, rare at many campgrounds, can be found here. Recreation options include biking, boating, fishing, and hiking, plus an easy, one-mile access trail to the Pacific Crest Trail.

Campsites, facilities: There are five walk-in tent sites and 25 sites for tents or RVs up to 30 feet long. Picnic tables and fire grills are provided. Drinking water, garbage service, flush toilets, a store, café, firewood, and ice are available. Boat docks, launching facilities, boat rentals, showers, and a dump station are nearby. Some facilities are wheelchair accessible. Leashed pets are permitted.

Reservations, fees: Reservations are not accepted. Sites are $16 per night, $8 per night per additional vehicle. Open mid-May–late September, weather permitting.

Directions: From Medford, drive northeast on Highway 62 for five miles to Exit 30 and Highway 140. Turn east on Highway 140 and drive 30 miles to the campground on the right.

Contact: Rogue River National Forest, Butte Falls District, 541/865-2700, fax 541/865-2795, www.fs.fed.us; Rogue Recreation, 541/560-3900, www.fs.fed.us.

238 FISH LAKE RESORT

Scenic rating: 7

on Fish Lake

Map 5.7, page 279

This resort along Fish Lake is privately operated under permit by the U.S. Forest Service and offers a resort-type feel, catering primarily to families. This is the largest and most developed of the three camps at Fish Lake. Bicycling, boating, fishing, and hiking are some of the activities here. Cozy cabins are available for rent. Boat speed on the lake is limited to 10 mph.

Campsites, facilities: There are 12 sites for tents, 46 sites with full hookups for RVs up to 38 feet long, and 11 cabins. Some sites are pull-through. Picnic tables, fire rings, drinking water, and garbage bins are provided. Restrooms with flush toilets and coin showers, propane gas, dump station, recreation hall, convenience store, café, coin laundry, ice, boat docks, boat rentals, and launching facilities are available. Leashed pets are permitted.

Reservations, fees: Reservations are accepted at 541/949-8500. Tent sites are $18–40 per night, and RV sites are $32–34 per night. Some credit cards are accepted. Open year-round, weather permitting, with limited winter facilities.

Directions: From Medford, take I-5 to Exit 30 and go to Highway 140. Turn east on Highway 140 and drive 30 miles to Fish Lake Road. Turn right (south) and drive 0.5 mile to the resort on the left.

Contact: Fish Lake Resort, 541/949-8500, www.fishlakeresort.net.

239 LAKE OF THE WOODS RESORT

Scenic rating: 9

on Lake of the Woods

Map 5.7, page 279   BEST (

On beautiful Lake of the Woods, this resort offers fishing (four kinds of trout, catfish, and bass) and boating in a secluded forest setting. It's on one of the most beautiful lakes in the Cascade Mountains, surrounded by tall pine trees. A family-oriented campground, it has all the amenities. In the winter, snowmobiling and cross-country skiing are popular. Attractions in the area include the Mountain Lakes Wilderness and the Pacific Crest Trail.

Campsites, facilities: There are 27 sites with full or partial hookups for tents or RVs up to 35 feet long and 26 cabins. Picnic tables and fire rings are provided. Restrooms with showers, a dump station, coin laundry, ice, snacks, a restaurant, lounge, and propane gas are available. There are also a boat ramp, dock, marina, boat and mountain bike rentals, and a barbecue area. Leashed pets are permitted.

Reservations, fees: Reservations are accepted at 866/201-4194. Sites are $28–35 per night, $7 per night per additional vehicle, and $1 per pet per night. Some credit cards are accepted. Open during summer season; call for winter schedule.

Directions: In Medford on I-5, take Exit 14 to Highway 62. Go six miles on Highway 62 to Highway 140/Lake of the Woods. Drive 59.6 miles on Lake of the Woods Road to the resort on the left.

Contact: Lake of the Woods Resort, 541/949-8300, fax 541/949-8229, www.lakeofthewoodsresort.com.

north for several miles, meandering around Fourmile Lake and extending into the Sky Lakes Wilderness. Other trails nearby head into the Mountain Lakes Wilderness. Boating, fishing, swimming, and waterskiing are among the activities here. Note that of the 60 campsites, 20 are available by reservation; the rest are first-come, first-served.

Campsites, facilities: There are 18 single sites and two double sites for tents or RVs up to 55 feet long. Picnic tables, garbage bins, and fire grills are provided. Drinking water, a dump station, and flush toilets are available. Boat docks, launching facilities, and rentals are nearby. Some facilities are wheelchair accessible. Leashed pets are permitted.

Reservations, fees: Reservations are accepted at 877/444-6777 or www.recreation.gov ($10 reservation fee). Single sites are $16–17 per night, $34 for double sites, and $8 per night per additional vehicle. The group sites is $90–95 per night. Open late May–early September, weather permitting.

Directions: In Ashland on I-5, take Exit 14 to Highway 66. Drive east for less than a mile to Dead Indian Memorial Road. Turn left (east) and drive 40 miles to Lake of the Woods. Continue along the east shore to the campground turnoff on the left.

Contact: Fremont-Winema National Forests, Klamath Ranger District, 541/885-3400, fax 541/885-3452, www.fs.fed.us.

240 ASPEN POINT

Scenic rating: 8

on Lake of the Woods in
Winema National Forest

Map 5.7, page 279   BEST (

This campground (at 5,000 feet elevation) is near the north shore of Lake of the Woods, adjacent to Lake of the Woods Resort. It's heavily timbered with old-growth fir and has a great view of Mount McLoughlin (9,495 feet). A hiking trail just north of camp leads

241 SUNSET

Scenic rating: 8

near Lake of the Woods in
Winema National Forest

Map 5.7, page 279

Sunset campground (at 5,000 feet elevation) near the eastern shore of Lake of the Woods is fully developed and offers a myriad of recreation options. It's popular for both fishing and boating. Of the 67 sites, 20 are available by reservation.

Campsites, facilities: There are 67 sites for tents or RVs up to 50 feet long. Picnic tables, garbage bins, and fire grills are provided. Drinking water and flush toilets are available. Boat docks, launching facilities, and rentals are nearby. Some facilities are wheelchair accessible. Leashed pets are permitted.

Reservations, fees: Reservations are accepted at 877/444-6777 or www.recreation.gov ($10 reservation fee). Sites are $17 per night, $8 per night per additional vehicle. Open late May–early September.

Directions: In Ashland on I-5, take Exit 14 to Highway 66. Drive east for less than a mile to Dead Indian Memorial Road. Turn left (east) and drive 40 miles to Lake of the Woods. Continue along the east shore to Forest Road 3738. Turn left (west) and drive 0.5 mile to the camp.

Contact: Fremont-Winema National Forests, Klamath Ranger District, 541/885-3400, fax 541/885-3452, www.fs.fed.us.

242 CANTRALL-BUCKLEY PARK & GROUP CAMP

Scenic rating: 8

on the Applegate River

Map 5.7, page 279

This county park outside of Medford offers pleasant, shady sites in a wooded setting. Encompassing 88 acres of land, the camp has 1.75 miles of frontage along the Applegate River, which has good trout fishing.

Campsites, facilities: There are 42 sites for tents or self-contained RVs up to 25 feet long and one group area for 60–100 people. Picnic tables and fire pits are provided. Drinking water, restrooms with flush toilets and coin showers, and a picnic area that can be reserved are available. Recreational facilities include horseshoes, a playground, and a recreation field. Leashed pets are permitted.

Reservations, fees: Reservations are accepted only for the group site at 541/774-8183. Sites

are $12 per night, $1 per pet per night, and $65 per night for the group site. Some credit cards are accepted with reservations only. Open mid-April–mid-October.

Directions: In Medford on I-5, take the Jacksonville exit to the Jacksonville Highway. Drive west on the Jacksonville Highway (Highway 238) for seven miles to Jacksonville. Bear left on Highway 238 and drive to Hamilton Road. Turn left (south) on Hamilton Road and drive approximately 0.4 mile to Cantrall Road. Turn right on Cantrall and drive approximately 0.5 mile to the campground.

Contact: Jackson County Parks, 541/774-8183, fax 541/774-6320, www.jacksoncountyparks.com.

243 THE WELLSPRINGS

Scenic rating: 5

near Ashland

Map 5.7, page 279

This wooded campground has mineral hot springs that empty into a swimming pool. Hot mineral baths are available in private rooms. Massages, sauna use, and swimming are also available for a fee. This is an old Native American birthing ground. Nearby recreation options include a bike path, a golf course, hiking trails, and tennis courts. Boating, fishing, and waterskiing are within 10 miles.

Campsites, facilities: There is a large grassy area for tents, 28 sites with full hookups for RVs of any length, and five tepees. Some sites are pull-through. Picnic tables and fire rings are provided. Restrooms with flush toilets and showers, coin laundry, ice, volleyball, massage therapists, a soaking pool, a swimming pool, and a sauna are available. Propane gas is within one mile. Leashed pets are permitted with deposit.

Reservations, fees: Reservations are not accepted. Tent sites are $15 per night, RV sites are $20 per night, $3–6 per person per night for more than two people, and tepees are $25 per night. Some credit cards are accepted. Open year-round.

Directions: From Ashland, drive north on I-5 to Exit 19. Take that exit and drive west for 0.25 mile to the stoplight at Highway 99. Turn right and drive 500 feet to the campground on the left.

Contact: The WellSprings, 541/482-3776.

244 GLENYAN CAMPGROUND OF ASHLAND

Scenic rating: 7

near Emigrant Lake

Map 5.7, page 279

This campground, located within seven miles of Ashland and less than one mile from Emigrant Lake, offers shady sites. Recreation options in the area include a golf course and tennis courts. It's an easy jump from I-5 at Ashland.

Campsites, facilities: There are 22 tent sites and 46 sites with full or partial hookups for tents or RVs of any length. Drinking water, fire rings, and picnic tables are provided. Restrooms with flush toilets and showers, propane gas, a dump station, wireless Internet service, firewood, a recreation hall, convenience store, coin laundry, ice, a playground, and a seasonal heated swimming pool are available. Leashed pets are permitted.

Reservations, fees: Reservations are accepted at 877/453-6926. Sites are $29–32 per night, plus $2 per person per night for more than five people. Some credit cards are accepted. Open year-round.

Directions: From Ashland, drive east on Highway 66 for 3.5 miles to the campground on the right.

Contact: Glenyan Campground of Ashland, 541/488-1785, www.glenyancampground. com.

245 DALEY CREEK

Scenic rating: 6

on Daley Creek in Rogue River National Forest

Map 5.7, page 279

Daley Creek campground is a primitive alternative to some of the more developed spots in the area. Situated at 4,500 feet elevation, the camp borders the banks of Daley Creek near the confluence of Beaver Dam and Daley Creek. Sites are scattered among old-growth Douglas and white fir, and the Beaver Dam Trail heads right out of camp, running along the creek. Fishing can be decent downstream from here.

Campsites, facilities: There are six sites for tents or RVs up to 18 feet long. Picnic tables and fire grills are provided. There is no drinking water, and garbage must be packed out. Some facilities are wheelchair accessible. Leashed pets are permitted.

Reservations, fees: Reservations are not accepted. Sites are $8 per night, $4 per night per additional vehicle. Open early May–mid-November, weather permitting.

Directions: In Ashland on I-5, take Exit 14 to Highway 66. Drive east for less than a mile to Dead Indian Memorial Road. Turn left (east) and drive 22 miles to Forest Road 37. Turn left (north) and drive 1.5 miles to the campground.

Contact: Rogue River National Forest, Ashland Ranger District, 541/552-2900, fax 541/552-2922, www.fs.fed.us.

246 BEAVER DAM

Scenic rating: 5

on Beaver Dam Creek in Rogue River National Forest

Map 5.7, page 279

This campground sits at an elevation of 4,500 feet along Beaver Dam Creek. Look for beaver dams. There's not much screening between sites, but it's a pretty, rustic, and quiet spot, with unusual vegetation along the creek for botany fans. The trailhead for the Beaver Dam Trail is also here. The camp is adjacent to Daley Creek Campground.

Campsites, facilities: There are four sites for tents or RVs up to 16 feet long. Picnic tables and fire grills are provided. There is no drinking water, and garbage must be packed out. Leashed pets are permitted.

Reservations, fees: Reservations are not accepted. Sites are $8 per night, $4 per night per additional vehicle. Open early May–early November, weather permitting.

Directions: In Medford on I-5, take Exit 14 to Highway 66. Drive east for less than a mile to Dead Indian Memorial Road. Turn left (east) and drive 22 miles to Forest Road 37. Turn left (north) and drive 1.5 miles to the campground.

Contact: Rogue River National Forest, Ashland Ranger District, 541/552-2900, fax 541/552-2922, www.fs.fed.us.

247 HOWARD PRAIRIE LAKE RESORT

Scenic rating: 7

on Howard Prairie Lake

Map 5.7, page 279

This wooded campground is located along the shore of Howard Prairie Lake, where boating, fishing, hiking, and swimming are among the recreation options. This is one of the largest campgrounds in over 100 miles.

Campsites, facilities: There are 150 sites with full or partial hookups for tents or RVs of any length and 20 furnished RV rentals. Some sites are pull-through. Picnic tables and fire rings are provided. Restrooms with flush toilets and showers, propane gas, a dump station, firewood, 24-hour security, a convenience store, café, coin laundry, boat docks, boat rentals, moorage, and launching facilities are available. Leashed pets are permitted.

Reservations, fees: Reservations are not accepted. Sites are $20–29 per night, plus $5 per person per night for more than two people. Some credit cards are accepted. Open mid-April–October.

Directions: In Ashland on I-5, take Exit 14 to Highway 66 and drive for less than a mile to Dead Indian Memorial Road. Turn left and drive 17 miles to Hyatt Prairie Road. Turn right and drive 3.5 miles to the resort.

Contact: Howard Prairie Lake Resort, 541/482-1979, fax 541/488-7485, www.howardprairieresort.com.

248 HOWARD PRAIRIE LAKE: LILY GLEN

Scenic rating: 6

near Howard Prairie Lake

Map 5.7, page 279

Set along the shore of Howard Prairie Lake, this horse camp is a secluded, primitive getaway. Trout fishing is available. Tubb Springs Wayside State Park and the nearby Rogue River National Forest are possible side trips. There is also nearby access to the Pacific Crest Trail. The elevation is 4,500 feet.

Campsites, facilities: There are 26 sites for tents or self-contained RVs and two group sites for up to 75 people. Picnic tables and fire grills are provided. Drinking water, vault toilets, and corrals are available. Some facilities are wheelchair accessible. Leashed pets are permitted.

Reservations, fees: Reservations are accepted for group sites at 541/774-8183 but are not accepted for family sites. Sites are $16 per night, $6 per night per additional vehicle, $1 per pet per night, and $2 per horse per night for more than two horses; group sites are $75–150 per night. Some credit cards are accepted for reservations. Open mid-April–October, weather permitting.

Directions: In Ashland on I-5, take Exit 14 to Highway 66. Drive east for less than a mile to Dead Indian Memorial Road. Turn left (east) and drive 21 miles to the campground on the right.

Contact: Howard Prairie Lake Recreational Area, Jackson County Parks, 541/774-8183, fax 541/774-6320, www.jacksoncountyparks. com.

249 HOWARD PRAIRIE LAKE: GRIZZLY

Scenic rating: 7

near Howard Prairie Lake

Map 5.7, page 279

One of a series of four county campgrounds at Howard Prairie Lake, Grizzly features well-spaced campsites amid a forest and lake setting. The lake level is known to fluctuate; in low-water years, this camp is sometimes shut down. It gets moderate use. The elevation is 4,550 feet.

Campsites, facilities: There are 29 sites for tents or RVs (no hookups). Picnic tables and fire rings are provided. Drinking water, vault toilets, and garbage bins are available. A boat ramp is nearby. A store, café, laundry facilities, and boat rentals are available within two miles. Some facilities are wheelchair accessible. Leashed pets are permitted.

Reservations, fees: Reservations are not accepted. Sites are $14 per night, $6 per night per additional vehicle, and $1 per pet per night. Open mid-April–October, weather permitting.

Directions: In Ashland on I-5, take Exit 14 to Highway 66. Drive east for less than a mile to Dead Indian Memorial Road. Turn left (east) and drive 17 miles to Howard Prairie Road. Turn right (south) and drive eight miles to Howard Prairie Dam Road. Turn left (east) and drive 0.25 mile to the campground.

Contact: Howard Prairie Lake Recreational Area, Jackson County Parks, 541/774-8183, fax 541/774-6320, www.jacksoncountyparks. com.

250 HOWARD PRAIRIE LAKE: WILLOW POINT

Scenic rating: 7

near Howard Prairie Lake

Map 5.7, page 279

Willow Point is the most popular of the four county campgrounds on Howard Prairie Lake. Similar to Grizzly, it offers flat tent sites in an area well covered by trees. The lake is stocked with about 100,000 trout annually.

Campsites, facilities: There are 40 sites for tents or self-contained RVs. Picnic tables and fire rings are provided. Drinking water, vault toilets, and garbage bins are available. A boat ramp is nearby. A store, café, laundry facilities, and boat rentals are available within four miles. Some facilities are wheelchair accessible. Leashed pets are permitted.

Reservations, fees: No reservations are accepted. Sites are $16 per night, $6 per night per additional vehicle, and $1 per pet per night. Open mid-April–October.

Directions: In Ashland on I-5, take Exit 14 to Highway 66. Drive east for less than a mile to Dead Indian Memorial Road. Turn left (east) and drive 17 miles to Howard Prairie Road. Turn right (south) and drive three miles to the reservoir.

Contact: Howard Prairie Lake Recreational Area, Jackson County Parks, 541/774-8183, fax 541/774-6320, www.jacksoncountyparks.com.

251 HOWARD PRAIRIE LAKE: KLUM LANDING

Scenic rating: 7

near Howard Prairie Lake

Map 5.7, page 279

Klum Landing is one of four county campgrounds on Howard Prairie Lake. A bonus at this one is that coin-operated showers are available. Sugar Pine Group Camp is more primitive and is situated away from the lake.

Campsites, facilities: At Klum Landing, there are 32 sites for tents or self-contained RVs. Picnic tables and fire rings are provided. Drinking water, garbage bins, and restrooms with flush toilets and coin showers are available; some facilities are wheelchair accessible. Sugar Pine can accommodate up to 100 people in tents or self-contained RVs. Vault toilets are available, and the facilities are not wheelchair accessible. A boat ramp is nearby. A store, café, laundry facilities, and boat rentals are available at Howard Prairie Lake Resort. Leashed pets are permitted.

Reservations, fees: Reservations are not accepted for Klum Landing. Sites are $18 per night, $6 per night per additional vehicle, and $1 per pet per night. Reservations are accepted for Sugar Pine Group at 541/774-8183. The group camp is $150–200 per night. Open mid-April–October.

Directions: In Ashland on I-5, take Exit 14 to Highway 66. Drive east for less than a mile to Dead Indian Memorial Road. Turn left (east) and drive 17 miles to Howard Prairie Road. Turn right (south) and drive eight miles to Howard Prairie Dam Road. Turn left (east) and drive 0.25 mile to Sugar Pine Group Camp on the right. Continue 0.75 mile to reach Klum Landing.

Contact: Jackson County Parks, 541/774-8183, fax 541/774-6320, www.jacksoncountyparks.com.

252 EMIGRANT CAMPGROUND

🚶 🚲 ⛵ 🎣 🚍 🐕 🛶 ♿ 🚐 ⛺

Scenic rating: 8

on Emigrant Lake

Map 5.7, page 279

This camp is nestled among the trees above Emigrant Lake, a well-known recreational area. Activities at this park include boating, fishing, hiking, swimming, and waterskiing. There are also two 280-foot water slides. The park has its own swimming cove (unsupervised). Side-trip possibilities include exploring nearby Mount Ashland, where a ski area operates in the winter, as well as visiting Ashland's world-renowned Shakespeare Festival, the Britt Music Festival, and historic Jacksonville.

Campsites, facilities: There are 42 sites for tents or self-contained RVs, 32 sites for RVs of any length (50-amp full hookups), an overflow area, and one group camp area for up to 100 people. Restrooms with flush toilets, coin showers, a dump station, snacks in summer, and a barbecue are available. A group picnic and day-use area that can be reserved are also available. Recreational facilities include horseshoe pits, volleyball, and a playground. Two boat ramps are provided. Laundry and food are within six miles. Some facilities are wheelchair accessible. Leashed pets are permitted in designated areas only.

Reservations, fees: Reservations are accepted for RV sites and the group site at 541/774-8183. Tent sites are $18 per night, RV sites with full hookups are $26 per night, $6 per night per additional vehicle, and $1 per pet per night. The group site is $125–175 per night. Some credit cards are accepted for reservations. Open mid-March–mid-October, weather permitting.

Directions: From Ashland, drive east on Highway 66 for five miles to the campground on the left.

Contact: Jackson County Parks, 541/774-8183, fax 541/774-6320, www.jacksoncounty parks.com.

253 HYATT LAKE

⛵ 🎣 🚍 🐕 🛶 ♿ 🚐 ⛺

Scenic rating: 8

on Hyatt Lake

Map 5.7, page 279

Hyatt Lake campground is situated on the south end of Hyatt Reservoir, which has six miles of shoreline. Fishing is good for brook and rainbow trout and smallmouth bass. The boat speed limit here is 10 mph. The Pacific Crest Trail runs next to the campground. Another campground option is Wildcat, about two miles north, with 12 semi-primitive sites.

Campsites, facilities: There are 54 sites for tents or RVs up to 40 feet long, five horse campsites, one group site for up to 50 people, and 12 walk-in tent sites. Picnic tables and fire grills are provided. Drinking water, restrooms with flush toilets and showers, garbage service, dump station, fish-cleaning station, group kitchen, day-use area, softball fields, volleyball, a playground, horseshoe pits, and two boat ramps are available. Some facilities are wheelchair accessible. Leashed pets are permitted.

Reservations, fees: Reservations are accepted only for the group camp or horse camp at 541/482-2031 or 541/618-2306. Sites are $12–15 per night, $3 per night per additional vehicle, with a 14-day stay limit. Campsites with horse facilities are $10 per night; the group site is $95 per night. Sites at nearby primitive Wildcat Campground are $7 per night. Pacific Crest Trail hikers pay $2 per person per night for camping. Open late April–October, weather permitting.

Directions: From Ashland, drive east on Highway 66 for 17 miles to East Hyatt Lake Road. Turn north and drive three miles to the campground entrance on the left.

Contact: Bureau of Land Management, Ashland Resource Area, 541/618-2200, fax 541/618-2400, www.blm.gov.

254 TOPSY

Scenic rating: 7

on the Upper Klamath River

Map 5.7, page 279

This campground is on Boyle Reservoir near the Upper Klamath River, a good spot for trout fishing. Swimming is not recommended because of the murky water. This is a top river for rafters (experts only, or non-experts with professional, licensed guides). There are Class IV and V rapids about four miles southwest at Caldera, Hells Corner, and Satan's Gate. I flipped at Caldera and ended up swimming for it, finally getting out at an eddy. Luckily, I was wearing a dry suit and the best

lifejacket available, perfect fitting, which saved my butt.

Campsites, facilities: There are 13 sites for RVs up to 40 feet long. Picnic tables and fire grills are provided. Drinking water, vault toilets, garbage service, and a dump station are available. Boat-launching facilities are nearby. A camp host is on-site in season. Some facilities are wheelchair accessible. Leashed pets are permitted.

Reservations, fees: Reservations are not accepted. Sites are $7 per night, $4 per night per additional vehicle, with a 14-day stay limit. Open mid-May–mid-September, weather permitting.

Directions: From Klamath Falls, drive west on Highway 66 for 20 miles to Topsy Road. Turn south on Topsy Road and drive 1.5 miles to the campground on the right.

Contact: Bureau of Land Management, Klamath Falls Resource Area, 541/883-6916, fax 541/884-2097, www.blm.gov.

255 JACKSON

Scenic rating: 7

on the Applegate River in
Rogue River National Forest

Map 5.7, page 279

Jackson campground is nestled in an old mining area at 1,700 feet elevation. Situated between the Applegate River and the road, under a canopy of ponderosa pine, it features a swimming hole and good trout fishing. An interpretive trail is across the road from the campground. Mine tailings can be seen from the camp. Trailers and large RVs are not allowed.

Campsites, facilities: There are eight sites for tents. Picnic tables and fire rings are provided. Drinking water (summer only), garbage service (summer only), and flush toilets are available. Some facilities are wheelchair accessible. Leashed pets are permitted.

Reservations, fees: Reservations are not accepted. Sites are $10 per night, $5 per night per additional vehicle. Open year-round, weather permitting, with limited winter services.

Directions: In Medford on I-5, take the Jacksonville exit to the Jacksonville Highway. Drive west on the Jacksonville Highway (Highway 238) for seven miles to Jacksonville. Bear left on Highway 238 and drive eight miles to the town of Ruch and Upper Applegate Road (County Road 10). Turn left and drive 10 miles to the campground on the right.

Contact: Rogue River National Forest, Siskiyou Mountains District, 541/899-1812, fax 541/899-3888, www.fs.fed.us; concessionaire, 541/899-9220.

256 BEAVER SULPHUR GROUP

🏊 ⛴ 🐕 ♿ ⛺

Scenic rating: 7

on Beaver Creek in
Rogue River National Forest

Map 5.7, page 279

This group camp is well hidden along the banks of Beaver Creek. It is set at an elevation of 2,100 feet and situated in an area with mixed tree cover, including tall Douglas fir, live oak, and maple. The camp is about nine miles from Applegate Reservoir, features attractive shaded sites, and offers easy access to the creek. Some recreational mining is done here; access is provided with a campground reservation.

Campsites, facilities: There is one group site for up to 50 people. Picnic tables and fire grills are provided. Vault toilets and garbage bins (summer only) are available. There is no drinking water. Some facilities are wheelchair accessible. Leashed pets are permitted.

Reservations, fees: Reservations are accepted at 877/444-6777 or www.recreation.gov ($10 reservation fee). The site is $50 per night. Open May–mid-September, weather permitting.

Directions: In Medford on I-5, take the Jacksonville exit to the Jacksonville Highway. Drive west on the Jacksonville Highway (Highway 238) for seven miles to Jacksonville. Bear left

on Highway 238 and drive eight miles to the town of Ruch and Upper Applegate Road (County Road 10). Turn left (south) and drive 9.5 miles to Forest Road 20. Continue three miles to the campground on the right.

Contact: Rogue River National Forest, Siskiyou Mountains District, 541/899-1812, fax 541/899-3888, www.fs.fed.us.

257 HART-TISH RECREATION AREA WALK-IN

🚶 🚴 🏊 ⛴ 🚐 ⛵ 🐕 ♿ 🚗 ⛺

Scenic rating: 7

on Applegate Lake,
Rogue River National Forest

Map 5.7, page 279

This concessionaire-managed campground on Applegate Lake has shaded sites and a great view of the lake. Bald eagles and osprey nest in the area, and it's a treat to watch them fish. A nearby boat launch and boat rentals are available. The walk-in sites are only 200 yards from the parking area.

Campsites, facilities: There are eight walk-in tent sites and eight parking-lot sites for RVs up to 45 feet long. Picnic tables and fire pits are provided. Drinking water, flush toilets, garbage bins, and firewood are available. A day-use area is nearby. A small general store and kayak and bicycle rentals are nearby. Some facilities are wheelchair accessible. Leashed pets are permitted.

Reservations, fees: Reservations are accepted at 877/444-6777 or www.recreation.gov ($10 reservation fee). Sites are $10 per night, $5 per night per additional vehicle. Open mid-April–September, weather permitting.

Directions: In Medford on I-5, take the Jacksonville exit to the Jacksonville Highway. Drive west on the Jacksonville Highway (Highway 238) for seven miles to Jacksonville. Bear left on Highway 238 and drive eight miles to the town of Ruch and Upper Applegate Road (County Road 10). Turn left (south) and drive 15.5 miles to the campground on the left.

Contact: Rogue River National Forest, Siskiyou Mountains District, 541/899-1812, fax 541/899-3888, www.fs.fed.us; concessionaire, 541/899-9220.

258 WATKINS

Scenic rating: 6

on Applegate Reservoir in
Rogue River National Forest

Map 5.7, page 279

On the southwest shore of Applegate Reservoir at an elevation of 2,000 feet, this campground, like Carberry Walk-In and French Gulch, is small and quite primitive—yet pretty—and offers all the same recreation options. Few campers know about this spot, so it usually doesn't fill up quickly. There are good views of the lake and the surrounding Siskiyou Mountains. The Seattle Bar day-use area at the lake is approximately two miles away.

Campsites, facilities: There are 14 walk-in sites for tents. Picnic tables, garbage bins, and fire grills are provided. There is no drinking water. Vault toilets are available. A general store, boat docks, and launching facilities are within two miles. Leashed pets are permitted.

Reservations, fees: Reservations are not accepted. Sites are $10 per night, $5 per night per additional vehicle. Open late May–early September.

Directions: In Medford on I-5, take the Jacksonville exit to the Jacksonville Highway. Drive west on the Jacksonville Highway (Highway 238) for seven miles to Jacksonville. Bear left on Highway 238 and drive eight miles to the town of Ruch and Upper Applegate Road (County Road 10). Turn left (south) and drive 17 miles to the campground.

Contact: Rogue River National Forest, Siskiyou Mountains District, 541/899-1812, fax 541/899-3888, www.fs.fed.us; concessionaire, 541/899-9220.

259 CARBERRY WALK-IN

Scenic rating: 5

near Applegate Reservoir in
Rogue River National Forest

Map 5.7, page 279

You'll find recreational opportunities aplenty, including boating, fishing, hiking, mountain biking, and swimming, at this campground on Cougar Creek near the southwest shore of Applegate Reservoir. Dense forest covers the campsites, providing much-needed shade. This camp is similar to Watkins Walk-in.

Campsites, facilities: There are 11 walk-in sites for tents and three spaces in the parking lot for RVs up to 25 feet long. Picnic tables and fire grills are provided. Vault toilets and drinking water are available. A general store, firewood, boat docks, and launching facilities are within two miles. Some facilities are wheelchair accessible. Leashed pets are permitted.

Reservations, fees: Reservations are not accepted. Sites are $10 per night, $5 per night per additional vehicle. Open late May–early September, weather permitting.

Directions: In Medford on I-5, take the Jacksonville exit to the Jacksonville Highway. Drive west on the Jacksonville Highway (Highway 238) for seven miles to Jacksonville. Bear left on Highway 238 and drive eight miles to the town of Ruch and Upper Applegate Road (County Road 10). Turn left (south) and drive 18 miles to the campground parking area. A short walk is required.

Contact: Rogue River National Forest, Siskiyou Mountains District, 541/899-1812, fax 541/899-3888, www.fs.fed.us; concessionaire, 541/899-9220.

260 SQUAW LAKE HIKE-IN

Scenic rating: 10

on Squaw Lake in Rogue River National Forest

Map 5.7, page 279   **BEST (**

"Paradise Found" should be the name of this campground. Numerous trails crisscross the area around this camp (3,000 feet elevation). The setting—the shore of spectacular Squaw Lake—is more intimate than that of larger Applegate Reservoir to the west. This spot has a mix of developed and primitive sites and is also more popular. In fact, it's the only campground in the district that requires reservations. This area attracts the canoe/kayak crowd. Be sure to call ahead for a space. Campers with disabilities are welcome, but arrangements should be made in advance with the local U.S. Forest Service office.

Campsites, facilities: There are 17 walk-in sites for tents and two family group sites that can accommodate up to 10 people each. Picnic tables and fire grills are provided. Vault toilets are available. Drinking water is available at one end of the camp during the summer only. Garbage must be packed out. Leashed pets are permitted.

Reservations, fees: Reservations are accepted at 877/444-6777 or www.recreation.gov ($10 reservation fee). Sites are $10 per night and group sites are $20–30 per night. Open mid-May–mid-September, weather permitting.

Directions: In Medford on I-5, take the Jacksonville exit to the Jacksonville Highway. Drive west on the Jacksonville Highway (Highway 238) for seven miles to Jacksonville. Bear left on Highway 238 and drive eight miles to the town of Ruch and Upper Applegate Road (County Road 10). Turn left (south) and drive 15 miles to Forest Road 1075. Continue eight miles to Squaw Lake and the trailhead. Hike one mile to the campsites.

Contact: Rogue River National Forest, Siskiyou Mountains District, 541/899-1812, fax 541/899-3888, www.fs.fed.us.

261 WRANGLE

Scenic rating: 10

near the Pacific Crest Trail in Rogue River National Forest

Map 5.7, page 279

This campground is located at the headwaters of Glade Creek in the Siskiyou Mountains at an elevation of 6,400 feet. The Pacific Crest Trail passes near camp. Dutchman Peak Lookout, built in the late 1920s and featured in the National Historic Register, is within five miles. This lovely campground, in a beautiful, high country setting, boasts huge Shasta red firs and views of the Siskiyou Mountains. Wrangle is along the Scenic Siskiyou Loop driving tour.

Campsites, facilities: There are five sites for tents. Picnic tables and fire grills are provided. Vault toilets, a pole shelter, and a community kitchen are available. There is no drinking water, and garbage must be packed out. Leashed pets are permitted.

Reservations, fees: Reservations are not accepted. There is no fee for camping. Open early July–late October, weather permitting.

Directions: In Ashland on I-5, take the Jacksonville exit. Drive east on the Jacksonville Highway to Jacksonville and Highway 238. Bear left on Highway 238 and drive eight miles to the town of Ruch and County Road 10 (Upper Applegate Road). Turn left and drive 9.5 miles to Forest Road 20. Turn left and drive 21 miles to Forest Road 2030. Continue one mile on Forest Road 2030 to the campground.

Contact: Rogue River National Forest, Siskiyou Mountains District, 541/899-1812, fax 541/899-3888, www.fs.fed.us.

262 MOUNT ASHLAND

Scenic rating: 8

on the Pacific Crest Trail in
Klamath National Forest

Map 5.7, page 279   BEST (

Set at 6,600 feet elevation along the Pacific Crest Trail, this beautiful camp is heavily wooded and has abundant wildlife. On a clear day, enjoy great lookouts from nearby Siskiyou Peak, particularly to the south, where California's 14,162-foot Mount Shasta is an awesome sight. Mount Ashland Ski Resort is one mile east of the campground.

Campsites, facilities: There are nine sites for tents or RVs up to 15 feet long, with extremely limited space for RVs. Picnic tables and fire grills are provided. Vault toilets are available. There is no drinking water. Garbage must be packed out. Leashed pets are permitted.

Reservations, fees: Reservations are not accepted. There is no fee for camping but donations are accepted. Open May–late October, weather permitting.

Directions: From Ashland, drive south on I-5 for 12 miles to Mount Ashland Ski Park Road (County Road 993). Turn west and drive 10 miles (the road becomes Forest Road 20) to the campground.

Contact: Klamath National Forest, Happy Camp/Oak Knoll Ranger District, 530/493-2243, fax 530/493-1796, www.fs.fed.us.

263 JACKSON F. KIMBALL STATE PARK

Scenic rating: 7

on the Wood River

Map 5.8, page 280

This primitive state campground at the headwaters of the Wood River is another nice spot just far enough off the main drag to remain a secret. A trail from camp leads to a nearby spring. Fishing from canoe is good on the Wood River.

Campsites, facilities: There are 10 primitive sites for tents or self-contained RVs up to 45 feet long. Picnic tables, fire grills, and garbage bins are provided. Vault toilets are available. There is no drinking water. Leashed pets are permitted.

Reservations, fees: Reservations are not accepted. Sites are $6–10 per night, $5 per night per additional vehicle. Open year-round, weather permitting.

Directions: From Klamath Falls, drive north on U.S. 97 for 21 miles to Highway 62. Turn left (northwest) on Highway 62 and drive 10 miles to Highway 232/Sun Pass Road (near Fort Klamath). Turn right (north) and drive three miles to the campground.

Contact: Collier Memorial State Park, 541/783-2471 or 800/551-6949, www.oregonstateparks.org. (Jackson F. Kimball is managed by Collier Memorial State Park.)

264 CRATER LAKE RESORT

Scenic rating: 6

on the Wood River

Map 5.8, page 280

The campground at Crater Lake Resort is dotted with huge pine trees on the banks of the beautiful, crystal-clear Fort Creek. It's located just outside Fort Klamath, the site of numerous military campaigns against the Modoc people in the late 1800s.

Campsites, facilities: There are 14 sites with full or partial hookups for RVs of any length, six tent sites, nine cabins, and one log cabin. Drinking water, picnic tables, and fire rings are provided. Restrooms with flush toilets and showers, modem access, a recreation hall, and coin laundry are available. Propane gas, a store, café, and ice are within one mile. Leashed pets are permitted.

Reservations, fees: Reservations are accepted. RV sites are $25 per night, $2 per person per night for more than two people, and $2 per pet per night. Tent sites are $5 per person per night. Some credit cards are accepted. Open mid-April–mid-October.

Directions: From Klamath Falls, drive north on U.S. 97 for 21 miles to Highway 62. Bear left on Highway 62 and drive 12.5 miles north to the resort (just before reaching Fort Klamath).

Contact: Crater Lake Resort, 541/381-2349, www.craterlakeresort.com.

265 COLLIER MEMORIAL STATE PARK

Scenic rating: 7

on the Williamson River

Map 5.8, page 280

This campground sits at the confluence of Spring Creek and the Williamson River, both of which are superior trout streams. An area for equestrian campers is situated at a trailhead for horses. A nature trail is also available. The park features a pioneer village and a logging museum. Movies about old-time logging and other activities are shown on weekend nights during the summer.

Campsites, facilities: There are 18 sites for tents or self-contained RVs up to 50 feet long (no hookups), 50 sites for tents or RVs of any length (full hookups), and an area for up to four groups of equestrian campers. Some sites are pull-through. Picnic tables, fire grills, garbage bins, and drinking water are provided. Restrooms with flush toilets and showers, a dump station, firewood, coin laundry, playground, and day-use hitching area are available. Some facilities are wheelchair accessible. Leashed pets are permitted.

Reservations, fees: Reservations are not accepted. Tent sites are $11–18 per night, RV sites are $13–21 per night, $5 per night per additional vehicle. The equestrian area is $12–18 per night and $1.50 per night per horse. Some

credit cards are accepted. Open year-round, weather permitting.

Directions: From Klamath Falls, drive north on U.S. 97 for 28 miles to the park (well signed).

Contact: Collier Memorial State Park, 541/783-2471 or 800/551-6949, www.oregonstateparks.org.

266 WILLIAMSON RIVER

Scenic rating: 6

near Collier Memorial State Park in Winema National Forest

Map 5.8, page 280

Another great little spot is discovered, this one at 4,200 feet elevation, with excellent trout fishing along the banks of the Williamson River, a world-famous fly-fishing river. Mosquitoes are numerous in spring and early summer, which can drive people away. A map of Winema National Forest details the back roads and trails. Collier Memorial State Park provides a nearby side-trip option.

Campsites, facilities: There are 10 sites for tents or RVs up to 30 feet long. Picnic tables, garbage bins, and fire grills are provided. Drinking water and vault toilets are available. A restaurant is within five miles. Some facilities are wheelchair accessible. Leashed pets are permitted.

Reservations, fees: Reservations are not accepted. Sites are $8 per night, $2 per night per additional vehicle. Open late April–late November, weather permitting.

Directions: From Klamath Falls, drive north on U.S. 97 for 30 miles to Chiloquin. Continue north on U.S. 97 for 5.5 miles to Forest Road 9730. Turn right (northeast) and drive one mile to the campground.

Contact: Fremont-Winema National Forests, Klamath Ranger District, 541/885-3400, fax 541/885-3452, www.fs.fed.us.

267 POTTER'S PARK

Scenic rating: 6

on the Sprague River

Map 5.8, page 280

This park on a bluff overlooking the Sprague River is in a wooded setting and bordered by the Winema National Forest. Canoeing and rafting are options here. For the most part, the area east of Klamath Lake doesn't get much attention.

Campsites, facilities: There are 17 tent sites and 22 sites with full hookups for RVs of any length. Drinking water, picnic tables, and fire pits are provided. Restrooms with flush toilets and showers, firewood, a convenience store, coin laundry, pay telephone, and ice are available. Leashed pets are permitted.

Reservations, fees: Reservations are accepted. Sites are $15 per night, plus $2.50 per person per night for more than one adult. Monthly rates are available for RV sites. Open year-round, with limited winter facilities.

Directions: From Klamath Falls, drive north on U.S. 97 for 27 miles to Chiloquin and Sprague River Highway. Turn right (east) on Sprague River Highway and drive 12 miles to the park on the right.

Contact: Potter's Park, 541/783-2253.

268 WALT'S RV PARK

Scenic rating: 7

on the Williamson River

Map 5.8, page 280

This heavily treed campground, across the highway from the Williamson River near Collier Memorial State Park, is one of three camps in the immediate area. The Williamson River has excellent trout fishing. For those looking for a more remote setting, head east to Potter's Park.

Campsites, facilities: There are 20 tent sites and 16 sites with full or partial hookups for RVs up to 40 feet long; some are pull-through sites. Drinking water, picnic tables, and fire pits are provided. Restrooms with flush toilets and showers,

firewood, coin laundry, and ice are available. A café is within 0.25 mile, and there is a store in Chiloquin. Leashed pets are permitted.

Reservations, fees: Reservations are accepted. Sites are $13.75–17.75 per night, $1 per person per night for more than two people, and $1 per night for air-conditioning. Open year-round, weather permitting.

Directions: From Klamath Falls, drive north on U.S. 97 for 24 miles to Chiloquin Junction. Continue north for 0.25 mile to the campground (adjacent to the Chiloquin Ranger Station) on the left.

Contact: Walt's RV Park, 541/783-2537, www.waltsrvpark.com.

269 AGENCY LAKE RESORT

Scenic rating: 5

on Agency Lake

Map 5.8, page 280

This campground sits along Agency Lake in an open, grassy area with some shaded sites. The resort has more than 700 feet of lakefront property, offering world-class trout fishing. Look across the lake and watch the sun set on the Cascades. Note that some sites are filled with monthly renters.

Campsites, facilities: There are 15 tent sites and 25 sites with full or partial hookups for tents or RVs of any length, three cabins, and one rental trailer. Drinking water and picnic tables are provided. Restrooms with flush toilets and showers, a general store, ice, boat docks, launching facilities, and marine gas are available. Leashed pets are permitted.

Reservations, fees: Reservations are accepted. RV sites are $16–20 per night; tent sites are $12–13 per night. Some credit cards are accepted. Open year-round, weather permitting.

Directions: From Klamath Falls, drive north on U.S. 97 for 17 miles to Modoc Point Road. Turn left and drive about 10 miles to the resort on the left.

Contact: Agency Lake Resort, 541/783-2489, www.agencylakeresort.net.

SOUTHEASTERN OREGON

© LINDSAY DOUGLAS/123rf.com

BEST CAMPGROUNDS

◖ Families
Drews Creek, page 415.

◖ Fishing
Drews Creek, page 415.

◖ Waterfront Campgrounds
Campbell Lake, page 412.
Dog Lake, page 415.

◖ Wildlife-Viewing
Jackson Creek, page 408.

Some people think that southeastern Oregon is

one big chunk of nothing. They are only half right. True, this high-desert region is dry and foreboding, with many miles between camps in several areas. However, because this part of Oregon is so under-visited, often you'll have vast areas of great land all to yourself.

Among the southeast's highlights are the Newberry National Volcanic Monument, with East and Paulina Lakes set within its craters; Paulina is one of the best lakes in the western United States for a chance to catch big brown trout. Other great spots include trailhead camps that provide access to Gearhart Mountain Wilderness in Fremont National Forest and camps at Steens Mountain Recreation Lands. Here are also some of the most remote drive-to campgrounds in Oregon, particularly in underused Ochoco and Malheur National Forests, as well as the launch point for one of the best canoe trips, the Owyhee River. This watershed is like nothing most have ever seen. It looks like a miniature Grand Canyon, with steep, orange walls and the river cutting a circuitous route through the desert. I have paddled a canoe through most of it, lucking into a permit from its most remote stretches below the Jarbridge Mountains in Nevada through Idaho and then into Oregon.

Be aware, though, if you tour this area of Oregon; keep an eye on your gas tank and know how far you are from the coming night's campground. You can cover a hellacious number of miles between chances for gas or a camp.

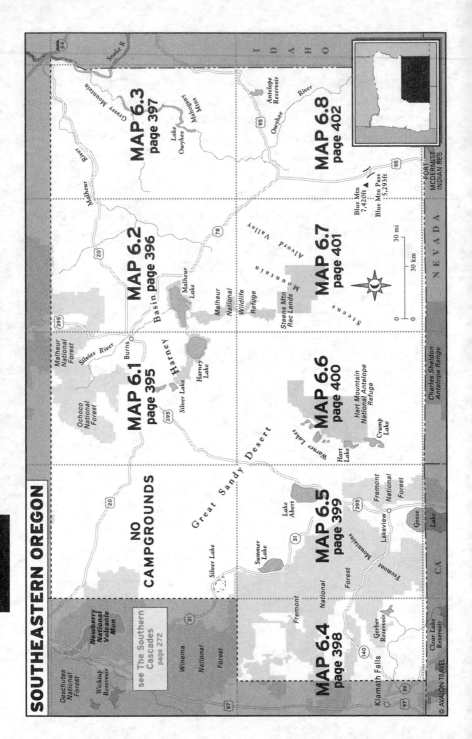

SOUTHEASTERN OREGON

NO CAMPGROUNDS

see The Southern Cascades
page 272

MAP 6.1
page 395

MAP 6.2
Basin page 396

MAP 6.3
page 397

MAP 6.4
page 398

MAP 6.5
page 399

MAP 6.6
page 400

MAP 6.7
page 401

MAP 6.8
page 402

IDAHO

NEVADA

CA

FORT McDERMITT INDIAN RES

Snake R

Grassy Mountain

River

Malheur

Lake Owyhee

Mahogan Mtns

Owyhee River

Antelope Reservoir

Blue Mtn 7,420ft ▲
Blue Mtn Pass 5,293ft

Malheur National Forest

Silvies River

Burns

Harney

Silver Lake

Harney Lake

Malheur Lake

Malheur National Wildlife Refuge

Alvord Valley

Steens Mountain

Steens Mtn Rec Lands

Ochoco National Forest

Great Sandy Desert

Warner Lakes

Hart Lake

Crump Lake

Hart Mountain National Antelope Refuge

Charles Sheldon Antelope Range

Silver Lake

Lake Abert

Summer Lake

Fremont National Forest

Lakeview

Fremont Mountains

Goose Lake

Deschutes National Forest

Newberry National Volcanic Mon

Wickiup Reservoir

Winema National Forest

Fremont National Forest

Klamath Falls

Gerber Reservoir

Clear Lake Reservoir

30 mi
30 km
0
0

© AVALON TRAVEL

Map 6.1

Campgrounds 1-5
Pages 403-404

Malheur
National Forest

Ochoco
National
Forest

Silver Creek

Emigrant Creek

SILVIES RIVER RD

Silvies River

41

45

41

SILVER CREEK RD

HINES LOGGING RD

Chickahominy
Reservoir

Burns

Hines

SPUD
FARM RD

Moon
Reservoir

Silver
Lake

Iron Mtn
5,367ft

Malheur
NWR

Harney Lake

0   5 mi
0   5 km

© AVALON TRAVEL

Foster Lake

Map 6.2

Campgrounds 6-9
Pages 405-406

© AVALON TRAVEL

Map 6.3

Campgrounds 10-13
Pages 406-407

Map 6.4

Campgrounds 14-19
Pages 408-410

6.5

4 5 6 7 8 / 1 2 3

Crater Lake National Park

see The Southern Cascades page 272

Winema National Forest

97

SLM MTN. RD.

Winema National Forest

River

62

Williamson River

Chiloquin

Agency Lake

97

Winema National Forest

Modoc Point

Upper Klamath Lake

140

Long Lake

Klamath Falls

140

Altamont

Round Lake

66

97

39

Merrill

OREGON

14

Fremont National Forest

Williamson River

15

16

27

Thompson Reservoir

17

28

18

Winema National Forest

Sycan River

Fremont National Forest

Sprague River

140

140

Fremont National Forest

Bonanza

GERBER RD.

19

Gerber Reservoir

0   5 mi
0   5 km

© AVALON TRAVEL

Map 6.5

Campgrounds 20-36
Pages 410-417

Map 6.6

Campgrounds 37-38
Pages 417-418

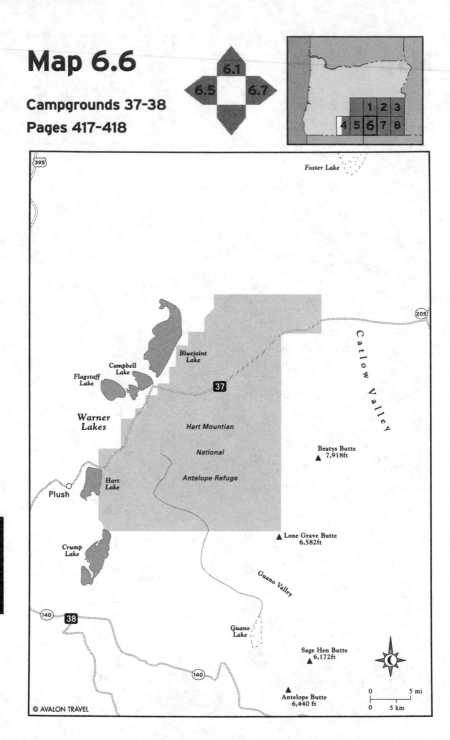

© AVALON TRAVEL

Map 6.7

Campgrounds 39-45

Pages 418-421

Map 6.8

Campgrounds 46-48

Pages 421-422

6.3
6.7

1 2 3
4 5 6 7 8

Jordan Valley
95
Jordan Creek
47 Antelope Reservoir
78
46 Rome
95
Burns Junction
Owyhee River
48 Whitehouse Butte 5,010ft
OREGON IDAHO
Big Grassy Mtn 5,445 ft
Rattlesnake
Battle
Creek
Sacramento Hill 5,375ft
Basque Station
95
Antelope
Creek
River
Owyhee
Blue Mtn 7,420ft
Battle Mtn 6,493ft
Blue Mtn Pass 5,293ft
Horse Hill 6,495ft
Defeat Butte 5,546ft
Oregon Canyon Creek
Little
West
FORT McDERMITT INDIAN RESERVATION
0   5 mi
0   5 km

© AVALON TRAVEL

1 DELINTMENT LAKE

Scenic rating: 7

on Delintment Lake in Malheur National Forest

Map 6.1, page 395

This very pretty, forested camp skirts the shore of Delintment Lake. Originally a beaver pond, the lake was gradually developed to its current size of 62 acres. It is now pretty and blue and is stocked with trout, providing good bank and boat fishing. Note that electric motors only are allowed on the lake. Insider's note: Rainbow trout here average 12–18 inches.

Campsites, facilities: There are 29 sites for tents or RVs up to 30 feet long. Picnic tables and fire grills are provided. Drinking water, vault toilets, garbage service, a group picnic area, and boat-launching facilities are available. Some facilities are wheelchair accessible. Leashed pets are permitted.

Reservations, fees: Reservations are not accepted. Sites are $10 per night, $5 per night for an additional vehicle. Open May–October, weather permitting.

Directions: From Burns, drive southwest on U.S. 20 for three miles to County Road 127. Turn right (northwest) and drive 11 miles to Forest Road 41. Turn left on Forest Road 41 and drive about 26.5 miles (staying on Forest Road 41 at all junctions, paved all the way) to the campground at the lake.

Contact: Malheur National Forest, Emigrant Creek Ranger District, 541/573-4300, fax 541/573-4398, www.fs.fed.us.

2 EMIGRANT

Scenic rating: 4

near Emigrant Creek in Malheur National Forest

Map 6.1, page 395

One of two camps in the immediate area, Emigrant is set at an elevation of 5,200 feet in Malheur National Forest, in a meadow near Emigrant Creek. You'll get peace and quiet here, because this spot is usually not crowded. There's good fly-fishing in the spring and early summer, and several nearby backcountry dirt roads are fun for mountain biking. Falls camp, two miles away, is busier but has drinking water.

Campsites, facilities: There are seven sites for tents or RVs up to 28 feet long. Picnic tables and fire grills are provided. Vault toilets and garbage service are available. There is no drinking water (but drinking water is available nearby at Falls campground). Some facilities are wheelchair accessible. Leashed pets are permitted.

Reservations, fees: Reservations are not accepted. Sites are $8 per night, $4 per night for an additional vehicle. Open May–October, weather permitting.

Directions: From Burns, drive southwest on U.S. 20 for three miles to County Road 127. Turn right (northwest) and drive 25 miles (passing Forest Road 41 on the left) to Forest Road 43 and the junction for Allison Guard Station, Delintment Lake, and Paulina. Turn left on Forest Road 43 and drive 9.75 miles to Forest Road 4340. Turn left and drive on Forest Road 4340-050 to the campground.

Contact: Malheur National Forest, Emigrant Creek Ranger District, 541/573-4300, fax 541/573-4398, www.fs.fed.us.

3 YELLOWJACKET

Scenic rating: 8

on Yellowjacket Lake in Malheur National Forest

Map 6.1, page 395

This quiet and crowd-free campground is set at an elevation of 4,800 feet in the ponderosa pines along the shore of Yellowjacket Lake. Fishing for rainbow trout can be very good in the summer; boats without motors are allowed.

Campsites, facilities: There are 20 sites for

tents or RVs up to 22 feet long. Picnic tables are provided. Drinking water, vault toilets, and garbage service are available. A boat launch is nearby. Leashed pets are permitted.

Reservations, fees: Reservations are not accepted. Sites are $10 per night, $5 per night for an additional vehicle. Open late May–October, weather permitting.

Directions: From Burns, drive southwest on U.S. 20 for three miles to County Road 127. Turn right (northwest) and drive 32 miles to Forest Road 47. Turn right and drive three miles to Forest Road 3745. Turn right and drive one mile to the campground on the right.

Contact: Malheur National Forest, Emigrant Creek Ranger District, 541/573-4300, fax 541/573-4398, www.fs.fed.us.

4 FALLS

Scenic rating: 5

near Emigrant Creek in
Malheur National Forest

Map 6.1, page 395

Falls camp is set in a beautiful meadow next to Emigrant Creek and is surrounded by ponderosa pine forests. This is a great place to see wildflowers in the early summer. A short trail leads to a small waterfall on the creek, which gives the camp its name. Fly-fishing and mountain biking are good here, as well as at nearby Emigrant, located two miles down the road. The elevation is 5,200 feet.

Campsites, facilities: There are six sites for tents or RVs up to 28 feet long. Picnic tables and fire grills are provided. Drinking water, vault toilets, and garbage service are available. Some facilities are wheelchair accessible. Leashed pets are permitted.

Reservations, fees: Reservations are not accepted. Sites are $8 per night, $4 per night for an additional vehicle, except for towed vehicles. Open May–October, weather permitting.

Directions: From Burns, drive southwest on U.S. 20 for three miles to County Road 127. Turn right (northwest) and drive 25 miles (passing Forest Road 41 on the left) to Forest Road 43 and the junction for Allison Guard Station, Delintment Lake, and Paulina. Turn left on Forest Road 43 and drive eight miles to the campground on the left.

Contact: Malheur National Forest, Emigrant Creek Ranger District, 541/573-4300, fax 541/573-4398, www.fs.fed.us.

5 CHICKAHOMINY RESERVOIR

Scenic rating: 4

on Chickahominy Reservoir

Map 6.1, page 395

While a good spot for group camping, this camp is located in the high desert with no shade. Weather conditions can be extreme, so come prepared. The camp is used primarily as an overnight stop for travelers driving through the area. Boats with motors are allowed on the reservoir. There is an access road on the northwest side of the reservoir for day use. The nearest services are five miles east (via U.S. 20) in Riley.

Campsites, facilities: There are 28 sites for tents or RVs up to 35 feet long. Picnic tables, garbage bins, and fire grills are provided. Drinking water (summer season only, subject to fluctuations) and vault toilets are available. A fish-cleaning station is available nearby. Some facilities are wheelchair accessible. Leashed pets are permitted.

Reservations, fees: Reservations are not accepted. Sites are $8 per night per vehicle, with a stay limit of 14 days. Open year-round, with limited winter facilities.

Directions: From Burns, drive west on U.S. 20 for 30 miles to the campground on the right.

Contact: Bureau of Land Management, Burns District, 541/573-4400, fax 541/573-4411, www.blm.gov.

6 JOAQUIN MILLER HORSE CAMP

Scenic rating: 5

in Malheur National Forest

Map 6.2, page 396

Set among mature ponderosa pines and adjacent to a meadow, campsites here are spread out, and there's a fair amount of privacy at this camp. It does receive some highway noise, though. Lots of old logging roads are available for biking, horseback riding, and walking. The camp gets low use, and while it caters to horse campers, all are welcome. Campers with horses are strongly advised to arrive early, before the weekend, to claim the campsites nearest to the corrals.

Campsites, facilities: There are 12 sites for tents or RVs up to 28 feet long. Picnic tables and fire rings are provided. Drinking water, vault toilets, and garbage service are available. Stock facilities include four corrals and hitching rails. Leashed pets are permitted.

Reservations, fees: Reservations are not accepted. Sites are $8 per night, $4 per night per additional vehicle. Open mid-May–November, weather permitting.

Directions: From Burns, drive north on U.S. 395 for 19 miles to the campground on the left (this turnoff is easy to miss; watch for a very small green sign on the right that says Joaquin Miller Horse Camp).

Contact: Malheur National Forest, Emigrant Creek Ranger District, 541/573-4300, fax 541/573-4398, www.fs.fed.us.

7 IDLEWILD

Scenic rating: 8

in Devine Canyon in Malheur National Forest

Map 6.2, page 396

This campground sits at an elevation of 5,300 feet in Devine Canyon, a designated winter Sno-Park that's popular with locals for snowmobiling and cross-country skiing. Several hiking and biking trailheads start here, including the Divine Summit Interpretive Loop Trail and the Idlewild Loop Trail. Since it provides easy access and a pretty setting, it's also a popular spot for visitors traveling up U.S. 395 and in need of a stopover. Bird-watching for white-headed woodpeckers and goshawks is popular. Expect to hear some highway noise. But the ponderosa pine forest and area trails are so beautiful that this area can feel divine, even if Devine Canyon and neighboring Devine Ridge were named back in the good old days when nobody worried about spelling.

Campsites, facilities: There are 26 sites for tents and five sites for RVs up to 28 feet long. Picnic tables and fire grills are provided. Drinking water, vault toilets, picnic areas, and garbage service are available. A group shelter can be reserved. Some facilities are wheelchair accessible. Leashed pets are permitted.

Reservations, fees: Reservations are not accepted. Sites are $10 per night, $5 per night for an additional vehicle, except for towed vehicles. Open late May–mid-October, weather permitting.

Directions: From Burns, drive north on U.S. 395 for 17 miles to the campground on the right.

Contact: Malheur National Forest, Emigrant Creek Ranger District, 541/573-4300, fax 541/573-4398, www.fs.fed.us.

8 CHUKAR PARK

Scenic rating: 7

on the north fork of the Malheur River

Map 6.2, page 396

Chukar Park campground hugs the banks of the north fork of the Malheur River. The general area provides habitat for chukar, an upland game bird species. Hunting can be good in season during the fall but requires much hiking in rugged terrain. Trout fishing is also popular here. BLM asks that visitors please respect the surrounding private property.

Campsites, facilities: There are 18 sites for tents or RVs up to 28 feet long. Picnic tables, fire grills, and garbage service are provided. Drinking water (May–October only) and vault toilets are available. Firewood is not available. Leashed pets are permitted.

Reservations, fees: Reservations are not accepted. Sites are $5 per night per vehicle, with a 14-day stay limit. Open year-round, with limited winter facilities.

Directions: From Burns, drive north on U.S. 395 for three miles to U.S. 20. Take U.S. 20 east and drive 55 miles to Juntura and Beulah Reservoir Road. Turn northwest and drive six miles to the campground.

Contact: Bureau of Land Management, Vale District, 541/473-3144, fax 541/473-6213, www.blm.gov/or.

9 OASIS MOTEL & RV PARK

Scenic rating: 6

in Juntura

Map 6.2, page 396

One of the only camps in the area, this well-maintained RV park is close to Chukar Park. The general area provides habitat for chukar, an upland game bird species. Hunting during the fall and trout fishing are recreation opportunities here.

Campsites, facilities: There are 22 sites with full hookups for RVs of any length, two cabins, and seven motel rooms. Some sites are pull-through. Picnic tables are provided. Restrooms with flush toilets and showers, a café, and ice are available. Leashed pets are permitted.

Reservations, fees: Reservations are not accepted. Sites are $17 per night and $6 per night per pet. Some credit cards are accepted. Open year-round.

Directions: From Burns, drive north on U.S. 395 for three miles to U.S. 20. Turn east and drive 55 miles to Juntura (a very small town). The park is on the left along U.S. 20.

Contact: Oasis Motel & RV Park, 541/277-3605, fax 541/277-3434.

10 LAKE OWYHEE STATE PARK

Scenic rating: 7

on Owyhee Lake

Map 6.3, page 397

There are two campgrounds here: McCormack and Indian Creek, which are located 1.5 miles apart. This state park is situated along the shore of 53-mile-long Owyhee Lake, a good lake for waterskiing in the day and fishing for warm-water species in the morning and evening. Owyhee is famous for its superb bass fishing; the place even has floating restrooms. Other highlights include views of unusual geological formations and huge rock pinnacles. Bighorn sheep, coyotes, golden eagles, mountain lions, mule deer, pronghorn antelope, and wild horses live in the area.

Campsites, facilities: McCormack has 31 sites with partial hookups for tents and RVs of any length, eight tent sites, and two tepees. Indian Creek has 26 sites with partial hookups for tents or RVs up to 50 feet long and nine tent sites. Drinking water, picnic tables, and fire grills are provided. Vault toilets, garbage bins, firewood, a dump station, and a picnic area are available. Restrooms with flush toilets and showers are available at McCormack. Boat docks, launching facilities, fuel, and ice are available at the park. Marine fuel is available at Indian Creek. Some facilities are wheelchair accessible. Leashed pets are permitted.

Reservations, fees: Reservations are accepted at 800/452-5687 or www.reserveamerica.com ($8 reservation fee). RV sites are $12–20 per night, tent sites are $12–17 per night, tepees are $27–36 per night, and $5 per night for an additional vehicle. Some credit cards are accepted. Open April–October.

Directions: From Ontario (near the Oregon/Idaho border), drive south on U.S. 20/26 for six miles to the Nyssa exit. Turn south and drive eight miles to Nyssa and Highway 201. Turn left (southeast) on Highway 201 and drive eight miles to Owyhee. Turn east and drive about 20 miles to road's end and the entrance to the park, approximately 33 miles from Nyssa.

Contact: Lake Owyhee State Park, 541/339-2331 or 800/551-6949, www.oregonstateparks.org.

11 COW LAKES

Scenic rating: 6

near Cow Lakes

Map 6.3, page 397

Cow Lakes is a little-used campground adjacent to an old lava flow. The lake is shallow and murky, which makes fishing popular here. The campsites are open and treeless, and the road is rutted and rough in places.

Campsites, facilities: There are 10 sites for tents or small RVs. Picnic tables and fire rings are provided. A vault toilet and a primitive boat ramp are available. No drinking water or firewood is available, and garbage must be packed out. Leashed pets are permitted.

Reservations, fees: Reservations are not accepted. There is no fee for camping. Open year-round, weather permitting.

Directions: From Burns Junction, drive east on U.S. 95 for 30 miles to Danner Loop Road. Turn left (north) and drive 14 miles (past Danner) to Cow Lakes and the campground.

Contact: Bureau of Land Management, Vale District, 541/473-3144, fax 541/473-6213, www.blm.gov.

12 LESLIE GULCH

Scenic rating: 6

on Owyhee Lake

Map 6.3, page 397

This campground sits on the eastern shore of Owyhee Lake, about 20 miles from the Oregon/Idaho border. Hiking, warm-water fishing, and waterskiing are among the recreation options in this high-desert area. Lake Owyhee State Park provides the other developed recreation destination on the lake.

Campsites, facilities: There are 12 sites for tents or RVs up to 20 feet long. Picnic tables and garbage service are provided. Vault toilets are available. There is no drinking water. Boat-launching facilities (for boats less than 17 feet long) are available on-site. Leashed pets are permitted.

Reservations, fees: Reservations are not accepted. There is no fee for camping. Open mid-March–mid-November.

Directions: From U.S. 95 where it crosses the Idaho/Oregon border, drive north for five miles to McBride Creek Road. Turn west and drive 10 miles to Leslie Gulch Road. Turn left (west) and drive 15 miles to the campground.

Contact: Bureau of Land Management, Vale District, 541/473-3144, fax 541/473-6213, www.blm.gov.

13 BIRCH CREEK HISTORIC RANCH

Scenic rating: 9

near the Owyhee River

Map 6.3, page 397

This is one of the most remote campgrounds in Oregon. When I stayed here, it was known as "Hole in the Ground." The official name, Birch Creek Ranch, is the collective name for two ranches founded about 100 years ago. The remote setting is an oasis in the arid, scenic Owyhee River Canyon, its green fields contrasting strongly with the sun-drenched cream- and chocolate-colored formations and the red and black volcanic rocks that soar up from the edges of its narrow meadows. This section of the Owyhee River holds Class III, IV, and V+ rapids. Hiking options include the Jordan Crater, a 4,000-year-old caldera offering domes, kipukas, lava tubes, trenches, and more. The Owyhee Canyon rim looks like a miniature Grand Canyon. This camp/ranch's stone walls, water wheel, and barn contribute to its inclusion on the National Register of Historic Places. I canoed nearly the entire length of the Owyhee, from the headwaters below the Jarbridge Mountains in Nevada, through Idaho and into Oregon.

Campsites, facilities: There are five sites for tents or small RVs. Picnic tables and fire rings are provided. A vault toilet is available. There is no drinking water, and garbage must be packed out. A camp host is on-site. There is access to the Owyhee River by reservation for non-motorized boats only. Leashed pets are permitted.

Reservations, fees: Reservations are not accepted. There is no fee for camping. Open mid-March–mid-October, weather permitting.

Directions: From Jordan Valley, take U.S. 95 north for 10 miles to Cow Creek Road at the Jordan Craters sign. Turn left (west) on Cow Creek Road and follow BLM Owyhee River access signs 28 miles to campground. High-clearance 4WD vehicles recommended. Road may be impassable when wet.

Contact: Bureau of Land Management, Vale District, 541/473-3144, fax 541/473-6213, www.blm.gov.

14 JACKSON CREEK

Scenic rating: 8

on Jackson Creek in Winema National Forest

Map 6.4, page 398   **BEST**

Jackson Creek is a remote campground in a beautiful stand of old-growth ponderosa pine

at an elevation of 4,600 feet. Horseback riding and mountain biking are popular. Wildlife-viewing can be outstanding some years. Note that there are many mosquitoes in spring and early summer, so bring repellent.

Campsites, facilities: There are 12 sites for tents or RVs up to 25 feet long. Picnic tables and fire grills are provided. Vault toilets are available. There is no drinking water. Garbage must be packed out. Leashed pets are permitted.

Reservations, fees: Reservations are not accepted. There is no fee. Open year-round, weather permitting.

Directions: From Chemult and Highway 97, drive south for 25 miles to Silver Lake Road (County Road 676). Turn left (northeast) and drive 22 miles to Forest Road 49. Turn right (southeast) and drive five miles to the camp.

Contact: Fremont-Winema National Forests, Chemult Ranger District, 541/365-7001, fax 541/365-7019, www.fs.fed.us.

15 SILVER CREEK MARSH

Scenic rating: 4

near Silver Creek in Fremont National Forest

Map 6.4, page 398

A trailhead and terminus for segments of the National Recreational Trail are located at this small, quiet, and primitive camp that gets little attention. It's a short walk to the creek, a popular fishing spot, and the camp is also close to a wildlife area boundary.

Campsites, facilities: There are 14 sites for tents or RVs up to 50 feet long. Picnic tables and fire grills are provided. Drinking water, vault toilets, garbage bins, and hitching rails and corrals for horses are available. Note that drinking water and garbage service availability is uncertain. Firewood is available nearby. Leashed pets are permitted.

Reservations, fees: Reservations are not accepted. Sites are $6 per night, $2 per night per additional vehicle. Open May–mid-

November, weather permitting. There is a 14-day stay limit.

Directions: From Bend, drive south on U.S. 97 for 32 miles to Highway 31. Turn southeast on Highway 31 and drive 48 miles to County Road 4-11 (one mile west of the town of Silver Lake). Turn right and drive six miles (the road becomes Forest Road 27). Continue south for five miles to the campground entrance road on the left.

Contact: Fremont-Winema National Forests, Silver Lake Ranger District, 541/576-2107, fax 541/576-2450, www.fs.fed.us.

16 THOMPSON RESERVOIR
🚶‍♂️ 🏊 🛶 🚤 🎣 🦌 🚐 ⛺

Scenic rating: 3

on Thompson Reservoir in
Fremont National Forest

Map 6.4, page 398

Located on the north shore of Thompson Reservoir among black-bark ponderosa pines the height of telephone poles, this simple and pretty camp features shaded sites close to the water. The area is popular for fishing and boating. Water in the reservoir fluctuates and sometimes nearly dries up altogether in late summer.

Campsites, facilities: There are 19 sites for tents or RVs up to 22 feet long, plus a separate group camping area. Picnic tables and fire grills are provided. Drinking water, garbage bins, and vault toilets are available. Boat-launching facilities are nearby. Leashed pets are permitted.

Reservations, fees: Reservations are not accepted. Sites are $6 per night, $2 per night per additional vehicle. Open May–mid-November, weather permitting.

Directions: From Bend, drive south on U.S. 97 for 32 miles to Highway 31. Turn southeast on Highway 31 and drive 48 miles to County Road 4-11 (one mile west of the town of Silver Lake). Turn right and drive six miles (the road becomes Forest Road 27) and continue

south for nine miles to the campground entrance road. Turn left and drive one mile to the camp.

Contact: Fremont-Winema National Forests, Silver Lake Ranger District, 541/576-2107, fax 541/576-2450, www.fs.fed.us.

17 EAST BAY
🚶‍♂️ 🏊 🛶 🚤 🐕 ♿ 🚐 ⛺

Scenic rating: 3

on Thompson Reservoir in
Fremont National Forest

Map 6.4, page 398

This campground on the east shore of Thompson Reservoir has paved roads, but it's still a long way from home, so be sure to bring all of your supplies with you. A day-use area is adjacent to the camp. Nearby Silver Creek Marsh Campground provides an even more primitive setting along a stream.

Campsites, facilities: There are 17 sites for tents or RVs up to 50 feet long. Picnic tables and fire grills are provided. Drinking water, garbage bins, vault toilets, and a fishing pier are available. Boat-launching facilities are nearby. Some facilities are wheelchair accessible. Leashed pets are permitted.

Reservations, fees: Reservations are not accepted. Sites are $10 per night, $4 per night per extra vehicle. Open May–mid-November, weather permitting.

Directions: From Bend, drive south on U.S. 97 for 32 miles to Highway 31. Turn southeast on Highway 31 and drive 49 miles to Silver Lake. Continue east a short distance on Highway 31 to Forest Road 28. Turn right on Forest Road 28 and drive 13 miles to Forest Road 014. Turn right on Forest Road 014 and drive two miles to the campground.

Contact: Fremont-Winema National Forests, Silver Lake Ranger District, 541/576-2107, fax 541/576-2450, www.fs.fed.us.

18 HEAD OF THE RIVER
🎣 🐕 🚲 ⛺

Scenic rating: 8

on the Williamson River in
Winema National Forest

Map 6.4, page 398

Almost nobody knows about this small, extremely remote spot on the edge of a meadow in the lodgepole and ponderosa pines, though hunters use it in the fall. The only camp for miles around, it's set at 4,500 feet elevation along the Williamson River headwaters, where you can actually see the beginning of the river bubbling up from underground springs.

Campsites, facilities: There are five sites for tents or RVs up to 30 feet long. Picnic tables, garbage bins, and fire pits are provided. Vault toilets are available. There is no drinking water. Leashed pets are permitted.

Reservations, fees: Reservations are not accepted. There is no fee for camping. Open Memorial Day weekend–late November, weather permitting.

Directions: From Klamath Falls, drive north on U.S. 97 for 30 miles to Chiloquin and Sprague River Highway. Turn right (east) on Sprague River Highway and drive five miles to Williamson River Road. Turn left (northeast) and drive 20 miles to Forest Road 4648. Turn left (north) on Forest Road 4648 and drive 0.5 mile to the campground.

Contact: Fremont-Winema National Forests, Klamath Ranger District, 541/885-3400, fax 541/885-3452, www.fs.fed.us.

19 GERBER RESERVOIR
🚶 🛶 🚤 🐎 🐕 ♿ 🚲 ⛺

Scenic rating: 6

on Gerber Reservoir

Map 6.4, page 398

This camp can be found at an elevation of 4,800 feet alongside the west shore of Gerber Reservoir. Off the beaten path, Gerber attracts mainly locals. Recreation options include

boating (10-mph speed limit), fishing, and hiking. Swimming is not popular here because the water is murky with algae.

Campsites, facilities: There are 50 sites for tents or RVs up to 30 feet long. Picnic tables and fire grills are provided. Drinking water, a dump station, vault toilets, two boat ramps with docks, and a fish-cleaning station are available. Garbage service is available in summer only. Some facilities are wheelchair accessible. Leashed pets are permitted.

Reservations, fees: Reservations are not accepted. Sites are $7 per night, $4 per night for an additional vehicle. Open year-round, with drinking water and garbage service available May–mid-September, weather permitting.

Directions: From Klamath Falls, drive east on Highway 140 for 16 miles to Dairy and Highway 70. Turn right (south) on Highway 70 and drive seven miles to Bonanza and East Langell Valley Road. Turn left (east) on East Langell Valley Road and drive 11 miles to Gerber Road. Turn left on Gerber Road and drive eight miles to the campground on the right.

Contact: Bureau of Land Management, Klamath Falls Resource Area, 541/883-6916, fax 541/884-2097, www.blm.gov.

20 LEE THOMAS
🚶 🛶 🐎 ♿ 🚲 ⛺

Scenic rating: 6

near the north fork of the Sprague River in
Fremont National Forest

Map 6.5, page 399

Lee Thomas is located near the trailhead that provides access to the Dead Horse Rim Trail. Nestled along the north fork of the Sprague River in the interior of Fremont National Forest, this small, cozy camp is a genuine hideaway, with all the necessities provided. It is set in a meadow at an elevation of 6,306 feet and, like Sandhill Crossing Campground (two miles downstream), it's popular with anglers and hunters in the fall.

Campsites, facilities: There are seven sites for

tents or RVs up to 16 feet long. Picnic tables and fire grills are provided. Drinking water and vault toilets are available. Garbage must be packed out. Some facilities are wheelchair accessible. Leashed pets are permitted.

Reservations, fees: Reservations are not accepted. There is no fee for camping. Open June–late October, weather permitting.

Directions: From Lakeview, drive north on U.S. 395 for 23 miles to Highway 31. Turn northwest and drive 22 miles to Paisley. Continue on Highway 31 for 0.5 mile to Mill Street. Turn west on Mill Street and drive 20 miles (the road becomes Forest Road 33) and continue to the T intersection with Forest Road 28. Turn left on Forest Road 28 and drive 0.5 miles to Forest Road 3411. Turn right and drive one mile to the campground on the right.

Contact: Fremont-Winema National Forests, Paisley Ranger District, 541/943-3114, fax 541/943-4479, www.fs.fed.us.

21 SANDHILL CROSSING

Scenic rating: 6

on the north fork of the Sprague River in Fremont National Forest

Map 6.5, page 399

If you're looking for a combination of beauty and solitude, you've found it. This camp (6,306 feet elevation) sits on the banks of the designated Wild and Scenic North Fork Sprague River, where fishing is superior. Although a low-use camp, it is popular with anglers and hunters in the fall. A nearby trailhead leads into the Gearheart Wilderness.

Campsites, facilities: There are five sites for tents or RVs up to 25 feet long. Picnic tables and fire grills are provided. Vault toilets and drinking water are available. Garbage must be packed out. Some facilities are wheelchair accessible. Leashed pets are permitted.

Reservations, fees: Reservations are not accepted. There is no fee for camping. Open June–October, weather permitting.

Directions: From Lakeview, drive north on U.S. 395 for 23 miles to Highway 31. Turn northwest and drive 22 miles to Paisley. Continue on Highway 31 for 0.5 mile to Mill Street. Turn west on Mill Street and drive 20 miles (the road becomes Forest Road 33); continue to the T intersection with Forest Road 28. Turn right and drive 11 miles to Forest Road 3411. Turn left and drive eight miles to the campground on the left.

Contact: Fremont-Winema National Forests, Paisley Ranger District, 541/943-3114, fax 541/943-4479, www.fs.fed.us.

22 DEAD HORSE LAKE

Scenic rating: 9

on Dead Horse Lake in Fremont National Forest

Map 6.5, page 399

The shore of Dead Horse Lake is home to this camp sitting at 7,372 feet elevation; it generally fills up on most weekends and holidays. A hiking trail winds around the perimeter of the lake, hooking up with other trails along the way. One original Civilian Conservation Corps canoe, a relic of the 1930s, remains in the lake. No gas motors are permitted on the lake, and a 5-mph speed limit is in effect. Nearby Fremont National Forest provides good side trips.

Campsites, facilities: There are 16 sites for tents or RVs up to 25 feet long and a separate group area for up to 40 people. Picnic tables and fire grills are provided. Drinking water and vault toilets are available, but garbage must be packed out. A boat launch and day-use area are nearby. Leashed pets are permitted.

Reservations, fees: Reservations are not accepted. Sites are $6 per night, $2 per night per additional vehicle. Open July–October, weather permitting.

Directions: From Lakeview, drive north on U.S. 395 for 23 miles to Highway 31. Turn northwest and drive 22 miles to Paisley.

Continue on Highway 31 for 0.5 mile to Mill Street. Turn west on Mill Street and drive 20 miles (the road becomes Forest Road 033); continue to the T intersection with Forest Road 28. Turn right and drive 11 miles (watch for the turn to Campbell-Dead Horse Lakes) to Forest Road 033. Turn left and drive three miles (gravel road) to the campground.

Contact: Fremont-Winema National Forests, Paisley Ranger District, 541/943-3114, fax 541/943-4479, www.fs.fed.us.

23 CAMPBELL LAKE
🏕 🏊 🚣 🛶 🐕 🚙 ⛺

Scenic rating: 9

on Campbell Lake in Fremont National Forest

Map 6.5, page 399   BEST (

This campground on the pebbled shore of Campbell Lake is located near Dead Horse Lake Campground. These high-elevation, crystal-clear lakes were formed during the glacier period, evidence of which can be found on the nearby Lakes Trail system. Both camps are very busy, filling up most weekends in July and August. No gas motors are permitted on Campbell Lake, and a 5-mph speed limit is in effect. A U.S. Forest Service map details the back roads.

Campsites, facilities: There are 16 sites for tents or RVs up to 25 feet long. Picnic tables and fire grills are provided. Drinking water and vault toilets are available. A boat launch and day-use area are adjacent to the camp. Boats with electric motors are permitted, but gas motors are prohibited. Garbage must be packed out. Leashed pets are permitted.

Reservations, fees: Reservations are not accepted. Sites are $6 per night, $2 per night per additional vehicle. Open July–late October, weather permitting.

Directions: From Lakeview, drive north on U.S. 395 for 23 miles to Highway 31. Turn northwest and drive 22 miles to Paisley. Continue on Highway 31 for 0.5 mile to Mill Street. Turn west on Mill Street and drive

20 miles (the road becomes Forest Road 33) and continue to the T intersection with Forest Road 28. Turn right and drive eight miles to Forest Road 033. Turn left and drive two miles to the campground.

Contact: Fremont-Winema National Forests, Paisley Ranger District, 541/943-3114, fax 541/943-4479, www.fs.fed.us.

24 MARSTER SPRING
🏕 🎣 🐕 🚐 ⛺

Scenic rating: 6

on the Chewaucan River in Fremont National Forest

Map 6.5, page 399

The largest of several popular camps in this river corridor, Marster Spring sits right on the banks of the Chewaucan Riverr at an elevation of 4,845 feet. This pretty campground is set among ponderosa pine trees in a good fishing area, yet is close to the town of Paisley. The Fremont National Recreation Trail is accessible at the Chewaucan Crossing Trailhead, 0.25 mile to the south.

Campsites, facilities: There are 10 sites for tents or RVs up to 22 feet long. Picnic tables and fire grills are provided. Drinking water and vault toilets are available. Leashed pets are permitted.

Reservations, fees: Reservations are not accepted. Sites are $6 per night, $2 per night per additional vehicle. Open May–October, weather permitting.

Directions: From Lakeview, drive north on U.S. 395 for 23 miles to Highway 31. Turn northwest and drive 22 miles to Paisley. Continue on Highway 31 for 0.5 mile to Mill Street. Turn west on Mill Street and drive 7.5 miles (the road becomes Forest Road 33) to the campground on the left.

Contact: Fremont-Winema National Forests, Paisley Ranger District, 541/943-3114, fax 541/943-4479, www.fs.fed.us.

25 CORRAL CREEK
🥾 🚣 🐎 ♿ �m ⛺

Scenic rating: 4

near the Gearhart Mountain Wilderness in
Fremont National Forest

Map 6.5, page 399

Set along Corral Creek, this camp is adjacent
to a trailhead that provides access into the
Gearhart Mountain Wilderness, making it a
prime base camp for a backpacking trip. Access is also available from camp to the Palisade
Rocks, a worthwhile side trip. Another option
is Quartz Mountain Sno-Park, which is 14
miles east of the campground. The elevation
is 6,000 feet.

Campsites, facilities: There are six sites for
tents or RVs up to 22 feet long. Picnic tables
and fire grills are provided. Vault toilets are
available. There is no drinking water, and garbage must be packed out. Stock facilities include hitching posts, stalls, and corrals. Some
facilities are wheelchair accessible. Leashed
pets are permitted.

Reservations, fees: Reservations are not accepted. There is no fee for camping. Open
mid-May–late October, weather permitting.

Directions: From Klamath Falls, drive east on
Highway 140 for 53 miles to the town of Bly.
Continue east on Highway 140 for one mile
to Campbell Road. Turn left and drive 0.5
mile to Forest Road 34. Turn right and drive
15 miles to Forest Road 012. Turn right and
drive to the campground.

Contact: Fremont-Winema National Forests, Bly Ranger District, 541/947-6300, fax
541/947-6375, www.fs.fed.us.

26 DAIRY POINT
🚣 🐎 �m ⛺

Scenic rating: 6

on Dairy Creek in Fremont National Forest

Map 6.5, page 399

This campground, elevation 5,200 feet, is situated next to the Dairy Creek Bridge in a stand

of ponderosa pine and white fir at the edge of a
large and open meadow. The setting is beautiful and peaceful, with a towering backdrop
of mountains. In the spring, wildflowers are
a sight to behold; bird-watching can also be
excellent this time of year. Fishing and inner
tubing are popular activities at Dairy Creek.
Warning: This campground is suitable for
large groups and is often full on holidays and
most weekends.

Campsites, facilities: There are four sites for
tents or self-contained RVs up to 25 feet long.
Picnic tables and fire grills are provided. A
vault toilet and drinking water are available.
Garbage must be packed out. Leashed pets
are permitted.

Reservations, fees: Reservations are not accepted. There is no fee for camping. Open
mid-May–October, weather permitting.

Directions: From Lakeview, drive north on
U.S. 395 for 23 miles to Highway 31. Turn
northwest and drive 22 miles to Paisley. Continue on Highway 31 for 0.5 mile to Mill
Street. Turn west on Mill Street and drive 20
miles (the road becomes Forest Road 33); continue to the T intersection with Forest Road
28. Turn left and drive two miles (crossing
the Dairy Creek Bridge) to Forest Road 3428.
Turn left and drive to the campground (just
past the intersection on the left).

Contact: Fremont-Winema National Forests,
Paisley Ranger District, 541/943-3114, fax
541/943-4479, www.fs.fed.us.

27 HAPPY CAMP
🚣 🐎 �m ⛺

Scenic rating: 6

on Dairy Creek in Fremont National Forest

Map 6.5, page 399

Here's a pleasant spot with open sites along
Dairy Creek, though only one site is close
to the water. The camp features some old
1930s Civilian Conservation Corps shelters,
preserved in their original state. Fishing is
available for rainbow trout, though the creek

is no longer stocked. The camp sits at 5,289 feet elevation.

Campsites, facilities: There are nine sites for tents or RVs up to 16 feet long. Picnic tables and fire grills are provided. Vault toilets, picnic shelters, and horseshoe pits are available. There is no drinking water (drinking water is available 1.5 miles west on Forest Road 047 at Clear Spring). Garbage must be packed out. Leashed pets are permitted.

Reservations, fees: Reservations are not accepted. There is no fee for camping. Open mid-May–late October, weather permitting.

Directions: From Lakeview, drive north on U.S. 395 for 23 miles to Highway 31. Turn northwest and drive 22 miles to Paisley. Continue on Highway 31 for 0.5 mile to Mill Street. Turn west on Mill Street and drive 20 miles (the road becomes Forest Road 33); continue to the T intersection with Forest Road 28. Turn left and drive two miles (just before Dairy Creek) to Forest Road 047. Turn right and drive two miles to the campground on the left.

Contact: Fremont-Winema National Forests, Paisley Ranger District, 541/943-3114, fax 541/943-4479, www.fs.fed.us.

28 LOFTON RESERVOIR

Scenic rating: 6

on Lofton Reservoir in
Fremont National Forest

Map 6.5, page 399

This remote campground sits on the shore of Lofton Reservoir, a small lake that can provide the best trout fishing in this region. Other nearby lakes are accessible by forest roads. This area marks the beginning of the Great Basin, a high-desert area that extends to Idaho. A large fire burned much of the surrounding forest about 20 years ago, making this campground an oasis of sorts.

Campsites, facilities: There are 26 sites for tents or RVs up to 25 feet long. Picnic tables

and fire grills are provided. Vault toilets and garbage bins are available. Garbage service may be discontinued, so prepared to pack out your trash. There is no drinking water. Boat docks and launching facilities are nearby. A camp host is on-site. Some facilities are wheelchair accessible. Leashed pets are permitted.

Reservations, fees: Reservations are not accepted. Sites are $6 per night, $2 per night per additional vehicle. Open mid-May–late October, weather permitting.

Directions: From Klamath Falls, drive east on Highway 140 for 54 miles to Bly. Continue east on Highway 140 for 13 miles to Forest Road 3715. Turn right and drive seven miles to Forest Road 013. Turn left on Forest Road 013 and drive one mile to the campground.

Contact: Fremont-Winema National Forests, Bly Ranger District, 541/947-6300, fax 541/947-6375, www.fs.fed.us.

29 COTTONWOOD RECREATION AREA

Scenic rating: 6

on Cottonwood Meadow Lake in
Fremont National Forest

Map 6.5, page 399

Cottonwood Recreation Area, along the upper shore of Cottonwood Meadow Lake, is one of the better spots in the vicinity for fishing and hiking. The camp is set at an elevation of 6,130 feet in a forested setting with aspen and many huge ponderosa pines. Boats with electric motors are allowed on the lake, but gas motors are prohibited. Three hiking trails wind around the lake, and facilities for horses include hitching posts, feeders, water, and corrals.

Campsites, facilities: There are 12 sites for tents or RVs up to 35 feet long and nine tent sites. Picnic tables and fire grills are provided. Drinking water and vault toilets are available, but garbage must be packed out. A camp host is on-site. Boat docks are nearby. No gasoline motors are allowed on the lake. The boating speed limit is 5 mph. Leashed pets are permitted.

Reservations, fees: Reservations are not accepted. Sites are $6 per night, $2 per night per additional vehicle. Open early June–mid-October, weather permitting.

Directions: From Lakeview, drive west on Highway 140 for 21 miles to Forest Road 3870. Turn right and drive about 10 miles to the campground.

Contact: Fremont-Winema National Forests, Lakeview Ranger District, 541/353-2700, fax 541/947-6375, www.fs.fed.us.

30 MUD CREEK

Scenic rating: 4

on Mud Creek in Fremont National Forest

Map 6.5, page 399

Remote and quiet, this camp sits at 6,600 feet elevation in an isolated stand of lodgepole pines along the banks of Mud Creek. Fishing in Mud Creek is fairly good, and Drake Peak (8,405 feet elevation) is nearby. There are no other camps in the immediate vicinity.

Campsites, facilities: There are seven sites for tents or RVs up to 16 feet long. Picnic tables and fire grills are provided. Drinking water and vault toilets are available. Garbage must be packed out. Leashed pets are permitted.

Reservations, fees: Reservations are not accepted. There is no fee for camping. Open June–mid-October, weather permitting.

Directions: From Lakeview, drive five miles north on U.S. 395 to Highway 140. Turn right on Highway 140 and drive eight miles to Forest Road 3615. Turn left and drive seven miles to the campground.

Contact: Fremont-Winema National Forests, Lakeview Ranger District, 541/353-2700, fax 541/947-6375, www.fs.fed.us.

31 DOG LAKE

Scenic rating: 5

on Dog Lake in Fremont National Forest

Map 6.5, page 399   BEST (

This campground is located on the west shore of Dog Lake at an elevation of 5,100 feet. Native Americans named the lake for its resemblance in shape to the hind leg of a dog. The lake provides a popular fishery for bass, crappie, and perch. Boats with motors are permitted, though speeds are limited to 5 mph. Prospects for seeing waterfowl and eagles are good.

Campsites, facilities: There are 17 sites for tents or RVs up to 40 feet long. Picnic tables and fire grills are provided. Vault toilets are available. There is no drinking water. Garbage must be packed out. A boat launch is nearby. Leashed pets are permitted.

Reservations, fees: Reservations are not accepted. Sites are $6 per night, $2 per night per additional vehicle. Open mid-April–mid-October, weather permitting.

Directions: From Lakeview, drive west on Highway 140 for seven miles to County Road 1-13. Turn left on County Road 1-13 and drive four miles to County Road 1-11D (Dog Lake Road). Turn right and drive four miles (the road becomes Forest Road 4017) into national forest. Continue on Forest Road 4017 for 12 miles (two miles past Drew Reservoir) to Dog Lake and the campground entrance on the left.

Contact: Fremont-Winema National Forests, Lakeview Ranger District, 541/353-2700, fax 541/947-6375, www.fs.fed.us.

32 DREWS CREEK

Scenic rating: 9

near Lakeview in Fremont National Forest

Map 6.5, page 399   BEST (

This exceptionally beautiful campground is set along Drews Creek at 4,900 feet elevation. Gorgeous wild roses grow near the creek, and several unmarked trails lead to nearby hills where campers can enjoy scenic views. A great spot for a family trip, Drews Creek features horseshoe pits, an area for baseball, and a large group barbecue, making it equally popular with group campers. Fishing is available in nearby Dog Lake, which also provides facilities for boating. Waterskiing is another option at Drews Reservoir, two miles to the west.

Campsites, facilities: There are five sites for tents or RVs up to 25 feet long. Picnic tables, fire grills, vault toilets, and drinking water are provided. Garbage must be packed out. Leashed pets are permitted.

Reservations, fees: Reservations are not accepted. There is no fee for camping. Open early mid-May–mid-October, weather permitting.

Directions: From Lakeview, drive west on Highway 140 for 10 miles to County Road 1-13. Turn left and drive four miles to County Road 1-11D. Turn right and drive six miles (the road will become Forest Road 4017) to the bridge that provides access to the campground.

Contact: Fremont-Winema National Forests, Lakeview Ranger District, 541/353-2700, fax 541/947-6375, www.fs.fed.us.

33 JUNIPERS RESERVOIR RV RESORT

Scenic rating: 6

on Junipers Reservoir

Map 6.5, page 399

This resort on an 8,000-acre cattle ranch is situated in a designated Oregon Wildlife Viewing Area, and campers may catch glimpses of seldom-seen species. Many nature-walking trails meander through the park, and guests can also take driving tours. Fishing for catfish and trout can be good and, because it is a private lake, no fishing license is required. The summer climate is mild and pleasant. Antelope and elk can be spotted in this area.

Campsites, facilities: There is a grassy area for tents and 40 pull-through sites with full or partial hookups (some 50-amp) for RVs of any length. Picnic tables are provided. Drinking water, restrooms with showers, a dump station, Wi-Fi and computer modem access, coin laundry, community fire pit, and ice are available. Recreational facilities include a recreation hall, a volleyball court, and horseshoe pits. Some of the facilities are wheelchair accessible. Leashed pets are permitted.

Reservations, fees: Reservations are recommended. Tent sites are $20 per night, and RV sites are $23.50–28.89 per night; weekly rates are available. Open May–mid-October.

Directions: From Lakeview, drive west on Highway 140 for 10 miles to the resort (at Milepost 86.5) on the right.

Contact: Junipers Reservoir RV Resort, 541/947-2050, fax 541/947-6788, www.junipersrv.com.

34 GOOSE LAKE STATE PARK

Scenic rating: 7

on Goose Lake

Map 6.5, page 399

This park is situated on the east shore of unusual Goose Lake, which lies half in Oregon and half in California. The fishing at the lake is poor, but better fishing is available in nearby streams. Waterfowl from the Pacific flyway frequent this out-of-the-way spot, as do many other species of birds and wildlife, like the mule deer that frequent the shaded campground. Note that only 15- and 20-amp service is available for RVs.

Campsites, facilities: There are 47 sites with partial hookups (water and electricity) for tents or RVs up to 50 feet long. Picnic tables, fire grills, garbage bins, and drinking water are provided. A camp host is on-site. Restrooms with flush toilets and showers, a dump station, ice, and firewood are available. Leashed pets are permitted.

Reservations, fees: Reservations are not accepted. Sites are $12–20 per night, $5 per night for an additional vehicle. Open mid-April–mid-October.

Directions: From Lakeview, drive south on U.S. 395 for 14 miles to the California border and Stateline Road. Turn right (west) and drive one mile to the campground.

Contact: Goose Lake State Park, 541/947-3111 or 800/551-6949, www.oregonstateparks.org.

35 WILLOW CREEK

Scenic rating: 4

near Willow Creek in Fremont National Forest
Map 6.5, page 399

This campground (at 5,800 feet elevation) is situated in a canyon among tall pines and quaking aspen not far from the banks of Willow Creek. Campsites are private, and some are located along the creek. Watch for wildflowers blooming in the spring. A hiking trail offers access to the Crane Mountain Trail, and a nearby dirt road heads north to Burnt Creek.

Campsites, facilities: There are eight sites for tents or RVs up to 22 feet long. Picnic tables and fire grills are provided. There is no drinking water, and garbage must be packed out. Vault toilets are available. Leashed pets are permitted.

Reservations, fees: Reservations are not accepted. There is no fee for camping. Open June–mid-October, weather permitting.

Directions: From Lakeview, drive five miles north on U.S. 395 to Highway 140. Turn right (east) on Highway 140 and drive seven miles to Forest Road 3915. Turn right and drive nine miles to Forest Road 4011. Turn right and drive one mile to the campground on the right.

Contact: Fremont-Winema National Forests, Lakeview Ranger District, 541/353-2700, fax 541/947-6375, www.fs.fed.us.

36 DEEP CREEK

Scenic rating: 8

on Deep Creek in Fremont National Forest
Map 6.5, page 399

Shaded by huge ponderosa pines and cottonwoods and nestled on the banks of Deep Creek, this pretty, little-used campground is the place if you're after privacy. Deep Creek is a good fishing stream. Magnificent spring wildflowers are a highlight here. The camp sits at an elevation of 5,600 feet.

Campsites, facilities: There are six sites for tents or RVs up to 22 feet long. Picnic tables and fire grills are provided. Vault toilets are available. There is no drinking water, and garbage must be packed out. Leashed pets are permitted.

Reservations, fees: Reservations are not accepted. There is no fee for camping. Open June–mid-October, weather permitting.

Directions: From Lakeview, drive five miles north on U.S. 395 to Highway 140. Turn right (east) on Highway 140 and drive six miles to Forest Road 3915. Turn right on Forest Road 3915 and drive 14 miles to Deep Creek and the campground entrance road on the right (Forest Road 4015). Turn right and drive one mile to the campground on the right.

Contact: Fremont-Winema National Forests, Lakeview Ranger District, 541/353-2700, fax 541/947-6375, www.fs.fed.us.

37 HART MOUNTAIN NATIONAL ANTELOPE REFUGE

Scenic rating: 6

near Adel
Map 6.6, page 400

The U.S. Fish and Wildlife Service operates very few areas with campgrounds—Hart Mountain is one of them. This unusual refuge features canyons and hot springs in a high-desert area. There are three primitive campgrounds: Hot Springs Campground, Post Meadows Horse Camp, and CCC Camp. Hot Springs gets the highest use in the summer. Some of Oregon's largest antelope herds roam this large area, and the campground is popular with hunters in the fall.

Campsites, facilities: Hot Springs Campground has 25 primitive sites for tents or RVs up to 20 feet long. Post Meadows Horse Camp has six primitive sites with corrals, hitching posts, and stock water (100 yards away) available; pellet feed is required for horses. CCC Camp has 20 primitive tent sites. Some sites have fire rings. Pit toilets are provided. There is no drinking water (but it can be obtained at headquarters, which you pass on the way in). Garbage must be packed out. Supplies are available in the town of Plush. Some facilities are wheelchair accessible. Leashed pets are permitted.

Reservations, fees: Reservations are not accepted. There is no fee for camping. Open year-round, weather permitting.

Directions: From Lakeview, drive north on U.S. 395 for five miles to Highway 140. Turn east on Highway 140 and drive 16 miles to the Plush-Hart Mountain Cutoff. Turn left (signed for Hart Antelope Refuge) and drive north for 43 miles (first paved, then gravel) to the refuge headquarters. Continue 0.5 miles to CCC Campground, four miles to Hot Springs Campground (the road is often impassable in the winter). For the Post Meadows Horse Camp, follow the above directions to the refuge headquarters. At headquarters, turn onto Blue Sky Road and drive 10 miles to the camp.

Contact: Hart Mountain National Antelope Refuge, 541/947-3315 or 541/947-2731, fax 541/947-4414, www.fws.gov/refuges.

38 ADEL STORE AND RV PARK

Scenic rating: 5

in Adel

Map 6.6, page 400

Remote Adel is the only game in town, so you'd better grab it while you can. Recreation options in the area include hang gliding, rock-hounding, and visiting hot springs at the Hart Mountain National Antelope Refuge, 40 miles north of Adel.

Campsites, facilities: There are eight sites for tents or RVs up to 40 feet (full hookups). Barbecues are provided. A store, a small café, gasoline, and ice are available. Leashed pets are permitted.

Reservations, fees: Reservations are accepted. Tent sites are $10 per night and RV sites are $18 per night; weekly rates are available. Some credit cards are accepted but not for the purchase of gasoline. Open year-round.

Directions: From Lakeview, drive five miles north on U.S. 395 to Highway 140. Turn right (east) on Highway 140 and drive 28 miles to Adel (a very small town). The RV park is in town along Highway 140 on the right.

Contact: Adel Store and RV Park, 541/947-3850.

39 STEENS MOUNTAIN RESORT

Scenic rating: 9

on the Blitzen River

Map 6.7, page 401

The self-proclaimed "gateway to the Steens Mountain," this resort is bordered by the Malheur National Wildlife Refuge on three sides, and it has great views. The mile-high mountain and surrounding gorges make an excellent photo opportunity. Hiking and hunting are other possibilities in the area. Fishing is available on the Blitzen River, with easy access from the camp.

Campsites, facilities: There are 25 tent sites, 37 pull-through sites with full hookups (30 or 50 amps), and 39 sites with partial hookups for tents or RVs of any length, plus eight cabins and one rental home. Picnic tables and fire pits are provided. Drinking water, restrooms with showers, a dump station, coin laundry, limited groceries and fishing supplies, and ice are available. Leashed pets are permitted.

Reservations, fees: Reservations are accepted at 800/542-3765. Sites are $15–30 per night and $5 per person per night for more than two people. Some credit cards are accepted. Open year-round.

Directions: From Burns, drive east on Highway 78 for two miles to Highway 205. Turn right (south) on Highway 205 and drive 59 miles to Frenchglen and Steens Mountain Road. Turn left (east) and drive three miles to the resort on the right.

Contact: Steens Mountain Resort, 541/493-2415, fax 541/493-2484, www.steensmountainresort.com.

40 PAGE SPRINGS

Scenic rating: 7

near Malheur National Wildlife Refuge

Map 6.7, page 401

Page Springs campground lies adjacent to the Malheur National Wildlife Refuge at an elevation of 4,200 feet. Sites are shaded by juniper and cottonwood, with some near the Donner und Blitzen River. Activities include hiking on the area trails, bird-watching, fishing, hunting, and sightseeing. The Frenchglen Hotel (three miles away) is administered by the state parks department and offers overnight accommodations and meals.

Campsites, facilities: There are 36 sites for tents or RVs up to 35 feet long. Picnic tables and fire grills are provided. Drinking water, vault toilets, a day-use area with a shelter,

and garbage bins are available. Some facilities are wheelchair accessible. Leashed pets are permitted.

Reservations, fees: Reservations are not accepted. Sites are $8 per vehicle per night, with a 14-day stay limit. Open year-round.

Directions: From Burns, drive east on Highway 78 for two miles to Highway 205. Turn south on Highway 205 and drive 60 miles to Frenchglen and Steens Mountain Loop Road. Turn left (east) and drive three miles to the campground.

Contact: Bureau of Land Management, Burns District, 541/573-4400, fax 541/573-4411, www.or.blm.gov/burns.

41 FISH LAKE

Scenic rating: 8

on Fish Lake

Map 6.7, page 401

The shore of Fish Lake is the setting for this primitive but pretty camp. Set among the aspens at 7,400 feet elevation, it can make an excellent weekend-getaway spot for sightseeing. Trout fishing is an option, made easier by the boat ramp near camp.

Campsites, facilities: There are 23 sites for tents or RVs up to 20 feet long. Picnic tables and fire grills are provided. Drinking water, garbage bins, and vault toilets are available. Boat-launching facilities are nearby (non-motorized boats only). Some facilities are wheelchair accessible. Leashed pets are permitted.

Reservations, fees: Reservations are not accepted. Sites are $8 per vehicle per night, with a 14-day stay limit. Open June–October, weather permitting.

Directions: From Burns, drive east on Highway 78 for two miles to Highway 205. Turn south on Highway 205 and drive 60 miles to Frenchglen and Steens Mountain Loop Road. Turn left (east) and drive 17 miles to the campground.

Contact: Bureau of Land Management, Burns

District, 541/573-4400, fax 541/573-4411, www.or.blm.gov/burns.

42 JACKMAN PARK

🏃 🐕 🏕

Scenic rating: 8

near Fish Lake

Map 6.7, page 401

One of four camps in the area, Jackman Park sits at 7,800 feet elevation in the eastern Oregon desert. This scenic campground, with its aspen and willow trees, is known as one of the best places to view the golden aspen leaves on Steens Mountain in the fall. Fish Lake is 2.5 miles away. Note that trailers and RVs are not recommended in the campground.

Campsites, facilities: There are six primitive sites for tents. Picnic tables and fire rings are provided. Drinking water and vault toilets are available. Leashed pets are permitted.

Reservations, fees: Reservations are not accepted. Sites are $6 per vehicle per night, with a 14-day stay limit. Open July–late October, weather permitting.

Directions: From Burns, drive east on Highway 78 for two miles to Highway 205. Turn south on Highway 205 and drive 60 miles to Frenchglen and Steens Mountain Loop Road. Turn left (east) and drive 22 miles to the campground.

Contact: Bureau of Land Management, Burns District, 541/573-4400, fax 541/573-4411, www.or.blm.gov/burns.

43 MANN LAKE

🎣 🚤 🐕 ♿ 🚐 🏕

Scenic rating: 8

on Mann Lake

Map 6.7, page 401

Mann Lake sits at the base of Steens Mountain. This scenic, high-desert camp is mainly used as a fishing camp—fishing can be very

good for cutthroat trout. Wintertime ice fishing and wildlife-viewing are also popular. Sites are open, with sagebrush and no trees. There are two small boat ramps and a 10-horsepower limit on motors. Weather can be extreme. Nearby Alvord Desert is also an attraction.

Note: Please respect private property on parcels of land next to the lake.

Campsites, facilities: There are dispersed sites for tents or RVs of up to 35 feet long, and open areas on each side of the lake. Vault toilets are available. No drinking water is available. Garbage must be packed out. Some facilities are wheelchair accessible. Leashed pets are permitted.

Reservations, fees: Reservations are not accepted. There is no fee for camping. A 14-day stay limit is enforced. Open year-round.

Directions: From Burns, drive southeast on Highway 78 for 65 miles to East Steens Road. Turn right (south) and drive 22 miles to the campground at Mann Lake.

Contact: Bureau of Land Management, Burns District, 541/573-4400, fax 541/573-4411, www.or.blm.gov/burns.

44 SOUTH STEENS

🏃 🚣 🐕 ♿ 🚐 🏕

Scenic rating: 6

near Steens Mountain Wilderness

Map 6.7, page 401

This campground hugs the edge of the Steens Mountain Wilderness. The area features deep, glacier-carved gorges, volcanic uplifts, stunning scenery, and a rare chance to see elk and bighorn sheep. Redband trout fishing is a mile away at Donner und Blitzen Wild and Scenic River and its tributaries, a designated reserve. This campground is also good for horse campers, providing them with a separate area from the other campers. Trails are accessible from the campground.

Campsites, facilities: There are 36 sites for tents or RVs up to 25 feet long; 15 of the sites are designated for horse campers. Picnic tables, corrals, hitching posts, and fire grills are provided. Drinking water and vault toilets are available. Some facilities are wheelchair accessible. Leashed pets are permitted.

Reservations, fees: Reservations are not accepted. Sites are $6 per vehicle per night. There is a 14-day stay limit. Open May–October, weather permitting.

Directions: From Burns, drive east on Highway 78 for two miles to Highway 205. Turn south on Highway 205 and drive 60 miles to Frenchglen. Continue south on Highway 205 for 10 miles to Steens South Loop Road. Turn left (east) and drive 18 miles to the campground on the right.

Contact: Bureau of Land Management, Burns District, 541/573-4400, fax 541/573-4411, www.or.blm.gov/burns.

45 WILLOW CREEK HOT SPRINGS

Scenic rating: 7

near Whitehorse Butte

Map 6.7, page 401

A very small campground with no privacy, Willow Creek features campsites about 100 feet from the hot springs, which consist of two connected, smaller pools. This campground can be difficult to find, and only the adventurous should attempt this trip. Despite being out of the way, it still attracts travelers from far and wide. The surrounding scenery features rocky hills, not a flat expanse.

Campsites, facilities: There are four sites for tents or small RVs. Fire rings are provided. A vault toilet is available. Drinking water and firewood are not available, and garbage must be packed out. Leashed pets are permitted.

Reservations, fees: Reservations are not accepted. There is no fee for camping. Open year-round, weather permitting.

Directions: From Burns, drive southeast on

Highway 78 for 105 miles to Burns Junction and U.S. 95. Turn right (south) on U.S. 95 and drive 20 miles to Whitehorse Road. Turn right (southwest) and drive 21 miles (passing Whitehorse Ranch); continue for 2.5 miles to a fork (look for the telephone pole). Bear left and drive two miles to the campground.

Contact: Bureau of Land Management, Vale District, 541/473-3144, fax 541/473-6213, www.blm.gov.

46 ROME LAUNCH

Scenic rating: 6

on the Owyhee River

Map 6.8, page 402

Rome Launch campground is used mainly by folks rafting the Owyhee River and overnighters passing through. A few cottonwood trees and sagebrush dot the camp with some sites adjacent to the Owyhee River. Rome Launch is also good for wildlife-viewing; mountain lions and bobcats have been spotted, and there are some farms and ranches in the area.

The Owyhee Canyon is quite dramatic, like a miniature Grand Canyon. I have canoed most of the Owyhee from the headwaters in Nevada below the Jarbidge Mountains all the way through Idaho and into Oregon, and I would rate this river as one of the top canoeing destinations in North America. Note: No motorized boats are allowed on the river.

Campsites, facilities: There are five sites for tents or small RVs. Picnic tables and fire rings are provided. Drinking water, vault toilets, and a boat launch are available. No firewood is available. All garbage must be packed out. Leashed pets are permitted.

Reservations, fees: Reservations are not accepted. There is no fee for camping. Open March–November, weather permitting.

Directions: From Burns Junction, drive east on U.S. 95 for 15 miles to Jordan Valley and the signed turnoff for the Owyhee River and

BLM-Rome boat launch. Turn south and drive 0.25 mile to the campground.

Contact: Bureau of Land Management, Vale District, 541/473-3144, fax 541/473-6213, www.blm.gov.

47 ANTELOPE RESERVOIR

Scenic rating: 3

on the Antelope Reservoir

Map 6.8, page 402

This campground gets little use, except during hunting season. An open area on a slope above the reservoir, the camp has no tree cover—be prepared for extreme weather. Water levels fluctuate at shallow Antelope Reservoir and it can dry up.

Campsites, facilities: There are four sites for tents or small RVs. Picnic tables and fire rings are provided. Vault toilets and primitive boat access are available. No drinking water is available, and all garbage must be packed out. Leashed pets are permitted.

Reservations, fees: Reservations are not accepted. There is no fee for camping. Open year-round, weather permitting.

Directions: From Burns Junction, drive east on U.S. 95 for 36 miles to the signed turnoff for Antelope Reservoir. Turn south and drive one mile to the campground on the left.

Contact: Bureau of Land Management, Vale District, 541/473-3144, fax 541/473-6213, www.blm.gov.

48 THREE FORKS

Scenic rating: 9

near the Owyhee River

Map 6.8, page 402

This remote camp is set along the east bank of the Owyhee River, where several warm streams snake through tall grass to the river. The area offers fishing for brown trout in the river and day hiking to secluded springs and a waterfall pool in the upper Owyhee Canyon (swimwear optional). Clusters of 95°F springs are located on both sides of the river, and the rugged Owyhee Canyon forms a magnificent backdrop. To the west are a number of wild horse herds. (The BLM recreation map has the general locations of the herds.)

Campsites, facilities: There are four sites for tents or small RVs. Picnic tables and fire rings are provided. Vault toilets are available. There is no drinking water, and garbage must be packed out. There is access to the Owyhee River by permit for non-motorized boats only. Leashed pets are permitted.

Reservations, fees: Reservations are not accepted. There is no fee for camping. Open year-round, weather permitting.

Directions: On U.S. 95 (15 miles southwest of Jordan Valley), turn south on Three Forks Road and drive 35 miles to the campground. High-clearance vehicles recommended. Road may be impassable when wet.

Contact: Bureau of Land Management, Vale District, 541/473-3144, fax 541/473-6213, www.blm.gov.

RESOURCES

NATIONAL FORESTS

The U.S. Forest Service provides many secluded camps and allows camping anywhere except where it is specifically prohibited. If you ever want to clear the cobwebs from your head and get away from it all, this is the way to go.

Many Forest Service campgrounds are remote and have no drinking water. You usually don't need to check in or make reservations, and sometimes there is no fee. At many Forest Service campgrounds that provide drinking water, the camping fee is often only a few dollars, with payment made on the honor system. Because most of these camps are in mountain areas, they are subject to winter closure due to snow or mud.

Dogs are permitted in national forests with no extra charge. Always carry documentation of current vaccinations.

Northwest Forest Pass

A Northwest Forest Pass is required for certain activities in some Oregon national forests. The pass is required for parking at participating trailheads, non-developed camping areas, boat launches, picnic areas, and visitors centers.

Daily passes cost $5 per vehicle; annual passes are $30 per vehicle. Combined recreation passes for Washington and Oregon are also available. You can buy Northwest Forest Passes at national forest offices and dozens of retail outlets and online vendors. Holders of Golden Age and Golden Access (not Golden Eagle) cards can buy the Northwest Forest Pass at a 50 percent discount at national forest offices only, or at retail outlets for the retail price. Major credit cards are accepted at most retail and online outlets and at some Forest Service offices.

More information about the Northwest Forest Pass program, including a listing of retail and online vendors, can be obtained at www. fs.fed.us/r6/passespermits. You can also phone 503/808-6008.

An Interagency Pass is available for $80 annually in lieu of a Northwest Forest Pass. The Interagency Pass is honored nationwide at all Forest Service, National Park Service, Bureau of Land Management, Bureau of Reclamation, and U.S. Fish and Wildlife Service sites charging entrance or standard amenity fees. Valid for 12 months from the month of purchase, the America the Beautiful Pass is available at most national forest or grassland offices or online at http://store.usgs.gov.

National Forest Reservations

Some of the more popular camps and most of the group camps are on a reservation system. Reservations can be made up to 240 days in advance and up to 360 days in advance for groups. To reserve a site, call 877/444-6777 or visit www.recreation.gov. The reservation fee is usually $10 for a campsite in a national forest, but group site reservation fees are higher. Major credit cards are accepted. Holders of Golden Age or Golden Access passports receive a 50 percent discount on campground fees, except for group sites.

National Forest Maps

National Forest maps are among the best you can get for the price. They detail all backcountry streams, lakes, hiking trails, and logging roads for access. They cost $9–12 or more and can be obtained in person at Forest Service offices or by contacting:

U.S. Forest Service
National Forest Store
P.O. Box 8268
Missoula, MT 59807
406/329-3024
fax 406/329-3030
www.fs.fed.us/recreation/nationalforeststore/

Forest Service Information

Forest Service personnel are most helpful for obtaining camping or hiking trail information. Unless you are buying a map or Adventure Pass, it is advisable to phone in advance to get the best service.

For further information on individual national forests, contact the following offices:

U.S. Forest Service
Pacific Northwest Region 6
333 SW 1st Avenue
Portland, OR 97204-3440
503/808-2468
www.fs.fed.us/r6
or
P.O. Box 3623
Portland, OR 97208-3623

Deschutes National Forest
1001 SW Emkay Drive
Bend, OR 97702
541/383-5300
www.fs.fed.us/r6/centraloregon/

Fremont-Winema National Forests
HC 10 Box 337
1301 South G Street
Lakeview, OR 97630
541/947-2151
www.fs.fed.us/r6/frewin/

Malheur National Forest
P.O. Box 909
431 Patterson Bridge Road
John Day, OR 97845
541/575-3000
www.fs.fed.us/r6/malheur/

Mount Hood National Forest
16400 Champion Way
Sandy, OR 97055
503/668-1700
www.fs.fed.us/r6/mthood/

Ochoco National Forest
3160 NE 3rd Street
Prineville, OR 97754
541/416-6500
www.fs.fed.us/r6/centraloregon/

Rogue River-Siskiyou National Forest
3040 Biddle Road
Medford, OR 97504
541/618-2200
www.fs.fed.us/r6/rogue-siskiyou/

Siuslaw National Forest
P.O. Box 1148
4077 SW Research Way
Corvallis, OR 97339
541/750-7000
fax 541/750-7234
www.fs.fed.us/r6/siuslaw/

Umatilla National Forest
2517 SW Hailey Avenue
Pendleton, OR 97801
541/278-3716
www.fs.fed.us/r6/uma/

Umpqua National Forest
2900 NW Stewart Parkway
Roseburg, OR 97471
541/672-6601
www.fs.fed.us/r6/umpqua/

Wallowa-Whitman National Forest
P.O. Box 907
1550 Dewey Avenue
Baker City, OR 97814
541/523-6391
www.fs.fed.us/r6/w-w/

Willamette National Forest
3106 Pierce Parkway, Ste. D
Springfield, OR 97477
541/225-6300
www.fs.fed.us/r6/willamette/

NATIONAL PARKS AND RECREATION AREAS

The national parks and recreational areas in Oregon are natural wonders, varying from the spectacular Columbia River Gorge to the breathtaking Crater Lake National Park. Reservations are available at some of the campgrounds at these parks and recreation areas. Various discounts are available for holders of Golden Age and Golden Access passports, including a 50 percent reduction of camping fees (group camps not included).

For information about each of the national parks in Oregon, contact the parks directly:

**Columbia River Gorge
National Scenic Area**
902 Wasco Avenue, Suite 200
Hood River, OR 97031
541/308-1700
www.fs.fed.us/r6/columbia/forest/

Crater Lake National Park
P.O. Box 7
Crater Lake, OR 97604
541/594-3100
www.nps.gov/crla/

Crooked River National Grassland
813 SW Highway 97
Madras, OR 97741
541/475-9272
www.fs.fed.us/r6/centraloregon

Hells Canyon National Recreation Area
Wallowa Mountains Visitor Center
88401 Highway 82
Enterprise, OR 97828
541/426-5546
www.fs.fed.us/hellscanyon/

Oregon Dunes National Recreation Area
855 Highway Avenue
Reedsport, OR 97467
541/271-6000
www.fs.fed.us/r6/siuslaw/

STATE PARKS

The Oregon State Parks system provides many popular camping spots. Reservations are often a necessity during the summer. The camps include drive-in numbered sites, tent spaces, and picnic tables, with showers and bathrooms provided nearby. Although some parks are well known, there are still some little-known gems in the state parks system where campers can find seclusion, even in the summer.

State Park Reservations

Many of the state park campgrounds are on a reservation system, and campsites can be booked up to nine months in advance at these parks. Reservations can be made for 44 Oregon state parks through Reserve America at 800/452-5687 or online at www.reserveamerica.com. A nonrefundable reservation fee of $8 and the first night's fee will be required as a deposit, charged to a MasterCard or Visa credit card (debit cards linked to MasterCard or Visa also accepted).

**Oregon Parks and
Recreation Department: State Parks**
725 Summer St. NE, Ste. C
Salem, OR 97301
800/551-6949
www.oregon.gov/OPRD/PARKS/index.shtml

STATE FORESTS
Oregon Department of Forestry
2600 State Street
Salem, OR 97310
503/945-7200
egov.oregon.gov/ODF

Tillamook State Forest,
Forest Grove District
801 Gales Creek Road
Forest Grove, OR 97116-1199
503/357-2191
http://oregon.gov/ODF/TSF/tsf.shtml

Tillamook State Forest,
Tillamook District
5005 3rd Street
Tillamook, OR 97141-2999
503/842-2545
http://oregon.gov/ODF/TSF/tsf.shtml

U.S. ARMY CORPS OF ENGINEERS
Some of the family camps and most of the group camps operated by the U.S. Army Corps of Engineers are on a reservation system. Reservations can be made up to 240 days in advance for family camps and up to 360 days in advance for groups. To reserve a site, call 877/444-6777 or visit www.recreation.gov. The reservation fee is usually $10 for a campsite, but group site reservation fees are higher. Major credit cards are accepted. Holders of Golden Age or Golden Access passports receive a 50 percent discount on campground fees, except for group sites.

Portland District
333 SW 1st Ave
Portland, OR 97204
503/808-4510
www.nwp.usace.army.mil/
or
P.O. Box 2946
Portland, OR 97208-2946

BUREAU OF LAND MANAGEMENT (BLM)
Most BLM campgrounds are primitive and in remote areas. Often, there is no fee charged for camping. Holders of Golden Age or Golden Access passports receive a 50 percent discount at BLM campgrounds with fees (group camps excluded).

Oregon Office
333 SW 1st Avenue
Portland, OR 97204
503/808-6008
www.blm.gov/or
or
P.O. Box 2965
Portland, OR 97208-2946
503/808-4510

Burns District
28910 Highway 20 West
Hines, OR 97738
541/573-4400
fax 541/573-4411
www.blm.gov/or/districts/burns

Coos Bay District
1300 Airport Lane
North Bend, OR 97459
541/756-0100
www.blm.gov/or/districts/coosbay

Eugene District
3106 Pierce Parkway, Ste. E
Springfield, OR 97477
541/683-6600
fax 541/683-6981
www.blm.gov/or/districts/eugene
or
P.O. Box 10226
Eugene, OR 97440

Lakeview District
1301 South G Street
Lakeview, OR 97630
541/947-2177
fax 541/947-6399
www.blm.gov/or/districts/lakeview

Medford District
3040 Biddle Road
Medford, OR 97504
541/618-2200
fax 541/618-2400
www.blm.gov/or/districts/medford

Prineville District
3050 NE 3rd Street
Prineville, OR 97754
541/416-6700
fax 541/416-6798
www.blm.gov/or/districts/prineville

Roseburg District
777 NW Garden Valley Boulevard
Roseburg, OR 97471
541/440-4930
fax 541/440-4948
www.blm.gov/or/districts/roseburg

Salem District
1717 Fabry Road SE
Salem, OR 97306
503/375-5646
fax 503/375-5622
www.blm.gov/or/districts/salem

Vale District
100 Oregon Street
Vale, OR 97918
541/473-3144
www.blm.gov/or/districts/vale

OTHER VALUABLE RESOURCES
Oregon Department of Fish and Wildlife
3406 Cherry Avenue
Salem, OR 97303
503/947-6000
www.dfw.state.or.us

Oregon State Department of Transportation
888/275-6368
www.oregon.gov/ODOT/

U.S. Geological Survey
345 Middlefield Rd.
Menlo Park, CA 94025
650/853-8300 or
    888/ASK-USGS (888/275-8747)
www.usgs.gov

Index

Acknowledgments

The following state and federal resource experts provided critical information and galley reviews regarding changes in reservations, fees, directions, and recreational opportunities. I am extremely grateful for their timely help and expert advice.

U.S. Forest Service

Ronda Bishop, Deschutes National Forest, Bend-Fort Rock Ranger District

Bob Hennings, Deschutes National Forest, Sisters Ranger District

Larry Hills, Fremont-Winema National Forests, Bly and Lakeview Ranger Districts

Doug Uran, Fremont-Winema National Forests, Silver Lake Ranger District

Phil McNeil, Klamath National Forest, Happy Camp/Oak Knoll Ranger District

Shannon Winegar, Terry Rittner, Malheur National Forest, Prairie City Ranger District

Jacquelyn Oakes, Mount Hood National Forest, Clackamas River and Zigzag Ranger Districts

Katherine Martin, Ochoco National Forest, Paulina Ranger District

Nancy Schwieger, Siskiyou National Forest, Gold Beach Ranger District

David Wickwire, Siskiyou National Forest, Galice Ranger Districts

Diana Dunn, Siuslaw National Forest, Central Coast Ranger District-Oregon Dunes National Recreation Area

Vicky Mugnai, Siuslaw National Forest, Waldport Ranger District

Kathy Rankin, Umatilla National Forest, Heppner Ranger District

Janelle Lacey, Umatilla National Forest, North Fork John Day Ranger District

Jeff Bloom, Umatilla National Forest, Walla Walla Ranger District

Dennis Scott, Umpqua National Forest, North Umpqua Ranger District

Mike Montgomery, Wallowa-Whitman National Forest, LaGrande Ranger District

Yvonne Santiago, Wallowa-Whitman National Forest, Wallowa Valley Ranger District/Eagle Cap Ranger District/Hells Canyon National Recreation Area

Annie Moore, Wallowa-Whitman National Forest, Whitman Ranger District

Jennifer McDonald, Willamette National Forest, McKenzie Ranger District

Bureau of Land Management

Dennis Byrd, Ashland Resource Area

Kevin McCoy, Brett Paige, Baker City Office

Trish Lindemann, Medford District

Greg Currie, Prineville District

Greg Morgan, Roseburg District

Traci Meredith, Salem District

Deb Drake, Tillamook District

David Draheim, Vale District

National Parks, Recreation Areas, and Refuges

Edan Lira, Columbia River Gorge National Scenic Area

State Parks

Chris Havel, Oregon State Parks media services

Rick Duda, Milo McIver State Park

Linda Brege, Deschutes State Recreation Area

Larry Moniz, Goose Lake State Park

Mary Nulty, Carl G. Washburne State Park

Other

Bill Doran, Metro Regional Parks and Green Spaces

Kirsti Cason, Morrow County Parks

Clara Johnson, Crook County Parks and Recreation

Kristi Mosier, Lane County, Richardson Park

Lynn Studley, Portland General Electric

Christie Harris, Linn County Parks

Jill Hammond, Jackson County Parks

Ken Hill, Port of Siuslaw

Kathy Hammons, Douglas County Parks

Alisha Howard, Josephine County Parks

www.moon.com

DESTINATIONS | ACTIVITIES | BLOGS | MAPS | BOOKS

MOON.COM is ready to help plan your next trip! Filled with fresh trip ideas and strategies, author interviews, informative travel blogs, a detailed map library, and descriptions of all the Moon guidebooks, Moon.com is all you need to get out and explore the world—or even places in your own backyard. While at Moon.com, sign up for our monthly e-newsletter for updates on new releases, travel tips, and expert advice from our on-the-go Moon authors. As always, when you travel with Moon, expect an experience that is uncommon and truly unique.

MOON IS ON FACEBOOK—BECOME A FAN!
JOIN THE MOON PHOTO GROUP ON FLICKR

MOON OUTDOORS

"Well written, thoroughly researched, and packed full of useful information and advice, these guides really do get you into the outdoors."

—GORP.COM

MOON OREGON CAMPING

Avalon Travel
a member of the Perseus Books Group
1700 Fourth Street
Berkeley, CA 94710, USA
www.moon.com

Editor and Series Manager: Sabrina Young
Senior Research Editor: Kathie Morgan
Research Editor: Glenn Mayeda
Copy Editor: Valerie Sellers Blanton
Graphics Coordinator: Elizabeth Jang
Production Coordinator: Elizabeth Jang
Cover Designer: Elizabeth Jang
Interior Designer: Darren Alessi
Map Editor: Mike Morgenfeld
Cartographers: Michelle Trame, Brice Ticen,
    Kat Bennett
Indexer: Sabrina Young
Illustrations: Bob Race

ISBN-13: 978-1-56691-841-1
ISSN: 1557-2587

Printing History
1st Edition – 2002
3rd Edition – April 2010
5 4 3 2 1

Printed in Canada by Friesens

Keeping Current

We are committed to making this book the most accurate and enjoyable camping guide to the state. You can rest assured that every campground in this book has been carefully reviewed in an effort to keep this book as up-to-date as possible. However, by the time you read this book, some of the fees listed herein may have changed and campgrounds may have closed unexpectedly.

If you have a favorite gem you'd like to see included in the next edition, or see anything that needs updating, clarification, or correction, please drop us a line. Send your comments via email to feedback@moon.com, or use the address above.